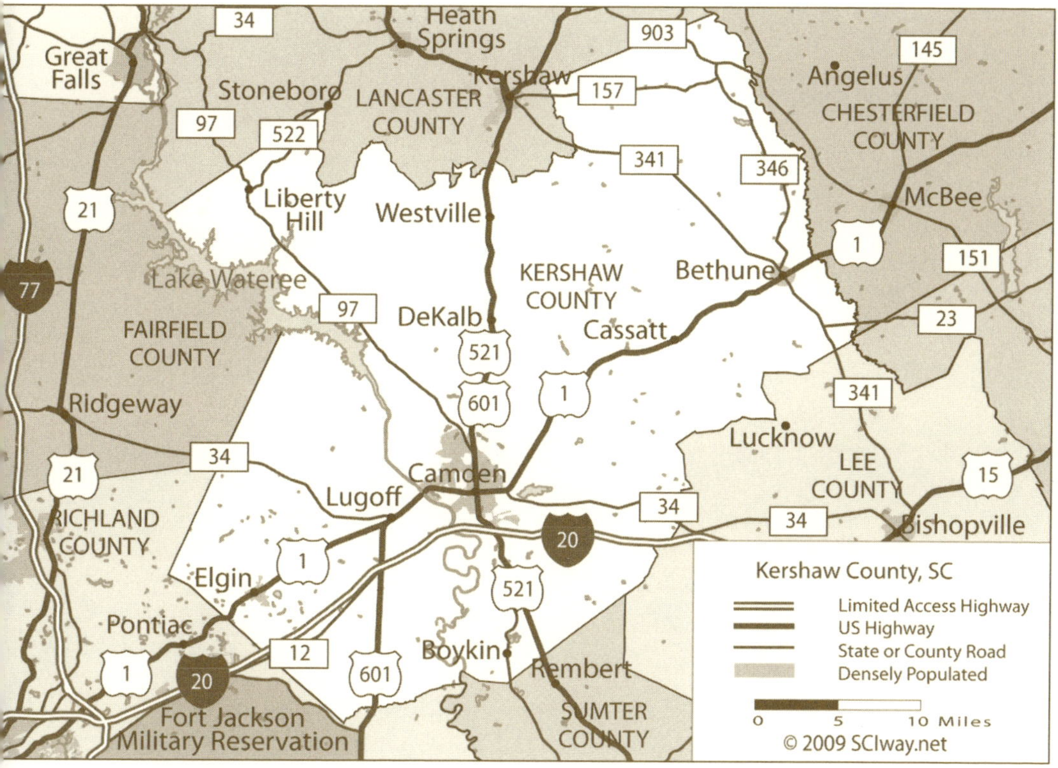
Kershaw County, SC
Limited Access Highway
US Highway
State or County Road
Densely Populated
0
5
10 Miles
© 2009 SCIway.net
Great Falls
Heath Springs
Kershaw
Stoneboro
LANCASTER COUNTY
Angelus
CHESTERFIELD COUNTY
McBee
Liberty Hill
Westville
Lake Wateree
KERSHAW COUNTY
Bethune
DeKalb
Cassatt
FAIRFIELD COUNTY
Ridgeway
Lucknow
LEE COUNTY
Camden
Lugoff
Bishopville
RICHLAND COUNTY
Elgin
Pontiac
Boykin
Rembert
SUMTER COUNTY
Fort Jackson Military Reservation
34
903
145
157
97
522
341
346
21
1
151
77
97
23
521
601
341
34
15
34
20
12
20

A History of Kershaw County, South Carolina

A History of

KERSHAW COUNTY

South Carolina

Joan A. Inabinet

L. Glen Inabinet

for the

Kershaw County Historical Society

The University of South Carolina Press

Published by the University of South Carolina Press
Columbia, South Carolina 29208

www.sc.edu/uscpress

Manufactured in the United States of America

20 19 18 17 16 15 14 13 12 11 10 9 8 7 6 5 4 3 2 1

Library of Congress Cataloging-in-Publication Data

Inabinet, Joan A.
A history of Kershaw County, South Carolina / Joan A. Inabinet and L. Glen Inabinet for the Kershaw County Historical Society.
p. cm.
Includes bibliographical references and index.
ISBN 978-1-57003-947-8 (cloth : alk. paper)
1. Kershaw County (S.C.)—History. I. Inabinet, L. Glen. II. Kershaw County Historical Society. III. Title.
F277.K3I53 2011
975.7'61—dc22

2010025221

Endsheets: maps of Kershaw County in 1926 (left; from Kirkland and Kennedy, *Historic Camden: Nineteenth Century,* 1926) and in 2009 (right; by permission of Sciway)

For the people of Kershaw County—past, present, and future

CONTENTS

ILLUSTRATIONS

Unless otherwise credited in captions, photographs were taken by L. Glen Inabinet.

ACKNOWLEDGMENTS

Many people over the years have been part of the process that has resulted in the publication of *A History of Kershaw County.*

The Kershaw County Historical Society, the primary contributor to the efforts for this publication, has long worked toward the goal of a comprehensive countywide history. To all who have participated in the planning and support of the project, we can only say repeatedly: thank you. The names of society presidents and members who rendered special efforts are among those listed below. We recognize especially, with gratitude, the constant and invaluable assistance of our colleague and dear friend Harvey S. Teal, chairman of the society's publication committee, whose personal and professional guidance has been wise and useful through all stages. We gratefully thank our editors at the University of South Carolina Press.

We lovingly acknowledge the inspiration of our parents and other kin and elders, who took us as children and later to see natural sites, monuments, old houses, churches, cemeteries, farms, gins, and country stores, at times pointing out where something used to be and sharing with us colorful recollections of folk they had known and how they lived, worked, worshipped, and played. We also lovingly express appreciation to our children—Julie Putnam, Bill Inabinet, and Greg Inabinet—and their families (and to extended family members) for the long years they have lived with and supported our dedication to this project with their own talents, interests, and labors. Likewise we thank the young people, too numerous to name, who taught us much in the more than three decades we were teachers in high school classrooms, and who sometimes explored the community with us for special projects.

For all their interested acts of assistance, which went far beyond expectations of mere professional responsibilities, we thank the staffs of the South Caroliniana Library, the South Carolina Department of Archives and History, the Camden Archives and Museum, and Historic Camden—especially Allen Stokes at the South Caroliniana Library, Agnes Corbett and Howard Branham at the Camden Archives, and Joanna Craig at Historic Camden, who were among the readers of our drafts. We also especially thank the *Camden Chronicle-Independent* for allowing us access to their extensive collection of bound volumes of almost a century of local newspapers.

It is impossible to name everyone who assisted us in this endeavor. With abject apologies for any unintentional omissions, we wish to thank people (some of them now deceased) who helped us by granting interviews, providing information, or giving assistance in other ways over the years. These individuals include Cornell Adamson, Dot Anderson, Helen Anderson, Lewis and Lottie Anderson, Robbie Anderson, Frank Babbitt, Carlyle Baxley, Charles Baxley, Boykin Beard, Meta Beard, Davie Beard, Likkie Beleos, Conney Bell, Gaffney Blalock, Mary Ann Blaskowitz, John Bonner, Alice Boykin, Baynard Boykin, Henry Boykin, Henry Brown, Martha Bruce, Claude Campbell, C. C. Canada, Walker Canada and his ATEC students, Darlene and Ralph Cantey, Clay Carruth, Margie Carter, John Caylor, W. D. Chivers, Margie Clarke, Jack Corbett, Alvin and Nellie Creed, Richard Creed, Mary Cunningham, John and Martha Daniels, Marty Daniels, Sam and Bobbie Jo Daniels, James DuBose, Shannon DuBose, Mary B. DuVal, Max Ford, Phyllis Gale, Miles Gardner, Elsie Goins, Frank Goodale, Val Green, Ann Hinson, J. E. Horton, Elizabeth Hough, John H. Jackson, Joe and Mary Ellen Jenkins, Steve Kelly Sr., the family of Ronald Kirkbride, Richard Lloyd, Clarence Mahoney, Paula Marcus, Larry McCaskill, Marvin and Esther McCaskill, Perry McCoy, Charles McGuirt, J. B. McGuirt, Jim McGuirt, Mike McClendon, Thomas McLester, Carol McNaughton, Vivian Metze, John Miller, Rachel Montgomery, Sam Montgomery, Don Morrison, Beebe Myers, Jade Northrup, Peggy Ogburn, Dallas Phelps, Bill Reasonover, David Reuwer, Barbara Rogers, Bert Rush, Barbara Russ, Alfred Smyrl, Jak and Betty Smyrl, Kathee Stahl, Andee Steen, Carl Truesdale, Joe Upchurch Jr., A. F. Watts, Tom Webb, Paul White, Alden Wooten, and Lois Zemp.

Certainly this project would not have come to fruition without financial support from the community. The Kershaw County Historical Society is most appreciative for grants and donations from the Frederick S. Upton Foundation; the John T. Stevens Foundation; the South Financial Group; the Humanities Council^{SC}; the Kershaw County Endowment / Central Carolina Community Foundation; Mr. and Mrs. D. Carlyle Baxley; Sheheen, Hancock & Godwin, LLP; Dr. John W. Bonner Jr.; Blue Cross–Blue Shield of South Carolina; and Mr. William T. Miller. The society is also extremely grateful for contributions from Savage, Royall & Sheheen, LLP; First Palmetto Savings Bank, FSB; Kennedy Insurance Agency; Mr. John R. Speaks; Dr. and Mrs. M. Michael Bonner; Dr. Shannon DuBose; Mrs. Elsie Goins; Senator Donald H. Holland; the Camden Garden Club; Colonel Frank K. Babbitt Jr.; Russell and Jeffcoat Realtors, Inc.; Ms. Evelyn Wooten; Mr. and Mrs. J. W. Martin Jr.; Mr. Stewart Lindsay; Cantey, Tiller, Pierce & Associates, LLP; Mr. and Mrs. Pierce W. Cantey; Mrs. Virginia Davidson; Mr. Sam Boykin Hay; and Mrs. E. B. Beard.

1

Landscapes

An Overview

First named and set apart in 1791, Kershaw County lies on a diagonal within the upper South Carolina midlands. Presently about 726 square miles in size, the county once extended a few miles further on both its upper and lower boundaries. Its map location is broadly generalized as "a hundred miles to the mountains and a hundred miles to the ocean." For countless generations human beings have made their homes in the area. Threads of the lives of past and present inhabitants are woven throughout the broad tapestry of America's story.

Thousands of years before written records, nomadic bands of native people seasonally inhabited the hills, woodlands, and river bottoms of the present county area. Relics they left behind testify to their presence. Centuries ago European adventurers to the newly claimed continent of America encountered tribal dwellers during brief forays into local areas. Only within the past two hundred to three hundred years, newcomers of European and African heritages began to transform the primal landscape with the settlements that evolved into the present way of life. A succession of traders, farmers, families, laborers, soldiers, preachers, teachers, merchants, and other builders of enterprise had distinctive impact. Not all changes were peaceful ones. A rich texture of struggle, loss, and accomplishment underlies the history of Kershaw County.

Natural Regions

Before the area was home to any man, the land took shape over long geologic ages, and different sections developed distinct natural characteristics. Landforms of upper and lower sections of the county identify them as parts of two different geographic regions, Piedmont and Coastal Plain. The Sandhills section and other distinct areas along the fall line between the two regions add to a noteworthy range of diversity.[1]

Piedmont

According to geologists, several hundred million years ago, in the Paleozoic era, the continents divided, drifted apart, collided, and reshaped. In that era and under volcanic influence, the underlying crystalline bedrock of Kershaw County formed. Much of it is granite, partially crossed by a belt of slate that some believe

Rock outcroppings on high hills along the roadside just south of Liberty Hill

was transferred here during continental shifting. Conditions for valuable water and mineral resources resulted during these formations.

In the northwestern quarter of the county, where high hills are prominent, the soil is richly colored clay that tends toward red and is especially favorable to native hardwood trees. Ancient rocks lie close to the surface, and large boulders or expanses of flat weathered rock often protrude from the variously textured strata. Picturesque outcroppings are visually striking along precipitous banks of the upper Wateree River, in areas around Liberty Hill and toward Westville, and along boundaries with Lancaster and Fairfield counties. These Piedmont features are characteristic of the South Carolina Piedmont Plateau, which stretches gradually upward to the Appalachian Blue Ridge Mountains.

Coastal Plain and Sandhills

The South Carolina Coastal Plain, which includes most of the state, descends from the Piedmont edge toward the Atlantic Ocean. Much of the plain formed from sediments of an ancient ocean that once reached much higher. In the warm climate of the Cretaceous period, when dinosaurs died out, the ocean was at its height and lapped across part of present Kershaw County. A narrow divisional belt of disconnected sandhills appears between what is observed of the Piedmont and Coastal Plain environments. Sandhills are dry, sandy, infertile rolling hills that have long been regarded as remnants of coastal dunes and delta deposits left behind millions of years ago on the edge of the old seacoast.

Sandhills loop irregularly through Kershaw County from its northeastern boundary with Chesterfield County to its southwestern boundary with Richland County, extending from Bethune to Cassatt, Camden, Lugoff, and Elgin. Dominant native growth of loblolly and longleaf pines long ago gave the Sandhills region the name "the pine belt." Bottomlands and flatlands of the Coastal Plain environment are more often obvious southward around Boykin and areas bordering Lee and Sumter counties.

Fall Line

The geologic edge where Piedmont and Coastal Plain formations meet is the fall line. Extending from New Jersey to Georgia, the Atlantic coast fall line bisects Kershaw County irregularly, although its map position is generally oversimplified as a straight line. Fall-line regions are most obvious along rivers and creeks, where waters flowing down swiftly from higher areas of harder Piedmont rock

Narrow marks of wagon wheels on an old Lugoff route, circa 1915, passing through the sand and longleaf pines of the region. Courtesy of Camden Archives

eroded softer Coastal Plain formations over time and created shoals or falls. Here shallows and rocky protrusions provided early people with convenient fords for crossing riverbeds. Locally such areas gave access to important fishing and hunting grounds for Native Americans who were attracted by an abundance of resources from two differing environments. The same advantages appealed to colonial settlers.

In early days river craft from the coast could not safely navigate beyond the fall line. At this point early travelers typically unloaded goods they had brought by river from lower regions and continued their journey by land. For a return trip by river they reloaded their vessels below the fall line with goods from upper regions. Because of such exchanges at the fall line, settlements that later grew into cities tended to form at such locations. About one mile from the flooding lowlands of the Wateree River, along prehistoric trading paths and just below the fall line, the eighteenth-century settlement at Camden developed into a commercial gateway of coastal and inland exchange.[2] In frontier days natural energy at the fall line was harnessed for flume and waterwheel industries and later, notably at Wateree Dam, for hydroelectric power.[3]

Rivers

Two river systems pass through or edge Kershaw County in northerly to southerly directions—westward the Wateree and eastward the forked Lynches. In addition, just inside the county's eastern boundary, swamp waters near the Sandy Grove community collect as tributaries to the head of a third river, the Black River, which rises in neighboring Lee County.

In the lower parts of the county, the Wateree and the Lynches flow more slowly and grow darkly stained from tannins leached from trees and decayed matter. Here they become, like the Black River, blackwater rivers. Elsewhere their nature differs.

The upper Wateree River is associated with Piedmont terrain. Along the Blue Ridge near Asheville, North Carolina, trickling mountain waters give rise to the Catawba River, which flows downward into South Carolina. As the waters of the Catawba pass from Lancaster County into Kershaw County, the name of the channel changes to the Wateree River. The Catawba and the Wateree are in reality the same river; the same body of water bears one name in Lancaster County and northward and another name in Kershaw County and southward. The individual names are remnants of early times and identify specific Native American tribes that once lived on the respective banks.

Until 1919 the Wateree River was the county's upper northwestern boundary line. Since completion of the Wateree Dam for hydroelectric power, the upper river channel has been submerged in the deep backwaters of Lake Wateree, the present boundary. Below the dam the river returns to a natural channel, passing

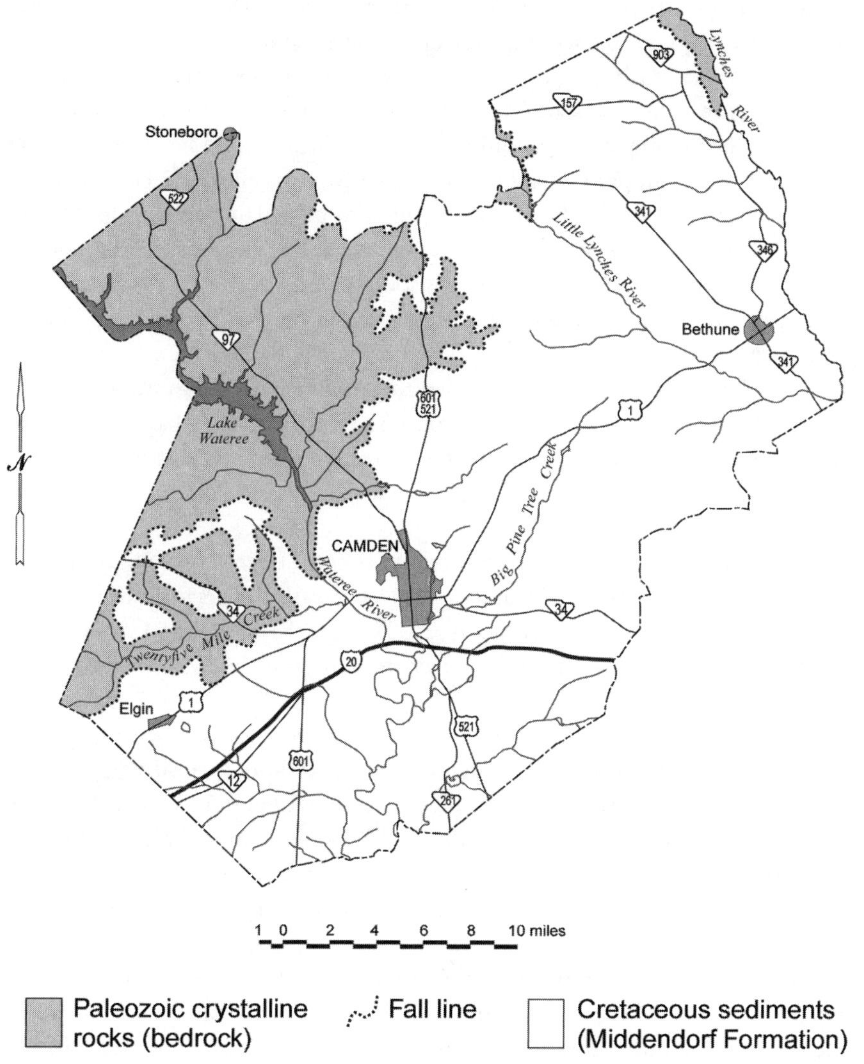

A precise rendering of the fall line in Kershaw County. Courtesy of the South Carolina Department of Natural Resources

over rocky shoals through some Piedmont banks and changing as it descends southward. Below Camden the Wateree is a Coastal Plain river and meanders snakelike through the sandy mud and hardwood swamps of the county's southwestern flatlands. In 2009 local and national conservation groups opened the first phase of the Wateree River Blue Trail, planned as a seventy-five-mile water trail for canoeing and kayaking. From the Wateree Dam and to the river's confluence, the trail was designed to encourage the appreciation and conservation of nature.

The Big Lynches River, lately identified as simply the Lynches River, rises just above the North Carolina state line and travels along most of the eastern boundary of Kershaw County in predominantly sandhill terrain. The Little Lynches River originates in upper Lancaster County, where it is called a creek. The Little Lynches at first collects Piedmont waters but also travels through sandhills most of its way through Kershaw County. In an area early designated as the Fork of the Lynches, the Big and Little Lynches join as one body in the swampy lowlands below the town of Bethune and continue the sinuous journey of a Coastal Plain river.[4]

As the river systems leave Kershaw County and continue seaward, they eventually become part of two of South Carolina's three great ocean-basin rivers. The Wateree joins the Congaree to form the Santee, and the Lynches becomes part of the Pee Dee, which the Black also joins. The Santee and Pee Dee rivers empty into the Atlantic Ocean.

Historically throughout Kershaw County the most agriculturally productive soils have been those affected by alluvial deposits near its rivers and creeks. These areas include the bottomlands along the Wateree River below Camden and around Boykin and the bottomlands near Bethune and the Lynches fork.

Natural Curiosities

Within each section of the county, natural oddities pique curiosity. An inaccessible sandstone "mountain," easily visible from long distances southwest of Lugoff, rises two hundred feet above the level floodplains of the Wateree Swamp. The eye-catching prominence has been called, after various owners, Nixon's Mount, English Mount, Dunn's Mount, and Black's Mount. In some areas east of Camden, ball-sized bubbles of hollow rock with colored powders inside are picked up from the sandy soil. Tradition holds that native warriors long ago decorated their bodies with colors made from contents of these ancient "paint rocks." Neighborhood development in recent decades has smoothed out the extreme edges of the Paint Hill bluff, later called the Precipice, a high ridge overlooking eastern Camden with long views over the Wateree Valley. Older citizens recall the steep eroded banks and exposed colors of the clay that gave the landmark on the town's edge its former names.

Early in the age of aviation, aerial photographs drew attention to specific isolated wetlands in Atlantic coastal states, mostly the Carolinas and Georgia. Known as Carolina bays, the elliptical depressions, which are home to rare and endangered species, are also found in Kershaw County. In the Shepard community between Camden and Cassatt, two adjoining bays are protected as the Savage Bay Heritage Preserve. It is believed that other such bays once existed in the local area. Despite many theories, including effects of ancient meteorites striking Earth, bay origins remain a mystery.[5]

Sportsmen who boat along the lower Wateree River are familiar with other watery landmarks, including various bends or "necks" and oxbows such as Devil's Elbow. The fork area of the Lynches has also been known by the same colorful nickname. Throughout the county all but a few once-familiar springs have been drained or closed off in modern times. They are remembered today only through place names: Brevard Springs, Brewer Spring, Cedar Spring, Cold Spring, Cool Springs, Green Spring, Jumelle Spring, Mineral Spring, Muster Spring, Rock Spring, Sandy Spring, Spring Branch, Spring Lake, Spring Village, Springdale, Springhill, and Springvale. Of these springs, the largest one was aptly known as Big Springs. Lying along the Lynches River bordering Chesterfield County, it was successfully promoted for several decades as a health resort.

Built by nature rather than by man, White Pond near Elgin has been a constant landmark on maps since the early 1800s. Always known by the same name, the sizable natural pond was historically observed to lack sustained inflow, and by old tradition it was rumored "bottomless." However, it was also known at times to go dry and remains threatened by drought and shrinking water tables. In recent years scientists from around the world have studied core samples from

A Carolina bay in the Savage Bay Heritage Preserve

the bottom of the privately owned and protected pond. Studies of Ice Age temperatures for nonglaciated areas and of plant and animal life in ancient times have cited data from relatively undisturbed White Pond.

In the upper sections of the county, several rock formations are individually distinctive. The Wateree Dam stretches far beneath its rugged eastern promontory, a towering granite bluff known as Eagle's Nest, which affords long views of the river system. Another rocky landmark that has impressed visitors from earliest times is the balanced boulder Hanging Rock, whose area was once on the Kershaw County border and is now in Lancaster County. Further inside the county a sheltering formation called Kelly Rock was named for a Civil War objector said to have hidden there. Near Liberty Hill a large expanse of exposed granite was better known in earlier days when the unpaved road that passes over it was more heavily traveled. Here curiously twisted trees and varied mosses grow from cracks in several acres of weathering rock. Exposed solid granite expanses in another part of the upper county prompted the name of the old community of Flat Rock, where the rock has been quarried extensively since early times. Smooth-veined, pink-hued granite of the area now adjoining Lancaster County was selected for the main features of the World War II monument dedicated in 2004 in Washington, D.C.

Directions of Settlement

A sense of terrain and direction has long helped identify the area of Kershaw County and the sections within it. By common reference the originally settled lower coast of South Carolina was early known as the "lowcountry." Frontier communities further inland—such as Camden, which claims title as the state's oldest inland (interior) city—lay in what was called the "backcountry" during colonial days and the "upcountry" afterward. In modern times central Carolina counties, including Kershaw, have popularly adopted the descriptor "midlands."

Local colloquial speech exhibited a familiar sense of direction. From the county seat at Camden people traveled "up the country" (northward to the high hills along the Wateree) or "down the country" (southward to the flatter lands along the river). They went "out to the country" (to the sandhills) when traveling eastward or "over the river" if they crossed the Wateree. Traveling further westward required going "over the river and out to the country." Hunters went "out in the woods" and "down in the swamp." Historian Harvey Teal has pointed out to the authors that early modes of travel by foot or on horseback made people keenly aware of going uphill or downhill. Agricultural tasks called attention to soil, rocks, watersheds, and geographical features, such as directional flow of streams. These are details that modern people with desk jobs and automobiles seem less likely to notice.

The elevations of Kershaw County that served as early direction markers continued in use as place names, many still familiar. The largest number of them identify communities, schools, churches, plantation homes, voting precincts, or post offices by names of high points. Some are Belk Hill, Broom Hill, Buck Hill, Cantey Hill, Carter Hill, Chalk Hill, Flint Hill, Funderburk Hill, Green Hill, Hobkirk('s) Hill, Jumelle Hill, Knights Hill, Liberty Hill, Lizard Hill, Magazine Hill, Malvern Hill, McCaa's Hill, Meroney Hill, and Nelson's Hill. Others are Paint Hill, Pindar Hill, Pine Tree Hill, Plane Hill, Pleasant Hill, Red Hill (two different areas), Rock Hill, Sandy Hill, Shaylor's Hill, Springhill, Stoney Hill, Sunny Hill, Sunnyhill, Thorn Hill, Tickle Hill, Trent Hill, and Zion Hill.

In many cases the "hill" designation referred not to a single high spot but to a general elevation that included several rises and denoted a community area rather than a single prominence. Twentieth-century subdivision names are more precise when describing large areas and use plural forms: Hillsdale, Kirkover Hills, Precipice Hills, Sandwood Hills, and Wateree Hills. Other names in the county suggestive of elevations are Mt. Joshua, Mt. Moriah, Mt. Pisgah, Mt. Pleasant, Mt. Prospect, and Mt. Zion, as well as Belmont, Branham Heights, Claremont, Forest Heights, Kirkwood Heights, Norris Heights, and Windsor Heights.

Far fewer names celebrate low points. These include Gillies Ditch, Green Valley, Gully Branch, Indian Ditch, Jumping Gully, Muddy Bottom, Rattlesnake Bottom, Sip Hole, and Springvale. Even fewer names mark level places: Flat Branch, Flat Creek, Flat Rock, Pine Flat, and Sandy Level. Midway, which might sound like a level place, was instead named as a halfway point.

County Boundary Lines

Before 1791 when the specific name Kershaw County was given by the state legislature, the area inside those original boundaries already had a history as part of larger entities. More than a century earlier the area lay within Craven County, and shortly before the Revolution it was within Camden District. Its ecclesiastical position was within the vast St. Mark's Parish. Under the new Whig government the opposite sides of the Wateree River voted in different districts, designated the District Eastward of the Wateree and the District Westward of the Wateree. The areas were then rejoined as part of newly created Lancaster County, before being divided somewhat similarly to present boundaries and being set aside as Kershaw County (or for many years as Kershaw District). Boundary-line adjustments up to modern years since have resulted in alterations and annexations, so that some borderline sections of the original county—Ionia, Lucknow, Stoneboro, parts of the old Tiller's Ferry settlement, and the entire town of Kershaw—now lie within neighboring counties.[6]

Travel Routes

Since early times the main directions of travel through the Kershaw County area have followed similar patterns. Prehistoric people wore down the first human paths as hunters followed animal trails along waterways and naturally weathered ridges. Rivers and winding footpaths, often merely faint traces in the wilderness, gave access for explorers and their followers to blaze their way into the interior of America. Pioneer settlers of European and African ancestry struggled to build roads for wheeled transport. These routes generally followed the natural directions of the native paths and followed ridges for convenience of drainage and exposure.

A maze of modern highways connects to straightened, paved versions of ancient trails and pioneer roadbeds. Early roads led directly onward to major interior or coastal areas, southward toward present Charleston and Georgetown, northward toward present Charlotte, eastward toward present Cheraw, and westward toward the present capital city of Columbia. Modern versions of these main roads pass within or at the edge of Camden, the county's first settlement and nearly always its seat, except for the few years the area was part of old Lancaster County. The first national highway, U.S. Highway 1, is one arm of Camden's main intersection at Broad and DeKalb streets, "the crossroads of the county." The superhighway Interstate 20 (I-20) connects at the city's southern entrance. Both these modern routes at or near Camden also bridge the Wateree River, itself once a major route of transportation.

Communities

For most of the county's history, the agricultural lifestyles that developed in the early area of Kershaw County did not foster growth of commercial towns, even small ones, aside from its one center at Camden. Instead trading posts or country stores and mills developed one by one along main travel routes. The rustic enterprises became social centers, even post offices and voting polls. As churches and schools collected near the places where people met, communities grew up. Some passed away in only a short time; some lasted for generations.

After trade was established at colonial Camden, a second pre–Revolutionary War trading post developed at Granny's (Grannies) Quarter Creek along the main road to the interior. Likely a store also operated along the eastward route in the lower Lynches River area that became Tiller's Ferry. In the early nineteenth century, near the upper Wateree River, Liberty Hill grew into a residential village of wealthy planters who cultivated surrounding areas before the Civil War ended their prosperity. Overall commercial communities were still few by 1883, when the Board of Agriculture of South Carolina reported: "Kershaw County has three towns and trading settlements, with eighty-four stores, to-wit: Camden, seventy-eight stores; Flat Rock, five stores; Welche's, one store. Of this number six sell liquors, two hardware, six dry goods, twenty-one miscellaneous articles, and forty-nine general merchandise. Four are kept by colored persons. The estimated wealth of the store keepers is $380,000."[7]

The economic portrait of the county soon changed, however. By the turn of the twentieth century prospects had improved as new railroad lines began drawing scattered businesses and country dwellers closer to station stops. The present towns of Bethune, Cassatt, Elgin (then named Blaney), Kershaw, and Lugoff had such origins. Other citizens saw improved opportunity in the cotton mills developing concurrently with the railroads and moved into newly organized mill villages. In eastern Camden the Wateree (Kendall) and Hermitage mill villages provided homes and communities with strong ties among employees of those pioneering industries. As modern industrial expansion continued in the following decades, Bethune, Kershaw, and Lugoff increased in size and opportunities.

By the late twentieth century the county's population growth had shifted to rapid development of suburban homes west of the Wateree and within commuting distance of jobs in urban Columbia, sprawling toward Kershaw County. Economic and social trends of early-twenty-first-century America have been quickly altering the face of Kershaw County. Environmental challenges have arisen as home development and recreational use have increased in natural settings such as Lake Wateree and as industrial needs have created ever-growing waste deposits in the atmosphere, soil, and waterways. Conservation and preservation organizations provide perspectives to balance present needs and long-term ideals.

The tourism industry in Kershaw County promotes old homes, antique markets, and equine traditions of the past, such as the steeplechase races, polo, and the hunt club. Other popular sports—such as golf, fishing, and hunting—also actively encourage natural preservation. The Historic Camden Revolutionary War Site, an outdoor museum complex of more than one hundred acres, is the area's most encompassing educational and preservation activity. Historic Boykin seeks to keep alive rural ways, and preservation of historic homes is encouraged throughout the county. In collecting historical materials for the use of modern researchers, the Camden Archives and Museum covers all Kershaw County, as well as other areas that were once part of the old Camden District.

The varied natural features that formed in ancient times have continued to influence historic and present times. Rocky highlands, sandhills, arid plains, and watery swamps have offered agricultural and developmental assets as well as challenges. Bottomlands of rich soil once bred disease-bearing insects. Swift-moving rivers and creeks that provided transportation and waterpower once flooded both seasonally and unpredictably, periodically isolating communities and threatening lives. Draining wetlands, building bridges, and industrializing the economy have solved some dilemmas and have created others.

Overall the process of settling Kershaw County has been a complex pattern of loss and gain. It has included displacement of native peoples, cultural adaptations of European and African newcomers, struggles of slavery, economic

Architect Henry D. Boykin II's sketch of the county seal he designed in the 1960s for the front of the new Kershaw County Courthouse at Camden. The seal depicts river, hills, and pines overlooked by Native American protector King Hagler. Courtesy of the Camden Archives

fluctuations, migrations in and out, and irreversible environmental alterations. Local roles in the conflicts of the American Revolution and the Civil War, both of which brought invading armies onto local soil, played a part in the defining of national identity and national destiny. The area's people have since continued significant and responsible roles. The stories of Kershaw County's history, complex and diverse, continue to unfold in its daily life.

2

Footpaths

The First Inhabitants

By twelve thousand years ago, perhaps earlier according to recent findings, human beings may have been living in the area that would become Kershaw County.[1] Relics, fossils, and ancient remains reveal the local presence of nomads and dwellers of prehistoric millennia. Archaeologists and anthropologists continue to identify and interpret artifacts that are the only records of people who did not leave written accounts.[2] These findings enlarge descriptions of Native American cultures here prior to the written records of outsiders, the European explorers who encountered the early people less than five hundred years ago.

Paleo-Indians

The wanderers who made early incursions into the local area are called Paleo-Indians, meaning "ancient," by anthropologists. These people were hunters and gatherers who ranged broadly for survival in a rugged world of harsh climates. By the end of the last Ice Age, some Paleo people in small groups were following southeastern river valleys and exposed upland animal trails to gather plants and hunt game. They sheltered in naturally protected areas such as riverbank overhangs and rock outcroppings. A history of the Stoneboro community describes several rocky sites along the boundary of present Kershaw and Lancaster counties that these ancient people may have used, such as Hanging Rock and Kelly Rock.[3]

Paleo-Indian hunters are believed to have come here following trails of both small and large animals, including some that became extinct as the earth's climate changed. Fossil remains of ancient creatures such as woolly mammoths, mastodons, giant ground sloths, saber-toothed tigers, and large bison have been uncovered in South Carolina. Extensive excavations have not been done in Kershaw County, but it is reasonably presumed that such animals also roamed here.[4]

Cooperating in small bands, hunters are believed to have driven large prey over high ledges or surrounded prey that were feeding or drinking, especially in low bottoms. Here they attacked from higher ground by hurling large rocks, wielding clubs, and thrusting with sharpened spears, often tipped with bone or stone points. Stone tools of Paleo design, including spear points, knives, and scrapers, have been found in Kershaw County.[5]

A circa 1950 photograph of relics collected by C. D. Cunningham, Liberty Hill postmaster. Courtesy of the Rachel Montgomery family

Archaic Indians

By ten thousand years ago the climate had warmed, and plants and animals more similar to modern ones had adapted to temperatures not much different from present conditions. Deciduous and pine forests were expanding. People of this period, which lasted until about three thousand years ago, are called Archaic Indians ("survivors of an earlier time") for their traditions, which developed out of the Paleo way of life. Not constantly wandering, they alternately settled and moved in families or small bands, likely according to season, in order to gather plants, to fish, and to hunt at advantageous times. Deer and small wood bison fed here on plains and grassland floors of the spreading forests. Along the shoals of the Wateree, Archaic people could club or spear large fish lazing in low rocky pools and use bone hooks and traps to catch smaller ones.

Polished stone tools, such as axes, improved old technology. Archaic hunters enhanced spear-throwing ability by use of stone weights with a device called the "atatl," and they shaped stems on many projectile points to attach them more easily to shafts. First attempts at making clay pottery yielded rough, undecorated containers strengthened with plant fibers. For cooking stews, women dropped heated rocks into hollowed-out stone vessels. A hole bored in such a rock allowed a cook to lift it with a stick.

Archaic people also developed use of grinding stones, or mortars, to process seeds and nuts. Both shells and kernels were ground or pounded together, perhaps mixed with water to separate some of the woody particles, and were consumed in the diet. Grinding stones and other rocks worn by fire-making processes have often been found locally. Mortars carved into fixed rock are also still in existence, such as one near the Stoneboro crossroad. Although they cannot be precisely dated, the artifacts are believed to be of Native American origin. The most widely known, Mortar Rock, is a county-owned site at Liberty Hill. The round circle precisely hollowed in the granite outcropping is artistically surrounded by an incised eyelike decoration. It has long been speculated that the site held ancient ceremonial significance.

Prearranged meetings, usually in high places visible from a distance, brought together various bands or tribes for purposes of trade, courtship, and social exchange. Thus early people who were frequently isolated from one another exchanged bloodlines, natural materials, works of their hands, and ideas of various cultures and places. Gradually over time newer traditions evolved from older ways, many of which also continued in practice.

Woodlands Indians

From the end of the Archaic period until about 950 C.E., the prominent culture was that of the Woodlands period, named for the forest-dominated landscapes surrounding the natives' pole-and-bark homes. By now gradual transition had been made toward more permanent villages and a lifestyle based on the cultivation of plants in forest openings and in clearings near rivers and streams. Crops included vining squashes, pumpkins, gourds, and beans, as well as corn, edible sunflowers, and tobacco. Baskets woven with grasses, vines, or flexible wood strips provided means of collecting and storing crops, and weaving techniques also fashioned fish traps for river shoals and creeks.

Hunting improved with the development of the all-important bow and arrow. Hunters typically shaped points for their arrows from locally available material, such as milky quartz, white stone locally called "flint rock," distinctive in upper parts of the county. More-skillful, decorated pottery also emerged. Clay vessels, tempered with sand and decorated before firing, were fashioned for food storage, for cooking, and for burial urns. Many stone and clay relics have been found in Kershaw County, sometimes in location patterns that suggest sites of camps and travel paths of the native peoples. Varied designs and decorations of pottery samples and sherds, or broken pieces, also reveal interactions and exchange of ideas with other locales. Relics of different periods overlap at many sites, revealing long-term use of advantageous areas.

Although initial use of the dugout canoe predates the Woodlands period, vessels continued to have important use during this time and on through the

A reconstructed piece of Native American pottery on display at the Camden Archives

historic colonial and plantation periods. Fashioned of a single trunk of a durable tree, often cypress, each canoe was carefully crafted. Slowly burning fires, fueled by strategic applications of resins, were skillfully tended to break down fibers on the inside of the trunk while wet clay protected areas not to be burned. The native builders employed stone implements as they "dug out" the shell and completed the final shaping. With the narrow, shallow-draft canoes, boatmen skillfully maneuvered uneven-bottomed, log-jammed river sections like those in the Kershaw County area.[6]

Fire was a tool of major importance to Woodlands people, as well as a force of power to earlier man. Fire not only warmed outdoor dwellers but also cooked food and herbal medicines, preserved animal skins for clothing and protection, tempered wood and pottery, cleared areas for settlement and agriculture, and purified remains of illness and death. Once or twice yearly hunters set forest floors afire. Observing results of natural fires begun in woodlands by lightning or combustion, native peoples used routine burnings to keep the forest floors where they hunted and lived relatively clear of underbrush. They were thus able to observe both game and potential human enemies from some distance, as well as more easily track either of them from prints impressed in the soil.

The burning of forests and agricultural fields returned certain nutrients to the soil and promoted specialized growth. Regular, low burnings, sometimes extending for miles and lasting for days, were favorable to longleaf pines and wire grass, both of which adapted well to sandhill soils. Thus the towering woodlands of Kershaw County that were traveled by explorers and early colonials had long been influenced by human as well as natural design.

Mississippian Mound Builders

According to prevailing interpretation, around 950 C.E., in the middle of the Dark Ages in Europe, a different group of people moved into the Wateree Valley. They brought to prominence a separate, complex culture that lasted here for more than six centuries, enduring through the time of early European contact.[7] The Mississippian people, to whom the later historic Creek Indians are believed to be related, pushed aside for some time the Siouan-speaking Piedmont Woodlands people, to whom are related the later historic Catawba and Wateree Indians known to English settlers.[8] The Mississippians had separate art forms, customs, and religion, and they possibly had a dissimilar language. Their government consisted of related chiefdoms controlled from temple mound complexes.

Although some mound burials in the Southeast have been associated with Woodlands traditions as well, the Mississippians are often referred to as "the mound builders" because of the prominence they gave in daily life and government to their ceremonial earthen works. Almost a dozen local "ancient monuments" or "mounts," as they were also sometimes called, attracted the attention of explorers and settlers in historic times. Recent studies of the few existing Kershaw County mounds, although incompletely explored, connect them with Mississippian origin. This culture early occupied Belmont Neck, a meandering loop of the Wateree River below Camden, and over time developed a series of mound complexes and villages within the floodplains throughout the river valley. The well-preserved site called Adamson Mound, on private property at the edge of present Camden, was one such early complex.

Migrating descendants of the great culture that had waned in the middle Mississippi Valley at places such as Cahokia near modern St. Louis, Missouri, apparently found their way here through Alabama and Georgia and are more particularly identified as South Appalachian Mississippians. Similar traditions existed at Moundsville in Alabama, at Etowah and Ocmulgee National Monument in Georgia, and at Town Creek in North Carolina, among other southeastern sites. All occupied floodplains for agricultural benefits, produced intricate artwork that included elaborate pottery, and surrounded town residences and central mounds with palisade walls for protection.

Coordinated toil was required in building the mounds, which served various purposes. Dirt dug with sticks and stone implements was carried basketful by basketful to the top of the heap and trod until firm by workers' feet. Residences of elite rulers topped some mounds, as did temples or other public structures with thatched roofs and rounded, clay-covered log walls. Most of the people lived in villages nearby, tending crops, fishing, hunting, and pursuing specialized crafts.

Present scholarship suggests that the major mounds in Kershaw County were part of the powerful chiefdom of Cofitachiqui, described by sixteenth-century Spanish explorers and associated with a way of life already endangered by the time it was first being written about. The Cofitachiqui belonged to times both prehistoric and historic, but the only contemporary written records of these people were penned by those who were a threat to them, observers sometimes ignorant of or insensitive to the meaning of what they saw.[9]

For centuries and on separate continents both Native American tribes and European countries had warred among themselves for survival and ascendancy. Therefore, when factions of both continents met at the same place, conflicts and struggle were inevitable. As deadly as warfare was, the effects of European diseases proved even deadlier to Native Americans. Diseases never encountered before

The ancient Adamson Mound rising above the floodplain near downtown Camden

decimated large numbers of natives, even whole tribes, because of lack of immunity and inexperience with treatment. Some of the earliest records describing native people in the Kershaw County area reflect their decreasing population—the beginning of their end.

European Contacts

In the centuries following the early contacts with Europeans, diverse theories about Spanish explorers' first routes through the uncharted wilderness emerged as attempts were made to trace their ancient travels onto modern maps.[10] Gradually clearer pictures have emerged regarding an extensive chiefdom in which the present area of Kershaw County once lay. Most interpretations since the 1980s locate the central power of Cofitachiqui in the Wateree River Valley, and some suggest that the mound complex on historic Mulberry Plantation, a short distance south of Camden, was its main city at the time of the first documented European visitation in the area.[11]

Hernando de Soto

By the first of May 1540, less than half a century after Columbus's arrival in the New World, the Spanish conquistador Hernando de Soto and his men reached the west bank of the river opposite the main town of the chiefdom they had been seeking. In Florida captive Indians had described a vast region in the northeast where Cofitachiqui, a large area of considerable wealth, was ruled by a female chief. Expecting to find gold there, De Soto had traveled northward, foraging supplies as he led his army of six hundred hungry men, three hundred horses, black slaves, and Indian captives along native paths and inland rivers. If interpretations are correct, the river he reached was the Wateree River, and the people he was looking for were living near present Camden.

De Soto's scribes give details of his encounter with the ruler, or the ruler's female relative as emissary—"La Cacica," the "Lady" or "Queen" of Cofitachiqui. Carried to the shore on a decorated litter, the young, attractive leader, dressed in delicate white, was paddled in a canopied canoe to welcome De Soto. Speaking to him with poise and regal bearing, she presented him in good will with a string of river pearls she had removed from around her neck.

The Indians then provided transportation across the river and gave the guests gifts, food, and lodging. Half of the dwellings in the village were given over to house them, indicating a town of extensive size. After first accepting hospitality, the Spaniards then began their intended search for precious metals among tribal holdings. They explored nearby public and private areas and rummaged through Cofitachiqui's mound-top platform temples. Some reports describe finding sacred burial structures where larger-than-life-sized wooden statues guarded bones of ancestors.

When the invaders also came upon articles of European manufacture, including beads and rosaries, they concluded that the people had made previous contact with the Spaniard Vásquez de Ayllón, who had led an expedition to South Carolina a dozen years earlier. Some of De Soto's men apparently examined other local mound areas they found vacated, possibly including Belmont Neck and the Adamson Mound. Reportedly, the young leader told De Soto that her people had been visited for several years by a mysterious epidemic, and many had died. Some scientists believe that effects of European diseases had already been spread to the Cofitachiqui.

Throughout their searches the Spaniards reported finding decorations of shells and freshwater pearls, sheets of mica, and hammered copper, but not the gold or silver they had expected. When food supplies were exhausted, the hosts told De Soto about a province further inland beyond the mountains. There, they said, was much food as well as gold and silver to be found. Almost two weeks after their arrival, the Spanish gathered for themselves the portable treasures of Cofitachiqui and went in search of alleged riches further away. As protection, De Soto forced the lady-queen to accompany them as guide and interpreter. However, after some days or weeks the young captive escaped, reportedly taking with her the most valuable box of pearls the Spaniards had ransacked from her people.[12]

Juan Pardo

Other European countries were also seeking to establish hold in the New World, just as they rivaled Spain in the Old World. In 1562 France established the first European colony in what became South Carolina, a part of the vast territory Spain claimed as "La Florida." Charlesport, the fledgling French settlement on Port Royal Sound, lasted only one year, but Spain reacted quickly to protect its interests. In 1566, on the same location at present-day Parris Island, South Carolina, Spaniards built a fort and town they named Santa Elena, capital of La Florida. Juan Pardo that year led an exploration of 125 men inland from the new settlement to seek an overland route to Mexico. Then, and again two years later in 1568, his mission took him on various visits among the Cofitachiqui and thus, according to interpretations, into present Kershaw County.

In addition Pardo in various places further inland visited groups of indigenous people who would in later generations rise to prominence in the Kershaw County area—the Guatari (Wateree), then ruled by a female chief, and the Ysa, Issa or Iswa (Catawba). He found both these tribes in present-day western North Carolina. Although Pardo never penetrated beyond the Appalachians, along the way he set up forts and attempted to spread Christianity to the Indians, efforts which endured only briefly. The Wateree, for example, soon killed the party of seventeen soldiers and a corporal Pardo had left behind with them. Eventually in 1587 Santa Elena, like Charlesport, was abandoned. In recent years scholars have found help in pinpointing the route of De Soto's expedition by tracing the more specifically described route of Pardo, who visited several of the same Indian towns in the same order that De Soto traveled.

The last Spanish explorer known to have documented a visit to Cofitachiqui was Pedro de Torres in 1627–28. He reported that the chief, who entertained him well, commanded the respect and obedience of all his vassal chiefs. Yet the presence of Spain by now was beginning to fade in this area of the continent, and the Spanish withdrew from outlying areas to concentrate on the stronghold at St. Augustine, Florida, from which they remained a formidable though more distant threat.

Henry Woodward

If the native people felt themselves more securely in control again after the withdrawal of the first French and Spanish settlers from the coast, these feelings did not long endure. Soon English ships appeared, looking for a site to establish a colony. In 1666 one of the Englishmen, a young surgeon named Henry Woodward, remained behind to minister to Indians at Port Royal Sound and to learn their language. He was so successful in beginning trade with them and with interior tribes that twice the Spaniards at Fort Augustine sent out expeditions to capture him to protect territory they claimed as their own. When the English returned to begin a colony at Port Royal, Woodward cited Spanish threats to encourage his countrymen to settle instead sixty miles up the coast. Thus was Carolina's first permanent settlement, Charles Town (the genesis of later Charleston), begun in 1670.

Woodward, known as South Carolina's first settler, remained important in lowcountry history, only one example being as an instigator of rice planting, the crop which brought the new colony's first agricultural wealth. He also made visits inland to the area of present Kershaw County. From just-established Charles Town, in the summer of 1670 Woodward trekked northwestward for fourteen days, visiting a number of smaller chiefs along the way, to meet with the Cofitachiqui chief whom he called the "Emperor" at his town of a thousand "bowmen." At Woodward's invitation, the emperor visited Charles Town a few months later, in mid-September. The chief visited again on an unknown mission in spring 1672.

Shortly after this time, for reasons and destinations still unclear, the people of Cofitachiqui apparently permanently vacated their territory, a mysterious "disappearance" that anthropologists continue to investigate. Theories being studied include voluntary migration away from European encroachment, involuntary rapid depopulation by disease from European contact, warfare with outlying tribes coming into the vicinity, and absorption into other tribal groups.

An old private drive at Mulberry Plantation that was once a footpath for the Catawba and other native travelers. Courtesy of Peggy Ogburn

Whatever the cause of their absence from their former homeland, no outside visitor to the area from this time forward reported finding lifestyles or cultures as complex as the former ones.

John Lawson

In 1700 the Lords Proprietors, in whom the king of England had vested title to the royal lands of Carolina, commissioned a surveyor to visit their holdings and describe them with an eye toward economic development. Thus on December 28, 1700, a young Englishman named John Lawson left Charles Town with a party of five other Englishmen and five Indians. Traveling through central and upper Carolina, Lawson kept a detailed journal to describe the inhabitants and natural resources he encountered.[13]

Modern examinations identify some of Lawson's route and descriptions with locations in the present Kershaw County area.[14] Much of the way his party traveled along an ancient native trading path known in local record and elsewhere as the Catawba Path, which linked the coast to the deep interior and roughly traced a major route still followed. For example, today's Broad Street in Camden, the center of its main business district, overlies part of the old Catawba Path.

When Lawson arrived, the Cofitachiqui were apparently no longer in the area, for his journal makes no mention of them or their culture in the places where they formerly lived. Along both sides of the Wateree River he found scattered native "plantations,"[15] including old fields and villages. He described a Siouan group, Congaree Indians, in an area below present Camden living in oval wattle-and-daub houses built of mud, sticks, and woven mats and topped with bark roofs. He was told that smallpox had taken the lives of many of the local people. The chief's wife, the "Queen," fed Lawson's party while the chief and his men were off hunting. The journal describes tame fowl six feet tall, perhaps sandhill cranes or whooping cranes. Above the area of Camden, Lawson's group consumed lunch on a quarter-acre-sized rock outcropping, possibly the Flat Rock area, and commented on the abundance of "marble" (granite).

In further travels Lawson encountered the Wateree ("Wateree-Chicaknee") Indians in present Lancaster County and the Catawba ("Esaw") Indians in the North Carolina area. At a later time the different names given the same continuously flowing body of water—the Wateree River in Kershaw County and the Catawba River in Lancaster County—show that the tribes found living along those respective bodies had moved further south than where Lawson encountered them. Both groups would later also be found living within the Kershaw County area.[16] The native name of the Lynches River is said to have been Kadapaw, and the Indians along that body are sometimes called the Kadapaw Indians. Although they at times have been reported as a separate tribal group, the name "Kadapaw" is often considered a pronunciation variation of "Catawba."

In 1709 Lawson's journal was published in England and became a popular travel book that encouraged interest in migration to Carolina and investment in its development. Within only a few decades the area of present Kershaw County would become part of an English plan to develop the backcountry and to attract European settlers to make their homes there.[17]

3 Axes and Boundaries

Frontier Settlement

Ways of life changed dramatically during the 1700s. At the beginning of the century the territory to become Kershaw County was part of that known as "the Waterees." The county area was clearly the home of indigenous people known by that name and dwelling alongside fields they tended on both sides of the Wateree River and possibly on parts of the Lynches.[1] By midcentury people of European and African descent began living in many of those locations, as well as in new clearings and along upper creeks. By the late 1700s the English government, which allowed removal of Native Americans and initiated opportunities for white prosperity, would itself be overthrown by the settlers and the new government of the United States of America instituted.[2] To understand the local story of the American Revolution and its consequences, it is necessary to consider conditions of the eighteenth-century people who became its participants. In the first half of that century the wilderness frontier dominated.

The Edge of Danger

The first wealth made in Carolina, as in the rest of America, grew from trading with the native people. For some time the only Europeans in the backcountry of Carolina were those in that enterprise. The historian Robert L. Meriwether describes some of the early 1700s paths by which traders and natives sought one another in the area of present Kershaw County: "The main path to the Catawbas ran nearly north from the Congarees [present Columbia area] to the west bank of the Wateree, and followed the stream to the [Indian] towns. Another crossed the sandhills from the Congarees to the Wateree villages, and joined a less used path up the eastern side of the Santee and Wateree. Above Pinetree Creek this eastern path forked, one route following the river, the other the ridge between the valleys of the Wateree and Lynches River."[3] Extensions of trails on the west side of the Wateree also connected traders with a main path from the coast to the Cherokee in the upper part of the state.[4]

Along these and similar old native routes, traders led single-file trains of loaded packhorses, harnesses jingling with distinctive bells to identify their businesses. Native people, who had engaged in trade among themselves, were quite willing to trade with the white men and rapidly grew dependent on their goods. Indians were eager to acquire guns and powder, horses, woven fabrics, colored beads and trinkets, metal knives and axes, and strong drink. In exchange, traders accepted mostly deerskins and other hides but also foodstuffs, raw materials, handiwork, services, and sometimes even captive Indians as slaves.[5]

Various tribes welcomed traders as friends and offered lodging near or within their villages. Lawson observed that the traders "travel and abide amongst the Indians for a long space of time; sometimes for a Year, two, or three." Furthermore, he said, "These Men have commonly their Indian Wives . . . instructing 'em in the Affairs and Customs of the Country." Tribes being matriarchal, however, in all unions the children belonged to the mother, and in cases of separation it was "impossible for the Christians to get their Children." However, Lawson claimed, "we often find, that English Men, and other Europeans that have been accustom'd to the Conversation of these savage Women, and their Way of Living, have been so allur'd with that careless sort of Life, as to be constant to their Indian Wife, and her Relations, so long as they liv'd, without ever desiring to return again amongst the English."[6]

Not all traders assimilated into domestic harmony, however, and unscrupulous profiteers among them created irrevocable damage. Exploitation and enslavement of free Indians for debts provoked retaliation in the outbreak of the Yamassee War. In 1715 the coastal Yamassee (Yemassee) Indians, recent allies who had assisted the colonials against the Tuscarora in North Carolina, went to war against the English in order to take revenge for offensive trading practices and for British tolerance of abusive traders.[7] The Wateree and the Catawba, with other Piedmont tribes, sided with the Yamassee, attacking and killing the traders in their territory and joining in the warfare on the coast. There unsuspecting settlers fell sudden victims to ax, knife, rifle, or fire.

During the bloody confrontations nearly four hundred whites died before safety was restored and the Indians were soundly defeated. A peace treaty negotiated in 1717 controlled hostilities through most upper-middle sections of South Carolina by 1718, although isolated outbreaks continued over a few more years. For several decades the English tenuously balanced peace between themselves and still-powerful tribes in the mountains, the Creek and the rival Cherokee. The latter had been the only British ally in the Yamassee War. At the Congarees a garrison and fort operated from 1718 to 1722 to protect trading interests and to shelter area dwellers should there be future attacks.[8] The old path from the Congarees to the Waterees maintained communications between the present areas of Columbia and Camden, still a vital modern link.

After the Yamassee War and a widespread smallpox epidemic that followed in 1718, the Wateree Indians were greatly reduced in number and maintained a much-weakened presence on their lands of which Kershaw County became a part. The Catawba too were seriously reduced but continued for a long period to absorb remnants of other tribes decimated by the triple enemies: war, smallpox, and rum. Though recalled for their ferocity in the Yamassee War, the Catawba now cultivated a different reputation by remaining thereafter allied to the government favored by their white neighbors.[9] To secure their safety the Catawba assumed a peacekeeping role that eventually aided colonial settlement of Kershaw County. Like the Wateree people, whom they eventually assimilated into their tribe, the Catawba hunted, fished, and traded in the county area for many years, returning to traditional camps from season to season. Sites once used by the Wateree became identified with the Catawba.

A Lynches River Barony

Amid the unsettled times some men foresaw the eventual march of English-style civilization into the wilderness and seized opportunities to invest in it. In 1725 Thomas Lowndes, an Englishman, was provost marshal of South Carolina. In 1726 the Lords Proprietors granted him a "barony" (a land grant of about twelve thousand acres or more) that included chunks of the Kershaw County area around the Lynches River. This was but one of four baronies Lowndes received in Carolina, and it was nearly half a century before the local area was surveyed for his descendant Edward Lowndes.[10]

Legal entanglements were complicated. In 1719, following complaints from Carolinians that proprietors failed to assist them with defense debts of the Yamassee War, the king agreed to accept Carolina as a royal colony. Lowndes claimed to have encouraged him to do so. The transition period of buying out proprietors' rights took a decade to settle, during which time Lowndes's barony was granted. It is unclear if profit resulted from later attempts to acquire titles to the ancestral grants. Much of the land then may have been settled under other titles.

Planning for Fredericksburg Township

One legacy of the Yamassee War was the heightened sense of coastal insecurity that encouraged the settling of backcountry areas such as Kershaw County. Lowcountry planters and investors were threatened on all sides—Indians from the wilderness, foreigners by sea, and a rapidly growing African slave population in their midst. In 1730 royal governor Robert Johnson advocated a plan, approved by King George II, for settling the backcountry with Protestant Europeans to buffer coastal communities from inland attacks and to provide white allies in other emergencies. Within part of present Kershaw County, Fredericksburg was laid out as one of the eleven planned "townships," each with space for an English-style town surrounded by outlying acreage to be owned and worked by individual townspeople.[11]

Although no town grew at the designated location in Fredericksburg, the township plan was the impetus for subsequent area settlement and the later trading

Fredericksburg Township and Lynches Fork on a segment of James Cook's 1773 "Map of the Province of South Carolina," which shows early local place names and travel paths in use in Revolutionary times. Courtesy of the Camden Archives

center nearby that became Camden. Throughout most of the colonial era the township name, sometimes later the misstated "Fredericksburg Parish," was used to identify the vicinity. The township name and boundaries remained on land records and some maps for a number of years.[12]

Planning for Fredericksburg had begun on paper and at a distance. As the township plan slowly unfolded on-site in the wilderness, however, its design and intended operation underwent significant alteration. In June 1733, a little more than a year after the birth of the future first American president, George Washington, in Virginia, instructions were written to lay out Fredericksburg at the mouth of the Wateree River. This location would have been in the area where the Wateree and Congaree join to form the Santee River, in the vicinity of the juncture of present Richland, Sumter, and Calhoun counties.

However, the surveyor James St. Julian, engaged in December and given his choice of location, selected instead a Wateree River site thirty-five miles upstream. In February 1734, consistent with the model design to provide each township with a navigable river landing, he laid out "Fredericksburgh" along the east bank of the Wateree, with the location for a town centered at the mouth of Pine Tree Creek, a few miles below present Camden. As his plat shows no indication of Indian habitations, native sites in the area must have been vacated at the time. St. Julian's ink drawing on linen cloth, fragile and almost completely faded, is preserved in the South Carolina Archives.[13]

A prominent feature running the full length of the plat is labeled "Catawba Path." Within township boundaries the path roughly parallels the river at a short distance. On the plat a single line crosses the Catawba Path below Pine Tree Creek, perhaps an intended town street extending to a river landing at its west end and angling at its opposite end along another probable street directed northward toward the creek. Beyond the upper township boundary the Catawba Path continues northward and inland as the river gently curves away westward. Along this upper stretch farther from the river is the part of the path on which the present Broad Street of Camden lies.

The survey markers for the township indicated river-bottom growth of sycamores and water oaks, along with pinelands further away. Near the southeastern boundary a "Beaver Dam" lay at the supposed head of Swift Creek, which otherwise did not lie within the township limits. The "Swamp" indicated above Swift Creek and along the lower township boundary has ever since been blamed for the fact that a settlement did not subsequently thrive at the planned location. In the cold, dry winter season when the surveyor was at work, problems of swamp "miasma" (largely mosquito-borne illnesses) and seasonally flooded lowlands did not present the obstacles they later proved in warm, humid weather.

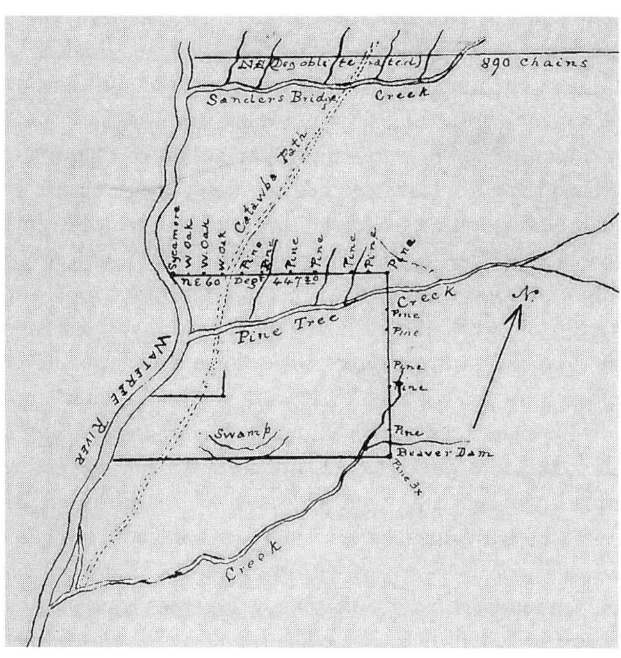

James St. Julian's plat of Fredericksburg in 1734. Copy drawn for Kirkland and Kennedy, *Historic Camden: Colonial and Revolutionary,* 1905

For various miles on the three sides of the township east of the river, St. Julian's plat briefly represents a few features, some with names. "Sanders Creek," with its mouth at the upper outer edge of the area, was marked with "Bridge" where the creek crossed the Catawba Path. The "Creek" at the lower outer edge, believed to be Swift Creek, was marked with a distinctive forking of the stream at the point where the Catawba Path crossed near its mouth.[14] The northeastern corner of the plat edges a waterway that later maps identify as the present Little Lynches River, and the lower portion of the eastern edge "runs in a swamp 340 chains."

Early Place Names

According to tradition, those place names on the map did not originate with the surveyor, although they were possibly given about the same time. The name of Sanders Creek, with its "advanced" feature of a bridge, lends credence to stories of an Indian trader, William Saunders (Sanders), thought to have kept a post there. According to an article citing old sources, Saunders blazed the first road through central Carolina, "between Georgetown and the large Indian Town . . . very near the present site of Camden." The road merged with the Indian trail most of its length. Saunders's home lay between the High Hills of Santee in present Sumter County and Indian Town.[15] The creeks he named lay between his home and his post.

Supposedly, "from local associations and incidents occurring on his first journey to Indian Town," Saunders named creeks in his path. Among those nearby, for example, Rafting Creek (in present Sumter County) was named for the method of transporting his goods safely. In present Kershaw County, Swift Creek was named for its current; Town Creek, for the Indian town on its banks; Pine Tree Creek, "because he cut a tall pine on its bank to assist him in crossing"; and Saunders (Sanders) Creek, north of Camden, for himself.[16] Some accounts, however, indicate that a pine-log crossing was in even earlier use at Pine Tree Creek, possibly placed there by native people. Surely the bridge at Sanders Creek would not have been much more elaborate.

A Trader's Deal

Another nearby Indian trader about that time was Thomas Brown, in the vicinity of present Columbia. In 1743, according to a state record, Brown unsuccessfully petitioned for a government refund for a March 13, 1735, purchase: "a body of land between Santee and Wateree Rivers, inhabited by Wateree Indians, not settled, inhabited or claimed by any white person."[17] It is unclear what Brown or the Wateree Indians knew of the survey of Fredericksburg that had taken place along the river lands the year before his land deal.

Since several years prior to 1735, the claim states, Brown had been "a lycensed trader to the Cattawba Indians" and lived near Congaree Old Fort, where "there are very few inhabitants in that remote part of the country besides your petitioner's family." He purchased the lands, he said, "to introduce whites" into the area. In trading he "used frequently to pass and repass . . . to the Cattawbaw

Nation" and came to know the "goodness" of the Wateree lands, of which "the Wateree Indians were the natural, rightful owners and possessors."

Although the Commons House of Assembly refused to reimburse Brown for the land deal outlawed ex post facto, his bill for £1,172 reveals trade items that natives valued. One-fourth of the bill was for heavy yard goods, primarily "strouds" (closely woven woolen broadcloths), "plains" (denimlike fabrics), and white blankets.[18] Provisions for feasting were typically included in important trades, and Brown's list included small amounts of beef and corn, a bushel of salt, and fifteen gallons of rum. In addition the trader gave three guns with gunpowder and bullets, presumably for hunting, as well as forty doeskins for their "worth in ammunition for war." Arms, alcohol, land, and mention of war—it was a typical trading mix, and a recipe that continued to formulate unrest.[19]

Struggles of Settlement

The Wateree Indians still laid claim to their Kershaw County lands even while the colonial government was offering incentives to Protestant European settlers to take up property in Fredericksburg Township. Each prospective family was promised a bounty (such as food and tools), a half-acre lot in the proposed town, and outside the town fifty additional acres per household member (including each indentured servant or slave), with ten years of freedom from quitrents. Takers did not come quickly, however, apparently delayed by cumbersome colonial property procedures as well as by backcountry unrest.

Land acquisition took time and money, even when some fees were waived as encouragement for settlement. Legal papers had to be filed with Charles Town authorities, adding to the slow process. As the first step, on marked boundaries a prospective claim holder filed an intent form, variously a precept, entry, claim, petition, or application. If the land proved available, a warrant was issued, after which a surveyor drew up a plat, or survey, that became part of the final documents. A grant, patent, or title was then issued. Securing titles typically involved a number of years, some expense, and a large degree of trouble and patience. Some early dwellers, of whom there are reports but few records, by necessity or choice bypassed the process and took up, without formality, unoccupied land on the fringes of settlement. Some of these "squatters" moved on; some filed later claims.

Kirkland and Kennedy report that "the very first landowner in the vicinity of Camden was one James Ousley, who obtained a precept for 300 acres on the western side of the river, nearly opposite Camden, on January 17, 1733."[20] Orders to lay out Fredericksburg had not yet been issued, however, so Ousley was probably merely speculating on land and did not settle on it.

Only a few persons—perhaps Indian traders, pelt hunters, or squatters—were dwelling in the Kershaw County area in late 1736 when a group of Cheraws living with the Catawba killed a family near Pine Tree Creek. "Neighbours" mentioned in the report sent word to Charles Town in alarm. Authorities ordered a lieutenant with eight men to range the back area for a short time and appealed to the Catawba to control the troublesome band.

Kirkland and Kennedy suggest that the unnamed victims may have been associated with the first group of families who obtained precepts in Fredericksburg Township on February 8, 1737. The two historians therefore consider the following group of family heads, listed with household size in parentheses, to be "the original prospectors of Camden": Adam Strain (4), David Alexander (2), James McGowan (6), Hugh McCutchin (2), Michael Harris (1), William Seawright (5), and Robert Seawright (1). Meriwether says that the first group probably originated as "part of the Scotch-Irish movement which founded Williamsburg" on the Black River, but he thinks that, despite their warrants, "it is not certain that they actually settled on the Wateree."[21]

In 1737, when warrants were given to the first group, the Wateree Indians were loudly protesting settlement on their lands. Colonel Henry Fox, in command of six rangers, was sent as an agent to deal with their "flagrant and insolent Behaviour." By invitation their chief men traveled at least twice to meet with authorities in Charles Town. Although Governor Bull recommended to the Commons House of Assembly that the Wateree be compensated for their claim, there is no record of the result.

After the final meeting in 1739, their remaining numbers moved from the local area to live in their own town within the Catawba Nation on the North Carolina–South Carolina border. According to Kirkland and Kennedy, the Waterees periodically returned to their old homelands to hunt, however, especially along Pine Tree Creek.[22] In the late 1730s Colonel Fox, who had dealt with the protesting Waterees, established his home along the river near Fredericksburg, apparently on the west side since Colonel's Creek in present Richland County is said to have been named for him. By 1741 another militia leader with large holdings, James McGirt, had established a home on the east side of the Wateree River near the lower boundary of Kershaw County.

The primary land takers in the early Fredericksburg area were speculators or planters. One was "Alexander Rattray, Gentleman," who between 1739 and 1741 moved from the lowcountry and settled near Swift Creek with his wife and eight slaves. Fredericksburg was not attracting the shopkeepers and small farmers who had been visualized by the distant planners of a town there. That type of lifestyle did not fit the frontier setting any more than the swampy boundaries of the proposed town suited prospective settlers. About that time references to town lots disappear from records, and the planned town area was eventually held as public property. Scattered homesteads and large-acreage investments instead became the pattern.

Concern grew in the lowcountry that the concentrated population numbers desired in the backcountry would not materialize with scattered large holdings. In fact, isolated plantations would only increase some of the problems that the township plan was designed to alleviate. African slavery in remote areas presented dangers since runaways there had more opportunity to escape their bonds and perhaps to join with troublesome Indians sympathetic with their condition. Some tribes already adopted and sheltered black runaways. However, the prospects of large tracts, virgin soils, and less-fever-prone settings appealed to planters and would-be planters willing to take their chances.

In 1739, to entice settlers expected from Scotland, the lieutenant governor placed a two-year reservation on lands east of the Santee and Wateree rivers from Jacks Creek to Fredericksburg, an area called "the North Britain tract." The group did not come. Meanwhile conditions on both sides of the Atlantic interrupted local concerns. After three violent lowcountry slave uprisings in 1739, in 1740 fifty black slaves were hanged in Charles Town for another insurrection plot. Later that year the city burned to the ground in an accidental fire. In 1739 England declared war on Spain, and hostility increased between Carolina and Florida. From 1740 to 1748 "King George's War" was under way in Europe, eventually allying France and Spain against England and extending conflict into the colonies.

For a time, as the English engaged in warfare and as Charles Town turned destruction to advantage by building a finer, more modern city, records reflected little about conditions at Fredericksburg. In 1743, however, George Haig was appointed deputy surveyor to make surveys in several townships, including Fredericksburg. From then on there was a flurry of paperwork, beginning with nine applications for land in Fredericksburg in 1743–44.

Both Charles Radcliffe (Ratcliffe) and Paul Harrelson presented petitions for land and bounty to build mills in 1744. The need for mills was considered so vital for community survival and future commerce that payments from the township fund were promised to men who would complete such enterprises. Radcliffe completed his dam at "Sims Creek," a name recorded for Town Creek for a short time, but he appears to have moved before finishing the mill. Harrelson received payment from the township fund for his dam in 1745. A dozen years after the planning of Fredericksburg, area development was ensuing.

The Settlers

Several historians have examined early land records of the Fredericksburg area.[23] Their information and other records from the South Carolina Archives provide data from which conclusions may be drawn regarding settlers and investors up to midcentury. Thousands of acres by then had been taken up in large chunks along the Wateree River by investors such as the attorney James Michie of Charleston and by lowcountry planters. Inland land values rose after Eliza Lucas in 1744 distributed indigo seeds to produce Carolina's second great cash crop, one not confined to coastal tidelands as was rice, the first cash crop.

Instead of growing as a colony of new immigrants, the early Fredericksburg area was being settled by Carolinians and comers from the northern colonies. Carolinians arrived with diverse means. The planter Daniel McDaniel of Williamsburg brought thirteen slaves, and John McConnel(l) was forgiven his fees because of "poverty." Roger Gibson, also of Williamsburg, settled with large tracts on the west side of the Wateree. He was no doubt quite useful to the pioneer area since one record identifies him as a blacksmith, and he served as captain of the Wateree militia.

Settlers from colonies northward arrived in the area. Bryan Rork of West Jersey was a bricklayer whose skills must have been welcomed by the pioneers. Jeffrey Summerford came from Pennsylvania. John Todd, who had lived in Pennsylvania and then North Carolina, brought three slaves with him. Benjamin McKennie brought southward nine white and three black people, settling near Sims Creek (Town Creek); he added another tract to provide himself a river landing. John Collins of Long Island traveled for twenty weeks en route to this area, bringing his wife and five children. Edward Malloy arrived with his wife and one child, having left four children at home in Virginia. Patrick McCormick and his wife brought their four children from New Jersey. John Maddox, also with a wife and four children, came from Maryland. In 1749 more than sixty surveys for actual settlers were marked out in Fredericksburg and opposite that area on the west side of the Wateree.

Travel Routes

Some of the Carolinians no doubt traveled the land routes to Fredericksburg. Others likely came by the Wateree River, although at this time the river was blocked for a distance by a huge "raft," or logjam of submerged trees, about ten miles above its juncture with the Congaree River. The obstacle was formidable enough to be marked on early maps and to be known as "the Raft." A few Indians living nearby earned small fees for porting goods and ferrying travelers around the jam.

Porters and guides were needed at other times on the river as well, for when the river seasonally flooded, boaters could lose their way among the meanders and swamps. Between present Camden and the planned town of Fredericksburg, a streak of rocky shoals, later removed, posed another obstacle in low water but was probably also used to advantage as a ford from bank to bank. The settlers' consideration of the river's importance is indicated by a keen interest in property affording them landings.

At this time the easiest land route for settlers coming to Fredericksburg Township from northward colonies was by the "Fall Line Road," which branched from the colonial coastal route, the King's Highway, at Fredericksburg, Virginia, and followed eroded areas southward along the fall line and through the sandhills of the mid-Carolinas. Connecting with present sites of Raleigh, North Carolina, and Cheraw, South Carolina, the route led into present Kershaw County, crossing the Lynches River. Today U.S. Highway 1, following straightened roadbeds, connects these same cities. The "Cheraw road" through the years has remained a local travel reference.

Lynch's Creek and Kershaw-Sumter Borders

While early settlement was ongoing along the Wateree, few records pertain to the present Kershaw County section along Lynch's (or Linches) Creek, as the two-branched Lynches River was then designated. Its eastern prong, now Little Lynches River, was at times also called Little Creek or Fork Creek. The area lay not only outside Fredericksburg Township but also beyond Williamsburg Township on the Black River and below Queensborough Township, with the Welsh Tract, on the Pee Dee River. While the townships offered incentives to entice newcomers to their environs, there were no competing offerings to settle in the upper Lynches. The locations of any early grants made there are difficult to locate because of the lack of identifying place names.

Except for perhaps squatters or an occasional person appreciative of isolation, the banks of the Lynches were probably home to few settlers prior to 1750. However, Janie Revill's research reports that in the vicinity of the present county line between Kershaw and Sumter counties, the area from the Wateree River to Lynches Creek became home to some early founding families. Between 1732 and 1737 settlers from North Carolina—Jonathan Christmas, Abram Michau, and William Newman—received grants on land they occupied in this area, and Giles Cook had received a grant by the following year.[24]

Very early the sandy, open grasslands west of the Lynches area and in its fork became utilized in a profitable colonial enterprise—raising livestock. Here cattle were driven, branded, and left to range on the open savannas. Old stories testify that deer and buffalo had long favored the area, a traditional Native American hunting ground. Supposedly the last of the small woods buffalo native to the area were seen here by late-eighteenth century settlers. The names of Big and Little Buffalo creeks as well as the county's upper eastern division, Buffalo Township, recall this period.

Various archival records refer to "cowpens" along the Lynches, and some of these likely existed in the Kershaw County area in early years. Herdsmen of the day used natural boundaries such as creek banks, forks, gullies, and cane brakes, rather than artificial fencing, to confine the free-ranging livestock they rounded up for marketing. Jumping Gully is an equestrian-related Lynches-area place name surviving from the eighteenth century. Jumping Gully is also an old place name west of the Wateree River.[25]

One record shows that James McGirt(t), a Wateree River resident, in 1745 bought half of the cattle ranging in an area between Lynches and Black River. A 1748 record refers to a sale of horses, hogs, and cattle, the cattle being kept by John Fryerson in a cowpen on Lynches Creek. A map by William Faden researched prior to the Revolution depicts "Forks of Linches Creek" with this note: "Excellent Pasturage where many Thousands Heads of Cattle are bred Yearly."[26] The pathway that is depicted passing through the fork at present Bethune is a portion of the Fall Line Road.

Effects of Expansion

By 1750 the signs of settlement were spreading throughout the area to become Kershaw County. In 1744 the English acquired control of the Ancient Warrior's Trail, thus making safer the "upper road" that stretched from Pennsylvania through the Shenandoah Valley and along the hilly ridges of the upper Carolinas, and that joined on one side with the Catawba Path. Gradually widened as a wagon road, also called the Philadelphia Wagon Road, in the next

Still-visible wagon ruts marking traces of the old Peay's Ferry Road from Liberty Hill to the Wateree River

decade the route would become flooded with families entering from the back-country and filtering down into the Kershaw County area through the Waxhaws. The road in the local area has been known over time by many names, some mundane and some evocative of a complex history—the Waxhaw Road, the Lancaster Road, the Salisbury Road, the Philadelphia Road, the Old Wagon Road, the War (or Warpath) Road, and the Battle of Camden Road, among other names. An old stretch of this road today is the Flat Rock Road. Before 1750 a trickle of families was finding its way along the path.

With newcomers spreading out, many more of the creeks of Kershaw County had acquired their names by midcentury, or did so shortly thereafter, and also attracted early settlers. Records reveal colorful, descriptive names. In the upper sections there appeared names still in use: Beaver Creek, White Oak Creek, Granny's (Grannies) Quarter Creek, Flat Creek, Gum Swamp (a creek), and Camp Creek. On the west side of the Wateree were added Sawney's Creek, Spears Creek, Wright's (and Rice) Creek, and Jumping Run (later Gully).[27]

The expanded native paths that brought settlers to new homes, the same roads that drovers made dusty driving herds to market, were also the roads used by horse thieves. By 1745 thieves preying on settlers at Fredericksburg were, in turn, chased back up those roads by mounted militiamen. Danger threatened also from marauding visits of hostile northward Indians. Although the local area had established travel routes and place names recognized by today's residents, the end of the frontier had not yet arrived, and struggle remained essential for survival in the rest of the century.

4

Powder Horns and Homesteads

Steady Expansion

Pivotal events at the midpoint of the eighteenth century significantly influenced the expansion of settlement into the pre–Revolutionary War area that would become Kershaw County. For a time uncertainties among the Catawba cast a shadow on the security of the local frontier, also shaken by hostilities between the English and the northward Cherokee. The conflicts were part of the brewing mix of wilderness and European politics that erupted throughout America a decade later. The results were the French and Indian War from 1754 to 1763 and the Cherokee War from 1760 to 1761.[1] Amid the uncertainties settlers had practical concerns. They were occupied with clearing and securing their lands, building homes, protecting their families, starting profitable enterprises, beginning churches, improving transportation, and establishing a voice in government. These common human pursuits did not make them of one mind, however, since diversity of origin and outlook characterized the populace.

Friends and Foes

In 1750 the Catawba Nation was in crisis, a weakened target of Iroquois raiders. Governor James Glen seriously wondered if it could survive. In the previous year disease and warfare had carried off the former chief and fourteen other leaders. The inherited command fell now to a warrior relatively low on the original order of lineage but presently high in rank among survivors. For the next thirteen years the warrior sometimes called Nopkehe would prove a strong leader of his struggling nation, an effective diplomat, and a dependable ally to his colonial neighbors. He was known to them by the title and name of King Hagler, as his name was signed on documents in his time, or King Haiglar (Haigler), as his name has long been phonetically spelled in local histories and usage.[2]

While the rate of immigration to the Fredericksburg area slowed during 1750, there was soon need for the enlarged militia that had been built up in recent years. In the spring of 1751 the section known as the Waterees grew alarmed by Indian attacks in the upper part of South Carolina under the control of the Cherokee. Militia under Captain Roger Gibson on the west side of the Wateree River and Captain Alexander Rattray on the east side totaled more than 180 men. Not all militiamen could safely or effectively be called from home at once, so as was customary, special patrols were recruited among them as rangers with increased pay for hazardous duty, while other militiamen remained as home guards.

On May 9, 1751, Captain Gibson wrote Governor Glen of reports from his company that inhabitants from upper parts of the state "are fled to the Congaree Fort for safety because of the Cherokees and Norw'd Indians who have killed several white People." His concern was that his company was "the nighest to the enemy," the one "most in danger," and yet "at present altogether unprovided with ammunition." In urgently requesting sufficient gunpowder and bullets, he pointed out that "the people being mostly new settlers here, within these two years my Company [has] advanced from 35 to 83."[3]

Captain Rattray, appearing before the governor and council on May 13, reported that his neighbors were "fleeing from Indians," with ten families having gone to Virginia and others to Charleston.[4] He was "using both Perswation and threats" to keep others from leaving. He urged officials to deal radically with the Cherokees by "making them Presents & paying them Tribute, instead of their being Tributary to us." To emphasize to Governor Glen the impact of frontier dangers, Rattray wrote on May 24 that the "pretty well settled" area where he had lived for ten years would have even more inhabitants were it not for "constant alarms from the Cherokees almost every year." His affidavit reported that as a result of the present fear, "all the familys have left their habitations, and betaken themselves to Forts with their wives and children, and their most valuable effects." In consequence many would lose their crops, despite his caution of "sending parties of men from Plantation to Plantation . . . so while one party works the other party guards them."[5]

In the 1751 crisis the Commons House provided for two ranger patrols to scout from the Catawba Nation to the Congarees to Ninety Six. Captain Gibson led one patrol of twenty-two men, most of them landowners in the Waterees.[6] On July 22 Gibson sent the governor his men's complaints: "that to Ride in the Heat and often sleeping wett by Day and Night in the wilderness, 120 miles from their familys, having their Provisions to provide, and too farr to carry, their Horses Tyring and themselves often taken sick and no proper means to help them, as also Day and Night in danger of their Lives, requireth a better reward than £14 per month." Although Captain Rattray had warned the council that unless there was a solution to the Cherokee threats "there will be no Living in these out parts," the Cherokee remained far enough away not to cause serious danger in the Waterees.[7]

Settlers

Whether all families who fled the perceived Indian danger eventually returned is unknown, but it is likely that at least some did not. There were, however, some

Participants in a mid–twentieth century DAR program at the granite stone marking the location of the Quaker meetinghouse in Camden's Quaker Cemetery. Courtesy of the Camden Archives

settlers in the local area in October 1751, when the first families of a small group of Quaker immigrants from Ireland acquired land warrants on both sides of the Wateree in the area of Fredericksburg.[8] Friends Neck on the western side acquired its name soon after being settled by some of the new families.

Kirkland and Kennedy have proposed an "imperfect roll" of early settlers believed to have belonged to this early Quaker band, alphabetized as follows by their surnames: Belton—Jonathan (or John) and later (about 1770) Abraham; English—Robert and Thomas; Evans—Joseph and Robert; Furnass—John; Gaunt—Nebo, Zebulon, and Zimri; Kelly—Samuel and wife, Hannah Belton, and Timothy and Walter; Mathis—Daniel and wife, Sophia; Milhouse (Millhouse, Milhous)—Robert ("leader of the colony"), Henry, John and wife, Abigail, and Samuel; Russell—Samuel; Tomlinson—Josiah and William; Wright—John; and Wyly—Samuel and wife, Dinah Milhouse.[9] Meriwether adds Joshua English and John Dixon, who took out warrants in 1753.[10]

Several Quakers brought with them white indentured servants, some if not all of whom signed their bonds in Ireland.[11] Samuel Wyly had three servants; Samuel Russell, two; Timothy Kelly, two; Josiah Tomlinson, four; and Robert Milhouse, five.[12] Some of them, such as Samuel Kelly, owned black slaves, and others later acquired them. Both slaves and servants were included in the numbers on which land was granted to the household heads, but when servants worked out their time, they were not only released of obligation but also could claim unclaimed land on their own rights. For example, when Cornelius Melone and his wife completed their indenture to Wyly in 1755, they took up land on Twenty-five Mile Creek, where he became notable and respected.[13] Among the people associated with the Quaker settlement, contrasts of initial affluence as well as changes in status are as marked as those among the other settlers of the Kershaw County area.

According to reports, the Quakers settled peacefully and industriously among the other plantations and homesteads of the Fredericksburg area. Wyly, the most prominent among the Quakers, soon established a trading store, possibly kept an inn, and eventually owned a gristmill and a sawmill. He was surveying land by 1753 and served as justice of the peace. In his various capacities as trader and as government representative, Wyly acquired the acquaintance and confidence of King Hagler. Wyly became an Indian agent as well, serving as the Catawba chief's secretary for official correspondence and treaties. Thus the leading man among the early settlers and the leading man among the Catawba forged a cooperative understanding that protected the progressing colonial development of the Kershaw County area.

Building an Economy

In the Fredericksburg area all settlers, Quaker and otherwise, were engaging in agriculture for survival, and many hoped to do so for profit. In a 1752 petition to the legislature, local inhabitants described the crops and products they were then successfully producing: "wheat, barley, oats, rye, peas, flax, hemp, and indigo . . . also butter, cheese, pork, beef, and tallow."[14] Charleston advertisements showed that there were additional markets to aim for, products such as pitch, tar, and turpentine. For families who imported or brought bees with them, honey and beeswax had market demand.[15] Brewing, distilling, curing, and milling were also lucrative endeavors. Even hunting and fishing could be as profitable to colonials as it was to Indians. In fact, just about anything that could be gathered, grown, or otherwise produced and gotten to a market could be sold.

However, even as trial and error revealed what their lands could produce, many obstacles loomed in getting yields to markets. The historian Alexander Gregg points out that for persons raising livestock they had brought with them or who domesticated herds from cattle or horses found running wild, "energy, rather than capital," was required.[16] Settlers, sometimes accompanied by slaves, drove animals to market in the fall, following old European and African practices and foreshadowing legendary American cowboys. A cattle, horse, or hog drive to Charleston or to northern markets followed trails and spread through open forests, stopping overnight at clearings in the woods. Gregg states, "It was in this kind of life, habituated to the use of the saddle in the woods for days and weeks together, often in the dangerous adventures of the chase, that our early settlers became such expert horsemen, and so inured to exposure and hardship" as would be required of them in the national struggles ahead.[17] By the early 1750s turnpikes along the eastern edge of the mountains increased the ease and appeal of following the upper trail to the Philadelphia market.

Transportation Improvements

A 1752 legislative petition by area inhabitants successfully sought specific transportation improvements. A study of colonial Camden explains the petitioners' argument that "locally produced surplus, together with export items from places to the north and west . . . could be collected and forwarded to the Charleston market" and "would promote the development of South Carolina's interior at the same time that it would diminish the colony's traditional dependence on Pennsylvania and New York." The study points out that the local inhabitants considered "their settlement in the context of the commercial development of the colony as a whole, and . . . the role they could play in larger trade patterns and linkages."[18] The lure of lucrative profits for the lowcountry, more than sympathy for the aspirations of backcountry people, seems to have won support for the improvements.

One request of petitioners was the opening of a road from Beard's Ferry on the Santee almost all the way to the Catawba Nation, or as described in later terms in an old history, "from Eutaw Springs across the Santee to Manchester, Camden and Lancaster."[19] Wyly and Milhouse were among the appointed road commissioners authorized to coordinate a labor levy of inhabitants along the way to work on it. By 1755 this beginning of the "great road," overlying part of the old Catawba Path, was completed as far as present Camden, and in five more years it ran as far up as the Waxhaws. Although neither a smooth nor easy travel route, it would play an important role in the coming years, including those of the Revolution.

Another improvement resulting from the petition was to clear the Wateree River of its major obstacle between present Camden and the Santee River, which was the water route down to the coast. The raft of debris jamming the Wateree for some distance above its mouth was removed, probably with some other sunken trees along its length, and provisions were made for keeping navigation open. By 1754 a private ferry crossing the Wateree near the mouth of Pine Tree Creek was being operated by Anthony Wright, possibly one of the Quaker group.

Improved transportation and enlarged markets initiated vocations for hired wagoners to drive goods up and down the roadways, and eventually for boatmen to follow the waterways. The changes also decreased the isolation that bound black slaves to the limited boundaries of the specific land they had been brought to work. At midcentury in South Carolina, these slaves outnumbered white citizens two to one. Some slaves traveled with cattle drives, some worked as wagoners, and some labored as boatmen. Many others were set to tasks clearing roads, waterways, and swamplands; others were sent with militia patrols against warring Indians. A slave who ran away from his owner might find safety among settlers on remote wilderness fringes where work skills of a new dark-skinned neighbor could prove an asset. Outlaw bands also accepted runaways willing to follow their lifestyles. A transitory population of mixed nationality, race, background, and ambition increased just beyond the areas defined by warrants and land grants.

Frontier Disorders

Disruption stirred the frontiers in 1755. Fear of the Cherokee subsided that year when the tribe allied with the English in the French and Indian War. However, in a major setback on July 9, forces under the traditional-minded British major general Edward Braddock were soundly defeated on the Ohio. His volunteer aide, American lieutenant colonel George Washington, having had to surrender Fort Necessity the previous year at the opening of the war, had tried unsuccessfully to warn Braddock about the different nature of frontier warfare.[20] One of the officers wounded in the battle when Braddock was killed was British lieutenant Horatio Gates, who would play a future role in Kershaw County's Revolutionary War history.

Braddock's defeat left settlers of western Pennsylvania, Maryland, and Virginia exposed and unprotected. A tide of migration, mostly Scots-Irish, headed southward, an increasing stream that began pushing into the Carolinas. In the next few years a number of settlers who wound down the Philadelphia Wagon Road or filtered down the Fall Line Road settled along the creeks and in the forestlands of Kershaw County, joining earlier pioneers already homesteading there. When William Hood of Beaver Creek died at age seventy-eight, his obituary testified that he had been born in 1750 in a tent at the Waxhaws three days after his Irish parents arrived there. Hood became a farmer and blacksmith on Beaver Creek, where he reared all twelve of his children, seven sons and five daughters.[21]

One family coming down the upper route following Braddock's defeat was that of the former ranger Jasper Sutton and his wife, with her young sons, James and John Chesnut, whose father had died on the frontier. During the height of hostilities the family moved for safety to one of the wilderness forts and afterward began a southward trek. They paused from time to time as needed to plant and harvest food, to wait out a winter season, and to look about for new opportunities. They stayed put for a year or two in North Carolina, between Salisbury and present Charlotte, and then moved on down through the Waxhaws to take up land and establish themselves in the upper Kershaw County area on Granny's Quarter Creek. By the next year or two more would be heard of them.

Some of the migrating families set out with only what they could carry themselves or, if more fortunate, pack on horseback. Some arrived in orderly fashion and began to apply for lands to start new lives. Others existed in poverty and lived as squatters. Religious dissenters who had left northern colonies to avoid Anglican taxes brought strong views with them. Joining the southward tide were recent European immigrants who had reached northern port cities only to find land in those provinces unaffordable. Immigrants who had set out with old-country neighbors or church members were sometimes still together. The medley of backcountry society grew even more diverse, influencing the future direction of the Kershaw County area.

Spiritual Concerns

Faced with constant struggles of survival in the wilds and in frontier settlements, many people longed for the comforts of religious guidance and for participation in familiar rituals of faith. There was no midcentury church or minister close enough to provide regular attendance for residents of the Waterees or the section around it. Occasionally the clergyman over all Prince Frederick Parish traveled inland. In 1753 parish records show that on one such trip he baptized twenty-three children, most of them belonging to families of the Fredericksburg vicinity.[22] Persons who wished to be law-abiding, churchgoing citizens were forced to great extremes for the most basic family ceremonies of marriage and baptism.

In that same year of 1753 local Quakers officially organized the Fredericksburg Monthly Meeting, also known as the Wateree Meeting, to unite with other bands of their faith in America. They did not yet have a meetinghouse, and as with any other family or group who wished to observe religious practice, they had to gather in private dwellings or in the outdoors. The majority of the area settlers were not Quakers, however, and lacked ties to such associations.

No doubt devout persons of other denominations also observed family devotions and at times united with others in worship, although written records did not record their gatherings. All inhabitants by law were part of the civil structure of the established Church of England, but most of those in backcountry Carolina came from traditions of dissenters—persons by spiritual and/or political convictions disaffected from the Anglicans. By origin or by faith, the majority of early Kershaw County people were defined as Presbyterians, a group deemed lightly by Anglicans, much as people in England looked askance at other parts of the British Isles—Scotland, Ireland, and Wales. The largest segment of the Kershaw County settlers was made up of Scots-Irish people. Neither old-country prejudices nor resentments of this group entirely disappeared on new-country soil.

In 1756, to fulfill civil and church responsibilities, the Commons House of Assembly provided a salary of one hundred pounds sterling a year to an established clergyman who would preach regularly at "Fredericksburgh, Pine Tree Creek, or such other centrical part in the Waterees . . . and six times a year at least, at the most populous places within 40 miles of the same." The position went unclaimed for ten years. In 1757 St. Mark's Parish was formed from the western part of Prince Frederick's Parish. Its boundaries were vast, and the present Kershaw County area was only a small part. The parish extended from the northwest line of Williamsburg Township to the Pee Dee and Santee rivers and covered all territory northward. Even when the boundary was moved back to Lynches River, St. Mark's Parish still covered an overwhelming area of South Carolina all the way to the province line.

The parish operation began sluggishly as a religious influence, although immediately the allotted representatives were elected to the Commons House. The interest of many backcounty people for more and smaller parishes was less for religious privilege than for the political representation they would have in government. Conversely the Commons House, controlled by lowcountry men, dragged its feet in dividing the backcounty into parishes because the same designation that gave the people churches also gave them votes, lessening lowcountry domination.

With religious formalities relatively unavailable to them, the people of the interior were strongly affected by the Great Awakening, the revival movement that personalized religious experience throughout America. From the first wave in New England in 1730 an emotional religious current made its way down through the southern colonies, especially in the backcountry, traveling ahead of and along with the flood of new immigrants. In the absence of organized churches, stalwart personal religious faith supported many pioneers through the difficulties of settlement. However, spiritual emotionalism also gave rise to various sects and untutored leaders that distanced the sympathies of established church government.

Pine Tree Hill

Meriwether estimates that the population of the area around Fredericksburg, on both sides of the Wateree River, numbered about eight hundred in 1757, the same year that St. Mark's Parish was formed; by 1759 the population had grown to about nine hundred. In the latter year those numbers included about fifty slaves at Fredericksburg and about one hundred slaves on the west side of the river. Four companies of militia protected the length of the Wateree River in 1757. With Joseph McKerthlin as commander and Michael Brannon as lieutenant, the unit covering the township included seventy-seven white men and twenty slaves. James McGirt's unit on the west side of the river included sixty-three white men and sixteen slaves.[23]

The Fredericksburg area around this time presented an attractive situation for investment. Good land was available and relatively cheap. A river and significant roads were open. Indian danger was fairly remote; Catawba allies were at hand for protection and trade. Settlers were successfully producing crops, operating mills, and aware that their community had broader potential. Such was the situation when William Ancrum, the partner of a Charleston mercantile firm, on June 12, 1758, received a 150-acre grant on Pine Tree Creek. The attached plat was marked "Pine Tree Hill" and included a location marked "Indian camp" at the fork of the creek.

Joseph Kershaw's Store

On a site dominated by a prominent sandy hill marked by distinctive longleaf pines, the firm of William Ancrum, Lambert Lance, and Aaron Loocock financed a country branch store. It promptly opened here under the operation of thirty-year-old Joseph Kershaw, an English immigrant and a former Charleston clerk

Visitors at Big Springs on Lynches River, the eastern boundary of Kershaw County

who for the past year or two had been operating a country store with his brother Ely (Eli) at the site of present Cheraw. The energetic new arrival to the local area was shortly made a member of the Ancrum, Lance, and Loocock firm, which remained in Charleston. The local branch was operated as Kershaw and Co. and advertised in Charleston papers as "Pine Tree Store."

Kershaw's store became a nucleus of activity around which gathered the small community that for a decade was known as Pine Tree Hill and later as Camden. Kershaw was persistently active in acquiring additional property for the firm and in building up its operations. Shortly after the store opened, Lambert Lance withdrew from the firm, and Kershaw's brother Ely became a partner. By 1760 the *South Carolina Gazette* carried advertisements of "fine Carolina flour" from Kershaw's mills on Pine Tree Creek.

Early in the operation of his store Kershaw also apprenticed a clerk, an energetic and capable young man who soon rose to a partnership. This was John Chesnut, whose mother and stepfather had settled on Granny's Quarter Creek after Braddock's defeat. Chesnut too became a leading man in the new community. It was for Joseph Kershaw that Kershaw County would later be named, though for Revolutionary War contributions more dramatic than his encouragement of early economic development.

A Treaty at Pine Tree Hill

For some time struggles during the ongoing French and Indian War sparked friction in areas around Pine Tree Hill. Contention rose between free-roaming Catawba allies and the increasing numbers of settlers encroaching on the lands where the Indians had traditionally been at home. Ongoing negotiations to settle discontent were interrupted when disaster struck the Catawba in 1759. Some of their warriors returning from fighting for the British against the French brought back smallpox, which rapidly decimated the Catawba people. What had been a thriving nation was transformed into grieving, disoriented ghost towns. A modern study concludes: "in a single season the Nation's total population dropped from perhaps 1,500 people to 500 or so."[24]

In February 1760, the same month that some Cherokees rose to slaughter families at Long Canes in western Carolina, King Hagler and a small band of smallpox survivors took refuge for a time on the outskirts of Pine Tree Hill, where Joseph Kershaw had always welcomed them in his store. Here they negotiated a treaty through Samuel Wyly that the Catawba refer to as the "Treaty of Pine Tree Hill," although the document has since been lost and its contents are revealed only through contemporary references. The Catawba gave up their claim to Kershaw County lands. Their chief had come to believe that a defined reservation was the best way to secure the peaceful safety of his people and was working toward that end. Merrell explains: "The Nation had little choice: if

A closeup, circa 1950, of the 1826 effigy of the Catawba chief Hagler atop the Camden clock tower. In 1995 the aging weather vane was removed to the Camden Archives and replaced with an exact replica. Courtesy of the Rachel Montgomery family

it was to interrupt the sequence of dependence, decline and dispersal that had already extinguished so many eastern Indian people, it had to erect a barrier against colonial Americans."[25] The Cherokee War, which lasted until 1761, was the kind of bloody encounter that Hagler hoped to avoid for his people.[26]

In February 1764 Wyly completed drawing up the survey of 144,000 acres that defined the Catawba's traditional lands.[27] However, in December 1763 at the Treaty of Augusta, which officially gave those fifteen square miles to the Catawba, Wyly signed the name "Hagler" symbolically and out of respect.[28] Hagler himself was dead, randomly slain on August 30, 1763, in an ambush by a Shawnee hunting party.

Once initial panic subsided among settlers of the Kershaw County area following King Hagler's death, the Catawba chief began to be elevated to legendary status. Reflecting on the long French and Indian War and the bloody Cherokee War, it was comforting for storytellers to reflect romantically on an illustration of peace between men of different backgrounds.[29] Otherwise, despite cessation of Indian hostilities, the ensuing years in the backcountry were far from peaceful.

5

"A mix'd Medley"

Vigilantes to Revolutionists

Ten years after a salary was first offered for a Church of England clergyman to serve from a center near Pine Tree Creek to areas forty miles around, one showed up. On September 16, 1766, an optimistic Reverend Charles Woodmason rode into Pine Tree Hill with light baggage. His books and other household goods he expected to follow from Charleston by wagon. With him the clergyman brought his English serving man, whom he had recently brought over, and a journal in which to record experiences as a newly ordained minister of the Church of England. Woodmason's journal, sermons, correspondence, and miscellaneous writings provide a rare, firsthand view of backcountry life during a significant half-dozen pre-Revolution years.[1] Although Woodmason's words must be considered in light of his strong religious, cultural, and personal biases, the writings also reflect his growing sympathy with backcountry political struggles and his efforts to amend the people's difficulties.[2] In the search for justice citizens repeatedly victimized by extremes of indifference and outright violence took both church and law into their own hands.

A "Wild Country"

To Woodmason's dismay, he found at Pine Tree Hill, the intended center of his itinerancy, not a single room he considered decent to rent. The people, he recorded, were "all new Settlers, extremely poor" and lived "in Logg Cabbins like Hogs . . . as rude or more so than the Savages." Woodmason quartered his first three months at the tavern, where he complained of exposure to rough behavior and habitual intoxication. His servant contacted a fever shortly after arrival and soon abandoned the minister's service.[3]

Woodmason doggedly pursued duty: "I came to this Wild Country to support the Interests of the Church of England and the People of our Communion, trodden under foot by the Herds of Sectaries [dissenting religious sects]." An educated Englishman and a former lowcountry merchant, he had returned to England to be ordained for the religious mission to a backcountry he had never before seen. He apparently expected to be greeted by people grateful for his services. Instead he found "the People around, of abandon'd Morals, and profligate Principles—Rude—Ignorant—Void of Manners, Education or Good Breeding—No genteel or Polite Person among them—save Mr. Kershaw an

English Merchant settled here. The people are of all Sects and Denominations—A mix'd Medley from all Countries and the Off Scouring of America."[4]

As Woodmason soon learned, Pine Tree Hill had two meetinghouses, one Quaker and the other Presbyterian, the latter representing the great majority.[5] His first Sunday there he officiated from the Presbyterian pulpit to 200 listeners. The people were no doubt curious to size up this first voice of both religion and law among them, but they quickly rejected the clergyman's offer to preach twice each Sunday. The following week Woodmason's audience was down to about 150 persons. Yet, regardless of class or sect, all the people, he said, signed his legislative petition to build an Anglican chapel in their midst. The Quaker Samuel Wyly was attentive to the new minister, riding with him through the area to introduce him to the community. On Christmas Day, Woodmason addressed a congregation of 100 persons, though none participated in the Anglican communion.

On December 28 Woodmason had only eighty hearers. He had been unable to purchase property in fee simple for a chapel or a parsonage, but the citizens presented a signed legislative petition to make several hundred acres of public land a glebe, or church property. Woodmason had written enthusiastically about this prospect to the bishop of London two months earlier, describing the land as "originally laid out for the town of Fredericksburg, but abandon'd as too low for a Settlement."[6] He expressed the belief that the land was worth five hundred guineas and would appreciate in a decade to four times that. It is unclear whether others agreed on the value of land that earlier had been shunned and whether indeed the people intended such an offering to honor the church.

In December, Joseph Kershaw took Woodmason into his home while the minister awaited the preparation of suitable quarters. Meanwhile, John Cantey, the keeper of the tavern from which the preacher had moved, made a stable out of the space that Woodmason had offered to use as a free school for twenty poor boys. Only three had ever agreed to attend. The preacher's goods, by way of tedious land haul from Charleston, arrived near the end of January 1767, four months after his own arrival and about the time he moved to new rooms in the house of an old Dutch widow. However, while he was away preaching, thieves broke into his rooms and made off with many items. It was only the first of a number of times he encountered crime.

By mid-February, Woodmason's congregation was reduced to sixty or seventy hearers, although he claimed that the populace was large enough to have supplied a service of five hundred. He complained of competition from different sects, such as "a Gang of Baptists or New Lights over the River" and a "Methodist" on Swift Creek.[7] He also mentioned several times that the people were wrought up over the Stamp Act, and having found out that he was to be one of the distributors of stamps, he believed them to be retaliating against him.

Area Congregations

In accordance with law Woodmason officiated at least every other Sunday at Pine Tree Hill, but most of his time was devoted to riding out on missionary visits to surrounding areas, many far beyond present Kershaw County. Within the local area he gathered congregations and preached quarterly at Beaver Creek and White Oak Creek. He preached monthly at each of the following places (variously spelled): Rafting Creek, Granny's Quarter Creek, Hanging Rock Creek, Little Lynches Creek (including Flat Creek and other areas), and two places on Great (Big) Lynches Creek. By the following year he was also preaching monthly at Graves Ford and Sawney's Creek. Out of more than one thousand people he numbered in the total potential congregation of just those places, he reported only twenty-three communicants, or persons eligible or willing to participate in the Anglican communion.

Conditions of Poverty

Woodmason encountered face-to-face the families who had come to the backcountry for multiple reasons and needs, although he does not discuss them. His initial reactions to the people were not always sympathetic. He was shocked by their poverty, and at times he blamed the people themselves for their condition. He describes "open Cold Cabbins—unfloored and almost open to the Sky." Even in cold weather, he found, "Their Cabbins [are] quite open and expos'd" with "little or no Bedding, or anything to cover them. . . . And all their Cloathing, a Shirt and Trousers Shift and [illegible] Petticoat. Some perhaps a Linsey Woolsey. No Shoes or Stockings—Children run half naked. The Indians are better Cloathed and Lodged. All this rises from their Indolence and Laziness."[8]

Woodmason berates the food he found: "Nothing but Indian Corn Meal to be had Bacon and Eggs in some Places—No Butter, Rice, or Milk—As for Tea and Coffee they know it not." He describes one group from Ireland as living "wholly on Butter, Milk, Clabber and what in England is given to the Hogs and Dogs." At one point he summarizes general conditions:

> In this Circuit of a fortnight I've eaten Meat but thrice and drank naught but Water—Subsisting on my Bisket and Rice Water and Musk Melons, Cucumbers, Green Apples and Peaches and such Trash. . . . Very few can read—fewer write—Out of 5000 that have attended Sermon this past Month, I have not got 50 to sign a Petition to the Assembly. They are very Poor—owing to their extreme Indolence for they possess the finest Country in America and could raise but ev'rything. They delight in their present low, lazy, sluttish, heathenish, hellish Life, and seem not desirous of changing it. Both men and Women will do any thing to come at Liquor, Cloaths,

> furniture, &c. &c. rather than work for it—Hence their many Vices—their gross Licentiousness Wantoness, Lasciviousness, Rudeness, Lewdness, and Profligacy they will commit the grossest Enormities, before my face, and laugh at all Admonition. . . . It is very few families whom I can bring to join in Prayer, because most of them are of various Opinions the Husband a Churchman, Wife, a Dissenter, Children nothing at all.[9]

The Blame of Others

At other times Woodmason laid elsewhere some of the blame for the problems of the people: "For thro' want of Ministers to marry and thro' the licentiousness of the People, many hundreds live in Concubinage—swopping their Wives as Cattel, and living in a State of Nature, more irregularly and unchastely than the Indians." He found the people "being eaten up by Itinerant Teachers, Preachers, and Imposters from New England and Pensylvania—Baptists, New Lights, Presbyterians, Independants, and a hundred other Sects—So that one day You might hear this System of Doctrine—the next day another. . . . And among the Various Plans of Religion, they are at Loss which to adapt, and consequently are without any Religion at all." Some backcountry people, who were "the Major Part Episcopals," wanted to participate as Anglicans, but "being oblig'd to be in perpetual Motion, I cannot have Time to instruct them, which is a great grief to me. . . . All [are] very poor and extremely ignorant—Yet desirous of the Knowledge of God and of Christ. Their Case is truly pitiable, but out of my power to amend and the Legislature turn a deaf Ear to all Remonstrances on this Subject."[10]

A Swarming Medley

Woodmason's journal reflects a backcountry more teeming with people than land records indicate, possibly because many of the people were transients or squatters of whom no record was made. At times he seems to have been overwhelmed with their numbers, stating, "I could not conceive from whence this vast Body could swarm—But this Country contains ten times the Number of Persons beyond my Apprehension." He was surprised by their variety of backgrounds. Sometimes his hearers included Indians, well-behaved ones. At Beaver Creek he "baptiz'd several Negroes and Mullatoos," and at Rocky Mount he preached "to a numerous Audience of various degrees, Countries, Complexions and Denominations." He describes his congregation of one hundred at Granny's Quarter Creek as "such a Pack I never met with—Neither English, Scots Irish, or Carolinian by Birth—Neither of one Church or other or of any denomination by Profession, not having . . . ever seen a Minister—heard or read a Chapter in the Scriptures, or heard a Sermon in their days."[11] Somewhere amid all his frustration Woodmason's later actions suggest that he gained some insight into the people's problems.

Decrying Lawlessness

Woodmason was not the only person to decry lawlessness in the backcountry. Remoteness from government proved a fertile seedbed for the increase of crime and violence following the traumas of the Cherokee War. Contemporary accounts testify to details not only of theft and destruction of property but also of kidnapping, rape, mutilation, torture, and murder—acts committed indiscriminately and with coldhearted intent to terrorize.

The historian Richard Maxwell Brown points out that in such a climate, "men born of decent property-holding parents sometime found their way into a life of crime."[12] Among the leaders of outlaw bands that preyed on area residents were the Black brothers—Govey and George—and their half brothers—Thomas and James Moon. These men were born in Fredericksburg Township to respectable families, the Moons being part of the Quaker band. The brothers inherited property, which they sold at good profit before embarking on lives of crime. Well known to those they openly preyed upon, these audacious outlaws held in terror the local community as well as distant areas.

A few officials, such as Lieutenant Governor William Bull and Chief Justice Charles Shinner of the Charleston court, attempted to provide courts for the interior, but efforts were frustrated for a number of years.[13] In 1766 Shinner personally traveled to Pine Tree Hill to organize citizens against gangs of horse thieves there, including the Blacks and the Moons. However, his friend Woodmason reported, the efforts failed.[14] Victims of the lawless elements feared further deprivations from those enemies so near. Shinner represented a distant court with little meaning for the people and was unable to rally them. The ousting of the rogues among them would occur only when the victims themselves were emboldened to take action.

On the night of July 11, 1767, a gang broke into and robbed John Pane's Pine Tree Hill blacksmith shop. They stole his stallion and took Joshua English's horse. Six miles down the Lynches Creek road, the gang seized and tied up a man named Davis. Torturing him with red hot irons, they forced him to reveal his hidden money, after which they set his house on fire and left him, still tied, to watch it burn.

The Regulators

By 1767 some backcounty men had had enough of the outlaws whose tactics of fear and intimidation virtually controlled the land. Spontaneously individuals began to unite to resist the villains. Their efforts were encouraged when Governor

Charles Montagu offered rewards for outlaw leaders to be brought to the Charleston jail. To area residents, this must have seemed license to bring the lawless to justice.

However, in early October the governor changed tactics when a large number of settlers between the Santee and Wateree rivers committed "riot and disturbances," burning houses alleged to be havens for horse thieves and threatening to come together to the capital to deliver complaints. Governor Montagu and the council issued a proclamation ordering the "Regulators," as they were being called, to disperse. Within a month Montagu was entreating for legislation to "suppress those licentious Spirits."[15]

The account of Mark Nettles, of the Pine Tree Hill area, is an example of the confusion in the backcountry movement. Nettles, assisting a constable, shot and killed a horse thief. Justices of the Peace Joseph Curry and Thomas Bond questioned whether Nettles had been legally authorized, and they issued warrants for his arrest. Nettles sought protection from Justice Shinner, then at Pine Tree Hill. Shinner sent a party of men to Curry with a message not to bother Nettles, but Bond disregarded it and attempted to arrest Nettles. In the resulting melee to protect Nettles, one participant had an ear bitten off and Bond had a tooth knocked out. Nettles, not arrested, was later pardoned. The use of group force to thwart processes that were legal but perceived as unfair would become a feature of the Regulator movement.

Before long, having been persuaded by the Regulators' cause, Woodmason began serving as secretary and spokesperson for them. On November 7, 1767, he presented to the Commons House of Assembly an important "Remonstrance" explaining the Regulators' grievances. Reputedly backed by four thousand of their number, the document contained their threat to invade Charleston unless the government moved quickly to remedy complaints. Within four days a legislative committee recommended three measures: the establishment of courts in the backcountry; the passage of a vagrancy act; and the creation of two companies of soldiers for three months to provide order.[16]

Within two weeks the Commons House authorized two companies of rangers, each with a captain, a lieutenant, and twenty-five privates. When the troops were formed, both captains, one of the lieutenants, and many of the privates were Regulators. In essence the government operation legitimized the Regulators' attempt at suppressing disorder.

The troops of rangers rendezvoused south of Pine Tree Hill at Swift Creek before Charles Woodmason's pulpit, where the clergyman gave the mission his blessing: "I know," he said, "that many among You have personally been injur'd by the Rogues. Some in their Wives—Others in their Sisters, or Daughters—By loss of Horses, Cattle, Goods and Effects."[17] The rangers rode off to hunt down outlaws across South Carolina and to trail them into Georgia, North Carolina, and Virginia. They recovered more than one hundred stolen horses and a number of stolen slaves, and they returned thirty-five young women to their homes. Although the rangers killed many of the outlaws who resisted, including Govey Black, court records reflect that their primary intent was to capture their quarries and bring them to public justice.

The Naming of Camden

At the height of emotion surrounding attempts to secure public safety, the name of Pine Tree Hill was changed to one reflective of citizens' rights—Camden. The name honors Charles Pratt, Lord Camden, one of the British champions of colonial rights then popular with the American people. Woodmason notes the change in his July 3, 1768, journal: "Officiated at Pine Tree Hill (now to be call'd Camden in Honor of Lord Cambden . . . the Americans being very fond at present of all who declar'd in their favor against the Stamp Act)."[18]

Kirkland and Kennedy point out that the first use of the name Camden is in a legislative act of April 12, 1768, that called for a court at Camden, "lately called Pine Tree Hill."[19] It would take until November of the following year, however, and tedious negotiations between Charleston and England before the later Circuit Court Act of 1769 finally established seven district courts, one of them at Camden. In the interim the backcountry continued on its own.

Issues of Morality

By March 1768, when the ninety-day ranger campaign ended, the crime spree had been checked. To assure stability of improvements, Regulators turned efforts toward addressing other problems of disorder created by "those who failed to measure up to respectable standards of morality and industry."[20] Their objects included idle and unproductive vagrants, irresponsible hunters, and immoral women. Still awaiting courts, the Regulators enacted their own system, "the Plan of Regulation," based on the vagrancy laws of surrounding colonies. A large group of backcountry people assembled at the Congarees in June 1768 and adopted a plan of correction that included flogging, work for those suitable of reform, and eviction of those who were not. For a time the Regulators appeared on the way toward achieving their goals.

When some victims of Regulator "corrections" brought lawsuits against them in the Charleston court and won, Regulators vowed to stand together to resist the serving of processes against any of them. Several such attempts resulted in verbal and physical abuse against the servers. Lieutenant Governor William Bull, forced to take action in place of the absent governor, issued two proclamations in August 1768: the first, to stifle the Regulators; the second, to pardon those who agreed to keep the peace.

Oral reading of a proclamation was the standard way of disseminating public information in the backcountry. Ministers and military leaders were frequently sent announcements that they were expected dutifully to read at gatherings. Sometimes a leader chose not to read a message if he personally disagreed with it or if he feared the reaction of an audience. Two men in the vicinity of Camden—Colonel Richard Richardson and the Reverend Woodmason—received Bull's proclamations. Richardson refused to read it to his militia. Woodmason read it but thereby so infuriated Anglican Regulators that they took their children to the Presbyterian meetinghouse to be baptized.[21] Woodmason traveled to Hanging Rock Creek on August 25 to read the proclamation to an assembly of Regulators but left without doing so when he sized up the crowd. Fearing personal injury, Woodmason sent the proclamation to be read at a Regulator meeting at Lynches Creek on August 26. Two days later he read it to the Wateree Creek congregation without incident, but when he attempted the same at Sawney's Creek, the congregation refused to listen.

The government had several inducements to allow Regulator control in the backcountry. First, many in the government, including Bull, acknowledged the legitimacy of most Regulator grievances. Second, the government recognized that sending troops from the lowcountry to put down resistance would leave that area vulnerable to slave unrest. Thus the government tolerated backcountry disorder that had some redeeming consequences in order to avoid potential chaos in other parts of the province. Meanwhile, Regulators continued to address basic issues of inadequate backcountry representation in the government.[22]

Establishing Law

Although Regulators provided many needed changes, eventually they went too far. Having taken on, without authority, many of the functions of government, they sometimes rendered brutal and capricious punishments and tried to control community morals, interfering in family life. Another group of backcountry settlers, known as Moderators, began to resist their control.

The Moderators used many of the tactics against their rivals that had served the latter so effectively. Conflict between the two factions seemed headed to a bloody conclusion in present Newberry County in late March 1769 when armed counterparts were brought to agreement by three persuasive messengers—Daniel McGirtt, Richard Richardson, and William Thomson, who would play major roles in the impending Revolution. Ten leading men of Camden in fall 1769 petitioned the governor to explain how well-intended zeal had been caught up in the movement's public clamor. Cooler heads prevailed.

The Court Act of 1769

In late November 1769 when the king gave his assent to the "Act for establishing Courts, building Gaols, and appointing Sheriffs, and other Officers, for the more convenient Administration of Justice in this Province," the main grievance of the Regulators was resolved. The new law provided that seven districts, including Camden, should have courthouses. Two judges were to ride the northern circuit of Camden, the Cheraws and Georgetown. The Commons House also appointed commissioners to supervise construction of courthouses and jails. Some of those appointed were former Regulators, including Benjamin Hart, Robert Stark, Joseph Kershaw, and John Chesnut in Camden District, and Ely (Eli) Kershaw in the Cheraws District. The public construction projects were a boon to the settlements in which they occurred, and they personally enriched some of the commissioners.[23]

Even as the Commons House was establishing the court system, prominent men of the backcountry were petitioning for amnesty for former Regulators. A committee headed by Joseph Kershaw and established to consider such a petition agreed in principle but withheld action, yielding to royal authority. John Chesnut and John Cantey led a group of Camden-area men in an effort to secure the governor's pardon. In 1771 Montagu granted amnesty to seventy-five former Regulators.

The Camden District Courthouse

As designated, the newly formed Camden District was a very large area. It began above Georgetown District and stretched all the way to the North Carolina border, bounded on the west by the Broad and Saluda rivers and on the east by the Lynches, a territory in present time encompassing nine counties. The hard-won courts in the new South Carolina districts could not begin functioning until completion of their jails and courthouses, the construction of which began in summer 1770.

The Camden District courthouse was completed in Camden in 1771, but the first session was not held there until November 5, 1772. Chief Justice Thomas Knox Gordon and Judge John Murray, both from Britain and appointed by Lord Hillsborough, presided. Among the first sheriffs appointed by Governor Montagu was Roger-Peter Handasyde Hatley for Camden District. Serving after his death was Joseph Kershaw, followed by John Wyly. The first grand jury in Camden included Joshua English, Matthew Singleton, Henry Hunter, and Joseph Kirkland, all former Regulators. They and their cohorts in other communities thus continued to push for change, although now using legal rather than illegal or extralegal means.

At the first term of the Camden court, the grand jury presentment complained that some district inhabitants were still 140 miles away from a place of worship and thus "subject to many evils too notorious to be overlooked in a Christian part of the world." Jurors in that term and at the following court in April 1773 also referred to the absence of schools, inadequate protection of law, "villainies and Roberies," numerous "beasts of Prey, such as Wolves, Tygers, Bears &c.," and "idle and disorderly vagrants" whose nocturnal deer hunting

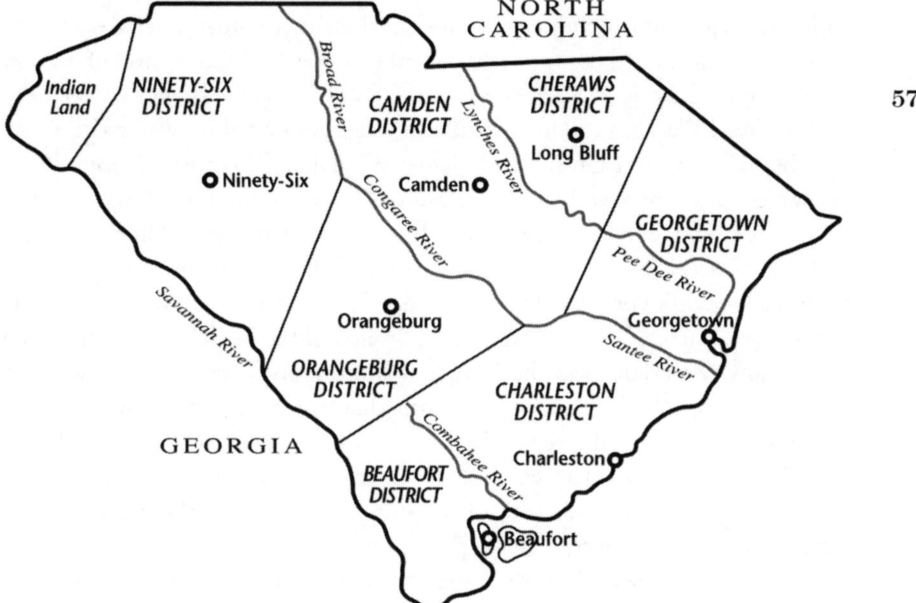

South Carolina districts, 1769–84. Courtesy of the South Carolina Department of Archives and History

also destroyed cattle and endangered settlers. The first jurors in that court included Robert Belton, James Cantey, John Cantey, Robert Carter, Glass Caston, John Chesnut, James Cook, Joshua English, John Gamble, Moses Gordon, Joseph Kirkland, James McGirtt, George Sanders, Thomas Sumter, Jasper Sutton, and John Witherspoon.[24] The needs and desires of the inhabitants were strained in seeking both more protection within the British system and more self-determination.

A New Focus

By the beginning of the 1770s, with the cessation of Indian hostilities, the curtailment of major outlaw activity, the end of the Regulator and Moderator movements, and the institution of local courts, backcountry settlers could turn their attention from survival to economic betterment. New arrivals continued to take up lands in the area around present Kershaw County. One huge group that had a significant backcountry impact consisted of five shiploads of Scots-Irish Presbyterians who emigrated from Ireland with the Reverend William Martin in 1772.[25] More than four hundred families from Ulster landed in Charleston and started on foot to lands allotted them in the Wateree–Catawba Valley areas.

Of these interrelated families who began with industry to organize churches and remained in touch with one another as they began life in the backcounty, a number moved into the upper areas of present Kershaw County. Half a dozen families spread along the Lynches, and a few settled on Sawney's Creek and Twenty-five Mile Creek. Jennet Peden took up land on the "Water Eye River" on a branch of Beaver Creek, while James Breden and John Riddle took claims on White Oak Creek and nearby locations. Tracts on Granny's Quarter Creek were settled by Thomas Creighton Jr., Robert Dunlap, William Dunlap, William McKee, Daniel McMullen, and Hugh Thomson. On "the great road from McDonald's Pond leading to Camden," John Blear found a home. Many of these areas in a few years would be embroiled in the battles and skirmishes of Revolutionary warfare, and the Reverend Martin would be a fiery spokesman.

The historian Walter Edgar points out that during the 1770s, while coastal communities developed a revolutionary spirit in reaction to changes in British imperial policies, the inhabitants of the interior "concentrated on their farms, orchards, herds, mills, and stores." Even subsistence farmers, the majority of the settlers, were beginning to increase their property holdings. Some had acquired slaves and were moving into the category of substantial planter, concentrating on cash crops such as indigo, wheat, hemp, and tobacco. Edgar points out that a backcountry indigo planter with nine to twelve hands could earn an income equivalent to from twenty-two thousand dollars to forty-four thousand dollars in modern currency.[26]

In addition to agriculture, mills were processing increasing yields of wheat and other grains, with industrious millers either supplementing their farming incomes or subsisting wholly on the tolls charged their customers. Some harnessed waterpower to run sawmills to furnish building materials for a developing area. Well-used roads, especially where two or more intersected, became the sites of mercantile establishments, set up by men who gambled their investments that the area would continue to grow and their stores would prosper.

Rugeley's Mills

By the mid-1770s a significant backcountry center of commerce was operating at Clermont, the estate of the Englishman Henry Rugeley, at Flat Rock Creek and Granny's Quarter Creek along the Waxhaw wagon road. This great road between Camden and Salisbury, North Carolina, was on a transportation route with Philadelphia at one far end and Charleston at the other. An account book for the trading post in 1776–78 reveals activities there related to banking, livestock trading, milling, shipping, and repair work.[27] Furthermore a tavern provided refreshment and lodging and served as a communications center for locals and travelers. "Charleston merchandise" was being ordered and delivered by Clermont wagons. "Sundries"—likely farm produce and manufactures—some from the Clermont plantation, were bartered and sold.

The Clermont tanyard processed "hides," and trade in "beeves" suggests slaughtering also. Other entries show business in flax seed, rice, honey, Indian corn, wheat, tobacco, hemp, and tallow. The saw and grist mills for which Clermont became known were especially active. Grinding wheat and Indian corn yielded several thousand pounds in profit annually. Payments also cited earnings from the labor of slaves, possibly porters or mechanics performing repair tasks for farmers and travelers. The trading post, frequently called "Rugeley's Mills," would play a role in several Revolutionary War actions.

Pottery Manufacture

A new manufactory—one requiring expertise different from usual agricultural operations—began operating in the early 1770s at Camden. This factory was a pottery operated by John Bartlam, who by July 1772 had arrived in Camden from England after a sojourn in the lowcountry, where he had operated a pottery at Cainhoy. One history states the following about the local enterprise, believed to have been set up at Paint Hill, a forty-foot bluff overlooking Pine

An old building, razed in 1958, with "Entertainment for all—Man and Beast," carved over the door. Local people trying to save the building believed that it was once a pre-Revolutionary inn serving visitors at the nearby courthouse. Courtesy of the Camden Archives

Local frontier settlers depicted in Claude Buckley's mural—now at Pine Tree Hill Elementary School—illustrating the various peoples and cultures that came together near the Wateree River to found Pine Tree Hill, later renamed Camden. Courtesy of the artist and the school

Tree Creek, east of present Camden: "When Bartlam arrived in the early 1770s, Camden could boast a Quaker Meeting House, a Presbyterian Church, saw mills, grist mills, flour mills, a brickyard, a large store operated by Joseph Kershaw, a boat landing and a courthouse and governmental seat for Camden District bounded by the Congaree and Saluda Rivers on the west and the Pee Dee River on the east. Bartlam would have viewed Camden as a growing, progressive town where a business venture such as his pottery stood a good chance of success."[28]

The accounts of Kershaw's store prior to the Revolution show brisk sales for jars, jugs, dishes, and chamber pots, some in large quantities and many of which must have been of Bartlam's manufacture.[29] Twentieth-century investigation has recovered several hundred sherds from this era at Camden. This evidence led the archaeologist Kenneth Lewis to state of Bartlam's production: "The pottery includes grey, red, and white paste ware in a number of vessel forms reminiscent of contemporary British ceramics. A number of glaze and glaze combinations are present . . . indicat[ing that] a wide variety of wares were manufactured here."[30] Lewis classified ten types of wares, including paste ware, earthenware, creamware, and bisque—in all an advanced operation for the colonial backcountry.

The Citizenry

As the Revolution neared, small incidents rippled the surface of backcountry calm. In one incident at Camden a youthful "boy evangelist" named Richard Furman was scheduled to preach in the courthouse, where itinerant preachers had often spoken since the public building had been erected. When asked for the key to the building, the sheriff refused to surrender it, stating that the young Baptist from the High Hills of the Santee was not a member of the Church of England. An angered crowd offered to break down the door, but Furman declined and then led the people a short distance away, where he spoke in the outdoors. His calm control and forceful speech won him adherents that day, after which the courthouse was never again denied him. Furman soon became a leading patriot spokesman.

Baptist preaching led by the High Hills church, south of present Kershaw County, had influence locally in the early 1770s, but other denominations too were present. Almost all services were outside those of the established church, in congregations formed among the people by initiatives other than those of the parish government. The Quaker meetinghouse still stood in Camden, as did that of the Presbyterians, where services of the Church of England were occasionally conducted by the Reverend Theophilus Drage on itinerant visits. Beaver Creek, in the upper part of the present county, had a Presbyterian and a Baptist meetinghouse. Perhaps as an outgrowth of the latter congregation, a Baptist church formed at the fork of Big Lynches and Red Oak Camp creeks under Jeptha Vining, a noted organizing preacher whose name is found several times on the account books of Joseph Kershaw in Camden. Along Sawneys Creek west of the Wateree, Baptist and Presbyterian churches formed beyond the boundaries of the present county. The pulpits of the various churches gave voice to spirited opinions preceding and during the Revolution.

Kirkland and Kennedy reconstructed the names of some families living in or near Camden at the time of the Revolution:

Adamson
Beattie (a dealer)
Belton, John (probably)
Brisbane, Adam Fowler
Brown, James
Cantey, John
Carey, James
Castelo (a shoemaker)
Charlton, Thomas
Chesnut, James and John
Clay, Joseph
Cook, John
Jones, Thomas
Kershaw, Eli and Joseph
Lang, William
Martin, James
Mathis, Israel, Mary and Samuel
Milhouse
Morong, P (in Log Town)
Murchison (a tailor)
Murrell, William (a schoolteacher)
Nettles, William

Postell	Tomlinson, Richard and William
Sutton, Jasper	Wadison, Richard
Thompson (a blacksmith)	Wyly.[31]

These must be viewed as only a beginning indication of the many inhabitants—including slaves, immigrants, and transient dwellers—who were part of the Kershaw County–area population at a crucial point in the nation's history.

Thus during the 1770s, as considerable agitation and then war erupted between England and the colonies, inhabitants of the South Carolina interior were laboring to improve their conditions. A short but productive period of backcounty peace had vanished by the end of the decade. Again dwellers of the present Kershaw County area found themselves fearing for property and possessions, for family and friends, and for their lives. As they had done before, they were willing to fight to defend the choices that they made.

6 Redcoats and Homespun

The Revolution

On the eve of the Revolution the inhabitants of the present Kershaw County area lived in an isolated, loosely organized, and comparatively ignored territory of the American colonies. Within sprawling St. Mark's Parish the extensive territory of Camden District had but one town—Camden—in an area that is presently divided into nine counties. Here a single jail and a courthouse, both rustic and recently built, served the entire district as the only evidence of government. Within a few years, however, colonial events would overwhelm the lives of the people and leave the countryside in smoldering ruins.

From the onset of the Revolution, local citizens were involved. Many were ignited by an appeal in November 1774 from Judge William Henry Drayton, presiding at the district court in the Camden courthouse. Kirkland and Kennedy have called the grand jury presentment at that session a "veritable 'Declaration of Independence'"; it was one of several presentments made in locations where Judge Drayton presided.[1] Settlers in the interior of South Carolina, though concerned with local problems, could be as outspoken as persons in more settled regions. Meanwhile events in the colonies churned toward spirited elections for a unifying Continental Congress and for the organization of provincial congresses in each of the rebelling colonies.

Movements toward Separation

In January 1775 the Province of South Carolina formed its first "congress," as the state's representative body was to be called, ignoring the wrangling of the royal governor William Campbell for continued British control. Elections were conducted according to parish divisions, so that men from the local area were among legislators elected from St. Mark's Parish—Samuel Boykin, Robert Carter, John Chesnut, Ely Kershaw, Joseph Kershaw, Aaron Loocock, Robert Patton, Richard Richardson, William Richardson, Matthew Singleton, Thomas Sumter, and William Wilson.[2] Various committees, most notably the Council of Safety and the Secret Committee, were appointed to assist the Provincial Congress in securing control of South Carolina.[3]

In the spring of 1775, when the S.C. Congress began raising troops, Francis Boykin, Thomas Charlton, and Ely Kershaw were chosen as military officers;

later Isaac DuBose was also chosen. When the provincial body on June 1 drew up a "Declaration of Association," its signers pledged willingness to sacrifice all, including their lives, to provide liberty to South Carolina. Among those signers John Chesnut and Joseph Kershaw represented St. Mark's Parish on the Committee of Continental Association.

In order to urge the people of the interior to sign and support the Declaration of Association, in August 1775 the Council of Safety sent Judge William Henry Drayton, chairman of the Secret Committee, and the Reverend William Tennant, a Presbyterian minister, as spokesmen to the backcountry. Meanwhile, the British governor had remained in communication with backcountry loyalists, also known as Tories, persons whose sympathies lay with Britain. Instead of supporting the Association, therefore, loyalist leaders—such as Patrick Cunningham, Robert Cunningham, Colonel Thomas Fletchall, and Moses Kirkland—were urging other backcountry men to arm in order to quell the rebellion against the Crown.

Joining Drayton and Tennant in supporting the cause of those who became known as the patriots, partisans, rebels, or Whigs were the Baptist clergyman Oliver Hart, Joseph Kershaw, and Richard Richardson of the High Hills. Yet even this respected group converted few other backcountry men to pledge support. Frustrated, Drayton took drastic action, ordering that some "Nonassociators" be arrested and their homes burned. In a compromise with Drayton's group at Ninety Six on September 16, 1775, Nonassociators agreed to remain neutral if the Council of Safety would leave them alone. The previous day Governor Campbell had officially dissolved the Commons House, the representative body under the British government, and withdrawn to asylum aboard a British warship in the Charleston harbor. The government of South Carolina was now in the hands of the Provincial Congress.

At the beginning of strife in the backcountry, two representatives of the Catawba Indians near Camden traveled to Charleston to learn the cause of the controversy surrounding them. The Council of Safety explained that the British wanted to take the land and asked the Catawba to join them in preventing that from happening. The council also requested that the Catawba seek the assistance of the Cherokee. Additionally the council sent Lieutenant Thomas Charlton and a detachment of rangers to escort wagons of powder and lead to woo the Cherokee, who were being stirred up by the British. The Cherokee, however, never received the supplies for they were intercepted at gunpoint by a band of Tories under Patrick Cunningham.

Not all Tories had accepted the tenuous neutrality of the Treaty of Ninety Six, and the backcountry stirred with unrest after Governor Campbell's defection. In November 1775 patriot and loyalist militias clashed at Ninety Six. The patriot Colonel Richard Richardson afterward raised some four thousand troops and in

December defeated the loyalist militia in the upper Piedmont during the Snow Campaign, so-called because it was waged during sleet and snow coverage of more than fifteen inches. Richardson then pursued and captured additional Tories. With pro-British sentiment effectively restrained, the Provincial Congress could now turn attention to other matters.

Tensions heightened when the British Parliament passed an act on December 31, 1775, to confiscate the land of colonists who chose to rebel. Most of the members of the South Carolina congress at first hoped for reconciliation with the Crown. At the beginning of March 1776 they drafted a new constitution for use until grievances were settled, but near that month's end they moved toward separation. On March 26, 1776, the members of the congress adjourned and then reconvened as the first General Assembly of South Carolina.

Attack on Charleston

The former colony was now an independent state, headed by John Rutledge as president. Joseph Kershaw was a member of the Legislative Council, forerunner of the modern Senate. Persistent rumors circulated that the British in retaliation were preparing to attack the provincial capital of Charleston and to incite the interior Indians to attack in the backcounty.

In anticipation of attack on Charleston, local militiamen from the present Kershaw County area went forward with other backcountry men to protect the city. Among local leaders at the defense of Charleston against the British were Lieutenant Francis Boykin, John Chesnut, and Captain Samuel Boykin, the captain at the head of a company of Catawba Indians.

Rumored assault became fact on June 28, 1776, when an eleven-ship British fleet and nearly three thousand men attacked Sullivan's Island. Here Colonel William Thompson's and Colonel William Moultrie's men capably defended an unfinished sand-and-palmetto log fort. By day's end the attackers pulled back. South Carolina's patriots were also cheered when the Continental Congress declared independence on July 4, 1776, a week after the British pulled back from Charleston. The palmetto became a proud emblem of South Carolina.

While the British fleet remained anchored off the Charleston coast until August, they made no further assault, although their proximity and the stirrings of internal intrigue set off a Cherokee uprising in July.[4] There was chaos in the backcounty, although the present Kershaw County area did not suffer the depredations of the upper sections. Apprehension remained keen, however, until the following year when the Cherokee were defeated and forced to relinquish their vast South Carolina lands. The ousting of the Cherokee, coupled with the failure of the British to capture Charleston, resulted in the area of present Kershaw County and most of South Carolina enjoying an interim of relative peace. For a time there was no British molestation and little Tory activity.

The Southern Campaign

For the next few years British military strategy paid little attention to the South as a whole. However, after the king's army suffered a disastrous defeat at Saratoga in 1778, the British took a new tact and began to plan the Southern Campaign.[5] In 1780, after nearly five years of fighting in the northern colonies, the British concentrated military efforts in Georgia and the Carolinas. Here, where Americans were otherwise occupied with Indian troubles on their frontier, the British reasoned that there was no large concentration of Continental soldiers to oppose them. Most important was the British belief that a large number of inhabitants were loyalists who would rally to the support of the Crown.

A key part of the British plan was to capture coastal capitals. Consequently, Charleston once again fell under attack, and backcountry militias hurried to its defense. The shift in British strategy to the South was to place Camden and surrounding areas in the forefront of the war.

Preparations at Camden

Although there was no overt military activity in the Kershaw County area before 1780, preparations had been made earlier for anticipated hostilities. Records show that in 1777 at a cost of nine thousand pounds Joseph Kershaw superintended the building of a brick powder magazine for the state, located at the foot of what was afterward known as Magazine Hill. When the fall of Charleston seemed imminent in February 1780, the ammunition and supplies stored in the Camden powder magazine were moved further inland to Charlotte, North Carolina, as a precaution, an effort requiring seventeen wagons. Additionally the magazine was fortified and enclosed with earthworks.[6] When the Historic Camden Revolutionary War Site was being developed in 1966, the foundation of the powder magazine was excavated and partially reconstructed.[7]

Seizure of Camden

On May 12, 1780, Charleston fell. General Benjamin Lincoln surrendered the city and his army of more than five thousand defenders, too many men for the British to imprison or punish. Instead militiamen were given paroles and sent home on the pledge not to fight again. A number of local men were among those paroled at Charleston. The British then moved troops into the interior. Between May and October fighting shifted eastward into areas of present Spartanburg, Cherokee, Union, York, Chester, Fairfield, Lancaster, and Kershaw counties (with isolated action in Marlboro, Marion, and Clarendon counties and on the Williamsburg-Georgetown line).

On June 1 the British general Charles, Lord Cornwallis, led his army to Camden. Residents, under a flag of truce, met the British at the entrance to the town and, following protocol, asked for protection. Cornwallis responded less agreeably and accorded them the status of prisoners on parole. According to several accounts, including his own, a local resident named James Cary (Carey) offered his services to Cornwallis at this time and soon afterward accepted a commission as a major in the British militia, First Regiment, Camden.[8] John Adamson and Henry Rugeley too at some point accepted commissions.

Upon entering Camden the British immediately seized private property for their use, including the newly built and yet unfinished hilltop home of Joseph Kershaw, which Cornwallis and his immediate subordinate, Lieutenant Colonel Francis, Lord Rawdon, took as their headquarters. Leaving Rawdon in command, Cornwallis returned to Charleston four days later to replace Sir Henry Clinton as the top British commander in the South.

Rawdon set about converting Camden into a secure military post. The British stronghold was surrounded by a palisade wall and defended by five earthen redoubts, one of which positioned cannon overlooking Wateree Ferry. Cary, now a colonel, also constructed a small redoubt on the west side of the river on the Camden-Congarees road, overlooking the approach to the Camden ferry over the Wateree. The redoubt was referred to as Cary's Fort. The British posted sentries on both sides of the river, and all boats were moved to the east side.[9]

Buford's Defeat and Tarleton's Quarter

When the British captured Camden, Colonel Abraham Buford's regiment was the only Continental force still in arms in South Carolina. Having arrived from Virginia too late to reinforce Lincoln at Charleston, Buford's troops had remained on the north bank of the Santee until the city surrendered. Buford then began retreating northward.

Colonel Banastre Tarleton, sent in pursuit of Buford, used forced marches and overtook the retreating Continentals on May 28, 1780, in the Waxhaws settlement above present Kershaw County. Because the ground on which Buford made his stand was not well suited for defense against cavalry, he soon realized that resistance was useless and ordered his struggling troops to surrender. By some accounts Tarleton's dragoons ignored the flag of truce, and by other accounts they failed to see it, but a slaughter of American troops ensued. Of the 350 Continental soldiers, 113 were killed and 150 were severely or fatally wounded. The battle, fought about nine miles from modern Lancaster, is commonly known as Buford's Massacre or the Battle of the Waxhaws, not to be confused with a later Tory raid through the Waxhaws.

The British capture of Charleston in May 1780 undoubtedly encouraged loyalists throughout South Carolina. Tarleton's decimation of Buford's regiment two weeks later served as a model for Tory bands bent on mayhem and likewise instructed patriots that if British "gentlemen officers" would commit such apparent acts of barbarism, they could expect no less from marauding bands of Tories and other lawless groups. Instead of cowering the backcountry into submission as the British had intended, however, the slaughter inflamed the passions of many men determined not to be overcome. The countryside was consequently consumed by frontier guerrilla warfare, Tory against Whig, neighbor against neighbor. Individual homes were fortified against attackers, as they had been earlier for protection from Indians and outlaws. A few frame houses with rammed earth construction that fortified inside walls gave more secure protection.

A new expression emerged from Buford's defeat. "Tarleton's Quarter" terrified anyone with the temerity to defy the British. Although some recent scholarship addresses the issue of exaggerated vilification of Tarleton and his men and questions whether Buford's defeat was more the predictable result of his own errors and the inexperience of his men than a "massacre" caused by Tarleton's vengefulness, the fact remains that at the time news of the affair in the Waxhaws inflamed backcountry patriots and emboldened its Tories. The image of Tarleton's Green Dragoons riding their horses nearly to death in pursuit of the enemy and, when encountered, riding into their ranks bloodily slashing away with their sabers, neither offering nor giving quarter, became the common symbol of British barbarism then and served as the standard for American historians during most of the next two centuries.

Rugeley's Fort

Along the heavily traveled Waxhaw Road to Camden in upper Kershaw County, the plantation of loyalist colonel Henry Rugeley figured in a number of military encounters. At a strategic point on Granny's Quarter Creek at the Flat Creek juncture, the colonel's dwelling, Clermont, stood near Rugeley's Mills and his trading post. Also at the site stood "Rugeley's Fort," actually a large fortified barn. Built of stout logs with loopholes cut through the walls, the barn had been modified for defense with a platform erected inside for a second tier of musketry. Surrounded by a strong abatis, it was invulnerable to a detachment of soldiers without artillery.

In November 1780 patriot colonel William Washington, with a small band and no artillery, approached the fort, cognizant of its strength. Without other means than surprise and a pine log shaped to resemble a cannon, he persuaded the forces within to surrender the fort without firing a shot. This incident of trickery with a "Quaker gun" bemused colonials and infuriated the British. Cornwallis had been considering promoting Rugeley, but this incident caused him to write Tarleton in disgust: "Rugeley will not be made a Brigadier. He surrendered without firing a shot, himself and 103 rank and file, to the cavalry only."[10]

"Bloody, nasty business"

"The war really was nasty, brutish, and long," summarized the historian Walter Edgar when speaking on December 1, 2001, at the site of the old British headquarters, now the Historic Camden Revolutionary War Site. "Especially in the South, it featured guerilla tactics by the American rebels and disregard for the rules of war by the British, who considered the conflict a compound of war and treason, and by militias loyal to the British." War in the backcountry developed into civil war—between families and neighbors. Edgar continued, "The war in South Carolina was bloody, nasty business. There was tremendous loss of property. British strongpoints controlled by day; colonials controlled at night. Hacking with sabers and bayonets was common." A study by Anthony J. Scotti Jr. confirmed the brutality of war in the backcountry: "By 1780, the gentleman's war had ended. Hardliners like Tarleton held sway; robbery and sexual assault were routine."[11]

Soldiers' Problems

Life was harsh even during times when there was no fighting. Providing life's necessities had always been difficult in the backcountry. For soldiers on the move and living off the land, the task was even more complicated. Not only were soldiers concerned for themselves, but they were troubled with thoughts that their homes and families of women and children, struggling with the daily problems of survival, were surrounded by roving bands of marauders. Problems of camp life were many: shortages of food and other provisions, lack of good drinking water, disease, "camp fever," and smallpox. Accounts have become legendary of the effects on General Horatio Gates's hungry troops who were fed green corn and molasses while marching to engage British troops at Camden.

Imprisonment

Soldiers taken prisoner faced uncertain treatment, and many were brought to the Camden jail, which the British enlarged and fortified with a redoubt covering the northern end of the town on the main road. Here too civilians were intimidated and incarcerated as part of British efforts to bring the people under control. The Reverend William Martin was imprisoned in the Camden jail for prorevolutionary preaching. The Reverend Richard Furman eluded Cornwallis by escaping to North Carolina. Robert Wilson, the father of six or more sons in patriot service at various times, was being taken with ten other prisoners from the Camden jail to Charleston when they tricked the guards with rum and escaped in the face of British dragoons.

One prisoner in the Camden jail, Joseph Wade, was sentenced to one thousand lashes on his bare back for breaking parole. About to be shackled with a leg iron for attempting to escape, Wade scornfully asked that the other leg be chained also, and as it was manacled, he "created amusement by playing Yankee Doodle with his fetters."[12]

Suffering was the common experience in the jail. Conditions were generally crowded; illness and wounds were common. After Tarleton defeated Buford in the Waxhaws, he brought to the Camden jail all who could be moved, which included fifty-three prisoners, many with serious injuries.

In British hands after the Battle of Hanging Rock, a young teenage courier from the Waxhaws, the future U.S. president Andrew Jackson, had encountered wrath for refusing to shine an officer's boots. An angry swipe of a saber in retaliation left a permanent scar on the forehead of the young militiaman. Jackson and his brother Robert were among the wounded who were marched forty miles and imprisoned in the Camden jail, where they contracted smallpox. Their mother, Elizabeth Jackson, secured their release shortly before Robert died. Going on to nurse prisoners on ships in the Charleston harbor, Elizabeth died there of "ship's fever."[13]

Other survivors also forever recalled sufferings at enemy hands. Tarleton's name was linked to additional heinous deeds when his men killed the young Quaker Samuel Wyly at his home. Between two different accounts of Wyly's death, the common thread is that he was ruthlessly and unjustly murdered. He may have been mistaken for his brother, John Wyly, who as sheriff had enraged the British by carrying out legal punishments to some convicted Tories. Young Wyly's body was said to have been drawn, quartered, and posted on roadside pikes, and family tradition tells that his sister Mrs. William Lang vainly pleaded with Rawdon for his body.[14]

Rawdon too was accused of excessive cruelty. Approaching Camden in May 1780, he captured two youths who had shot at his troops at the High Hills of the Santee. He had Kit Gales hanged from a tree and had Sam Dinkins shackled and brought in to the Camden jail. In Camden, Rawdon seized the home of John Chesnut, who had returned there on parole after the fall of Charleston. The British "drove his family to Knights Hill and put [Chesnut] in the Camden prison." Until his death Chesnut bore on his ankles the marks of the irons that chained him to the floor, and he never forgot his treatment. About two months after the British took possession of Camden, Rawdon had more than 160 citizens incarcerated, 20 of them manacled, "in the intense heat of the dog days," the dread season of fever. These citizens had refused his demand that all males in and around Camden join the British to fight against Gates's approaching army.[15]

Kirkland and Kennedy cite a description of the Camden jail from the work of the historian Elizabeth Ellett, who collected many interviews to document *Women of the Revolution.* The wife of Thomas McCalla visited the Camden jail to see her husband, who was taken captive at the Fishing Creek battle: "The sight of the prison-pen sickened her. It was an inclosure like those for cows or pigs, and within, sitting or stretched on the bare earth, with no protection from the ardent September sun, were hundreds of unhappy prisoners, some of them with smallpox." On a later visit she found her husband in handcuffs and chained to the floor, along with other men she recognized: John Adair (later governor of Kentucky), Nicholas Bishop (the eighty-year-old deaf father of several patriot fighters), Thomas Gill, Joseph Wade, and William Wylie. Parson Mason Locke Weems's *Life of Marion* tells of the wife of a poor Quaker noncombatant in this area, Peter Yarnall, who "lost her reason at the gruesome sight" of her husband's body "hanging dead on a beam from an upper window."[16]

By various tactics the British brought the local area under tenuous control. The historian Robert Stansbury Lambert points out, "During the ten months that Cornwallis and Rawdon held the town of Camden, a number of local people . . . made their peace with the British by taking protection or accepting commissions in the militia."[17] Faced with suffering in jail, where they were of no use to country or family, some men accepted "protection"—agreeing not to resist the British without agreeing to serve on their behalf—in order to be of aid at least to their families. Some protectionists also quietly aided families of fighting men.

Among citizens incarcerated and sent as prisoners to Charleston was Joseph Kershaw, deported with his brother Ely Kershaw to British Honduras. The latter died of putrid dysentery aboard the ship as it reached the harbor of St. George, and Joseph remained in Bermuda until the war's end. Their brother William Kershaw accepted protection in Charleston and from that position maintained contacts with his brothers' families.[18] Young Samuel Mathis, paroled after the fall of Charleston, remained in the Camden area during British occupation to look after his sister, the wife of Joseph Kershaw, and her younger children. His diary of that period offers interesting insight into conditions during occupation.[19]

Patriot resentment of imprisonment was strong, and the Camden jail engendered resistance as well as forced submission. However, the British were not the only ones to use it. Patriots had used the same jail to hold their prisoners before the British arrival. One such prisoner was Colonel John Phillips, a friend of Cornwallis and an active loyalist in the area of present Fairfield County.[20] Lambert explains:

> John Phillips was a confirmed loyalist from the beginning of the conflict. Confined in irons in an Orangeburg jail in 1778 after an abortive attempt to flee to St. Augustine, he later spent four months in the Camden jail for refusing to take the oath to the state. Phillips had come to South Carolina

> from northern Ireland in 1770 and settled with his large family on Little River north of the Broad. When the British came to Camden, Phillips rallied his neighbors near the town of Winnsboro on Jackson's Creek and offered their services to Cornwallis. Known as the Jackson's Creek Regiment, they performed more arduous service for the British than perhaps any loyalist militia unit raised in South Carolina.

Citing four loyalist regiments raised near Camden—Rugeley's, Cary's, Turnbull's/Floyd's, and Phillips's—Lambert observed that men in only Phillips's group demonstrated "consistent zeal for the cause."[21] However, a Fairfield historian credits Phillips with being "instrumental in obtaining pardons for the seventy or more Whigs . . . condemned to death" in a drumhead court at Winnsboro during British occupation.[22]

Dilemmas of Slavery and Dependability

The British at times offered freedom to slaves who would defect to their side. Sometimes, however, the British officers would sell the slaves who had sought their protection. Tarleton reported that upon the approach of the British, slaves would sometimes quit their masters to follow their "liberators." He considered them a "nuisance." Some British officers used escaped slaves as washerwomen, cooks, or sexual servants.

Some local slaves visited the British camps out of curiosity, some with intent to stay. Correspondence and records of the period refer to concerns with slave behavior. The presence of a potential "domestic enemy" added to insecurities of the time, and slaveholders, sometimes with British assistance, used strong measures to keep slaves in line. Samuel Mathis recorded in his diary in March and April 1781 several instances of runaway slaves he found in British employ. He found "wicked Jin" in "Mr. French's employ" at the General Hospital and claimed her with an order, afterward having her "well whiped." A few days later, having hired two soldiers for help, Mathis also claimed Caesar and Punch from the hospital and "tied them" before proceeding homeward. The slave Esther visited the British camp on a Sunday and was whipped when she returned home late. Two days later Esther took her children and clothes and ran away. She was found, "being hidden in an officer's room," but Mathis could not get her back. Especially vexing to the British was the problem of slaves deserting owners who were loyalists. Cornwallis gave orders to discourage them from coming to British camps and tried to send them back to their owners, whose goodwill was of special concern to him.

Both the British and the Americans had problems with dependability of their soldiers. Desertion was not uncommon; furthermore soldiers would sometimes change allegiances; men taken prisoner and paroled then turned up on the field at ensuing encounters. The historian Lawrence E. Babits has cited the case of

Michael Dorkerty, for example, who was listed as killed at the Battle of Camden but who was actually a prisoner of war. Dorkerty changed sides five times during the war.[23]

Local Engagements

Battles or skirmishes occurred all over the area of present Kershaw County. On July 20, 1780, at Flat Rock, Major William Richardson Davie destroyed a shipment of provisions. Thirteen-year-old Andrew Jackson was a courier under his command. On July 21, 1780, in the vicinity of Beaver Creek, Davie's troops captured a British convoy and confiscated provisions intended for the British at Hanging Rock. As the Americans were en route back to camp with their British captives, another British force ambushed them, but with unexpected results. The Americans suffered only one death and two injuries, but nearly all the British prisoners were killed or wounded. Davie's men managed to escape.

On August 6, 1780, at the Battle of Hanging Rock, a site now in Lancaster County, a part of Colonel Thomas Sumter's troops under Davie, Colonel Robert Irwin, and Colonel William Hill attacked and nearly destroyed the crack British Prince of Wales Regiment, which lost 269 of its 278 men during the three-hour battle. The colonial troops were on the verge of decimating their foe when officers mistook a group of approaching buglers for British reinforcements and retreated. Andrew Jackson was among the patriot band that day also. This was the second encounter between the British and Americans at Hanging Rock. Five days earlier Davie had led a group of Sumter's men to victory over a British force there.

Gates at Camden

On June 14, 1780, without Commander in Chief George Washington's approval, the Continental Congress appointed General Horatio Gates, "the hero of Saratoga," to replace Lincoln as commander in the South. On July 25 Gates arrived at the colonial camp near Coxe's Mill in North Carolina and assumed command of the army of Maryland and Delaware Continentals that Washington had dispatched from New Jersey in April. The men there were under the command of General Johann Baron de Kalb, a seasoned French soldier of German birth who had joined the American cause along with the noted Gilbert du Motier, Marquis de Lafayette.

Gates was anxious to take away the momentum that Charleston's fall had given the British. A letter from Sumter in late July convinced Gates that he could achieve his objective at Camden, where only seven hundred British troops held the post.[24] The new commander began marching the sorely ill-equipped troops toward that purpose. They crossed the Yadkin at Mask's Ferry and headed directly for Rugeley's. Having crossed Big Lynches, he encountered strong fortifications at the Little Lynches and was forced to detour before joining the present Flat Rock Road to Rugeley's. The area today is still called Gates Ford.[25]

By August 13 the Americans had reached Rugeley's Clermont, where they were joined the next day by General Edward Stevens and seven hundred Virginia militiamen. These men had been joined earlier in the month by Lieutenant Colonel Charles Porterfield's Virginia Light Infantry and General Richard Caswell's North Carolina militia. The presence in South Carolina's interior of a gathering American army had prompted Rawdon two days earlier to withdraw from Lynches Creek to his base in Camden. Rawdon abandoned most of his outlying posts, massing his troops in Camden.

The British assembled some twenty-three hundred men. Like their American counterparts, they ranged from seasoned regulars such as Lieutenant Colonel James Webster's Twenty-third and Thirty-third regiments and Tarleton's Legion to two groups of North Carolina loyalists. Some of the British forces, like the Americans, were sickly. It was, after all, the annual fever season in the heat of summer.

Gates's plan was not to assault the entrenched enemy bastion directly, but rather to interfere with British strategic and logistical operations and thus to force Rawdon either to retreat or to come outside of Camden to fight. If Rawdon chose the latter, he would presumably be at a disadvantage since he would be attacking the Americans at a defensive position of their choosing. General Cornwallis, having been apprised of the circumstances by Rawdon, left Charleston and arrived in Camden on August 14. Assessing the situation, Cornwallis ordered his troops to march out at 10:00 P.M. the next night, with the plan of attacking Gates at Rugeley's the following morning.

The Battle of Camden

Unknown to Cornwallis, Gates's forces also began a march at exactly the same time. Unaware of British movements, the Americans had the intent of moving closer to Camden to harass the enemy operations. At 2:30 A.M. on the morning of August 16, the lead elements of both armies collided just north of Gum Swamp, a creek near present Flat Rock Road. After a brief skirmish both sides withdrew and prepared for the battle that would come at dawn. Gates learned from captured prisoners that the enemy before him included Cornwallis and Rawdon with three thousand men, far more than expected.

At sunrise the battle commenced. Cornwallis ordered his forces positioned under Rawdon on the left side of the road to attack. He simultaneously instructed Webster to do likewise on the right. The intensity of the assault by Webster's Twenty-third and Thirty-third caused the weaker colonial forces in front of them, Stevens's Virginia Militia, to break lines. The units flanking the Virginians—the North Carolina militia on the American right and Porterfield's Light Infantry on the left—quickly followed suit. All efforts to rally the routed soldiers were unsuccessful, including a final effort by Gates, who had fallen back to Rugeley's. Gates surmised from the swarm of panicked troops that his entire army had fled, and he too turned up the road northward in retreat to Charlotte, North Carolina, not realizing that the Delaware and Maryland troops on the other side of the road were still engaged on the battlefield.

The departure of the North Carolina and Virginia militias allowed British troops to flank the remaining Continentals, who were putting up a gallant fight. Sensing a quick victory, Cornwallis also committed his reserves, the Seventy-first Highlanders, to the fray. The Americans could not withstand the tremendous assault of fire and bayonet. De Kalb himself suffered eleven gunshot and bayonet wounds.

Those who were able fled to the swamps to avoid death or capture. Cornwallis, ordering his main army back to Camden, continued up the road to Rugeley's, along with the light infantry, Legion infantry, and the Twenty-third Foot. Tarleton's Dragoons pursued the fleeing Americans as far as Hanging Rock, returning to rendezvous with Cornwallis at Rugeley's later that day.

The Americans had suffered a devastating defeat. In addition to equipment and supplies, their losses totaled an estimated 900 killed and wounded, and 1,000 taken prisoner. The combined British casualty figure of killed, wounded, and missing was 324. Wounded men of both sides were taken to Camden, which was ill equipped to care properly for the sheer numbers of casualties. Some, like De Kalb, who suffered three days before dying, were so severely injured that they stood no chance of survival even if medical supplies and personnel had been available.

Cary's Fort (Wateree Ferry) and Fishing Creek

The day before the Battle of Camden, an American victory had been achieved in the strategy to harass British operations outside their stronghold. On the west side of the Wateree opposite Camden, Colonel Thomas Taylor, under Sumter's command, had attacked and captured Cary's Fort, a redoubt overlooking the road to the ferry. At the time that Gates moved toward Gum Swamp, he had not yet received Sumter's letter dated August 15, 1780, from Wateree Ferry. In capturing the fort and Commander Cary too, Taylor had also taken possession of an arriving convoy of some forty loaded wagons and seventy recruits bringing rum and other supplies from Ninety Six to Camden. Sumter took his captured prisoners and provisions and moved up the west side of the Wateree River.[26]

Ironically it was while Gates was fleeing toward Charlotte that one of Colonel Sumter's officers caught up with him the next day to deliver the news of success at Cary's Fort. Meanwhile, moving slowly with prisoners and captured wagons, Sumter continued up the west side of the river and camped on the night of August 17 at Rocky Mount, some thirty miles from Camden. Having evaded British lieutenant colonel George Turnbull, who was searching for him, Sumter

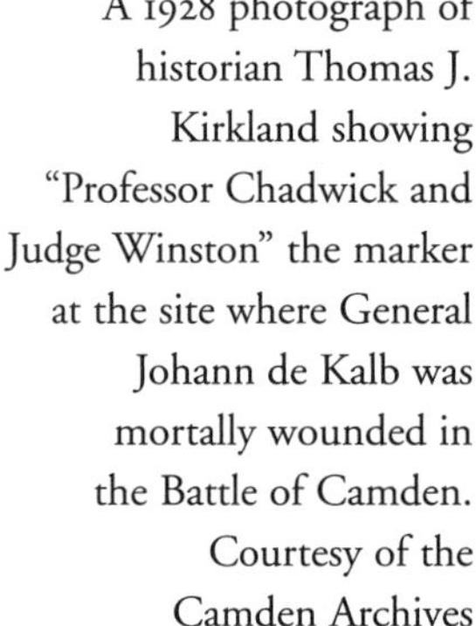
A 1928 photograph of historian Thomas J. Kirkland showing "Professor Chadwick and Judge Winston" the marker at the site where General Johann de Kalb was mortally wounded in the Battle of Camden. Courtesy of the Camden Archives

apparently felt secure enough to move only eight more miles to establish a camp at Fishing Creek.

Here the Americans relaxed their guard; some began cooking, eating, swimming, or sleeping. On the afternoon of August 18 Tarleton's Legion and an accompanying detachment of infantry caught up with the Americans and attacked the casually guarded camp. The brief encounter resulted in 150 of Sumter's men being killed or wounded, more than 300 captured, and the rest dispersed throughout the countryside. Sumter himself had been sleeping and barely escaped, bereft of hat, coat, and boots. In contrast, Tarleton's losses were only 9 dead and 6 wounded. The British captured 800 horses, 2 three-pounders, 2 ammunition wagons, many small arms, and 44 carriages of baggage, rum, and other supplies.[27] In addition they liberated James Cary and the other Tory and British prisoners.

Guerrillas in the Interim

After the devastating loss at Camden, afterward considered the worst defeat of the Revolution, and the sound whipping at Fishing Creek, it might have seemed that the British held undisputed control of this section of the backcountry. Yet guerrilla actions continued defiantly. The exploits of leaders such as Francis Marion, "the Swamp Fox," and Thomas Sumter, "the Gamecock," and men who served with them were local lore in later years.

Most of the military actions were not large-scale encounters like the Battle of Camden but smaller contacts. On March 6, 1781, Sumter and a British detachment from Camden under Major Thomas Fraser fell in together "between Scape Hoar and Radcliffe's Bridge," according to Rawdon's report, reprinted by Kirkland and Kennedy, who identify the site in present Lee County, "formerly in Kershaw County." Rawdon states, "A smart action ensued, in which the enemy were completely routed, leaving 10 dead on the field and about 40 wounded." The Americans also claimed it a victory, for at the end of the running fight Sumter burned the bridge and escaped over the Lynches.[28]

The researcher Lyman C. Draper learned an episode of the encounter from Edward M. Boykin, by report of Joseph Tiller, who lived with his father at Tiller's Ferry, just below the "Fork of the Creek" (Lynches). Following the fight, some of Sumter's men, pursued by the British, knocked at the Tillers' door at night. Young Tiller's father showed them a secret ford into the fork of Lynches Creek, facilitating their escape. British soldiers soon arrived but, having lost their quarry, camped overnight in Tiller's yard.[29] American retellings of such encounters focus on the wiliness of guerrilla fighters, who despite losses escaped to come back and fight again and again, sometimes with the aid of helpful citizens.[30]

The ferocity of guerrilla warfare is also recalled in other old stories. The 1842 memoir of James Jenkins, as a youth one of Marion's men and later a local minister, states:

> When the British were in possession of Camden, under Lord Rawdon, Marion sent a small company to make observations. The British had charge also of the mills near Camden . . . where they got grinding done for their army, and had stationed a company of men to defend it. This scout of Marion's approached in the night, and my brother, with one or two more, was in the act of setting fire to the building, when M'Pherson, contrary to orders, shot down their centry. This roused the men in the house, who came swarming down like bees; and alarmed the horse in Camden, whose feet roared like thunder, as they came to their relief; so the scout had to retreat.
>
> After they left Camden, they came upon a party of Tories, dancing, and ordered them to surrender; they did so; but when Maj. Downes, their leader, came out and saw so few, not knowing that there were more just behind, he ran back, shut the doors and commanded his men to fire. Here the brave M'Donald was shot down in the yard . . . the squad came up, rushed in, and killed every man. Downes was shot last, under the bed. His

daughter was wounded, and remained a cripple near Camden. . . . After M'Donald fell, he begged not to be left; but the Camden horses were pursuing; hence, they had to escape for their lives.[31]

Hobkirk's Hill

Entries in Samuel Mathis's diary beginning in mid-April 1781 refer both to guerrilla movements and to the Battle of Hobkirk's Hill, a major engagement about which he later wrote a historical account from interviews and an examination of the field. Still on parole and at the head of his sister's household at Kershaw's Burndale place west of the Wateree, Mathis was planting potatoes with slave help on April 25 when he heard actions of the battle: "very heavy fire of Cannon and Musketry lasting 15 minutes."[32]

With the Americans having experienced victories at Cowpens and Kings Mountain, the tide was beginning to turn when General Nathanael Greene, who replaced Gates as commander in the South after the Battle of Camden, moved his army into the area of present Kershaw County. On April 19–20, skirmishing with British pickets, he encamped between Camden and Hobkirk's Hill at Log Town, and from that height he surveyed the British fortifications only half a mile before him. Surprise attack was impossible since the British had cut down all the trees from that point forward and had left the trees lying on the ground to thwart approach.

Finding that Major Thomas Fraser had reinforced Camden, Greene deemed an attack improvident. The next day he moved to Hobkirk's Hill, a mile northward on higher ground and a better position to defend. Captain Robert Kirkwood was sent to skirmish British and Tory troops that had moved into Log Town as an outpost. On April 20 William Washington and his dragoons joined Kirkwood's Delaware infantry, and the next day they raided Camden's west side. They "burned a fortified house and redoubt near the Wateree River" and also seized "more than 50 cattle and 40 horses . . . desperately needed by Greene's . . . army."[33]

Two days later Greene directed his men to lay a corduroy road through the swamp and throw a bridge over a crossing on Big Pine Tree Creek, a location thereafter called Greene's Bridge. By this means Greene shifted position to the southeast of Camden near Paint Hill. From there he could block the exchange of aid between Rawdon and Colonel Watson, who was en route from the Santee, besieged by Marion and Colonel Henry Lee.

Receiving word that Watson had withdrawn to Georgetown, Greene on April 24 retraced his route and once again established a position on Hobkirk Hill. His supplies running low, he deployed his forces in anticipation of a fight. From left to right were the following regiments: Second Maryland (Lieutenant Colonel Ford); First Maryland (Colonel Gunby); Second Virginia (Lieutenant Colonel

Hawes); and First Virginia (Lieutenant Colonel Campbell). Captain John Smith's light infantry of Marylanders and Colonel Reid's North Carolina militia were in reserve. Behind Smith on the right was Colonel William Washington's cavalry. Captain Robert Kirkwood's Delawares were about half a mile away on Greene's left. A half mile beyond Kirkwood, Greene placed two companies of pickets, Captain Morgan's Virginians and Captain Benson's Marylanders, "where the 'Bye Road' [present Mill Street] crossed the highway from Camden to Cheraw."[34]

For five days Greene had been moving around Camden on various sides, his presence challenging the enemy. Rawdon, with a fort of men sick with fever, knew too that Marion was en route following the collapse of Fort Watson. On the night of April 24 a defector from the American camp brought Rawdon information inducing him to make an aggressive move the next day. The informant assured Rawdon that Sumter had not yet arrived to aid Greene and that Greene lacked both provisions and artillery.

That information was true at the time, but the next morning, unknown to Rawdon, the American quartermaster Colonel Edward Carrington arrived in Greene's camp with supplies and three cannons. These were quickly set, two

A tour group in 2008 following guide Charles Baxley's explanation of battle-line positions at the Battle of Hobkirk's Hill, an area that is now a neighborhood of historic homes

covering the Waxhaw road and the other placed between the First and Second Maryland regiments. With artillery and supplies in position, Greene and his men relaxed a bit: "After the morning's exercises, arms were stacked in ranks, and the troops with delight hastened to appease the cravings of an appetite whetted by many fatigues and two long days of fasting. A gill each of rum—a luxury long denied them—was allowed. General Greene, with his officers, was reveling in a dish of coffee. Pots were boiling merrily, and the 'feasting' . . . was at its height. Some soldiers were bathing, or washing their clothes, in the neighboring brooks. The horses were tethered nearby to graze, with saddles, as a precaution, not removed."[35]

Meanwhile, unknown to Greene, that same morning of April 25, 1781, Rawdon left Camden in the hands of the sick and wounded and set out on a silent march to engage the enemy. At 10:00 A.M., with a force of nine hundred, every able-bodied man in the garrison, Rawdon began secretly moving his army, not proceeding on the main road but heading east to Little Pine Tree Creek. The British moved quietly along the west bank, shielded from sight by the bluffs and woods. When they were about parallel with Log Town, they angled west to intersect the main road near the base of Hobkirk's Hill, where they would form their battle lines. They were not detected until their vanguard reached the Cheraw road and received fire from Greene's pickets. The sound of musketry was the first notice of the enemy. The American scene immediately altered: "Men rushed to arms, some barefoot, most, we are told without coats; the baggage was hurried off to Saunders [Sanders] Creek."[36]

The pickets fought a slow retreat to Captain Kirkwood's position, but their combined strength was inadequate to stop the British advance. They did slow Rawdon's progress, however, thus allowing the main body of Greene's army to form its lines. Because Greene had already organized the lines and the men lay on their lines, order was maintained despite the surprise arrival of the British.

The British also received a surprise, however, for upon forming their lines, they were hit with fire from artillery that was not supposed to exist. Their startled reaction led Greene to think that the British lines were on the verge of collapse, and he ordered a flanking maneuver on each end—Ford on the left and Campbell on the right. Washington's cavalry was ordered to go around to the enemy's rear to seal off any retreat.

The wily Rawdon, however, ordered a counter flank tactic. Colonel John Gunby's regiment panicked. This began a chain reaction among the other (Second) Maryland regiment. By the time the brigade reformed several hundred yards to the rear, the British had reached the top of the hill. Greene was with the Second Virginia Regiment (Hawes), which was advancing against the enemy, but when he realized their vulnerability because of the situation with the rest of his forces, he ordered the Virginians to fall back as well.[37]

A dramatic struggle ensued to rescue the valuable artillery pieces atop the hill. The sacrifice of Captain John Smith's hard-fighting company—all forty-five men killed, wounded, or captured—held the enemy at bay until Washington's cavalry arrived to save the cannons from capture. Washington covered the withdrawal of Greene's army, which in good order proceeded to the north bank of Sanders Creek. The American's composure coupled with heavy casualties by the British prevented the latter from venturing far beyond the battleground. Rawdon did not pursue the retreating Americans but returned the main body of his army to its garrison in Camden, leaving a small force in control of the hill. That night Washington's cavalry took possession of Hobkirk's Hill after driving the British from the field. "Perhaps in no other battle of the Revolution," say historians, "were the forces engaged so largely composed of Americans on each side."[38]

Greene stayed at Sanders Creek until April 27 and then moved to Rugeley's. For the next three weeks he remained in or near the present Kershaw County area, during which time he and Rawdon played cat and mouse. Several times—at Rugeley's and at Sawney's Creek—they came near one another but backed off from risking an engagement. By the second week of May, Greene was far from overconfident, however. Overestimating the strength of Rawdon in Camden, and in fact the strength of the British in the South, he glumly predicted to Davie on May 8 that the southern colonies were doomed.[39]

British Departure

Contrary to Greene's assessment, continued harassment of Rawdon's supply lines coupled with eminent British setbacks had prompted the British commander to give up Camden. On the morning of May 10 Rawdon moved out, destroying much of the town as he retreated. He left behind prisoners taken at Hobkirk's Hill as well as his own wounded who were unable to travel, but he took with him a number of Tories, their families, and slaves. Chaos and dismay attended many of the civilians who accompanied the British, knowing they faced an uncertain future but fearful of being left behind. Those who could took slaves with them. No doubt some slaves were willing to go and others were distressed. James Cary, for example, took slaves he had with him at the time, some belonging to others such as Joseph Kershaw, "in exchange," he later claimed, for slaves of his own that he left behind.[40] Many of the refugees, lacking financial means to secure lodging in Charleston, constructed a shantytown, which they named "Rawdontown," outside the city. Hunger and illness afflicted many. A number of loyalists sailed with the British when they evacuated Charleston, and some almost immediately began efforts to clear their names and reclaim the property they left behind.

Just under two weeks following British evacuation, Samuel Mathis noted in his diary on May 23, "I had our family moved into Mr. J K's large new House

A 2009 Revolutionary War reenactment at Historic Camden Revolutionary War Site, presented in front of the reconstructed Kershaw-Cornwallis House, home of patriot Joseph Kershaw and headquarters of Lord Cornwallis

[former British headquarters] in Camden." With his sister and children secured, Mathis abandoned his parole and on July 1 recorded his next action: "Joined Genl. Marion at Singleton's Mill." Actions to establish control continued until British evacuation of Charleston in December 1782.

Perspectives

Historians frequently have subscribed to John Adams's assertion that during the Revolution colonials were divided by thirds: one-third remaining loyal to England, one-third favoring independence, and the final third expressing indifference. It is fairly easy to find references to the patriots whom local histories have long revered. It is only slightly more difficult to learn of the Tories whom they denigrated but also frequently misunderstood. The third group is more difficult to identify locally. In the present Kershaw County area it would appear that there was only a small passive faction; however, it is also problematic to label some individuals as consistently supporting either group. Cornwallis stated that "in a civil war, there is no admitting of neutral characteristics, and . . . those who are not clearly with us must so far be considered against us." Political, economic, social, religious, or other differences among backcountry settlers notwithstanding, the British presence in the backcountry had made it difficult, if not impossible, for its people to be neutral. No matter which side a citizen chose, he often paid dearly.

The war had also destroyed the legal system, which now had to be rebuilt. During the British occupation of South Carolina, the provincial court system had ceased to function. In its stead the British established a board of police at Charleston that replaced the court of common pleas and also served in an advisory capacity to the commandant. This board of police also had jurisdiction over property disputes and debt settlement. The board followed the procedures of the now-defunct civil courts as closely as possible in an attempt to minimize resistance to its control. Kershaw County citizens who needed recourse through the courts once again had to travel to Charleston and appear before an alien bench, just as had been necessary before the Circuit Court Act of 1769. Local justices of the peace could hear only servants' complaints against their masters and civil cases involving less than three pounds sterling. Justices could also issue warrants for criminals, who when arrested would be taken to Charleston for trial.[41] Many of the criminally inclined in the backcountry are said to have sided with the British because of the greater latitude of tolerance with which their crimes were treated as a result of their loyalties. Justice, order, and trust now had to be restored.

An uncertain future lay before the residents of the present Kershaw County area at the end of the Revolution. Yet the citizens who remained or returned there were risk takers. They or their forebears had risked their lives and fortunes in migrating to America, where stakes had been raised to defy the greatest world power of the time. Surely area citizens savored the taste of hard-earned victory as they faced the challenges of rebuilding.

7

New Ways

Post-Revolution

At the close of the Revolution's warfare in 1781, the area to become Kershaw County lay in ruins. Peace-time disorder followed the chaos of war. Walter Edgar states of South Carolina: "Both patriots and loyalists had torched their opponents' homes and barns and carried off everything of value. The only real inland town, Camden, had been almost completely destroyed. Joseph Kershaw's mills, probably the most extensive commercial operation in the backcountry, had been burned to the ground."[1] Despite their trauma, people of energy were determined to build or rebuild what they had fought to secure, including homes, churches, courts, and schools as well as personal, economic, and political freedoms. These struggles did not end when the peace treaty of 1783 was signed.

Kirkland and Kennedy point out that the hub of Camden "immediately after the war . . . attracted . . . many of the Revolutionary soldiers who had come within its influence during military operations."[2] In the common struggle to rebuild lives and to reconcile differences, survivors and newcomers alike embraced patriotism for the new country. In the final decade of the eighteenth century Kershaw County was officially born.[3] Challenged soon afterward by the invention of the cotton gin, the county would face the nineteenth century tempered by aspiration and compromise.

The inhabitants who profited least from victory over England were the slaves, over whom both sides had wrangled. The British had held out promises of freedom to slaves who joined them, and some had been forced into labor or had willingly provided services with such hopes. Some other blacks had served among the partisans, enduring camp and battlefield dangers, in order to improve their condition. At home slaves and other civilians alike had shared wartime miseries of insecurity, upheaval, labor, and deprivation.

At war's end, however, rewards of personal liberty were not extended to bondsmen in general.[4] A few free persons of color lived in the area of present Kershaw County by the 1790s. For example, Bonds Conway, a skilled carpenter, bought his own freedom with his earnings in 1793.[5] Store account records of that decade reveal names of other free blacks: Ned Harris, Buck Jackobs, Tom Martin, Jim Pemberton, Tom Pemberton, Scipio Stanley, David Sweat, John Webb, and Jim Wickham. Although some persons of color were able to take advantage of new opportunities, such cases were not typical. Nor was slaveholding typical for inland white families at the time. In 1790 three out of four families owned no slaves, and of those who did, two out of three owned fewer than five. However, agricultural and economic conditions following the war would perpetuate the system of slavery for more than eight more decades.

Spiritual Rebuilding

When the British were defeated, another kind of war resumed. For a desolated people, the crusade for spiritual salvation brought to the front a mixture of religious warriors, including both independent messengers and denominational appointees. Although churches and meetinghouses had been destroyed and congregations scattered, records document that in 1782 religious meetings were held locally by Baptist, Lutheran, Presbyterian, and Quaker leaders.[6] A few years later Methodist preaching was also heard.[7]

Despite the wide variety of messengers at work, rebuilding congregations and houses of worship took a number of years. Although leaders reported believers hungry for the word of God and nonbelievers in desperate need of it, day-to-day burdens prevented many people from immediately addressing spiritual concerns. In 1782 local Quakers were so reduced in number that they voted to lay aside their monthly meetings and ceased to hold regular worship.[8] The losses and demands of wartime survival had especially strained the practices of those who had aspired to live in peace. In Camden the British during occupation had dismantled the only meetinghouse, Presbyterian, to raise a barracks for soldiers.[9] Likewise in the countryside meetinghouses had suffered from abuse and neglect, although some of the simple log structures were repaired or replaced from materials at hand.

Religious meetings were sometimes held in dwellings or the outdoors, but almost all were conducted by itinerants or by ministers who rode long distances to serve various congregations. Records show that the following among preachers held one or more religious meetings in or around the Kershaw County area in 1782 or 1783: Baptist—Lewis Collins, James Fowler, Richard Furman, and Joshua Palmer; Lutheran—Christian Theus; Presbyterian, John Logue and Thomas Reese. In 1786 the Methodists Beverly Allen and Richard Swift were here, and Bishop Francis Asbury was there the following year.

In 1782 there were meetinghouses in various directions from Camden—at Flat Rock, on Twenty-five Mile Creek, and at High Hills. On record was a "church at Salem" by 1784 and a meetinghouse at Swift Creek by 1786. It appears from a later source that the meetinghouse at the fork of the Lynches was built around this time. Some currently active churches claim descent from the roots of these old congregations.

Some settlements went without houses of worship for a time after the war. Both Hanging Rock and Singleton (Singleton's) Creek are on record as "congregations" in 1782. It is not shown whether the old Beaver Creek meetinghouse survived the war, but one of that name was in use again later. The Quaker assembly gathered "near Camden" in 1782, their historic meetinghouse no longer standing. The area around the old site with its attached burial ground, now known as Quaker Cemetery in Camden, has remained a community place of burial since the late 1790s.[10]

There were no formally organized church bodies or houses of worship in the boundaries of Camden during the poverty of early postwar years, although a "congregation" met there in 1782. Two years later Joseph Kershaw sold a town lot in trust to the High Hills Baptists to build a daughter church in Camden, although the property went unused and a church was not erected on another lot for a quarter of a century. In his will of 1788 Kershaw provided land to "God's Antient people, the Jews," although no house of worship was built there either. Presbyterians, the largest prewar denomination, by 1790 had rebuilt at their earlier site at Meeting and Church, but the structure disappeared from record, perhaps lost to fire, sometime later in the decade.

After the Camden courthouse was rebuilt in 1792, for many years the various congregations shared it for religious meetings, as it apparently was open to the community at large. James Kershaw, in the diary he kept from 1791, refers to a town meeting on January 4, 1793, to discuss acquiring the regular services of a clergyman. The eldest son of Joseph Kershaw, the diarist at various times refers to the preachers John Logue, Richard Furman, and Thomas Adams. (Adams was a Congregational minister who served the Presbyterian Church here eight years.) The building of the first Methodist church in Camden may be dated 1798 by a reference of Bishop Francis Asbury, and his journal in 1794 refers to a rural chapel of unspecific denomination at Granny's Quarter.[11]

Whether in town or the countryside, gatherings of congregations fulfilled secular as well as religious functions and were forums for public announcements and for private socializing. Participation in the practice of religion offered slaves and other persons of color more equitable status than did other aspects of society at the time. Whites and blacks, free and enslaved, male and female—all worshipped in the same meetinghouse.

Regaining Security

In 1784 Judge William Drayton kept a journal of a trip to the South Carolina interior. His descriptions of Camden and its surrounding countryside reflect contemporary isolation and postwar desolation. From the area of present Columbia, where Judge Drayton left the home of Colonel Thomas Taylor, his traveling party first lost its way to Camden and was forced to turn back and hire a guide before proceeding the following day. The judge describes traveling wholly through "Pine barren, chiefly high & very sandy"; passing "a large circular Pond or Lake, containing at least 30 acres" (now White Pond); going over "remarkably high Ridges"; and reaching gravel near the Wateree River.

There, the judge says, "The Ferry cross the Wateree [near the present I-20 bridge] is from one high Bluff to another, about 200 yards. From the River to Camden is about 1 mile; along the Road have been left, in clearing the adjacent Fields, several large Oaks, which form a pretty avenue & afford a most agreeable Shade to Passengers." Observant of areas susceptible to epidemic fevers, he describes the town: "Camden is laid out upon a rising ground; but has some very low Land between it & the River, & a Cypress Swamp on one Side of it. From these Circumstances I should judge it not so healthy as Ninety Six." Judge Drayton then gives evidence of Revolutionary War destruction: "There are some good Houses in Town, particularly Col[onel] Kershaw's, but there are marks of the British having been here, as well as in many other Parts, through which we pass'd. They burnt the Court House, Gaol, & the greatest Part of the best Houses. They cut down all the Fruit Trees; and destroyed all the Furniture, which they could not carry away. These evident Proofs of their wanton Barbarity & Desolation were strong Evidences of the Truth of many Relations we had of their cruelty to the Persons of Men, Women & Children. In our Progress, after this from Camden to Charleston we could trace their last Retreat by the stacks of chimnies, that appear'd along the Road."[12]

A Court System and a New County

In such disordered surroundings for town and countryside, with economic security broken and courts in shambles, lawlessness was a common reality stronger than the influence of scattered churches. Thievery was rampant, and violence often accompanied it. The redress of conditions was difficult, and stressful circumstances continued even after courts and constables were reestablished. British occupation had dismantled the backcountry court system, replacing it with a board of police at Charleston. Once more citizens from the interior had to travel to that city for legal processes. After the war local courts again became a high priority of the "interior" or "upcountry"—a more forward-looking designation eventually replacing "backcountry." Organization took some time, however, and courts faced additional problems bringing to order a headstrong and often unruly postwar society.

On November 3, 1781, Governor John Rutledge established the first court of record for Camden District, the expansive territorial designation of the prewar decade. Wood Furman, appointed ordinary, held court at his home at the High Hills of the Santee until 1783, when Colonel Henry Hampton was appointed and held court at his plantation near Winnsboro. The following year the office was moved to Camden, and in 1785 Henry Beaumont was the deputy ordinary.

In 1785—four years before the United States Constitution would be ratified—South Carolina was divided into counties to create more manageable local government and more accessible courts. The expanses of Camden District were divided into seven counties, designated Chester, Claremont, Clarendon, Fairfield, Lancaster, Richland, and York. A court was established for each county, although the Camden District Court of Ordinary also continued to function two more years. Additionally state judges traveled to hear district-level cases at the old seats, so that Camden remained a district court site even though it was not at first a county court site.[13]

For half a dozen years, 1785–91, the area to become Kershaw County lay divided among four of the early counties—Claremont, Fairfield, Lancaster, and Richland.[14] Most of present Kershaw County, including the old boundaries of Camden, lay within Lancaster County, although some edges of territory lay in the three other bordering counties. The upper border of Claremont County, for example, was Pine Tree Creek, just below the town of Camden.

With "equality" as a democratic measure, an effort was exerted to place seats of government at midpoints.[15] Under the requirement that county court sessions be held at a central location, the Lancaster County court met in the house of John Ingram at the Hanging Rock, that is, in the old settlement near the familiar natural landmark. The area later became part of Kershaw County but is now again part of Lancaster County. Seven justices were appointed in 1785: Isaac Alexander, Andrew Baskins, Adam Fowler Brisbane, John Craig, Robert Dunlap, Samuel Dunlap, and John Marshall. Among others who also later became justices of that court were Richard Champion, John Chesnut, and Benjamin Haile.

Appointed in 1785 as justices of other counties in which some parts of present Kershaw County lay were the following, preceded by their respective counties: Claremont—James Armstrong, George (J——?), Elijah McCoy, Thomas McFadden, William Murrell, William Richardson, and William Wright; Fairfield—John Buchanan, James Craig, Henry Hampton, William Kirkland, Philip Pearson, John Winn, and Richard Winn; and Richland—Andrew Allison, Richard Brown, Wade Hampton, Joel McLemore, William Myers, Arthur Brown Ross, and Thomas Taylor.[16] Among those listed are recognized men whose activities affected the area to become Kershaw County.

Shortly after the new counties were laid out, discussions were under way to address inconveniences and dissatisfactions. In 1787 a large number of "Inhabitants In and Around the Town of Camden" petitioned the legislature for a separate county with Camden as the center. The public economy would be served, the petitioners argued, because the new county and the Camden District could share one courthouse. Their appeal complained of present problems of jurisdiction since "the dividing Lines . . . are running within two Miles from the

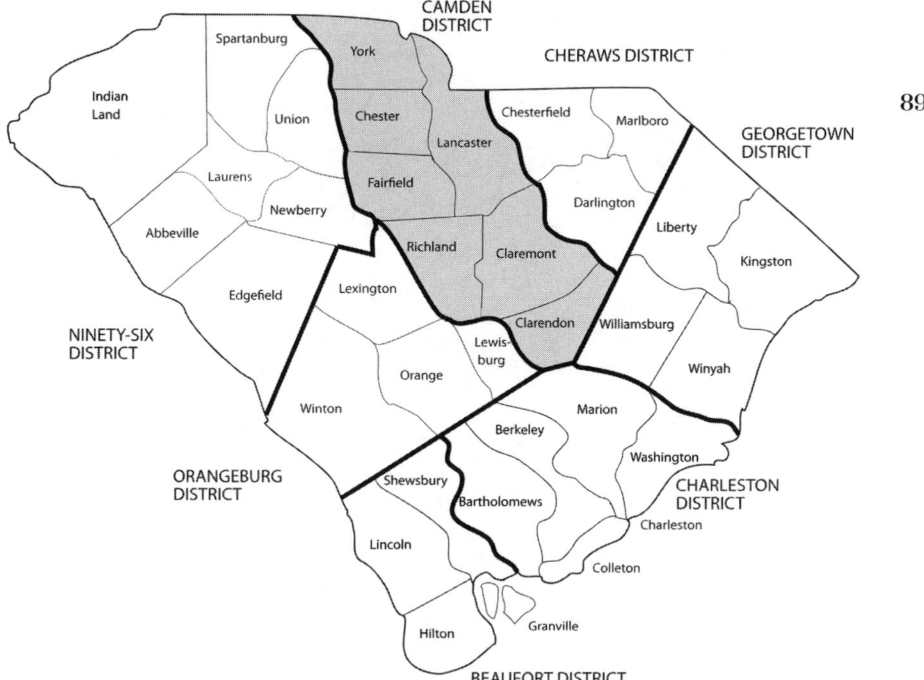

South Carolina districts, 1785–90, with most of present-day Camden in Lancaster County and some parts of present-day Kershaw County in neighboring counties. Adapted by permission of the South Carolina Department of Archives and History

Town of Camden." Describing the area, they said, "The Town of Camden, with the fertile Lands of the Wateree River adjoining make perhaps one of the most populous and promising Settlements in the middle or back Parts of the State." An appended statement said that the petition had been signed by Joseph Kershaw, John Chesnut, and "about 350 others," a number that may give some sense of the white male population of the area at the time.

The petition proposed the name "DeCalb" (DeKalb), but by 1790 a different name, Kershaw County, was in tentative use, although the county was still in its formative stages and not yet officially designated. The election for representatives of the Constitutional Convention of South Carolina, the body selected in 1790 to consider the ratification of the Constitution of the United States of America, must have illustrated the awkwardness of the voting districts at the time. Most of present Kershaw County lay in the far-flung District Eastward of the Wateree, which elected the following: Adam Fowler Brisbane, Richard Champion, John Chesnut, George Cooper, Isaac Dubose, John Kershaw,

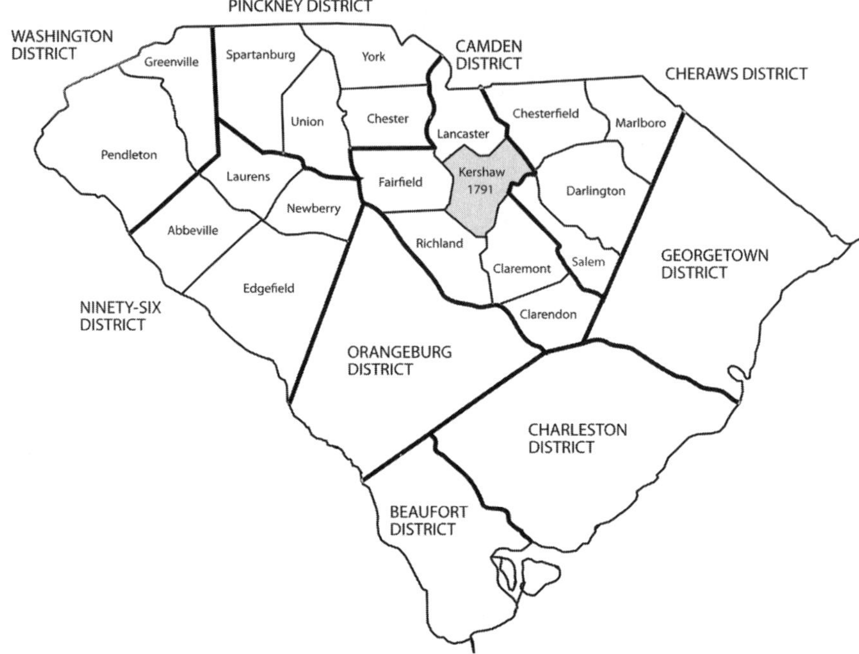

South Carolina districts, 1791–99, showing Kershaw County, set apart in 1791 (with Camden as its seat), and Salem County, set apart in 1792. Adapted by permission of the South Carolina Department of Archives and History

Laurence Manning, John Marshall, Isham Moore, Thomas Sumter, and William Welch.[17] Citizens on the west side of the Wateree no doubt felt far removed from them, voting and being represented in the District Westward of the Wateree, which stretched expansively in the opposite direction.

In January 1791, citing the greater convenience of conducting their business in Camden, 110 "Inhabitants of Beaver Creek and White Oak Settlements" and an unknown number of "Inhabitants Residing on the West Side of the Wateree River" approved petitions to have their communities included within the boundaries of Kershaw County.[18] A petition of 34 inhabitants of Claremont County suggested some adjustments to run the line near Swift and Raften Creek at the river to opposite the mouth of Spears Creek in Richland County. Furthermore that same month inhabitants of Camden successfully petitioned to incorporate their town for the encouragement of trade and the preservation of peace, order, and good government. The subsequent incorporation gave rise to Camden's long-standing claim of being the state's oldest inland town.

In February 1791 the South Carolina General Assembly by legislative act officially designated "Kershaw County" out of defined portions of Claremont, Fairfield, Lancaster, and Richland counties, naming it in honor of the patriot Joseph Kershaw. Camden was made the county seat. Here later that year, on December 28, 1791, Kershaw died at the age of sixty-four years at his hilltop home that a decade earlier had been headquarters to the now-vanquished British commanders. By the time of his death, the community Kershaw had helped to start was definitely beginning to rebound from destruction.

Courts in Action

From their beginnings both district and county courts were flurries of activity—verifying property ownership, settling estates and debts, providing for orphans and indigents, regulating slaves and free blacks, redressing grievances, meting out justice against thievery and villainy, licensing taverns and distilleries, and overseeing improvements of public roads and bridges.[19] The decisions of the courts, however, were not always welcomed in a debt-ridden society where citizens by necessity had been accustomed to handling grievances with personal justice. Edgar points out, "In 1784 in Camden, Hezekiah Maham, upon being served with a writ, forced the sheriff's deputy to eat it and three others. The following year debtors closed Camden's courts to prevent foreclosures."[20]

Illegal interruptions, however, did not persist with the approval of citizens who desired improvements. In 1786 Joseph Kershaw was foreman of the grand jury, which urged more support for the sheriff's office, stating that "offences are committed with impunity" and it was too easy "to defy the Sheriff; to escape from him, or break prison, and to be screened from punishment by one means or another." The jury's presentment assured the court: "The laws and constitution of the State are very dear to the freemen of Camden district; we value them the more, as they cost us so much of our property, our toils, and our best blood. And whatsoever . . . the misconduct of one or two people at the Court before the last, the citizens of this district will unite with the Legislature in the same zeal and firmness to support the honor and authority of the Republic, which they formerly exerted in rooting its enemies out of the country." Persistence and cooler heads over the long run countered temporary upsets, although complaints continued and other adjustments followed to establish a system of justice among people largely unaccustomed to its formal workings.

New positions opened for judges, lawyers, clerks, sheriffs, constables, jailers, and others. Josiah Cantey became surveyor in 1786. Henry Beaumont, Daniel Brown, and Jacob Brown were in practice by 1786, "the first attornies to hang up shingles in Camden."[21] They were followed by Benjamin Perkins in 1787, Samuel Mathis in 1790, Joseph Brevard in 1792, Benjamin Bineham (Bynam) in 1794, and John Brown in 1798. Abram Blanding was reading law here in 1799 and in practice the following year. An additional number of literate men added "esquire" to their names as justices of the peace. In the newly formed Kershaw County court system in 1791 Francis Boykin began a long term as clerk, while John Kershaw served as justice and Joseph Kershaw Jr. served as sheriff. The two Kershaws were sons of the patriot for whom the county was named.[22]

Retaliations following court cases were sometimes violent or even fatal. In April 1789, following a disputed court case, the Camden attorney Jacob Brown took out a peace warrant against Captain Thomas Baker of the Winnsboro area. The latter, according to testimony, in other previous conflicts had bitten an ear and gouged an eye. The peace warrant did not end the issue, however, for one month later at the Camden race track Baker and Brown paced off with pistols and turned and fired, each man killing the other. This duel, the "earliest and bloodiest recorded," according to the description of Kirkland and Kennedy, illustrated the violence that legal processes endeavored to prevent.[23] Frequent grievances against county courts, including concerns about untrained judges, led to reforms over time.[24]

The old court days were rampant with emotion. Besides the tensions of high stakes with much to be satisfied or lost, diversion entertained spectators, and a holiday atmosphere prevailed. Curious crowds gathered, some seizing opportunities to barter or to pilfer. Stray cattle, horses, and hogs that were found on a landowner's property by law had to be "tolled" and brought before the court for identification or sale. Auctions to settle estates or debts were conducted; slaves were rented; workers were contracted; and aside from business, wagers were placed on horse races.[25]

The entertaining atmosphere encouraged various indulgences that spilled over into the courtroom. On March 1, 1793, a state witness, William Houston, reported to the county court drunk and "behaving insolently." He was "committed to Close prison" until further order. That same day a ruling issued that hereafter the sheriff, or deputy in his absence, "Shall always When in Court Wear a Sword." In May, James Bowles was jailed for twenty-four hours for "Insolent and Contemptious behavior in presence of the Court." In August 1794 the widowed Mrs. Johnson, "Comeing into Court Disguised in Liquor," was jailed until sunset for flagrant contempt.

In the sequence of rebuilding public buildings, the jail and whipping post preceded the local courthouse. In July 1791 the sheriff was ordered to have built "a pa[ir] of Stocks before the Goal [*sic*] on one side of Broad Street," the jail (gaol) standing at its old site at the southeast corner of Broad and Bull. The courthouse, opposite in its old location on the southwest corner, was standing in 1792 when the July 5 *South Carolina Gazette* described a July 4 dinner held there. The courthouse building was a practical and simple structure, as indicated

On the site of the earliest courthouse, built when Kershaw County was set apart in 1791, this courthouse designed by Robert Mills was constructed in 1826 and used until 1906. Shown here in an early photograph, this building is presently the Kershaw County Chamber of Commerce and Visitors Center. Courtesy of the Camden Archives

from later references as well as from complaints of a 1790 grand jury over the too small appropriation that had been allotted for it by the state.

The public whipping post served justice largely to the improvident guilty. Several punishments carried out in 1793 indicate some of these sentences. William Norris, convicted of petit larceny, was ordered "taken to the Publick Whipping Post immediately after the adjournment of the Court this day there to Receive Twenty Lashes on his Bare Back and pay Costs of Prosecution before discharged." Zachariah Martin, brought to trial for cattle stealing, was sentenced to a fine of forty pounds or thirty-nine lashes on his bare back. A "riot" erupted during the case of John Phillips, Shadrack Phillips, and Isaac Williams on three indictments of cattle theft and resulted in additional fines for them and two spectators. The only one of the three to plead "not guilty" received the most severe sentence—a fine or twenty-five lashes per indictment. While physical punishment entertained vulgar crowds with violence and incurred resentments because wealthier offenders could avoid the pains that poorer ones suffered, such public displays were intended to deter would-be lawbreakers.

After the notorious horse thief Gray Briggs was executed in Camden on December 5, 1794, a Charleston newspaper commented on December 13: "He died as he lived a hardened wretch, for before he was turned off, he addressed himself to the surrounding spectators and told them he dared say that if a number of them had their dues, they deserved the punishment about to be inflicted on him." The gallows was possibly even then at the "hanging tree" that became part of local lore. Kirkland and Kennedy state that the tree was a gum "in the hollow just east of Fair street, about the middle of the area inclosed by Laurens, Mill, Boundary and Fair streets."[26] Its location remained a tradition through most of the twentieth century.

Aside from the effect of local courts, in a larger sense the organization into counties was, according to Edgar, "one of several political hushpuppies tossed to the backcountry."[27] Under the state's 1790 constitution, counties did not become election districts, so the old parish units still served for selection of representatives, and legislative power remained skewed in favor of the lowcountry. A reform group to address the inequity organized in 1794 among men from the old backcountry, including Wade Hampton of Richland County and John Kershaw of Kershaw County.

Losses, Reparations, and Restitutions

In courts and legislative bodies from local to international levels, for decades following the Revolution, claims arose from debts and losses surrounding the war. The new state of South Carolina struggled to pay soldiers and to settle with civilians entitled to compensation, making some payments with land, slaves, or other assets confiscated from loyalists. Counterclaims attempted to clear names and to reclaim property, and complications ensued over mistaken or disallowed seizures. In addition some individual efforts were made to secure the return of or compensation for slaves carried off by the British during the evacuation of Camden.

After the war Joseph Kershaw was able to recover only a small part of his fortune, the greatest portion of which went to pay for personal debt he had assumed in support of the patriot cause. While exiled in Bermuda, Kershaw had signed notes to merchants there mortgaging his lands in and around Camden in order to purchase nine thousand pounds' worth of clothing and military supplies to aid the colonials. The ship was captured en route by the British, and because his expenditures had not been authorized by the American government, they were not recoverable after the war. The records of Kershaw's settlements reveal extensive holdings of about thirty thousand acres of land and more than three hundred lots, especially in interior South Carolina, that had been mortgaged.[28]

Proportional losses fell to other area patriots as well. Local merchants owing debts to Charleston and English merchants had first to collect notes from local planters and farmers. They in turn had to collect debts from one another. Some citizens had assets in receipts issued them by the British during their occupancy, which they hoped would be made good by that government. In many cases receipts, accounts, and deeds had been scattered or lost in what one plea called "the Confusion and troubles attending the late Revolutionary War."

A variety of fates and circumstances befell area loyalists after the war. James Cary recovered none of his local property and received paltry compensation from the British government, although he traveled to Jamaica, Canada, and even England in search of redress.[29] Cary never returned to America, although after his death his wife, Mary, lived out her years with her kinspeople in Virginia. Robert English remained in the West Indies, although two of his daughters married locally. Daniel McGirtt reportedly retired to a quiet old age at the country homes of patriot kinsmen, including his Cantey relatives in this area. Henry Rugeley regained some portions of his assets, although payment of debts incurred by his brother Rowland consumed much of the amount. The treatment of loyalists after the war often depended on the relative treatment that local patriots believed they had received at the hands of given individuals during the war. Local lore has passed down traditions of secretive aid from certain loyalists, such as a rumored warning by McGirtt before a Tory attack, and suspicions of Rugeley's complicity in the surrender of his fort.

On December 1, 1782, Rugeley petitioned the General Assembly with regret to hear that he had been banished and his property confiscated, as the "only crime alledged . . . is his having taken a Commission in the British Militia which he assures . . . was merely in Compliance with the Request of some principal Neighbours (now Subjects of this State) to prevent its falling into the Hands of a person whose intent it was well known was to oppress the Inhabitants of the District in which he Resided." More than two dozen signatures, of local patriots, were attached in testimony by those "impressed with Gratitude for his humanity to them, when they Laboured under the Severe treatment of the British Officers, during their Domination."

A noted loyalist restitution is that of John Adamson, whom Kirkland and Kennedy call "the honored Tory." A Camden merchant before the war in partnership with the patriots John Chesnut and Duncan McRa,[30] the Tory militiaman Colonel Adamson successfully returned home from exile following a 1783 appeal of area inhabitants that "whilst he had any Influence, he ever exerted that Influence in behalf of Distressed Americans." One incident often repeated is that Adamson saved the life of Mrs. Martha Bratton of York when a Tory inquisitor, in search of her husband, threatened to decapitate her with a reaping hook. Adamson quickly regained status after the war, resumed his mercantile-planting interests, and rebuilt a large fortune.

Grappling with the Economy

Financial difficulties were common among citizens at all levels. The burdens of debt that created distress under the Sheriff's Sale Act of 1785 were made more moderate in 1787 by a replacement act that allowed payment of old debts to be divided into three annual payments. One of the difficulties in paying off debts and financing new beginnings, however, was the lack of a common measure of money. A sum indebted at a prewar or wartime rate of exchange had to be repaid in that amount despite a much dearer pound value after the war. In 1788 "Inhabitants Eastward of the Wateree" petitioned the senate with "Deepest concern and Heartfelt grief" regarding "the vigorous operation of the Act enforcing payment from Debtors." They urged a valuation bill to "avert the Distress, Ruin and Confusion" and to "establish Justice, Equity and Moderation on the behalf of Creditors."

Without a national bank or uniform currency, both counterfeiting and uncertain exchange rates added to the problem of a general shortage of reliable currency, especially in interior areas, where many urged minting a "paper medium." The variety of money systems in actual use after the war is illustrated in area court records. Three kinsmen over five years sold three similar-sized plantation tracts in related local areas, each using a different monetary system. In 1787 James Love and his wife, Margaret, sold 300 acres on "Hanging Rock Creek a Branch of Lynches Creek," for "six hundred pounds old currency." The following year John Love and his wife, Jane, sold 250 acres on Little Lynches Creek for "five pounds sterling." In 1791 Hezekiah Love sold 300 acres on Hanging Rock Creek for "300 pounds of Good & lawful money of the State."[31] Out of necessity a variety of currency continued in use for some time. On November 21, 1795, James Kershaw, then owner of the Camden Ferry, totaled his ferriage receipts in three systems: "By cash 10 dol. & a French crown—£2-5-11."[32]

In many cases new expenses were discharged by bartering or through exchange of produce. Court records reveal some of these terms. In 1789 Joseph Coates and Daniel Kirkland agreed to repay a note of sixty pounds with "Tobacco, Pork or Indigo delivered at Camden . . . at Market price." That same year John Mickle agreed to pay "1100 wt. Tobacco" to build a road at his plantation. In 1793 Clement Stewart made provision of horses and cows to provide for the schooling expenses of his four children. When metal value exceeded face value, coins were melted into useful items, such as spoons ("coin silver"). Records from 1788 and 1789, for example, show mortgages being undertaken with down payments of silver spoons, in one case "one spoon part."

In 1790 Judge J. F. Grimké's charge to the grand jury of the Camden District Court was optimistic of "bright prospects" since Congress had recently acted to assume a large part of the war debt, relieving local governments from "difficult alternatives of overburthening our constituents with taxes, or of ruining . . . sufferers by withholding . . . payment from them." One of the pleas for relief filed in 1793 shows that not all types of burdensome taxes ended, however. Twenty-three names are attached to "The Petition of John Morris, William Morris and other Inhabitants in Camden District in behalf of themselves and others who come under the description of Free Negroes Mulattoes and Mustizoes." Stating that earlier "your petitioners, who were Freeholders or Tradesmen, paid a Tax only for their Lands, trades, and other valuable property," they pointed out that since March 1789 several taxes had been added per head on blacks, mulattoes, and mestizos—resulting in double what they once paid.[33] The legislative committee recommended to "exempt free people of colour from pole Tax where they pay any other part of the public Tax paid of the people of this State." People of color, after all, did not vote. However, capitation taxes continued to burden people of color throughout the antebellum nineteenth century.

Cash Sources

The struggle to find a reliable cash source was one part of the economic issue. After the Revolution there was a return to many of the prewar sources of income. Stockmen, for example, sought to reestablish cattle and swine herds and eagerly registered distinctive brands with the courts. The identifications ranged from relatively simple markings such as a slash or a hole in a specific ear section to more complicated ones. In 1789, for example, William Sprunt registered a "cross and hole in right ear and cross and slit in left ear." In 1790 Andrew Baskins registered a swallow fork and fish hook in each ear, with horses additionally branded with *AB* and cattle with *A* only. The same year a female cattle owner, Mary Marshel, registered a cross and fish hook in the right ear and a figure *3* in the left ear, with an additional brand of *27*. It may be presumed that the complicated markings were designed to thwart rustlers who were changing marks. In fact, the greatest number of charges brought before the county court were for theft—especially of cattle. Vying with those cases in number were charges for assault and battery.

Just after the war planters again turned to indigo as a money crop, but the lapse of the bounty that Great Britain had been paying soon proved that endeavor no longer lucrative for export, although it was still grown for domestic use. Indigo was an exacting crop, however, even toxic in long-term effects on workers. Unbruised, blooming plants had to be steeped to a certain hue and then the liquid poured off and beaten to a froth as it fermented. At a precise point lime was added, and the sediment was collected, strained, pressed, cut into blocks, and dried for market.

Soon replacing indigo's dominance as a major market crop, tobacco too was difficult to handle. Leaves had to be sun dried, were heavy to transport, and had to be kept dry. Wheat required milling, and corn needed grinding, so mills had to be rebuilt to make these products profitable for market. Grain and corn were also distilled into spirituous liquors, and homegrown fruits were fermented into brandies. A number of early farmers and planters complied with the required court process to acquire distilling licenses.

Transportation by Land

For crops to be profitable, usable roads and safe transport to market were required. The names of many citizens and areas of local settlements can be derived from court appointments of overseers, or managers, of specific roads and bridges, for by law all property holders owed a given time of service to labor on (or to provide labor for) the upkeep of public transportation routes near them. Overseers who failed to call citizens to work and those who failed to provide labor when called were subject to penalty of law, and yet weather and soil conditions made some areas nearly impossible to maintain.

Moving market crops challenged the placement and upkeep of roads. Heavy loads of corn or wheat weighed down wagons, as did beef and pork whether cured or pickled, and dug narrow wheels into sand or clay roadbeds. Wheelless sleds or litters dragged under the burdens of heavy loads were also destructive to road maintenance. Tobacco, which had to be kept dry so as not to be ruined, was often rolled down the road in a huge hogshead (barrel container) to which an axle was attached and pulled by a horse. According to Kirkland and Kennedy, Joseph "Squire" Patterson remembered "hogsheads of tobacco rolled down the road past his residence on White Oak Creek from North Carolina to the Camden warehouses."[34] The old Georgetown Road was an important "rolling" road from North Carolina to Georgetown, passing the length of present Kershaw County along ridges and between creeks so that even in rainy seasons crops could be taken to market without crossing waterways.[35] Along the routes cattle were also driven to market, further challenging roadway maintenance.

During the Revolution, to suit their defense and transportation needs, the British had made changes to some of the old roads, widening some, hacking out additional routes, and blocking others. Such roads provided postwar advantages and disadvantages. The roads that gave access to markets also gave ready ingress and egress to thieves and outlaw gangs who preyed on victims and made hasty getaways.

Waterway crossings were major obstacles to land transportation. Smaller waterways were simply forded, sometimes at peril to travelers and cargo. Graves Ford on the Wateree River was one crossing long in use, near the mouth of Sanders Creek. Revolutionary correspondence mentions Elkins Ford on the Wateree. The area of the upper Lynches crossed by American forces in the Revolution has ever since been known as Gates Ford. Also found in postwar references are Wells Ford on Twenty-five Mile Creek, Brevard's Crossing Place, Carter's Crossing, and Kingston's Ford.

Only crude materials existed to build bridges, which were feasible only over relatively narrow waterways, and these quickly decayed or were swept away with periodic flooding. Ferries were preferred for crossing wider bodies. Over the Wateree River the Camden (Wateree) Ferry that had been in operation long before the Revolution was quickly back in business after the war. Also crossing the river, about halfway between the mouths of Beaver and White Oak creeks, Mickle's Ferry had begun operation during the war. First vested in 1778 to Joseph Mickle, it was in 1792 vested to John Mickle.

After the war additional ferries crossed the Wateree at other points. In 1787, about midway between the mouths of Camp and Sanders creeks, John Chesnut established Chesnut's Ferry at his Knight's Hill plantation, ferry rights being vested in 1788.[36] In 1791, below the Camden Ferry, English Ferry was authorized on the plantation of Joshua English, on the west side of the river.[37] In 1795, north of Mickle's Ferry, at the request of inhabitants of Fairfield, Kershaw, and Lancaster counties, Rugeley's Ferry was vested in the name of Henry Rugeley, possibly a nephew of the Tory colonel.

An important public ferry "at the fork of Lynches Creek" was vested in 1791 after the petition of the private ferry owner Joseph Tiller, who pointed out "that the Long wished for Road from the Town of Green's Ville [originally Long Bluff, then Greeneville, now Society Hill] On the Pee Dee to Camden is At length Accomplished."[38] The following year it was a link on the national post road from Peterborough, Virginia, to Fayetteville, North Carolina, to Augusta, Georgia, through Cheraw, Camden, Columbia, and Cambridge in South Carolina. A

Remains of an old plank road in a swamp near Sandy Grove community. The road was on a route used by the British and part of the old wagon road between Camden and the Bishopville area.

Flatboat crossing the Wateree River at Peay's Ferry, near Liberty Hill, 1911.
Courtesy of the Camden Archives

horseback mail carrier needed more than four days to travel one way between Fayetteville and Augusta.

Locally the post road united the judicial center of Cheraw District with the judicial center of Camden District. Cantey's Bridge crossed the road from Tiller's Ferry to Camden Ferry. The post-road traffic promoted settlement at Tiller's Ferry as well as along the way. Lynches-area residents signing Tiller's 1791 petition were (William) Chamber, Frederic Evans, Daniel Horten, Benjamin Moseley (L.D.M.), Joshua Palmer, Henry Sanders, Thomas Sherly, Richard Stratford, and Jesse Wall.

A change was ordered to the Camden ferry over the Wateree on November 7, 1794, following the petition of James Kershaw "that the present Landing on the South side of Camden Ferry is not so proper as if changed to about 300 yards lower down the River." The legislature approved, therefore, for commissioners "to fix on a place more proper than the present for a landing, and also for laying out the road therefrom the nearest & Most convenient way to cross Wrights branch."[39] The movement may have been prompted by changes in the river or its banks, or by related transportation links.

Transportation by Water

Attention was also being paid to facilitating waterway transportation to move crops to market. To provide dry storage, especially for tobacco, and to facilitate shipping on the Wateree River, large warehouses were built on both sides of its banks in order to take advantage of navigable stages. On the west side of the river opposite Camden, Joseph Kershaw had earlier laid out a town he called Westerham. Although the name survived for some time, a town did not develop at the location, possibly because the rich soil of the area was soon in greater demand for agriculture.

From early times transportation issues, both local and broader, were woven into larger schemes to tie the area to state, national, and international communication. In 1786 the merchant-agriculturalist Elkanah Watson, who had spent five years working in Europe, where he studied canals, visited Camden during a business trip. His *Memoirs* reported fifty houses in the town where tobacco, indigo, flour, beef, and deerskins were the valuable commodities of interior trading. These, he said, were sent to Charleston "by a circuitous and expensive water carriage, down the Santee and by Bull's Island."[40] Watson, later a noted promoter of the Erie Canal, was not the only man of his time to envision internal improvements by water.

In March 1787 the Company for Opening the Navigation of the Catawba and Wateree Rivers incorporated under legislative act, with John F. Grimké as president. Also in March the General Assembly ratified an act to open navigation of "Lynche's Creek" as well. The state chief engineer Colonel John Christian Senf, who had been a military engineer under General Gates at the Battle of Camden, shortly began work as a civil engineer for the Catawba and Wateree company as well.[41] The desire to improve navigation seemed a logical one if only because the richest lands lay along the waterways and the greatest number of citizens resided in these areas.

In the 1790s nationally there was a fever of canal-building schemes to improve waterway transportation. In this state work began on the twenty-two-mile Santee Canal in 1793 and continued through the decade to link midlands and coastal water routes. In 1795 a legislative report approved plans to extend navigation of the Catawba into North Carolina as a "great and manifest advantage" to South Carolina, and plans were under way that would lead to canal building on the Wateree and Catawba rivers.

No less a personage than George Washington accepted the vision of which the Wateree Canal was intended to be a part. Washington referred to the arsenal being built in the "vicinity of Rocky Mount on the Wateree in South Carolina," stating, "It is expected that a canal will ere long effect a good navigation between the Wateree and the Catawba; which whenever it shall happen will render the vicinity of Rocky Mount extremely convenient to the supply of North Carolina by inland navigation." Arthur Wade states of Washington: "He had kept abreast of plans to link the widely-separated regions of the new country by roads, rivers, and canals, and by 1798 he was fully aware of South

Carolina's project for a series of canals to supplement its rivers and to provide trade waterways from central North Carolina's rich iron region to the Atlantic at Georgetown and Charleston. In selecting the tiny settlement of Rocky Mount, Washington was relying on a project already under way to link the Catawba with the Wateree, bypassing the falls near Rocky Mount, and thus providing a route to the ocean by way of the Santee and Cooper rivers."[42]

Milling

Once mills were repaired and operating again after the Revolution, often at old seats, milling was again very profitable. Thomas Broom of Maryland had been in Camden with Lee's Legions during the war and had seen Kershaw's mill seats then. In 1794 Broom moved to Camden with a large mercantile stock and became partner with two other Revolutionary War veterans and previous Kershaw partners—Duncan McRa(e), who moved from the Pee Dee, and the local Zach Cantey. Broom, introducing new processing, bought the mill sites on Pine Tree Creek below the city limits and operated profitable water-powered mills there.

Low water conditions exposing shoals in areas where people used to cross the Wateree River near the plantation of early settler Richard Champion at the mouth of Granny's Quarter Creek, now within sight of the Wateree Dam. Courtesy of the Camden Archives

Moving with Broom from Elkton, Maryland, were families of men closely kin to him—Harmon and Johannes Arrants, James Syng Murray, and Zebulon Rudulph—and who also engaged in milling or mercantile activities. The widower Broom married the widow of Samuel Boykin and died of yellow fever on a visit to Charleston in 1799. Milling enterprises continued, however. McRa in 1798 had bought the site of the old Indian camp at the confluence of Big and Little Pine Tree creeks, where he erected the first of the grist and flour mills successfully operated for a number of years.

At Swift Creek, where the county's only working gristmill operates today at Boykin Mill Pond, milling started as early as this era under the planter Burwell Boykin. Among other Kershaw County mills of various types in use in the post–Revolutionary War eighteenth century are these: Archer's Mill (between Hanging Rock and Mickle's Ferry); Chambers Mill (in the area of the county line and English Ferry); Chesnut's Mill (below Camden); English Mills (below Camden); Marshal's Mill (between John Lockhart's plantation and Lynches Creek, called also "Col. Marshal's old Saw Mill"); Moore's Mill (past English Mills below Camden); and Peoples Mill (between the Lynches and Camden).[43]

The potential for exploiting water transportation appealed to local entrepreneurs of the Pine Tree Navigation Company. In 1796 the partners Broom, Cantey, and McRa, along with James and John Kershaw, chartered the company for the purpose of making Pine Tree Creek navigable. By the following year they had opened the creek as far as Broom's Mills and attempted to recharter with additional investors to extend water transportation "to the foot of the hill, on which Camden is Situated."[44] The company proposed to add locks and to build a tobacco warehouse and inspection station at the head of the canal at Camden. Investors espoused savings for North Carolina tobacco farmers currently using costly land carriage to Wilmington or Charleston.

The ambition, engineered under Colonel John Christian Senf, never proved successful.[45] Although the company gained rights of land acquisition and control, similar to the controversial rights accorded to the separate company for Wateree-Catawba navigation, some citizens appeared disgruntled about public authority over private holdings. Furthermore, in various areas the increasing numbers of mills, canals, and plans for such did not please all people, and petitions ensued from citizens in the state concerned about obstructions to fishing and waterway transportation caused by dams, sluices, and mill houses. It is likely that the flood-prone nature of lower Pine Tree Creek also helped to doom the efforts.

Specialists and Craftsmen

Specialized skills of workmen were required for planters, farmers, and their supporting network of millers and merchants to build a flour-based agricultural economy. From court records, store account books, and various other documents may be gleaned the names of many craftsmen in building professions at work in the Camden or Kershaw County area in the 1780s or 1790s. These include the following: bricklayer—William Cook; carpenters, house carpenters, or house joiners—James Cook, William Deans, Drury Harrington, Robert Hood, John Hutchins, Robert Robinson, Adam Swan, Lewis Wallis (Wallace), and Enouch Wind; and cabinet (furniture) maker—Thomas English II. In 1793 an industrious slave carpenter about thirty years of age, Bonds Conway, purchased his freedom with his own money and from that trade made a comfortable livelihood, purchased property, and raised a large family.[46]

There were additional specialized builders. Men described as boatbuilders, ship carpenters, or shipwrights included John Kirkpatrick and Richard Stradford (Stratford). Zebulon Gaunt was described as a millwright. Absolam Blanchard of Camden was variously called a coach maker, a mechanic, or a chair (carriage) maker, while John Burns on Twenty-five Mile Creek was simply termed a wagon maker.

Other craftsmen in the 1780s or 1790s included blacksmiths: Thomas Berry, Thomas Cougher ("of Beaver Creek"), Joshua Grayham ("lives near James Perry"), Hugh McDowall, John Payne, Andrew Prestly Jr., "the Negro Randy," Samuel Russell, and Niclolass Swilley (Swilla). References gleaned from James Kershaw's diary indicate that Robin Hood and Paul Smith, likely also blacksmiths, were possibly gunsmiths. From court records Joshua Palmer was a cooper (barrel maker), and Thomas Burns was a silversmith. William Martin was a cordwainer (leather worker); Peter Rush, a rope maker; and Benjamin McKensie, a saddler. An account book names James Perry as a saddler, and Kershaw's diary says that one "Kent" shoed a horse and one "Patterson" fixed a clock. "Patterson" is given the label watchmaker by one account book.

Some other occupations of record in that time period included the following: "taylors"—James Betty, Samuel Bried, and Alexander Goodall; shoemakers—James Berry, William Whitaker, (?) Young, "Shoemaker John," and "Stumpy Jim"; and weavers—Molly Bass and Prissy Evans. Customers well attired by these persons might have sought out the portrait artist Belzons. John Fisher, William Parker, and John Reid (Reed) with his wife, Sarah, were innkeepers; Fisher owned "the yellow house," Parker had a house behind the courthouse, and the Reids' place may have operated near the river. The taverners John Dinkins and John McCaa were owners, respectively, of Dinkins Tavern and MaCaa's Tavern.[47] John King was a butcher, and John Plunkett and "Daniel the baker" were bakers.

Jacob Greenuff, a "Meriner" (mariner), was possibly involved in river transportation; John Smith "of the Wataree" described himself simply as a "Labourer." An unidentified account book names Clarke and John Jacobs as "working on boats." Spencer Brummitt was a miller, and Jesse Minton, whose father owned a mill he later inherited, called himself a "Mechanic." Records also mention the wagoneers P. Walker and W. Wallace, and the surveyors McWhilly and William Turrno. Several plantation names are found in account books: Bettie's Neck, Crab Apple, Hopewell, Payne, and Red Hill. Overseers named were Joseph Holliday (Duncan McRa[e]'s), James Hunter (John Kershaw's), William McKay (Martin's), John Martin (at Crab Apple plantation), and Thomas Williams (Robert Lee's).

Additionally slaves, apprentices, or hired workmen assisted many of the craftsmen, providing a busy workforce in the community. James Kershaw put his valuable slave Guinea Catoe to work with the boatbuilder Kirkpatrick.[48] In other enterprises the Kershaws owned a brickyard and a brew house, both of which over time had various owners.[49] Isaac Alexander owned a brickyard. Benjamin Carter in his lifetime earned a fortune tanning and finishing fine leathers; his tanyard vats operated near the creek swamp below York and Mill streets.[50]

The various crafts and especially boatbuilding in the area increased the local demand for production of rosin and turpentine from sandhill pines as well as timber from the various forest trees. No specific names are associated with specialization in these natural products, suggesting widespread availability and probable use of slave or poor white labor in their collection. Turpentining as a cash business was at the time largely carried out in North Carolina and may have been brought to Camden from that area.

Along the river area near the boatyard, where "Camden-built boats" were constructed and launched, wharves and warehouses increased in the late eighteenth century. The boats were advertised in Charleston as sizable enough to carry 120 barrels of rice or 15 to 20 cords of wood. Camden's Samuel Mathis in 1786 was running two boats monthly to James Mouzon's store near the mouth of the Santee, where goods were transferred to Mouzon's schooner for the rest of the trip across Bull's Bay to Charleston. Later, "Coleman's boat" traded between the coast and Camden. In his diary Kershaw mentions the local construction of a bateau, of the flat used as his ferry, and of a canal boat. Riverboats for merchant trading, many of them built at the Camden boatyard and with names such as *La Belle Catherine, Schrive, Polly Brisbane,* and *Venture,* plied the Wateree. An account book cites boat names in the late 1790s; one is simply *Rebecca,* but other names suggest political allusions: *Republican, Wolsey,* and *Sanscullotte*—terms associated with the ongoing French Revolution.

An industrialist of his day, Richard Champion, who had managed a highly skilled factory producing hard-paste porcelain at Bristol, England, sold the patent in 1781 and immigrated with his family to South Carolina in 1784.[51] In the Kershaw County area he took up the life of a planter, although he may have

Surviving brickwork for gates that once raised and lowered water levels for rice fields of merchant-planters south of Camden

aspired to engage in manufacture in the future. Before his death in 1791 of fever, he likely discussed with local men technical changes of the Industrial Revolution—division of labor, assistance of machinery, and improved roads and canals to carry products to market. Richard Lloyd Champion, his elder son, served as clerk of court from 1790 to 1808.[52]

Mercantile Enterprises

That business prospects were promising is suggested by a 1786 Charleston ad to rent the Camden store Chesnut & Co. (formerly Kershaw's), which was "upwards of 60 feet in front . . . where about forty wagons have been dispatched in a day." Postwar mercantile enterprises in or around the hub of Camden were operated by men of diversified backgrounds, including Charleston investors, local planters, and northern, immigrant, or Jewish merchants. While business interests continued under prewar merchant-planter names such as Adamson, Cantey, Chesnut, and Kershaw, court records of the 1780s include as well the names of newly arrived Camden merchants: David Bush, Claude Jean Baptiste LeDroit DeBussy, Samuel Levy (Levi), Mordecai Lion, William Parker, Joachim Gottfried Schutt, and Solomon Woolf. Nathaniel Cary, believed to have been a kinsman of the Tory colonel James Cary, was also an area merchant and planter of the time.

From 1793 to 1800 four eventual brothers-in-law of varying backgrounds became separate merchants in Camden. They were, in order of arrival, Dan Carpenter of Massachusetts, Phineas Thornton of New Jersey, James L. Clark of Scotland, and Jonathan Eccles of Ireland. Other merchants who came in the decade were Alexander Matheson of Scotland and Lewis Ciples, an Englishman from the Carolina lowcountry representing Charleston merchants. James Kershaw's diary adds the surnames of two other local merchants, "Scot" and "Young." In rural areas peddlers' carryalls—covered wagons lined with shelves and cubbyholes to secure widely varied merchandise—visited locales around mills and other natural stopping places, such as taverns, ferries, fords, and bridges. Here, over time, general stores would be established in a number of settlements.

Helping to battle the fevers, ailments, and injuries that carried off so many citizens at untimely ages were medical men variously guided by a smattering of training, some scientific readings, folk traditions, and a large dose of intuition. Among local medical men practicing in the postwar era were Dr. Isaac Alexander, a Princeton graduate from North Carolina and a Revolutionary War surgeon who attended the wounded Baron de Kalb; Dr. Robert Brownfield; Dr. James Martin; and Dr. John Trent of Trenton, New Jersey. Two late-century references in Kershaw's diary mention a "Dr. Perkins" and a "Dr. Davaur."

Apprenticeships

At the end of the Revolution, when local opportunities for education were few, one practical way for a young person to become productive was through apprenticeship to a skilled master. Records of the 1780s–90s reveal that in exchange for education and job training, a young apprentice agreed not only to provide faithful service but also to abide by strict codes of behavior.

In 1787 Zachariah Bell and his wife bound their six-year-old son Thomas to the county justice Robert Dunlap to learn his occupation—that of planter. Thomas was to serve until age twenty-one, at which time of release Dunlap was to give him "one Horse and Saddle and one suit of cloathing"; until then he was to provide the boy "sufficient Meat Drink Washing lod[g]ing and cloathing fitting for an apprentice" and to "learn him to Read and Write." In return, young Bell was to keep his master's secrets, obey his lawful commands "gladly," treat him honestly, and keep him from harm. In addition the boy's contract dictated: "at Cards Dice or any other unlawful games he shall not play, Taverns or Alehouses he shall not frequent, fornication he Shall not commit." Neither was he to buy or sell, to contract matrimony, or to move away without his master's permission. Such terms were typical.

In 1787, when opportunities were promising in the carpentry trade, Dr. Isaac Alexander apprenticed his brother Ezra Alexander to John Wallis (Wallace), a house joiner. In 1789 Magdalene De Bussy signed an apprenticeship agreement for her nephew Lewis Cabass(y) for three and a half years with the same master craftsman. In 1792 Mary Baxley of Anson County, North Carolina, apprenticed her son Edward Baxley to the "house carpenter" Enouch Wind.

Young females as well as males became apprentices, and education was also promised them. In 1786 Richard Dawkins, with the consent of Ferraby Dawkins, a minor female, contracted her apprenticeship until 1791 to the innkeepers John and Sarah Reid (Reed) of Camden. In 1790, about the time that Dawkins's term of service was ending, Elizabeth Jones, an orphan, "with the consent and approbation of the worshipful Justices of the Court," apprenticed herself to the Reids for eight years "voluntarily and of her own free will and accord." Jones's contract was typical of the chance given young females: "to be taught to read and write English as becometh one in her station and also plain Needle Work."

Placing an orphan as an apprentice was an approved function of the court, both to relieve the community of the burden of indigent support and also to offer an unfortunate child a chance in life. Information shows that courts actively sought placements for needy or abandoned youngsters, although by law no one could be bound as an apprentice against his or her will—as a forced contract echoed the ties of slavery. Other circumstances sometimes led courts to place young people as apprentices. In 1787 a court at Hanging Rock bound out four children of a late planter from the Pee Dee whose widow was accused of having "greatly neglected" her children, ages five to eleven, "by living a disorderly life." Richard Champion apprenticed the two young boys and two young girls. The boys were to be trained as planters until age twenty-one; the girls would be trained as weavers until age eighteen. All were to be taught reading and writing. At the time of freedom each boy would be given two suits of clothes and linens as well as plantation tools; each girl would receive two suits of clothes and a spinning wheel.

Besides the apprenticeships recorded in court, other children were probably placed to work in less formal circumstances—especially on farms and in households. Private agreements may not have bound the children legally, but neither did they assure delivery of benefits, such as education, that might have been perceived as more useful to the apprentice than the master. Furthermore, even under a formal contract, the length and extent of training was not described. Just as contracts promised food and lodging "appropriate for an apprentice," educational skills "appropriate for an apprentice" would likely be minimal.

Schools

In the colonial world the education of young people was not considered a responsibility of government but rather was a function of the home. Backcountry families, a far distance from schools and schoolmasters, and often with small means to afford them, had only slim opportunities for educating their children. The few "free" schools, basically charities to keep destitute orphans from prolonged public dependency, often had incompetent instructors. Those families who could pay hired whichever tutors they could find; families of more ample means sent their children to other places, even abroad, to be educated. James and John Kershaw, for example, were educated in England. Most backcountry children, however, received little or no education. The new republic was unable to finance any bold departure from traditional expectations. However, individuals who recognized the importance of capable instruction took the lead in organizing schools in the postwar years.

Records are limited regarding area post–Revolutionary War schools. None is known of in the rural areas, and only a few references survive for Camden. A 1786 Charleston newspaper ad offered to rent the Red House residence in Camden, "formerly a Boarding School for Young Ladies (which is at present much wanted there)." Joseph Kershaw's will of 1788 mentions an "old schoolhouse" on a downtown Camden lot.

Much more is known about a local institution that bore influence through much of the next century. The Camden Orphan Society was organized on July 4, 1786, and opened its first school in 1791. One of its charter members, William Lang, with his wife, Sarah (Wyly), gave eight lots in Camden to establish the "public school." A charitable, educational, and social organization, the Orphan Society stated its purpose to erect school buildings and to promote the schooling of "poor orphans and other poor children in distress," as well as the "moderate relief of such members as may want it." The society supported four orphans annually, and the other students, often children of prominent families, paid tuition. In a modern sense, the school would be described as "private" rather than "public." Kirkland and Kennedy discuss in detail the institution's history.[53]

The first principal of the Orphan Society School, Robert Dow from Scotland, served for more than a dozen years, emphasizing practical English branches above the "dead languages" of Latin and Greek. For one year, 1793, the Reverend Thomas Adams, pastor of the Presbyterian church in Camden, was principal. Charter members of the society were John Adamson, Isaac Alexander, Joseph Brevard, Adam Fowler Brisbane, Benjamin Carter, William Carter, James Cook, James Kerr, William Lang, John Reid, Robert Reid, and William Tate.

At least one other late eighteenth-century school operated for a time in Camden. In the *Columbia Gazette* of May 8, 1794, "Mrs. Jervoise" advertised having opened "a boarding school at Camden, for young ladies, in which they will be taught the Harpsicord, and a variety of needle-work; also reading and spelling; and a proper Master will attend to teach Writing and Arithmetic."[54] In the same year James Kershaw noted that he took his young brother Geoffrey, age twelve, to enroll in "college" at Mt. Zion Institute in Winnsboro. A number of young Kershaw County males were educated at this notable institution, established in 1777.

Public Assistance

Assistance to the needy of society extended to others besides orphans. Just as orphans through education were provided means of eventually earning their own keep, so assistance in general attempted to restore the needy to self-reliance. The group Commissioners of the Poor, headed for some time by Samuel Mathis, administered public assistance to the very needy. Only a few names at a time were on lists of public aid, and even fewer were often repeated. Procedures for out-of-wedlock pregnancy required mothers to divulge names of partners, and cases of bastardy brought before the courts required men to post bonds or pay fines to assure the support of illegitimate children. At times physicians were paid by the court for treatment of the poor, especially when public health might be endangered otherwise. For a period of time one financially struggling father received public funds for "two Idiots his Sons" since lunacy prevented their working to support themselves. Assistance was often given the poor in allotments of corn rather than coinage.

National and International Contacts

Despite the continued relative isolation of Kershaw County, national and international issues became of concern and special interest when they were brought to the area. Perhaps the greatest public excitement of the postwar years resulted from the visit made to the area by George Washington, the first American president and Revolutionary War commander in chief.

Washington's Visit

In 1791 Washington arrived as part of a tour of southern states during his second term of office. Traveling from Savannah, the furthest point he visited, Washington reached Columbia, the capital city with its new statehouse, on May 23. Two days later he and his party set out for Camden at 4:00 A.M., traveling slowly because of a foundered horse. Washington noted in his diary that they ate breakfast at "an indifferent house 22 miles from the town—the first we came to." To avoid obligation or offense to individual citizens, the president preferred public accommodations when possible. The unnamed house where he breakfasted was about two miles within the present bounds of Kershaw County. Known locally as Holliday's Tavern, for many years it was a familiar accommodation for travelers along the route.

"The Road from Columbia to Camden, excepting a mile or two at each place, goes over the most miserable pine barren I ever saw, being quite a white sand and very hilly," wrote Washington. "On the Wateree, within a mile and a half of which the town (Camden) stands, the lands are very good; they culture Corn, Tobacco, & Indigo. Vessels carrying 50 or 60 Hhds. of Tobo. come up to the Ferry at this place, at which there is a Tobacco Ware-House."[55] Throngs of eager citizens, said to have included nearly the whole town of Camden, awaited the president's arrival at the river.

Texts of the formal welcome and response speeches have been preserved, as were the seventeen toasts raised at the public banquet in Washington's honor that evening.[56] Ladies retired after the third toast; the president retired about midnight, after the fifteenth toast, which was one he offered: "The town of Camden, and prosperity to it." The house in which Washington was entertained stood originally at the corner of King and Fair streets but was later moved to Mill Street, where it is known today as the Washington House. The president slept at the public inn kept by John and Sarah Reid.[57]

The day after the banquet Washington rode out early on horseback to visit the grave of Baron de Kalb and to inspect remains of British works in Camden.[58] Accompanied by a number of citizens who rode with him, Washington viewed with interest the battlefields at Hobkirk Hill and at Gum Swamp, site of the Battle of Camden. His journal comments on each with interest. Washington separated from his Camden well-wishers at Gum Swamp and rode fourteen miles up the Waxhaw Road to stop at "one Sutton's" and then twelve miles more to James Ingram's at Hanging Rock. From there, continuing along that time-worn route, the president journeyed on to Charlotte, to Salisbury, and then to his Mount Vernon home.

A Frenchman's Appeal

The next year, not long after the beginning of the French Revolution, the village of Camden welcomed another celebrity—the first minister from France to visit America since the Revolution. Arriving at Camden by stage from Charleston on April 17, 1793, "Citizen-Minister Genet" was met at Town Creek by the Camden Troop of Horse, escorted to a residence provided in his honor, greeted with a formal speech by the intendant Isaac DuBose, and honored at a public dinner. It was afterward learned that in Charleston, in direct violation of this country's treaties and neutrality, Edmond Charles Genet was enlisting American seamen to man privateers preying on British ships. Before Genet reached Washington, the government he represented had been overthrown in France. Rather than return home to face beheading, he sought political asylum and lived the rest of his life quietly in America.

Federalists, including George Washington and many of the lowcountry planters, opposed risking another war with England by becoming involved in alliances with France. Backcountry men, however, followed the beginning of the

French Revolution with great interest because of sympathy for ideals of freedom and equality, appreciation for a people who had supported this country in its own struggle, and for lingering antipathy for the British. The diary of James Kershaw reveals that the enthusiastic annual celebration of the Fourth of July, observing American independence, for a few years was followed with local celebrations of the anniversary of French independence, July 14, Bastille Day.[59]

Lingering British antipathy was provoked in 1794 when English ships intercepted American ships to seize French supplies. Concern was widespread that weaknesses of the treaty that ended the Revolution would lead to another war. That local citizens took seriously the need for readiness is suggested by a Charleston newspaper report that year that the Kershaw County Regiment at Camden had elected officers with 646 votes in attendance. A Camden Company of Militia is also mentioned later.[60] Kershaw's diary of July 1795 notes that two town meetings, the second one including county residents, were held to discuss the disappointing Jay Treaty, which failed to strengthen the first treaty but did postpone for a while a second war with England.

Sophistication

Despite the remoteness, smallness, and newness of Camden society, the diary of James Kershaw reveals that in the last decade of the eighteenth century some of its citizens lived with a high degree of sophistication. He, at the age of eight, and his brother John, at seven, had been sent to their grandfather in England to receive education. James Kershaw did not return to Camden until 1784 when he was twenty. A cultured and sociable man of energy and inquisitiveness, he possessed an alert mind and a strong sense of public responsibility. He was actively involved in managing his plantation in the 1790s, and his notes refer to the planting of crops, the beating and cutting of indigo, the marking of cattle, the gathering of honey, and the operation of a "pumping machine."

Kershaw regularly made meteorological observations, recording earthquake tremors, noting directions of sounds from long distances, and carefully watching freshets. He wrote that the river flooded so high in 1796 that his sister Mary rode with others on a flatboat all the way up to the "Indian mounts" (Adamson mounds). In addition Kershaw surveyed or had surveyed significant parts of the community—the Indian camp that became a mill site, areas around the courthouse, Quaker Cemetery, and DeKalb Street—and helped plan other town areas.

Kershaw clearly had passions for theater, art, and music and was able to enjoy these in Camden society. He frequently participated in Thespian Society meetings, painting backdrops, acting and reading roles, and attending dramatic productions. The courthouse, according to his reference, served as a community theater as well as a church building and the seat of justice. Some refined musical instruments had been brought to the area, for Kershaw tuned "M Chesnuts

Piano Forte" and "Miss Eliza's Spinnet." In addition he met regularly with the St. Cecilia Society for performing music and was active in many dances, balls, and assemblies in homes and taverns. The hosts were men, married or bachelors, or social organizations such as the Assembly and the St. Cecilia Society.

Kershaw drank tea with friends and neighbors, enjoyed their weddings, and attended lectures, religious services, and "exhibitions" (traveling shows of curiosities, one of them wax works) that came to the local community. He escorted his sister and later his wife to attend quilting frolics for women. Outdoor activities included attending the Light Horse (later the Light Dragoon) military musters and militia parades, firing a cannon salute, playing a game of cricket, hunting at Westerham, fishing at Belton Spring, and hauling seine at Ross's Fishery on the Wateree. Kershaw visited "town" (Charleston) in the winter for business and pleasure and also vacationed near Charlotte at the Catawba Springs, a natural mineral springs, for health and pleasure in the dog days of summer.

Kershaw's diary shows that he gave personal attention to family and to public responsibilities. He oversaw smallpox inoculations and discipline for slaves, sat up night after night to nurse his youngest brother through fever, attended town meetings, followed politics, entertained visiting ministers and public guests in his home, and sat as a court judge.

While a cultured lifestyle was exceptional in the 1790s, and only a few local citizens had the background or opportunity for such a range of activities, Kershaw's success no doubt set a tone for community aspiration. In many events—in church, town meetings, the tavern, the sporting field, and the muster ground—Kershaw and his set rubbed elbows with ordinary persons of good intent. Up-and-coming citizenry in the expanding democratic society of the new republic found positive models among those who exercised public responsibility, respected the law and religion, valued education and the arts, and engaged in politics, agriculture, and business.

An Emerging New Economy

By the closing years of the decade, significant change was on the horizon. The cotton gin, patented in 1793 by Eli Whitney to separate cottonseed from cotton fiber, had immediate impact in the lowcountry, where long-fiber Sea Island cotton was being cultivated. That type of cotton was fairly easily separated from the seeds by hand labor. However, the gin's greatest impact was in the upcountry, where short-fiber cotton, more stubborn and time-consuming to separate by hand, was the only type that could be grown profitably. Prior to 1793 cotton had been planted in the upcountry only for domestic purposes. Because the seeds stuck so stubbornly, like ticks, to the short fibers, many families—women and children alike—had previously spent night-time hours sitting around the fire painstakingly picking out the white fluff for home spinning and weaving.

Even as word spread about the new cotton gin and various mechanics sought to duplicate or improve its workings, upcountry farmers set about learning how to plant and manage the promising new crop. In 1796 "Sundry Inhabitants of Camden District" petitioned the legislature to establish an inspector of cotton in their section. The request was turned down on December 10, however, as being "premature & improper," citing as reasons "the very late Introduction" of cotton in the state, the uncertainty about how to conduct a cotton inspection, and "the inconsiderable Quantity as yet reared for market in the part of the Country from which the petition comes."

At the end of 1796 the production of Camden District cotton may yet have been of "inconsiderable Quantity," but the upland planters were learning fast. James Kershaw noted on April 24, 1797, that he had "Planted the cotton round the Warehouse, Westerham." Open land all over was being converted to try the new crop. Planters with large holdings and ample slave workers had the jump on agricultural experimentation, but a steady stream of other farmers would soon be joining the planting ranks. Furthermore landowners were not the only ones to establish themselves through cotton. Before 1800 William Nixon began work as a laborer in cotton and at other manual jobs, eventually building wealth as opportunities expanded before him. By the dawn of the nineteenth century, the rapid transition to a cotton-crop economy, set in motion by a mechanical invention, had led to an extended slave system being declared essential to fulfill the promise of a new age.

8 Cotton and Complexities

1800–1860

By 1800 the foundations were in place for the society of the pre–Civil War nineteenth century. A clear view of the often-fabled antebellum period is sometimes obscured by the perspectives of various storytellers, often veiled with dark clouds of impending judgment or with mists of romanticism. Records reveal times much more complex than they have been typically perceived. The people of 1800–60 were far more diverse than the stereotypical images by which they are often portrayed.

Since Kershaw County was not set apart until 1791, the year after the first federal census, it was the second national census in 1800 that provided the first population data on the specific area by then called Kershaw District.[1] John Fisher, a district census taker, reported in 1800 that the population total of 7,340 consisted of 4,706 white inhabitants, 104 "other free persons," and 2,530 slaves. In 1810, according to district census taker Matthew C. Wiggins, the total population had increased to 9,822. While the white population had grown by less than 5 percent in the decade (to 4,911), the number of slaves had almost doubled (to 4,832) and nearly equaled the number of whites. The category of "other free persons," totaled as "colored," had decreased by 25 percent.

The demand for laborers to cultivate cotton, the future "king" of southern cash crops, had spurred the increased acquisition of slaves. Some growth before 1810 had possibly resulted from "last-chance" speculation: the slave trade was outlawed in the British Empire by 1807, and Congress had closed American ports to slave imports from Africa by 1808. Population shifts continued in Kershaw District throughout the antebellum period despite restrictions on importations. Various accounts from throughout South Carolina refer to planters' concerns for the health of the slaves, for their "breeding," and for their natural increase in numbers. By the 1840 census the district included more than twice the number of slaves (8,043) as whites (3,988), a disparity further widened by the time of the next census.

At the turn of the century, according to his 1800–1801 diary, Arthur Brown Ross was successfully farming on the west side of the Wateree River and conducting the Camden Ferry from that direction. A justice, he was involved in diverse local affairs and was growing several crops for domestic use. Ross personally labored on and supervised his plantings, made and sold whiskey, tended his cattle and hogs, fished the Wateree (dragging nets for shad and sturgeon), hunted (deer, hogs, bears, turkeys, and waterfowl), and took rides or long walks through the fields with his wife, Hannah Conger (affectionately called "the old lady"). Their social lifestyle, less outgoing than that of James Kershaw, focused on home and family. Ross grew some flax and cotton, at least for his own use.[2]

By 1800 local planters had begun turning their focus to growing cotton, gradually abandoning the diversity that many had practiced earlier.[3] The cultivation of the white fiber drove the economy in the coming decades, past the Civil War and into the next century. It would also vastly alter the environment as well as the social structure. Since heavy-feeding cotton quickly depleted the soil's fertility, planters purchased new land and more slaves to clear additional fields. The farming practice of the day was to leave exhausted fields fallow until they were renewed by nature, but this subjected much district land to erosion and environmental change. Large-scale effective fertilizers were then unavailable, and crop rotation was less immediately profitable than cotton cultivation.

Ironically the market for raw cotton, grown in the agricultural South with manual labor under the ancient system of slavery, had been spawned by a modern mechanical revolution that had economized cloth manufacturing in England and in the North. Thus, in the interdependent production of cotton fabrics, the distant manufacturer focused on labor-saving mechanization, while the local planter relied on intensification of human labor. Like the rest of the agricultural South, the economy of Kershaw District was additionally influenced by seasonal ups and downs and by fluctuating foreign markets that helped determine personal fortunes and swayed local, state, national, and international politics.

A Focus on Faith

While an early chance of profit from cotton was high, so was the risk of loss from weather-induced crop failures, damage during shipping, market vagaries, or overextension of credit. It was an era when ambition, energy, and luck were all visible players in an individual's fortune. Great wealth and poverty coexisted. Coinciding with the times, evangelical religious revivals caught fire throughout the country and focused attention on divine rewards and punishments. A number of Kershaw District churches originated in the early decades of the nineteenth century, the time of the Second Great Awakening, and bore influence throughout the antebellum period.[4] Similar influences throughout the South resulted in the region's eventual acquisition of the title "the Bible belt."

This time religious enlightenment was not brought from settled regions into backcountry darkness but rather was sparked, in 1800, during camp meetings that began on the frontiers of Kentucky and Tennessee. The fervor that eventually spread throughout the nation reached Kershaw District by 1802, brought to

The Drakeford House, circa 1810, a log cabin dismantled and reassembled on the grounds of Historic Camden Revolutionary War Site. Courtesy of the Camden Archives

its most inland border downward from the Waxhaws and Hanging Rock. The Reverend James Jenkins on June 30 wrote Bishop Asbury from Camden: "Hell is trembling, and Satan's kingdom is falling." His letter described a "general meeting" at the Waxhaws at the end of May, conducted by five Methodist, five Baptist, and twelve Presbyterian ministers: "Sinners were converted on all sides, and numbers found the Lord."[5]

From this nearby major revival, ministers of various denominations—both together and independently—fanned the "warming" of personalized religious experience. Camp meetings, itinerant and circuit preachers, home prayer meetings, and witnessing by local converts had their effects among all classes throughout the district. In 1804 a regular camp meeting place became established on Swift Creek, eight miles below town. The place was so frequently used for this purpose that it became known as the Camden Camp Meeting. Along various creeks revival meetings drew attendance—at Hanging Rock, Granny's Quarter, Sanders, Lynches, Sawney's, and Twenty-five Mile creeks—and within this and the coming decade a number of churches were built throughout the district. Older churches were spurred to new vigor, and new congregations drew together. Meetinghouses evolved into consecrated churches served by denominational ministers.

The Upper District

Strong influences came from the congregations in the upper portion of the district, where the first meetings were held. The old Beaver Creek Presbyterian Church developed three branches during the antebellum period: Tolerant Presbyterian Church, established on a branch of Singleton Creek; Mt. Bethel Presbyterian Church, begun as a mission to replace the former Miller's Meeting House near Russell Place; and Liberty Hill Presbyterian Church, organized in 1850. So strong was the denomination in Liberty Hill that an old saying declared that even the dogs there were Presbyterian.

Baptists too were strong in the upper portion of the district, if not on "the hill." The old Beaver Creek Baptist Church was mother to the Flat Rock Baptist Church, organized in 1809. Flat Rock in turn influenced the founding of at least two other churches eastward and southward. One was the early Beaver Dam Baptist Church in the area of the current church of that name near present-day Cassatt. Another was Bethsada/Bethesda Baptist Church between Flat Rock and Camden; its covenant was signed in September 1827 "at flinthill," and in 1830 the body moved to the "Schoolhouse in the Sand hill." Another church in the upper area of the county, Mt. Pisgah Baptist Church, was organized in 1837 and met for its first ten years in a schoolhouse.

Besides their stronghold at still-active Hanging Rock Methodist Church, where area camp meetings began and continued, Methodists extended their work into remote areas of the upper district. The property deeds in the courthouse reflect isolation but show that the area was opening up. In 1816 Friendship Meeting House was located "on the Ridge that divides the Waters of Sanders Creek from those of Grannies Quarter Creek on the said Ridge called Chesnut's road"; in 1820 Ebenezer Meeting House sat "on the road that leads from Cornelius Quinlays to Camden"; and in 1829 a possible meetinghouse existed "on the Waters of Flat Rock Creek."[6]

The Eastern Portion

Eastward in the district all denominations spread influence in the slowly growing Lynches River area. In the early part of the century several families originally from Scotland came down from North Carolina and settled near the area of present Bethune. The community they formed retained many Old Country ways. In 1812 the Presbyterian minister Colin McIver from Scotland, preaching in English and Gaelic, began itinerant work among these people, of whom Scotch Cemetery is a reminder. Pine Tree Presbyterian Church was first organized among them in 1820 on Benjamin Perkins's Pine Tree Plantation on Big Pine Tree Creek, between Camden and present Bethune in the area known as Hyco. Because the church was built on No Head Branch, it sometimes appears in records as No Head Church. About 1850 Pine Tree Church moved to the head of Bell Branch, which was more central to the congregation. From this second location a daughter church, Turkey Creek Presbyterian Church, was organized in 1858 closer to the Tiller's Ferry settlement, which was once part of Kershaw District but now is in Lee County.

In 1815 land for Tiller's Church, an old congregation, was deeded to Methodist trustees; by 1831 the name had been changed to Bethany Methodist Church. In 1853, about four miles from Tiller's Ferry and nearer present Bethune, Pleasant Hill Baptist Church was organized. Northwest of present Bethune the interdenominational Bethel Meeting House, built in 1827 by an old congregation, took the name Bethel Baptist Church of Christ (later Macedonia Baptist Church) in 1832, following a three-day protracted meeting. Above that area in the mid-1800s the present Timrod Baptist Church was organized as Lizard Hill Baptist Church, thought to have been located in the area of Minton Pond, now Horton Pond.

Southern and Southeastern Areas

Congregational influences crossed neighboring district boundary lines, making connections with Methodists around Lodebar and old Rembert Hall, Baptists in the High Hills, Presbyterians around Salem, and Episcopalians at Stateburg. Within Kershaw District, on the "Road [by McRa(e)'s mill] from Camden to People's Mill," Methodists in 1812 were deeded "the Meeting House hitherto called Melone's Meeting house but which probably hereafter may be called Marshall's Meeting House." The property on which the present building known as Marshall's Methodist Church stands, just across the line in present Lee County, was deeded in 1836. Also in the southeastern section Antioch Baptist Church was organized in 1824 at Poplar Branch, the result of a brush-arbor revival (so named for the temporary shelter built to protect worshippers from the elements). Baptists were also active in the old Swift Creek congregation, establishing Swift Creek Baptist Church earlier than can be shown by extant records, which begin in 1827. The church building of that date is preserved at Boykin Mill Pond. Frequent camp meetings, attended by all denominations, were held nearby.

West of the Wateree

More thinly populated by antebellum settlement than the rest of the district, the area west of the Wateree River sustained fewer individual churches. Depending on where a planter and his family lived, they might travel for services across the river to Camden or across to upper Kershaw District settlements such as Beaver Creek or Liberty Hill. Alternately they might travel northward to Longtown, Ridgeway, or Winnsboro in Fairfield District, where Presbyterians held early dominance; or westward to Columbia or Blythewood in Richland District. Preachers from these areas also itinerated into the West Wateree area.

Methodists were active on Sawney's Creek by 1810, when church trustees bought land adjoining a "Meeting House," detailed on a plat. Some believe that this purchase was the origin of Ebenezer Methodist Church, still active in what is now Lugoff. On Twenty-five Mile Creek, also in 1810, Methodists were deeded land on which the following year they built a sanctuary that is still part of Smyrna Methodist Church. Smyrna was founded by members who had been worshipping at a nondenominational Fairfield District church called the Wolf-Pit, where James Jenkins was then preaching. Following a camp meeting at Sanders Creek, across the river in Kershaw District, Methodists desired their own church and thus built Smyrna. Another active church with early roots on Twenty-five Mile Creek is Harmony Baptist Church, near the present town of Elgin. The Twenty-five Mile Creek Baptist Church in Richland District formed several branches and met at various locations, two of them being Sawney's Creek and Bear Creek. In 1858 the church at Bear Creek moved to Kershaw District to form Harmony Church, presently in Tookiedoo community, Elgin.

Camden Churches

At the turn of the century the only church building within the town of Camden was still the Camden Methodist Church, standing in a pine grove in the present area of King Street between Campbell and Church streets. In two separate memoirs written at midcentury, the original structure is recalled by early members. According to Mrs. Isaac (Sarah Thornton) Alexander, it was "a plain structure in accordance with the primitive habits and appearance of the people of that day."[7] Mrs. Phineas (Elizabeth Williams) Thornton describes an 1807 enlargement: "by advice & aid of Bishop Asbury it was lengthened in the rear making quite a walk to enter at one end to go up through to the other."[8] In 1828 the increasing congregation completed a new hilltop church on DeKalb Street and sold its old building to Dr. William Blanding, who memorialized it in a sketch.[9]

In 1805 the Presbyterians of Camden, apparently without the church they rebuilt after the Revolution, met in the courthouse to organize as Bethesda Presbyterian Church. Afterward they again rebuilt on Meeting Street at the end of Church Street, where the old Presbyterian cemetery is today a part of Quaker Cemetery. A northward movement of the town had been under way sometime before the Presbyterians left their old site. In 1822 construction was completed for the notable sanctuary still in use on DeKalb Street, at the head of Market Street. Its design, setting, and history have made Bethesda Presbyterian Church an area landmark.

In 1809 the congregation that became Camden Baptist Church, today the First Baptist Church of Camden, completed its first sanctuary at the northeast corner of York and Market streets, and it was officially constituted in 1810. In its early years the church was often enriched by the services of ministerial students from the Roberts Academy and the Furman Theological Institution at the High Hills of the Santee. In 1836 the church moved to a larger sanctuary at the site presently 1111 Broad Street. Baptisms were conducted in outdoor locations, frequently Factory Pond.

In post–Revolutionary War years interest was cool toward the Episcopalian denomination, which was associated in the public mind with prior Anglican domination. In 1813 the Reverend Andrew Fowler, an Episcopal missionary, found only four communicants in Camden and was withdrawn in 1817. Episcopal worship languished until 1830 when Grace Episcopal Church was constituted under the Reverend Edward Phillips and a church was dedicated on the west side of Broad Street. The congregation strengthened during the rectorship of the Reverend Thomas Frederick Davis, bishop of the Diocese of South Carolina, who chose Camden as his headquarters. In 1859 the only Episcopal Theological Seminary that the state ever had began operating across the street from his home, the Bishop Davis House, today a local landmark.

While persons of Catholic or Jewish faith did not build places of worship in Kershaw District during the antebellum period, a small number of these believers are said to have observed private worship in homes and to have traveled on occasion to services in Columbia or Charleston. The predominant strength of Protestant churches was clearly visible in Camden, as one history points out: "By 1836, four main Protestant denominations had built substantial churches within a short distance in each direction of the Broad and DeKalb street intersection. On the second block to the west of the intersection stood the Methodist church; on the second block to the east, the Presbyterian. Within the block to the south of the intersection stood the Episcopal church; within the block to the north, the Baptist."[10]

Slave Worshippers

Slaves, who began attending camp meetings and worship services with their owners, became generally permitted, as convenient, to attend services and join churches of their denominational choice. This practice was later made legal only as long as some white people were in attendance at the meetings, a law rendering impractical the founding of separate all-black churches. Free or enslaved people of color were original members in all local churches of record founded at the time. The Camden (First) Baptist Church, for example, had twenty-five members, nine of whom were black.[11] In 1824 one of the slave members, Monday (Mrs. Ray's), requested to take his letter from that church in order to become a constituting member at Antioch Baptist. Liberty Hill Presbyterian was constituted with thirty-six white and ten slave members,

As rural planting operations increased in number and size, the Reverend (later Bishop) William Capers in 1830 organized "Plantation Missions" to minister to slaves through the Missionary Board of the Methodist Church. By 1833 the Wateree Mission was being operated in Kershaw District, supported by planters of various denominations. The missionary preacher paid scheduled visits to preach, to assist in church discipline, and to officiate at baptisms and weddings in plantation churches.[12] A local Methodist minister's wife said of the planter Colonel James Chesnut in 1853: "He has been from the beginning one of the most intelligent and liberal patrons of the Wateree Mission to the blacks. He took a personal interest in the matter, attended the Mission Church, and worshipped in the midst of his people."[13]

In town churches, as well as on plantations, black leaders developed among congregations and served as deacons and elders to their people. Records remain of several devout Camden Methodist slaves who earned licenses to preach: David (Ancrum's), Hector (Alexander's), William (Whitaker's), Charles (Reynolds'), Abram (Cantey's), and Quash (Chesnut's). Only one of their slaveholders was himself a Methodist. In 1833, on property adjoining the Methodist church on DeKalb Street, a separate building was erected—a prayer house where black members could hold class and prayer meetings. West of the Wateree in 1857 slaves near the Perkins plantation sought and received permission to sing and conduct prayer meetings in a brush arbor they had built. The history of the postwar era makes clear the significance of black leadership that developed in the antebellum churches.

The Lingering Past

While day-to-day necessities absorbed most citizens and others kept an eye turned toward the future of this world or the next, some early nineteenth-century glances lingered on diminishing signs of the ancient past. An 1816 letter in the first sustained local newspaper, the *Camden Gazette,* referred to local Indian mounds ("Artificial Mounts"), "*tumuli* [burial mounds] . . . on the banks of the Wateree river, near Camden." According to the unnamed writer, several of the mounds had "sensibly diminished within the last twenty years, by cultivation and the effect of rains." Comparing them to raised burial places in other parts of the world, he described "a lofty conical mound, like that on Ogilvie's neck, in the plantation of Col. James Chesnut on the Wateree" and wondered "what might be related . . . if the Indian tradition had been preserved, or if the Catawbas and Waterees had produced a Herodotis [or] a Homer."[14]

The comment by one who may have observed the mounds in the 1790s reveals long interest and shows that cultivation of the mounds by local farmers had begun very early. Indications are that it continued at various times throughout the nineteenth century. Mound positions above floodplains and the nature of the soil and humus composing them made them useful to agriculturalists. In some cases mounds were leveled and scattered to manure fields. It is interesting that the 1816 observer associates the earthen works with the tribes who had inhabited the area, for many scholars in that century presumed American Indians incapable of such constructions.

Dr. William Blanding, who moved to Camden about 1806 from Rehoboth, Massachusetts, observed a number of such mounds and other remains. Along with his studies as a naturalist and with his practice of medicine and pharmacy, Dr. Blanding mapped and described fifteen sites of "Ancient Works" he found during visits over the years along both sides of a twenty-five-mile stretch of the Wateree valley, mostly in Kershaw District. Sites included several mounds or mound groups, a rock mortar, fortifications, ditches, embankments, dwelling sites, and a rock pile. He reported mounds being used for agriculture and dwelling places in 1806 and others leveled to manure fields in 1826, as well as sites rich in "aboriginal relics," including Hobkirk Hill and Paint Hill. In 1848 the Smithsonian Institution published Dr. Blanding's descriptions and map, a rare document of major significance.[15]

Dr. Blanding viewed Native Americans with respect. His papers, for example, describe a seedless peach given him by the Cherokee, and he sent samples to Philadelphia scientists for study. He also sent northward Native American relics, along with other outstanding botanical and natural specimens from the local area. According to the archivist of the Philadelphia Academy of Natural Sciences, the present records of Dr. Blanding's contributions over many years reveal "a steady stream of specimens . . . plants, minerals, birds, shells, entomological specimens and miscellaneous invertebrates." The Smithsonian today is unable to determine from early record keeping which artifacts in its collections were contributed by Dr. Blanding, although evidence of his contributions is recognized by that institution.[16]

Other locals in Kershaw District too became intrigued by the ancient sites. It was probably the editor Thomas J. Warren who wrote "American Antiquities" for the *Camden Journal* of December 24, 1850: "We saw in the shop of Mr. [Isaac B.] Alexander [jeweler and portrait artist] the other day, a Pot, dug from the large mound two miles from here. It is quite large . . . there were two taken up—the other larger than this. The mound, we understand, is about sixty feet high, and near three hundred yards in circumference."[17] It would be intriguing to think that the pioneer photographer Alexander exposed some images of the pots and objects, but the camera was in a state of infancy, and there is no evidence that he utilized it except for human daguerreotypes.[18] Warren was eloquent pondering questions still being asked:

> The question naturally arises, who made these mounds? They are scattered over our country, and if you ask the Indian who made them, his answer is, they were here before us. Where are they who built them, and for what

> purpose were they made? . . . For what were they used? were they [the builders] worshippers in high places, and thronged they in deep devotion the lofty summit of these elevated places as they sent up their orisons to the great spirit? or were they [the mounds] watch towers, upon which were kindled the beacon fires to warn their tribe of the approaching foe? Or were there astronomers even then, who watched in the grand and stilly night, the wandering Pleaides?

Antebellum memory of the past century elevated admiration of the historic Catawba chief King Hagler to a position of public honor. In 1826 a gilded iron weather-vane effigy idealizing the eighteenth-century leader was raised atop the steeple above the Camden market, at that time on the corner facing the new courthouse at Broad and King streets. The commemorative, functional effigy was a gift to the community from its maker, silhouette artist J. B. Mathieu. From its first location the effigy and steeple were removed in 1859 to stand at the new town market, the site presently designated as 1011 Broad Street, on the opposite side of the street from the present town tower, to which the effigy was removed in 1886. Contemporary with the Indian figure were the four-sided town clock, made by Lukens of Philadelphia, and the large signal bell, cast by John Willbank of Philadelphia in 1824, both also part of the lofty tower. No logo has been more closely identified with Camden and Kershaw County over the years than the effigy of King Hagler.

While some Kershaw District citizens may have romanticized the real or imagined past of Native Americans, contemporary tribal descendants were impoverished and generally regarded as in cultural decline. The popular South Carolina novelist William Gilmore Simms in 1833 published a fanciful tale entitled "Haiglar, a Story of the Catawba," a chivalric and unrealistic episode that reveals almost nothing of fact about its purported subject.[19] Simms's opening, however, reflects a romantic attitude toward their past and recent treatment:

> The Catawbas, now a miserable tribe of some three hundred persons, occupying a territory of fifteen square miles, in the upper part of the state of South Carolina, was, at one period of American history, the most chivalrous of the savage nations. To the warmth and courage of the southern character, they added all the capacity of endurance peculiar to the north; and among the Indians, bore a reputation, which for their qualities, had no competitor among them. They were a lively, generous people and fast friends and allies of the Carolinians when the infant white settlements were surrounded on all hands by deadly enemies. The Carolinians were not ungrateful, and have nothing with which to reproach themselves in their treatment of this people. They have been maintained in the state with a tolerance at once due to humanity and former service, and grateful to the now decaying but once powerful nation.

In 1840, in fact, under a new treaty with South Carolina, the Catawba ceded all their lands to the state and moved to North Carolina, where they expected to obtain new lands. North Carolina would not sell them land, however, and after eighteen months the tribal remnant returned to South Carolina and negotiated possession of eight hundred acres, a small portion of their former land.[20]

No tribal lands were held in Kershaw District during the antebellum period, although local individuals or families of Indian blood or of mixed descent appear variously on records of the time. Some influences derived from Native American life were so assimilated into common usage or so blended with similar African American and European influences that their origins were obscured to the general public. Canoes, fishing baskets, clay vessels, and tanned hides were among everyday useful objects; corn and pumpkins were staples; and native herbs were part of household and apothecary cures of the time.

James Kershaw's and William Blanding's diaries comment occasionally on nineteenth-century visits of Indians to Camden, probably to trade. A statement in Blanding's Smithsonian publication points to the quiet survival of ancient tradition well into that century. He states that at the mouth of Town Creek, a point of ancient habitation, "A very fine description of clay is found at this spot, which is resorted to by the Catawba Indians every spring and autumn, for the purpose of manufacturing pottery from it."

A few individual Indian names turn up in records, and a few individuals were known by personality. Chunkey Bone, for example, an exceptionally tall Catawba, was the ever-present attendant of the district nullification-era leader of the Union Party, General James Blair, himself six feet six inches in height. Some families took pride in recording Indian ancestry, although their stories tend to refer romantically to connections such as "a full-blooded Cherokee" or "a chief's daughter." Such stories are repeated among both black and white families, despite some nineteenth-century writers who claimed (contrary to evidence) that local Indians intermarried only with whites. Indians were said to have accompanied the militia that tracked down runaway slaves in the Wateree and Santee swamps in 1823, beheading one of the slaves and placing his head on a pole as a warning.[21] It is likely that antebellum tales of lurking Indian ferocity were circulated among slaves to discourage their attempts to escape into area swamps and woodlands. Thus, in many ways, lingering traces of the past remained a part of the antebellum period.

The Cotton-Based Society

When cotton cultivation began to prove profitable, the market town of Camden—already positioned with merchants, financial agents, and shipping operations—quickly evolved into a major cotton-handling connection between the upcountry and the lowcountry. On November 25, 1810, William Blanding commented in his diary on valuable produce traveling to the lowcountry: "This day 60 Wagons passed thro' this town [Camden] for Charleston—on an average each wagon had 9 Bales—Equal to 480 Bales; each Bale 300 lbs. Total amount of Cotton, perhaps lb 144000 and at 15¢ would be $21600." Northward-bound produce was noted in the diary of James Kershaw on February 25, 1815: "12 waggons with cotton passed here to Baltimore." Kershaw's comment was dated just five days after he remarked on news received in Camden about "Peace"—that is, the signing more than two months earlier of the Paris Peace Treaty on December 24, 1814, ending the War of 1812. The ending of hostilities with England brought further opportunities for increased prosperity in cotton exportation.[22]

In May 1816 the *Camden Gazette* reported "upland cotton" selling at twenty-seven cents a pound in Charleston and twenty-three cents in Camden. Prices by June had risen to thirty cents in Charleston and twenty-four cents in Camden. Although per-pound prices fell considerably in later years, as production increased with larger plantings and extended operations, profits continued rising overall in the early decades. According to Robert Mills's 1826 *Statistics of South Carolina,* 20,000 bales of cotton were sold in Camden in 1825. This was a sizable figure, considering the fact that in 1822 the Board of Public Works reported to the state legislature that annually about 130,000 bales were shipped from Charleston, and 70,000 of them were raised above the present head of navigation in the state.[23] A significant proportion of that cotton was therefore being sold in Camden, and no doubt more passed through the town on wagons en route to being sold in Charleston.

Robert Mills's *Atlas of the State of South Carolina,* published in 1825, reflects extensive development under way in the growing economy. The atlas's map of Kershaw County, surveyed in 1820 by John Boykin, is likely representative to that date rather than the publication date, but it shows a number of places that figure in the contemporary history and lifestyles.[24]

A Grand Lifestyle

In the early decades cotton profits supported a lifestyle that was comfortable and sometimes even grand for successful planters and their associates.[25] For a number of family lines, the profits established a base of wealth and high expectations that piqued the ambition and imitation of rising generations. Fine homes and more extensive plantations spread throughout Kershaw District, while people of plainer taste and less concern with style also lived more comfortably on modest homesteads. Patterns of leisure and refinement were established among persons of affluence, or at least of reputable credit. They made summer retreats to sandhills homes of improved style, to fashionable springs, or to northern or European resorts. There were more elaborate traditional entertainments of hunts, horse races, dinners, and balls. Also, to prepare family youths for suitable roles in these lifestyles, appropriate educational institutions were founded.

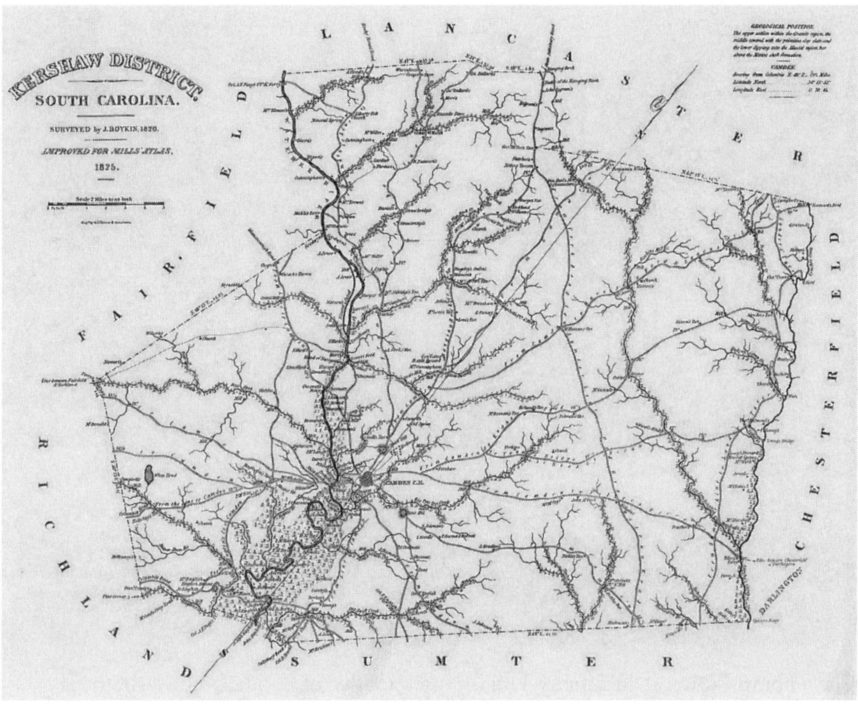

Map of Kershaw County in Robert Mills's 1825 atlas.
Courtesy of the Camden Archives

In the hilly, pine-covered vicinity of the Revolutionary War Battle of Hobkirk's Hill above Camden, a summer-retreat community named Kirkwood grew into a small village where substantial and impressive dwellings eventually took prominence over the first small, plain cabins.[26] A number of the antebellum homes in Kirkwood, now long embraced within the Camden city limits, are modern showplaces. In the highest rural hills of Kershaw District, the planters of the Beaver Creek plantations and surrounding areas began building summer homes and sizable mansions at Liberty Hill, which grew into a substantial and close-knit antebellum village with its own stores, churches, schools, and social organizations.

During the annual hot-weather "sickly season," retreats to cooler hills and spring waters were enjoyed for social as well as health reasons. Depending on circumstances, various families gathered at springs to camp out in nature or established themselves to live simply in rustic cabins; other families chose springs with commercial establishments where they could indulge in luxurious accommodations. Kirkwood, for example, had several cool-water springs. North

The Thompson home in Liberty Hill is representative of houses built in the rural village during the era of antebellum agricultural prosperity.

of Kirkwood and Camden, Cool Spring(s) (sometimes called Cold Spring) became another summer retreat for several families. The 1825 Mills map shows Mineral Spring at Liberty Hill, and one of the elegant summer homes in that area also took the name Cool Springs.

In the Lynches River area the Chesnuts and other families south or east of Camden utilized "Joseph Brevards Mineral Spring," as it appeared on the Mills map, and elsewhere was also called Mineral Spring(s), Brevard's Mineral Spring(s), Brevards Spring(s), and eventually Big Springs. James Chesnut was said to have developed a spot for bathing there during the antebellum period. On the west side of the Wateree, Muster Springs and White Pond were natural areas long known. Throughout the district many families no doubt had favorite summer camps along the many creeks.

Names of some popular or fashionable watering holes that local citizens enjoyed socially outside Kershaw District emerge from contemporary sources: Bradford Springs, in the Springhill–High Hills area of Sumter District; Glenn Springs, near Spartanburg; Lightwood Knot Springs, near Columbia; Limestone Springs, near Gaffney; Mineral Springs, which became known as Heath Springs in Lancaster District; and Rice Creek Springs, between Camden and Columbia.

For those who went out of state, mountain foothills appealed, including Catawba Falls near Asheville, North Carolina, and Catawba Springs near Hickory, North Carolina. Various springs in Georgia, such as Warm Springs, and in Virginia, such as White Sulphur Springs, were also patronized.

The Plain People

From the generally rising affluence of the cotton economy, material conditions appear also to have improved among the "plain people," the relatively infrequently described middle class that probably included more than half of the white populace of Kershaw District. Neighbors in settlements throughout the area aided each other in common activities such as raising barns and bringing in crops, quilting, seining fish from the river, and driving livestock. They joined together in social activities rising from their shared work and their worship experiences. Small slaveholders among the plain people often labored in fields, households, or shops alongside their slaves. The historian Rosser H. Taylor includes among the plain people "independent farmers, merchants, small tradesmen, teachers, artisans and mechanics."[27]

Although not given the status of the "genteel" or the aristocrats, the plain people or yeomanry in their time were generally noted for steadiness and accorded respectability in the community. They served faithfully at musters, on beats, and in the military; they formed churches, educated their children, and took pride in "doing for themselves." Some persons affluent enough to have afforded a grander lifestyle chose a simpler way of existence and counted themselves among the plain people.

Plain people held themselves apart, through industry and reputation, from the less fortunate "poor whites," marked by chronic poverty. Justly or not, all levels of society, including the slave population, viewed poor whites as shiftless and disreputable. Taylor points out, "About the only records left by the poor whites were those involuntarily deposited in the county courthouses as evidence of reprehensible conduct."[28] Yet all classes in Kershaw District included members who became marked with notoriety or with celebrity, and fluctuating fortunes sometimes made class lines fluid and blurred distinctions at various levels. The potential that one might rise from class to class was kept before youths as a motivating factor. To this purpose an article in the August 14, 1855, *Camden Journal* urged "virtue, honesty, and perseverance" upon "humble youth" that they might rise in wealth and position as had the presidential candidate James K. Polk, born a poor boy in North Carolina.

"Bad eminence"

By different behavior, however, some in Kershaw District rose to "bad eminence," an expression of the time. One example, among accounts before the district court in the antebellum years, is a rowdy white female named Mary. She was known to the courts by a trio of surnames or aliases—Cunningham, Scanlin (also Scatling), or Wests—but was unconnected with other local family lines of those names. A resident of Gum Swamp, she was identified to the court in 1812 as the "wife of William Cunningham" and by 1815 as his "widow." Many papers in the state archives relate to a dozen indictments in Camden courts and to charges and countercharges involving Mary between 1812 and 1833. A Mary Cunningham is a listed as a head of household in the 1820 census, and a residence labeled "Mrs. Cunningham" appears on the 1825 Mills atlas map just below the site of the Battle of Camden.

In 1812 Mary and a young man were charged with beating a man and stealing his corn and fodder. In 1815, then a widow, she brought seven witnesses to court to clear her of the charge that she stole a neighbor's sheep and changed the brand. In 1816 she was charged with slander. In 1818, with all three of the various aliases connected to her name, Mary was back in court under three separate charges, with some persons who had previously testified on her behalf now testifying against her. This time the grand jury indicted her for "a Nuisance in keeping a house of ill fame" where "certain persons as well men as women of evil fame . . . at unlawful times as well in the night as in the day . . . remain drinking tippling whoreing and misbehaving themselves . . . offending to the corruption of the publc [*sic*] morals." A second case charged her with selling illegal liquor by the drink at her home, and a third with passing counterfeit or forged money.

For more than a dozen years, many charges were brought against Mary for physical assaults on neighbors, travelers, and other persons in the community as well as for trading with slaves and sending out her slave woman, also named Mary, to steal for her. Sometimes the white Mary was accused of attacking individual women or men by herself—with a whip or a dirk or with sticks, stones, or brickbats. In 1825 the Camden grocer James McEwen, for example, charged her with stabbing him with a dirk and with cutting him several times on the face. At other times she was accused of attacking with a group.

In 1830 Mary brought charges against her feisty neighbor Squires McDonald for "beating her with a stick and also with his feet" when, he said, she tried to stop him on his horse on the public highway. A petition on his behalf was signed by a dozen leading men asking the court to consider "the infamous & turbulent character of the prosecutrix Mary Cunningham" and to excuse him from the guilty charge that would imprison him as he was an "Industeres & a hardworking man" responsible for the support of a large family that would suffer in his absence. A feud apparently resulted, for in 1833 McDonald testified to the robbery of his home by Mary, accompanied by a half dozen other individuals he named, some with her surname, who set upon his place "with knives hatchets Dirks and Clubs" and since then had "waylaid the Road to murder him."[29]

It is interesting to ponder the origins of the scofflaw-matriarch as well as to question why such reputed outrageous behavior was allowed to endure so long on a major public road in antebellum Kershaw District. Perhaps her rural location near the edge of the old battlefield with its bullet-blasted trees put her beyond the pale of constant legal intervention. Perhaps remains of a fallen heritage or accumulation of ill-gotten gains afforded her financial security. Or perhaps a culture that prided itself on polite treatment of genteel women could not relegate to the anomalous female offender the whipping post, jail cell, or hangman's noose assigned notorious male offenders. Ironically, while some women felt constrained by the restricted role that society accorded their gender, this antebellum woman, clearly without the status of a lady, may have been able to turn the societal mind-set to her advantage.

Distinctions of Color

The legally least-advantaged people of the antebellum period were clearly those held in slavery, whose own words of their experiences have only rarely survived. More than seventy years after the end of slavery, as part of the Federal Writers' Project, a few people from Kershaw District were among surviving former slaves interviewed in other places about their memories of slavery.[30] In Raleigh, North Carolina, T. Pat Matthews interviewed ninety-two-year-old Henry James Trentham, a former slave of Dr. John I. Trantham and his wife, Elizabeth, in Kershaw District. At Winnsboro, South Carolina, W. W. Dixon interviewed eighty-eight-year-old Delia Thompson, a former slave of Jesse Kilgore and his wife, Alethea Lois Collins, who had lived at Red Hill plantation on White Oak Creek in Kershaw District and who had been neighbors of Dr. Trantham.[31]

Dixon also interviewed eighty-five-year-old Rosa Starke of Winnsboro, a former slave of Nick Peay, whose family had Liberty Hill connections. Dixon used the custom of dialect spelling to reproduce the sound of her voice as she explained the complex racial and class distinctions that slaves recognized: "Dere was just two classes to de white folks, buckra slave owners and poor white folks dat didn't own no slaves. Dere was more classes 'mongst de slaves." She listed in the first class the house servants—butler, maids, nurses, chambermaids, and cooks; In the next class down were carriage drivers, gardeners, carpenters, barbers, and stablemen; then came wheelwrights, wagoners, blacksmiths, and slave foremen. "De nex' class I 'members," she continued, "was de cow men and de [ones] dat have care of de dogs. All dese have good houses and never have to work hard or git a beatin'." The next group included "cradlers of de wheat, de threshers, and de millers of de corn and de wheat, and de feeders of de cotton gin." In the lowest class, below all others, were the common field workers.

The 1850 census provides more detailed information than did previous censuses about a class of people that did not figure in Rosa Starke's list—free persons of color. In enumerating them the census taker listed each individual's name, age, and occupation and designated that person as black or mulatto. The census taker appears to have relied on physical appearance rather than racial descent since children of the same family were sometimes variously described within the same household. Overall about half of the free people of color were listed as black and half as mulatto. Any relative advantages for an individual to have a mixed-blood or an African appearance could be variously interpreted.

In 1850 free persons of color headed thirty-three separate households; of these, nineteen heads were female and fifteen male. Free persons of color were also living in twenty-one households headed by white persons. In these white households almost two-thirds of them were listed as black rather than as mulatto, almost two-thirds were male, and only a few were thirty years of age or older. In addition about half of those under thirty were twelve years of age or younger. Conclusions may be drawn that the majority of free persons of color lived in separate households and that those who lived in white households were mostly black male workers or serving children. It may be noted that of the white householders, three were slaveholding farmers surnamed Bowen, whose separate households employed a total of ten freemen.

Most freemen in 1850 lived in urban rather than rural settings. Of freemen whose occupations were listed, one was a wagon driver (Isaac Rodgers), four were brick makers or bricklayers (Henry Brown, Jack Cleveland, Monday Cook, and Thomas Pettifoot), and four were carpenters (Peter Conway, M. Heathcox, Manson House, and C. Vaughan). Additionally there were one blacksmith (Edward Conway), five mechanics (Thomas Conway, Donn Coples, A. Dixson, Peter Hunter, and Francis Shaler), and an apprentice (Joseph Conway). Richard Chesnut Sr. was listed as a barber, and Andrew Henry Dibble Sr. and Eli Jacobs were tailors.

Only two freemen were listed as farmers—James Pettifoot, who was living in a white household, and Elijah Bass, an eighty-year-old mulatto householder living west of the Wateree River. Bass was a householder in Kershaw District by the 1810 census and the owner of two slaves. He was, in fact, the only slave-owning person of color then enumerated in the district. By 1809 he owned five hundred acres on the "waters of Beaver Dam and Bell Branch, waters of Twenty Five Mile Creek of the Wateree River." His mother, Molly Bass, was a white woman, according to documents she filed in the district court, and a woman of property who bequeathed slaves and two plantations in her will filed in 1829. Bass's wife too was white, a native of North Carolina, and Bass described himself as a "freeman of Color" in his will, recorded in 1854.

The Bass family was part of a precedent-setting antebellum court decision that addressed legal definitions of race. In 1846 a daughter or granddaughter of Elijah Bass, "Mrs. White," filed suit against a state tax collector who tried to have her pay the capitation tax placed on free blacks. In *Mrs. White v. Tax*

Collector testimony was given that Bass's mother was a mulatto; his father, a Revolutionary War soldier; and Bass, a "dark quadroon if he was one." The reason the decision favored Mrs. White, however, was that the Kershaw District court had previously allowed Bass to testify in a property suit, thus treating him as white since it was illegal for persons of color to testify against whites. The decision in *Mrs. White v. Tax Collector* influenced state courts at the time to allow white legal status for those who, by community acceptance, had been permitted to participate in the activities of whites. Thus evidence of having owned land, having paid property taxes, having acquired education, or having joined military groups provided ways that persons of color could "pass" the racial barrier, if they also cultivated appropriate speech, manners, and appearance to maintain community acceptance. Because of such rulings, some South Carolina whites grew more cautious about permitting persons of color to "act white," and tensions might flare in any situation that questioned an individual's family heritage or social acceptance.

To preserve their freedom unchallenged in an increasingly divisive society, most free persons of color were cautious in maintaining appropriate records of their status. A person of African American heritage who could not produce proof of his freedom could be legally assumed to be a runaway and could be sold into slavery by the state. One certificate of freedom issued in the Charleston court in 1860 was especially distinctive in being signed by high-ranking officials, the governor and secretary of state, and in documenting the free heritage of Andrew Dibble, thirty-six, "a Tailor now residing in the Town of Camden." He was identified as the son of Mindah, whose mother, Beck, was the daughter of Catherine Cleveland, who by an 1807 affidavit was certified as "a native of Africa . . . born free on the Island of Bannanoes" and in 1764 was "brought into the State . . . by Elizabeth Cleveland (now Hardcastle)," a free mulatto kinswoman.[32]

Some certificates of freedom were issued in the courts at Camden throughout the antebellum years. Here too other records document occasional orders for the selling of suspected runaways who could not produce such freedom papers. One local man, in fact, petitioned the court to relieve him of completing his contracted payment for the purchase of one suspected runaway who had subsequently run away from him also. Thus, for various reasons, many persons in the antebellum period—both blacks and whites—learned with zeal to identify their class and family connections.

Dueling

The Kershaw District Grand Jury, headed by Burwell Boykin, foreman, in September 1804 presented the following grievance: "the prevalence of Dueling; which contrary to all law Human and Divine, sweeps off many useful citizens."

A circa 1925 photograph of a Kershaw County woman following the African custom of balancing heavy burdens on the head. Courtesy of the Camden Archives

The customs of the plantation system, under which the property owner or slaveholder reigned as supreme master, created a society in which many separate worlds revolved—and sometimes collided. By old feudal ideals a man of character would behave with charitable responsibility to those weaker than himself, and they in turn would honor him with deference to his decisions. Thus a man's "name," which represented his "honor"—or that of his family, was a tangible aspect to defend, since by that name his position and thus his livelihood were upheld in his world. Ideally, it was believed, a man's desire for honor would prompt him to kind, moral behavior. Ideality and reality, however, did not always match. Some masters became bullies to subdue underlings. Furthermore men undisputed in their own territory often grew to expect their names and reputations to garner them respect and deference in other spheres of influence as well, and they were offended when others saw things differently.

Defense of honor led to a number of local duels in the antebellum period. Dueling was rife in the tensions just prior to the outbreak of the Civil War and was also reported in camps during the early months of conflict among officers eager to establish status. From surviving records it seems that dueling was guided by the formal "code duello," which was drawn up in Ireland in 1777 and regarded as terms for a fair fight in most of the English-speaking world. In 1838 former South Carolina governor John Lyde Wilson published an updated version of the code that became accepted reference in America. In principle, duels were means of settling insults or personal affronts, not for securing property or possessions. Duels of honor were fought only among men who considered one another social equals; persons of a lower class were considered beneath notice and could be ignored or simply caned or whipped. A duel was supposedly a last resort to resolve an offense; therefore friends of the parties involved at first acted on their behalf to adjust the difficulty between them. Duels by the code of honor were fought by prescribed steps, not in the heat of a moment of offense but following deliberate and controlled procedures over a stage of time and in the presence of peers. The very premise—that a separate, private justice by mortal combat was acceptable and exclusive to the elite—appealed to some persons and repulsed others.

Opponents of dueling argued that such contests were arrogant, cold-blooded, illegal, and even immoral; and such opponents formed antidueling societies. The historian Taylor points to a popular defense of dueling in 1822, which held that the duel "tended to preserve the amenities of life, that it was an incentive to virtue and a shield of personal honor—honor which the courts were powerless to defend." Thus, outside of the law and the public eye, dueling persisted among certain members of the educated class otherwise most dedicated to law and its institutions. Taylor points out, "Men who guarded their honor, but deplored the practice of dueling, found it exceedingly embarrassing to decline a challenge because the challenger reserved, and sometimes exercised, the privilege of publicly posting [announcing orally or writing about] the challenged party as a poltroon and a coward for refusal to fight."[33]

On May 20, 1812, an article headed Columbia, South Carolina, and printed in the Salem, Massachusetts, *Essex Register* reported that a duel had been fought in Camden between two officers of the Third U.S. Regiment of Infantry. Lieutenant Timothy Spann had been killed and Lieutenant William Laval wounded. Kirkland and Kennedy place the site two miles below Camden and describe details from oral tradition.[34]

On January 15, 1829, the much-lamented death of Henry George Nixon, son of William Nixon, in a duel with his friend Thomas A. Hopkins brought an outcry from the community. The duel had taken place at Sand Bar Ferry near Augusta, Georgia, with a former governor of South Carolina, John L. Wilson, acting as second to the deceased, state legislator Nixon. Kirkland and Kennedy detail many of the stories long passed down about the duel. One of the duelists reportedly practiced in Quaker Cemetery by firing at the 1822 tombstone of "Neal Smith, merchant, and his wife Mary McLehose." After the encounter

Nixon's grief-stricken father erected a high, solid wall around his son's grave at the old Presbyterian burial ground, now part of Quaker Cemetery. Within nine months after the duel Hopkins too had died, "pined away of grief," and was buried at old Swift Creek Church.[35]

The Kershaw Anti-Duelling Society organized in response to the Nixon-Hopkins event. The February 21, 1829, *Camden Journal* published the society's constitution, wherein members pledged "to use every honorable means to suppress the unlawful practice of Duelling; viewing it as an unjustifiable exposure of human life, uncalled for by the legitimate laws of honor, and capable by a prudent and timely interference of a just and amicable arrangement." The society president was James S. Deas; the vice presidents were John Boykin Sr. and James Chesnut; the secretary and treasurer was Dr. George Reynolds; and standing committee members were Dr. E. H. Anderson, John Cantey, John Carter, John Chesnut, James C. Doby, James K. Douglas, and William McWillie.

Most duels or threatened duels remained in the private sphere, away from newspapers and courts but rampant in rumors. Perhaps their drama made them seem more numerous than their actual number, but tradition persists that they intensified in the political height of the nullification period of the late 1820s and 1830s. One of the many causes advanced for the Nixon-Hopkins duel was politics, the reason given in the Charleston papers.

Kirkland and Kennedy researched the oral traditions of an 1845 encounter about which no published contemporary accounts existed. The duel fought in the present Lugoff area between James P. Dickinson and John Smart was the outgrowth of remarks following another near-duel between others adjusted "on the field." It ended bloodlessly, although both opponents were "crack shots." When the challenger Smart, by rules of the code, was asked, "Are you satisfied?" he responded, "Disgusted." Reportedly, "jocularity produced good humor and ended hostility."[36]

An artifact of the Dickinson-Smart affair survives in the form of a metal target fashioned by Dickinson for his practice. Called "the Iron Man," the target is shaped like the silhouette of a man standing to fire at an opponent. Following the bloodless duel the Iron Man was discarded in the Factory Pond. After the pond water was drained in postwar years, the target was discovered and again put to use for practice.

Education and Social Improvement

"The four pillars of the social order in South Carolina were ancestors, possessions, occupations and education," states Taylor. He also contends, "So socially desirable was the station of planter that non-slaveholding whites in the cotton belt anticipated the time when they could boast of the ownership of slaves and cotton fields."[37] Upward mobility was definitely possible. Education was one means by which families attempted to maintain or to improve social standing, as well as to train youngsters for acceptable occupations and professions in addition to suitable social roles. It was an institution that by law excluded the formal participation of persons of color. Although a glance at many advertisements for schooling opportunities may give the impression that there was no shortage of educational institutions for whites in the antebellum period, it must be remembered that as private endeavors, many places were sustained for only a few short sessions and often were irregularly attended.

Orphan Society Schools

In Camden the social and benevolent endeavors of the Orphan Society continued from the previous century to provide both private and some charity schooling throughout the antebellum period. The society sponsored various schools and academies, coordinating both public and private funding. It supported education by charging tuition for private students, who composed the largest body, and by receiving from the county proceeds of escheated property—that of deceased persons without heirs, by conducting one or two annual lotteries, and by accepting allocated state allotments for individual indigents. Camden young people attended as day students; youths from rural parts of the district and beyond boarded with local families to attend the school sessions.

Names of schoolmasters and schoolmistresses echo through local history, remembered for various influences on community youths. Of local denominational influences on education, those of the Presbyterians were here, as elsewhere, especially strong. Robert Dow continued as principal (main teacher) of the Orphan Society school until 1805, when the Presbyterian minister Andrew Flinn assumed the role. In that year William Lang, an original donor, bought back the old school property, and the house that had been used by Cornwallis, the former Joseph Kershaw home now in a state of disrepair, was purchased for one thousand dollars and converted into an academy. Apparently the curriculum was enlarged as well as the space. Latin and Greek were part of academy studies that prepared students for college and sometimes extended into early college curricula. The Camden Orphan Society schools maintained a highly respected reputation throughout their history.

In 1809 the Baptist minister William Brantley was principal, and he was followed in 1810 by the Presbyterian minister B. R. Montgomery.[38] That year the society ran a separate free school, which operated for two years until the state of South Carolina extended free public education through an act of 1811. In 1811 the Presbyterian minister George Reid was Orphan Society principal, with C. J. Shannon as assistant (second teacher). Political conditions that year, leading to the War of 1812, no doubt encouraged the organization of the boys of the academy into an artillery company with uniforms and simulated cannons. From 1819 to 1823 the Scotsman John McEwen was principal. During his term in 1820 the Kershaw-Cornwallis site was exchanged for property on DeKalb Street immediately east of where Bethesda Presbyterian Church was to stand. In 1822 the church and two brick academies, one for males and one for females, were completed. Throughout six more decades the society sponsored schools at this location.

In 1823 and 1824 schools here were conducted by "Messrs. Thayer and Hart," followed in 1825 by Reverend Jonathan Whitaker, his wife, and his son Daniel K. Whitaker, with "Mrs. and Miss Jumelle" in charge of music. The Whitakers also offered, for additional charge, lessons in ornamental needlework; "Painting on Velvet and in Oils, Crayon and water colours"; and private instruction. Reverend Raynolds Bascom, whose wife likely also assisted, took charge in 1825 but died in 1827 and was succeeded by Ebenezer P. Niles through 1829.

In 1830 Henry P. Hatfield assumed the principalship until 1836, when because of ill health he took up a school at Bradford Springs. Dr. Moses Holbrook, in most years with his wife also teaching, served as head of the Orphan Society School from 1836 to 1845. In 1838 the society moved an old schoolhouse from the lower end of the town to the wooded edge of present Hampton Park to serve as an auxiliary building, reportedly to separate a class of rowdy boys that year. The building became known as Pine Grove Academy. From 1839 to 1846 it was privately leased by Leslie McCandless as a classical English school.

From 1845 to 1846 Orphan Society academies were taught by George S. Walker and Miss C. W. Ellis. Leslie McCandless was principal from 1846 to 1849, teaching variously with Miss Clarrisa Brittain, Mrs. A. H. Hart, and Miss Frances Augusta Coleman, the third of whom became his wife. In 1849 McCandless resigned but rented the brick academy buildings to continue a private school there with his wife. The classical school conducted in 1849 in the Cunningham house opposite them on DeKalb Street by Reverend Thomas B. Russell was probably an Orphan Society school. The 1850 census shows that the Presbyterian minister Samuel Donnelly was Orphan Society principal that year. In 1853 William Steadman was principal for the society school, and from 1859 Charles H. Peck conducted the male academy as a semimilitary school and Miss Maggie DeNoon conducted the female academy. The war period had clearly begun in April 1861 when the local newspaper reported that at Peck's school, "Mons. C. Metzler Von EeKelen" had instructed cadets in broadsword practice and "in the new and very efficient Zouave Drill."

Other Private Schools

In the first issue of the 1816 *Camden Gazette,* Samuel Mathis offered to board "four or five orderly schoolboys" at his Camden home, and Mrs. Campbell advertised a "Female Boarding School" at Bradford Springs in Sumter District. By 1816 Joshua Reynolds was conducting a school, probably in his home still standing on Broad Street just south of the present Camden Archives. Kirkland and Kennedy name several private schools that operated in Camden between 1815 and 1820, names also found elsewhere. The "Misses Carpenter" had a boarding school on Broad Street, and "Mr. A. Carpenter" taught for the Camden School Association. Mrs. William Langley, "lately of Lodebar Academy" in Sumter District, had a school here, as did the Camden Baptist preacher Jesse Pope. Joshua Reynolds operated a female boarding school, and a Frenchman noted for fencing skills, Michael Rudolph, operated a school for boys.

Various sources show that in the 1820s an academy for males and females was conducted by "Dr. Cleary and Lady" in "Mr. Whitaker's rooms" on Broad Street, and the Misses Salmon operated a female seminary opposite Lafayette Hall. Mrs. Esther Clarkson and Miss Clarkson conducted a school where the subjects were reading, writing, orthography, geography, grammar, and arithmetic, with drawing lessons or boarding resulting in extra charges. This school closed when Mrs. Clarkson married Ebenezer Niles, another local educator.

In the decade of the 1830s Mrs. Bascom, widow of the Presbyterian minister Raynolds Bascom, and Miss Legare conducted a winter school in Camden and a summer school in Kirkwood, offering boarding for female students. P. McCaskill had an English school on DeKalb Street, and "Monsieur Godefroy" ran a French school. Misses Henrietta and Rebecca DeLeon in this period operated an acclaimed girls' school opposite Lafayette Hall, probably the former female seminary. An institution that Kirkland and Kennedy term "one of the best schools for girls ever maintained in Camden" began in 1833 under Misses Stella Phelps and Mallory in Ebenezer Niles's old schoolroom. As a child, Mary Boykin Chesnut studied for two years in Miss Phelps's class and recalled her with praise. Miss Phelps began a long tradition of May Day ceremonies that became part of community custom. In 1841 she married another local educator, Henry P. Hatfield, who operated another school in Camden.

In 1839 Leslie McCandless, then eighteen years old and a recent graduate of South Carolina College, opened his first Camden school with a Mr. Leland and began a half-century-long career in the course of which McCandless became the leading name in community education. In 1842 Mrs. Charles Spann was conducting a very large school in Camden, with fifty boarders, and charging $350 per session. In the summer she conducted her school at her Kirkwood residence. In 1845 Miss Frances Augusta Coleman of Vermont took over the outstanding girls' school of the former Miss Phelps, now Mrs. Hatfield, and she was teaching at the time she married McCandless. Like him, she continued for many years as a prominent local educator.

Camden Free School

Few records of the education offered by the state at the Camden Free School from 1812 survive, although its operation was headed by leading citizens serving as school commissioners. Some of the teachers' names survive from newspaper and court references. In 1831 Antharies Purviance was schoolmaster, and William Nixon was head of the commissioners. Newspapers explained, "Those who wish to send [students to the school] must get a ticket from one of the Commissioners." Because inability to pay for education was equated with attendance at the free public schools, many citizens were too proud to apply, and thus the potential of public schools languished. Throughout the state they bore the stigma of paupers' schools.

For local youngsters who did attend the public school, however, the rudiments of a basic English education gave many a start in life. In 1833 the Camden Free School was under the charge of Moreau Naudin, and parents wishing to send their children applied for tickets to Everard Cureton or William Nixon. In 1834 the school was again headed by Purviance. In 1860 well-to-do friends of the longtime merchant C. J. Shannon, who had taught years ago, were amazed when he returned to the profession to take charge of the free school. Various well-meaning citizens, recognizing the value of the public school for the benefit of society in general, helped at times to sustain its operation.

Upper Kershaw District Schools

In the upper part of Kershaw District in 1816, ambitious planters of the Beaver Creek settlement twenty miles north of Camden organized the first formal school of that area. The historian Andrea Steen says that the building was constructed two stories high, thirty-three feet by twenty-two feet, with four partitions and was used for Presbyterian worship on Sundays. Trustees were Joseph Cunningham, John Fletcher, Adam McWillie, George Miller, Joseph Patterson, George Perry, and John Russell (replaced the next year by his son Ferguson Russell).[39] In the *Gazette,* Principal G. G. MacWhorter advertised the Beaver Creek Academy, opening on January 1, 1817, next to the Presbyterian congregation, with both male and female departments, the latter taught by Mrs. Britton. In 1820 the school changed its name to Russell Place Academy. In 1840, with John G. Bowers as a teacher, it advertised in the *South Carolina Temperance Advocate* as being twenty-four miles north of Camden. In 1850 a new building was constructed near the county line with Lancaster, and here the school was called the Russell Place Line School.

At Liberty Hill, according to information compiled from the separate histories by Louise Johnston and Mary Ellen Cunningham and from various other sources, early teachers named "Spencer" (probably Samuel Spence) and "Gore" are mentioned, as well as a noted educator of the period, James Wilson Hudson, who in 1834 left to become principal of the Mt. Zion Institute at Winnsboro. Samuel Spence, an Irish weaver who immigrated to South Carolina in 1828, found no work of that type here but turned to teaching and settled in upper

Kershaw District. One source states that he educated "a number of men who became prominent in the professional world."[40] On December 31, 1850, Samuel Spence with J. T. Cauthen inserted an ad in the *Camden Journal* for their operation the following year of Hanging Rock Academy, "26 miles north of Camden, near the stage road from Camden to Charlotte . . . located in a healthy, moral and religious community, remote from vice or immorality of any kind." Cauthen, "a South Carolinian by birth and education," and Spence, "so well known in the community" that no more need be said, offered to prepare "Young men of studious habits . . . to enter any college in the United States."

In 1850, when the *Journal* advertised for a teacher for the Female Academy at Liberty Hill, the trustees were H. R. Brown, William Dixon, and J. S. Thompson. In 1851, when George MacMaster was teaching at Liberty Hill, the trustees were the same. Before that year an old log building had served as a schoolhouse, near the site of the present Presbyterian school, but plans were under way for improvements. In 1852 James B. Cureton deeded two acres on Peay's Ferry Road near the Presbyterian manse. Here a four-room, two-story frame structure with wide porches on three sides was built for an academy. Among teachers during the antebellum period and for a time afterward were "Capt. and Mrs. Orchard" and a northern teacher named "Mr. Fenn" who espoused a southern position.[41] According to an 1851 *Camden Journal,* the Liberty Hill Male Academy included instruction in Latin and Greek and was directed by a South Carolinian, John Rennie Blake of Abbeville.

A "Southern" Education System

By the beginning of the 1850s growing political tensions that strained relations between the North and the South grew more polarized. On January 2, 1851, *Camden Journal* editors Thomas J. Warren and C. A. Price made strong editorial comments regarding the education of local youths: "We call attention to the Schools advertised in our columns. They are Southern—and by that we mean, have no Northern Teachers—a School with a Northern Teacher is not a Southern School no matter where located. The able Teachers, the healthy locations, their cheapness, &c. we hope will secure them an ample patronage. We hope the Teachers will admit no Northern book to be used. . . . They are all poisonous springs from which Southern pupils should never drink." In fact northern teachers had long been numerous in local schools as throughout the rest of the South, where educated native males were generally more profitably employed in other fields and educated native females were generally discouraged from seeking employment outside the domestic sphere.

One effort to provide native teachers for South Carolina classrooms included the organization of a training school in upper Kershaw District, which was announced on December 30, 1850, by Samuel Donnelly, the Camden Orphan

Society principal. In the *Camden Journal,* Donnelly advertised the January 20, 1851, opening of the South Carolina Normal School near Russell Place (today Stoneboro). The boarding school would provide both English and Classical education and was open to all, but it was designed "primarily for the training of teachers" and especially for "those desirous of becoming teachers, whose means are limited." The ad explained, "In the higher, or teacher's class, every one shall be entitled to free tuition who shall sign an obligation to devote, at least two years after leaving the institution, to the business of teaching within the State,—the preference being given to the district from which the pupil comes."

Schools Abroad

Some families sent their young people "abroad" for education—not often to another country, as the term is often construed, but to a place outside the home district. While Charleston was a favored city in South Carolina and Philadelphia a favored city outside the state, a large number of students educated outside their home area attended schools within the interior of the state. Mt. Zion Institute at Winnsboro, where the Camden schoolmaster Leslie McCandless at one time served, was a frequent choice for Kershaw District males. A number of district females attended the Barhamville school near Columbia under Dr. Elias Marks; the school was also known as the S.C. Female Institute and the Columbia Female Academy.

Summertime Schools

Many families took advantage of their summer retreats to surrounding springs to educate their children at the same time. Some Kershaw District schoolmasters taught at summertime academies, some of which also operated year-round. Eliphant Peck, for example, in the 1830s taught at Richland School in Rice Creek Springs, twenty miles from Camden and thirteen miles from Columbia. In the 1840s Henry P. Hatfield did summer teaching at Bradford Springs in Sumter District. Rembert Settlement Academy and Lodebar Academy also operated not far from Bradford Springs. In 1860 Harmony Female College operated the Bradford Springs Institute.

Social Graces

Teachers of the social graces found pupils among adults and young people. Whereas various country reels could be learned and enjoyed at home as children grew up, polished instruction in ballroom dances with attendant manners and fashionably changing steps set apart the instruction of the affluent and elite from that of the masses. Formal instruction provided initiation into the fine points of social compatibility with upper-status persons in other communities. Dancing schools were in popular proliferation, random examples of which included

"Messrs Walcott & McCauley in HA McAdam's Long Room," Mr. Kingsbury's dancing school (at one time with Ilai Nunn) at the Camden Hotel, cotillions and fancy dances taught at Mr. Welsh's Ball Room, and dancing instruction at William Nixon's tavern. Other social skills included vocal music, taught, for example, by Johnathan S. Jenkins and Mrs. Jumelle; French, by Monsieur Godefroy; and penmanship, by "Coe & Strong." John B. Morin, a recent arrival from Paris, offered "small sword practice in Havis' Ball-Room" at John Havis's tavern. Fencing, like horseback riding, was considered a desirable practice for improving the carriage and physical grace that could set the aristocrat apart from the commoner.

Societies of Educational Nature

Adults who wished to continue their learning had opportunities through social organizations that included educational activities. Kershaw Lodge no. 29, Ancient Free Masons, was organized in 1811 and was one of the state's first Masonic orders, wherein members advanced step-by-step through learning and service. Other organizations were less structured. The DeKalb Lyceum, for example, presented many lectures of a scholarly nature. Members of the Wateree Agricultural Society listened to scientific talks and conducted experiments useful in their own planting operations. The Flat Rock Literary Society enjoyed readings and discussions and may have been associated with the Library Society of the Flat Rock Baptist Church. In the same area the Flat Rock and Beaver Creek Temperance Society focused their information sharing on social issues and likely related political and religious ones. It is not clear whether this society was separate from or evolved into the Total Abstinence Society of Beaver Creek and Flat Rock as perhaps the result of continued focus. The Washington Temperance Society, which organized in Camden, undertook a controversial move to admit women as well as men as participating members in 1844.

Sabbath Schools

The origins of modern Sunday schools that provide denominational religious teaching, early Sabbath schools were often interdenominational and sometimes provided elementary reading and perhaps writing instruction to help persons of all ages and backgrounds understand the Bible and apply its teachings. The teachers were typically educated persons, often local school personnel. In Camden various denominations met together on the Sabbath in "union" classes, some of them held regularly in the town hall. Music and singing instruction were also provided to help members more fully participate in worship services. Some Sabbath schools built up sizable lending libraries and distributed Bibles and tracts in the community. Sabbath schools were also instituted among free and enslaved persons of color, although instruction had to be varied since teaching them to read was contrary to South Carolina law. Occasionally individuals, however, believing in the necessity of Bible reading, quietly disregarded that law to make literacy skills part of religious education.

Children of Color

On the whole, while children of color were trained in practical work skills, relatively few acquired "book learning." Some slave children picked up basic literacy from white playmates or in households where their education was seen as an advantage to the slaveholders, and slaves sometimes passed their knowledge on to other slaves. However, free children of color were naturally more likely to have opportunities to acquire literacy since many of their parents worked in crafts or trades where such knowledge was needed. Reportedly, parents able to do so quietly hired tutors for their children. In what was perhaps an exceptional rather than a typical situation, Bonds Conway's granddaughter Ellie, later the wife of Andrew H. Dibble, was as a young girl taken to Charleston by her father, Moreau Naudin, "to attend an underground Quaker school for free persons of color."[42]

Planting Operations

Whatever its assets and its debits, the cotton economy around which all lifestyles revolved had at its base the operations of individual planters. By the 1820 federal census the total population of 12,429 in Kershaw District included 5,147 persons (mostly slaves) "engaged in agriculture." James Chesnut was the district's largest planter, with 210 such workers. Three other planters reported statistics of 100 or more engaged in agriculture: Mary Boykin (150), Zachariah Cantey (100), and Duncan McRa (161). Planters who had 40 or more agricultural workers but fewer than 100 were a more sizable group: William Ancrum (93), James Blair (53), Joseph Brevard (81), John Carwell (55), Joseph Cunningham (45), James S. Deas (70), Joseph English (62), Benjamin Haile (48), Elizabeth Hopkins (47), William W. Lang (42), Powell McRa (50), Adam McWillie (57), Benjamin Perkins (47), Reuben Starke (40), and Mary Whitaker (60).

An even larger number of planters reported at least 15 but fewer than 40 engaged in agriculture. These included John Adamson (22), David Archer (15), Benjamin Bineham (36), Alfred Brevard (35), John Brown (16), John Cantey (22), Harriet Chesnut (27), John Chesnut (20), Lewis Ciples (32), Robert Coleman (18), Thomas Crim (16), Arthur Cunningham (19), Everard Cureton (20), William Daniel (19), William Dixon (18), Charles Ellis (15), Joshua English (25), Sarah Flake (16), William Guphill (22), Richard Hunley (17), Abram Jones (20), John Kershaw (18), Jesse Kilgore (26), Francis Killingworth (24), James W. Lang (26), Thomas Lang (35), Joseph Patterson (20), Philip Pitman (16), James C. Postell (26), John Reed (25), George Stratford (20), John Truesdell (18), Archibald Wadkins (20), Nancy Watson (15), James Williams (15), Robert Williams (18), and Lovick Young (17).

In comparison to a modern business of 15 workers, 1820 planting operations that size might be considered substantial.[43] It should be noted also that a number of the planters were merchants or professional men as well, so that planting was only part of the business they carried on. The presence of a half-dozen female planters suggests that increased status was accorded to that gender in the presence of wealth. The planter role of females in these cases was usually acquired by inheritance, most often from a deceased husband. The largest female planter, and also the second-largest planter in the district, was Mary Whitaker Boykin, the second wife of Burwell Boykin, who died in 1817. Although education and social position were advantageous assets, women in the male-dominated culture had to exercise special individual abilities in order to maintain success as antebellum planters. The widow Boykin, according to Kirkland and Kennedy, "was left with the care of their fourteen children—most of them young—a charge to which she was fully equal, for she is noted in the family tradition as a woman 'Planned / To warn, to comfort and command.'"[44]

By report of the 1830 census, the district's largest slaveholder was still James Chesnut, listed as head of a household including 333 slaves. The two next-largest slaveholding households were headed by women. Mary Boykin held 295 slaves, and Mary McRa, daughter of John Chesnut and second wife of Duncan McRa, who died in 1824, held 280 slaves. William Ancrum's household included 208 slaves. Fourteen households included between 100 and 200 slaves: William Adamson (146), Benjamin Bineham (112), James Blair (100), John Chesnut (183), Joseph Cunningham (186), James S. Deas (120), Ben T. Elmore (116), Ann P. English (111), Benjamin Haile (90), Abram Jones (100), John McRa (105), William McWillie (198), William Nixon (151), and John Taylor (134).

From the 1830 census Priscilla T. Oliver calculated that "The 8,333 slaves in Kershaw County in 1840 were owned by approximately one-half of the 'householders' listed, for an average of 17 slaves per owner. Eighteen householders owned more than 100 slaves for a total of 3,056 slaves and an average per 'large' owner of 179. Of the remaining 5,277, the average would be 10.3 slaves each slave-holding household."[45] The figures also mean that approximately one-half of the households owned no slaves. Furthermore, since the dollar-value of slaves represented the greatest "property" worth in the area, a net-worth gulf stretched between slaveholders and nonslaveholders.

Winds of Change

While schools, churches, and the law increased their prominence in the expanding society, clouds gathered about the image of its golden prosperity. Discovery was made in 1816 of a local plot for a slave insurrection intended to begin on July 4, a day of feasting, festivity, and patriotic celebration. The plan for a bloody end to their owners was revealed by a slave of Colonel James Chesnut, who warned his master. Following apprehension and the trials of a number of suspects, six of the conspirators were executed.[46]

The discovery roused disquieting fears and doubts. Attitudes of racial distrust or disliking increased among some citizens; among others sympathies were stirred. Dr. William Blanding's wife, Rachel Willetts of Philadelphia, wrote two letters to a cousin there expressing fear ("I think it is Time for us to leave a County that we cannot go to bed in safety") and realization ("Their thirst for revenge must have been great").[47]

Decreased Fertility

The agricultural demands of heavy-feeding cotton took a heavy toll on local soils, and the diminished fertility of unreplenished fields reduced planting yields and profits. As availability of new land decreased locally and land prices increased, many residents turned their ambitions toward distant acreage—in Georgia, Florida, Alabama, Mississippi, or Texas. The Louisiana Purchase of 1803 and the settlements of the War of 1812, as well as a series of treaties and removals of Native Americans, opened more and more unclaimed territory.

Out-Migration

Migrations from Kershaw District began increasing in the 1820s, and by the 1830s they surged into an outward flood steadily draining off local talent and resources. Oliver points out, from the 1830 census, "The white population of Kershaw County, after enjoying a steady increase for the previous three decades, dropped from 5,625 persons in 1820 to 5,016 in 1830. The number of family units decreased by 102. The slave population, however, increased substantially—from 6,692 in 1820 to 8,333—and the free blacks from 112 to 196."[48] Overall out-migration was driven by desire for new land, although the movement was also prompted by the political and personal controversies related to hotly contested issues of slavery, states' rights, and nullification.

Southward and westward migrations had long been a part of the history of central Carolina. Arthur Brown Ross, a planter on the west side of the Wateree River, described in his diary for February 20, 1800, the departure of his son-in-law's family for Mississippi: "This day David Simms is to move for the western country." Ross and his wife accompanied the packed wagon as far as Horsepen Branch before they turned back, and he recorded poignantly, "I heard my daughter cry a quarter of a mile, I think." Only five years later the Rosses joined the direction of the younger family members, migrating permanently to Mississippi.[49] Many families who separated never saw one another again.

While many family names disappeared from the local area because of migration, many of those most commonly present at the time of the 1830 census are still found within the county. The most frequently repeated surname of a household head in what was then Kershaw District was Williams, a name that recurred in that position twenty separate times. There were eleven households each headed by the surnames of Brown, Gardner, or Jones. Surnames recurring between seven to nine times each as heads of households were Ballard, Cook, McCaskill, McLeod, Parish, and Sanders. Names of household heads recurring four to six times each were Anderson, Blair, Boykin, Campbell, Cantey, Carter, Clinton, Coats, Cunningham, Daniels, Davis, Dixon, Dunlap, English, Gaskin, Gillis, Goff, Goodwin, Graham, Hall, Hogan, Hood, Horton, Ingram, Irwin, Johnson, Kelly, Kershaw, Love, Lowry, Marshall, McDonald, McDowell, McKee, McRa, Miller, Moseley, Nelson, Parker, Perry, Pettyford, Robinson, Scholfield, Schrock, Scott, Smith, Sowell, Taylor, Thomson, Tiller, Turner, West, White, Wilson, and Young.

By February 22, 1834, the *Camden Journal* lamented: "The rage for migration southwesterly has we think increased during the past year beyond all calculation. We daily see extensive caravans of movers, many of whom carry with them a considerable portion of the needful." Within one week nearly two hundred such migrants had passed through the local area. Furthermore, the paper noted, "From our own district the number is really so great as to make one melancholy, whole families disposing of their possessions here for little or nothing and migrating to the West with the hope of improving their condition." In fact, these were not local poor, according to the paper, for the majority were "from their pecuniary circumstances we would suppose able to live comfortably anywhere."

The "tremendous tide of emigration flowing westward" continued. The November 28, 1835, *Journal* reported, "During the week not less than eight hundred persons, white and colored, passed through Camden, three hundred in one party." What the paper found most disturbing was that "many of them are our own people, friends and neighbors."

Among those leaving for western areas of America were persons with hopes of greater affluence elsewhere and those discomforted by political and social concerns in a slave-dominated population and a politically dissident society. In varying degrees all such concerns no doubt affected a majority of movers to some extent.[50] Especially influential among the emigrants of the mid-1840s was the Liberty Hill native and Camden lawyer-banker William McWillie, one of Kershaw District's steady voices of the Union Party and a leading temperance advocate. In the new territory of Mississippi to which he moved with his extended family in 1845, McWillie rapidly rose politically. In a few years he was elected as a congressman, and in 1857 he became governor of Mississippi.

Investments Elsewhere

Although many large planters remained in Kershaw District and continued to thrive, some of them also invested heavily in lands elsewhere and carried on more successful operations there under the management of employed overseers.

Estate records show too that some provident locals also invested with varying success in steamboats, western banks, mining operations, railroads, and the like. Thus some of those who remained at "home" and appeared to be thriving here were in fact at least partly supported by profits from elsewhere.

The Gold Rush

Another influence driving some antebellum migration, an influence that had in fact begun at home, was the lure of mineral gold—that original dream that had for so long driven the exploration of America and that was awakened in the local vicinity of Kershaw District each time nuggets turned up in local creeks. The *Camden Journal* for December 17, 1831, referred to the largest of the area prospects, that which became known as Haile Gold Mine:

> We have seen more gold lately, than is quite pleasant to look at unless a man owned it himself, or had some prospect of fingering a modicum. Capt. Benj. Haile, of this town, owns a mine upon Lynch's Creek, partly in this district and partly in Lancaster, which we have no doubt is one of the richest in the southern states. He had already taken from it about 10,000 dollars, and the ingots which we have looked at to-day amount to something more than 5,000—the produce of only two months. Capt. Haile only works upon the surface, and that too upon a small scale. Two masses which appear evidently to have been deposited while in a state of fusion, were among the specimens exhibited to us, and are of the value of about $50.

With close-hand knowledge that a lucky find meant immediate profit, some people from the local area were lured westward, especially in 1849 when news broke of gold discoveries in California. In fact the *Camden Journal* printed several letters from William J. Lemmond of Lancaster, one of the forty-niners who was seeking his fortune on the California goldfields.[51] The day his ship arrived in that state, Lemmond was surprised to meet two brothers from Camden, Albert and Augustus Tryon, also new prospectors who had arrived there the previous day by another ship. "I and the Tryon boys will stick together," he wrote, "go to the mines and I hope the next news you heare from me will convey the delightfull inteligence that I am making money." The gold rush thus added encouragement to the promises of western migration.

International Shipping

Some of the local struggles to maintain profits and power at home were attended by influences not locally controllable. Charleston, by geographic positioning, had lost status as a port in international shipping. Its former market position was challenged by Savannah and had been overshadowed by the quantity of cotton at the ports of Mobile and New Orleans. The percentage of cotton production in the small state of South Carolina could not keep up with that of the huge new western-territory fields. In the 1840s cotton prices reached an antebellum low, around three cents a pound in Camden and five cents in Charleston, but confidence remained among many growers, and by the 1850s cotton seemed on a rebound, selling again at ten, twelve, and fourteen cents per pound.

Local Enterprises

By the final decade of the antebellum period, the populace of Kershaw County was firmly committed not only to maintaining a cotton economy but also to defending it as far as necessary. However, throughout the whole of the antebellum period, whatever the occupation of a citizen—from merchant to mechanic, teacher to tavern keeper, lawyer to moneylender—no one was ever entirely removed from connection with the cotton-planting economic base and its reliance on the slave system.

Cotton Gins

The gin makers who crafted and repaired the equipment were vital to the processing of cotton. These technical specialists had been busily employed in Kershaw District from early in the century. At the beginning of the mechanical era, cotton was separated from its seeds with a small hand gin manually operated by a single worker. Afterward, powered by horses and later water, larger ginning operations were set up. Each early plantation gin was hand-built, one by one, to suit the individual planter's specifications. Once ginned, cotton was packed into bales with a large outdoor press utilizing a wooden screw turned by horsepower.

In the early part of the nineteenth century two enterprises at work in Camden advertised making and repairing gins. These were the firms of Allen Jones & Drury Campbell on King Street and William Atkinson & John Workman "at the sign of the Sheaf, Rake & Hoe." For most of the antebellum period the name John Workman was consistently associated with selling gins, selling parts, and working on gins. Others, for example Joseph M. Gayle & Co., sold gins later. Over the years some Kershaw District planters also dealt with the longtime Sumter District gin maker William Ellison of Stateburg, a former slave who had been apprenticed to the early Winnsboro gin maker William McCreight. With his earnings in the lucrative new field Ellison purchased his freedom, established his own business and a large family, acquired substantial property, and became one of the area's largest slaveholders. About 1846 McCreight's son Robert moved to Camden and also sold gins here.

Blacksmiths and other mechanics, including specialized slaves on plantations, also became proficient in repairing gins and the other farm equipment involved in cotton production. Some who had been blacksmiths in the eighteenth century continued their work, and others included James B. Berry, John Cole, Edward Conway, William O. Rives, Moses Roundtree, Charles J. Shiver, Samuel Shiver, T. L. Shiver, Robert L. Tweed, and William Worth. The Kings Mountain Iron

Company of York District advertised ore sales locally, and along with groceries and dry goods general stores often sold both iron and steel for the use of plantation blacksmiths.

By the 1850 census listings for "mechanics" outnumbered those for blacksmiths. Nathan Broom Arrants, listed earlier as a wagon maker and blacksmith, was listed in 1850 as a mechanic. The designation now likely included workers of various skills with technical knowledge for mills and gins as well as for farm equipment and transportation vehicles. Many mechanics of necessity probably also did some blacksmithing. Those called mechanics in 1850 were Thomas Banks Sr., Drury Campbell, Thomas Conway, Donn Coples, A. Dixon, A. Rice Dulin, William Gardner, Levi R. Grey, William Hotchkiss, Peter Hunter, John P. Kirkland, Robert Jackson McCreight, Douglas Minton, John A. Moore, William C. Moore, Munroe Naudin, Archibald Nelson, James Nelson, John Nelson, William Nelson, Alfred Selzer, Francis Shaler, John Sinclair, Robert L. Tweet, and H. Whitaker.

Mills and Other Operations

Like the cotton gins, the many gristmills and most sawmills of the era continued water-powered operation in the manner of those of the previous century. The names by which mills were known continued to be informal, changing as owners changed and sometimes referring to the owner, sometimes to the miller, and occasionally to the location.[52] Most operations were fairly small, designed to serve neighborhood convenience rather than volume. McRa's multistoried flour and grist mill at Camden, however, had grown from the past century to such a size that the many workers there were described in the 1830s as living in "tenements." The first steam mill in the county, according to advertisements at the time and newspaper statements afterward, was the Love sawmill in the DeKalb area, in operation by the early 1850s.

A sampling of mill types in just one section of the district is suggested in the June 7, 1828, *Camden Journal*, wherein John C. Donavan offered lumber sawing at his Sandy Run Mills, James Kershaw was selling lumber at the Marengo Mills, Chapman Levy offered "to clean Rice on Toll" at "My Rice Mill on Little Lynches Creek," and a saw and grist mill were operating on M'Cullom's Ferry Road, fifteen miles from Camden. It was probably in the upper part of the county that Lewis Hogan and William D. Hogan operated an innovative feed mill, about which they issued notice: "The subscribers having purchased the right to prepare mills to grind corn with the shuck & cob, into food for stock, for the District of Kershaw, Sumter and Fairfield, will enforce the law against all persons that prepare and use mills for that purpose, unless they obtain a written permission from us."

While not water-powered grinding operations, turpentine stills were other rural manufacturing ventures, informally named, that also increased in number and size during the late antebellum period. A number of persons who planted cotton in their richer fields made use of their longleaf pine stands in sandy soils by distilling turpentine.

Textile Manufacturing

DeKalb Factory, the district's first cotton mill for textile manufacturing, was in operation in Camden by 1838 at the old Factory Pond, for a long time in the next century the site of Wateree (Kendall) Mill. The water-powered factory, which early used slave operatives effectively, ran at first with one thousand spindles for yarn making. The number of spindles had doubled by 1846 when about forty looms were daily turning out yarn and cotton osnaburgs (sturdy fabrics). The use of slave operatives was abandoned when the demand for labor lessened their availability. In 1849 about twenty women, all whites, tended these looms at a salary range of twelve to twenty dollars monthly.

In 1853 Mrs. Margaret Maxell Martin, wife of Camden's Methodist minister, published in the local newspaper a series of articles entitled "Rides about Camden," one topic of which described a visit to the DeKalb Factory.[53] She described the operatives as "comfortably housed" with "temporal and spiritual interests . . . both well-cared for." In one room Mrs. Martin spoke with a spinner who earned $10.14 a month and who reported, "That is more than I could make any other way." The spinner continued: "Some folks look down upon factory folks, but I have had to work hard all my life. I think that a female is better paid for work and less exposed here . . . it is not so hard as field work. I am thankful to be as well off as I am."

In addition to its textile manufacturing, DeKalb Factory operated at the same location a gristmill, a tannery, and a shoe manufactory, which produced thousands of pairs of pegged and sewn "Negro shoes" yearly. Kirkland and Kennedy cite an 1849 source in stating, "The factory village was pleasantly situated, the one hundred and fifty-four white inhabitants living in neat cottages, with thriving gardens, 'indicative of comfort and refinement.'"[54] Both a day school and a Sabbath school were conducted at the factory, and at one point a house of worship was erected there and served by ministers from town.

At the end of 1855 the factory burned, and by the following year most of the workers had moved away. A twist of fate may have brought an unexpected benefit from the much-lamented disaster, however. One source points out: "Seeing devastating effects of the great factory fire may have spurred on the work and investment of mechanical-minded [Camden postmaster] John N. Gamewell, then a Sunday School leader at the DeKalb Factory and a local telegraph employee. Gamewell, with the backing of . . . James Dunlap [later Camden mayor] as a business partner, marketed the Gamewell Fire Alarm Telegraph, acquiring international patents. This public alarm system eventually cornered the market for decades and saved untold lives in industries and municipalities around the world."[55]

Financing

In the early Camden newspapers cotton factors—for example, William Clarkson; N. B. Mazyck and David Bell from Charleston; and local merchants—advertised credit in financing and marketing on commission. James McEwen advertised locally as a cotton buyer in the 1830s, and Hayman Levy and Thomas McMillan did so in later years. With the encouragement of merchants in 1844 to reorganize the manner in which auctions and private sales were conducted in random areas, both a public cotton market and a public slave market were established. The latter was placed east of the town market that was then operating at the old jail site facing the courthouse. Some local sales of slaves were advertised with financing through James Adger & Co. of Charleston, owner of Adger's Wharf, although generally such arrangements were rarely openly mentioned in ads.

Most local general stores offered credit and barter under "liberal terms," although later some stated that they served as "bank agents," suggesting that financing was arranged through separate lending institutions. Some merchants who accepted payment in cotton became speculators, holding and selling at advantageous times. A few stores advertised as "cash stores," offering "cheaper" prices, but of these some advertised also with liberal terms; these stores may thus have sold at discount for cash. In the antebellum economy communities urged the local organization of banks, not because citizens, even their most affluent, had extra cash to "bank" and invest or save, but because they wanted credit to finance agricultural operations. At its base credit ran the cotton economy.

General Stores

Most antebellum general merchant enterprises operated under the names of their individual owners rather than by titles, and the main part of their business was based within the town of Camden. In about the first quarter of the antebellum period groceries or dry goods or both, often including hardware, could be purchased in Camden from various merchants, including these (often followed by "& Co."): Henry Abbott; John Adamson; John G. Ballard; Uriah Blackmon; Francis Blair; John J. Blair; William Brown; General Zack Cantey; Dan Carpenter; Alphonso Catonnet; Charles Emile Catonnet; Lewis Ciples; James Clark; Coleman & English; James B. Coleman; Everard Cureton; M. H. DeLeon; John Doby II; Joseph Doby; James Kennedy Douglas; Jonathan Eccles;

David Foster; Alexander Hodges; James Jenkins; William E. Johnson; Charles Jugnot; Jesse Kilgore; Robert Latta; (Joseph) Lee & DeLeon; Hayman Levy; Mordecai M. Levy; Samuel Lopez; J. Lyon; Alexander Matheson; Christopher Matheson; William Matheson; J. B. Mathieu; Samuel Mathis; John McCaa; Hugh McCall; John McCants; Charles Meugy; John Meugy; Robert Mickle; J. S. Murray; Murray Robinson & Co.; Stuart Perry; Rowland Rugeley; Thomas D. Salmond; Charles John Shannon; Levy Solomon; Isaac Smith; Mendel Smith; Neal Smith; Joseph Thornton; Phineas Thornton; Trapp, Patterson, & Wilie Vaughn; John Charles West; and John Workman.

Antebellum stores were stocked with imported merchandise and also with "Country Produce," as described in the March 17, 1832, *Camden Journal.* At that date cotton was being sold at 8½¢ to 9¾¢ a pound; corn, 50¢ a bushel; and wheat, 75–80¢ a bushel. Flour milled at the Camden Mills was sold at $6.00 a barrel; flour milled in the country, $4.25–4.50. Fodder, per cwt. (100 pounds), was $1.00–1.25. Whiskey was sold at 35–40¢ gallon; apple brandy, 35–45¢; and peach brandy, 40–62¢. Advertised as "country merchandize" were bagging and ball rope, coffee, and mackerel by the barrel. Three types of iron, priced about the same, were sold by the pound—Swedish, English, and North Carolina (a little cheaper).

Country Stores and Mail

Because stores that operated in rural areas did not advertise often in newspapers, which were centered in town, specific information about merchants outside Camden is less easily available.[56] References in court records show that by 1811 Dr. Peter Garlick's store was in operation in the area that later became Liberty Hill, settled around that merchant enterprise. Wyatt Patterson ran a store within Liberty Hill by 1830. At least between 1816 and 1821, and probably longer, Daniel S. Bailey & Co. operated a tavern-store at Hanging Rock. The ledger from that period documents sales of household goods and alcoholic beverages, in quantity as well as by the drink. Russell's store above Beaver Creek was in operation by 1820. Goodwyn's (Goodwin's) store at White Oak Creek was a polling place from the 1820s and was known through the antebellum years. A store was probably also operating in that decade near Young's Bridge on the Lynches and Cureton's Mill west of the Wateree. When Jesse Truesdel in the 1831 Camden newspaper advertised the "Store now occupied by me at Flat Rock," the enterprise was already long established as "being the place for holding Elections, battalion musters, etc." By 1854, when the *Southern Business Directory* was published in Charleston, that publication gave the Kershaw District population as 14,473 and included merchants of small communities: Liberty Hill, with John Brown, Matheson & Gibbons, and R. C. Patterson; Flat Rock, with W. G. Kir(k)land, W. B. Fletcher, and W. B. Fletcher Jr.; and Lynch(es) Creek, with William M(u)ngo.[57]

The November 31, 1816, *Camden Gazette* announced that it would be operating a private mail service as it delivered its newspapers every Sunday morning from its office as far as Beaver Creek. The places of deposit were probably sites of local enterprises within area communities: "Mrs. Arledge's [tavern], Hughe's [*sic*] Store, Garlick's store, Warrenton, Bec[k]hamville, Mr. Millers, & Flat Rock." Hughes's store may have been a forerunner of Goodwin's store or of an operation later known as Hughes Mill.

The first federal post office established outside of Camden operated in Jesse Truesdel's store at Flat Rock in 1823. The likelihood is high that other rural post offices in the district were also placed at sites where merchandising was carried on—most typically general stores, merchant mills, ferry operations, or plantation stores. The rural post offices that followed in the district were these: in 1828, Lynchwood; 1829, Russell Place; 1830, Liberty Hill; 1834, Turkey Creek; 1837, Red Hill; 1838, Tiller's Ferry; 1839, Sandton; 1844, Granny's Quarter; and 1844, Hanging Rock. Not until 1849 was a post office opened south of Camden, at Boykin's Depot. Bee Tree post office opened in 1850 west of the Wateree River. That was followed in 1853 by Elm Grove and Palmetto and in 1857 by Anniedell.[58] Since rural stores and post offices were placed in concentrated population areas—first in the upper part of the district and at Lynches Creek; later south and west of Camden—their locations reflect the pattern of district growth and development.

Town and Country Public Houses

Rugged, time-consuming travel conditions made necessary the operation of public houses in town and countryside for the lodging and refreshment of travelers. During the first quarter of the century, Camden tavern and innkeepers included at various times Ballard & Dye, John G. Ballard, Uriah Blackman, Henry DuBose, John Havis, J. B. Matthieu, (H. A.) McAdams & Drakeford, M. M. McCullock, Colonel William Nixon, Welsh & Smythe, and Thomas Welsh. A few of their establishments had simple, functional names: Camden Hotel, Planters Hotel, and Travellers Hotel. Most, however, in a time when literacy skills were low, were identified by signs that hung outside: the Sign of the Bell, the Sign of the Buck, the Sign of the Eagle, and the Eagle & Harp. The Nixon Hotel, named for its owner, had as a sign a representation of "Old Hickory," Andrew Jackson, and in later years it became known as the Jackson Hotel.

The 1820 survey that was the basis of Mills's 1825 map depicts a number of rural taverns and inns along main transportation routes. North of Camden, at the fork of the Liberty Hill and Lancaster roads, near a similar intersection in the present Dusty Bend area, stood (David) Carwell's (variously spelled) Tavern. Taking the right-hand road at that point and going northward by "the road to

Hanging Rock"—that is, the old route by the Battle of Camden site toward Salisbury—the traveler encountered in order six public houses: Love's Tavern, Mrs. Love's Tavern, Noxe's Tavern, Burge's Tavern, Miller's Tavern, and George Miller's Tavern. Taking the left-hand route from Carwell's Tavern, "the road from Camden to the [county] line"—that is, the old Beaver Creek route—the traveler reached L(ewis) Cook's Tavern and Mrs. Aldridge's Tavern.

East or northeast of Camden, on various routes that intersected with the old Georgetown Road and crossed the Lynches River, lay two places named McKinnon's Tavern and two places named Dixon's Tavern, as well as Holland's Tavern, Debrules Tavern, and Sanders Tavern. Southeast of Camden on the road to Schrock's Mill, probably past the present county line, were Nickle's Tavern and L(ewis) Peebles Tavern. West of the Wateree River, Cuzack's Tavern lay on the Winnsborough road, and Holliday's Tavern and Hughson's Tavern were on the Columbia road.[59]

In comparison with the many taverns, dramatically fewer country stores are indicated on the 1825 map. Crap's Store and Russell's Store, both above Beaver Creek, are the only rural stores named. However, since a plantation store was

The McDowell home, photographed in the 1950s, in the upper part of Kershaw County. The house is said to have been enlarged from an early 1800s log structure, Mrs. Aldridge's (or Arledge's) tavern, which was rolled on logs to the present site. Courtesy of the Camden Archives

often part of the routine business of a planter, at some of the various plantations marked on the map stores likely existed as a matter of course. For example, nearby "Red Hill or Kilgore's old store," one of the locations named in 1834 legislative papers describing Liberty Hill Militia Co. Beat no. 1 in upper Kershaw District, is not indicated on Mills's map.

After 1825 a few older public establishments in Camden continued to operate, but additional inns, taverns, and hotels came into existence before the Civil War. Keepers during this period included John Bailey, J. B. F. Boone, R. P. Boyd, Joseph Goodman, Mrs. J. B. Mathieu, S. A. Mathieu, Mary (Mrs. H. A) McAdams, Hiram McCants, John McColl, William McKain, E. G. Robinson, A. S. Rogers, A. R. Ruffin, and William Watson. With more distinctive styles of naming apparently now in vogue, establishments included four named for patriots of Camden's historical past: DeKalb Hotel, Jackson Hotel, Kershaw House, and Sumter Hotel. Goodman's Hotel (Sign of the Golden Ball) and the McAdams House (also Hotel) were named for their owners, and two others, Bell Inn and Cross Keys, were named for signs. The Traveler's Inn also identified itself as the Sign of the Heart. The remaining four were Camden House (later Hotel), Mansion House, Planters Hotel, and Temperance House (later Hotel), the last of which eliminated the usual spirits from its table. Joseph Goodman operated a "boarding house," and E. P. Niles advertised to board "gentlemen." At Sandton, a stage and mail stop in upper Kershaw District, twenty-one miles from Camden and eighteen miles from Lancasterville, John Fletcher advertised his tavern at the Sign of the Eagle.

Merchant Specialties

As time passed, some Camden merchants aimed for special niches or combined specialized sales with general merchandising. In 1844 newspapers, for example, the long-time storekeeper Moses Drucker was advertising a "New Cash Store." One midcentury memoir recalls that Drucker had purchased the old courthouse when the new one was built and, apparently after moving the old wooden structure, had long used it for a store.[60] In 1844 Christopher Matheson advertised that he was selling "Family and Plantation Supplies," would serve as an "agent at either of the Banks," and even offered to rent his dwelling house. Private papers show that he cosigned mortgages related to slave sales, probably a typical practice of merchants.[61] In 1844 the merchant George Alden, in addition to manufacturing and selling shoes, especially sturdy "Negro shoes," advertised a selection of "Piano Fortes." While far more merchants were men, in 1844 a local ad announced, "Mrs. E. Warren will continue to keep . . . a general assortment of *Fancy Goods.*"

Other, more-exotic offerings to catch the consumer's eye appeared in 1844 in J. M. Gamewell's ad for "Ice! Ice!" and "Green House Plants." In 1850 F. Schneider, a butcher, advertised "meats of all kinds," apparently freshly cut.

Daniel Beaufort was also a butcher, and William B. Campbell, Mrs. Crosby, and Augustus Massebeau were bakers. Keith S. Moffat's announcement in 1850 that he was opening the "Southern Store" not only heralds a period in which a boycott of northern-manufactured goods was begun as a political protest but also signifies one of the first local stores to operate under a separate title of its own, unrelated to its owner's name. In other words, political identification rose above individual reputation. In 1860 "Meroney & Boswell" advertised "a Bath House" in their new store with a choice of "shower or plunge" baths, and they also sold extra fine flour on consignment. J. S. Meroney advertised to purchase "green and dry hides." Interestingly the latter fact shows that, after more than two centuries, the earliest of local products were still viable market items.

Other town or country merchants also operated in Kershaw District generally after the first quarter of the antebellum.[62] Among those not already mentioned were the following: A. Elias Allen; J. H. Anderson; William Douglas Anderson; Samuel M. Benson; Thomas Bonnell; Eli Whitney Bonney; John Baxter Frazier Boone; John Brown; Dan Carpenter (Jr.); Benjamin W. Chambers; Joseph Charlesworth; Stephen Craig Clyburn; Stephen Franklin Clyburn; W. Clyburn; Benjamin Cook; John M. Cooper; James B. Cureton; DeLeon & Levy; Jacob Samuel DePass; Doby & Gilman; Anthony Douglas; George S. Douglas; James Kennedy Douglas; Moses Drucker; George H. Dunlap; James Dunlap; James J. Dunlap; R. M. Dunlap; Joseph Fenet; William C. Gerald; William J. Gerald; John Ingham; John Irwin; William Johnson; W. B. Johnston; James Jones; Thomas Jones; Anthony McMillan Kennedy; Robert MacMillan Kennedy; William Kennedy; (Bernard) Koopman & Sommers; A. T. Latta; Robert Latta; James D. Lemiere; Hayman Levy; Solomon Levy; Henry G. Loper; Love & Love; Charles Marechal; Matheson, Anderson & Co.; C. F. Matheson; Farquhar Matheson; James Matheson; Nathan Mayblum; Daniel McCall; McCall & McIntosh; M. McCaskill; P. McCaskill; William Douglas McDowell; James McEwen; William McKain; Thomas McMillan; Perry Moses; James S. Murray; John D. Murray; Niolan & Fenet; John M. Niolan; Stuart Perry; (?) Rich; P. Robinson; Rosser & Ingram; John Rosser; C. J. Shannon; T. E. Shannon; George W. Shaw; Lemuel Butts Stephenson; J. S. Stewart; George Stradford; Enoch Tryon; L. A. Tryon; Robert L. Tweed; William Vernon; James Irwin Villepigue; Paul Francis Villepigue; Paul Thomas Villepigue; Mrs. E. Warren; T. J. Warren; H. C. Wellhaven; Daniel Wheeler; George Wilson; James M. Wilson; Robert Wilson; T. Wilson; Winn & West; (?) Wolfe; John Workman Jr.; John Workman Sr.; William C. Workman; Young & McKain; and Alexander Young.

Tradesmen and Craftsmen

Tradesmen and craftsmen continued to be vital contributors to community growth and comforts. Persons in Kershaw District who wished to build or improve homes in the expanding economy of the first quarter of the century could obtain materials from John Kershaw's lumber mills, hire a house carpenter such as William Robinson, arrange bricklaying or plastering with Francis and John Cook, and have painting done by James Williams or Thomas E. Baker, the latter of whom also advertised sign painting and gilding. Furniture could be purchased from McFeat & Thompson, and books and stationery were available from the bookbinder George Forbes, the Camden Book Store, or Alexander Young (later Dr. James A. Young).

Candles to light the home were handmade and sold by Mrs. Carpenter or the Camden Candle Manufactory. The auctioneer Alexander Rogers was a source of previously owned goods, specialty items, and goods sold in quantity. Tinwork could be provided by Edward M. Bronson and Sylvester Bronson (the surname was also spelled Brunson); gold and silver work, by William Parker or Alexander Young. Watches and clocks could be obtained from John Parker or from Alexander Young, who also sold jewelry. Leather goods were available from the tanyards of Benjamin Carter or (Christopher) Kohler & (David) Miller. Carriages were made and repaired by H. R. Cook.

Somewhat later in the antebellum years lumber was sawed and sold at many mills, such as those of John C. Donavan, John Love, J. J. Sanders, Andrew C. Stratford, and Joseph N. Williams. Brick makers or bricklayers included Henry Brown, Jack Cleveland, Monday Cook, George Parker, Thomas Pettifoot, and Joseph Winges. In an 1828 advertisement Anderson & Lee offered brick at their kiln at "prices, size, & quality equal to that of Columbia," which was $7.50 per 1,000, with discounts for cash or large orders. In the business of building and repairing wagons and other conveyances were Robert Mann, John R. Smith, and Moses Wages.

House carpenters included David Carpenter, Charles L. Chasten, Peter Conway, R. Francis, M. Heathcox, Manson House, D. R. Kennedy, S. W. Love, Samuel Love, Tenant Bowen Lucas, James McDaniel, Thomas Nelson, Levi Polk, William Reid, Henry C. Roberts, Benjamin Robinson, William Robinson, and C. Vaughan. Cabinetmakers included William Thomas Burchmore, William Cooper, James Francis Sutherland, and William Tarber. Furniture could also be bought from the merchant C. L. Chatten, while in 1835 W. Gardiner advertised selling "Cabinet Furniture" such as bureaus, bedsteads, washstands, and writing desks "manufactured by himself." Coopers were John H. Henson, James Roach, John Young, and four men surnamed Munn—Angus, Daniel Jr., Daniel Sr., and John.

Additional tinners were Benedictus D. Bronson and Francis B. Root Sr., and Charles Thomas Mason was a silversmith. Painters or glaziers included G. W. Strickland and Charles Whittemore. W. B. Campbell sold toys, and I. F. Bremer bound books. Printers included, among others, G. W. Addison, George Howell,

Robert McNight, Thomas William Pegues, and G. W. Tarbox. Living in the Pegues household in 1850 were Howell and three other men, also printers: G. W. Bell, James Little, and J. J. Lyons.

Styles and Personal Refinements

Specialists served basic needs and also provided refinements to individuals interested in style and personal improvements. Boots and shoes were manufactured or sold by George Alden, L. F. Breaker, A. Burr, W. Olds, Peter Warren, M. J. Wheeler, J. & S. White & Co., Thomas MacCartney Wilson, William Wilson, Wilson & Shegog, and Workman and Boone. The manufacturer George Alden bought leather locally, making mostly "Negro shoes," which were advertised by the hundreds. Liberty Hill's one manufactory, the tanyard of John Brown, processed leather for shoes sold at Alden's. In 1842 Alden & Co. paid for "dry or green hides" or exchanged hides for shoes, "at cash prices." J. & S. White advertised a variety of shoes: "walking, dancing gentleman's pumps, ladies seal skin, white silk, etc."

Mrs. C. F. Carpenter and Miss Holmes advertised "Millinery and Mantua-making," while F. J. Oakes, Dinah (Denah) H(ouston) McEwen, Susannah McEween (Mrs. James) Tweed, and Matilda Wilson (later Mrs. T. B. Walker) offered millinery also. Tailors included Francis Allen, Gilkeyson & Blair, J. J. Davis, C. A. McDonald, Mr. Monroe, J. C. Palmer, and I. Wood. That tailoring services were in demand is suggested by McDonald's advertisement in the October 27, 1824, *Southern Chronicle and Camden Aegis* to hire two or three experienced journeymen tailors, with good recommendations, and two or three apprentices. Barbers and hairdressers included William C. Adams, who also advertised shaves, and John B. Morin. For the well-turned-out as well as citizens of plainer tastes, the services of the photographers Isaac B. Alexander, J. P. Boswell, and H. B. McCallum promised lasting records. Alphonese Catonnet sold treats at his confectionary store.

Medical Practitioners

Addressing health needs, members on one early list of the Camden Medical Association included Edward H. Anderson, William Blanding, Alfred Brevard, B. W. Carter, Abraham DeLeon, John McCaa, and W. B. Whitaker.[63] Others in practice at the time were the dentist E. Hurley and the physician Shubel Blanding, who later devoted himself to dental surgery. Dr. William Langley was also an editor of the 1816 *Gazette,* the first sustained local newspaper, and medical advice made its way onto those pages as well as into talks he made locally. On June 27, 1816, an article in the *Gazette* discussed the wintertime epidemic catarrh, or influenza, advising medical authorities to treat it with bloodletting and cathartic purging. To keep healthy, citizens were advised during the winter to move into warm, well-ventilated houses; to avoid exposure to night air and to cold or rain; to wear appropriate clothing, including flannel next to the skin; to abstain from intemperance in ardent spirits; to avoid excessive exercise; to keep the bowels open; and to discharge small amounts of blood whenever spirits became too excited.

From November 1 to December 8, 1820, Dr. William Blanding kept a diary during his treatment of his brother James Blanding, sick with fever in Charleston. The doctor left Camden on November 1 and arrived in Charleston the afternoon of November 3, having crossed two ferries and spent two nights in taverns on the way. It was as hasty a trip as could then be made. Noting "My Brother very sick," he describes repeated dosages: "Once more begun with the Calomel, Opium & Camphor every 2 hours, with the Antimonial Wine & Sencka Snake Root Tea." Purgatives, bloodletting, narcotics, and herbal teas or tonics were common medical treatments by early doctors, who attempted to rid the body of illness and to keep patients calm for recuperation and rebuilding with attentive nursing.

Pharmacists

Early doctors generally kept at hand the medicines they prescribed their patients, and some, including William Blanding, Abraham DeLeon, and Mordecai DeLeon, developed specialties and operated businesses as pharmacists. Customers who patronized drugstores to procure medicines for self-treatment probably received advice along with the purchase. George Reynolds and William Reynolds later took over Blanding's drugstore, and Joshua Reynolds too was long noted in the profession. Advertising as patent medicine vendors was done by the businesses Jumelle & Young and Alexander Young, the latter of whom also sold jewelry and, in later years, advertised a bookstore. Other druggists of note during the period were Z. J. DeKay, John J. McKain, W. J. McKain, and Francis L. Zemp. At least one local doctor was said to have had his career ruined by an opium addiction. Such problems were not uncommon among the public either, as alcohol and narcotics were parts of many popular patent medicines as well as those medically dispensed.

Dentists

Some medical practitioners specialized as dentists. Shubel Blanding, for example, traveled widely in the area and maintained a practice in Camden. In 1832 he advertised making "incorruptible teeth" of porcelain. In an age without preventive care, dentists regularly lanced infected gums and pulled painful or decayed teeth. For persons of means, dentists attempted to construct oral mechanical apparatuses to help in chewing food. Other antebellum dentists or dental surgeons were M. W. Bissell, Jacob W. DePass, Francis S. Lee, Joseph Lee, T. Berwick Legare, and D. M. Rogers.

Midwives, Root Doctors, and Home Medicine

Although by reference midwives were numerous and more commonly consulted than doctors, since no license or training was required, their names rarely survive on official records. Proof that Mary Arledge (Aldrige) of upper Kershaw District was a midwife survives from her having been called as a witness in an 1836 court case. Other folk practitioners, among slaves as well as free people, are known to have existed, although the record of their names is dim. For personal care, not all people preferred or could afford services by members of licensed medical professions. "Indian cures" were popularly referred to, as were African remedies and other treatments handed down from the Old Country. Among standard prescriptions, Camden drugstores sold "Thompsonian medicines," popularized by the New Englander Samuel Thompson, who focused on herbs and steam baths rather than the bleeding, blistering, purging, and vomiting techniques of the "scientific medicine" of the day.

The Camden merchant and postmaster Phineas Thornton collected material from various sources and published a book of medical advice, home remedies, and folk wisdom, which also included recipes and tips for housekeeping and gardening. *The Southern Gardener and Receipt Book* by P. Thornton, circa 1840s, has been reprinted more than once in modern times for its interesting contents.[64] Thornton begins the section entitled "Receipts for the Cure of the Diseases of Man" with this advice: "If every morning, and, when the heat is oppressive, every evening, the whole surface of the body were bathed in water, fresh from the pump or well, with a sponge or rubbed well with the hands, so that the pores of the skin are rubbed open, and cleansed or rubbed dry with a crash towel (better than a flesh-brush), the population of the city and country in which so excellent a custom prevailed would be remarkable for health, let the climate be as it might." Other advice includes applying soot to fresh wounds to stop bleeding and to ease pain; bathing a nosebleed with vinegar; giving parsley tea, from roots and tops, to stop vomiting; and bathing in warm beef pickle to treat frostbite.

Gunn's Domestic Medicine, subtitled *Poor Man's Friend,* was one of the American home medical tomes in use in Kershaw District in the 1840s.[65] It includes advice favoring heroic medical methods on one hand and herbal ones on the other. The book speaks with concern of the increasing prevalence of the debilitating and generally fatal respiratory disease known as consumption (tuberculosis). In part the advice for treatment is as follows: "If possible, consumptive patients should remove to a warm climate the moment a predisposition is discovered; a change to a warm or temperate atmosphere during the winter months, may be the means of removing . . . this complaint." Also the pleasant "fumigation or vapour, constantly inhaled or breathed" from "burning tar" "is considered by physicians a valuable remedy in consumption." Furthermore, "As nothing tends more to aggravate the symptoms of a consumption, at an early stage of it, than a desponding mind . . . every thing should be done to cheer the spirits, such as cheerful society, music, &c. . . . The consumptive patient should daily take as much exercise as his strength will admit of. . . . The best exercise will be riding

on horseback." Such medical advice illustrates why the warm-weather colony of scenic Kirkwood, north of Camden, with its pleasant society and pine-scented, temperate areas for riding, became valued and sought out as a healthy location in the winter as well as in the summer.

Prejudice against Hospitals

In the antebellum search for good health, a general prejudice prevailed against hospitals. Probably because only the most desperately ill sought help in such institutions, they were associated in the public mind with suffering and death. For a short time Doctors Charles John Shannon and Wiley Jackson McKain attempted to operate a local infirmary in Camden to treat chronic diseases, but it closed for lack of support. While most doctors kept offices where they could see patients, doctors also rode long distances to visit patients in times of illness. References describe their crossing the Wateree both in the Camden area and in the upper part of the district to treat sickness on the western side. People living in boundary areas also sought medical aid in other districts if neighboring communities were closer.

Medical Doctors

Several medical doctors were located in upper Kershaw County. David George was at Russell Place, Ezekial Mayhew at Beaver Creek, and Alexander McDowell at Flat Rock. In the sections around Red Hill and present Flint Hill, James W. Ford, Hugh McDowell, and John Isaac Trantham were in practice. Robert B. Johnson, William Kilgore, and Wiley Jackson McKain were at Liberty Hill during at least part of their practice. Miles McInnis from Scotland treated the people of the Lynches River area before his death in 1810, and later Benjamin Simons Lucas practiced at Tiller's Ferry.

In addition to those earlier mentioned, area medical doctors included Isaac Alexander, Edward H. Anderson II, Richard Anderson, Edward M. Boykin, Daniel Pomeroy Bush, William Carlisle, Lynch Horry Deas, Daniel Louis DeSaussure II, Louis McPherson DeSaussure, Lucian Dinkins, William Ross Dye, F. E. Gordon, Hayman Levy, William A. Love, John Mackey, Benjamin McCaa, John McCaa Sr., Thomas W. McCaa, William McCulloch, R. S. McDow, John Milling, Albertus Adair Moore, William L. Pickett, Edward Anderson Salmond, Thomas Whitaker Salmond, John J. Shropshire, William Thorn, John Trent, Benjamin Fleming Watkins, Thomas J. Workman, and James A. Young. A few of the men of the time who held medical degrees practiced only in limited circles, primarily among family members and slaves, in conjunction with their responsibilities as plantation masters.

Bethesda Presbyterian Church, dedicated in 1822, and the monument to De Kalb, with its cornerstone laid by Lafayette in 1825. Courtesy of the Camden Archives

Public Improvements

In the 1820s several important public structures were erected in Kershaw District during that influential early period of affluence and ambition. The most imposing of the structures were designs by Robert Mills, nationally noted as the federal architect and designer of the Washington Monument. He is thought likely to have assisted in the design of the stately brick home at Mulberry Plantation (1820), constructed under the master builder David Bartling. While superintendent of public buildings for South Carolina, Mills was the architect of Camden's Bethesda Presbyterian Church (1822), which was flanked with the male and female academies of the Orphan Society School, and the architect of the public monument to Baron de Kalb (1825) fronting the church's DeKalb Street entrance. One of Kershaw District's most enthusiastic welcomes was given in 1825 to the Marquis de Lafayette, who came to Camden in March to lay, in solemn Masonic ceremony, the cornerstone to the monument dedicated to his former Revolutionary War comrade De Kalb.[66]

The Kershaw District Courthouse (1826) erected under Mills reflects the characteristic, classical features of its architect. The old wooden courthouse replaced by Mills's grand design had been described in petitions as "in a very defective state, never having been completed" and "little more than a frame weatherboarded, with coarse board partitions for two or three rooms . . . no office kept within, nor . . . accommodations . . . for the officers." The new public building gave dignity and status to the community. Presently the renovated courthouse, with many old features preserved, is home to the Kershaw County Chamber of Commerce and Visitors Center.

Other era milestones also strengthened Camden's position as a market town and increased opportunities within Kershaw District. These included the opening of the Camden branch of the South Carolina State Bank (1822) and the first successful bridging of the Wateree River (1828). The latter project was first approved by the legislature in 1825 when rights to the Camden Ferry were granted to a local group—Alfred Brevard, James W. Lang, Thomas Lang, Lawrence Whitaker, and Thomas Whitaker—who were also permitted the authority to construct and maintain a "covered toll bridge." Investors proceeded with the project organized under the name of the Wateree Bridge Company.

Navigation Improvements

The ambitious project to make the Wateree-Catawba system navigable from seacoast to the upper state line had begun earlier under private enterprise. State control prompted additional work in Kershaw District to clear the Wateree River channel and to proceed with building the Wateree Canal. Most of the latter effort took place on the western side of the river between 1821 and 1827. Efforts were attempted also to improve navigation of the Lynches system to slightly beyond the fork of Big and Little Lynches creeks, although the work seems never to have been completed for the intended distance.

River Boats

From the 1820s shallow-draft steamboats could navigate the Wateree within a short distance above Camden, although their success depended on water levels and expensive upkeep of the river channels. Some use was made too of team boats, with animals harnessed on deck to walk turning a propeller shaft for power. Match boats, using a man-powered system, employed two vessels, one slightly smaller than the other. Each traveled heavily loaded to deliver crops downriver, and when emptied, the smaller boat was fitted inside the larger for the return trip upriver against the current. Flatboats, basically rafts steered by poling and often simply discarded or sold for lumber downstream, remained in common use. The Camden boatyard, near the present junction of Wild Turkey Lane and Old River Road and in the vicinity of the present city water treatment plant, steadily operated to build, repair, and outfit the various rigs.

Steam Railroad

In 1827 the state granted a charter to the South Carolina Canal and Rail Road Company to build what then was said to be the world's longest railroad, a line from Charleston to Hamburg. The charter included commitment to extend a branch from the main line to Camden, but it was 1842 before work on that section began and October 27, 1848, before the railroad extension from the Kingsville junction finally reached Camden. Merchants were eager for the increased business related to shipping and loading cotton.

The railroad abruptly lessened dependence on water transportation, although for some time the river was still relied on to bring crops down from upper areas to meet the railroad and also continued for other transport-to-market use. The South Carolina railroad station at Camden stood on King Street, three blocks from the terminal point of a canal intended for freight barges to reach Camden from the Wateree River. Freshets threatened stability all along the railroad line, however, especially as tracks through swamplands were constructed on trestles. More than once moving trains en route to or leaving Camden tumbled into the Wateree Swamp when trestles gave way.

The Wateree Canal

Despite vast state expenditures on construction of the Wateree Canal in the upper western Kershaw District, modern knowledge of the canal's location has been obscured by the relatively inaccessible river area in which it was built and later by the twentieth-century submersion of much of its remains under Lake Wateree.[67] In fact reproduction maps of the canal typically mislead in duplicating its position on the Mills map published in 1825.[68] That map depicts a canal a little more than four miles long, its lower end entering the river slightly north of the mouth of Sawney's Creek. At the time the Mills map was being prepared, only "the upper section" of the eventual five-mile canal had been completed, and there was question about which of two routes "the lower section" should take, although both choices included placing works below Sawney's Creek to compensate for obstacles near Graves Ford. Construction on the lower section of the canal continued at least two years past the publication date of the map, with a cost in excess of that of the upper section. The upper section of four miles, from 1821 to 1827, cost $71,161.27, while the lower section of just more than one mile, from 1823 to 1827, cost $87,693.50, for a total expenditure to date of $158,854.77.[69]

An understanding of the operation of the Wateree Canal may in modern times be gained by examining still-standing portions of similar works at Lancaster County's Landsford Canal, today a state interpretative park. An 1828 summary report to the legislature by the state superintendent of public works Abram Blanding, formerly of Camden, described the completed canals. The Wateree Canal, according to Blanding, was "about five miles long, overcoming fifty two feet fall" and included "four granite, three wooden lifting, and one brick guard lock." The Landsford Canal was "two miles long . . . overcom[ing] thirty-two feet fall, by four lifting and one guard lock, of granite." Along with the five-mile Rocky Mount Canal and the three-mile Catawba Canal, the four canals of the Wateree-Catawba system overcame a total fall of 256 feet with thirty-six locks, so that "with the other operations, on the lower part of this stream and the Santee river, the navigation is extended from the sea board to North Carolina a distance by land, of one hundred and eighty miles."

The ambitions of water navigation were, however, countered by unpredictable forces of nature—from droughts that left canals inaccessible, to freshets that washed destructive debris into the works—and by wearisome upkeep and contention. For example, it was found that canal banks had to be fenced to prevent their destruction by hooves of water-seeking cattle and hogs, and yet area farmers and fisherman resented such unneighborly intrusions on traditional access rights. Apparently some workings of the Wateree Canal were soon found defective, for an advertisement in the March 3, 1832, *Camden Journal* opened bidding for workmen to replace three wooden locks at Grave's Shoal with three granite ones and to construct three dams for those locks within eighteen months of the contract. However, by the time the grand scheme of canal transportation had soured as a costly delusion, a model railroad had already been exhibited in Camden (1831) in hopes of encouraging such a construction, and public interest was seeking new directions.

Gleaned from various records are the names of some of the men who worked on the Wateree Canal or provided other services. Abram Blanding, Walter Izard, and Robert Mills all served in various state administrative capacities dealing with work on the project in the district. The contractor David Grafton, of the firm Kibbe and Grafton, died during work on the Wateree Canal in the early summer of 1822. "Messrs Clark, Cleverly and Couty" were hired afterward. Because slave labor was difficult to obtain, being considered too valuable at the time to hire out for the dangerous and exhaustive digging, Irish immigrants were imported for some of the manual work.[70] Most of these workers being Catholic, they received ministerial services from the priest of St. Peter's Parish, founded in central Carolina in 1821 as an outreach to the canal workers. Record shows that in 1827 the Camden merchant John Baptiste Meugy sold a DeKalb Street lot to the Catholic Church of South Carolina, a single statewide diocese organized in 1820, although a church building was not completed at that site. Little is known of the canal diggers except that a number suffered from exposure to the fevers and diseases of the unfamiliar climate.

Random records identify the names of some Kershaw District citizens who received payments related to the Wateree Canal. In 1822 John Whitaker was paid $1,500 for land to be used for the canal. The following year Abram Jones was

Remains of the Wateree Canal near the western side of the dam.
Courtesy of David Reuwer

compensated for constructing "counter drains," and Abram Childers was paid wages as a "bank ranger." Darling Jones, "through whose race and under whose mill, the Wateree Canal runs," negotiated $4,200 in compensation for land and lost income. In 1827 the "estate of Watson" was paid for land. In 1827–28 a number of other payments were made: to Stephen Boykin for surveying public lands for the Wateree Canal; to James W. Cantey for cleaning the canal; to Thomas Crim for reconstructing three bridges over the canal; to Charles Bailey for wages as "lock keep"; and to William Anderson and William Clark for other "work on the canal." Bailey was still keeper in 1832, and Samuel Shaylor was a keeper sometime afterward.

Walter Izard, state assistant engineer, reported to the legislature that "from the first of October 1826, to the first of October 1827, there has passed through the . . . Wateree Canal—3,144 bales of cotton." A total of 149 boats "loaded and empty" had used the canal, along with 15 rafts, and of these, 68 boats had been carrying cotton. The gross amount of toll was $327.84, not a huge profit for a costly venture even considering that the canal may not have been fully operational during the whole of the year. Presumably a number of thrifty upland planters continued shipping their crops the way they always had, by waiting for high water. Even the report to the Board of Public Works in 1822 had observed that "although the shoals at Loves and Grave's are difficult, yet when there is a small swell in the river, boats carrying from 30 to 40 bales of cotton can pass them; and at the present time most of the cotton raised as high as Rocky Mount, descends the Wateree river in boats." It is likely that just as some citizens tended to avoid state toll roads in favor of rougher but free local roads, many planters at opportune times preferred to take their chances on open waters. As late as 1844, however, citizens of Fairfield County were petitioning to have the Wateree Canal repaired for their access southward.

Landings and Boatyard

However the boats arrived in the Camden area, competition was keen for their business. Rival ads in the *Camden Journal* of December 15, 1827, touted the respective advantages of the Camden Ferry landing, under J. D. Winn and William Kennedy, and the "Boat Yard," under Everard Cureton, Christopher Matheson, John J. Blair, and William E. Johnson. The leasees of the Ferry Landing, which lay south of town, announced the recent completion of "a wharf with a crane . . . to facilitate the unloading and loading of boats" and cited rates of wharfage "the same as heretofore, *viz:* two dollars" for unloading or loading all or part of a load. The same rates were to be charged for boats that tied up on the opposite bank, as that land, they pointed out, was also under their control.

The advertisement for the boatyard, which lay north of town, was a strong reaction to the ferry-landing terms: "The attempt to preclude us and others from the use of the river bank opposite their landing, is as illiberal as it is illegal and violent. Common sense should have taught them that the right to fasten to the banks is incident to, and inseparable from, the right to navigate the river." Writers of the ad also questioned how their competitors justified "the same charge for merely fastening to their ground, or for putting on board one bag, as 100 bales of cotton." Boatyard wharfage was one dollar for a full load "and for less, in proportion," and while the company also had rights to their opposite bank, interfering with public use of it was "contrary to the established custom here, and every where else." Boatyard proprietors challenged, "To show our regard for their threats upon this subject, we mean to fasten to the other side, and perhaps to this too, whenever it shall be necessary or convenient."

The Wateree Bridge

A major engineering venture was undertaken in 1827 when work began on the challenge of building a bridge across the Wateree River near Camden. Ferries were hard-pressed to handle the weight and the numbers of loaded farm wagons that needed to cross the temperamental divide, which was now also being plied by increasing numbers of merchant watercrafts making their way up and down the river and inevitably crisscrossing paths with the bulky ferries. A spirited, red-headed Connecticut Yankee from New Haven named Ithiel Town provided a plan to local investors. He had been promoting and building bridges for nearly a decade when his distinctive, patented design was adopted by the Camden Bridge Company.

Town had a sound reputation. In 1818, near Salisbury, he had built North Carolina's first covered bridge, one that spanned the Yadkin River, which frequently flooded like the Wateree. In North Carolina he developed a truss design of his own: "Making use of the pine planks available at any sawmill, Town fashioned a lattice web of timbers connected by wooden pins at the points of intersection. He termed it his 'Town lattice mode of bridge construction,' and patented the invention in 1820."[71]

The Wateree Bridge was built by Town's lattice-trussed, covered-bridge design—a wooden, self-supporting upper body over substantial stone piers. An advertisement in the *Camden Journal* of June 7, 1828, reveals one local source of lumber supplies. John C. Donavan of "Sandy Run Mills, Kershaw District," reported himself ready to serve the public as he had finished sawing for "the Bridge over Camden Ferry." Petitions show that the ferry at this time had been operating in the vicinity of—to about three hundred yards south of—the original ferry dating to pre–Revolutionary War times. One of the stone land piers of "the Bridge over Camden Ferry" still stands on private property on the western shore, a location from which the present I-20 bridge can be seen.[72] Extensive abutments and roadwork were also necessary to lift the approaches and exits of the bridge above the swampy floodplain.

Construction on the bridge began in October 1827 under the local contractor Colonel William Nixon, who from 1819 to 1822 had been paid nearly ten thousand dollars by the state for work clearing the bottom of the Wateree River of obstructions from as far north as Graves Ford eight miles above Camden to some twenty miles below the town. In order to prepare for safe passage of steamboats, Nixon had opened the channel one hundred feet wide, trimmed all the banks, and cut down or girded trees likely to fall into the water. Town probably worked with Nixon in choosing sound footing for the piers and adapting the position and width of the bridge to the river site. Although sustaining damage at times and requiring repairs, the bridge was used for half a century before being destroyed and replaced by another bridge in a new location about a mile north of the old one.

The wooden Town bridge was roofed to protect its flooring from the weather, and its sides provided support, stability, and further protection from the elements. The sides of the covered bridge also blocked the sight of rushing waters that might frighten horses or other draft animals as well as timid travelers. The entrance to a covered bridge has been described as barnlike and welcoming to

A stone pier from the 1828 Wateree bridge, on the west bank of the river, dwarfing the truck on the left

skittish animals. A typical Town design featured latticed side supports covered halfway up with board siding that increased the sense of security, and with the upper latticed sides left uncovered for light and ventilation.

Although operated as a toll bridge to recoup its expense, the newly completed bridge in 1828 was made "free" for wagons that were loaded with cotton. Town merchants clearly wanted to encourage business. From state payments that year to Everard Cureton and John Blair "for removing the shoal at Wateree Ferry," it is learned that at the point near the bridge, these men excavated rock barriers that prevented boat passage in low water.[73] In 1828 on one day thirty-three river boats arrived at Camden landings ready for business. No complaints at that time were recorded of difficulties in navigating past the bridge, although periodically debris, sediment, sand, and loose rock deposits continued to require removal from various locations in the shifting channels of the river. Ironically the cleaner the banks were made of potential debris that might wash into the river, the more rapidly sand and clay eroded into the water. Extensive embankments dug by slaves to protect agricultural fields from high waters also leeched soil into the channels at times of freshets. River water, once a clear dark brown, began more often to run clay-colored and opaque.

Sorrowful Contrast

Tragedy rather than public achievement marked the spring of 1860, perhaps an ironical foreshadowing of the sorrows that would break forth with the advent of war in the spring of the following year. On May 5 the Sabbath schools of various churches from Kershaw and Sumter districts met for a joyful picnic at a traditional old gathering place, Boykin Mill Pond, nine miles south of Camden. Late in the afternoon some sixty persons—both adults and youths—casually boarded an old flatboat to take a pleasure trip around the pond. Not far from shore, however, the boat hit a snag, and panic ensued that it was sinking. The boat did not sink, but many frightened occupants jumped toward shore or were pushed into the mass of writhing humanity in the water. As a result twenty-four people were drowned in a tragedy of only a few minutes duration.[74] Although the incident wracked the community with grief at the time, those losses were soon to be overshadowed by even larger numbers in the war years ahead.

Military Traditions

Romanticized views of military heroism were prevalent in Kershaw District throughout the antebellum years, stemming in the early 1800s from praise for the local Revolutionary past from notables such as Washington and Lafayette. Later the Seminole War (1837) and the Mexican War (1846–48) were supported by slaveholding cotton growers, who favored U.S. territorial expansion. Local men quickly volunteered to serve in both wars. The men were heralded on leaving and treated as public heroes on return.

In 1836 Colonel John Chesnut's regiment responded enthusiastically to a call for three-months' duty in Florida, where they followed orders to burn the Everglades villages of a "Negro-Indian" called Abram and the Seminoles' head chief, Micanopy. Although later the war was questioned for actions against civilians, the local men returned to widespread approbation. None died in combat, but some afterward suffered ill effects of camp life and exposure. Unable to regain his health, Colonel Chesnut died in 1838 and was beautifully eulogized.

When President James Knox Polk called for volunteers against Mexico in 1846, the first South Carolina company to respond was the DeKalb Guards of Camden, under Captain Keith Stuart Moffat. As the Kershaw Guards, they served in the Palmetto Regiment, engaging the enemy from Vera Cruz to Mexico City. Newspaper correspondents described their actions effusively. About half of the men leaving from Kershaw District died from wounds or disease. Public subscriptions contributed to raising large and impressive monuments to two of the war dead: Lieutenant J. Willis Cantey in Quaker Cemetery and Colonel James Polk Dickinson in Monument Square. Military tradition and public attitudes strongly influenced the way men of Kershaw District later reacted to the eruption of conflict between the North and the South.

9

Broken Ties

War Brought Home

When South Carolina seceded from the Union on December 20, 1860, residents of Kershaw District were jubilant, and by the following spring they popularly anticipated a short and glorious war to confirm their independence. By the conclusion of that war, four long, bloody years later, Kershaw District had paid dearly. Its economy had been crippled, its infrastructure ruined, many of its people killed or maimed, and its lands overrun by invading foes under General William T. Sherman and General Edward E. Potter. Throughout the war years and immediately afterward, hardships befell both those who struggled to defend the old way of life and those who gained freedom after the failure of that struggle. In the beginning, however, patriotic enthusiasm and emotional excitement heralded a "second war for independence." Immediately following the election of Abraham Lincoln to the presidency, James Chesnut resigned his U.S. Senate seat and returned home to help draft South Carolina's Ordinance of Secession. Within the next six weeks half a dozen other states followed that lead. With Joseph B. Kershaw and Thomas J. Withers, Chesnut represented Kershaw District at the Secession Convention in Montgomery, Alabama, where representatives from rebel states organized the Confederate States of America.

In Alabama with her husband, James, at the formation of the Confederacy, Mary Boykin Miller Chesnut on February 18, 1861, began a diary that she continued during the next four years as she variously returned home to Kershaw District or accompanied her husband on his posts of duty. Historians today consult as major resources the remains of her original day-by-day jottings, as well as the various drafts she afterward expanded from them, perhaps with an eye toward publication. In the first few sentences of her earliest dated entry in her private diary, Mary Chesnut proclaims, "We have risked all, & we must play our best for the stake is life or death."[1]

Spirits of Resistance

Between Lincoln's election and South Carolina's secession, men in various communities of the state formed rifle clubs or minutemen clubs, "extra-legal local militia organizations separate from the South Carolina Militia."[2] The constitution of the Minute Men Club of Camden called for the election of a captain and

Mulberry Plantation, the winter residence of Colonel James Chesnut's family from 1820 and a home of the Civil War diarist Mary Boykin Chesnut and her husband, General James Chesnut

other officers and made provisions similar to those of social clubs: one-dollar initiation fees, meetings every Saturday, fines for absences, and music at demonstrations. Rules required wearing a blue cockade on the left side of the hat and at parades a red scarf across the chest and a black cap, both emblazoned "M.M." The seriousness of the organization lay in its last article, requiring members "as soon as possible to procure a Colt's Revolver, a Rifle, or some other approved firearm." Mary Chesnut recorded in her diary February 18, "Camden was in unprecedented excitement. Minute men arming with immense blue cockades & red sashes, soon with sword & gun, marching & drilling."[3] Reminiscent of the Revolution, a three-member Committee of Correspondence was stirring other communities to form similar groups.

Fort Sumter

By spring the threat of war came to a head over federal attempts to resupply Fort Sumter in the harbor of Charleston. Amid much fanfare militia volunteers from Kershaw District rallied to the defense of the port city. Crowds of citizens, led by young cadets of Professor C. H. Peck's Academy, escorted Captain John D. Kennedy and the Camden Volunteers to the local depot on April 9 for a special train to Charleston. The unit arrived in time for the first guns of the war. Camden people so heartily cheered on Lancaster District militia passing through the area that the men dubbed the community "the Cockade town."

In Charleston, Mary Chesnut awaited the results of the tense negotiations in which her husband was involved. In her expanded account she describes the night of the April 12 ultimatum: "I do not pretend to go to sleep. How can I? If [Union major Robert] Anderson [commander at Fort Sumter] does not accept terms—at four—the orders are—he shall be fired upon. I count four St. Michael chimes. I begin to hope. At half-past four, the heavy booming of a cannon. I sprang out of bed. And on my knees—prostrate—I prayed as I never prayed before."[4] From Charleston rooftops in the dark of early morning, she with other

Boy cadets, circa 1861, at Mr. Peck's Academy, which stood at the rear of the Presbyterian church in Camden. Courtesy of the Camden Archives

anxious civilians watched the colorful lights of artillery fire in the opening engagement of the war.

Another witness from Camden was the daughter of the future general Joseph B. Kershaw. Eleven years old at the time, Harriet DuBose Kershaw Lang later described the attack on Fort Sumter through a child's experiences: "I recall our trip to Charleston to be with father as long as possible. We, with many other officers' families boarded at the Charleston Hotel, where we daily looked for the opening of hostilities." When "the dread sound of the booming cannon" awoke the children at dawn, they gathered around their mother and prayed for safety for their father and success for the troops: "We soon gathered on the roof of the hotel, which was flat on top, and being very high, was a good observatory. Here we watched the 'Battle of Fort Sumter.' The firing continued, as I remember, until quite late in the afternoon, when Anderson raised the white flag. Our people were wild with excitement, and every one thought the war would soon end, and our dear ones be at home again."[5]

In Kershaw District too civilians awaited word on the unfolding of events. The *Camden Journal* of April 16 reported, "It is a well ascertained fact that the sound of the cannonading was distinctly heard in Camden and ten miles above. From the market steeple, on Friday night [April 12], between eleven and twelve o'clock, we saw what was supposed to be repeated flashes from the volleyed thunder of Charleston harbor." Local stories of great-distance sound and light transmission, impossible to imagine in the modern world, were also asserted in later years.

When word reached Camden the next afternoon on the outcome of the cannonading, the *Journal* declared, "A thrill of joy went through every heart and the streets of Camden rang with the loud acclaim, 'Fort Sumter is ours.'" In the war enthusiasm that followed, according to Kirkland and Kennedy, "within a year some eight hundred out of one thousand voters had volunteered. A little later these were increased by two or three hundred more, until more than eighty per cent of the entire white male population above the age of eighteen had enlisted."[6]

Records in Ink

"We stood on the bare hills men without a country," recalled Kershaw District's Lieutenant Colonel Edward M. Boykin in his memoir *The Falling Flag,* written nine years after he numbered with his men among the tattered forces of General Robert E. Lee at the 1865 surrender at Appomattox, Virginia.[7] Among other military memoirs of active participants, the 1899 *History of Kershaw's Brigade* described the exploits of the command in which many local men served under General Joseph B. Kershaw and in which General John D. Kennedy also rose to prominence.[8] Although many public documents and private papers were lost or destroyed in wartime, a number of letters and memoirs survive to record the experiences of those years, both on the battlefront and on the home front.[9]

Valuable resources exist in surviving issues of contemporary local newspapers. Every Friday the editor J. T. Hershman published four pages of the *Camden Confederate,* the newspaper that lasted the greatest length of wartime. Its presence largely replaced but was not connected with the previous *Camden Journal,* whose editor T. J. Warren left for service at the head of the Kershaw Guard.[10] Near the end of the war two papers circulated—the *Camden Weekly Confederate* and the *Tri-Weekly Journal.* When Union invaders destroyed their pressrooms, the two merged their salvaged type into the *Journal and Confederate.*

The first issue of the *Camden Confederate* on November 1, 1861, rang with a spirit of resistance, repeating from the *Charleston Mercury* excerpts from the *New York Times* that called for Union vengeance on South Carolina. The northern paper asked: "Is it not more than poetic justice, that South Carolina, so flagrant in sin, should be made to feel the earliest and heaviest penalties of war? If a Southern city must fall, let Charleston be razed to the ground, and salt sowed on its ruins. If Southern fields must be desolated by the invasion of Union armies, let South Carolina's cotton and rice plantations be marked by the conquering advance. . . . Let the prayer of Unionists in all thirty-four States be heard for the early and unsparing chastisement of South Carolina." Readers had little doubt what to expect should the enemy reach their homes. Fears of coastal invasions were strong, with federal ships riding outside of Charleston and other ports, and readers closely followed military news.

Military Units

The military units most frequently encompassing Kershaw District men first organized with militia and volunteers. These local units were among the first to join in the defense of Virginia, home of the Confederate capital at Richmond, signing up for one year. Many of the men provided their own weapons, gear, clothing, and even horses, and some also brought along personal body servants, trusted slaves who shared camp and battlefield dangers. Men aged fifteen or fifty were not uncommon. Neither were hired substitutes who were paid by individuals unable or unwilling to serve in the field. Conscription and Confederate States of America regulations affected changes as the war wore on.

Companies

The Second South Carolina Volunteer Infantry Regiment, which became part of Kershaw's Brigade, was one of the longest-serving units of the war and one of the first out-of-state groups to report to Virginia. Companies in that regiment with captains from Kershaw District were Company E, the Camden Volunteers—John D. Kennedy and William Zack Leitner; and Company G, the Flat Rock

Guards—Columbus C. Haile, Joseph P. Cunningham, and Jesse Erasamus Truesdel. The Camden Volunteers were "the first company in Kershaw's original regiment that volunteered for that service," according to the 1862 newspaper. Also joining Kershaw's Brigade was the Fifteenth South Carolina Volunteer Infantry Regiment, Company D, the Kershaw Guards, under Captains Thomas J. Warren and C. Benton Burns.

The first local militia company to leave for Virginia, the DeKalb Rifle Guards, under Captain Thomas L. Boykin, soon disbanded and dispersed to other commands. Company C, the Kershaw Troop, in the Sixth South Carolina Volunteer Infantry Regiment, had organized as a cavalry unit but volunteered as infantry under Captains Edward M. Cantey and R. M. Cantey.

Five independent companies in November 1861 organized into the Seventh South Carolina Infantry Battalion, which was largely involved in coastal defense until transferred to Virginia late in the war. A number of district men enlisted in these units under local captains: Company A, the Lucas Guards—L. W. R. Blair (later battalion major) and B. S. Lucas Jr.; Company D, the Kershaw Grays—John L. Jones; Company E—Burwell E. Boykin; Company F, the Lucas Rifles—Dove Segars; and Company G, the Moffat Rifles—William Clyburn. In the Third South Carolina Artillery Battalion, W. L. DePass was captain of Company G, the DeSaussure Light Artillery, which aided in coastal defense.

Three cavalry companies with many local men served in the Army of Northern Virginia under captains from Kershaw District. In the Second South Carolina Cavalry Regiment, Company A, the Boykin Rangers, were Captains Alexander Hamilton Boykin and John Chesnut. In two units of the Seventh South Carolina Cavalry Regiment the following were captains: William M. Shannon and James L. Doby in the Kirkwood Rangers; and in Company K, the Wateree Mounted Rifles, Edward M. Boykin, later lieutenant colonel of the regiment. District men were also actively recruited to serve in 1863 in Virginia and later in South Carolina with Hampton's Legion, under General Wade Hampton of Columbia.

Conscripts

The first conscription act, in April 1862, called up able-bodied white men ages eighteen to thirty-five. William M. Shannon, chief enrolling officer for Kershaw and Lancaster districts, ordered conscripts to report on July 21 to the instruction camp at Columbia "under pain of being arrested" if they did not. Two weeks later he reported that of the 113 Kershaw District men reporting, 51 had been exempted by surgeons' certificate, 27 were appealing conflicts in the law, and 35 had enrolled. By September a second act extended the upper age of conscription to forty-five.

Home Guards

In 1862 Edward M. Boykin helped organize men ineligible for service abroad into the Kershaw District reserves, the Twenty-second Regiment South Carolina Militia, stating that "if the enemy should get a foot-hold in force anywhere on our mainland, every available man will be needed to keep him from the interior." John Thompson was captain of the Upper Battalion; A. M. Kennedy, the Lower Battalion. Men exempted because of age or physical disability were organized into beats to patrol town and countryside in order to keep peace and order and control the slaves, who colloquially called the patrollers "paddy-rolls." The April 18, 1862, *Camden Confederate* printed a list of 112 names organized by the eight beats of the district—Buffalo, Camden, Cureton's Mills, Flat Rock, Goodwin's, Liberty Hill, Lizenby's, and Schrock's Mill.

In late 1863 Governor Milledge Luke Bonham expounded to the S.C. General Assembly the difficulty of assembling home defense units because the Confederate conscription age had been increased. He requested for home defense every available able-bodied male from sixteen to sixty, even those who had procured exemption by hiring substitutes. Persons in the home guard who had military training were often seriously disabled, so that home guard duties most typically fell to the young and the elderly, those who lacked training. In Kershaw District sign-up lists for home defense were posted in Camden at James Dunlap's store and in Flat Rock at L. B. Stephenson's store.

In February 1864, when the third conscription law broadened regular military ages to seventeen to fifty years, James Chesnut, who had been serving on the staff of Confederate president Jefferson Davis, returned to South Carolina as a brigadier general to organize the state's reserves, which became known as Chesnut's Brigade. The Senior Reserves of Kershaw District were placed under Captain John Thompson as Company D of the Fifth Battalion, South Carolina State Troops. In September, Junior Reserves from Lancaster and Kershaw districts were mustered in as Company I in the Third Regiment South Carolina State Troops, the regiment that was headed by Colonel A. D. Goodwyn.[11]

Slave Labor

At various points, especially when Charleston was under siege, the governor called for "slaves liable for road duty" to report to the nearest depot with three days' rations and spades or shovels for thirty days' labor on fortifications. In Kershaw District slave owners were asked to supply one-fourth of their road duty workers, although in 1863 more were urgently requested when numbers proved insufficient. Home guards were called to discourage raiders from stealing workers for Union purposes. Governor Bonham in October 1863 appealed to the General Assembly to double the length of slave time on coastal defenses and to include free blacks as well. Also letters and oral accounts have preserved references to slaves who accompanied masters to the battlefield and sometimes took up arms in defense, although official records rarely documented such cases. Many accounts credit enslaved persons with helping manage plantations and businesses during the absence of owners.

Hazards of War

A sampling of newspaper obituaries from late 1861 and early 1862 reveals that varied hazards of military service quickly presented themselves. Not far from home there were deaths in training camps. In Captain Warren's company at the Fair Ground, H. Corbett died of congestive chill, while Sidney B. Capell and Tira Kemp died of measles raging there. Serving in the Carolinas, Sergeant A. Sommers of the same company drowned in a lowcountry bay, and Harmon Arrants of Captain Cantey's company died of typhoid pneumonia.

In Captain Kennedy's company in Virginia, Jesse Nettles died of wounds received at Manassas, while John Team, unscathed in that battle, died in Lynchburg of typhoid fever, which "swept away thousands." W. W. Turner and Lewis M. Vaughan, in the same company, likewise survived Fort Sumter and Manassas to die of disease in Lynchburg.

Most of the deaths above were of men eighteen to twenty-one years of age, presumably in the prime of health. As the war continued, combat deaths increased, but deaths from disease, deprivation, and exposure continued to decimate the ranks with even greater ferocity. The more extreme the age of the soldier, the more likely prey he was to adverse conditions.

The increasing occurrence of battles with unbelievable carnage changed the presentation of death notices in local papers. At first lengthy obituaries lauded individual deaths, but death notices soon were reduced simply to long rosters of names. In a memoir written in 1911, Esther Reynolds (Mrs. F. Bruce) Davis of Camden detailed the shift from idealism at the time of secession to solemnity following each succeeding battle with its toll on the human resources of the community.[12]

Home-Front Struggles

Since most of the volunteers and conscripts throughout the war were simple farmers or laborers without financial reserves or slaves, not only did they have trouble supplying their own needs at the front, but also their absences left their families with scant means of existence at home. At the beginning of the war many men expected to be back in time to work the next crop. However, when the war dragged on, many other men hesitated to leave their families with no one to provide for them. As early as May 1861 committees organized to relieve families in want. A tax was levied, and boards of relief were established to help meet the needs of soldiers' wives and children. These needs increased with time.

As the war continued and Confederate currency depreciated, the money tax was replaced by taxes "in kind." Farm animals, foodstuffs, and other usable goods were given over to satisfy taxes and to supply war efforts. At the end of 1861 property subject to taxation included real estate, slaves, livestock, merchandise except for agricultural products, railroad and financial stock, cash, notes and securities except for Confederate bonds, and "gold watches, gold and silver plate, pianos and pleasure carriages." Tax liabilities later extended to foodstuffs, agricultural tools and implements, all wheeled vehicles, musical instruments, domestic articles, jewelry, books, works of art, as well as "value of all other property not enumerated in the foregoing." The Camden Town Council added local taxes for items sold within its boundaries.

In 1863 the Soldiers Board of Relief met weekly at the store of its secretary-treasurer, W. D. McDowell. An example of its organization is seen in the June 5 newspaper. Following a meeting of district citizens at Camden's town hall, called to discuss food shortages of soldiers' families, the board raised 220 bushels of corn to distribute without compensation and 544 bushels to sell to the families at $1 each, half the price recently agreed on to sell to the army. A sum of $193 was contributed to purchase more corn and wheat. The corn was deposited at three mills: those of John Gaskins, Granny's Quarter Creek; J. H. Vaughan, Sanders Creek; and Captain E. Parker, "over the river." Soldiers' families could apply to board chairman John DeSaussure or Camden intendant James Dunlap or to one of the following: Jesse Truesdale, Flat Rock; J. Ross Dye, Liberty Hill; or James Team, over the river.

The February 12, 1864, *Camden Daily Journal* appealed to citizens to help with transportation for indigent families receiving corn raised by the tax in kind. Being "without slaves, and rarely having a horse," according to the paper, "some of these females may now be seen walking the public roads with their allowance of meal on their heads, carrying it for miles. Their male relatives are in the army doing military duty and periling their lives to secure the property and the lives of the men at home."

To increase essential food production for all citizens, the planting of cotton was legally restricted from early in the war, first to three acres and finally to one acre per hand. Households with only one or two workers were thus nearly eliminated from cotton production and cash acquisition. Women, elderly men, and children, in addition to carrying out their usual responsibilities, took over farm and field labors that had been performed by males now absent.

Large plantations with many slaves faced different but serious problems of labor care and management. Draft exemptions that were granted for supervisors of slaves were often derided as unjustly favoring wealthy slaveholders, although supervision of large numbers of workers was critical for public security as well as crop production. As battlefield demands increased, the jobs at home once performed by white overseers were filled by women, elderly men, and trusted slaves. From time to time local ordinances restricted slave movements to reduce supervisory demands, although in some instances slaves carried out responsibilities with which they had never previously been entrusted.

Harriet Lang recalled, "During the first year or two of the war, people managed to get on very well, for many had saved supplies, such as sugar, coffee and tea, to last for a short while. These supplies soon gave out, and then a cup of coffee or tea was an unheard of thing, sugar could not be obtained at all."[13] As commonplace items grew scarce or nonexistent, home folk improvised or did without. Kirkland and Kennedy give examples: "Wooden soled shoes were devised for the slaves. Magazines of salt had to be established. The soil under old houses was scraped for manufacture of salt-petre, essential to gunpowder. The bells of the Camden churches were taken down for casting cannon."[14] In March 1863 Camden's town council forbade injuring trees on public streets and squares "by stripping them of bark to make dye stuff." Typical of many ersatz articles, the *Journal* of June 3, 1864, described a process of making sugar from sorghum syrup.

Aid to Soldiers

Folk at home sought to aid those at the front. Spiritual help was immediately summoned. Preachers led revivals and special prayer meetings at home and in camps. Soldiers' Bible societies organized in Camden, Flat Rock, and Liberty Hill to send Bibles and religious tracts to men in service. The Episcopal seminary that had begun under Bishop Davis in Camden shortly before the war broke up while the student-preachers went to war, most of them as chaplains. Methodist preachers, who had been especially active preaching among slaves before the war, continued preaching to them during the war, urging them to maintain peaceful and obedient behavior.

In the same communities that organized Bible societies, ladies' aid associations also organized and were considered of such importance that newspapers broke tradition to mention by name the women who headed them. In Camden, Sally Chesnut was president of the district organization; in Flat Rock this role was served by Ellen E. Perry. Newspapers frequently published letters from captains at the front thanking ladies' aid groups for donations of clothing, blankets, and other supplies. Sewing and knitting circles met weekly, and most women kept needlework daily at hand. Fund-raising was frequent and sometimes fun. In May 1862 at the town hall "patriotic young ladies of Camden" presented a tableaux exhibition, with tickets sold as a benefit for the soldiers. The newspaper often acknowledged contributions of cash and supplies by individual donors.

Aid associations were also kept busy supplying hospitals with bandages, covers, and medicines, including homemade wines and cordials. Camden furnished a soldiers' rest for traveling men and a wayside hospital that expanded in numbers as trains brought in evacuees and battle casualties. Disease sometimes took a greater toll than combat wounds. Smallpox in 1863 spread into the community, with Intendant Dunlap urging citizens to be vaccinated, at public expense if they could not pay.

Women volunteered long hours tending to sick and wounded soldiers arriving in Camden, most of whom were strangers. Harriet Lang recalled, "Our hospitals were filled . . . the poor fellows were looked after as well as our small means would allow."[15] More than two hundred patients were reported being cared for at times, with various buildings used when needed. Private homes also helped with convalescents. The April 5, 1865, *Journal and Confederate* reported causes of deaths in the First South Carolina Hospital at Camden for March 12–31: asthma / typhoid fever, pneumonia, softening of the brain, and chronic diarrhea. A local woman helping at the hospital, Martha Lyles, met there and married a Confederate surgeon from Kentucky, Dr. George R. C. Todd, whose sister Mary was the wife of Abraham Lincoln. Dr. Todd, who remained adamant in Confederate views after the war, lies buried in Quaker Cemetery.

Opposition

Not all persons chose to support the war and those fighting it. Lack of support was evidenced in various ways. The August 8, 1862, *Camden Confederate* denounced as traitors "some in this community—as we have heard of elsewhere—who are endeavoring to depreciate the Confederate bills, by trying to put them at a discount in exchange for the bills of the bank of the State." Accusations of price gouging increased in times of dearth. A writer to the newspaper in January 1863 responded to complaints about the high cost of shoes by asking why the paper did not also criticize planters who withheld corn from the market "until they could get an excessive profit." A letter in March complained of "speculators riding from the lower end of Camden, past the outside limits of Kirkwood, in order to meet the country wagons—so as to buy up poultry, provisions, &c for the purpose of speculation."

Not all of those called up for military or guard duty were willing to serve, despite warnings of arrest and court-martial with threats of execution for defaulters. The March 20, 1863, *Camden Confederate* reported that the bodies of two deserters, brothers, had been found at a camp in the woods some eleven or twelve miles from Camden. The pair, of which one was "a conscript of this district," had eluded authorities for several months while preying on neighbors in the sandhills, killing stock and stealing produce.

For men who sought to avoid military service, the district's rugged terrain offered many places where they could go into hiding. One local tradition states that a deserter named Kelly made his home in a rock shelter hidden in a remote part of upper Kershaw District. The site continues to be known as Kelly Rock.[16]

Daily Routines

In the midst of chaos and uncertainty, communities routinely attempted to follow familiar patterns. Although rural schools were generally disrupted during the war, Camden, swollen by the presence of many refugees, many of them lowcountry gentry, advertised several schools. In 1863 C. H. Peck operated his "Private and Select School for Boys." Also resuming that year were the schools of Mr. and Mrs. McCandless as well as Mrs. Peck's School for Boys, Miss (Maggie) DeNoon's School for Boys and Girls, the Reverend L. R. Staudenmayer's school "next to the Presbyterian Church," and a Mrs. Dawson's School. Some families continued to employ tutors. Most of the teachers from the North had chosen to return home when war seemed inevitable; others had departed when fighting began.

However, these notices of "normal life" were overshadowed by the war. Political, economic, religious, and social notices all reflected the war. The September 25, 1863, *Camden Confederate* notice of the arrival of "Mr. Chammond, the landscape gardener employed to lay out the grounds of the Cemetary," no doubt brought sadness that the project had to accommodate the casualties of war. John C. West, a Camden native who had gone to Texas in 1855, visited his birthplace on furlough in March 1864, reporting in his journal that he found the cemetery "much enlarged and improved."[17] Even ordinary advertisements reflected the times, such as the February 20, 1863, *Camden Confederate* notice for sale of "a good strong cavalry or work horse."

Another sign of the war's toll on civilians was the local influx of coastal dwellers fleeing anticipated northern attack on that area. The September 18, 1863, *Camden Confederate* printed a notice from the board of directors inviting "refugees from the Low Country residing in Camden or the vicinity" to use the bridge over the Wateree River free of charge. Many of the refugees were transient residents who returned home as soon as they were able. Among those who remained permanently was the lowcountry family of the Charleston dentist Miller W. Bissell, who refugeed, as the expression went, "in front of Sherman." Settling with his family in Camden, Dr. Bissell became an integral part of the local medical community.

Sherman's Invasion

The last extant issue of the *Camden Weekly Confederate,* February 8, 1865, reflects the keen alarm of home preparations in anticipation of invasion by Sherman's troops, whose movements had been closely followed since the burning of Atlanta. The newspaper pledged not to withhold information regarding the enemy's whereabouts and actions. At the time the Union army had crossed the Salkehatchie River and was meeting resistance at River's Bridge in present Bamberg County. In Kershaw District defenders were gathering from all groups of available males—those "not yet assigned," those recommended for light duty, those "transferred to the invalid corps," and those disabled for field service.

Esther Davis described the fear in Camden: "On the morning of the 17th of February, 1865, we heard terrific explosions and knew that Sherman had reached Columbia. That night the Western sky was lurid with the glare of the burning city and we felt that in twenty-four hours Columbia's fate might be ours." She detailed the hiding of valuables, the daily afternoon prayer services at Camden churches, the arrival of refugees from Columbia, and the daily scouts' reports pinpointing the enemy's location and expected arrival.[18]

For a time Camden was protected from invasion by prolonged heavy rains and a freshet rising in the Wateree River that was long recalled as "the Sherman freshet." Floodwaters forced the Federals to avoid the lowlands around the town and instead to cross higher up the river. Among Sherman's men who crossed at Liberty Hill, Major Thomas W. Osborn, artillery officer in the U.S. Army of the Tennessee, kept a journal that recorded Union activities in the district. On February 22 he reported Sherman's army on the opposite bank of the Wateree at Peay's Ferry, where retreating pickets had "destroyed all means of crossing." Across the three-hundred-foot river with a rapid current, the Federals floated a squad of men on a makeshift raft to "secure a line for a ferry so a bridge could be built."[19]

At Red Hill Post Office in Kershaw District on February 23, Osborne described the countryside as "very fine, the best we have seen since we left the coast," with large plantations and excellent buildings. "The little town of Liberty Hill is the finest I have seen in the State," Osborn said. There were twenty "large and beautiful" houses with "beautifully laid out and finely cultivated" yards. He portrayed the inhabitants as "very kind and highly cultivated," adding, "I have not been so much pleased with any town South."[20]

Bessie Clark Whitaker later recalled to an interviewer her experiences refugeeing in Liberty Hill at a house commandeered as Sherman's headquarters. She, a sister, and three companions crossed the Wateree River by boat, apparently as the Yankees were also crossing just a short distance upriver at Peay's Ferry. The five hid in the woods and swamps until they reached safety in the home of a friend. Awakened after a restless night by a bugle and the sound of galloping horses, Bessie Whitaker described the alarm: "Raising our eyes we saw eight or ten [soldiers] at the door. In the twinkle of an eye they were down and all through the house hunting silver and taking everything of value they could find." One of the soldiers told them they "would probably see thousands of Blue Coats before night. And indeed we did!!!! They simply poured in from sunrise to sunset."

She added, "About an hour before sunset Sherman sent some of his bodyguards in advance to say to Mrs. W. that he would make his headquarters in her house, please to have two rooms prepared for him. A little later on he came in grand style, beautiful horses and coach and a very heavy bodyguard of well dressed men." Sherman's behavior was that of "a gentleman." He moved out of the house the next morning: "Then came what we dreaded most—the stragglers. They were the ones that did the most harm."[21] Some other firsthand accounts have been collected in *Long Ago at Liberty Hill* by Mary E. Cunningham, who grew up in one of the houses that was occupied by the invaders for eight days.

For more than a week Sherman's troops remained in Kershaw District, their march onward frustrated by weather-related conditions. Some units were dispatched down the road into Camden with orders for strategic destruction. Other units remained with the vital "bridge train" engineers who started heading over through the Flat Rock area and down toward Tiller's Ferry with all the heavy supplies and mechanical parts necessary to effect whatever bridge, pontoon, or ferry was needed for the army to cross its next obstacle, the Lynches River. Additional soldiers were dispatched throughout the countryside with orders to forage for the supplies the army needed to keep itself fed and moving. Along the way all units encountered whatever defense could be mustered by Confederate remnants, home guards, and civilians—and found people already struggling with shortages of food and supplies.

On February 24 and 25 Major Osborn was further east in the district when he wrote his journal at Williams Crossroads. The federal officer said that the "upland, or plateau, east of the Wateree river" was "very sandy and covered with pine forest, which is used for the manufacture of turpentine," continuing, "there are some very large manufactories in this region." Osborn reported the enemy hanging "on our flanks with cavalry."[22] Some Confederate remnants, too small and ill-equipped to confront the enemy head-on, operated guerrilla-fashion to protect families at home by bedeviling the margins of the federal flanks to discourage foraging and to encourage a hurried exit of troops.[23]

Osborn was not with the Federals sent to Camden on February 23–25, but his account describes their work: Lieutenant (John A.) McQueen was sent to reconnoiter it and the vicinity, and General (William B.) Hazen's two regiments to destroy cotton and government stores there. Special Field Orders no. 48 (February 24) designated Captain William Duncan, Fifteenth Illinois Cavalry, and Captain John L. King, Fourth Independent Ohio Cavalry, to "destroy the depot and other railroad property and take whatever army supplies may be found."[24] When the local press restored publication, the destruction of government stores and public buildings was described. First the freight and passenger depots and then the Cornwallis house (used for government storage) and the commissary at the southeast corner of Broad and DeKalb streets were set afire. The latter spread a blaze that consumed the block of stores to Rutledge Street. Other stores and cotton sheds were also fired, along with Masonic Hall and the

Wateree River bridge.[25] The newspaper report continued, "They (invaders) broke and pillaged all stores, took what goods they wanted and threw the rest into the streets, whence it was carried off by the negroes, who were encouraged to appropriate whatever they needed or fancied." As a result of soldiers' visits to "nearly every house in Camden and Kirkwood," the article said, "many families have been stripped of everything they had in the world."[26] Firsthand local accounts speak of experiences at the hands of invaders that varied from outrage to courtesy, more the former than the latter.[27] Lieutenant McQueen was one who was spoken of with appreciation for his aid to local families.

Elsewhere in the district, on the night of February 24, after Union troops had been a full day in Camden, Confederate cavalry under Matthew C. Butler encamped near present Cassatt, on the left of Georgetown Road just west of its intersection with Porter Road. Nearby, Sherman's Fifteenth Corps was divided into two campsites, one a short distance east of the crossroad on the left of Holland Road and the other slightly north of Providence Road. Just north of West Crossroads to the left of present S.C. 42, the forces skirmished.[28] Major General John A. Logan wrote from West's Cross-Roads on February 25, "I have had 2 men killed and several wounded; have killed and wounded some 10 rebels."[29]

Osborn's journal for February 25 refers to a skirmish after which "two of our men who had been captured were brought out . . . and shot in cold blood. General [John E.] Smith . . . ordered two Rebels who he had just captured, out on our skirmish line, in plain view of the enemy and they were shot."[30] The previous day General Sherman had written Confederate general Wade Hampton regarding a report "that our foraging parties are murdered after capture and labeled 'Death to all foragers.'" Sherman warned that he had ordered reciprocal treatment of rebel prisoners in Union hands and advised Hampton to "give notice to the people at large that every life taken by them simply results in the death of one of your Confederates." Sherman was adamant that his army had an unquestioned right to forage. In his reply of February 27, Hampton retaliated that "there is right older, even, than this, and one more inalienable—the right that every man has to defend his home and to protect those who are dependent on him."[31] The actions and verbal exchanges between these ranking opponents while troops were in Kershaw District suggest the tension and violence that ran high during the invasion.

Osborn wrote his last three entries in Kershaw District on February 26, 27, and 28. His men lingered near Tiller's Bridge, their crossing of the Lynches delayed by rain-swollen waters. Two divisions of the Fifteenth Corps were at Tiller's and two at Kelly's (Kelley's) Bridge four or five miles below. The Seventeenth Corps was nine miles above at Young's Bridge. Osborn described the enemy they captured as "the most contemptible crowd I have ever seen used as soldiers. Most of them old, gray headed men, from fifty to sixty-five years of age," and "nearly all of them are infirm."[32]

Able-bodied men were few in number among remaining southern defenders. In recent months some Kershaw District reserves, mostly old men and youths not old enough for the battlefields or men too disabled for such service, had been among those detailed to guard Union captives at the Florence, South Carolina, stockade. For five months prisoners had been shuffled to Florence from prisons such as Andersonville that lay near Sherman's projected path. When Sherman approached Florence, prisoners again had to be dispersed. Conditions were stark in both northern and southern prisons. Mary Chesnut reflected on February 29 [*sic*], 1865, on Union refusals to exchange prisoners: "We must feed our army first. . . . If they [Federals] send our men back, they strengthen our army—and then their policy is to keep everything here to help starve us out. That is what Sherman's destruction means."[33]

Harriet Lang recollected the destruction of the raid on Camden: "The road for miles along the route of the army was a scene of desolation and destruction. The road was strewn from Camden to Lynch's Creek, and all along the route, with dead fowls, pigs, and food of all kinds, which our people needed sorely. . . . During this raid the soldiers would open a man's smoke house, take what they wanted, then open barrels of molasses, flour, meat, and pour the contents on the ground floor of the smoke house, making such a mess of it that it was of no use to the poor farmers. Starvation stared us in the face."[34]

Randall Lee, who was a slave child in Kershaw District during the Civil War, recalled in a 1930s interview the visit of Union soldiers to the plantation where he lived outside Camden. Although he had heard "talk about freedom," little was said "until Sherman's army came through notifying the slaves they were free." Lee's mind was "indelibly impressed with their doings." The soldiers "took all the food they could get their hands on and took possession of the cattle and horses and mules." They also put Lee's brother, Levi, on a mule, loaded the mule with provisions, and sent it to their camp a couple of miles away: "Levi liked that, for beside being well treated he received several pieces of money. The federal soldiers played with him and gave him all the food he wanted." Lee said that while the soldiers were camped in the area, his grandfather Levi had had a dream about hidden money in a certain spot, had found and dug up a cache at the spot one rainy night, and had buried it securely in his own cabin. Union soldiers, however, searched slave cabins as well as big houses and found and took his money. The old man "mourned a long time about the loss of his money and often told his grandchildren that he would have been well fixed when freedom came if he had not been robbed."[35]

Potter's Raid

The last organized confrontation in Kershaw District occurred one month after Sherman's troops passed over the Lynches. On April 5, 1865, Union general Edward E. Potter left Georgetown with some twenty-seven hundred white and black troops, including the Fifty-fourth Massachusetts and the 103rd United States Colored Troops (South Carolina). According to local accounts they came into Camden from the south on April 18 and broke into the banks and safes. Emma Holmes, who had come to Camden as a lowcountry refugee early in the war, recorded in her journal, "The Yankees . . . staid one night here, the 17th."[36] Potter wrote in an official correspondence that he occupied Camden without opposition, but finding that his main objective, the railroad trains, had been moved below Boykin's Mill, "we marched to that place on the 18th and found the enemy entrenched."[37]

As for Potter's brief occupation of Camden, Emma Holmes stated, "The whites encamped in the park, the negroes at the lower end of the town."[38] Joel Williamson wrote, "The slaves, perhaps noting the prominent presence of Negroes among the soldiers, welcomed the invaders."[39] Holmes added that "a regular camp meeting was held among the negro troops, of course attracting crowds. . . . Tremendous excitement prevailed, as they prayed their cause might prosper & their just freedom be obtained."[40]

Threatened by the assembly of a home guard, the federal soldiers left Camden the next morning. In an area near Middleton Depot in present Sumter County, Potter's men "discovered nine locomotives and approximately 200 cars from the rolling stock of the Wilmington & Manchester and South Carolina Railroads." The federals destroyed the trains and tracks.[41] The home guard, augmented by five hundred Kentucky cavalrymen, confronted Potter's men at Boykin's Mill.[42] First Lieutenant E. L. Stevens of the Fifty-fourth Massachusetts Infantry, mortally wounded, is considered the last federal officer killed in the war. After a brief skirmish the outmanned rebels retreated first to Dinkins's Mill and then to Stateburg, where they disbanded. Since General Lee had surrendered more than a week earlier, essentially ending the war, most of the southerners returned to their homes.

Potter started back to the coast with a much larger number accompanying him. Emma Holmes wrote that "great numbers of servants went off from town, really crazy from excitement and the parade," and Harriet Lang recalled, "As this raid passed through the country, the negroes from the plantations were carried off in wagons from the farms."[43] Joel Williamson puts the number at an estimated three thousand, while Walter Edgar states that "some five thousand black Carolinians" followed Potter.[44] According to David Duncan Wallace, Potter's "incomplete report of destruction included 1,000,000 feet of lumber, 32 locomotives, 250 cars, vast stores, 100 cotton gins and presses, 5,000 bales of cotton, and much railroad trackage."[45] Halfway to Georgetown, Potter received word of Johnston's surrender to Sherman in North Carolina; Potter ceased his destruction on April 21.

By the end of June the war was effectively over. The last significant Confederate army—that of General E. Kirby Smith, commander of the trans-Mississippi

A 1914 gathering of Confederate veterans at Bethune.
Courtesy of the Camden Archives

Department—had surrendered on June 2. On June 23 President Johnson declared an end to the federal blockade that had plagued the South for more than four years. In Camden at Bloomsbury on June 12, Mary Chesnut described the local condition: "We are shut in here—turned with our faces to a dead wall. No mails. A letter is sometimes brought by a man on horseback, traveling through the wilderness made by Sherman. All RR's destroyed—bridges gone. We are cut off from the world—to eat out our own hearts."[46]

War Years Recalled

The life that resumed at war's end was far from "normal," as the emotional events of the war—especially the ordeal of bringing home bodies from faraway battlefields—gave way to the problems of survival in a land of devastation and postwar military occupation. Many contemporary writers expressed sentiments similar to those of Edward M. Boykin, describing the interactions of former adversaries at the Appomattox surrender. Acknowledging that "success had made them [the victors] good natured," he remarked, "The Federal army officers and men bore themselves toward us as brave men should," adding that "much kindness and consideration were exhibited." He concluded, "Had the politicians left things alone, such feelings would have resulted in a very different condition of things."[47]

Aging Veterans

Over the following decades, especially when aged veterans were passing on, numbers of obituaries refocused attention on war service as well as later community contributions. A sampling of these notices, representative of many more, reflects the esteem that followed veterans after the war.[48] Some had fought through the four years without being wounded. One was John Player, Antioch section, who died in 1918 at the age of eighty-two. Sixteen-year-old Joseph W. Hyatt, Cassatt section, enlisted in November 1861 in the Seventh South Carolina Battalion, Company A, and served until the end without injury, dying at seventy in 1914.

Many veterans lived years with obvious war wounds. Joseph Walker Floyd's right arm was shot off at the shoulder at Chancellorsville. A Virginian, he moved to Liberty Hill in 1869, and until his death at seventy-five in 1915 he engaged in agriculture and the mercantile business. Floyd served as a Liberty Hill magistrate and a Kershaw County legislator and was a delegate to the 1895 constitutional convention and a trustee of the State Normal and Industrial College of Orangeburg.

A Kershaw resident, Labon C. Hough was wounded and lost the sight in one eye at the battle of Weldon Railroad. When he died at sixty-five in 1911, "the stores in Kershaw were closed and business was suspended for the funeral which was one of the most largely attended ever seen in Kershaw." Camden's J. W. Gardner was also wounded and captured at Weldon Railroad. In 1882 and 1884 he was elected county commissioner. Six of his former comrades served as pallbearers when he died in 1909 at the age of sixty-five.

According to his 1902 obituary, W. J. Fletcher, of the Flat Rock section, died of the slow effects of war wounds from which he never recovered. Ebin Neimus Yarborough of Lynchwood (Bethune), at Drewry's (Drury's) Bluff in 1864 "was struck by a ball which tore a hole in his right side and shattered a bone in his right arm." Yarborough was elected state commander of the United Confederate Veterans in 1934. A fellow member said that Yarborough "got our pensions increased in 1935 and . . . personally visited almost every veteran in the state during his commandership." Yarborough lived to ninety-seven, dying in the Confederate Home in Columbia. Thomas Wilson Brown died at the Confederate Home at age eighty in 1926.

Fifteen Camden veterans who died between 1881 and 1938 lived to an average age of seventy-two. W. L. DePass survived wounds at Manassas and Pocotaligo, practiced law in Camden, served as a county commissioner, and died in 1881 at forty-five. Isaac Holland, a farmer, merchant, and judge, died in 1938 at ninety-seven. After the war George Gilman Alexander spent seven years in New York City working as a printer on such publications as *Leslie's Weekly* before returning home to Camden. Before his death in 1913 at sixty-seven, Alexander edited the *Camden Journal*, served two terms as postmaster, and was city clerk and treasurer, Camden mayor, and a Kershaw County senator.

After the war Samuel B. Latham was a county commissioner and Camden warden before his death in 1904 at age sixty-two. George Washington Moseley, who lived to be eighty-three, represented the county in the state legislature. John Boone survived the war but died in 1910 of injuries suffered during a prison break while he was the Camden jail keeper. James L. Haile, present at Fort Sumter, reenlisted in the Kirkwood Rangers in 1862 and served until Appomattox. He was twice elected sheriff.

Three brothers from the DeKalb community served in the Seventh South Carolina Battalion. Stephen Craig Clyburn and his younger brother, Lewis Lee, were both officers in the company commanded by their older brother, William. After the war Stephen was Kershaw County clerk of court and a trustee and bank director before he died at sixty-seven in 1904. Lewis, also in banking, was one of the organizers and the first president of the Loan & Saving Bank of Camden as well as a stockholder and president of the Peoples Bank of Kershaw. He died at age eighty-four in 1925.

Samuel J. Benton, promoted from private to captain for bravery at Malvern Hill, operated the Benton Hotel in Kershaw following the war. Four former comrades served as honorary pallbearers at his funeral in 1923. W. J. Young, of the Hanging Rock section, was an overseer for large slave owners before the war. After four years of war service he returned home and farmed until his death in 1921 at age eighty.

In addition to Yarborough, three other Bethune veterans were N. A. Bethune, W. S. Marshall, and Daniel McLaurin. Bethune, a farmer, businessman, and Bank of Bethune president, died at age eighty-two in 1929. Marshall died in 1915 at age seventy-eight. McLaurin, who had been badly wounded at Cold Harbor and Battery Wagner, was a member of the county board of control. He was sixty-three years old when he died in 1904.

Five West Wateree veterans who died between 1905 and 1928 reached an average age of more than seventy-seven years. C. P. Bowen, a magistrate, died at sixty-four; his 1905 funeral was attended by "six bonified veterans who were pallbearers." William Branham of Rabon's Crossroads reached eighty-seven before his death in 1928. J. J. Bell, H. Frank Boykin, and Robert Easler all died in 1922, ages seventy-five, seventy-seven, and eighty-four respectively. Bell, a planter who became the first president of the Bank of Lugoff, had an unusual wartime experience. As a member of Captain Wheeler's Cavalry serving in Georgia, Bell took a Union prisoner who turned out to be Dr. Mary Walker, "the woman surgeon . . . who by Congressional enactment was allowed to appear in male attire." After she was identified, Bell was designated to escort her safely to Union headquarters.

Thomas A. Cauthen and Robert Turner were Westville-area veterans who moved to Kershaw, where they died, respectively, in 1921 at seventy-five and 1915 at eighty-one. Another Westville native, James T. Truesdell, was magistrate of Flat Rock Township for nearly half a century before his death in 1919 at age eighty-nine. W. D. Trantham, born near Flat Rock, joined the Flat Rock Guards when he was only thirteen and served until being sent home as underage. After the war he graduated from Wake Forest, read law, was admitted to the bar, and practiced law until 1905. He served as a state representative in 1879 and again in 1888, was chairman of the board of trustees for the Camden graded schools, and was elected probate judge before his death at sixty-three in 1911.

William Ferguson Russell returned to his birthplace, Westville, after the war and was elected as a trial justice of Flat Rock Township and as a state representative in 1890. He also served as auditor and coroner before his death at age eighty-five in 1930. Another Westville native, Samuel Young, served in the Seventh South Carolina Battalion and survived the war. He suffered a lingering death in 1893 as the result of an accidental burning of his face by turpentine. He left a wife and eleven children.

Records in Marble

Several memorials honoring veterans blend into the present landscape of the county. The Confederate Memorial, topped with a dove of peace, once stood in Camden's Broad and Laurens intersection but now centers the southeastern park of Monument Square. The Pantheon, a six-columned memorial dedicated on May 10, 1911, stands in another Camden park, Rectory Square, in recognition of the six generals born on native soil: James Cantey, James Chesnut, Zack Cantey Deas, John Doby Kennedy, Joseph Brevard Kershaw, and John Bordenave Villepigue. All but Villepigue survived the war. Deas was wounded at Shiloh. Kennedy, wounded many times, gained a reputation for quick recuperation and return to action. After the war Chesnut, Kennedy, and Kershaw returned to the district and continued as leading men in community affairs.[49]

Today the exploits of the generals are less frequently retold than the story of a humanitarian deed by an enlisted man from upper Kershaw District. Sergeant Richard Kirkland has been nationally as well as locally memorialized. Kirkland entered Kennedy's company as a private in 1861. On December 14, 1862, the day after the bloody Battle of Fredericksburg, Virginia, wounded and dying enemy soldiers had been lying all night on the battlefield before the stone wall that served as a Confederate line of defense. Moved with compassion by the groans of the wounded and their cries for water, Sergeant Kirkland requested permission from General Kershaw to go to their aid. Despite personal danger, Kirkland was not allowed to show a white flag, but once the enemy forces realized his mission, they held their fire. For an hour and a half Kirkland made many trips carrying water and giving what relief he could. He moved from man to man, exchanging empty canteens with filled ones, before returning to his post, taking up his rifle, and rejoining his comrades behind the stone wall.

For his deed Kirkland became known as "the Angel of Marye's Heights." He participated in every engagement of Kershaw's Brigade from Bull Run to

Beside a working grist mill, this monument at Boykin Mill Pond recognizes both Confederate and Union soldiers in one of the closing actions of the Civil War.

Chickamauga, where he died at the age of twenty-three. His last words were reported: "Save yourselves, men, and tell Pa I died right." Today a century-old fountain in Camden's Hampton Park commemorates Kirkland's humanitarian example.[50] On the Fredericksburg National Battlefield a monument sculpted by Felix DeWeldon re-creates a lifelike scene of Kirkland giving aid to a wounded soldier.[51]

In Boykin two markers recall one of the last engagements of the war. A historic sign describes the Battle of Boykin's Mill on April 18, 1865, between homeland defenders and General Edward E. Potter's Union forces. Potter's men, who proclaimed emancipation to area residents, included America's first organized African American troops, among them the Fifty-fourth Massachusetts. To recall sacrifices, in modern times the "Reactivated 54th" raised a stone obelisk at Boykin's Mill, on one side listing southern defenders and on the other Union forces. The other sides recognize individual participants: Burwell Boykin, a fifteen-year-old home-guard defender; and Lieutenant E. L. Stevens, the "last federal officer killed in the war."[52]

In 1865, however, monuments and storytelling of the war were as yet of little interest to the people of Kershaw District. All were too freshly connected with the adversities they had endured to be concerned with more than the struggles of daily life in a society recovering from devastation. Some eventually succumbed to the injuries of the body or emotion that they now bore; others overcame their wounds. Both those who had lately lost and those who had lately gained faced a changed way of life.

10

Festering Controls

Reconstruction

Despite the end of warfare in April 1865, disorder did not cease in Kershaw District—or, as it was called after the second postwar state constitution in 1868, Kershaw County. Reconstruction lasted a dozen years after the war's end, bringing fundamental changes to all aspects of life. Following the demise of the Confederacy, every government that had operated under it had to be reorganized. National, state, and local political changes coincided with economic and emotional upheavals. Postwar policies for a time disenfranchised many former Confederates who were experienced in leadership, while enactment of the Thirteenth, Fourteenth, and Fifteenth Amendments to the U.S. Constitution provided for participation of black males in the political process. Amid postwar upheavals a new electorate arose, the majority of them without education or experience in self-government. Opportunists, idealists, and realists all sought to steer the floundering ship of state.

The end of slavery inevitably altered the agricultural system that was the linchpin of the area economy. Farmland had been neglected or ravaged during the war. Fields, especially those in upper Kershaw District, were badly eroded by war's end. Few horses, mules, or other work animals survived. Furthermore telegraph lines, roads, bridges, water channels, and railroads linking suppliers and consumers had been neglected, damaged, or destroyed. The dismantled railroad and the burned bridge over the Wateree River presented tremendous obstacles, as did ruins of public buildings, mills, homes, barns, and fields throughout the district. Lacking viable capital, the local government was unable to repair or replace infrastructure; and merchants and mechanics, like farmers, lacked means of resuming business. Individual citizens stared hunger in the face. Attempts to restore economic stability through liens on farms and crops would continue to have devastating effects in the years ahead.

Distinctions within the social system—fragilely maintained before the war—grew precarious. While still mourning loved ones sacrificed to a "lost cause," some local whites attempted cooperation with the new order. A large number, however, resisted changes, especially attempts to enforce placement of former servants in roles of equal participation with or in charge of the former ruling class. Traditionalists resented what they viewed as defection of some of their own kind—called "scalawags"—and the infusion of Yankees they viewed as opportunists—called "carpetbaggers." Similar tensions existed within the black community as well, with some of the race urging cooperation and others urging separation or even retaliation. All groups struggled with the necessity of learning to trust and cooperate with one another—the blacks who had been free before the war, the newly emancipated blacks now called "freedmen," and the whites of various economic levels. In the interim there were scuffles, arsons, and even murders within Kershaw District/County, as there were within the rest of the conquered South.

Presidential Reconstruction

Advanced to the presidency following the assassination of Lincoln, Andrew Johnson was a southern Democrat who had remained loyal to the Union. He clashed almost immediately with Republicans in Congress who accused him of too-favorable treatment of recent enemy leaders. Presidential Reconstruction further suffered because of southern resistance to congressional policies regarding newly freed blacks. The many differences in northern and southern positions assured clashes among the president, Congress, and southern whites. At first, however, Johnson adopted Lincoln's policy of relative leniency in bringing conquered rebels back into the Union. In May 1865, when Johnson issued a virtual blanket amnesty to most former Confederates, southerners—including those in Kershaw District—anticipated regaining control of state and local governments with the ability to readjust the economy.

On May 15 the town of Camden reacted to the crippling money shortage by beginning to issue its own currency in denominations of twenty-five cents, one dollar, two dollars, and five dollars. This scrip, acceptable for taxes and all town dues, circulated at par, and at intervals it continued to be redeemed until 1877. The first extant issue of a Camden newspaper since the end of the war, the *Tri-Weekly Journal,* edited by D. D. Hocutt, appeared on May 29. Through the local press may be traced the day-to-day confusions and adjustments to the momentous as well as the ordinary occurrences in the resumption of life in Kershaw District in 1865.

The Kirkwood flour and grist mill resumed operation shortly following its wartime destruction, but such quick restoration of order was the exception. Strained tempers, violence, and accidents became ordinary. Some incidents ended in personal violence. The June 5 newspaper reported, "We regret to hear of a fatal receptee having taken place in this district, on Thursday evening last, between Mr. James Kirkland, Duncan McRae and Powell Kirkland, resulting in the death of the former. He received three balls in his body, and lingered but a few hours." Violence was commonplace—often spontaneous and unorganized but sometimes in the form of dueling, the "gentleman's" alternative to street brawling and country scuffling.

Attempts to restore property taken in raids and looting are revealed in the June 14 newspaper with a request for the return of "books taken from Mr. Bonney's store-house (Drakeford's old store)" in February. The request contended, "The servants of many families in Camden, and on the adjoining Plantations have Books in their possession which are of no use to them . . . old volumes of Greek and Latin and Standard works in [gilt] binding, also a Roman Misal, (illuminated) for which a reward will be paid."

For some time conflicts arose from some freedmen's definitions of "freedom." Although federal authorities stated that former slaves, while entitled to wages, must continue to labor as did other working classes in America, such an expectation countered the perceptions of some former slaves. Many bondsmen had seen "free" people simply as persons of leisure and property who did not have to work to provide for themselves and who could visit friends and family when and where they chose. Some slaves, after being told that they were free, had immediately taken to the road to experience their freedom. Some freely took food or objects they desired. A number of the freedmen traveled with one major goal—seeking out and finding loved ones from whom they had been separated in the past.

After roaming for a while, many former slaves soon returned to the plantations. The historian Joel Williamson has concluded, "Most migrants resettled themselves within a matter of days or weeks and within a few miles of the place which, as slaves, they had called home."[1] Hunger was common everywhere they went, and some former slaves began to recall former meals and shelter with longing. Walter Edgar describes the tendency to return to familiar places as "economic necessity" as well as "attachment to the land."[2]

The Federal Garrison

Both erratic mobility and the unrealistic expectations of former bondsmen had proven disruptive since the wartime invasions of Union troops. Yet, even for freedmen willing to work, landowners often lacked money for wages or provisions for support. Real hunger, in fact, was looming over Kershaw District by the time the area was garrisoned by the federal troops that arrived on June 14, 1865. This first detachment, commanded by Captain C. W. F. Ferguson, was composed of two companies of the Twenty-fifth Regiment Ohio Volunteers. It was replaced in a few months by two companies of the Thirtieth Massachusetts. Commanding the latter unit of seventy men was Captain E. A. Fiske, who was subsequently succeeded by Captain Samuel Place. Place would gain local confidence and remain in Kershaw District after his tour of duty to hold elective offices and even to serve as sheriff.

Harriet Lang provided a firsthand account of their occupation of Camden: "Just after the war, the South was put under martial rule. Camden is laid off in blocks, with wide streets and parks. In the park near our home the soldiers were encamped. I well remember the bugles sounding reveille at dawn, and Taps at bedtime."[3] Officers established headquarters for their operations in the Camden City Council chambers. Although town officials had to give up their space, they were allowed to continue to function in day-to-day operations.

Federal officers emphasized to all that slaves were free, but beyond this their status was less clear. Neither citizenship nor suffrage had yet been offered them. A series of orders in the June 16, 1865, newspaper was issued by the local commander Captain Ferguson and by the commander at Charleston, Brigadier General John P. Hatch. These quickly established the procedures of the temporary martial government.

From the Camden post came the promise of punishment for "armed bands of marauders infesting the country and committing depredations on the peaceful citizens." For the present time no liquors could be sold or given away, and mules, horses, and wagons had to be reported but could be retained and worked. Issued at Charleston, General Hatch's firm directions to planters extended in practice to landowners elsewhere. Planters "after taking the oath of allegiance" were instructed to "assemble the freedmen (lately their slaves) and inform them that they are free, and that henceforth they must depend upon their own exertions for their support."

Furthermore, Hatch stated, "Equitable contracts in writing will be made by the owners of the land with the freedmen for the cultivation of the land during the year." The recommendation for payment suggested "one half the crop." In addition he asserted that any owner refusing to cultivate the land "will be considered as endeavoring to embarrass the Government" and would have his land subject to seizure. From Orangeburg, General Hatch clarified that support of freedmen "from age or infirmity, unable to labor" would be the responsibility of the local parish, and that "until such provision is made, they will remain on and draw their support [from] the plantations where they now are."

The Camden newspaper, three days after printing General Hatch's decrees, on June 19 described the procedures for the local administration of the amnesty oath, including the fact that female property owners were also required to take the pledge of loyalty to the United States of America. The same issue included a solemn letter written by Brevet Brigadier General A. S. Hartwell, and dated ten days earlier from Columbia, to the former slaves regarding their new responsibilities, rights, and dignity:

> To the Freedmen:
>
> The time has come for you all to do your best to show that you are fit to be free men in this great Republic. Observe sacredly the marriage tie. Learn to read and write. No one must leave his wife, children or aged

> parents while he can assist them. Thieves and Idlers and people strolling about the country will be punished. Be prudent and quiet, and orderly. If you have trouble report it to the military authorities. This year you cannot do much more than get a living for yourselves and families; those will get the best pay next year who work the best now.
>
> Let no one be either proud or ashamed of the form or color that God has given him. Be proud of the chance to do for yourselves and for each other.

General Hartwell adamantly ordered that "no person shall turn off from his place or house those colored people who have lived with him and still desire to remain with him and do what they can."

Aside from the military's efforts to assure order, local citizens took action as well. On July 15, 1865, with "all industry . . . paralyzed and social life in chaos," Dr. Lynch Horry Deas presided in Camden over a meeting of citizens who, Kirkland and Kennedy say, urged President Johnson to appoint a provisional governor and reestablish the civil government. Johnson had in fact about two weeks earlier appointed B. F. Perry governor, but the news had not arrived here owing to the destruction of railway and telegraph lines.[4]

In the chaos of disorder many former Confederates felt discomforted accepting pardons or signing the required oath of allegiance necessary to reorganize their lives and livelihoods. To the "unreconstructed," accepting a pardon seemed an admission of wrongdoing, and promising allegiance to the United States seemed disloyal to those who had died in southern defense.[5] Although local citizens often chafed under the presence of outsiders, the military government provided valuable assistance to needy persons of all races and stations under the agency that became known as the Freedmen's Bureau.[6] Need was indeed great. The bureau appointed commissioners for each former Confederate state, directing them to meet the immediate needs for food, clothing, and shelter as well as to establish feasible systems of compensated labor and to establish schools.

The Constitution of 1865

President Johnson had ordered earlier "that a State convention be held to frame a new Constitution, composed of delegates to be chosen at an election at which only those could vote who had been qualified under laws in force *prior to the war*—which of course confined the ballot to white males."[7] In accordance a convention met on September 13, 1865, in Columbia's First Baptist Church, ironically the same location where secessionists had first convened. Kershaw District's two delegates, Major L. W. R. Blair and Colonel A. D. Goodwyn, were both former Confederates. In two weeks the convention completed its task. The new constitution repealed the ordinance of secession and acknowledged manumission of slaves but did not grant blacks the right to vote.

In addition to its provisions concerning freedmen, the 1865 constitution made several other significant changes that altered traditional political balances within the state. For one, it replaced the representative selection by lowcountry parishes, making the district unit instead the foundation for elections to the General Assembly. Office-holding was no longer restricted to property owners. The governor, now to be elected directly by the people, would have veto power. President Johnson approved this constitution, which was not submitted to the state's voters for ratification.

The constitution of 1865 was the criterion upon which the government was reorganized and elections were held in October. Kershaw District elected former Confederate generals J. B. Kershaw as state senator and W. Z. Leitner and W. L. DePass as state representatives. J. D. Kennedy was elected First District representative in the federal Congress. The new state legislature that convened in Columbia that same month generally resembled the legislatures that had met in the antebellum years. The newly elected senate and house met in the library and chapel at South Carolina College. Their only action in this special session was the ratification of the Thirteenth Amendment abolishing slavery.

Recollections

Local political and legal changes during Reconstruction were described in 1938 when W. W. Dixon interviewed Alexander W. Matheson, a member of a long-time Camden-area merchant family. Matheson recalled "when we had a military government in South Carolina."[8] Born in comfortable circumstances in Liberty Hill, this son of Alexander Matheson and grandson of John Perry was a young schoolboy in Camden from the beginning of the war until the school closed in January 1865. His family status was affected by the times, and he received no more formal schooling after the war and his father's death. Matheson instead "assisted about the farms, up and down both sides of the Wateree River, for a number of years." Interviewed at age eighty-three in the Longtown section of neighboring Fairfield County, where he had settled after marrying in 1875, he had been a magistrate for thirty years, was active in Democratic clubs for fifty-two years, and was described by the interviewer as "well informed of much of the State's political history."

Matheson's account of the changing periods of government shows a study of history and also occasionally reflects the attitudes of his times. Recalling the oath of allegiance required before voting for the constitutional convention, Matheson said: "This pardoning business was a sore spot to many of our wealthy and best people. Hot discussion of the subject was engaged in. Some never made the application for pardon; many did."

Black Codes

In December 1865 the second regular session of the postwar legislature formulated a controversial set of laws that became known as the "Black Codes." For the first time South Carolina law established a uniform definition of color in order to define the different rights accorded white persons and persons of color. Matheson recalled: "It was declared and made a law that all Negroes, mulattoes, mestizos, and all descendants through them were . . . persons of color, except that every such descendant who might have of caucasian blood 7/8, or more should be deemed a white person. . . . Marriage between a white person and a person of color was declared to be illegal and void." The codes established a special system of district courts that tried only blacks, allowing them rights to hold property and inheritance, to be a party to litigation, and to enter into contracts. However, the codes also withheld political and social rights, barring blacks from serving in the militia and prohibiting them from carrying firearms without a permit.

The Black Codes also virtually eliminated freedmen from participation in trades by requiring costly licenses, and a freedman who entered into a labor contract was treated much like a slave under the former system, required to have permission to be absent from the property. Regulations repetitively used the terms "master" and "servant," thus creating a de facto system of slavery in place of the outlawed de jure system. Camden's James Chesnut was one of the few legislators who cautioned that body that such discriminatory treatment of blacks was ill advised, but his warning was disregarded.

In other former Confederate states legislatures passed similar measures, outraging Congress that old southern elite factions were emerging stronger than ever. Even without suffrage rights, southern blacks would be counted in federal censuses equally with whites so that their numbers would allow southerners larger delegations to Congress and greater strength in the electoral college.[9] General Daniel Sickles, the new military commander in South Carolina, also reacted strongly, asserting that the state's laws must treat blacks and whites equally; he proclaimed the codes void.

"Conflicts were the order of the day in South Carolina," according to Matheson, with "the military authorities and the Freedmen's Bureau on one side and Governor Orr and the State courts on the other. In Washington, there was conflict between President Johnson and Congress."

Labor Contracts

All appeared calm, however, in early 1866 when the January 6 *Camden Journal* reported that "an immense concourse gathered in Camden at Call of Captain Fiske who addressed them and read the military orders regulating labor contracts." The newspaper described the meeting:

> The open square in front of the Court House and site of the old Market and the spacious cross streets were packed with a living mass of colored people. We observed present there also many of the largest planters. The orders were read and explained to them. Capt. Fiske's address was clever and unexceptionable. John Chesnut [sometimes Chestnut] and Harmon Jones, two intelligent freed-men, also made addresses and repeated the good advice they have given on several occasions. Let us hope the delusions so fondly cherished by the freed-men, that the government intended to give them land or support them in idleness have been dispelled.

Removal of the Garrison

On March 24, 1866, after occupying Camden for nine months, the federal garrison was removed and the provost marshal Captain Reed returned the keys to the arsenal and town hall to Captain J. A. Schrock, Intendant A. D. Goodwin, and Wardens J. A. Young, J. B. Alexander, Robert Mann, and Leslie McCandless. Perhaps this action led many whites to presume that matters would soon return to "normal." The military presence would be replaced, however, by an enlarged civilian bureaucracy.

Congressional Reconstruction

Irate over the Black Codes, a Radical Republican Congress in spring 1866 overrode Johnson's vetoes and passed the Freedmen's Bureau Act and the first Civil Rights Act. With human suffering still widespread in the South, the Freedmen's Bureau continued to provide food, clothing, shelter, medical needs, and education to the South's destitute of both races. The historian Harvey S. Teal has concluded, "Lines of authority involving the military, philanthropic organizations, the Freedmen's Bureau and South Carolina civil authorities were often blurred and fuzzy. In July 1866 these lines became less blurred when the Bureau was given more authority to supervise these matters."[10]

With passage of the Fourteenth Amendment, which was ratified two years later, states as well as the federal government had to uphold the rights of citizens. Other parts of the amendment barred former leaders of the Confederate government from holding state or federal offices and also punished any state that prohibited an eligible person from voting. Congress had proved its ability to override the president and could now institute its own policies.

While President Johnson and Congress were sparring for control in Washington, penury reigned in Kershaw District, where famine threatened following a prolonged drought. The grand jury in 1866 found "much Suffering throughout the District." The commissioners of the poor, who before the war had regularly served only a handful of district poor, generally fewer than a dozen, during August alone had "afforded aid to 512 Adults and Children." Local destitution was obviously great, similar to that documented in other districts. Captain Samuel Place of the Freedmen's Bureau received additional supplies to distribute to the indigent.

Under the protection of the district military commandant, all male citizens in South Carolina could register for an election of delegates to a new state convention. Matheson recalled that when local blacks were first registered, "they had but one name such as John, Jocky, Catoe, Solomon, Pompey, Wade, Tom and the like—some took the surnames of their former slave owners; others wanted such surnames as Pinckney, Manigault, Fernandez, Bonaparte, Washington, Guerard, Prince, Jefferson, Jackson, Lincoln, Sherman, and Grant."

Military Districts

In early 1867 Congress overrode Johnson's vetoes and passed three Reconstruction acts. This legislation divided the former Confederate South, excluding Tennessee, which had granted blacks the right to vote, into five military districts. In charge of each district was a Union general to function in effect like an appointed governor with troops at his disposal. Martial law could be enforced by bayonet, with offenders subject to military courts-martial. These acts also added additional requirements for states to be readmitted to the Union. States subsequently had to ratify the Fourteenth Amendment and to include in their constitutions a guarantee of the right to vote for all adult males without regard to color.[11]

Cooperative Politics

The *Camden Journal* of May 16, 1867, reported a public meeting for citizens of Camden—regardless of color—to discuss the political condition of the area and ways to improve it. One participant was Captain Samuel Place, representative of the Freedmen's Bureau.[12] Another participant was John A. Chesnut, a freedman who later would gain prominence in the community as a Republican and then lose it by switching to the Reform ticket in 1870. The optimistic goals of many persons in attendance were probably best expressed by the Reverend Ben Lawson, who was quoted by the newspaper as stating that "the freedmen have only to obtain education to enable them to make their mark high."

The newspaper reported another biracial political gathering at the town hall a week later, which drew a crowd of about three hundred with nearly equal racial balance. Former Confederate generals Chesnut, Kennedy, and Kershaw were among white attendees. Among freedmen attending was John A. Chesnut, who made an impromptu speech upon request. Many examples of such meetings indicate, as General Chesnut expressed it, that "all have common interests." Further evidence of racial cooperation was given in a May 1867 resolution by blacks of the Swift Creek Church, who thanked General J. D. Kennedy for donating "a beautiful place, in a high and healthy location" for establishing a school for their children.

If the *Camden Journal* is representative of white attitudes, public reaction for a while remained outwardly calm, even with the July 25 publication of General Orders no. 60 naming the board of registration for the district of Kershaw. As anticipated, African Americans would now be registered to vote. The newspaper blandly described the board as being "as fair a selection as could be made. There is no reason to apprehend fraud or partiality in the discharge of their duties, on the part of this board."

Restraint is seen in letters to the editor, such as one dated August 8, 1867, and signed "CAUTION," which urged other white citizens to let freedmen, Yankees, and their allies have their way without opposition. It exhorted them to deal fairly with people of color because, in a matter of time, blacks and whites would be battling together "against crushing Yankee *taxation* and *rapacity*."

Meanwhile white conservatives were meeting to discuss the state of political affairs in the embryonic stages of the "straight-out" movement.[13] The *Journal* reprinted articles from other states about black citizens who had realized that the Union League (Republican Party) was "against peace" and were now withdrawing from it. Other articles from out-of-town papers indicated that black laborers were desperate and would settle for much less than the league was demanding for them.

A Civilian Tried by Military Court

In 1868 the attorney William M. Shannon argued before a formal military court in the trial of the white civilian Isaac Owens, charged with the murder of the freedman William Mickle. Shannon's published summary of his arguments in the case reveals the volatility of the times.[14] Shannon attempted first to show that the local court, not the military court, should have jurisdiction in the case.[15] The court turned down the argument of jurisdiction, found Owens guilty of manslaughter, and sentenced him to five years of hard labor.

In the published case Shannon reviews the events that began in upper Kershaw District and ended in a near riot in Camden when Mickle was shot—accidentally, it was argued—as he and another suspect were being taken into the jail. On January 12, 1868, Owens and a son were visiting a neighbor when the two freedmen admitted they had robbed his smokehouse and set a diversionary fire beside Owens's home, with his elderly parents and small children inside. (Owens's father, Richard, ill at the time, died within a week of the fire.)

Neighbors who were called to help apprehend the culprits included two freedmen. A. J. McDowell rode "sixteen miles to Camden, and back home that night" to obtain the legal warrants for the party to act as officers of the law: "They proceeded quietly, orderly, peaceably, no threats, no violence" to arrest the suspects and take them into Camden. Sheriff Edward E. Sill, whom they met en route, directed them to deliver the prisoners to the jailer Sheorn. At the gate of the jailhouse, amid a gathering crowd of townspeople, Owens was "lifting the bar—his attention was necessarily turned from the prisoners." There was confusion, a jostling, or an attempt to run. Owens's gun was cradled in his arm and fired, unintentionally it was claimed, and the firing of a second, unidentified gun also sounded. A confusion of riotous events followed.

Shannon argued that had violence been intended, no such efforts to follow the law or to travel the exhausting trip into town would have taken place. The prosecutor pressed his case of intentional malice because in court Owens's testimony included an offensive pronunciation. Shannon's rebuttal argued that the word was "only a matter of taste and sentiment, a mere corruption of the word negro, which neither you nor I would use, because we know what the correct word is . . . but . . . the accused . . . only spoke as he had spoken all his life."

The case that ended in Owens's conviction aroused white residents at the time to distrust the military court system to protect them and their families in cases that involved persons of color. It likely contributed to the tensions of other situations that followed in the area. Theft, arson, hunger, safety of home and family, protection under the law—all were matters of deep concern to blacks and whites alike.

The Constitution of 1868

As mandated by Congress, a convention to draw up a new state constitution assembled in Charleston in January 1868, with representatives chosen by the new electorate, now including black voters. Almost immediately came voices of concern that fears of corruption in the state were materializing. Even the *New York Herald* editors, quoted in the Camden paper on February 6, were sharply critical in comparing a state delegate's daily expense allotment of eleven dollars plus mileage to that of a federal congressman's eight dollars. The cooperative outward restraint of Kershaw District political relations wore thin as the closely watched convention was followed by the election of 1868.

Alexander Matheson, a Liberty Hill native and lifelong Democrat, recalled in a 1938 interview the time when "a Negro majority" resulted in new representation and a new constitution had to be written. Matheson said, "Then it looked like every sharp cunning rascal who could get a carpetbag and transportation from above the Mason and Dixon line put out to the State in quest of political adventure. These carpetbaggers and a few South Carolina white scalawags organized the Federal Union Republican Party and laid plans to control the Constitutional Convention of 1868. They accomplished their purpose."

Matheson recalled "48 white men and 76 Negroes sworn in. . . . Of the whites, there were only 23 native South Carolinians; the other 25 were natives of

Massachusetts, Ohio, Rhode Island, Connecticut, New York, Pennsylvania, Michigan, England, Ireland, Prussia, Denmark, Georgia, North Carolina, and places nobody has ever found out." He pointed out some positive effects brought about by the work of the legislators: "As they knew nothing about society and constitutional law, it is a wonder that they gave us a constitution as good as they did. . . . We lived under its provisions till 1895. On the whole, it was an improvement over the Constitutions of 1791 and 1865, in that it prohibited imprisonment for debt; apportioned representation in the House of Representatives according to the numbers of inhabitants in a county; provided for the public free school system; provided compulsory attendance of children in the schools between the ages of six and sixteen years; and prohibited lotteries of every kind."

The Delegation of 1868

For the first election under the new constitution, the Democratic Association of Kershaw County, as the old district was hereafter called, organized in April and offered a traditional ticket with some of the area's most prominent white men—General J. B. Kershaw for senator and Colonel W. M. Shannon, Dr. E. M. Boykin, and Major W. L. DePass for representatives. A vigorous Democratic campaign directed propaganda to both races. To win blacks' support, the Democrats passed resolutions recognizing the freedom of citizens of color and investing them with civil rights. In the April 9 *Journal,* Democrats invited black citizens to join them, "the true friends of the colored people, no less by identity of interests in the future than by memories of the past."

Not content merely to praise their own candidates, Democrats launched vitriolic condemnations against the two white Republican candidates. The senate nominee Justus K. Jillson from Massachusetts was labeled a carpetbagger and the house nominee Solomon George Washington Dill from Charleston, a scalawag. The *Journal* urged all white and black citizens to go to the polls and vote, calling Jillson "a political scavenger" and declaring: "The nominee for State Senator by the League is a traveling, carpet-bag fellow, who loves them [blacks] for office and office sake alone."

The former Charleston resident was dealt with similarly: "Of Dill, what shall we say! He was the most blatant black man hater during and just after the war. He is a league man only for office. He is a crafty, designing, unprincipled traitor." Dill elsewhere explained his position: "I have always been a poor man, and always known to be on the side of the poor."[16] The Democrats made no attack on the black nominees—John A. Chesnut and Jonas Nash, both local freedmen.

Tension revolving around the election ran high in Kershaw County. Provost Marshal Samuel R. Adams wrote Governor Scott from Camden on May 26, 1868, that "strong antagonistic feeling" had persisted between whites and freedmen for the past three weeks. Adams urged Scott to send a detachment of troops or, Adams warned, because of the political climate "much evil will result." Talking was no longer enough, he assured the governor, as "Ku Klux" gossip was prevalent and freedmen were arming for emergency.[17]

On May 28, only two days after Adams's letter, the *Journal* reported that there had been much excitement over rumors of a "Ku Klux" visit, but "to the disappointment of some and gratification of others," no secretive white vigilantes had arrived. The press was mum on whether the organization that made its mark elsewhere (the Ku Klux Klan) was active locally at this time. Nevertheless the rumors and threats of such activity and the government's reaction to those threats affected local tensions.

At election's end, the Union Republicans had swept the field with a slate of two whites and two freedmen gaining control of the county delegation. A major change in political power became evident. The 1868 delegation was one of the most unusual ever to represent this—or any—county. Of the original four, S. G. W. Dill was murdered at his West Wateree residence before taking office, and Jonas Nash died in office, thus necessitating two special elections. A white man, John A. Boswell, replaced Dill, and the freedman William Adamson succeeded Nash. Senator Justus K. Jillson later became distinguished as the first South Carolina superintendent of education. Only one other delegation—Abbeville—had more changes than did Kershaw County; and perhaps no other delegation was as diversified, as it included at various times a carpetbagger, a scalawag, three freedmen, and a white of unknown background.

The Dill Murder

Less than a week after Adams's warning to Governor Scott about potential problems in the local area, tension erupted into a sensational murder. Representative-elect S. G. W. Dill was said to have angered local whites with his speeches to freedmen on the theme of "forty acres and a mule." Perhaps white fears of being dispossessed of their lands were fanned further by the fact that Dill, for forty years a resident of Charleston, was a southern white man seen as turning against his own kind. At his home in the Harmony section of western Kershaw County, reportedly a headquarters for black Union League members, Dill was carefully guarded by black Republicans in recognition of the strong feeling against him.

On the night of June 1, 1868, a volley of bullets, shot from the dark into his home, killed Dill and Nester Peay, his armed guard, and wounded Dill's wife.[18] Federal troops searched the countryside, making many arrests. At least twenty suspects were sent to prison in Charleston, but no shred of evidence was uncovered. Those arrested maintained their innocence and were eventually released.[19]

Hostilities apparently had quieted down in the local area by the following month because the *Journal* printed a notice on July 16, 1868, that the "Yankee soldiers, garrisoned in Camden since the 'Dill murder'" had returned to Columbia. Notice was made that the liberal-minded Dill and Nester Peay, his bodyguard, were buried separately in racially segregated cemeteries. By fall of that year the Democrats appeared to be gathering support. The *Journal* announced a mass meeting on September 8 with the popular former Confederate general Wade Hampton as an invited guest. The big parade included the Camden Colored Club and the Liberty Hill Colored Club, though in the last two positions of the procession.

The historian Walter Edgar explains that because of "terrorism that wracked the upstate in the fall of 1868" the governor "sent a message to Wade Hampton that if he did not speak out against the violence, the long-feared race war might erupt." Hampton's widely publicized response was successful in "appealing for 'the preservation of order'" in the face of potential federal intervention: "Almost overnight the KKK went underground, and for eighteen months the state was relatively peaceful."[20] The star of Wade Hampton's political power was rising.

Forty Acres and a Mule

The murdered Dill had possibly been arguing for land distribution to freedmen. At war's end rumors had spread among newly freed slaves that they could expect to be given allotments of enough land and supplies to be self-supporting. While white fears of having their personal land seized and given to former slaves did not materialize, South Carolina was the only southern state to benefit freedmen with a land-distribution plan. In 1869 the South Carolina Land Commission was funded to buy large tracts at public expense, subdivide them, and resell them at reasonable cost and lenient terms to the homeless poor of both races. Of the twenty-eight counties in which land was purchased for this purpose, in only five other counties was more land bought than in Kershaw County (6,360 acres).[21]

One of the two large tracts purchased here was known in the Reconstruction records as "the Burroughs tract" (the name was "Burrows" on the plat) for a purchaser who had acquired and resold it. It lay in the sandy southeastern part of the county on Swift Creek. The second large tract, referred to in state records as "the Cyples Tract," lay in the upper part of the county along the Wateree River and White Oak Creek. It had formerly operated as the plantation of Lewis Ciples and then his widow Sarah Ciples, who had died during the war.[22] Much of the land in both areas was afterward said to have been exhausted or eroded, not fertile enough for small tract farming.

The historian Carol Bleser states that "Major Sam[uel R.] Adams, who had served under [General] Scott during the war, seemed a reliable agent to investigate the Burroughs tract in Kershaw County. Adams, in his evaluation of the tract, seems to have relied heavily upon the opinion of the freedmen as to the land's value." On Adams's word the advisory board of the Land Commission hastily purchased it for $22,500 but then "discovered that the market value of the tract had been fixed at $8,000, and that the notorious 'scalawag,' Franklin Moses, Jr. . . . had purchased the land at a reduced price from the original owner and then employed Adams to act as his agent in deceiving the board as to the land's actual worth."[23] How Adams's involvement was explained locally is unclear, but apparently no disfavor remained attached to his name in Kershaw County, where he afterward made his permanent home.[24]

Bleser contends, "The history of the Land Commission during the period 1869–72 is an example of the moral slump that was characteristic of government at all levels during the Grant era." The Republican administration of U.S. president Ulysses S. Grant, 1869–77, is viewed by historians as marked by scandal, graft, and a general decline in ethics in government. In all South Carolina counties, Bleser continues, "although the land experiment was humanitarian in concept, in practice it was sabotaged by internal dissension, riddled with corruption, and harassed by the criticism from the Conservatives."[25] Yet some small farms in Kershaw County (ten to one hundred acres in general) had a start as Land Commission tracts, sold mostly to blacks. Some parcels were sold later when remaining, reclaimed, or escheated tracts went into the state sinking fund. Some of the Cyples (Ciples) tract now lies under the impounded Lake Wateree. Local complaints about the land program during Reconstruction stemmed from the belief that the taxes citizens were hard-pressed to pay were being squandered to buy near-worthless land, the profits for which were filling the personal pockets of politicians.

Black Militia

As a result of the violence against blacks the previous year, a new state militia was created in 1869, and since blacks were allowed to serve in it, whites refused to join. The resulting units, nearly all black, placed the use of force in the hands of those who had previously lacked it. At first the black militia contributed to peacekeeping, although Edgar points out that "the spoils system that weakened so many other Reconstruction programs corrupted the militia as well." Edgar also states that "in 1870 violence exploded and never fully abated until the Republican regime collapsed in 1877."[26]

A riotous disturbance in downtown Camden on the Fourth of July in 1871 involved black militiamen. According to Kirkland and Kennedy, "two colored companies, Sandy Stratford and C. Shiver, Captains" paraded the streets that day in celebration. In general during the postwar period freedmen but not former Confederates observed the anniversary of national independence. When a Camden white police marshal named John Smyrl arrested a reportedly unruly militia member, other members threatened the law officer. Monroe Boykin, a freedman who was then a Baptist preacher, along with Paul Wilson, a former Confederate soldier, stood side-by-side to prevent the other militiamen from stabbing Smyrl with bayonets. The one-legged former Confederate major William "Zack" Leitner arrived by carriage in time to help quell the swelling mob. Kirkland and Kennedy say that the tensions of the day were felt as far away as Kirkwood.[27]

Black Firemen and Policemen

Black fire units, unlike militia, drew general praise from the white community. Citizens seem to have taken great pride in the fire companies, as the *Camden Journal* described the firemen's parade on May 20, 1869: "The three colored companies performed to the satisfaction and delight of everyone. . . . We defy any town in the State to show a more efficient and well manned colored fire department than Camden." The newspapers made frequent references to parades and other public gatherings where these companies appeared along with white fire companies. As bodies of unarmed men acting to protect lives and property in town, black firemen were more readily trusted by white citizens than were black militiamen who were allowed weapons and a range of the countryside.

Likewise, Camden's having two positions for black men along with two for white on the police force seems to have satisfied and not disturbed townspeople. On May 27, 1874, the *Kershaw Gazette* commented on a display of the new uniform soon to be issued to the policemen. The "neat costume" was dark blue with brass buttons "similar to style of New York City police." The article referred to the police as "our knights of the club and stars." The same newspaper on April 15 found it quite appropriate that following a town election "colored firemen" paraded from the courthouse, "torches in hand" and "with drums and fife," and cheered before the homes of the newly elected intendant and wardens.

Black Vigilantes

All law-abiding citizens grew weary of lawbreakers. In 1872 a band of five "colored robbers" was preying on the area surrounding Camden. Sam Page, a black resident, was robbed within a mile of town "on the Chesterfield road, running back of what is known as the Factory Pond." After a similar robbery in broad daylight each of the next three days, "several colored men, among whom was Alderman [William] Deas, sallied forth armed to the teeth, intent upon the capture or annihilation of the gang." A search uncovered the gang's camp, which they had abandoned. The July 18 newspaper commended the black enforcers for endeavoring "to bring to justice those who are drawing down reflections upon their race."

Just a few years earlier the idea of armed black men roaming the countryside—even in pursuit of justice—was considered alarming rather than reassuring.

By now, however, the Camden police force was equally divided by race, so that men of both races at times served to restore order.

Arson

Along with robbers, arsonists created terror throughout the county. The frequency of the crime is suggested in the February 6, 1868, *Camden Journal* article "Another Barn Burnt." Destruction of the barn with two thousand bushels of corn belonging to A. H. Boykin on Swift Creek was "no doubt the work of an incendiary," the article concluded. Unexplained fires plagued the county into the next decade. The *Journal* reported on August 15, 1872, that an "incendiary fire" had destroyed Captain Eli Parker's new mill near the Kershaw-Fairfield boundary line. The December 5 issue described a 3:00 A.M. fire that destroyed a large two-story barn and its contents on Adam Team's Hermitage plantation, and on December 19 the newspaper commented, "Our list of burned gin houses grows larger every week." Such destruction in the time of postwar food shortages and crop failures indeed threatened the very survival of citizens. Frequent fires also endangered the town. The newspaper on October 12, 1872, referred to an odor downtown "in the burnt district."

Acts of arson were committed by persons of both races, sometimes out of meanness, spite, or retribution, but often arson was a distraction to cover other crimes—robbery or murder. The trail of an arsonist, who could inflict huge damage with a single spark, was generally consumed by the time the deed was discovered and was difficult to trace.

The "Ku Klux"

Frustration swelled against a government seen as corrupt and as indifferent to or incapable of providing protection against the outrages of disorder. Conditions provoked both individual and organized vigilante responses, and they strengthened determination to overtake political control. Actions attributed to "the Ku Klux" increased especially in upstate South Carolina. To quell resistance in other parts of the South, the federal government hastened to make an example of the state.

On October 12, 1871, President Grant ordered all armed groups to disband and surrender their weapons and disguises. Five days later the president suspended the writ of habeas corpus in nine counties in which Ku Klux Klan activity was most active. Kershaw was not included, but three counties on its borders were—Chesterfield, Fairfield, and Lancaster. Consequently, Kershaw's omission tends to confirm reportedly limited local Klan activity; yet Kershaw's proximity to the other counties suggests reasons that rumors and threats were so prevalent and were taken seriously. The November 9 Camden newspaper remarked, "The Ku Klux proclamation [of President Grant] has damaged trade everywhere." Presumably citizens felt their recourse to protection had been removed.

In the summer of 1872 the *Camden Journal* dealt with a variation of vigilante activity. An August 1 story entitled "A Colored Ku Klux Scrape" described a nocturnal assault against a "colored" resident of an area near "Englishes mills." A gang of fifteen or twenty men dragged the man from his West Wateree home, covered his head, bound his hands and feet, carried him into the woods, "deposited him upon the ground and taking sticks beat him until they thought he was dead, cut off a piece of his ear and untying him, left him there."

The victim survived the attack and told authorities that his head covering had slipped, allowing him to observe that his assailants were all of his own race. The newspaper cited as the reason alleged for the attack was that the victim had "bewitched his daughter-in-law, who had lately died." A later issue brought information "from reliable authority, that the real reason . . . was because he was a Democrat."

Adjustments to Changes

The turmoil of the postwar years made adjustments to change difficult for citizens. Yet from the very beginning changes inevitably resulted from the infusion of northerners, the emancipation of slaves, and the political and economic devastation of the times. Departures from traditional patterns of life immediately struck white citizens who had been accustomed to affluence and propriety. Shortly after the war Emma Holmes wrote sarcastically in her diary from Camden on August 15, 1865, about a woman who "has disgraced herself by her engagement to a Yankee Lieutenant of the garrison here. The only excuse to be made for her is that her father is Yankee born, & she has so little intellect & so few attractions save her wealth that her society was unsought anywhere." The diarist likewise treated news that two slaves of one family had married Yankees: "one a light colored mustee had property left her by some white man whose mistress she had been. She says she passed herself off for a Spaniard, & Mercier Green violated the sanctity of Grace Church by performing the ceremony. The other, a man, went north & married a Jewess."

Besides social changes, most residents of Kershaw District faced other significant adjustments in their lives. Emma Holmes, who remained in Camden for a time after the war, recorded on June 22, 1865, that she was applying for work with families with children. Holmes, who had lived a life of leisure in Charleston and afterward taught locally as a governess, added that "my pride is buried with the Confederacy, at least all false pride." She worked in 1865 as a seamstress, "taking in sewing to assist in paying for our washing, etc. . . . We are to be paid in sugar and soap, at 50 cents a garment. Of course, we should prefer money, but, that being scarce, barter is the order of the day." At various times servants taught Holmes and others like her to make butter, to iron a man's shirt, and to perform other housekeeping skills.[28]

Some people tried at first to take up life again as they had once lived it, behavior which offended Emma Holmes. Her journal for June 28, 1865, reported that "Thursday night, the Kennedys, Mathesons & Hailes, united, gave a ball at the latter's house, a hundred & odd persons there—tableaux & dancing, ice cream & hot supper being the order. I cannot understand how people can so soon cast off the memory of this bitter war & rush into gaiety, when the grass is scarce green over the sods that cover their brothers, cousins & uncles." She recalled discussion of a comment during the war: "We hear that some Camden youth remarked after a visit home on furlough, 'well, 'twill make no matter if we die, we won't be missed, the girls will still dance and be gay.'" Holmes wrote on October 12, 1865, that "a grand tournament, followed by a fancy ball at Col. [A. D.] Goodwyn's house took place here."[29]

In ways other than the temporary diversions of fancy balls, which affected a relative few, people of Kershaw County tried to adjust to new ways of living, or in some cases to revert to former ways. White residents alternated between practices of conciliation and alienation in regard to nonwhites. African Americans were allowed the use of public facilities for the first time. In addition to opening Camden's town hall for usual events, the council also offered it free to "the Colored People of Camden" for a ball and to the "Colored Members of the Baptist Church" for a supper. However, other actions were less agreeable. In May 1868 in West Wateree the Fraternal Democratic Club of Harmony passed resolutions against employing anyone in the Loyal Union League, that is, the organization supporting the Union Republican Party. At the same time there were rumors of local Ku Klux Klan activity.

A number of former Confederates migrated to Florida or to the west, turning their backs on burned homes, eroded fields, and political squabbling. Some blacks went north; others preferred to remain where they had always lived. Rather than work for a landowner, a lifestyle which too closely resembled slavery, many freedmen wanted to rent land and work it themselves. Since most white landowners were disinclined to rent to blacks, the dominant system that emerged was sharecropping. This system allowed the cropper, or tenant, to work for himself, at least in theory, but allowed the property owner to retain control of his land. The tenant worked the land and at harvesting time kept a share for his efforts. Both white and black farmers worked under varying forms of this system following the war. For most it offered a subsistence living.

Some whites asserted attitudes in line with the statement in the local February 6, 1868, newspaper that freedmen were unproductive laborers. The newspaper stated that in part this was because they took time off to attend political and religious meetings, adding that the "operations of the Union League have been detrimental to them." The article charged that black laborers did not work to their potential and that some left cotton "hidden in the field," for which they returned at night to collect and sell for their own benefit. The article further criticized "a class of white men [who] go about the country for the purpose of robbing the people, they get corn and cotton from the freed people, giving in

exchange . . . whiskey, and other unnecessary articles." However, other freedmen worked hard and received approbation from white neighbors.

Such were the conditions when the attorney William M. Shannon made a speech before the Camden Bar Association in 1869 or 1870, giving a history of old Camden and reflecting on current times: "We occupy now the position of new settlers in our country, with everything to achieve anew, with the increased difficulty that our lands are old & worn we are burdened with debt, that we have the heaviest scale of taxation, known to old & wealthy nations, that our habits & modes of life are unfit for the change, & that, what was our wealth & labor is now a tax & burthen."[30]

From Bondsmen to Freedmen

In a 1930s interview in his later years, the former Kershaw District slave Randall Lee remembered "paddyroles" after the war.[31] During the war, he explained, patrols "were sent by the Rebels to watch the slaves to prevent their escaping," and he recalled that such groups also "were very active after freedom." Lee said, "They intimidated the Negroes and threatened them with loss of life if they did not stay and work for their former masters." His old master, however, "did not want any of his slaves treated in such manner. He told them they were free and could take whatever name they desired." That is when Lee chose his name. His interviewer explained, "His brother Aaron took the name Alexander, not thinking how it looked for two brothers of the same parents to have different surnames."

Lee recalled that after the war "his father began farming on his own plantation, his mother remained home and cared for her house and children. She was of fair complexion, her mother having been the daughter of a half-breed Indian and a Negro woman. Her father was white. Her native state was Virginia and she bore some of the aristocratic traits so common among those born in that state of such parentage. She often boasted of her 'blue blood Virginia stock.'"

Lee's father was "very prosperous in early reconstruction days. He owned horses, mules and a plow . . . made of point iron with a wooden handle." As circumstances improved, the parents began "trying to give their children some education." Lee recalled, "It was very hard for those living in small towns and out in the country to go to school even though they had money to pay for their education. The north sent teachers down but not every hamlet was favored with such." Lee learned to farm, saved his profits, and years later moved to Florida, where he bought land of his own. His life after the war demonstrates some of the considerable movement of both black and white citizens in seeking opportunities elsewhere.[32]

A former slave family who became successful at home following the war is described in a 1930s interview conducted for the Federal Writers' Project in Columbia. Stiles M. Scruggs recorded the story of "a retired, and well educated Methodist Episcopal minister," the Reverend James H. Johnson, who had been born in 1855 "at the town servants' quarters of Alfred Brevart [Dr. Alfred Brevard] at Camden." His mother was a maid and his father an overseer. Reverend Johnson related what happened to his family during Reconstruction: "In 1866 my father bought four acres in the vicinity of Camden and improved it with a house and barn, and we lived there for several years. My father went into the mercantile business in Camden and prospered. There I went to the public schools. We had teachers from the North, and I finished all the grades."

Debts, Taxes, and Sheriff's Sales

For most people, black and white alike, the postwar period brought hard economic times and real threats to survival. The *Camden Journal* of February 6, 1868, printed a letter from General O. O. Howard, chief of the Freedmen's Bureau, to the bureau's assistant commissioner for South Carolina, Brevet Major R. K. Scott. Howard stated that he had allocated more relief funds to this state

A working farmer during the period of improved conditions in the early 1900s, with an ox and a wagon for transportation and a means of livelihood. Courtesy of the Camden Archives

than to any other because South Carolina was one of three states in which there was a likelihood of famine.

Harriet Lang recalled, "Our farmers, trying to make a living, were heavily taxed. Every bale of cotton was taxed five dollars, and no cotton could be sold until the tax was paid."[33] The record book of the town of Camden shows details of the "Ordinance to raise supplies for the year 1868." This action levied property, sales, and income taxes as well as set business license fees and charged a five-dollar capitation tax per male eighteen to sixty years of age. Each improved town lot was taxed at fifty cents per one hundred dollars assessed value, with ½ of 1 percent of the value thereof added for a tax supporting the public wells that were used for human and animal drinking as well as for firefighting.

When the traveling Robinson and Southern Circus refused to pay a town tax in Camden, saying that a state tax of fifty dollars had already been paid, the town council enacted a ten-dollar fine in addition and commissioned a special deputy to pursue the circus to Flat Rock with a magistrate to collect. Despite protests and attitudes about taxes, most citizens had to abide by the law.

The historian Harvey S. Teal concludes that the economic problems of the time resulted not mainly from the tax structure but from crop failures in 1866, 1867, 1869, and 1870. From detailed study of crop and tax statistics, Teal states: "Due in part to a severe drought, 1866 proved to be a very poor crop year. Many Negroes [and whites] owed more at year's end than they earned during the year. 1867 was an even worse crop year. The Freedmen's Bureau set up a crop lien system whereby rations were advanced to Negroes and some whites; their debts to be repaid when crops were harvested . . . 1868 was a good crop year, but was followed by bad years in 1869 and 1870, although not as disastrous as 1867."[34] The resulting agricultural depression that extended through the 1870s brought on hunger, deprivations, foreclosures, and sheriff's sales. Perhaps the longest-lasting effect was the establishment of reliance on the crop lien system that would haunt southern agriculture for years to come.

Offerings from the February 6, 1868, *Journal* are indicative of hard times that year. A notice of "U.S. Marshall's Sales" listed the "Camden Bank Building, situated on the south-east corner of Broad and Rutledge streets . . . levied upon as the property of the Bank of Camden." The auction also offered an eight-hundred-acre tract on Persimmon Branch. The same newspaper announced a "Sheriff's Sale" to auction fifteen hundred acres on Beaver Creek. R. M. Kennedy posted a notice: "I find it necessary for the current year, to confine myself to the CASH system."

Such notices continued into the next decade. For example, the June 6, 1871, *Camden Journal* printed a long list of forfeited lands being sold for taxes. Some were town lots or small parcels, but listings also included an 800-acre tract in Buffalo and a Flat Rock piece of more than 1,000 acres. The September 5, 1872, newspaper listed a sale of one parcel of some 12,000 acres. The December papers published bankruptcies and sales of tracts of 600, 800, and 2,623 acres, among

This 1976 sketch by artist Jak Smyrl illustrates stories from his grandfather about the lack of farm animals after the Civil War, when people pulled plows themselves or plowed with a milk cow. Courtesy of Jak Smyrl

smaller ones of 200 or 300 acres. John D. Kennedy's Doby Place and Rock Hill Plantation in West Wateree were auctioned, as were 5,000 acres on Lynches River belonging to Colonel L. W. R. Blair, divided into tracts for "smaller farms and the times." Small farms too fell under the auctioneer's hammer during hard times, and these were so numerous that they were not always individually advertised.

Several large turpentine farms had operated profitably in Kershaw County before Sherman's army came through.[35] After the war residents were encouraged to resume that industry to offset other agricultural losses. The June 29, 1871, *Camden Journal* reported the availability of "lands very near the Wateree River [that] can be rented for a mere song." The major obstacle to this venture was the same barrier to nearly every other endeavor in the postwar South—lack of capital. Many of those who turned to turpentining disregarded prudence and added forest-land destruction to the region's land woes.

Medicine and Mortality

The medical community required reorganization following the war to improve health care for Kershaw County patients. Doctors faced scores of indigent patients—veterans returning with diverse maladies and injuries, and freedmen accustomed to uncompensated medical care. Local doctors in 1866 proposed the postwar reorganization of the Kershaw Medical Association.

The association adopted medical ethics put forward by the American Medical Association and accepted the fee bill proposed by the physicians of Camden after some adjustments. For night visits after 10:00 P.M., the day visit fee would be doubled to four dollars. A proposed charge of two dollars per hour was determined to be too large, and they agreed to reduce the fee to one dollar per hour unless the doctor's time happened to be "particularly precious on the occasion," for which they were urged to use "conscientious discretion."

The doctors agreed: "No physician shall contract to attend any individual institution, or family by the year; nor take charge of any particular case for a specified sum, except such as are enumerated in the above mentioned Fee Bill adopted by the Association." They apparently passed the resolution that "members of this association . . . decline positively, attending upon any parties after thirty days notification, except when the fee is presented upon the solicitation of their services." In 1868 D. L. DeSaussure announced the resumption of his medical practice at his office in the rear of Dr. Zemp's Drug Store, and T. J. Workman offered his professional services to the community in his office "immediately above Baum's store, entrance on Rutledge Street."

A glance at the 1870 mortality census of Kershaw County reveals eighty-two deaths that year, largely among young children (twenty-five below the age of ten) and among the elderly (twenty-three above the age of sixty).[36] Likely the statistics reflect circumstances of the time. The largest number of deaths (sixteen) were attributed to the general designation of "fever," with thirteen more to the more serious typhoid fever (seven) and cholera (six). Additionally nine deaths were attributed to dropsy, a condition that sometimes developed as an aftermath of fever. Besides these, eleven deaths were attributed to pneumonia and ten to consumption.

More than half the deaths in 1870, therefore, were from ailments known to worsen in situations of exposure, displacement, and stringent living conditions, such as were reported after the war. Especially vulnerable were young black children (thirteen deaths) and young mulatto children (seven deaths), the latter group representing more than half of the total number of mulatto deaths reported (thirteen). Elderly blacks (over age sixty) experienced three times the number of deaths as did elderly whites, fifteen deaths compared to five. Two elderly mulattoes also died.

Sporting Activities

During Reconstruction sporting activities fulfilled a number of roles—survival, diversion, and even subterfuge. W. E. Johnson of Liberty Hill kept a diary in 1870 and 1871 in which he recalled many treks across Kershaw County and surrounding areas hunting and fishing. He brought home fish and game to feed his family, enjoyed his outings in the interim, and like a number of local men, was involved in political activities. Johnson recorded on August 25, 1870, that he "made a stand [speaker's stand, platform for Democratic political rally] prepared a place for Carpenter & Butler to speak." He recorded on September 27, "Carpenter & Butler Shannon. Tom Massey & others made speeches here today about 500 persons present Col Shannon Drs Trantham & Ford." Johnson had earlier, on September 17, stated that "Ann and myself went to Kirkwood to day—Radical Political meeting at Liberty Hill." In October he resumed bird and deer hunting.[37]

The September 5, 1872, *Camden Journal* refers to a new law governing hunting: "Monday last, being the first available day, under the new game law, for indulging in this fascinating sport, we heard of several different parties who took advantage thereof." The article specifically mentions a group of fifteen or twenty from Camden who hunted "in the vicinity of Mr. Ario Niles' plantation, a few miles above this place [Camden]." The city marshal J. M. Cantey killed "one fine doe," the group's only success for the day. Over the next few days perhaps either more people took to the woods or the hunting improved because the September 12 newspaper reported that "last week four unfortunate deer bit the dust."

The traditional southern lifestyle of hunting, which combined recreation with necessity, made the carrying of guns natural. Throughout the South sportsmen were able to combine their comings and goings on horseback, carrying guns, and traveling together in groups with political activities that evolved later into the formation of "rifle clubs" for political influence. Traditional outdoor activity was also a way in which white men of various stations maintained cordial comradeship with one another and with black men with whom they hunted. Hunting and fishing together, men valued the skills of individuals.

In an earlier time community militia meetings had offered opportunities for male bonding and social companionship with families and friends who watched militiamen drill together and compete in personal and team competitions. Under postwar strictures against displays of military enthusiasm, opportunities for competition and bonding experiences emerged through other outlets. The playing of baseball, begun in the North in the mid-1840s, is said to have been spread through America by Union soldiers in Civil War camps. In Kershaw County the sport caught on in the postwar years. Young and adult males formed bonds of friendship with the formation of local baseball teams. In 1874, for example, the *Kershaw Gazette* followed the sport in Camden through the summer. On May 27 young men were reported forming a baseball club to play in the afternoon, and on June 17 "the popular amusement of our town" doubled when another team, the Palmettos, was organized for juveniles. The newspaper printed the names of the officers of the Kershaw Club and the Camden Club on June 22, and two days later it announced a match game between the two. Reportedly informal teams were also playing one another in various parts of the county.

By July another match game was played, this one to settle the championship of the county. Although the newspapers discreetly refrained from reporting scores and winners, the enthusiastic reporting of events smacked of old militia meets or equestrian tournaments. The championship game was played at 3:00 P.M. in Kirkwood on the grounds of the Kershaw club. D. D. Dunlap was umpire, and T. J. Ancrum and W. R. McCreight served as scorers for the respective Kershaw and Camden teams. Ladies of the Grace Church Sewing Society served ice cream. With fanfare General James Chesnut presented to the winners a championship flag sewn by the ladies. Later in the month the Kershaw Club (probably the county champion) met a team from Orangeburg in a match game. Such games, in the way of militia meets, formed contacts and gave opportunities for political exchanges as well.

Efforts to Improve

Despite many problems throughout society, glimmers of hope emerged in efforts for improvements. The *Camden Journal* on November 9, 1871, discussed the revitalization of part of the riverfront: "The question of the opening of the old Boat Yard Road, that was under discussion at the time of our last issue, has become a fixed fact, as the commissioners have given the contract to Capt. Jeter of the *Isis,* and from the well known energy of the Captain, it may be considered as done. The old yard which was once an institution near Camden, will again be the scene of busy life, as the steamer *Isis* will be boarded, lodged and done for there. Possibly in the course of time's changes, some descendants of the old Tubal Cains of other days, may make the Welkin ring once more with the merry sound of the hammer and saw." The difficulty of securing labor, equipment, and funding for clearing the channels resulted in relatively limited postwar steamboat navigation, however.

The Wateree Bridge

On July 4, 1872, the *Camden Journal* reported on the progress of the "free bridge [over the Wateree River] now being built by Mr. J. B. LaSalle." Citizens were anxious that the bridge lost during the war be replaced, but hard times had delayed such efforts. A reporter who had recently visited the site found "quite a settlement down there" erected for LaSalle and the carpenters. Other documents reveal that the piers from the old bridge burned by Sherman were being reused to rebuild the new bridge where they stood. According to the newspaper, the bridge's piers were being raised about two feet higher. This effort to avoid ill effects of high water involved additional support at the top of the piers.

LaSalle advertised in August 1872 to hire "15 good, smart, active laborers," urging, "This is a good opportunity for steady employment at good wages." The necessity for the new bridge was expressed in the August 22 newspaper: "This will be a great Convenience to our [cotton] planting friends over on the west side and will enable most of those living comparatively near town to ship two loads a day, whereas by ferry it was not possible to make more than the one trip."

Such employment as the bridge construction offered was welcomed, but it came with risk. The November 14 issue reported a serious accident. LaSalle and three of his workers had been standing on the unfinished third span when it succumbed to the raging torrent of the river below. LaSalle was thrown to the safety of the completed part of the structure. One man was instantly killed, and the other two received bruises but swam to safety. After other problems and delays, the project eventually was completed. The February 3, 1874, *Kershaw Gazette* read, "The Bridge Commissioners having in charge the building of the Free Bridge across the Wateree river, report that they have accomplished the work—that it is a sound and substantial structure."

Other Bridges and Roads

Other bridges throughout the county were not reported sound. In the same year, 1874, the grand jury investigation revealed the county "roads and bridges almost impassable." This listing included the "Summerville Road from Liberty Hill to the Lancaster line and the River road from Liberty Hill to Vaughan's gin house, on Sander's Creek." The report also listed other problem areas: the bridge over Beaver Creek on the river road ("down for over a year"); the bridge across Granny's Quarter Creek, near the Canty place; the bridge across Sanders Creek at Vaughan's gin house; and bridges across Little Lynches Creek (Jones' Bridge), on the Bishopville road (Green Bridge), across Pine-tree Creek, and over the Big Lynches (Tiller's Bridge). The grand jury concluded: "These roads are the main highways of the county, and lead directly to the county market, and demand prompt and effectual attention." The May 6 newspaper reported that several planks were still required to finish the Beaver Creek bridge.

Not only was travel perilous out in the countryside, but conditions were also at times unsafe for pedestrians in town. A notice in the November 9, 1871, *Camden Journal* called attention "to the condition of a foot bridge on the west side of Market street between Rutledge and DeKalb streets, as its present condition makes a pitfall for the unwary traveler, who has to pass that way before the gas is lighted." On March 11, 1874, the *Kershaw Gazette* reported, "That rough, ragged and rocky place just this side of Chesnut's Ferry, which everyone who has passed well remember, has been worked upon . . . and is now a safe, smooth and satisfactory road." However, by 1876 the same paper was again complaining of the "unsightly condition of the public road leading from Camden to Chesnut's Ferry."[38] As ever, use and weather continued to strain road conditions and to burden the public purse.

Railroad Travel

While offering an alternative to overland roads, restored railroad travel was not without problems. Even at its best, railroad service was slow and cumbersome—perhaps as long as four and a half hours between Camden and Columbia. The

September 5, 1872, *Camden Journal* criticized railroad management: "Just after the war, when in their wisdom in the management of the S.C. Railroad had our track taken up for 13 miles [apparently to reuse rails elsewhere because of post-war shortages], Sumter took a good portion of our legitimate trade from us." The newspaper on October 10, 1872, printed a new schedule for service between Camden and Columbia. A train left Camden about 7:20 A.M. daily with arrival in Columbia expected between noon and 5:00 P.M. The Camden-bound train left Columbia at 2:10 P.M. with an estimated arrival between 5:00 and 7:00 P.M. For some time neither river, highway, nor railroad travel was efficient enough to support efficient economic development.

Education

One crucial reform during Reconstruction was in public education. Largely nonexistent before the war except for children of the privileged, basic educational opportunities expanded after the war for children, and sometimes adults, of both races. In addition to local advocates, outsiders also spearheaded such efforts, a number of them under the Freedmen's Bureau. Private schools operated as well for families who could afford them or at the impetus of northern benevolent or missionary societies.

Research by Harvey S. Teal indicates that nine schools for Kershaw District freedmen were in operation in 1866.[39] The May 13, 1867, Camden town minutes include a request by Reverend B. F. Whittemore, superintendent of education, for a school site on the "Public Square" at the corner of DeKalb and Campbell streets.[40] A May 20 letter from Whittemore offers thanks "in behalf of the Freedmen." At least one school existed prior to this time. Teal points out that Justus K. Jillson, a teacher in Massachusetts before the war, had come to Camden a year earlier—in 1866—"to teach in a 'colored' school as an employee of the Freedmen's Bureau." A number of northern teachers and missionaries set to work almost immediately at war's end. One was Sarah Babcock, who before leaving Camden to return home to Massachusetts to marry the Reverend James Mather, purchased the old Lang family plantation home at DeKalb and Campbell streets. For several years after she left, the home and property were rented from her for school and residential use by the missionary teachers. Sarah Mather kept alive in her mind for many years the dream of a fine educational facility there to train young black scholars as teachers.

Jillson, who served as state superintendent of education from 1868 until 1876, left records from his first three years that shed light on education during that critical time. Apparently by this time public schools were not being staffed by the numbers of northern teachers reported earlier. Jillson's records identify thirty schools in Kershaw County—eighteen "white" and twelve "colored." They also name teachers and students, describe the length of school sessions and types of school buildings, and identify the owners of the buildings. In the case of the Stephenson School "located six miles below Camden on T. L. Boykin's land," one report indicated the school's owner as "the M.E. Church," while another stated it to be "owned by 'Freemen.'"

The eighteen white schools were one-teacher schools with an average of twenty-four students per class. All the teachers were white southerners, but only two were female. The reported sessions ranged from 1 month to 10 months and averaged 4.2 months; a "month" was considered twenty days. There were usually two sessions, which corresponded with the agricultural cycles of planting, cultivating, and harvesting crops.

Thirteen teachers and one assistant operated the twelve schools for blacks. Eleven of the employees were southern black males. Of the three white females, two were southern and one northern. Like their counterparts for whites, all buildings but one were single-teacher schools. Class size, however, was larger in the black schools, averaging forty per class. Sessions were shorter, averaging three months and four days, with two sessions reported as only fifteen days.[41] The combination of marginally trained teachers using outdated, hand-me-down books in less than comfortable buildings seems stark by modern standards, but it was a considerable step toward providing universal public education in Kershaw County.

In addition to tax-supported schools, individuals continued to open or reopen private schools. An advertisement in the *Camden Journal* on February 2, 1871, notified the community of the resumption of exercises with a "Great Reduction in price of Tuition." An institution conducted by W. Beaumont Clarkson and Mrs. M. Louise Clarkson offered French and music as well as English and mathematics. Mr. Joseph C. Nettles, "a one legged Confederate veteran," published a notice entitled "Public School" in the *Journal & Gazette* for July 26, 1877, that he had opened a "school for boys at the DeKalb House." A number of well-educated men and women lacking funds and seeking first-time employment in the postwar years turned a hand toward teaching. Private tutoring as well as private schooling were also available.

The cost of implementing public schools being high, many citizens resentfully associated them with the mismanagement and graft of state government. A taxpayers' revolt occurred in the present Bethune area in mid-1872. Voters considering a tax measure learned that their local teachers had been paid less than 60 percent of the money previously raised for their salaries and that there was no money left in the treasury to pay them the rest. Therefore, according to the July 18 *Camden Journal,* voters resolved "that we, the legal voters and tax-payers in School District No. 5, known by the local name of Lysenby . . . do agree, that until the free school law be intelligently, faithfully and honestly administered, that we will not lay any tax on our property, for the support of free schools in this district."

Religion

People of faith in postwar years confronted the current conditions by wrestling with the timeless issues of acceptance, blame, guilt, and revenge and by examining beliefs in rewards and punishments. With freedmen being encouraged to develop leadership abilities, in the early months after the war black believers withdrew from old houses of worship and formed separate churches that became centers of instruction for spiritual, political, social, and economic freedom. Educational opportunities, previously available only to children of the privileged, presented possibilities to those of both races and all economic levels. Both churches and educational institutions aided in overcoming economic and political woes.

The war and its aftermath had an impact on the religious community of the area just as they affected other aspects. Churches, after having split sectionally before the war, now divided racially. Northern missionaries accompanied the occupation troops that came into the district after the war; these missionaries assisted black churchgoers' efforts to form their own churches. At first glance it seems somewhat ironic that at a time when blacks were joining whites in politics and economics, facets of society previously denied them, they were withdrawing from the one component of culture in which they had previously participated. It appears that blacks were self-motivated to withdraw; northern missionaries aided their efforts, and white church members offered what assistance they could. As freedmen were moving into other areas where they would compete with whites, perhaps both races were eager for blacks to have one segment they could control apart from their former masters. The mind-set of most whites throughout the nation was still that blacks were a race subordinate in potential.

Church records, like other records during Reconstruction confusion, are often missing or incomplete. However, a Camden Methodist minute book that resumed on January 23, 1869, noted that in October of that year the trustees resolved to sell the Rock Spring (upper Kershaw District) and Pinder Hill (West Wateree) churches, both of which had been organized as part of the prewar Wateree Mission. African Methodist Episcopal (A.M.E.) churches were organized in the areas of those churches after the war. In addition the Camden Methodist Church voted in 1872 to sell its DeKalb Street property to the black congregation.[42]

Camden Baptist Church also suffered from the war and its aftermath. It suffered financial loss as well as membership loss. Few records have survived from the war years, but the church, like the rest of society, struggled along as best it could. Indicative of the hard times, the Baptists did not send a letter or any contributions to the Charleston Association in 1865, 1866, or 1867.

In 1866 its black members withdrew to form their own church. By the end of a day-long meeting on January 22, black Baptists, assisted by two northern missionaries serving as moderator and clerk, had crafted a resolution "that the time has come when our religious interests and the wants of our people demand that we form ourselves into a separate church." The clerk, Reverend James Hamilton of the American Baptist Missionary Convention, drew up a letter to the Camden Baptist Church requesting letters of dismissal for fifty-four male and fifty female members. The new church, Mt. Moriah, called the freedman Monroe Boykin as its pastor, a position he held for thirty-four years until his death. Reverend Boykin was also credited with founding most of the black Baptist churches in Clarendon, Lancaster, Sumter, and Kershaw counties.[43] On September 23, 1873, Liberty Hill Presbyterian Church granted permission to twenty-five black members to form their own church.[44]

Bethlehem Missionary Baptist Church, active in Lugoff, was founded in 1866 "to give the African-Americans in this community the opportunity to freely worship God in their own environment." Bethlehem "was the first African-American Baptist Church to be organized in the West Wateree section of Kershaw County."[45]

When the war ended, the plantation owner Callie Perkins gave her former slaves the property (several acres) in West Wateree at the head of the branch later known as Buck's Crossing, where they had been meeting for religious purposes "as long as they made no disturbances in the neighborhood."[46] They built a house of worship to replace the brush arbor they had been using and joined the South Carolina Methodist Conference. Their church, Ephesus, is still active.

The camp meetings that had been prewar evangelical traditions in many churches were popularly enjoyed by black denominations, although white enthusiasm dwindled. Whites, in fact, grew suspicious and even antagonistic about black camp meetings, where political speaking mixed with and often overshadowed spiritual teaching. In the electioneering period of 1872 the August 22 *Camden Journal* reported "a large colored camp meeting" near Liberty Hill, attended by many people from Camden. The October 15 newspaper reported that south of Camden, "A religious revival of considerable magnitude has been going on for several days at Town Creek, about four miles below town. The camp and tabernacle are situated in the midst of a swamp, Town Creek running around two sides of it, and an impenetrable canebreak on the West." The reporter attempted a cautionary warning: the possibility of an outbreak of fever in such conditions.

Temperance

Citizens grew widely stirred to join in a fight against what they held to be at the root of many of the community's problems—excessive use of alcohol. At an August 1872 "meeting of the colored citizens of Camden and vicinity at the colored Methodist Church," twenty-seven persons formed the Camden Temperance

Society for "action in the suppression of intemperance and the promotion of virtue and good morals in the community." John Chesnut, who chaired the meeting, was elected president. The group heard remarks from the invited guest

A. M. Kennedy of Wateree no. 9, the white temperance organization.

Kennedy also headed a temperance meeting at "Lynchwood Church" in August, reporting afterward that the church could not accommodate the large crowd. The benches were taken outside and arranged under the trees, to be occupied by the ladies and members of the Wateree Division. Following the meeting, those present "partook of a bounteous repast." Members of Wateree no. 9 continued to assist in the organization of other groups. In September a new division opened in West Wateree with Dr. William R. Nelson as worthy patriarch. In July 1874 the Sandy Hill Division formed six miles below Camden. In December a large two-night meeting at the town hall in Camden brought in the public to hear the famous temperance lecturer Edward Carswell of Canada.

Organizations for Improvements

Several gleanings from the 1872 Camden newspapers show other evidence of elected officials' and citizens' efforts to improve the community. The town council passed a resolution on April 15 to divide Camden into four wards. The intendant was Jno. M. Davis, and the wardens were John D. Kennedy, John Kershaw, William Deas, and Andrew Dibble. Two wards apparently were predominately white, two black. A list of the "Supervisors of Election" for the county's nine precincts indicated representation by both Democrats and Republicans.

Commercial improvements included "Capt." Wm. Clyburn's erection of three "neat and substantial buildings on Main Street" and "Capt." W. L. DePass's plan to construct four stores fronting on Broad Street "with many of the latest improvements for light, ventilation, and so on" to make it "one of the most attractive business resorts in town." These examples of up-to-date development contrasted with enduring older businesses. A concurrent advertisement by L. Rich of Camden, for example, offered to purchase any quantity of hides, sheep pelts, rags, wool, old copper, brass, lead, iron, and so forth. Rich was located in the Workman Building, Broad Street, the second door from the corner of Rutledge Street.

Various groups that came together for sociability or expediency in the postwar years also began to work for cultural, economic, or political improvements for the town and county. The Survivors Association of Kershaw County had organized among veterans by 1872, at least half a dozen years before a similar statewide organization. With General J. B. Kershaw as president, the group held regular meetings in the town hall, where concerns included efforts to relieve the contemporary difficulties of former Confederates and families.

Grangers

In July 1872 another town-hall meeting resulted in an influential step, the organization of a local unit of the National Grange of the Order of the Patrons of Husbandry, a national group organized after the war to restore "kindly feelings" among the people. William M. Shannon introduced the main speaker, D. Wyatt Aiken, who spoke urgently about the ways people in an agricultural society could work together for self-improvement. According to the newspaper, "He said the middle belt of South Carolina was the Paradise of the world: that nature had strewn her gifts upon us with lavish hand: that we all were complaining and restless and considered ourselves extremely poor." Aiken urged "redeeming our prosperity in an intelligent and educated manner."

At the first meeting of Wateree Grange no. 43, Shannon was elected master (president) and John Kershaw, secretary. Master of the Grange that formed at Flat Rock was Dr. J. I. Trantham. The following year W. K. Thompson was secretary of the Liberty Hill Grange. Representatives attended state and regional conventions, sharing ideas and becoming prompters of improvements that spilled from the fields into all aspects of life. The 1872 Wateree Agricultural Fair drew crowds to "the old fairground on Magazine Hill."

Unraveling Republican Control

Although Democrats would not yet regain power in the elections of 1872, a splintering within the Republican Party began locally as well as nationally. Some in the party attempted to change its direction from within, becoming known as "Bolters" and "Reformers," some seeking to return focus to the ideals of Lincoln. Area Republican "Regulars" such as Justus K. Jillson, Samuel Place, and C. Shiver were linked to the gubernatorial candidate F. J. Moses, whom others discredited for scandal. Local opponents—the Bolters—included C. C. Bowen and a man named Ferguson. Both factions waged lively campaigns. The Camden newspaper for September 12, 1872, referred to two separate days of politicking. The Bolters learned of a rally discreetly planned by the Regulars and "sent out runners to notify their adherents to come into town the same day." That Saturday being marked by "fiery heat," a throng began to gather in Camden. "The Regulars were taken by surprise, but could not decline to give the other side a hearing," continued the newspaper, "and at twelve o'clock, a motley crowd wended their way to the grove near the colored public school house," where speakers extolled their virtues and criticized their opposition.

The following Monday night the two factions held separate meetings complete with name-calling and "a huge amount of gas expended by both sides." The October 15 article added, "The Bolters had the best of the music this time as they engaged the services of the colored band and drew quite a crowd." The *Journal* commended the two factions for avoiding "disturbances of any note" but commented that "the rivals are becoming more and more irreconcilably separated." The town council, recognizing the possibilities for violence, voted to augment the regular four policemen by hiring an additional sixteen—eight whites, eight blacks—for election day.

Seventy-two delegates—eight from each precinct—attended the Regular nominating convention, which put forth the black candidates Henry Cardozo for senator and A. W. Hough, Reuben Gaither, and Frank Adamson for representatives. The delegates nominated for sheriff Samuel Place, who had come to the district in 1866 as a captain in command of a detachment of occupying federal troops. They also nominated R. E. Wall for clerk of court, Frank Carter for school commissioner, and John A. Boswell, Daniel Johnson, and David McCaskill for county commissioners.

Only five of the nine precincts—Camden, Flat Rock, Cureton's Mill, Swift Creek, and Red Hill—sent delegates to the Bolters' convention. Their slate included the following: representatives—John A. Chesnut, Scott Brown, and William Boykin; sheriff—J. S. Meroney; clerk of court—A. Dibble; school commissioner—James Whitaker; county commissioners—J. F. Sutherland, chairman, Frank Moses, and Daniel Harris.

The following week the newspaper carried notice of a meeting the next day. Urged by a circular from General J. B. Kershaw, the "conservative citizens of this precinct" were to meet at the town hall "to organize a Club to carry out the purposes put forth in that call." The notice carried the names Edward M. Boykin, Wm. M. Shannon, and J. D. Kennedy. Throughout the period local newspapers employed the name "Conservative" for Democrat and "Radical" for Republican, and they described the former with reserved dignity and used satiric ridicule in lengthy reports on the latter. Confrontations were detailed at political rallies, especially if they indicated Radical disturbances. In October near Bettyneck in West Wateree, an altercation with the clerk of court candidate R. E. Wall prompted Wash Benny to draw a pistol.

Election Results

The election of 1872, which many outnumbered white voters avoided, was immediately followed with complaints of irregularities. A local report on October 24 stated that Cureton's Mill had opened for a general election only once since the war and did not open for this election. Lizenby had not opened either as the managers failed to attend, the clerk having gone "coonhunting" instead. Lizenby voters had to travel six or seven miles further to Raley's Mill to vote. The Buffalo poll was also closed, necessitating its voters to travel twelve to fifteen miles further to Raley's Mill as well.

The Regulars carried the election, their closest call being the sheriff's race, which Place won by 260 votes. His Bolter opponent, John S. Meroney, lodged an election protest. His complaints were those above in addition to the fact that a new poll had opened at Liberty Hill and that no notices had been published about the election date. He further alleged that election commissioners and managers had not been sworn and that two commissioners of election were also candidates.[47]

The substantial reelection of Republican Regulars in 1872 was seen as an indication that the party associated with national and state spoils was not to be reformed within. Elected as governor was the Sumter scalawag Franklin J. Moses, who had been involved in Kershaw County land fraud and earned the epithet "the robber governor." Wade Hampton stepped to the forefront, calling for southern whites to band together to "dedicate themselves to the redemption of the South." The call would echo through the following four years into the explosive election of 1876.

Advertising Assets

One tactic of concerned citizens to counter the negative conditions under which they were living was to promote local assets in hopes of attracting worthy new inhabitants and investors. The *Camden Journal* for November 28, 1872, printed a lengthy letter from William M. Shannon designed to attract attention and investment. Shannon, who was a leader in the local Grange movement, shared many of the attitudes and approaches of the organization, although it was not part of the letter.

In his letter Shannon extolled the virtues of the local area, recalling its heritage from the Revolution through the "last, unhappy struggle." He heaped lavish praise upon the landscape—"the fertile valley lands" profuse with "corn, wheat, oats, peas, pumpkins, rice, and cotton." He appealed "to the Northern people to come in and settle." He presented opportunities for capitalists ("come and take these glorious water powers"), farmers ("come and be our neighbors in delightful homes"), laborers (who in a year or two could be "independently settled for life"), and "Gentlemen of ease and taste" ("come an[d] buy these mansions, whose owners want more contracted homes").

The July 17, 1873, *Camden Journal* contained an editorial similar to Shannon's letter. It pointed to the excellent location of Camden with many roads providing access to "ten thousand (10,000) acres of unused, unappropriated lands" within five miles of the town. Small farms of one hundred to two hundred acres could be bought for five to twelve dollars per acre, "water and timber being abundant on all, and every locality perfectly healthy, except on the 'Charleston Road' and the 'River Road,' and for these, sand-hill retreats are easily procured."

The July 24, 1873, Camden newspaper reported that to date, sixteen thousand bales of cotton had been shipped from the railroad depot. A week later the paper stated, "Even on Broad Street, we see attractive private residences surrounded by lots in the Sandhills of cotton, ranging in size from five to twenty acres, all of which promise a bale of cotton to the acre. This is a happy combination of the ornamental and useful for nothing is prettier than a well-cultivated cotton field. Surely, nothing, in this section, is more profitable than cotton."

The *Kershaw Gazette* on April 29, 1874, quoted the opinion of another local Granger, Dr. E. M. Boykin, on agriculture of the area: "Now these lands, by the change of the supply of labor, must necessarily be broken up into farms, and each man must cultivate his own holding with himself and his family, as the nucleus of his labor system. . . . The poorest of our native whites, who under the old system, could not get a footing on these lands are now a thriving people." It is interesting that Boykin was describing a system similar to the "forty acres and a mule" concept. It is also worthy of note that he referred to "the old system" but did not refer to slavery. Furthermore, while he was accurate that poor whites had been unable to "get a footing" on lands, it was overstating it to say that in 1874 they were "a thriving people."

An editorial in the May 27, 1874, *Kershaw Gazette* offered advice to improve the economy. The article advocated the developing of cotton mills in the county, which "offered one of the best localities in South Carolina." Camden, it stated, "set at the head of steamboat navigation on the Wateree River, and upon one of the termini of the South Carolina Railroad connected through it, with all the roads in the State," provided an ideal site for a manufacturing center. The article focused on Big Pine Tree Creek, which "never fails in the driest season," with its five mill seats, "the fartherest 10 miles from the town." The editorial offered considerable detail on four sites—the McRae estate, Marengo Mills, the Perkins tract, and the DuBose estate.

Some in the community were anxious to promote greater use of the Wateree River for transportation. The *Kershaw Gazette* on March 11, 1874, reported that since the previous December, Captain William Rush and the steamer *Lillington* had been running a regular schedule. On June 3 the newspaper printed the following account of a special excursion of the steamer entitled "A Trip on the Wateree":

> The party took boat just above the new bridge, about 9 o'clock in the morning, with the sun somewhat shaded by light clouds, and a delightful breeze; moving up stream to the head of navigation—Graves' Ford, seven miles up the river and about a mile above Chesnut's Ferry, past the old boatyard, and the warehouse established by the well known enterprise of Capt. Parker. After going as far up as was safe to do, on account of the shoals, the boat was made fast, and some two or three of the stock-holders took the yawl, and pulled up to the shoals themselves—looking out, we believe, for a way round them, so as to open up navigation to the fine stretch of river that runs up into the Liberty Hill country. Those left

> upon the boat consoled themselves it appears, SATISFACTORILY, during the absence of the party up stream, by making use of various appliances, heretofore concealed in boxes, baskets and possibly a jug or two, and then the deliciously clear, cool, running water suggested to some one a "bath," and soon the river was filled with a splashing cro[w]d that made up quite a scene . . . no doubt, made at the same spot, long before the white man knew the country; for it seemed especially adapted for an Indian bathing place.
>
> On the return of the yawl, the boat dropped down to "Parker's Landing," where in a shady spot a table was spread. . . . After dinner and a very pleasant time, enlivened by free intercourse and exchange of sentiment, and much good feeling, the party turned down stream and landed all "right" again at the bridge getting home in good time, and in good condition.

Perhaps the frequent advertisements of the area's positive features paid dividends. Certainly they may have encouraged residents. The *Kershaw Gazette* on February 3, 1874, reported the arrival of fourteen immigrants in Camden: "All of them were robust young men, of whom seven are Irish and seven English." The group was initially provided shelter in the town hall and then readily found employment on area plantations. Judging from the activity of the cotton growers and apparent ease with which jobs could be obtained, it does not seem that the Panic of 1873 that so adversely affected the commercial and industrial sections of the country impacted the local agricultural economy to a great extent.

Quite possibly publicity promotions additionally attracted the eventual attention of some of the northerners who invested locally later in the decade. Their most immediate effect, like that of similar efforts throughout the South, was to woo through favorable impressions of southern people in the northern press. Journalists in the North began ridiculing Reconstruction legislators as southern newspapers had been doing for some time. In the process of "redemption," Edgar concludes, "the white community won the propaganda war by successfully manipulating the Northern press."[48]

Continued Problems

Local complaints continued against conditions under the Reconstruction government. The January 22, 1874, *Camden Journal* reported a local court case and the judge's reaction afterward. In the case of *State v. Cyrus Clarkson* the black defendant was charged with grand larceny in stealing cattle: "The Jury, composed of colored men, brought in a verdict of 'not guilty,' contrary to overwhelming and conclusive evidence of the guilt of the prisoner. No one upon the Jury was able to write the verdict, and the Judge ordered the Clerk of Court to endorse it upon the record, and the foreman to make his 'mark.'" The article continued, "His Honor then commented upon the conduct of the Jury

Commissioners in drawing men grossly illiterate and incompetent to serve as Jurymen, rebuked the Jury for their total disregard of all law and evidence in the case, ordered that their names be stricken from the Jury list, and that the Sheriff furnish 24 men of intelligence and integrity from which another Jury might be selected." The judge added that to his regret, he could not set aside the verdict, which under law must stand.

Even minor incidents of legislative behavior were reported in local papers with satiric ridicule and likely some bias. For example, the May 3, 1876, *Kershaw Gazette* related that Ebenezer George, "the Honorable Member from Kershaw," had indicted the police officer Winyah Jones for assault and battery. The legislator and his party were "enjoying a spree and creating some disturbance unbecoming a citizen of this quiet and peaceable corporation" when he "had to be taken in limbo" by Officer Jones. Representative George "thought his dignity had been impaired by the arrest, inasmuch as he is a member of the Legislature of South Carolina," and "as soon as he became in a suitable condition he swore out a warrant for the arrest of Jones."

As in earlier periods of contention, fires continued to be serious problems. Even spontaneous ones seemed to raise the dreaded specter of arson. On January 5, 1874, the *Journal* printed letters of thanks from Camden merchants to the citizens and fire companies, "especially the colored portion of our population," who had responded to a postmidnight fire that had threatened "the very heart of the business centre of town." The March 18 *Gazette* article described "Terrible Flames" that destroyed a downtown building and burned seven houses. The *Gazette* on July 15 reported that John M. Perry of Liberty Hill had lost his dwelling, smokehouse, kitchen, and two outbuildings as a result of the "work of some rascally incendiary." Perry's loss, like that of most other victims of fire, was uninsured. The Camden post office burned on the night of February 19, 1875.

A curiosity and an ominous omen of violence emerged in 1875 from the bottom of Factory Pond where it had been discarded thirty years earlier. When water was lowered for a floodgate repair, Clark Williams recovered "the Iron Man," a prewar dueling target in the shape of the side silhouette of a standing man. After its retrieval, this figure was again put in use for another five years to hone the aim of men preparing for a duel. Williams kept the target on the front porch of his country home Cedar and Pines at Spring Hill.[49] Amid other contentions, dueling fever had not died out, although for a while those inclined toward dueling seemed united in ousting a common foe.

The End of Reconstruction

In the midsummer heat of 1876 violence rocked South Carolina in the election campaign between the incumbent governor, Daniel H. Chamberlain, and his opponent, Wade Hampton. Typical rhetoric emerged in the Democratic mass meeting in late July at Turkey Creek Church, about twenty miles northeast of Camden. Organizers, quoted in the *Kershaw Gazette,* derided the present government, which "under the pretense of being the poor man's friend, has ground him to the earth with a burden of taxes he cannot pay." They also indicted incumbents for "destroying the confidence of man in man," bringing "financial embarrassment upon the country," and disgracing "the judicial branch of the State by electing the worst men of both races, in order to enrich thieving officeholders and oppress the suffering people."

The Democrats invited "every person, of every race and color, who sincerely desires purity, honesty and economy in our State government, and consequent low taxation, to unite with us in an effort to redeem the State from the group of corrupt and unprincipled adventurers in this the centennial year of American

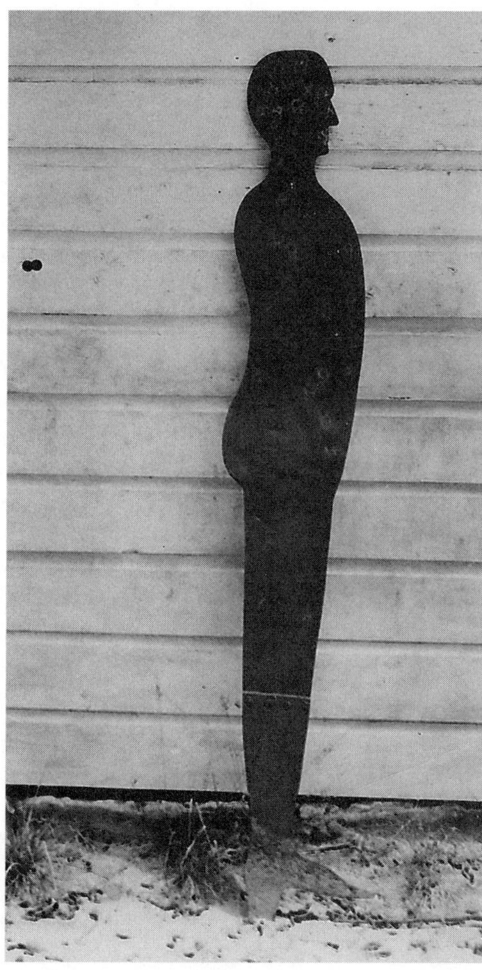

The life-sized "Iron Man" target used for dueling practice. Courtesy of the Rachel Montgomery family

independence." The campaign struggle proclaimed national identity with its heroic Revolutionary War references to 1776.

The period of hotly contested political struggles was marked by fires—acts of suspected or admitted arson committed by both sides and targeting both black and white citizens. In March near Knights Hill, two churches "belonging to colored people" were burned. In July arsonists targeted the house of "John Carlos (colored)" in Camden, and in late October there was an attempt to fire the residence of Dr. W. E. Aiken in Camden. The intensity of incidents increased in mid-November with the incineration of W. A. Ancrum's storehouse and a stock of goods near Camden and of Ancrum's store on Swift Creek the following day, the latter a two-thousand-dollar loss. A week later Jim Stuckey and John Anderson, two "colored Democrats" living southeast of Camden, were burned out. Dr. John I. Trantham of Flat Rock suffered a six-hundred-dollar loss in early December when his barn and stables were torched.[50]

The redemption movement locally reached a fever pitch on October 9, 1876, when a huge rally welcomed Wade Hampton to Camden. The boom of "rusty old Revolutionary cannon" that had been resurrected for the event awakened patriotic memories. As was the case everywhere he had gone during the campaign, Hampton was accompanied by and met by orderly bands of mounted men wearing red hunting shirts. So impressive was the effect everywhere in the state that the contest became known as "the Red Shirt campaign." The presence of mounted men unified in a common cause—with many former Confederates among them—also stirred recall of recent resistance in the "late unpleasantness."

The *Kershaw Gazette* described a torchlight parade of five thousand men that escorted Hampton to the speaker's platform at the town square, thereafter known by his name. Hampton Grove, bounded by DeKalb, Lyttleton, Fair, and Hampton streets, has also been called Hampton Square but is presently known as Hampton Park. Men from all over the county and from surrounding counties had come for support.

In contrast, the visit to Camden by Hampton's opponent, Chamberlain, appears to have been more somber. As Kirkland and Kennedy describe it, "throngs of negroes packed the sidewalks, and between these dark lanes, defiantly rode endless columns of mounted Red Shirts, gathered from this and adjoining counties. Perfect bedlam reigned for hours."[51]

The same day that Hampton visited Camden, Governor Chamberlain requested that federal troops be sent to South Carolina. On October 17 President Grant issued a proclamation that placed federal troops at the call of the governor. On October 27 Battery K of the Third Artillery, consisting of twenty-nine enlisted men and four officers under the command of Captain L. L. Livingston, established a camp at Camden near the railroad station. Furthermore, Grant ordered the disbursal of all southern white gun clubs and hunting clubs.

The fountain honoring Confederate soldier Richard Kirkland, who risked his life to take water to wounded enemy soldiers at the Battle of Fredericksburg. This memorial stands at the center of Hampton Park, a long-time site of social and political gatherings.

Southerners reorganized into "music clubs" and "baseball clubs," generally mounted ones. Men continued to wear red shirts and to ride horseback.

The election, like others during Reconstruction, was wrought with irregularity. Locally as in other parts of the state, many of the tactics employed by Regular and Reformer Republicans in the previous election surfaced in this one—some polls did not open, some opened in other places, voters were sent long distances to find an open poll, some voters were intimidated, some ballot boxes were stuffed with handwritten ballots, and some ballot boxes never made it to the places where they were to be counted. Red-shirted men milled about polls, some riding from poll to poll and voting at each place. Georgians migrated in and voted in the counties adjacent to the Savannah River, and some precincts recorded more votes than there were eligible voters. Hampton "won" by a little more than one thousand votes. Kirkland and Kennedy observe: "Camden went into ecstasy. Barrels of Rosen blazed in huge bonfires at every street corner; men embraced and leapt for joy."[52]

Chamberlain's supporters cried fraud; both Republicans and Democrats claimed victory. When the redeemers arrived at the State House, they were confronted by federal troops. Hampton convinced his followers to relocate, and there they convened as a body politic. Chamberlain and his supporters organized in the State House. For four months South Carolina had two rival governments. White taxpayers refused to pay their "legitimate" taxes, instead upon request voluntarily sending 10 percent of their previous year's tax to Hampton's government. With the Republican government's coffers depleted, state agencies turned to the rival regime for operating revenue.

Democrats and Republicans had other problems in the nation's capital. The Republican Rutherford Hayes had defeated the Democrat Samuel Tilden by just one electoral vote in an election equally as tainted as that in South Carolina. A special "election committee" had awarded all twenty-two disputed votes (seven from South Carolina)—any one of which would have awarded the presidency to Tilden—to Hayes. Democrats vowed to block Hayes's inauguration.

Anxious to have at least four more years in the White House, Republicans offered compromises. They would agree to federal subsidization of southern railroads and, most important, to withdraw the last of the federal troops from Florida, Louisiana, and South Carolina.

Thus, for political expediency, national Republicans abandoned southern Reconstruction, clearing the way for native whites to reclaim the government. After Hayes was inaugurated without incident, he was visited by both South Carolina "governors." Convinced that Hampton, not Chamberlain, controlled the state, President Hayes ordered the troop withdrawal on April 3, 1877, and a week later they began to leave. On April 11 Chamberlain, with no funds and no army to sustain him, withdrew from the State House, leaving Hampton unopposed. Federal Reconstruction was over.

The years 1865 to 1877—the Reconstruction period—were one of Kershaw County's most tumultuous eras, marked by victories and defeats, successes and failures, cooperation and conflict, renewal and destruction. Reconstruction had begun, as the war ended, with an enemy army present. It ended with white power, heralding an era of racist control under what became known as "Jim Crow" laws.[53] Although the era ended with the county divided, during the time, despite the trials and tribulations, there were some indications that northerners and southerners and blacks and whites could cooperate, and those signs offered hope for the future.

11

Iron Rails and Soil Rows

Toward a New Century

In the late 1800s an impoverished Kershaw County headed toward the twentieth century while struggling to stabilize economic, political, and social conditions. Across the county and the state agriculture devolved to even smaller farms dependent on sharecropping and a crop lien system under which many survived but few flourished. Camden expanded as a winter health resort for wealthy northerners and reincorporated as a city. Industrialization lagged, although east of Camden one cotton mill in 1890 and another in 1900 attracted some traditional farm families who sought the security of wages and homes in two adjacent mill villages. Late in the nineteenth century promises of railroad expansions would begin to affect tourism, business, and industrialization. At railroad stops scattered rural dwellers collected or would begin to collect into new communities. As the century wound down, Kershaw County had glimpses of future changes.

Following the 1876 "redemption," as contemporary lingo termed the election of Governor Wade Hampton, many citizens hoped that daily life would settle into a pleasant peacefulness, accented with benefits of public improvements. In some ways such changes appeared to be under way by the following year. A congenial *Journal and Gazette* column in July 1877 described life in the farming section of Granny's Quarter, where abundant rain was favoring good corn and cotton crops. A social highlight was a recent "seining frolic at the river" that "took in out of the wet 250 catfish" and served up a big stew and fry. Several days later, when high water thwarted the seining of the river, fishermen seined Granny's Quarter Creek, resulting in "a feast of gar [a boney fish] and a flow of stew." Rural dwellers appeared to be making their good-humored best of situations.

Although patterns of agriculture significantly shifted to a prevalence of small farms, Kershaw County retained some large-scale operations, mostly in areas that had experienced less wartime invasion. In the same 1877 newspaper issue, a journalist described a visit to a thirty-five-hundred-acre plantation of the Camden merchant-brothers Herman and Mannes Baum on the western bank of the Wateree. Here Lewis M. Watts, the manager, oversaw fifty top hands and twenty-seven mules. At the Big Level, Sikes' Neck, Shelter Piece, and Gibson's

Neck sections of the plantation, the writer viewed 150 of the "finest cattle we ever saw, and hogs innumerable," as well as crops of cotton, oats, peas, and two hundred acres of "as fine corn as ever grew anywhere."

Other planting operations in West Wateree were also extensive. A September 1878 newspaper reported that two of those planters sent to market twenty thousand bushels of rice that fall, although the recent freshet had seriously damaged corn crops. The heaviest losses were one thousand bushels to J. B. Hammond and two thousand bushels to J. L. Gettys.

Since farming acreage and labor were reduced in most parts of the county, interest in how to maximize crop yields was widespread. "Every town lot in Camden can be made to produce two crops of grain annually," advised the November 21, 1878, *Kershaw Gazette.* "Plant small grain now, reap in May or June, and then put in a crop of late corn. It is important that every edge be made to cut now-a-days." Rural communities held spirited competitions to improve yields. For example, growers at Shaylor's Hill in 1878 vied to produce the greatest number of sweet potatoes per one-fourth acre.

Agricultural production included more than row crops. Turpentiners in an expanding industry tapped mature stands of longleaf pines in natural forestlands across the county. The April 2, 1878, *Camden Journal* estimated that "$200,000 worth of turpentine will be produced in the county this year." The article stated that "most of it will go [down the Wateree River from Camden] by Steamer *Lillington* to Acton, and thence [by railroad] to Wilmington." The 1883 *Kershaw Gazette* announced a new enterprise opening on York Street in Camden: "A cooper shop, for the manufacture of turpentine barrels." The distinctive scent of pine pitch, or gum, wafted through many sections of the county where the bark of living trees was tapped to collect their slow drippings. Aromas also arose from turpentine distilleries and tar pits.

Transportation—Problems and Progress

Citizens who may have wondered where federal troops went in 1877 after they were pulled out of the South had only to follow national developments in local press reports: "The question now is, will the troops be sent to fight the Indians or the 'strikers'?" On one hand, the United States government was embroiled on the Great Plains, where General George A. Custer's Seventh Cavalry had been annihilated at the Battle of Little Big Horn the previous year. On the other hand, northern commerce and industry were being stymied by a crippling railroad strike "extend[ing] to all the great lines leading from the West to New York, Philadelphia and Baltimore, embracing engineers, firemen, brakes men, train hands, section masters, road hands and machinists." Because of bloody riots in Maryland and Pennsylvania, several state governors called on the president for assistance in preserving the peace.[1]

The Branch Railroad

Not connected to these great lines, the only railroad in Kershaw County faced no strikes but had its own problems. The line that reached Camden was still only a terminal branch of the financially strapped South Carolina Railroad (SCRR) and went nowhere except the direction from which it came. The July 26, 1877, *Journal and Gazette* complained that "discriminating and illiberal" railroad policy had "driven from Camden, and consequently from Charleston, several thousand bales of cotton annually" in favor of "Monroe, Charlotte, Ridgeway and points along the line of the Wilmington, Columbia and Augusta [WC&A] railroad."

The WC&A line, which competed with the SCRR's Camden-to-Charleston route, could be accessed near the Wateree River in lower Richland County at the Acton station near Kensington Plantation, Eastover. At the time, under favorable water conditions, the route of the *Lillington* ran between that point and Camden and on to some points northward. The steamboat service and related railroad connection both benefited and competed with the county's main commercial center at Camden.

In the same July 1877 newspaper, a letter signed "Merchant" described the area around Camden with "nearly three thousand people and sixty stores—some of them doing a large and extensive business, shipping some 15,000 bales of cotton to Charleston annually." Lamenting that cotton once received at Camden from Chesterfield and Lancaster was now going to Charlotte and Monroe for shipment, the writer urged the railroad to develop competing freight facilities in Camden. This improvement would "bring cotton from the vicinity of Sumter, Timmonsville, Mayesville, Bishopville—from Western Darlington, Chesterfield and Lancaster—increasing our receipts by five or ten thousand bales annually, with a proportionate increase of up freight."

The same writer addressed another reason to improve the railroad: "Northern tourists who would spend much of their time in our healthy sand hills, filling our superb dwellings with boarders, tell us that Camden is so difficult of access that they are forced reluctantly to seek less desirable places." The 1877 letter reveals early interest in using Camden's antebellum homes to attract a tourist trade and recognizes the need for railroad cooperation in this and other business endeavors.

Grumbling continued the following year against sluggish railroad management. The newspaper charged in April 1878 that "broken down engines and other dilapidated rolling stock" too often delayed passengers, mails, and freight. Although passenger trains traveled between Camden and Charleston daily except for Sundays, mails were delivered here only three days a week. The inconvenient timing of Camden arrivals and departures was said to encourage passengers to hire conveyances to other train stations at Columbia, Doko (later Blythewood), or Ridgeway.

The same issue described another type of breakdown on the Camden line. Recently the departing train was delayed twenty-eight hours and mail was received forty-eight hours late because of an accident near Boykin's Station. A train to Camden had plowed into four cows that had wandered onto the track. The cows were killed, the engine was derailed, and passengers "made their way to town as best they could."

A Railroad Extended—Origin of Kershaw

By 1877 northern investors had begun extending railroad connections from Camden to Marion, North Carolina. The line of the Charleston, Cincinnati, and Chicago Railroad that prompted a spurt of development in the upper part of the county was popularly called "the Three C's" (or "3C's"). Walter Edgar describes the change from state ownership: "By 1881 the South Carolina Railroad, the 'child of Charleston capital,' was controlled by New Yorkers."[2]

One upper Kershaw County native who took great interest in the railroad development was a former Confederate private and former Union prisoner named James V. Welsh. After the war he tried farming and keeping a store, and being on sandy terrain covered with black oaks and pines, he turned to lumbering. Now with the courtesy title of "Captain," Welsh saw a great opportunity for his sawmill if he could convince the railroad to alter the proposed route, which was originally to pass several miles away. To do this, according to one account, Welsh "offered tempting bait. He proposed to have a town laid out, to give the land needed for the streets, and to give every other lot in the business section to the railroad company. The railroad officials succumbed; a station was built, and the village of Welsh's Station came into being."[3] A short time later Welsh urged that the village's name be changed to honor a man he highly respected, Confederate general J. B. Kershaw, and thus the town of Kershaw resulted. Development rapidly followed.

The laborious process of building the railroad was later described by Melverda O. Gaskin: "The tracks first put down were laid by hard, back-breaking manual labor. Teams of men using horse-drawn pans to dig dirt for building solid bed foundations, worked from dawn to dark, clearing trees, blasting stumps from the ground, digging and hauling dirt to fill in the holes, hauling rough sawed timbers to construct bridges across streams or ravines, sometimes through swamp lands. There were no caterpillar tractors, no backhoes, no giant mechanical jaws to lift and place crossties and rails. Teams of men using spades, picks and mallets smoothed dirt beds, laid crossties, placed rails and anchored them with spikes, all by hand." After the line was completed, Gaskin said, "small stations, many of which had been way stations for wagon trains and stage coach

A postcard view of Kershaw in the early 1900s, after it became a prosperous railroad stop. Courtesy of the Camden Archives

routes, became railway stations. From Camden, there were railway stations at Dusty Bend, Sanders Creek, Shamokin, DeKalb, Clyburn Station, Westville [West], Three C's, Fifty Six, and possibly others now long since forgotten, before the stop at Kershaw."[4]

Bridges and Roads

Land roads and water crossings also required repair or extension in the later nineteenth century. The Wateree Bridge, which had taken so long to replace and repair after the war, failed to maintain public confidence. The original design by Ithiel Town in the 1820s, with trussed sides and roof helping to support the spans, seems to have been abandoned or misunderstood when the postwar bridge was rebuilt on the original spans. No doubt lack of funds and materials, as well as perhaps a lack of engineering knowledge, brought about the decision simply to lay spans atop the old bridge, possibly with rails but without side walls and cover. By oral reports, the sight of the wide, rushing waters of the river made man and beast timid about crossing the bridge, especially given its hazardous reputation acquired from the deaths associated with its reconstruction. After the county completed the bridge, officials applied to the state for a separate appropriation to construct a cover. Thus the sides and roof must have been considered "finishing" rather than basic to the bridge's support, and they were added after the flooring. Possibly the additional weight made the bridge unstable or the cover lacked sufficient support to stand sturdily, but reports of creaking and moaning made travelers and animals uneasy. According to reports, the reputation grew that the bridge was haunted.

Confidence was even shakier after flood damage in 1878, and despite some additional repairs the following year, the court before long determined the bridge to be a liability to the county and ordered it destroyed as a hazard.[5] The ferry operated at its old site near the bridge for at least two years, through 1883. A fragment of a *Kershaw Gazette* that year describes a substantial new flat constructed to operate for the Camden Ferry as twelve feet by sixty-eight feet, not including aprons.

In 1883, at a changed location about a mile above the old wooden bridge, a steel toll bridge (popularly called "the iron bridge") was constructed as a profit-making venture with private funding. The location of the new bridge was approximately at the end of present Old River Road, which ends at Wild Turkey Lane, and just above the property of the city wastewater treatment plant. The relocation of the bridge, with its access roads probably following the old ones to the former boatyard in the area, was compatible with the northward movement of the town from its original location. For a time the new bridge seemed secure.

The widespread poverty and disorganization of the postwar years had resulted in severe neglect of bridge maintenance on other bridges in the county as well, according to 1878 issues of the *Camden Journal.* For example, a February 26 article reported that the bridges over Lynch's Creek were in serious disrepair, being "mere skeletons, and the life of neither man nor beast is safe in crossing them." Since the war neighboring Darlington County had spent no money on the repair of Kelly's Bridge, Stokes Bridge, or Tiller's Ferry Bridge, although Kershaw County had appropriated a small amount to repair Kelly's Bridge. The bridges were "of great importance not only to planters living on both sides of the creek, but also to the town of Camden. The 'Darlington trade' is by no means an inconsiderable item in the business of our merchants." A Darlington resident who favored bridge repair complained of the inconvenience of traveling six or eight miles to have corn ground when "some of us can hear the gates hoisted at two or three mills on the west side of Lynches creek." He observed also a "merchant flour and rice mill" on the opposite side of the creek that those on the east would like to use and lamented, "We are cut off from Camden, our cotton market, which is the best inland market in the state."

In the May 21, 1878, *Camden Journal,* a Tiller's Ferry resident described Kelly's Bridge as "a miserable trap on which people often have to risk themselves and their property in attending to their legitimate business, and I am told that Gardner's and Stoke's [*sic*] are no better." On September 12 the newspaper addressed the dismal state of Stokes Bridge, in "so dangerous a condition, the farmers of Darlington who come to Camden to trade, have made it a practice to unhitch their teams before crossing the bridge, and pulling their wagons over by hand." Even that precautionary step could prove dangerous. Dove Gilbert and J. Lewis Bennett, "returning from Camden with a load of purchases, arrived at the bridge when it was quite dark. They went through the usual routine of unhitching, and had pulled their loaded wagon nearly over the bridge, when a plank tipped up and tumbled the wagon and contents into the creek."

County roads and town streets were also obstacles to travel. Members of the 1878 grand jury complained that since their last meeting no repairs had been made to the "very bad condition" they had reported on Camden Ferry Lane, McCords Ferry Road, Chesnut's Ferry Road, and the bridges and roads between Camden and Liberty Hill. The March 5 *Camden Journal* described the Lancaster road as "almost impassable" just north of Sanders Creek, especially on the hill beyond Gum Swamp.

The September 12, 1878, newspaper issued a commendation: "The [Camden] Chief of Police has the cart busy fixing the streets. During the past week several crossings have been made on lower Broad street, so that in wet weather a person can pass over without having to wade through the mud. Many of the side streets have been put in good repair." However, the same issue stated, "Farmers living below Camden on the Charleston Road are complaining bitterly of the dangerous condition of several of the bridges on that road."

Lewis P. Anderson, who moved to Camden in 1898, recalled in later years the problems of unpaved streets after a rain when "people and animals all sloshed along together in the mud. After a rain, all along Main Street people laid down boards so you could walk . . . but the horses and buggies would come along, dislocate the boards, and people would be slipping in the mud again." Problems were compounded by the weight of "teams of oxen and big cotton-loaded wagons," and when streets dried, they were left rutted.[6]

Stagecoaches

Stagecoaches continued as part of the transportation system in the latter part of the 1800s. Almost a century after the closing years of the stagecoach, Judge Edgar "Shorty" Marsh in 1983 recalled some tales of the "good old days" that had been related to him by his uncle, Sam Niles.[7] The stagecoach made a dramatic arrival in town: "The depot stood where the Camden post office is now [Broad and DeKalb streets]. The horses would come over the hill [Broad and Campbell streets] at a full gallop. Apparently their rest aboard the ferry over the river, gave them an energy spurt for their arrival." Marsh continued, "When passengers got off the stage, they were brushed with feather dusters to get rid of the dust. Then they could eat in a restaurant above the depot. They called it the tearoom."

Marsh also remembered his uncle's admiration for the profession of driver or mule skinner, "a professional handler, like a race horse jockey today." Niles had claimed, "A good one could hold the reins of six horses in one hand and direct each one to turn a corner on cue." Required to perform maintenance as well, a skinner could "remove the nut of a wagonwheel, pop it halfway out and grease it without allowing the stage[coach] to fall."

Water Travel—Steamboats

Despite intermittent complaints about railroad inefficiencies, the use of the railway ultimately hastened the end of not only the stagecoach but also another mode of shipping—the steamboat. Postwar inabilities to keep the riverbeds clear also contributed to the passing of water transport. An advertisement in the February 5, 1888, *Camden Journal* offered for sale to the highest bidder the "Steamer *Lillington* which has been plying between Camden and the W.,C.& A. Railroad bridge, on the Wateree river." As the Wateree was at high flood from a recent freshet, one wag suggested that "the steamer *Lillington* be put upon the line between Bateman's Bridge and Perkins' Hill, for the accommodation of the denizens of Western Wateree during the balance of the winter." Although the Camden Steamboat Company, under President James Jones, dissolved in September 1878, steamboat use continued for a time. A West Wateree resident complained to the *Camden Journal* on February 20, 1879, about the screeching "nuisance" of the steamboat whistle exhausting "enough steam to run it halfway to Acton, or some other country more distant" each time a rider crossed the Wateree Bridge.

Judge Marsh recalled his uncle's explanation that steamboats on the Wateree were not shaped like Mississippi River paddle wheelers but instead "resembled shrimp boats." The boats could travel as far up the Wateree as the Liberty Hill area, where they were stopped by rapids. Their decks were stacked with merchandise of all types, including wire, cloth, nails, axes, and barrels of cheese. Marsh stated that Niles, born in 1883, witnessed the last steamboat to arrive in Camden: "A merchant heard the whistle," and nearly everybody in town "headed down [present] U.S. 521 to a spot near the Indian Mounds." The public watched the captain hold the craft steady against the current as men cut poplar trees, with which they constructed a bridge from shore to the boat. According to Marsh, "It was an important day in the community."

Julian Rush, born in 1886, left memoirs of steamboats bringing fertilizer and other commodities to Camden and going back downstream, taking cotton to Charleston and Georgetown. Rush, whose father was an overseer at Mulberry Plantation, recalled, "I would run down to the river when we could hear it coming chugging up the river." Rush said that the boat's engine was louder straining against the current than when it headed downstream. He recalled, "It pleased us as all the crew waved at us."[8]

Floods

The bane of all travelers, floods damaged bridges and roads of all types and threatened human life. In January 1878 a man attempting to cross the freshet waters at the end of the Wateree Bridge was swept away in a swift current, and his body was later discovered caught in a fence on the flooded river road. In December a body was found beneath the water of the trestle crossing Hermitage Swamp. The victim had gone to Camden to get his Christmas goods, but because the river was up he had been unable to drive the wagon home. He had fallen to his death while attempting to walk the trestle.

Heavy storms in 1878 washed away a number of mill dams, including these named in the September 19 newspaper: "Both of Mr. J. H. Vaughan's and T. J. Smyrl's, on Sanders Creek, L. L. Clyburn's, on Granny's Quarter, S. R. Adams' on Big Pine Tree Creek, and Tiller's mill in the eastern part of the county." Smyrl, Vaughan, and Adams had just repaired their dams from damages in another storm a few weeks earlier.

The December 26, 1878, *Camden Journal* observed that the Wateree River had overflowed its banks four times since fall, and all crossings at Camden had been stopped. Rising backwater also covered the road to Sumter. The article continued, "Some people attribute the frequent overflows to the embankment built across the swamp by the Wilmington, Columbia, and Augusta Railroad . . . there has been at least twice the number of freshets in a season since the embankment was built than there was before."

The 1878 freshet also interfered with the contractor F. J. Hay's work repairing the Wateree Bridge. In the January 30, 1879, *Camden Journal* a resident west of the Wateree praised Hay's work. Alleging that six months earlier the bridge had been noted for "its careening appearance, its dilapidated condition, its continued evidence of decay," the writer declared it currently to be "a safe and accommodating means of a visit to Camden." In fact more flooding would continue to damage the structure.

During periods when the ferry instead of the bridge operated, the receding of flood waters caused other problems. In January 1881 there was no damage to the ferry operation when rain and melting snow caused the Wateree to rise and flood the bottomlands. However, the January 13 *Camden Journal* reported: "On Monday morning when the ferryman went to Camden ferry he found that the river had fallen during the night and left its flat high on the bank. It was late in the day before it could be got back in the river and some persons had to wait a good while before they could be put across."

Floods that often proved to be enemies of modern man's attempts to control his environment sometimes destroyed ancient man's efforts as well. In 1886 a heavy freshet washed out portions of the ancient village site at the Mulberry Indian Mound. It was reported that a number of ancient dog burials were uncovered at that time.[9] A June 1892 *Camden Chronicle* reported much conversation about Indian mounds. Many bones were excavated "in the edge of town on the railroad," which according to tradition was "on the Indian path from Catawba to Pee Dee river." The article stated that one could pick up arrowheads "almost anywhere in this section."

Politics

What may have seemed a slow-moving, only gradually changing rural existence was in fact being buffeted by the high spirits of political currents. Following the 1876 election, the flood of investigations and charges of corruption that were leveled against former state officeholders also stirred tensions among county politicians.[10] In late summer before the 1878 elections, Kershaw County was a hotbed. The victors of the last election were anxious not to lose hard-fought ground, and the losers were anxious to regain it. With victory as a goal few hesitated to resort to questionable means to achieve it. Republican Radicals and Democrats held meetings throughout the county, vying for support through appeal and intimidation.[11] Newspaper coverage, far from unbiased, made clear distinctions of party and race.

Racial Tensions

Racial tensions were part of the preelection atmosphere. The January 1, 1878, *Camden Journal* reflected white fears with the following complaint: "There are in this town about 20 young colored men, strong and able-bodied, and who appear to live well; but how they obtain their living is a mystery, for their only occupation appears to make both day and night hideous with their drunken rows and obscene behavior. . . . Under the present law they can only be arrested and imprisoned for 24 hours. . . . [They] give the police more trouble than the rest of our population. . . . We want . . . enforcement of the vagrant law and a chain gang." Again in March the newspaper complained about the number of "able bodied colored men who seem to have no employment." On the eve of the 1878 election, the October *Journal* reported apprehension over the report that six "colored companies with arms, would parade through our streets in defiance of the law and the orders of the adjutant general." Commissioned troops were sent to Camden, and the expected companies did not appear.

White apprehension about large gatherings of blacks continued, resulting in suspicions too of church gatherings and camp meetings. Emotional outdoor religious exercises were now generally abandoned by whites and attended almost exclusively by blacks. All knew that political speaking as well as preaching went on there. The October 31, 1878, *Camden Journal* reported the "annual camp meeting at Town Creek last week. On Saturday and Sunday every road leading to the camp was crowded with vehicles of every kind loaded with persons going to the meeting." The reporter estimated "between 4,000 and 5,000 negroes on the ground" at noon on Sunday. A related story reported that Nicodemus Brownfield, "colored U.S. Deputy Marshall, arrested several men on Monday for selling whiskey at Town Creek Camp Ground on Sunday last without a license." The writer expressed the opinion that "no man, licensed or unlicensed, ought to be allowed to traffic in whiskey at a camp meeting of Churches."[12]

Rifle Clubs

The 1878 preelection period stirred with the organization of political clubs and "rifle clubs," which had been banned during the Red Shirt campaign. These and other reminders of the former Confederacy abounded. Members of the Oakland Democratic Club, who organized a rifle club at Marshall's Church, chose "the old Marshall's Field" for their parade ground and selected gray uniforms. The Flat Rock Guards (Company G, Second South Carolina Volunteers) were reported "revived," and officers were chosen. Citizens of "upper and lower Granny's Quarter" met at L. L. Clyburn's store to form a cavalry company and reorganize the Granny's Quarter Democratic Club. Cureton's Mill and Swift Creek likewise held meetings "to organize for the campaign." President J. D. Dunlap called a meeting of the Camden Democratic Club at Jones Hall. In an obvious tactic of pressure, the February 5 *Camden Journal* promised to publish rolls of every club in the county because "every Democrat, white or colored, should see that his name is properly enrolled, so that it will appear upon which side he stands."

Hampton Day

The grandest rally of all, planned to equal "the biggest fourth of July the sun ever shown [*sic*] upon," was the 1878 Hampton Day, organized in the spirit of the last election. Governor Wade Hampton and other dignitaries were scheduled speakers in the square presently called Hampton Park. Despite the governor's absence owing to illness, the rally was a rousing event. Men and mounted riders from neighboring counties joined with local clubs in the enthusiastic gathering. Like the Camden Light Artillery, they turned out wearing red shirts. Any man who did not have such a shirt could have one furnished him. Red shirts were also given to black men.

For the rally march, Democratic clubs on foot rendezvoused at "Bank Corner," Broad and Rutledge streets, and the cavalry and clubs on horseback assembled at the courthouse. The line of march went up Broad Street to Laurens, east to Lyttleton, and down Lyttleton to Hampton Square. The militia companies of the Kershaw County Regiment mustered on Monumental (today Monument) Square, "fully equipped for inspection by [E. W. Moise] the Adjutant and Inspector general." The result was as the newspaper had predicted: "Such a sight as this . . . will carry many of us back to the good old days before the war."

Moise prevented some militiamen from assembling, however. "Four colored militia companies from the country" had come to Camden to join the Ellis Guards, the Camden black militia, in a battalion parade. They had "assembled in front of the colored school house, on west DeKalb street" and were ready to march when Captain Lemon Thomas was handed a dispatch from Moise: "Send companies home at once. You are violating the law." Captain Thomas, informed that it was illegal "for militia companies from other beats to drill in Camden," disbanded the country militia, some of whom scoffed at having to become spectators. Since the order did not pertain to his own company, Captain Thomas drilled them as planned.[13]

A source of great surprise that delighted some and frightened others was a small hot-air balloon. The newspaper pronounced the rally a success despite Hampton's illness: "As far as the eye could reach we could see the red shirts prominent in the moving mass."

Political Spirits

Printed reports of political meetings in the Democratic *Camden Journal* during the 1878 campaign were inevitably biased. W. D. Trantham, county Democratic chairman, was the *Journal* editor until fall campaigning began, when the editorship was taken over by his former business manager G. G. Alexander. Trantham's presence at Radical (Republican) meetings was intended to forge support for a ticket that would allow for some officeholders from both parties but maintain the dominance of mainline Democrats. The *Journal* quoted Governor Hampton at the beginning of the campaign: "Independents may be good men, but now they are our worst enemies."

The newspaper accounts reveal strategies and intimidation typical of the period. To attend a Radical meeting at "Holland Harris's School House" in West Wateree, Trantham and a small group from Camden crossed the river at Chesnut's Ferry in early September 1878. After "a long and dusty ride" they reached the site and were told that the meeting had been postponed, a ploy to have them leave unheard. However, when Dr. William R. Nelson of West Wateree arrived "at the head of a body of horsemen," organizers realized that the visitors were not going to leave. Radicals then called the meeting to order and introduced the speaker Wesley Salmond.[14]

Organizers voiced favor for a mixed ticket with some Democrats and some Radicals, when James Thompson called out for a straight Radical ticket. Described as "a white mulatto from English's Mill" and said to be well known in West Wateree, Thompson was reportedly intent on "inflaming minds of colored people against whites." Trantham countered, telling the Radicals that "they might come with us or not, as they liked; but in November we would roll up a majority that would place old Kershaw in the front rank of the Democracy, and show the radicals how fruitless would be any opposition in the future." The *Journal* reported that Trantham's speech met great enthusiasm, "and the rebel yell that followed carried us back vividly to the campaign of 1876." Later in the month the newspaper commented that the same group of Radicals had tried to hold a meeting at Cureton's Mill without letting the opposition party know but found themselves confronted by seventy-five red shirts.

Two Radical meetings were reported in early October. The *Journal* printed the names of organizers at the first one, held in Camden at the "colored school house" on DeKalb Street (Jackson School): Frank Adamson, William Boykin, Frank Carter (county chair), William Carter, Hampton English, Isaac English, Sam Page, Frank Pearce, Richard Price, Almond Reynolds, Lemon Thomas, Tony Thompson, Nathan Truesdell, and Paris Watts. The other gathering was at a far distance from town, at Bull Neck on the line between Fairfield and Kershaw counties.

At an especially spirited political meeting at Young's Shop in the Lynch's Creek section in late October 1878, Trantham, J. D. Shaw, and Joel Hough spoke to a mixed crowd. The newspaper asserted, "From the number of colored men present it would appear that they were all coming over to the Democratic party." A "home-made band" was featured with "a two-string fiddle and a one-string banjo, a cracked fife, and an old tin horn." The beat was provided by "two drums made out of cheese boxes . . . beating the double-quick while the men were going at the rate of a dead march."

On display was "a black sheep skin inscribed with the words: 'Old Efe's Hide,' captured November 5, 1878." The article continued: "About a hundred men, white and colored, went down to the old scalawag's house and asked him to come up and they would give him a chance to address them; but no persuasion could induce him to go—either to listen or to speak himself. They carried with them a banner with a wolf dressed in sheep's clothing drawn on. They said it was indicative of the scalawag's character." The "scalawag," presumably a white man unaligned with Democratic policy, was unnamed in the article. The most prominent Lynch's-area resident answering this description was L. W. R. "Rochelle" Blair, and "Efe" may have been a wordplay on the last syllable of the name he was called.

A former Confederate major and large planter whose political views in recent years had been voiced in the *Kershaw Gazette,* Blair had earlier opposed fusion efforts, asserting in 1875 that "one or the other of the two races must rule the State of South Carolina." Blair, however, had actively supported Hampton in his first bid for governor and voiced favor for mutual dependence and rights for black and white citizens. After the election, when money was still tight for farmers, Blair in print and speech supported a paperback money policy contrary to the Democrats' hard money views. Like some of his rural neighbors, he also favored traditional free-range practices for livestock, in opposition to fencing laws, which the majority supported. In the election of 1878 Blair's espousal of the Greenback Party was viewed as heretic by his former Democratic allies.[15]

Just after his successful reelection, Governor Wade Hampton fractured his leg in a serious hunting accident. The General Assembly elected him as a U.S. senator the same day his leg was amputated, and in 1879 he resigned as governor to begin service for two terms in Washington, D.C. The lieutenant governor who ascended to office and the next elected governor were, like Hampton, former Confederate officers. In 1880 the Republicans made no nomination for governor, but a convention of Greenbackers nominated Blair for the office.

In September the Antioch Democratic Club held a political meeting in Antioch Church, with Richard Brown presiding. Among the speakers were Trantham and Blair. According to the *Journal,* Blair condemned "so-called Democrats who failed to live up to the promises of 1876." The *Journal* in October described a Democratic rally of "tremendous enthusiasm" in the town of Kershaw. The reported four thousand attendees, with "Red Shirts everywhere," welcomed speakers including "Generals Hampton, Hagood, Kennedy, and Butler." The newspaper reported that the people were "as fully aroused as in 1876." In the 1880 election Democratic gubernatorial candidate General Johnson Hagood easily defeated Blair. Elected lieutenant governor was General John Doby Kennedy of Camden, another loyal Hampton supporter.

In national politics it was not until 1884, with Grover Cleveland's victory, that Democrats celebrated the party's first presidential win since the loss to Abraham Lincoln just before the Civil War. Kershaw County Democrats were well prepared that year for a victory celebration. According to the later recollection of the local historian Thomas Ancrum, "Barrels of rosin had been placed along Main street [in Camden] and when the news of the election was flashed, they were set on fire, lighting the town. There was much cheering and some shot pistols to add to the celebration."[16] It was a political milestone frequently recalled in later years. At the time of the national bicentennial observation in 1976, a number of local senior citizens dated their birthdays in relation to when Grover Cleveland was elected president.

The Farmers' Movement

In later years a former Kershaw County legislator of the period, Thomas J. Kirkland, reflected on political shifting that began within the Democratic Party in the final decade of the century: "Somewhat prior to 1890, when the 'Farmers Movement' was brewing, their meetings were attended by all shades of planters, big and little." There developed "a vague discontent, especially among the farm element, a majority of the population," to the old order that had resumed power: "They [farmers] had suffered years of low prices, five cents for cotton, and were in debt to the tradesmen. They had few schools, poor roads, and the towns had all the advantages." As Kirkland pointed out, "The agitation of 1890 has been generally regarded as an outbreak of the plain people against the culture or so-called aristocratic class, who had long exclusively held the higher offices and practically controlled the State Government—a condition which existed from early times."[17]

Elected as governor was a very different type of politician, Benjamin Ryan Tillman, later called "Pitchfork Ben." Some historians connect the events of this time with the Progressive or Populist movement that rose in national history. Kirkland says of Tillman: "His like we shall not see again. Those who came against him only with logic and facts were blown away like chaff. His self-confidence was supreme and his gall unlimited. His touch of the popular pulse was infallible and his consuming zeal for the common people seems to have justified in his and their eyes some of his shocking utterances and actions."

Despite receding even further at this time into the background of state politics, the Republicans too continued meeting. The September 23, 1892, *Camden Chronicle,* under the heading "Radical Convention," reported that "a convention of the republican party of Kershaw county was held at the court house yesterday, when," in the reporter's words, "the usual scenes of disorder were enacted." The account stated that W. E. Boykin was reelected as county chairman, and state convention delegates included E. Frasier, Charles McLanglin, and A. W. Powell. Delegates elected to the congressional convention were Jerry Brown, W. E. Boykin, I. S. Brown, and Frank Pearce. The newspaper stated, "There was [*sic*] no white men in the convention."

The political power wrested from postwar Republican hands was more and more firmly grasped by the new Democratic majority. Both racial and economic differences separated various political factions.

Social Effects of the Lost Cause

By the 1880s old soldiers and civilians alike were writing nostalgic memoirs, and efforts were unified on raising memorials to the Confederate dead. Memorial efforts had begun by 1873 when the Ladies Monumental Association, an outgrowth of the wartime ladies' aid and benevolent societies, started to collect money for a Confederate monument. Ten years of efforts were carried on under the terms of three successive presidents of that organization: Mrs. H. D. DeSaussure, Miss C. M. Boykin, and Mrs. Alfred E. Doby. During Mrs. Doby's term of office the organization wrote a constitution under the name of the Ladies Memorial Association. One accomplishment of the group was to replace, with engraved stone markers, the wooden markers labeled just "C.S.A." at Quaker Cemetery on the graves of twenty-two unidentified soldiers who had died in the Confederate army hospital at Camden.[18]

The degree of local reverence is reflected in the fact that, when the Confederate Monument was constructed in 1883, it was placed at the center of the intersection of Broad and Laurens Streets, and traffic traveled around it for a number of years.[19] Thousands attended the ceremonial unveiling on June 20.[20] The railroads offered special excursion rates, and far-distant visitors were among local attendees. Smaller efforts also were made as memorials. In 1896, for example, members of the Camp Richard Kirkland United Confederate Veterans arrived early for an encampment on the grounds of Cool Spring, bringing a scuppernong or other vine to start a vineyard. Confederate veterans had organized in this county before 1890 under General E. N. Yarborough of Bethune and L. L. Wittkowsky of Camden. Adjutant Joel Hough of Camp Richard Kirkland listed seventy members.

As veterans aged, public support was shown them in the form of pensions, for which veterans' groups also helped lobby. Following General Assembly legislation the Kershaw Board of Pensioners met for the first time in 1897 to plan elections for township boards of pensioners. Chairman N. A. Bethune approved a list of meetings: DeKalb Township at Camden, Buffalo Township at Lynchwood School House, Flat Rock Township at Westville, and Wateree Township at Rabon's Cross Roads. Efforts were made to see that every entitled veteran, or widow, got pensions.

Reacting to veterans' concerns and recognizing that some national textbooks reflected unfavorably on the South, local teachers met to discuss an important curriculum question concerning what children should be taught about the Civil War. According to the December 10, 1897, *Camden Chronicle,* teachers agreed that "nothing should be contained in the school history prejudicial to the honor of the men who followed the stars and bars from '60 to '65." The writer emphasized that "the doctrine of State rights is as firmly fixed in the minds of our people to-day as ever before" and that the southern "heroes" had struggled for their rights "as granted in our Federal Constitution." The column concluded, "Let the youth of South Carolina be taught that our fathers were not guilty of treason under the constitution when they attempted to assert their right to self government."

Educational Changes

The education or training of youths, once generally held to be the responsibility solely of parents (or slaveholders), began in the later part of the nineteenth century to be perceived as at least partly a public responsibility. Benevolent organizations, especially churches, sometimes assisted.

Private Black Education

The old Lang family plantation home, on the corner of DeKalb and Campbell streets, had been purchased during Reconstruction by the Freedman's Bureau

A Mather Academy historical program presented in the early twentieth century, part of a traditional curriculum. Courtesy of the Camden Archives

teacher Sarah Babcock. In 1877 the home became the nucleus of a noted institution that opened to offer quality education to black youths. What became the privately endowed Browning Home and Mather Academy was supported by the Woman's Home Missionary Society of the Northern Methodist Church, headquartered in Cincinnati, Ohio.[21] The institution that grew from one building to a campus of several buildings is described by a historical marker at its site: "Mather Academy was founded in 1887 by the New England Southern Conference of the Women's Home Missionary Society of the Methodist Church. It succeeded a Freeman's School opened during Reconstruction by Sarah Babcock, who returned to Massachusetts, married Rev. James Mather, and became the corresponding secretary of the Southern Conference when it was organized in 1883. The Methodists opened a 'Model Home and Industrial School' on this site in 1887."

Modern Graded School System

In 1885 South Carolina instituted the modern graded school system to organize separate white and black public schools into more efficient and effective educational opportunities. Under the system students had to meet specific learning standards to pass from grade to grade. It took a few years, however, for the graded system to begin functioning. Specific training for teachers was an essential aspect. Several small private white schools in Camden were eventually combined under the improved state guidelines to become part of the new public education system. The Orphan Society schoolhouses and the McCandless schoolhouse on Laurens Street, along with the private schools of Mrs. Mary A. Shannon and Mrs. Mary C. Thomasson, brought established reputations and experienced teaching practices into the public school system. From 1886 to 1888 a Mr. Turnipseed was in charge of the Camden schools. He was succeeded by A. C. Moore, 1888–90, who was credited with much of the groundwork of establishing the new graded system.[22]

When the graded schools in Camden began their fall 1892 session, the white school had 231 pupils enrolled, "an increase of about 40" above the previous year, requiring the employment of another teacher. Jackson, the "colored" school, opened with only 80 pupils since "so many of the colored children are at this time of the year at work in the cotton fields elsewhere," but by the end of the harvest, it had more than 200 students. A private school for white students was also open in 1892, headed by a returned Camden native, Professor Robert M. Kennedy. Open to both male and female pupils, it operated at the residence of the widowed Mrs. W. Z. Leitner.[23]

The trustees for school district no. 1, the Camden schools, successfully passed a bond referendum in 1893 for a new building for the Camden school, a substantial brick structure constructed for eleven thousand dollars on the grounds of the Camden Educational Society, facing north on Laurens Street. The McCandless schoolhouse on the site was sold and removed across the street to become a private residence.[24] The new domed, two-story school with raised basement included four large rooms downstairs and four rooms upstairs with central hallway, and upper rooms could be opened into larger spaces. Grades one to ten were accommodated in the single building. The trustees promised, "Modern sanitary and hygiênic plans will be observed throughout the building."[25] Many students had their first experiences with indoor plumbing in public schoolhouses.

School trustees advertised to acquire "the best pedagogic talent of the State" the following fall. For the new Camden Graded School, Robert M. Kennedy was elected principal with a monthly salary of seventy-five dollars. His male assistant, Leonard T. Baker, was paid sixty dollars. The three female assistants—Mrs. M. A. Shannon, Mrs. N. S. Withers, and Miss E. P. (Lizzie) Stoney—each received thirty-five dollars.[26]

Elected for the Jackson Graded School, with monthly salaries, were J. D. McLester, principal (thirty dollars), and assistants Eliza A. Reed and Rebecca E. Boykin (fifteen dollars each). The Knights Hill Colored School employed Reverend J. W. Moultrie for twenty dollars. Salaries of the time were based on subjective criteria, including assumptions and custom. Men were paid more than women; whites, more than blacks. It was customarily understood that men received more salary as they were presumed heads of households; women were paid less since male relatives should be helping support them. The perceived costlier expenses of a white lifestyle were the justification for higher compensation for whites than for blacks. As skewed as comparative salaries were, they were respectively considered good pay for their time.

Country schools in Kershaw County operated under a separate superintendent. A letter signed "teacher" in the March 1897 *Chronicle* praised the accomplishments of Superintendent L. L. Copeland but added, "We need more money, better school houses, better equipment, better trustees, better patrons, and better teachers." The writer suggested that school terms of longer duration would allow teachers better pay, which in turn would attract better-qualified teachers. The letter also advocated "a strict compulsory school [attendance] law." A public letter signed "Colored Teachers of Kershaw County" thanked Copeland for his assistance and praised the advancements in their schools during his administration.

Teachers of the county and city white schools unified in the 1897 organization of the Teachers' Association, which elected as president L. L. Copeland, as vice president Leonard T. Baker, as secretary and treasurer J. Willie Dunn, and as sergeant at arms P. T. Bruce. On December 10 the paper reported a current educational reform, "Writing in Schools," citing a study conducted by physicians concerned about "the sight and the general health of the children." Considering the increased requirement for writing in the schools, the doctors were concerned about the relation of desk size to student size and the effect of desk design on posture, which affected eye strain and might possibly "cause or aggravate errors of refraction."

Sunday Schools

Sunday schools, applauded not only as a religious influence but also for educational purposes, were active throughout the county. In 1893 C. W. Birchmore was secretary of the multidenominational Kershaw County Sunday School Convention. Birchmore, also editor of the *Wateree Messenger* and a county school superintendent, compiled a list of county Sunday schools, with superintendents and their addresses: Antioch Baptist, J. E. Davis, Antioch; Beaver Creek Presbyterian, (? D.) Ursery, Oakhurst; Beaver Dam Presbyterian, Allen McCaskill, Camden; Bethany Baptist, J. W. Gardner, Westville; Bethany Methodist, W. M. Kelly, Tiller's Ferry; Bethel Methodist, J. H. Hendrix, Lynchwood; Beulah Methodist, J. K. Murchison, Camden; Buffalo Baptist, E. S. Davis, Kershaw; Camden Presbyterian, Reverend W. W. Mills, Camden; Crescent Methodist, Mrs. Sarah Gray, Camden; Damascus Methodist, T. A. Cauthen, Westville; DeKalb Baptist, H. J. Munn, Kalb; Flat Rock Baptist, J. A. McDowell, Flat Rock; Flint Hill Baptist, A. C. Watts, Cantey; Gum Swamp Baptist, F. E. Sparrow, Antioch; Harmony Baptist (E[ast]), W. S. Corbett, Tiller's

The busy intersection of Broad and DeKalb streets in 1914, at the head of a business district with dirt streets and produce-laden wagons. Courtesy of the Camden Archives

Ferry; Harmony Baptist (W[est]), J. W. Perry, Blythewood; Hopewell Presbyterian, J. L. Gettys Jr., Camden; Liberty Hill Presbyterian, W. K. Thompson, Liberty Hill; L(y)ttleton Street Methodist, J. B. Phelps, Camden; Marshall's Methodist, J. B. Hall, Camden; Mt. Olivet Baptist, John Goff, Camden; Mt. Zion Baptist, C. U. Myers, Camden; Pine Grove Baptist, Newton Kelly, Camden; Pine Tree Presbyterian, N. A. Bethune, Lucknow; Reedy Branch Methodist, T. J. Davis, Antioch; St. John's Methodist, J. N. Jones, Camden; Sand Hill Union, James W. Taylor, Kershaw; Shiloh Methodist, D. M. Kirkley, Abney; Smyrna Methodist (no information); Stockton Union, J. C. Humphries, Camden; Turkey Creek Presbyterian, J. J. Josey, Tiller's Ferry; and West Branch Union, G. E. Philips, Abney.

The "New South"

Some community leaders had for some time already been touting the "New South" philosophy that was gaining attention in the region. The concept advanced the belief that a self-sufficient economy depended on economic diversity, industrial development, and improved methods of transportation. As early as 1872 William M. Shannon and other local visionaries had attempted to promote capital investment in Kershaw County. However, significant change was slow to materialize, and by the end of the nineteenth century agriculture, industry, and governmental structures had made some steps forward but still had a long way to go before becoming part of a new South.

Agriculture

County citizens whose incomes depended on the fortunes of cotton were busy and optimistic in the fall of 1880. In early October crops were large. Gins were crowded with cotton and running day and night. Cotton had risen to more than ten cents a pound. By January 1881 cotton was still more than eleven cents, "falling but still good." Yet many farmers lamented that a considerable amount of cotton was still in the fields, unpicked for lack of labor.

The shortage of labor was especially keen at harvest time when demand was high, but it also involved the fact that landowners and hired workers had different ideas about how long and hard the laborers should be willing to work. Farmers complained that a number of potential black workers were satisfied to work just long enough to earn sufficient money to get by on and then preferred going fishing to returning to the fields. Resentment was felt on both sides, with potential workers feeling it their right to exercise freedom in accepting work or not.

Other problems also bothered various farmers. In his journal J. W. Gardner of the Tiller's Ferry section recalled reactions to the 1881 "stock law" passed by the legislature. The law, requiring that cattle be fenced so that they ranged only on their owners' property, sought to end the old tradition of open-range grazing, which was bothersome to many and deadly to railroads. Barbed wire, patented in 1874, was changing the nature of the cattle industry across the county. According to Gardner, who was elected county commissioner in 1882 and 1884, farmers in "many Sections of Sand-hill country" were "not prepared [and] not willing to abide by [the law], they having large herds of Cattle & no fence pasture land, so most of the people living in the fork of Lynch's Creek agreed to let these streams be their boundaries and turn their cattle [out to graze] as before."[27]

Thomas Watts of the same area, however, wrote in an October 24, 1881, letter to John Malcolm Watts that there was "considerable excitement about the stock law. . . . Petitions circulating through the county for and against the fence." In contrast to Gardner's sentiment, Watts wrote, "The fence is largely in the majority in this part of the country" and added, "For the last 8 or 10 days we have been having some timber (cut) to start building."[28] Some farmers' petitions to the legislature complained that the cost of a fence would exceed the value of the land they would be fencing. Access to water was another problem for cattle owners whose own lands did not have a steady supply.

On the other hand, the new law was welcomed as fair and just by property owners who previously had had to bear the expense of fencing their land in protection against intrusions by free-ranging cattle belonging to others. Some of those who owned cattle, it was said, owned little or no land and thus had been profiting off the property and labor of others who were taxpayers.

Migration

Various farming conditions continued to encourage out-migration. In the January 20, 1893, *Camden Chronicle* the correspondent from Pisgah expressed worry over weather and future crops since "ice on the running streams is two to three inches thick" and "the small grain crop is killed." He reported, "A great many speak of going out West next year if things do not change for the better," and he continued with the opinion that "taxes are getting to be burdensome."

One variation of the out-migration movements was reported in the January 8, 1878, *Camden Journal:* "About a hundred colored persons embracing men, women and children, from Lancaster county, passed through Camden on their way to Charleston, where they said a ship was waiting to take them to Liberia." The newspaper continued, "The colored people of Camden, with few exceptions, regarded them as deluded beings, and the victims of sharpers, and they were advised to return to their homes." They found no vessel for them when they arrived in the port city. The *Charleston News and Courier* reported that people in different parts of the country were "duped and fleeced."

To balance out-migration, an editorial in the January 27, 1893, issue of the *Chronicle* urged new settlers to move into the county. The paper urged "thrifty and honest immigrants to come and settle amongst us," and added, "Kershaw county could give comfortable homes to a thousand more families." It cited the soil, climate, clear and pure water, and "heavily timbered" lands. The editorial said that the soil, "if not rich . . . by rotation in crops and proper cultivation, can be made to yield profitable crops." Turning from the county's assets to the type of immigrants desired, the writer stated, "We need a larger white population to increase all branches of business; to assist enterprises and to add to the general welfare." Becoming even more specific, the piece continued, "We want only people who can and will work, and who expect to work."

Farmers' Organizations

Farmers, traditionally independent as a group, began to incline toward forming organizations, first as social outlets and then as political forces. In 1878 a unit of the National Grange organized with twenty-four members at Sandy Grove Church in the neighborhood of Tiller's Ferry. Later the same year the Liberty Hill Grange included both male and female officers. The Granny's Quarter Grange organized in 1882 and by the following year had forty-eight members. From the Antioch section in 1897, "J. E." wrote a letter to the *Chronicle* praising the Grange. He reported that Gum Springs Grange, whose new hall was nearly completed, had "accomplished a great deal for our farmers," and he stressed that farmers united in the Grange could "advance their interests better" than they could acting individually.

A more widespread agrarian political movement, the Farmers Alliance, was active in Kershaw County by the 1890s. Three district or state officers attended the quarterly meeting in July 1893 at the courthouse. The group, under President James R. McGill, unanimously approved resolutions that denounced deflation as a cause of the depression and advocated the federal government's return to the "free and unlimited coinage of silver as well as gold."[29] The election of Governor Ben Tillman was a part of the outgrowth of the farmers' movement of the time.

In December 1897 the Kershaw County Cotton Growers Association organized at the courthouse with J. C. Rollings as president and the newspaper editors W. L. McDowell (*Camden Chronicle*) and C. W. Birchmore (*Wateree Messenger*) as secretaries. Additionally the following vice presidents were chosen to represent the four townships: W. A. Ancrum, W. F. Russell, D. M. Bethune, and H. F. Boykin. The organization unanimously passed a resolution that denounced "the theory of overproduction as proclaimed by the robbers, speculators and gamblers of Wall street." The resolution portrayed speculation in cotton futures, rather than excess production, as the dilemma. They asserted that the law of supply and demand, unhindered by "the present vile and dishonorable methods" employed by Wall Street, would adjust prices of cotton and other farm products for the benefit of sellers and buyers. A Mr. Russell spoke, praising farmers for their hard work and economy and denouncing "the infernal money sharks" who kept farmers from getting ahead. Concerning speculation, Russell sardonically advised that "it would be better for everybody to go into buying cotton futures as cotton can be bought for far less than it cost to make it."

Cotton Mills

Some steps toward industrialization attracted interest in the county. An article in the March 29, 1883, *Kershaw Gazette* reported on the proliferation of cottonseed-oil mills: "All over the State we hear of cotton seed oil mills being erected. It is an enterprise in which the investment will amply pay the 1st year." The article commented that prices varied from eighteen hundred dollars to three thousand dollars to purchase equipment to process the waste seed, the by-product of ginning, and render it further useful.

What would become a large change in production and in the lifestyle of workers was begun by the building of Camden's first postwar cotton factory. The Camden Cotton Mill (later called Hermitage) was constructed and incorporated in 1890 on the former site of McRae's flour and grist mill. The latter mill had operated by water transported one-half mile from McRae's pond via a canal. The water flow proved insufficient for the needs of a modern factory, and a considerably larger canal had to be dug in 1892. The mill, which had been rumored in the local press as early as 1878, began operations under president A. D. Kennedy with 150 employees operating ten thousand spindles and three hundred looms.[30] "The early history . . . included a cycle of organizing and going broke; this happened five times during 1890–1905," states Jean Wells.[31]

The first decade of postwar textile mill operation—cycles of hopeful beginnings and disappointing closures—was a disruptive one for investors, who were plagued by financial struggles, and for early employees as well. Some of the workers came with previous experience in mills elsewhere. Most who came, however, were area agricultural families who had sharecropped or who owned small farms of worn-out land. They came to the unfamiliar conditions not to avoid labor but to work, more profitably they hoped, and to improve life for their families. In a sense they were some of the first believers of the New South concept.

Loans and Banking

Financial institutions to promote economic progress gradually became reality. In 1883 the Enterprise Building and Loan Association was organized, the first of its type in Camden. After more than three decades of absence from the county, in 1888 a new Bank of Camden was chartered with H. G. Carrison as president. It is unclear where the bank began its operations since the old building had been sold at auction the previous year, but the August 26, 1892, *Camden Chronicle* reported a construction delay on the new bank building awaiting arrival of the metal front. The Camden merchant Marion H. Heyman recollected in a memoir that "Kershaw county at [the turn of the century] was served by two banks. The Bank of Camden with Mr. H. G. Carrison, Sr., as president and the Farmers and Merchants Bank with Mr. E. Miller Boykin as president." The latter bank was established in 1899 but closed in only four years.[32]

Cotton Buyers

Camden businessmen continued to try to improve the town's position as a cotton-buying center. The September 23, 1892, newspaper reported under the head "More Cotton Buyers" that E. Miller Boykin & Company, "representing several strong firms," had entered the Camden cotton market. Boykin & Company were "buying at Kennedy's platform" and were "prepared to pay the highest price for the staple." Another entry into the market, according to the newspaper, was "Capt. Wm. Clyburn," representing a Virginia cotton-buying firm. Clyburn was buying at the "Clyburn Block."

In 1896 the Sumter newspaper *Watchman & Southron* under the head "Why Cotton Leaves Sumter" expressed concern that cotton from that county had been going to the Camden market in increasing quantities for several years. The writer pointed out several reasons. Camden was not "bottled" like Sumter was;

Camden had competing railroad lines in or near the town and had the Wateree River; and furthermore Camden buyers who were expert graders purchased directly from the farmers, paying according to quality.

Businesses

A wide variety of businesses, mostly small and independent, operated in the county. The *Camden Journal* on September 23, 1880, printed the following advertisements: "Now that our farmers are gathering in their rice, they should know where to have it pounded and cleaned for market. Messrs. Metts and Player, two miles above Camden, have their mill in thorough order. . . . Don't send your rice to Charleston." L. M. Watts advertised, "My mill at Flat Rock is now in thorough repair and ready for ginning cotton." John Boykin announced that he had established "Town Creek Mills, a set of mills 3½ miles below Camden on the Charleston road" for cotton and corn.

The same newspaper also announced, "Mr. E. H. Shepard, photographer, has arrived, and will be ready for business in a short time." Other notices announced the reopening of the DeKalb House, with J. O. Sanders as proprietor, and the opening of S. B. Latham's remodeled and refurbished Latham House. A tenant could lodge at the former, which included a bar and billiard room, for $2.00 per day or at the latter for $1.50 a day. The newspaper also posted a notice signed by John R. Goodale, intendant, and D. C. Kirkley, clerk and treasurer, that the fee for a liquor license (retailing wine, cider, brewed or malt liquor) in Camden had been reduced from $125.00 to $50.00 a year. Three weeks later the October 14 newspaper commented, "A good deal more whiskey was flowing around town last Saturday than was good for the peace of the community."

Several advertisements posted in the June 16, 1893, *Camden Chronicle* provide a look at some aspects of life then and the businesses that sustained it. Dr. A. A. Moore's Drug Store offered a variety of services. He advertised, "Prescriptions properly compounded at all hours, day and night, by a qualified pharmacist." His drugstore offered too "a full line of GARDEN and FLOWER SEED" and sold "Glenn Spring Mineral Water by the bottle or by the case." He could provide "ICE during the incoming season" but cautioned that Sunday sales were "in cases of sickness only." A rival for the druggist Moore's ice business was W. Geisenheimer's Ice House, which also kept "a full supply . . . during the warm season." Geisenheimer said that he had "a car load of pure lake ice now on hand" and posted "Sunday hours from nine until twelve."

Blacksmiths provided another service that was essential for the majority of inhabitants in the 1890s. W. T. Hall notified the public that "I am no longer at the old Mett's stand, but have opened a NEW SHOP for blacksmith work and general repairing . . . in the rear of the store of J. J. Watkins & Son," with "entrance either from Main or DeKalb street."

Another advertiser was S. J. English, "The Fashionable Barber." A haircut was twenty cents, and a shave cost ten cents, with reduced rates for children's haircuts on Thursdays. English's shop was located "2 doors below G. G. Young's Book Store."

W. T. Lollis advertised his trade of gin repairing. Citing many testimonials from satisfied customers, Lollis offered "to repair and sharpen gins, repair gin brushes, and do all kinds of engine and boiler work." A different kind of repair service was offered by J. E. Rutledge. Dr. Rutledge, a dentist, was to set up shop for one week at Camden's Workman Hotel, where he would perform dental work on any local residents needing such.

Gins, such as those serviced by Mr. Lollis, and other factories could be dangerous places of employment, as was pointed out by a notice of the death of J. B. Gaskins in the April 9, 1897, *Chronicle.* The newspaper had reported the previous week that Gaskins, who operated the Swift Creek Mill for H. H. Boykin, had "one of his fingers mashed off" at the mill. The current edition of the newspaper expressed surprise and grief that Gaskins had died from the effects of his injury.

C. C. Vaughan advertised his ginning services in the September 9, 1897, newspaper. Boasting of having purchased completely new equipment, Vaughan posted the charge for ginning as $1.25 per bale. It might be pointed out that a year's subscription to the *Camden Chronicle* was $1.00.

Modernization and Diversification

Some established small businesses began modernizing in the latter part of the century. In later years an unsigned newspaper article titled "Our Town" recalled, "During the passing of years, the country stores turned into city stores with plate fronts, and the wooden fronts turned to brick fronts. Carpenters and brick masons were kept busy." Camden also witnessed the arrival of new businesses, owned and operated by proprietors of various ethnic and cultural heritage. The writer gave examples: "A wholesale grocery business was started and the first Greek to come to Camden was George Schaderassi. Then came Joe Chu Do to open a Chinese laundry, and the townspeople flocked there to get their first glimpse of a Chinaman. Next from abroad were the Sheheen brothers, Joe and Abraham, from Syria, and from Germany came Mr. Block, Jake and Gus Hirsch, and Mr. Henry Eichel."[33]

Nan Hough Forester in her memoirs pointed out that Camden's dry goods stores did not carry ready-made women's clothing. Instead, she noted, "Some women made their own clothes. Those who could afford it had their clothes custom-made by one of the three local artist-dressmakers. Two of these were blacks, one of whom had resided in the North before coming to Camden. She insisted that she be addressed as 'Madam.' The other served only those ladies she chose, and then if the type of dress desired appealed to her." Mrs. Forester recalled other leading black businesses around the turn of the century:

> Mr. English owned the barber shop patronized by the most influential men of Camden. Their personal shaving mugs lined his display shelves. Mr. English had his residence in a fine colonial cottage on Lyttleton Street, near that of Miss Sue Gibbs. He had several beautiful, always well-dressed, daughters. The English family lived quietly and were good citizens.
>
> Mr. Collins owned the only livery stable of note. His home on West DeKalb Street was a charming old house of the Louisiana-type "raised cottage" with broad, high steps leading to the first floor.
>
> Eugene Dibble owned a well-stocked general store on the western corner of Broad and DeKalb streets. Mr. Dibble was tall, slender, with perfect manners. I remember my father saying with profound respect, "Eugene Dibble is a black gentleman."
>
> In the early mornings all Camden awakened to . . . Billie, the town hawkster. He carted his fresh vegetables up the streets, calling "Butt-head cabbage, crosseyed peas" and so on, as he designated each variety of produce in some humorous way.[34]

Commercial Hotels

The Workman was one of Camden's two main hotels at the turn of the century, according to Marion H. Heyman. The other was the Commercial Hotel on the corner of DeKalb and Market streets, across from Bethesda Presbyterian Church.

Nan Hough Forester described the intersection of Broad and DeKalb streets around the turn of the century: "At the upper end of the business section, where the postoffice is now situated, stood the Workman House, a large three-storied brick hotel. The building was directly entered from the street where a long piazza, well-stocked with rocking chairs, extended its full length. These chairs were usually occupied by . . . 'drummers,' or traveling salesmen, their feet resting comfortably on the railing." Lewis P. Anderson recalled that from the porch drummers would spit tobacco into the street and try to engage the town girls in sweet talk.

Mrs. Forester said: "Mothers cautioned their young daughters to pass the Workman House on the opposite side of the street. However, should one have passed on the near side, she would have been well protected from unpleasantness; for there among the drummers sat Des Goodale, self-appointed protector of Camden's young ladies." The Camden residential section began on Broad Street a short distance north of the Workman House.

Effects of Railroad Development

Thomas Ancrum recalled that at the end of the 1890s, when railroad service to Camden was still limited, "Trains were usually met by crowds, who had nothing better to do, and a train was still a cur[io]sity. Many 'hacks' met the train to drive drummers to the hotels or citizens to their home for a fare of twenty-five cents. Camden's main hotel then was the Workman House, an imposing three story structure that stood where the post office is now located."

Two New Railroads—Seaboard and Coast Line

Tremendously important to the development of the county was the coming of two additional railroad lines about the turn of the century—the Seaboard and the Northwestern railroads (the latter a branch from Sumter of the Atlantic Coast Line).[35] Ancrum described the local excitement: "Camden had many thrills about the time of electric lights [becoming available in some homes in town], and when it was announced that the Seaboard Air Line was to come to Camden, people were as elated as they were over the announcement of the Du Pont plant years afterwards [mid-1900s]." Ancrum continued, "Hardly had the Seaboard announcement been made, when it was announced that the Northwestern Railroad was to come to Camden. . . that [soon afterward] gave Camden three railroads and many industries, and a highly developed tourist center."

The significance of obtaining these railroads was explained by the *Charleston News & Courier* of April 4, 1888: "One shall stand on Hobkirk's Hill before very long, and see railroad trains pass by on their way from Chicago to Charleston, and from New York to Columbia. Forty miles of the line of one of these railroads have just been completed, and the line is extending daily. The old historic town is in the throes of another revolution, and it will emerge from the latest one in such form, that neither Cornwallis nor its nearest neighbors will ever recognize it again."

By 1899 the Seaboard Air Line Railway had completed ninety-one miles of track from Cheraw to Columbia, the last segment of its north-south main line between Richmond, Virginia, and Tampa, Florida. Seaboard correctly predicted profits from shipping Florida produce to the North and from transporting northern tourists to the South. This railroad, which affected all Kershaw County, provided Camden—the largest and most established community on this new section—with direct connections to major urban markets. The *Camden Chronicle* declared that the railroad would "be a lasting blessing to our city" and optimistically told residents to expect large numbers of "tourists and pleasure seekers" and "a great influx of population." Completion of the Seaboard line was followed by further development in the twentieth century.

Thriving Tourism

Camden had already begun developing a reputation as a resort for northerners seeking a warmer climate for the winter, and expanded railway connections would increase that appeal by providing easy access to the community. Some of the first tourists came for health purposes. Kershaw County's mild climate and fresh air and water were considered therapeutic, an atmosphere that advertisements repeatedly described as "salubrious." Tuberculosis, the dread disease of the time, was rampant in the country, but many doctors recommended winter sojourns in climates such as this to avoid the illness or to strengthen the recuperating patient. Camden had four hotels operating by the 1890s with thousands of tourists visiting every winter.

In 1882 F. W. Eldredge, manager of Haile Gold Mine, acquired Pine Flat on upper Lyttleton Street, home of the late duel victim William M. Shannon, and converted it into Camden's first major tourist hotel, the Hobkirk Inn.[36] Eldredge's venture, begun as a way to house visiting gold mine executives and visitors, was quite successful. Connections to Camden by way of the Three C's Railroad made the location convenient for his original purpose. In 1884, with expansion plans in mind, Eldredge purchased another Kirkwood-area home, this one a short distance north on Lyttleton Street, from Mrs. Callie J. Perkins. Using his wife's nickname "Goodie," Eldredge dubbed this second house Goodie Castle. He operated it and Hobkirk Inn until he died in 1912. Mrs. Perkins meanwhile purchased Lausanne, the former home of John M. DeSaussure, and opened it in 1889 as a tourist resort under the name Uphton (Upton) Court. Caleb Ticknor acquired the property upon her death in 1898 and opened it two years later as the Court Inn.

Jane Starke Bauskett (Mrs. W. D.) Trantham recalled the charm of Upton Court: "Jersey cream and butter, along with a menu such as comes only from southern kitchens and southern cooks! The rooms were large and had wide windows and open fireplaces. There was no other form of heat, and there was no running water. But the gardens were full of lovely paths, as were the acres of giant pines in the background. The guests walked and rode horseback and drove various kinds of vehicles."[37] The setting and accommodations had similar appeal in the other residences converted into hotels.

Thomas Ancrum pointed out that tourism brought new sports to the community: "A golf course had been laid out behind the Hobkirk Inn about 1897, and there were few golf courses in America then." The author of "Our Town" stated that Camden was only "the second town in the South to have polo. Rogers L. Barstow, of Boston, and the late Captain K. G. Whistler succeeded in establishing polo as a Camden sport."

John Daniels, in his equestrian history *Nothing Could Be Finer,* states that the sport of polo began locally in 1898, but that the first team, with much to learn, played only sandlot polo its first two years. He identified the first polo field as "near the Hobkirk Inn on the east side of Broad Street." When that site had to be abandoned for a right of way for the new railroad, a second field was established "in the same location as today's Kirkwood Field."[38]

Equestrian sports were happily enjoyed by tourists and residents alike. Riding and shooting sports were local outdoor endeavors in which visitors were easily accommodated. Daniels refers to Camden's background that made the development a natural one: "Horse racing in Camden began at an early time and the Canteys and Singletons were, among others, well-known for their fine, well-bred winning thoroughbred horses. With this distinguished heritage the citizens of Camden possessed the traditions and the qualities to recognize the opportunity to develop into an outstanding winter resort and a highly regarded year-round residential community."[39]

Local Community Life

Although several towns would develop at the turn of the century from the coming of the Seaboard, only the town of Kershaw, on the Three C's line, had developed significantly before the end of the 1800s. Boykin remained a small stop in the rural community below Camden, but Kershaw, which had experienced much commercial growth in the upper county, incorporated in 1888.

The town of Kershaw had grown rapidly. The area's turpentine industry, farmers, and mining interests at three-mile-distant Haile Gold Mine quickly became leading customers of the railroad. The booming economy attracted people in great numbers. Construction of the railroad depot had been followed by the erection of stores and residences, but the building boom could not keep up with the population growth. The small, one-room schoolhouse on Matson Street was replaced by a larger frame structure in 1888, and ten years later the Kershaw Graded School was established with nine grades. The school's first trustees were R. L. Blackmon, J. V. Welsh, J. T. Stevens, E. D. Blakeney, and James M. Carson.[40]

Kershaw suffered a tragic fire the night of November 13, 1897. According to Miles Gardner, the fire apparently began in a bakery run by an Adams and James C. Hough. The bakery was busier than usual because of an overflow crowd in town to see the circus. David Jesse Gardner, sleeping upstairs in the building next to the bakery, awoke to the smell of smoke and gave the alarm, but the fire rapidly spread through the wooden buildings in both directions from its origin. Thirty-one buildings burned in just over three hours. There was approximately $14,000 of insurance coverage for the estimated $350,000 loss. As Kershaw rebuilt, it did so almost entirely of brick.[41]

Small Communities

A number of small communities enjoyed local closeness but had interest in connecting to events beyond them. The Camden newspapers secured the cooperation of various communities to include their local news on a regular basis. One of the more amusing entries is the following from the May 22, 1879, *Camden Journal:* "We are at a loss, for there is nothing to report. Those who are not sick are well, those who are not dead are alive, those who are not married are trying to be."

Other reports, in contrast, reveal much detail. A column signed "Josh" in the April 19, 1883, *Kershaw Gazette* reported on agricultural conditions and expectations, schools, public roads, and public health at Shaylor's Hill, in upper Kershaw County. It read, "There has been considerable sickness prevailing about recently" and named one resident "still sick with pneumonia." Area weather conditions had forced a delay in the planting of cotton and corn, but "farmers are going in for another big crop of cotton this year; and much more corn will be planted than there was last year." Oats, planted early in the fall, "are looking well and promise a good yield," and furthermore, "everybody is preparing for a big potato crop." There was also anticipation for "a few peaches this summer and lots of apples and blackberries."

The report also revealed, "There has been no white public school open in this locality this year" but added, "One colored school has been in operation for the past two months." On travel conditions, the writer stated, "Beaver Creek Road has recently been worked, but it is yet rather badly cut up," and suggested, "Why not have our public roads worked by contract and paid for by taxation, as suggested in your editorial on public roads a few weeks ago?"

The correspondent "Ajax" reported regarding West Wateree: "This section was once considered as the 'Lost Territory' of Kershaw county, but . . . we have built up wonderfully; improving our lands, building new churches, enlarging and improving our orchards, &c." He continued, "We are also beginning to 'wear off' from the lien system for our maintenance and support; many of us having plenty to eat at home, and some to spare, this year."

The column continued, "West Wateree can boast of the very best well and spring waters and the finest of mill streams; also two trial justices and two physicians." Turning to agriculture, the newspaper reported, "Cotton planting has commenced with a rush. Grain crops are looking better," but added, "Some of the river bottoms are too wet to plough."

Westville was originally referred to as "the West section" because of the large number of families of that name living there. After the Three C's Railroad established its line through the section, a post office was approved at "West," in response to an 1888 application from John C. West, who became postmaster. The mail was delivered over the post roads until the railroad began operations in 1890. That November the post office name was changed to Westville, which the community took thereafter.

The arrival of newspapers and mail was a big event in small communities. Beginning around 1891 Liberty Hill folk would congregate at the "Monkey Roost," a retaining wall of stacked granite slabs near the store that housed the post office. According to the historian Mary Cunningham, many local residents would gather there in the evening and socialize as they waited for the daily mail delivery, but "after the post office moved [1918], the tradition sort of ended."[42]

The November 9, 1887, *Camden Chronicle* gave news of Cantey and Killgo. Cantey lay about nine miles northwest of Camden along the ridge paralleled now by Gaines Church Road. J. E. Creed advertised a branch store in that community and another in the DeKalb community.[43] The newspaper reported that Henry George had a contract to carry the mail from Camden to Cantey and Killgo, about eighteen miles northwest of Camden, and back.

Various sources reveal glimpses of activities at Tiller's Ferry, where Daniel W. Gardner was postmaster from 1886 to 1897, followed by Benjamin L. Norwood. A portion of a letter from Thomas Watts to John Malcolm Watts on October 24, 1881, commented that the "county commissioners let out Tiller's Ferry Bridge to lowest bidder on last Friday. It was taken by a Mr. King of Darlington at 272½ dollars . . . a great reduction in bridge building since John Brannon built Young's Bridge some 8 or 10 years ago at 1000 dollars."[44] In 1884 Benjamin James Ratcliffe built a mill just off what is now called the Old Wire Road, alternately the Stagecoach Road, about ten miles east of Camden. Typical of its time, it was made of timbers hand-hewn with broadaxes. The operation consisted of a gristmill, a sawmill, and a cotton gin. The screw press that packed the ginned cotton into bales was turned by mules.[45]

Organizations and Entertainments

Within and among the different communities, people enjoyed a wide variety of organizations and entertainments. Traditional activities such as churchgoing and neighborhood socializing—including hunting and fishing—were as active as ever, although some organized activities seemed to attract universal interest.

Fraternal orders, for example, were widespread in the late nineteenth century. The January 8, 1878, *Camden Journal* reported the influence of members of Camden's Masonic lodge in helping organize other lodges in neighboring communities. The newspaper stated, "A few years ago, Kershaw Lodge, in Camden, was the only institution of the kind in the county, or within 25 miles of our town," but that "Bishopville, Flat Rock, Spring Hill, and Lynchwood Lodges—all the outgrowth of, or indebted for members, more or less, to Kershaw Lodge—have since been established." The March 5, 1878, newspaper reported a "flourishing lodge of Good Templars" formed by "the colored people." It met weekly "over the store of Mr. D. R. Kennedy." Other lodges such as Knights of Pythias, Odd Fellows, and Woodmen of the World also had devoted members. Additional groups organized as lodges primarily for eligibility for the insurance such groups offered and met less frequently than others.

The appearance of a circus never failed to cause excitement. In 1878 anticipation was keen for the arrival of Old John Robinson's Circus in Camden. The circus was to pitch its tents on the "vacant plot of ground rear of store of Messrs W. A. Ancrum & Company and C. J. Dunlap" and to appear in a grand street pageant the next morning before opening its acts in the afternoon. A popular, advertised feature of the circus was its four elephants. The March 5 newspaper described the scene Sunday afternoon when two hundred to three hundred people, eager to watch the circus enter town, "assembled at the Wateree Bridge to see the elephants come across." The crowd, growing weary, became distracted by a fight between two boys when "suddenly there was a cry that 'the elephants were coming.' Just then the largest one appeared at this end of the bridge, raised his trunk and gave a terrific snort like he was mad." Seeing no keeper with him, the crowd thought that the elephant had broken loose. The fight quickly broke up, and the frightened spectators scattered. Lewis P. Anderson recalled early circuses from 1898: "When I was a boy they held the circus right smack in the middle of Broad Street. They had side shows from the Workman House clear down to where Mt. Moriah Church is now, with elephants, lions, tents all in the street."

A September 5, 1878, *Camden Journal* article commented on baseball as a pastime in some Kershaw County communities. A team from Oakland played a team from Tiller's Ferry "at the Peebles place" with William Herron as umpire. The August 7, 1896, *Camden Chronicle* reported a match game between Columbia and Camden in which the local boys' 9–2 victory "fully sustained their reputation of being good ball players."

A writer in the April 5, 1883, *Kershaw Gazette* exclaimed, "The skating mania has attacked a good many of the young people of the town, and this pleasure is indulged in to a considerable extent." Roller skating is also referred to in a fragment of another 1883 *Kershaw Gazette.* "The ladies" were conducting this entertainment at the "hall of the YMCA" at the corner of Broad and DeKalb streets. Refreshments were served, and the admission was ten cents. The Young Men's Christian Association organized in Camden in 1881.

A regular football schedule began in Camden in 1894, and the sport quickly became popular with students and the public throughout the county. The first teams were intramural ones that year in the Camden Graded School under L. T. Baker, then a teacher and later dean of the faculty at the University of South Carolina. Their first game was played on Thanksgiving Day. The next year the Camden team played its first out-of-town game, with Columbia.

Baker, interviewed in later years, recalled that the first football field was a vacant lot between Lyttleton and Fair streets. "Later," he said, "the polo field was used for football and perhaps one of the first invading teams, the Lancaster high team, played a game against Camden on Christmas day afternoon."[46] The first available scores of Camden playing Lancaster, in 1899, show the home team winners both times, 18–0 and 11–5.[47] Winter tourists are said to have been enthusiastic fans who mingled with local supporters at Camden football games.

Governmental Changes

As communities grew or changed, they required alterations also to the structure of their governments. A General Assembly act of February 20, 1880, enacted the name change of Lynch's Creek to Lynch's River for both its branches. Today the spelling is officially "Lynches," the form often in use earlier as well.

County Lines

In the continuing pattern of more isolated areas seeking more opportunity for self- government, the Salem section that bordered and crossed over Kershaw and Sumter boundaries was part of an area by 1896 actively seeking to create a separate Salem County. Shortly before the November 17 election on the proposal, a letter to the *Camden Chronicle* urged the selection of Lucknow for the county seat, as it was more central and convenient than Bishopville.

Although voters failed to approve the new county, the issue was not dead. The December 18 newspaper reprinted the following from the Sumter paper: "The Salem County fight is to be carried to the Legislature . . . to induce that body to create the county which was defeated at the ballot box." The Sumter paper pointed out a potential conflict of interest with two individuals, a state legislator and the assistant attorney general, being attorneys hired by the Salem County Committee.

When the effort to create a new Salem County failed, supporters changed tactics. With the approval of Assistant Attorney General William Hutson Townsend, they proposed "to take fifty miles less from Kershaw County, thirty-five miles less from Darlington and seventy-five miles more from Sumter and also to change the name." In 1897, when the Salem issue was revised, the General Assembly complied. The following year boundaries were surveyed—mainly following old roads and waterways. In 1902 the voters gave approval for a new county drawn from part of Kershaw County and parts of Darlington and Sumter counties. With Bishopville as its seat, the new county was named in the nostalgic spirit of its time for the revered Confederate commander in chief—Lee County.

Municipal Development and a City Government

Despite some controversies, confidence in the government of Camden was generally stable, and business continued to expand. In mid-1877 a total of $5,292.30

in town currency of the $34,252.10 issued more than twelve years earlier was still outstanding. To redeem the currency the town council issued bonds at 7 percent interest. The council consisted of Intendant J. C. Rollings and Wardens Eugene Dibble, D. C. Kirkley, L. B. Latham, and R. E. Wall. Since town money had been reliable, however, many citizens did not want to surrender it, although by 1880 the scrip had become so worn- out that merchants would no longer accept it.[48]

Camden undertook an important civic improvement a few years later, the building of a new town hall combined with an opera house to enhance business, meeting, and entertainment facilities for area citizens. The town council at the time consisted of Intendant James Jones and Wardens John T. Nettles, M. A. Metts, H. G. Carrison, and John M. Smyrl. In July 1884 they agreed to purchase from Herman and Mannes Baum the property at the southeast corner lot of Rutledge and Broad streets for thirty-five hundred dollars. Here a cavernous old store dubbed "the Ark" had burned seven years earlier.

In June 1885, under Intendant J. C. Rollings, the town issued fifteen thousand dollars in construction bonds. Although in the previous municipal building on the other side of Broad Street the town hall and the town theater shared space above the town market, at this time a separate town market was built just south of the Camden Opera House, as the new building was called. The old town clock and distinctive King Hagler weather vane were moved from the other side of Broad Street and added atop the new structure. The tower still stands at that location.

To meet modern demands Camden sought a new legislative charter, which was granted on December 24, 1890, to replace the municipal charter of 1791 that had governed the town for one hundred years. Under the new charter Camden officially became a city, administered by a mayor and a city council instead of by an intendant and wardens. Dr. John W. Corbett, the administrator during this transition, entered office as intendant and left as mayor. Camden's first elected mayor was H. G. Carrison. The first city council consisted of four members—then called aldermen—D. C. Kirkley, J. C. Mann, J. E. Vaughan, and W. J. Jones.[49]

Marion H. Heyman recalled that Camden employed a lamplighter who went about the main streets lighting the post lamps that illuminated the city streets. Businesses, like homes, were lighted by kerosene lamps. Navigation of city streets was undoubtedly difficult, especially at night or during inclement weather. Heyman added, "The only sidewalks in Camden were those on Broad Street business blocks made of wide slabs of flagstones." Thomas Ancrum recalled the time before Camden had electrical lighting. There were "many dim kerosene lights along Main street and some of the prominent corners. The first electric lights on the streets were known as arc lights and burned a carbon stick, which had to be renewed every few days."

One step forward, which was interrupted by fire after the turn of the century but which had proved its merit and was later reestablished, was the organization of water and electrical utilities. In 1897 the Camden Water, Light and Ice Company, incorporated by Frank K. Bull and E. E. Mandeville, agreed under a twenty-year contract to furnish the city with water and electrical power from a private plant in Kirkwood. Utilities were a major issue in the reelection campaign of Mayor F. Leslie Zemp, who maintained that for about three and one-half mils additional tax the city could purchase lights and water and also maintain a reel company with horses for fire protection.

Another important service arrived in 1896 with the first telephone in Camden. Marion H. Heyman recalled, "Telephones were introduced around the turn of the century by Mr. T. Baxter McClain, coming to Camden from Yorkville, S.C." Camden residents viewed the new system of communication with both excitement and skepticism. The author of "Our Town" recalled that some residents "were very dubious about the claims of hearing a voice a mile or two away. The system had been installed several years before some citizens got up nerve enough to use the 'phone, particularly the older generation."

By spring 1898 a number of other improvements had been made in Camden. The artesian well near the depot was extended to a depth of 150 feet. A number of stores installed electrical wiring to tap the potential of electrical power. The night the power was turned on, Gladis, the young daughter of Superintendent James Hanlan, was the one to flip the switch. Workers hurried to finish the ice factory by summer; machine-made ice was presumed to be healthier than pond ice. In a public health effort, Camden's town minutes of May 24, 1898, recorded compulsory vaccinations in the city.

Four Camden streets were created around the turn of the century. In 1887 M. H. Haile donated land for the street that bears his name. Arthur Lane was created when W. L. Arthur and A. D. Kennedy conveyed land to the city in 1894 for that purpose. Two years later William Clyburn and A. T. Clyburn granted land for Clyburn Street. In 1901 Egmont von Tresckow provided the city with property for a street beside Lafayette Hall, which he had purchased, with the provision that the street be named in honor of the Marquis de Lafayette, who had been welcomed there.[50]

A Background of Violence

In the late nineteenth century Kershaw County stood poised between images of the Old South and the New South, set against a background of violence—violent deeds of nature and violent deeds of man. Some of the deeds of man that were then legal are no longer legal. Some were illegal then, as now. Jim Crow laws and racial intimidation through hints of, if not actual presence of, the Ku Klux Klan and similar groups increased tensions and rivalry.

Dueling

The tensions of political challenges and economic uncertainties strained relations among some who persisted in admiration for "spirit" and "defense of personal honor," values they associated with the southern past. Among whites episodes of dueling, which occurred despite laws to the contrary, dismayed many but for a while were tolerated by adherents of the old code of honor, ironically often the very class of men most opposed to excesses in the present society. Kirkland and Kennedy explain the period thus: "For some time after the Civil War, there seemed to exist a cordiality in the social life of Camden, due doubtless to the common misfortunes endured by all. But by degrees this good fellowship gave way to the poison of jealousies and feuds, leading to the epidemic of duels that for a time cursed this community." The writers also point out, "In two years, 1878–80, four of these affairs culminated here; several others were barely averted."[51] The four, related in various ways, may be summarized as follows:

September 5, 1878, W. B. (Boggan) Cash and S. Miller Williams met across the state line in Anson County, North Carolina. Result—both shots went astray.

December 30, 1878, W. B. (Boggan) Cash and James Cantey met at DuBose's (DuBois) Bridge on the Darlington side of Lynch's Creek. Result—bloodless, but a ball went through Cantey's waistcoat.

August 25, 1879, Thomas Henry (Hal) Clarke and C(harles) J. Shannon met in the vicinity of Hobkirk Hill. Result—both shots went astray.

July 5, 1880, E. B. C. Cash and William M. Shannon met at DuBose's Bridge. (Cash was the father of Boggan Cash; Shannon, the father of C. J. Shannon.) Result—Shannon died on the field.

Public sentiment—locally and beyond—arose instantly in response to the Cash-Shannon duel.[52] Outrage brought an avalanche of editorials and sermons against dueling throughout the South. A coroner's inquest led to an indictment against Cash, who was tried in Darlington for dueling and murder. A jury deliberated five hours but found Cash not guilty. Nevertheless his actions were reviled by many. The South Carolina General Assembly passed an enforceable statute against dueling. The new law required that all state officials take an oath that they never had taken and never would take part in a duel. Since traditionally the class of men most likely to duel was the class that also considered office holding a responsibility, the law and public sentiment proved to be deterrents. The antidueling oath remained in effect until 1947. The Cash-Shannon duel was the last accepted code-of-honor duel, sometimes referred to as the last legal duel in the state and effectively in the country.

Both the principals had served in the Civil War; both held positions of respect in their communities; both had Kershaw County kin and friends. Cash's home was Cash's Depot in Darlington County; Shannon's home was in Camden. Both had sons who had fought previous duels; both men had had roles in dueling also. Cash, grieving the recent loss of his wife, cited slights he perceived to her memory as the cause of the offense leading to the duel. Shannon at death left a wife and thirteen children.

Shannon had won local appreciation for legal defenses of Kershaw County men in Reconstruction conflicts and for his speeches and his written accounts of local history that recalled nostalgically days gone by. As a leader of the local Grange, Shannon had been an advocate encouraging a number of agricultural, business, and community improvements. He had alternately encountered some criticism in his handling of the Joseph Cunningham estate and most recently for his failure to provide financial accounting for costly county expenses related to repairs on the Wateree Bridge. In relation to the latter, Shannon's son had dueled the newspaper editor Clarke, who had raised questions in the issue. Emotions on all sides of the Cash-Shannon duel lasted for a long time.

A Shooting on Rutledge Street

The Cash-Shannon duel may have effectively ended dueling, but violence continued. On July 4, 1882, James L. Haile shot and killed L. W. R. Blair, once a staunch Democrat, who had become disenchanted with that party. Instead he had embraced the Greenback doctrine and such local causes as free pasturage, and he had emerged as an Independent candidate for governor. Blair had the support of most blacks and a small group of whites but had become a pariah to the Democratic Party. The Independence Day on which he was shot, Blair had been speaking to a crowd of blacks in a vacant lot at the southwest corner of Rutledge and Broad streets. Later his body, "pierced by five bullets from a rifle fired by Captain Jas. L. Haile," lay lifeless on Rutledge Street, according to Kirkland and Kennedy.[53]

Accounts differ about the circumstances of the shooting. One story, told by Nan Hough Forester, is that a group of politically prominent men met and reached a consensus that Blair's death would benefit the state. Each drew a card; the man who drew "the death card" was obligated to kill Blair. Haile gave his account at his trial in the Kershaw County court, according to Kirkland and Kennedy. His testimony claimed that Blair, "with right hand in the breast of his coat," approached him in an intimidating fashion. Haile's self-defense was successful; he was acquitted.

According to Kirkland and Kennedy, a sequel to Blair's death occurred a few weeks later with the death of his daughter near the Blair home: "The body of young Rochella Blair was found at the foot of the 'precipice' at Paint Hill. Beside it a vial of white powder, marked 'strychnine' told the story. The cause—grief at her father's death."[54] Nan Hough Forester recalled seeing the half-empty bottle of strychnine presented as evidence. Like the case of Cash and Shannon, the death of Blair brought many emotional reactions from his admirers and detractors.

Crime and Punishment

Newspapers were filled with gruesome details when Oliver Bristow on March 30, 1883, became the first person executed in Kershaw County since Reconstruction. Described as "a dark complected, heavy thick-set negro," Bristow had been convicted of complicity in the previous November 30 murder of Fred M. McDowall "about 10 miles above Camden." Another man said to have also been involved was killed at a ferry on the Catawba River. The murder of McDowall had alarmed many. The evidence against Bristow was circumstantial, but, the newspaper said, the circumstances pointed so clearly to Bristow's complicity that after a seven-hour trial the jury found him guilty. The hanging took place in the jail yard about noon, witnessed by only a few people.

The press gave many details of the execution. The gallows "consisted of two upright posts, capped with a beam, from which the rope was suspended. The trap was arranged with a double door, which was held in position by a pin resting upon the ground. The rope used was obtained in Camden, and was ¾ inch hemp rope." This scaffold "was erected in the jail-yard, on the southern side of the jail, and within a few feet of Broad street." Despite its nearness to the street, where "by 10 o'clock a dense crowd of people had assembled," curtains prevented the curious throng from witnessing the hanging. Before the trap was opened, the prisoner reiterated his claim of innocence. Bristow "ascended the gallows, accompanied by his spiritual adviser, the Reverend Monroe Boykin, who remained with him almost until the fatal moment."[55]

The newspaper reported, "It was not until 12 o'clock that life was found to be extinct; the body having hanged forty-three minutes." Dr. J. E. W. Haile had detected signs of life when he examined the body three previous times. The explanation for the duration was that, contrary to the sheriff's instructions, Bristow had turned his head after the noose was adjusted; as a consequence "the neck was not broken."

Mob Violence

In August 1897, according to local newspapers, more than one hundred masked men came from the West Wateree area through Camden to the Mt. Olivet Baptist Church community. There the mob was said to have removed two Mormon elders from James Dixon's home and to have beaten them severely. One report concluded, "The Mormons are charged with very immoral conduct in the West Wateree section and the people are determined to put a stop to it."[56]

On September 3 the paper identified the mob as "white cappers [Ku Klux Klan members] of Fairfield," who after exhaustive search found their two victims "about five miles below Camden." About forty of the attackers were reported to have been arrested. The writer stated, "The mormons [*sic*] have stirred up more animosity among neighbors than can be settled within a decade, yes, two decades."

Under a separate title, "The Mormon's Troubles," the newspaper reported that two elders "from the vicinity of Ridgeway" had sought protection from the assistant attorney general, presenting him a list of ninety-two persons they alleged had participated in the arson of their church. Among them, they claimed, was a minister. Mormons "out West" sent money to rebuild their house of worship, but the two elders said that they had been threatened with death "if they attempted to remove the materials from the depot at Ridgeway." The assistant attorney general did not take the names, but he wrote neighborhood magistrates to have county sheriffs execute warrants for "serious criminal offenses" against the Mormons. The newspaper stated that there were relatively few Mormons in the state, with the largest settlements in Fairfield, Chesterfield, Lancaster, and Kershaw counties.

The *Chronicle* also related details of the visit of "white cappers" to Camden on August 20, stating that 120 mounted, masked, and armed white men "rode quietly down Main street" about 9:00 P.M., heading toward the south. The report stated, "Others were also seen on the side streets." Two mounted and armed but unmasked men came along about 25 minutes later; they addressed the crowd gathered on Main Street, asking whether a group had come through earlier. When a citizen approached them, one "fired off his gun into the crowd and then galloped rapidly out of town."

Another account in the same column provided slightly different information. The riders, "coming in apparently from across the Wateree river," were said to number ninety-two. They passed through Camden's main streets about 9:15 P.M. "in good order and double file," moving "toward the southern end of the city." This account placed the shooting incident near the opera house, where the rider fired "into the ground." Neither police nor other witnesses recognized any of the vigilantes, but their dress indicated that "they were from the country."

The article cited rumors that these riders might have been the white cappers "who have been after the Mormons lately in Fairfield county." The writer pointed out that "a good many Mormons live a few miles below Camden in the direction taken by the white cappers." The article reported that police were augmenting their usual side arms with Winchester rifles and temporarily might add extra officers.

Problems of Alcohol Control

Many citizens were of the firm opinion that a large degree of general and serious crime, as well as social dissipation, was the result of overindulgence in too freely available alcohol. Recalling conditions in the early 1890s when Camden had nine bars selling liquor by the drink and riotous behavior was common at night and on weekends, F. N. McCorkle remarked, "Ladies were never seen on the streets after nightfall and especially on Saturday." Camden had three black police officers—Dock Carter, Theodore Campbell, and Jack McKain—who patrolled the downtown area. When a white citizen broke the law, McCorkle said, these officers "cautioned them, and if necessary, called their superior white officers."

Temperance had been a major moral guideline preached from pulpits and revival stands for the past half century. Some leaders called more severely for total abstinence from beverage alcohol. A growing number of people felt that moral injunctions would be better served by legislation. In 1892, in fact, statewide voters in a nonbinding referendum voted in approval of prohibition. Amid a variety of opinions, controversial legislation passed in the late hours of Christmas Eve in the heat of debate between whiskey interests and prohibitionists.

The law that created the South Carolina Dispensary, dubbed "[Governor] Ben Tillman's baby," was a compromise that caught people off guard. The law took liquor sales out of the hands of barrooms and merchants and made the state the sole dispenser of alcohol.[57] The Kershaw County legislator Thomas J. Kirkland, not a prohibitionist but a dispensary opponent, explained his concerns to his constituency in the January 27, 1893, *Camden Chronicle.* He found most objectionable "that it greatly concentrates the liquor elements directly upon and within the official life of the state. It adds a corrupting power to the political machinery of office in Columbia."

Camden, nonetheless, acted quickly to comply with the law in order to have a legal location for alcohol sales, a place that could be controlled and that would bring in tax revenues. It was first necessary to set up a local dispensary and to appoint a dispenser, who had to post a three-thousand-dollar bond. The dispensary, drugstore fashion, was to sell bottled alcohol over the counter to adult customers who signed for it but who could not consume the product on the premises or in public. The newly designated Kershaw County Board of Control considered petitions from two local grocers for appointment as dispenser, choosing D. F. Dixon since he had more signatures than H. E. Halsall did.[58] The dispenser received one hundred dollars per month and the assistance of a salaried clerk. At a monthly rent of twenty-five dollars, the dispensary was set up in the Wolfe Building on Broad Street, with Dixon allowed to sell groceries in another section of the space.

The Camden dispensary was one of only three in the state ready to open on July 1, 1893, the day the law went into effect.[59] By October there were more than fifty dispensaries in operation in the state. Churches favoring prohibition were not readily mollified by the new law. Dispenser Dixon's church, Lyttleton Street Methodist, disciplined him first with suspension and then with expulsion while he was selling alcohol.[60]

Barrooms, with no products to sell, automatically closed. The individual dispensary became known as an "Original Package" store. Consumption did not necessarily decrease, although money now flowed into the pockets of the state rather than those of individual sellers. Thomas Ancrum recalled, "Whiskey then was sold by the dispensaries, which were operated by the State of South Carolina and a half pint sold for 15 cents. A lot of 'Fuss X' corn liquor brought 50 cents a quart. It was more or less understood that ladies were not to be on the streets on Saturday afternoons, as there were many drunks on the streets, and the little police force was kept busy locking up the unruly drunks.[61] Many people carried pistols then and shooting scrapes or cutting scrapes were not uncommon."[62]

The asset most practical people recognized in the dispensary system, despite its shortcomings, was that money that flowed into public coffers was put to use for public good at state, county, and municipality levels. The fact that state profits went largely to public education did not, however, satisfy some citizens into believing that the system was in the moral best interest.

Looking Backward and Forward

The violence that remained a part of the background of the late 1800s reached all levels of society. Personal, political, religious, and racial elements were the roots for part of the violence, which was sometimes enacted individually, sometimes as a part of ritual behavior, and sometimes as a part of vigilante actions. Violence existed in contrast to, but was as real as, forward-looking aspects of the times.

Even in their own times, opinions of the closing years of the century were mixed. An article in the October 8, 1897, *Camden Chronicle* commented on southern agricultural and industrial development. Stating that "people are employed, mines, mills, and railroads are busy," the article also reported that, except for cotton and tobacco, farmers were experiencing good yields with prices higher than in recent years. The piece also commented on the gradual diversification of the region with the establishment of "new enterprises" and an influx of northern immigrants "of the best character." The article pointed out that from 1800 to 1897 southern mills had increased their share of the cotton consumed by American mills from 23 percent to nearly 87 percent.

That picture of prosperity, based on a conversation with a "land and industrial agent of the Southern Railway," conflicts with a newspaper article several months later, however. At that time the January 14, 1898, *Camden Chronicle* reacted to accounts of prosperity printed in northern journals that said that area banks had an excess of money to lend at low rates of interest. The newspaper, in referring to "this twaddle about returned prosperity," stated that it saw no tangible evidence of such. It asserted that locally the farming class that "comprises the bulk of our citizenship and furnishes the back bone of all commercial prosperity" was not experiencing prosperity. In the coming century the strain between the farming class and other economic groups would become even more pronounced.

12

Uneven Steps

The Progressive Era

As the twentieth century unfolded and the world moved toward the first of two encroaching world wars, still-agrarian Kershaw County moved in some ways with the rest of America into what is known as the Progressive Era. A prevailing belief during this time was that people who coordinated their efforts and applied knowledge and logical reasoning could solve long-standing problems of society. In some ways, like Progressives everywhere, citizens believed that they were moving forward energetically and positively into an improved future. In other ways, like the rest of the South, Kershaw County settled into divisions of racial segregation and of social and economic distinctions.

In the twentieth century prewar period, Kershaw County was visibly altered by the progress of railroad towns and the construction of agriculture-related industries. An expanded railroad system, central to the change, eased travel to, from, and within the area. An influx of tourists grew with increased accommodations and leisure activities, although visitors and the struggling farmers and mill workers who constituted the majority of the local population moved in different spheres within the same community. The advent of automobile travel necessitated improvements to the county's roads and bridges. Twice more during the period the forces of nature washed away the only bridge across the untamed Wateree River, leaving residents and travelers relying for lengthy spells on tedious ferry crossings.

The installation and expansion of electrical, water, and communications systems enhanced public health and safety and presented new demands on local government. Electrification and flood control became possible with the construction of dams on the Catawba-Wateree system, although the Wateree Dam, the final one in the chain, was not in operation until after a world war. Problems of crime and lack of education were still critical obstacles to the development of the county. Yet by 1917 when Kershaw County troops responded to the nation's call for defenders in the Great War, the area was being drawn into some aspects of a more modern time. Local efforts paralleled many national efforts for reform, especially those combating illiteracy, disease, and poverty.

Persistence of Old Ways

Agriculture—especially cotton—continued to be the main enterprise of the county in the early twentieth century. In downtown Camden a gin operated on

Arthur Lane, and the offices of several cotton brokers stood on Rutledge Street. Platforms and warehouses filled the interior parts of the block. Each fall farmers had their cotton ginned either in town or elsewhere and sold most of it in Camden. Other times of the year they came to town to purchase needed supplies and equipment—usually on credit—from local merchants. The credit was an open account extended throughout the growing season on a signed agreement to pay when the crop was sold. Besides liens on crops, banks and merchants accepted liens on land, homes, equipment, or even furniture and farm animals to assure repayment of debts.

Farmers made trips to town on weekends. Camden merchants remained open late Friday and Saturday nights, the streets illuminated by gas lamps. Some merchants also operated on Sunday mornings, and in fact, since many store owners or managers lived on the premises, some opened at any hour to accommodate arriving customers. Camden's merchants included those from a sizable Jewish community as well as black businessmen. Marion H. Heyman recalled that the following were leading merchants: Tom Arrants; Baum Brothers (Herman and Mannes); G. C. Bruce; James Burns; H. G. Carrison (later Rhame Brothers); Eugene Dibble; William Geisenheimer; Hirsh Brothers; A. D. Kennedy; John Man; John T. Nettles Sr.; Springs, Heath, and Shannon; M. Tobin; English Vaughan; Paul Villepigue S. M. Wilson; Adolph Wittkowsky; David Woolfe; George Young; F. Leslie Zemp; and Zemp and DePass Druggists.

Animals were still ever present in city life. In 1900 three liverymen, Evans Collins, Sam Latham, and George T. Little, operated their respective stables in downtown Camden. Both Collins and Little were on the south side of DeKalb Street—Collins in the block west of Broad, and Little in the block east of Broad. The Latham Stables stood on the east side of Broad Street in the block north of York. When these busy places ceased to operate in coming years, the cause was not sanitation concerns but the advent of the automobile.

Families in town kept household animals for reasons other than transportation. Thomas Ancrum recalled that in the early 1900s, "Nearly every home had a horse or cow or both. Cows were assembled daily during the summer months and driven [as a group by a young black boy to] pastures near town, at a cost of 25 cents a week. It was [a] common sight to see as many as one hundred cows being driven to Smyrls pasture, back of the cemetery. Mr. [John M.] Smyrl kept a bull in his pasture and if a calf was born later, the owner of the cow was to pay him a fee of one dollar." Until the advent of electricity and refrigeration, a family's cow remained their safest, most reliable source of milk and dairy products.

Contract Labor

The use of contracts binding labor to a landlord, a practice set up during Reconstruction, persisted into the new century. A. C. Watts of Cantey posted a notice in the September 6, 1901, *Camden Chronicle* naming two men who "are under contract to me and have left my premises without my permission." Watts warned the public "not to hire or in any way harbor" the two. Similar notices appeared in the following months and years. The Camden City Council in December 1905 declared it illegal for anyone to entice "any tenant, servants, or laborer, under contract with another . . . whether verbal or written" to leave the limits of the city. Violators would be guilty of disorderly conduct and subject to a fine not to exceed forty dollars per violation. In April 1913 one individual who lured ten laborers from Camden was taken off the train at Cheraw under warrant from the Davidson Lumber Company. Returned to Camden under the charge of "enticing labor from one state to another" and also wanted in Columbia, he was set to work on the chain gang, laboring on Kershaw County roads to pay off his fine.

Farm Distresses

Walter Edgar points out that the continuation of low crop prices and lean conditions on worn-out land led to decreases in farm sizes and landownership. Hardships of the lien system also contributed to these problems. The average farm in South Carolina in 1880 was 143 acres; ten years later it was 115 acres; and in 1900 it was only 90 acres. Furthermore, while one-half of farmers in 1880 owned their own land, by 1900 only 38 percent were landowners. In other words, six of ten farmers in 1900 were tenants or sharecroppers.[1] In general the statewide conditions reflected Kershaw County's situation as well. Most who worked the land had little chance to get ahead through agriculture, but lack of education and opportunity afforded little choice of any other vocation. Even traditional agriculturalists recognized the need for changes. Those who were forward-looking spoke of potential power systems, industrialization, and railroads.

Three Major Railroads

Three major railroad systems, all with eastern markets, had entered Kershaw County by 1900 and intersected at Camden. The new rail connections provided the infrastructure to diversify the county's agriculture-dominated economy and prompted other improvements. Tourists from many directions were soon making their way into the area, and residents were moving about with increased ease.

The Southern

The one railroad in existence before the turn of the century, the line from Charleston that eventually extended to Marion, North Carolina, continued operation as the Southern Railway.[2] Melverda O. Gaskin described "four to six trains daily moving between Camden, Kershaw and Lancaster" and said, "Residents could visit anywhere between these towns and be back at home in the evening." By various connections along the line, county citizens could travel in one direction to the Atlantic or in the other direction to major parts of the interior of America.

Passengers departed and arrived in Camden at the Southern Depot on the south side of DeKalb Street, between Mill and Rippondon streets. The freight depot was nearby on the northern side of DeKalb Street. The 1911 railroad map of South Carolina for the S.C. Railroad Commission shows two stops in the county below Camden—first Stockton and then Boykin—before Hagood in Sumter County. The map shows three stops north from Camden before the border town of Kershaw—in order, Cool Springs, Kalb (later DeKalb), and West (later Westville).

An Atlantic Coast Line "Short Line"

In 1900, in connection with the Atlantic Coast Line Railroad, the South Carolina lumber magnate Thomas Wilson reached an agreement to extend his Northwestern railroad line (which local wags nicknamed "the None Worse") from Sumter to join onto the Southern Railway at a point three and one-half miles south of Camden. Locally the road completed in 1901 was sometimes called "the Wilson short line" or "short cut." The Northwest junction was not far above the present intersection of Highways 521 and 261.[3] Between that point and present Rembert in Sumter County were small stops—in order, Frierson, Cantey, and Ellerbee. In 1900 the Atlantic Coast Line ran from Virginia into Georgia and was continuing to expand. In Camden passengers made their connections to the Atlantic Coast Line by boarding a Northwestern train at the Southern Depot.

The Seaboard

The Seaboard Air Line Railway from the turn of the century had tremendous impact throughout the county. Scattered rural dwellers collected at some of the county railroad stops and formed new enterprises in small communities and towns that developed—Bethune, Cassatt, Lugoff, and Blaney (now Elgin). Seaboard agents, anxious to increase use of their railroad, actively promoted business opportunities all along their line, from tourism to agriculture to industry.

The Seaboard also dramatically improved connections between Camden and Columbia. Earlier, via the old South Carolina Railroad, a local trip to the capital city took several hours and necessitated circuitous travel—first southward from Camden along the river down to Wateree and the Kingville junction just above the Congaree Swamp, and then by another line northward to Columbia. By 1901 the Seaboard had constructed a steel bridge trestle straight across the Wateree River at Camden and reduced the trip to less than an hour and a half.[4] As a result some Columbia businesses began to expand their interests to Camden and beyond.

The impact of railroad lines on the creation of towns such as Blaney (now Elgin) is recognized in this mural Brent and Colt Shirley painted for the Blaney-Elgin centennial celebration in 2008.

Camden passengers boarded at the Seaboard Depot at Chesnut and Gordon streets, near present Monroe Boykin Park, which was then called Seaboard Park. Freight was shipped from a depot at DeKalb and Gordon. J. T. Burdell's 1901 *Map of Kershaw County* depicts the Seaboard trestle over the Wateree at its present location. It stood north of the "iron bridge" then used by land travelers, south of the present U.S. Highway 1 bridge.

Along with the advantages of trains, dangers were also present for passengers and for people and animals along the tracks. Unpaved roads crossing the tracks proved troublesome. In January 1901 a boxcar en route to the Camden Cotton Mill turned over at the edge of town because the track was "covered with dirt from wagons crossing it." While encouraging improvements to old ways, railroads were also challenged by newer modes of transportation.

Competition from the Automobile

In 1900 the first automobile brought to the area rolled into Camden at the head of the parade for Field & Hanson's Minstrel Show. This "horseless carriage" created quite a bit of gawking and excitement. Thomas Ancrum recalled that the first person in town to own an automobile was Dr. John W. Corbett, and the second was the son of Dr. A. A. Moore. Marion H. Heyman described young Caleb Moore's auto as "a two cylinder underslung affair with high wheels and dashboard [similar to] buggies of the time with control lever on the right side and a long bar across the lap for steering." Encountering a fast Seaboard train on North Broad, the young man nearly died in a resulting crash that destroyed his vehicle. The crash was only the first of a number of serious accidents at the Dusty Bend crossing, for many years a notorious danger spot.

In the years before state licensing, one dollar paid the county for a white enamel auto tag. Heyman was issued tag number 14 for a red Maxwell runabout that he bought in Columbia but did not know how to drive. He hired Bob McCreight, one of the few locals who possessed driving skill, to drive the vehicle home to Camden for him. Heyman described the route before auto roads: "There were probably four or five miles of sand clay road out of Columbia on the Two Notch Road. All the rest was deep sand, hence I had to get out and stay out and push for more than twenty miles." A large crowd greeted them in Camden to view the car, which had no windshield, top, or lights. Heyman added, "A short time before the First World War Highway No. 50 from Columbia was 'paved' with sand clay and shortly after became part of Highway No. One with hard-surface paving."

New businesses organized to deal with the new equipment. Autos were such novelties that their sale was treated as a news story rather than as advertising. The May 3, 1912, *Camden Chronicle* carried a notice that Camden Motor Company had just received "one of the handsomest touring cars ever brought to this city." A representative of the J. I. Case Company was in town demonstrating it, "the latest model 40-horse machine." After a time motorized vehicles were put to work on farms and for businesses and were used in conjunction with railroads to transport deliveries. Eventually the need for improved highways to handle new transportation would alter the county landscape, as the building of railroads had done, and would decrease the isolation of individuals and communities. Such changes, however, came gradually.

Growth on the Southern Line

Kershaw

In the early twentieth century the town of Kershaw, bisected by the Southern Railway, continued rapid growth. By 1900 the area had its own newspaper, the *Kershaw Era,* edited by J. W. Hamel. There were fifteen hundred inhabitants and more than two dozen stores as well as a number of shops, a large planing mill, two banks, and several churches. Streets and sidewalks had been improved with packed clay, cooperatively brought in and laid down by inhabitants. There was a telegraph and telephone office; shops for machining, blacksmithing, and woodworking; three restaurants and two icehouses; two barbershops and two shoe shops; two livery stables and a marble works; and three drugstores and a dispensary for alcohol sales. In 1902 John T. Stevens founded the Kershaw Oil Mill, and the Kershaw Telephone Company was established with twenty subscribers. That same year Kershaw was incorporated and elected its first mayor, Osborne Floyd.[5]

After the establishment of Kershaw's cottonseed-oil mill, some area citizens grew restless under what they considered unfair taxation, the taxes in Lancaster County being higher than in adjoining Kershaw County. This faction worked to get the entire town in Kershaw County, asserting that the boundary line had been inaccurately surveyed. The Kershaw and Lancaster county legislative delegations contested the issue until 1907, when they reached a compromise giving each county approximately one-half of the town's business district.

A year after this border compromise, disaster struck Lancaster County's Haile Gold Mine, a major area employer. With periodic modifications the mine had operated productively until 1908 when a boiler exploded, destroying the sixty-stamp mill, killing Manager Ernest Thies, and ceasing operations. In a 1911 foreclosure John T. Stevens purchased the property, transferring it to Haile Gold Mining Corporation. A small, modern cyanide operation started two years later but was abandoned after several months.[6]

One multiple entrepreneur during Kershaw's growth was S. W. Heath. In 1900 he owned the Heath Banking and Mercantile Company and was a partner in the Clyburn Heath Mule Company, which hired out, sold, and traded horses and mules. He was also a partner in the Heath & Jones lumber operation at Flat Creek that worked twenty mules, was an organizer of the Kershaw Oil Mill and of the Kershaw Telephone Company, and was the founder of a granite company at Russell Place west of Kershaw.

Stoneboro

Russell Place, once a part of Kershaw County, is now known as Stoneboro and is just over the line in Lancaster County. The area was always known for its rock formations. However, it was not until 1900 that those characteristics were made profitable. That year Dr. T. J. Strait, owner of three thousand acres bordering both counties, met with a Southern Railway agent about a possible railroad route from Winnsboro to Heath Springs across his property. The agent noted the granite formations and sent them for testing.

As a result, by 1902 land had been leased and quarrying had begun. Andrea Steen detailed the companies that carried out extensive quarrying operations for a dozen years before hard times brought an end to the era. Part of the ambitious efforts, and likely a partial cause for its eventual demise, was the expense of a private spur line from Russell Place to join the railroad at Heath Springs. In 1907

S. W. Heath moved his business interests to the area, began operating a granite quarry and a store, and spearheaded the railroad building. He encouraged the community's name change to Stoneboro. In 1908 the post office officially became Stoneboro as well. By that year granite was being shipped by train to all parts of the country. Steen stated, "The quarry brought about many changes at Russell Place. The sleepy little community was becoming a bustling place." Many men, accustomed to farming, worked for paychecks for the first time in their lives.[7]

The very success of the quarry contributed to the industry's downfall. In order to keep up with orders it expanded and could not afford the expense, especially combined with upkeep on its railroad. In 1913 and 1914 the holdings were sold off, leaving only the Stoneboro name to live on.

Growth on the Seaboard Line

In late May 1900 the Seaboard Air Line Railway marked the completion of its line from Richmond, Virginia, to Tampa, Florida, with officials traveling its full length and back on two trains that stopped and celebrated along the way. Harvey Teal examined the impact of the Seaboard in a two-part article.[8] In the first part he quoted newspaper accounts describing the arrival of the celebratory trains: "There was quite a crowd at the station to greet the arrival of the train [from Richmond], and those on board reported that all along the line there had been great crowds at the stations, bringing flowers and showing their friendliness to the Seaboard in many ways. At Camden the ladies were out in full force and [railroad] President Williams was pleased with the cordiality of their welcome." Teal's article explains, "The two trains passed Camden about eight o'clock in the evening on a Wednesday as they journeyed to Tampa." He quotes the press, "The first train was composed of seven coaches and carried the distinguished party and the Seaboard's fine band! As soon as the train pulled in the band alighted and played 'Dixie' which was greeted with cheers by the large crowd who went out to witness the finest train that ever passed Camden."

The first part of Teal's article points out significant changes in the names and numbers of towns and villages that would locate along the Seaboard path: "About every seven to ten miles, the railroad constructed two sidetracks and in many places, built a station or 'depot' where a 'depot agent' handled mail, passengers, freight and other railroad business. Since the Seaboard was a single track line, these sidetracks were constructed to allow trains to pass and to serve as a place to park freight cars for loading and unloading. If not already present a village or town usually developed at these sidetracks and stations." As train schedules became more regular, farming families and even farm animals adapted the sounds of trains into their daily routines, especially if a train whistle coincided with a mealtime.

A northeastern county landmark between Cassatt and Midway is the long-used Seaboard railroad overpass above busy U.S. Highway 1, another significant transportation route.

Bethune

"With the coming of the railroad in 1900," according to the local historian Harriet Mays, "the people began to move inward and the community was thickly settled between the Lynches rather than on the river banks."[9] Teal's article states that "the post office of Lynchwood [as the area was then known] was moved three miles east to the railroad." The February 2, 1900, *Camden Chronicle* remarked: "We were shown a plat of the town of Lynchwood one day this week by that excellent gentleman, Mr. S. T. Gardner, who has laid off the town in streets and building lots, and is writing out titles to the various lots which sell for $50.00 per lot. The town is nicely laid off, Main Street running north and south, and the railroad running near the southern part of the town." By several accounts the property owner Daniel Murdock Bethune, a Confederate veteran and state legislator, gave the railroad the right of way through his land. For his favors and his position as a leading citizen, the name of the town was changed in his honor. As Mays stated, "The town was chartered as Bethune in 1900 with K. C. Estridge the first intendant."

Teal's article comments that the post office name changed also and that "in early July 1900, 800 to 1,000 new people from various places gathered to celebrate the birth of this new town with speeches by various dignitaries." The October 18, 1901, *Camden Chronicle* reported: "Since the arrival of the S.A.L. [railroad] here there has been a steady growth of this town. Stores and dwellings are continually going up. There are perhaps a dozen or more saw mills in or within hearing of the town. The new Presbyterian church here which is nearing completion, will be one of the most attractive churches in the county." Bethune also built a town hall and completed Bethune Graded School in 1902. The town suffered great loss by fire in 1907 but continued to develop with the organization of the first Bank of Bethune in 1908 and the completion of a hotel three years later.

Cassatt and Shepard

The railroad gave names to two county stops, Cassatt and Blaney, later towns at opposite ends of the county, in order to honor bankers or stockholders who helped to finance the Seaboard Air Line Railway. Cassatt lies seven miles south of Bethune. There is no record that Alexander Johnston Cassatt, for whom the stop was named, ever visited the area.[10] The second part of Teal's article begins with the explanation that Cassatt was granted a post office on December 24, 1900, and "lots and streets were laid out on both sides of the railroad, lots sold, and sidetracks and a depot constructed," but the community "has never grown beyond the village status." According to a Camden newspaper in 1913, Cassatt in that year had four stores, an express office, a post office, a rural route, a sawmill and gin, a shingle mill, and a nearby school. Seven miles south of Cassatt at another stop, "the Shepard community developed as a result of the railroad coming through. Sidetracks were built, but the community never received a post office." Cassatt's neighbor Shepard, therefore, never grew as a town.

Blaney

West of the Wateree River and a dozen miles from Camden, Blaney, another railroad stop named for a stockholder, slowly developed into the town that presently is known as Elgin. The town was originally called Jeffers after a post office was established there in 1898 and the community adopted the name of its first postmaster, William T. Jeffers. When the Seaboard came, Teal's article states, "the post office name was changed to Blaney. A town developed around the railroad depot and post office." By some reports "Mr. Blaney," whose first name is now lost, visited locally while the tracks were being laid. Blaney was incorporated on January 23, 1908, and a brick schoolhouse became the community pride in 1912. Jesse T. Ross and D. D. Evans owned the first store built in the town, and Ross served for forty-seven years as Blaney's first postmaster.

Lugoff

On the west side of the Wateree River about five miles west of Camden and seven miles east of Blaney, Lugoff gained its name from another type of railroad connection. One source cites Congressman W. F. ("Railroad Bill") Stevenson of Cheraw, a longtime attorney for the Seaboard, for the assertion that "the town of Lugoff got its name from Count Lugoff of Russia, who was one of the civil engineers who built the road from Richmond to Jacksonville."[11] Railroad records show that N. E. Lugoff, a Russian or Prussian native, was assistant chief engineer working on the line from Camden to Cayce. An old Camden newspaper column stated, "The railroad was built in the late Nineties, when only mules and men were available for the work. There was no such thing as bulldozers, drag lines, trucks, gasoline engines, etc. then, and the work was tedious. The older citizens recall that there were many Russian laborers working on the construction, and what became of them, no one can recall."[12] Teal's article explains that "the community of Lugoff developed on the railroad and received a post office on 18 July 1900. It grew slowly for many years."

The former Blaney railroad depot, moved and renovated as a feed-and-tack store outside Elgin. The telegraph operator and other personnel watched for trains from the bay windows at right.

Railroad publicists and promoters were anxious to point to examples of prosperity along their lines. The Lugoff area having been a significant farming section of the county and not as ravaged as other areas by Union invasions, its land had been in better shape than most after the war. The coming of the railroad gave development a boost in the area. Local newspapers and other publications widely promoted Lugoff for success in rural agriculture. They described a "progressive" agriculture—farming with modern equipment, up-to-date methods, and of course railroad access.

Careful reading shows that the farmers, farm sizes, and conditions described in Lugoff were far different from those typical in the county at the time. The specific Lugoff landowners described were businessmen, merchants, and bankers. They were educated, backed with capital from other sources, possessed of large acreage, and positioned to take advantage of railroad assets. They hired farm managers (overseers) with agricultural expertise and experience. Surely if New South agriculture were to prosper in Kershaw County, it would do so under these ideal conditions.

An article in the May 27, 1904, *Camden Chronicle* provided a promotional glimpse of the West Wateree section at that time. The area, connected to Camden and the east side of Kershaw County with an iron toll bridge and a Seaboard Air Line Railway bridge, had "majestic plantations" on which grew cotton, corn, and rice. The anticipated rice harvest would "take 20 [railroad] cars," nearly double the normal ten to twelve cars. The chief producers of rice were the plantations of Springs & Shannon and Mrs. H. R. Jordan. The plantations of the Baum brothers (Mannes and Herman) and of Henry Savage raised and baled "hay enough for several menageries," the area's total production of "30 to 40 car loads being forwarded . . . by wagon procession." A. D. Kennedy's estate, "with its cotton gin and saw mill, barns, and cottages," resembled a village. "Fifty car loads of cotton seed were forwarded last year and 6,150 sacks of fertilizers were shipped in this year." Wagons transported most of the cotton shipped to Camden, and some went by rail.

One and one-half miles from the bridge lay the village of Lugoff. In 1904 it had three stores owned respectively by Mrs. T. R. Team, J. N. Jones, and M. B. Rabon. All three proprietors also owned plantations. Jones owned the village site, served as postmaster, and operated a large "60-saw Van Winkle" cotton gin and a small sawmill. A mile away the planter J. S. Hammond operated a cotton gin and also bought cottonseed for the Southern Cotton Oil Company. C. P. Jones managed a gin on the J. K. Jones plantation.

Victor Ward engaged in many ventures. He had come three and one-half years before as Lugoff's first railroad agent, a position he retained along with that of express agent and telegrapher. Ward also was a buyer of cottonseed for the South Carolina Oil Company, manager of the Team warehouse, and operator of a lien business. The 1904 article continued, "Lugoff, besides mail each way by rail, has a rural route up river, and to Bellfield [an upper West Wateree post office], sending about 4,000 pieces of mail per month, and another route will soon be down the river." William R. Reasonover, a former carpenter and builder, served as mail carrier for the U.S. Rural Free Delivery (RFD) route.

A decade later forward-looking agricultural investors were looking for more profitable ventures than cotton. In 1914 L. I. Guion bought land in West Wateree that had been depleted by a century of cotton farming and converted it to the raising of Hereford cattle. Guion built a dike parallel to the Wateree River to prevent floodwaters from inundating the bottomland that made up his pastures. He planted the upland portion with corn and cotton, using manure from his cattle for fertilizer. He created seven essentially equal pastures "all coming to one point." Here he sunk a large well that would supply his cattle with water. He also built large sheds under which livestock could be fed and cared for during inclement weather. Henry Savage too experimented with raising beef cattle in West Wateree. The April 3, 1914, newspaper reported the rail shipment of twenty-seven Angus cattle—three bulls and twenty-four heifers—to his Westerham plantation.

Government agents had joined with cattle producers in Kershaw County in efforts to eradicate the cattle tick, a great concern statewide. Guion, for example, had a large dipping vat on his West Wateree farm. When he loaded sixty-nine cows, averaging 694 pounds each, into two cars at the Lugoff siding and shipped them to Baltimore, the January 1, 1915, *Camden Chronicle* deemed it "one of the largest shipments of cattle ever made from this county." The July 9 newspaper reported that Guion's Camden Beef and Cattle Farms had shipped another thirty-five cattle, this time to Richmond.

Government aid to fight the cattle tick was one of the first local effects of the 1914 Smith-Lever Act, which formed a partnership between the U.S. Department of Agriculture and the nation's land-grant colleges to develop the Cooperative Extension Service. By 1920 the farm demonstration agent W. L. Saunders was providing on-site assistance throughout rural areas in Kershaw County. Before long the two influential positions of county farm agent and home-demonstration agent, with aid from Clemson and Winthrop colleges, provided local leadership in research-based progress for farm and market and for home, school, and community.

Other Signs of Progress

An encouraging sign of progress in 1904 was the opening of a chartered savings bank in Camden, the Wateree Building and Loan Association. Its purpose was to encourage thrift by making savings easy and profitable. The bank in turn invested savings in local enterprises.

New Public Buildings

In 1901 Camden City Council voted in favor of an eighty-three-hundred-dollar contract to build a new two-story brick jail overlooking the town on the crest of the hill halfway between DeKalb Street and the area that became present Lafayette Street. The five-room facility, with residential space in the front for the jailer and his family, had capacity for forty prisoners. The crumbling conditions of the old jail had resulted in constant threats of escapes. There are no records showing concern about building a jailhouse in close proximity to business and residential areas, and its location may possibly have then been considered a visible deterrent to crime.

By early 1904 steps were under way to replace the existing Kershaw County Courthouse, deemed "out of date and out of repairs" as well as "unsafe for the records . . . cold, damp and unsafe for the health of officials and attendants." The February grand jury approved twenty-five thousand dollars in bonds, and by June building sites at the upper end of town were being examined. In mid-July an early morning fire destroyed a hilltop landmark on Broad Street, the revered old Lafayette Hall, and that site consequently proved to be the preferred location for the new courthouse.[13] By November 1905 the commissioners accepted the completed new courthouse building, and county officials occupied it the following month.

Economic Progress

Throughout the Progressive Era newspapers eagerly proclaimed the progress—or decried the lack of it—in their respective communities. A January 18, 1901, *Chronicle* article, "The Development of Camden," asserted that the local community was on the cusp of an economic boom. The writer cited as a major asset the rail lines with competitive freight rates linking the community to "every part of the Union." On the commercial side he pointed to the successful operation of the cottonseed-oil mill and to a new enterprise nearing completion, "E. M. Boykin's cotton factory."

Cotton manufacturing, in fact a touch-and-go operation, taxed both managers and operatives. In 1900 a second cotton factory, the third in Camden's history, had been constructed beside Factory Pond (now Kendall Lake), "very nearly on the site of the old DeKalb Factory" that had burned before the Civil War. Incorporated first as the DeKalb Cotton Mill, the $144,000 factory opened with 12,500 spindles and 300 looms. Its mill village had seventy houses. When corporation president E. Miller Boykin died in 1903, the factory closed for a year. It was reorganized and operated for four years as Pine Creek Mill and was then sold to other interests, who controlled it until 1916.[14]

Meanwhile the Camden Cotton Mill, which had struggled into existence in the previous decade, continued to operate while working to solve problems. In

February 1901 P. T. Villepigue resigned as president for health reasons. In 1905 the mill again closed and reorganized. R. B. Pitts Sr. began that year at the head of the operation that took the name Hermitage Cotton Mill. He slowly guided it into the black, beginning an association that linked the Pitts family for decades with Hermitage. Amid the struggles of managers and operatives, the potential of cotton manufacturing held promise.

In Kershaw the cessation of gold mining operations in 1908 combined with the depletion of most of the area's timber from cutting or turpentining led to community interest in a new industry. Kershaw's John T. Stevens had joined Lancaster's cotton mill magnate Leroy Springs in other ventures. The two partnered again to help provide Kershaw with a cotton mill in 1912. Springs became a major stockholder and president of the Kershaw Cotton Mill, while Stevens became its vice president. Some of the cotton mill's hundreds of employees lived in the surrounding countryside, and others moved into the area to live in company housing. Availability of jobs again encouraged workers and residents of upper Kershaw County.

Located in Camden beside the railroad on east DeKalb Street, on five acres originally part of the DeSaussure estate, a cottonseed-oil company began operation in fall 1900. The following spring the owners, the Atlantic Cotton Oil Company, sold the business to the Southern Cotton Oil Company. In addition to ginning and selling cotton, the new oil mill produced cottonseed oil, meal, hulls, and linters for the parent company Wesson Oil & Snowdrift, Inc. Cottonseed oil was shipped in railroad tank cars to the Savannah, Georgia, refinery that processed Wesson Oil and Snowdrift shortening for human consumption.

Another oil mill product, cottonseed meal, was an ingredient in livestock feed and also in fertilizer, some of which was distributed to local farmers. The lint went to munitions plants—a major consumer after 1914—and to factories producing cellulose and mattresses. Those products were shipped up the Atlantic seaboard as far as New England. Another product of the Camden plant, cottonseed hulls were largely consumed in this state. Farmers used these hulls, which have a nutritional value similar to that of hay, to feed beef and dairy cattle. Thus the railroad connections promoted industry, which in turn assisted area farmers.

According to "The Development of Camden," in the January 18, 1901, issue of the *Camden Chronicle,* other signs of contemporary progress were the improvement and painting of existing homes and the new construction of "pretty homes on lots which have been vacant for centuries." The writer noted work under way to develop the Lafayette Hall property of Egmont von Tresckow. The street he was cutting through the property would benefit the town as "the natural outlet from Main [Broad] street to the Seaboard passenger depot [Gordon Street at Chesnut]." Materials were already on-site for the first

The rear of the DeRoyal Textiles building, which looks much as it did when the building housed the Hermitage Cotton Mill

of many homes that would soon line the street. The writer described the area that became known as Lafayette Avenue as "high, dry and airy" and stated, "Being situated at the summit of the first ridges, the drainage is perfect." The continued northward movement of Camden was considered an advantage to overcoming health problems associated with the low-lying areas of earlier development.

The writer with the positive outlook for Camden cited as a major disadvantage to the town's progress the fact that the two local newspapers in 1901 wasted valuable space on gossipy comments such as who dined with whom or who owned a "Jersey cow with a crumpled horn." He stated, "Camden has outgrown these little matters." He urged businessmen to encourage—verbally and financially—the merger of Birchmore's *Wateree Messenger* and McDowell's *Camden Chronicle* presses into a daily newspaper that would be bold enough to print "something startling, theories and ideas that sparkle with progressiveness." Such a comment likely rankled rural readers fond of reading about their own communities as well as many local folk who enjoyed keeping up with small-town social events. The newspapers continued as they were for a number of years more, although they also contained effusive reporting on community changes. Birchmore especially championed educational and rural causes.

The January 25, 1901, *Chronicle* reprinted an article by D. A. Dickert from the *Newberry News and Herald.* The author of the memoir *History of Kershaw's Brigade* (1899), Dickert wrote of a recent visit in "What I Saw on My Trip to Camden." The writer praised Camden as "one of the most prosperous and progressive towns in the State." He mentioned the commercial and residential structures being built and the cotton mill that would soon be active with "hundreds of cottages that adorn 'factory town.'" Dickert also referred to large planing and lumber mills and to "a branch of the State's great moral institution, a distillery that turns out daily 200 gallons of 'chemically pure.'" It may be of significant interest that one of the revered old veterans viewed local Progressivism in such a positive light.

Marion H. Heyman described the profitable state-licensed distillery just west of Camden, a sizable operation using agricultural produce from the county: "A large legalized distillery located on what is known as Smyrl Hill was owned and operated by John Smyrl and its output was sold to the state dispensary and its product was considered good corn whiskey of high proof. On low bid it sold for one dollar and fifty-five cents per gallon including federal tax of one dollar and ten cents per gallon. None was sold at retail."[15]

The distillery was located on the Smyrl dairy farm, near the southwest corner at the intersection of present Ehrenclou Drive and the road to the wastewater treatment plant, near present Camden High School. The operation, according to Thomas Ancrum, was "licensed to make whiskies, and hundreds of barrels of corn and rye whiskies were manufactured there each year. Many c[a]rloads of shelled corn arrived in Camden and wagons hauled it out to the distillery. The distillery ceased operations when the state of South Carolina closed all its dispensaries, and got out of the liquor business [1907]." Present Smyrl Circle, a residential street nearby, is a reminder of that era.

Smyrl was also the local dispenser for several years, operating the "dispensary" where citizens made the only in-store alcohol purchases legal at the time. In other communities of the county too one dispensary was licensed per area to sell bottled alcohol. None was legally sold by the drink. The county board of control elected A. H. West as dispenser at Bethune in 1901. A. R. Hough was dispenser at Kershaw. In 1901 the *Kershaw Era* in the latter town reported, "The gross profits of the Kershaw dispensary for the week ending April 27, were $118.32" and wryly commented, "Pretty good for hard times, and a large proportion of men . . . if you ask them for what they owe you, will tell you that they are unable to pay you, and have at the same time a bottle in their pocket and the scent on their breath."

The effect of the dispensary system was to bring in immediately a great deal of money for government use—especially for schools and roads—but not especially to curb use of alcohol or related disturbances. While the distillery operated, the sale of agricultural corn and grains provided a good market for farmers. The distillery also provided local employment and railroad business. However, some political, some temperance, and all prohibition elements remained dissatisfied with the overall state system and were anxious for other reforms related to beverage alcohol.

A 1904 economic update of Camden reflected optimism about the city's status and future. The city had railroad lines leading to all points of the nation and handled eighteen thousand to twenty-one thousand bales of cotton annually; the Camden Lumber Manufacturing Company was operating; the Charles P. Rossignol mill was under construction near the electric plant to manufacture finishing materials for buildings—columns, brackets and moldings; the Camden Water, Light and Ice Company operated successfully; the Camden Bottling Company had added equipment; and the Camden Press Brick Works Company had added equipment and expanded to increase capacity to sixty-five thousand bricks a day. One hundred acres of the brick company's 216-acre tract were said to have sufficient clay for fifty years of production. Businessmen looked to the future as well as the present.

Public Health and Safety

Long-standing health and safety issues had to be addressed for community progress. Drainage in lower Camden was a major issue. Some sections, including parts of the main business section, had been built over former swampland, and these areas flooded following rains. To help alleviate the problem a system of ditches had been dug and expanded over the years. Ken and Boo DuBose wrote: "By the early 1900s, the ditches were three to four feet wide and five to six feet deep, necessitating the use of foot bridges and wagon bridges to gain access to and from the streets. The ditches ran along both sides of Market Street and most other streets in downtown Camden, and a large ditch ran along the east side of Main Street, now known as Broad Street, going under the buildings." From an interview with Mrs. Willa Harrison of Market Street, the DuBoses stated:

> During a heavy rainstorm the ditches would overflow and pedestrians had to be careful that they and their property were not carried away by the torrents of water . . . the ditches are remembered as collectors of trash, the breeding place of mosquitoes and a constant maintenance problem.
>
> The unpaved streets were also a problem. During dry periods they were dusty, and that was the best that could be said for them. During rainy weather they were kept in a mire by the horse and mule–drawn traffic, and with no sidewalks and a constant drainage problem, the pedestrian had to tiptoe across or had to find a board to throw across, or perhaps some bricks to throw into the mud and use as stepping stones.[16]

A June 1904 public health campaign by the Kershaw County Board of Health hauled tin cans, which collected rainwater, to the "dump ground" and urged citizens to drain low places and report water-filled ditches. While admitting that a link between malaria and mosquitoes was not universally accepted, the board recommended covering standing water with oil or disinfectant and installing "fly screens" on homes to keep out mosquitoes.

Camden city minutes of July 1907 document the issuance of five thousand dollars in bonds to install a sewerage system in most of the town. It was a major step in sanitation. Black neighborhoods, however, were rarely included in the first installations. In March 1908, when ordinances were passed to protect trees and shrubs in the city and to regulate the sewage system, the Commission on Lights, Water, and Sewage was set up to license and bond plumbers and to inspect connections. An ordinance also outlawed "cess-pools and dry closets" in the city. In April the council voted to regulate the butchering and sale of fresh meat within the city limits, consistent with federal Progressive legislation of the 1906 Pure Food and Drug Act and Meat Inspection Act. In May 1908 the council addressed garbage disposal by passing an ordinance prohibiting the deposit "on any of the parks, streets or sidewalks . . . any dead animal or fowl or any decaying animal or vegetable matter or any filth or sweepings of residences, stores, offices or other buildings or any waste paper, straw, hay, broken glass, tack, piece of tin or metal of any kind whatever" that could be a nuisance or an endangerment. Such materials were to be piled on the premises of property owners and to be collected by "agents or representatives" of the city.

Many people viewed the 1901 construction of an infirmary adjoining the Camden residence of Dr. John W. Corbett on Laurens Street as a sign of community progress. When Marion H. Heyman later recalled this as Camden's "first hospital," the home was then occupied by the W. Robin Zemp family. The same January 25, 1901, newspaper that announced Dr. Corbett's hospital also reported that "Dr. J. A. Lightner, colored, who has been practicing medicine for some time," was leaving Camden in a week or two and would be missed.

National reforms often touched on the treatment of those who could not care for themselves. In 1901 Kershaw County reported to the state that the local poorhouse was valued at $200.00, of which $125.00 was the real estate value of the establishment and its one hundred attached acres. Ten people were currently supported, with nine being the average most of the year. Since eight of the inmates were "unable to perform any kind or amount of labor," the county rented out the poorhouse farm. The average weekly cost to support each pauper was $0.60. Crops grown, in bushels, included 150 of corn, 100 of potatoes, and 20 of peas. Crops "retained for use on the farm" were valued at $125.00. Besides poorhouse inmates, the county aided seventy-five other persons, some of them with produce from the farm. Total charity expenses for the year were $300.00, including interest on the poorhouse itself. Clearly residence in the poorhouse was a resort of only the most desperate, and its facilities were quite basic.

Also addressed as a reform was the issue of business on Sunday. In June 1908 the city council passed an ordinance declaring it a misdemeanor for anyone to conduct business within the city on the Sabbath. Fines of ten to fifty dollars or imprisonment of five to twenty days were levied. Physicians, pharmacists, and operators of livery stables received exemptions. Ice deliveries were permitted until 1:00 P.M. Another ordinance one month later prohibited minors from loitering in or playing in billiard parlors or pool halls. Such places were believed to harbor "blind tigers," as illegal liquor operators were called, who could target youngsters. Some people encouraged but others resented legislation to enforce codes of moral behavior.

The Wateree Bridge and Dam

Maintenance of the Wateree River road had long been a concern because of dangers of floodwaters. In 1901 the county board of commissioners appropriated one thousand dollars for a major modification to raise the road one foot above the highest recorded flood level in order to preserve passage during times of freshets. In 1902 the King Bridge Company of Iowa contracted to raise the Wateree iron bridge about five feet higher and thus to place it "out of reach of all driftwood that always comes down the river with every freshet." Major S. R. Adams was awarded the contract "for the dirt work for the bridge." For a time the modifications seemed successful.

While the actual construction of a dam to provide flood control and power for electrification was more than a decade away, planning was under way early in the century. The site for building the Wateree Dam was purchased in 1904 but was not publicized widely. Agents for some time previously had been quietly approaching landowners in the upper Kershaw County area that promoters expected to be flooded. They offered what seemed to impoverished farmers to be a sweet deal—the Southern Power Company would pay their taxes and "lease" their land to be flooded if and when a dam could be constructed. In the meantime owners could continue to farm and use the land as usual.

One who remembered those sales later described them, pointing out that no landowners had heard of the plans to construct a series of dams to hold back the water at a number of points along the river. The only plans they were told of were those to build a local dam:

> The average citizen in this area was very unknowing of the end results at the time the power company decided to buy land and build a dam. The purchasing agents approached the land owners with a proposition to buy the land cheaply and allow the property owners to use the land as usual, tax free, until they backed water on their property. This was a good pitch because very few persons up and down the river ever believed that it was

> humanly possible to dam the river. If anyone had ever seen the high flood waters which were at times several miles wide in some areas, he could understand why they felt as they did. Times being hard, the landowners felt they were getting a little windfall from this deal. Thinking of the value of land today, the selling of this land could be considered as a gift to the power company.[17]

Thus years later some of the improvements of the time were viewed with a sense of loss by some of those whose lives were changed.

Kershaw County residents watched news accounts with interest as various dams were built upstream. The other impoundments along the Wateree-Catawba River were created before the final one, the dam in Kershaw County, was built. By its 1912 annual business meeting held at the Bank of Camden, the Wateree Power Company, a subsidiary of the Southern Power Company, owned "practically all land next to the Wateree River from near Knights Hill, five miles north of Camden[,] to Great Falls in Lancaster County." According to the March 29, 1912, issue of the *Camden Chronicle,* the company expected to develop a dam site at Cat Fish Creek, about ten miles north of Camden.

Three years later the April 16, 1915, *Chronicle* described the power facility that the Southern Power Company expected to complete in 1916 on Fishing Creek on the Catawba River, three miles above Great Falls. The new power plant would generate thirty thousand electric horsepower, added to thirty-two thousand horsepower being generated at the Great Falls plant and another thirty-two thousand horsepower at the Rocky Creek facility a mile from Great Falls. Hardaway Construction Company of Columbus, Georgia, would have no problem with delivery of materials since the power company during its development of the Great Falls and Rocky Creek facilities had already built a railroad that passed within a few hundred yards of the new site.

Once the people of Kershaw County saw that the formidable Great Falls had been successfully dammed, they knew that it would be possible to complete dam construction here. From other reports too they knew of the dangerous nature of the work. For example, the September 29, 1916, *Camden Chronicle* reported the death of five workers at Nitrolee "where Hardaway Contracting Company is erecting a great dam across the Catawba River for a hydro-electric plant for the Southern Power Company." The beginning of the Great War and the commencement of work on the Wateree Dam would soon be in competition for men.

Effects of Tourism

To a great extent tourism helped to counter the lingering effects of the Civil War and Reconstruction and especially the depressions of 1873 and 1893. In addition to both grand and small hotels, tourists rented private homes seasonally vacated by their owners for that purpose. From 1914 Camden and other southern resorts experienced increased patronage, the arrival of tourists who normally spent the season in Europe but who were prevented from traveling there because of the ongoing conflicts that eventually led to worldwide war.

To appeal to the tastes of their cosmopolitan visitors, some locals capitalized on re-creating appealing images of the "old South" elite, complete with the accoutrements of hospitality—teas, parties, dances, and hunts—for the enjoyment of guests. They retold and published local historical episodes and romantic legends. Resort associations with "old darkey" types and well-trained black serving people created a sense of order and comfort that matched the most favorable antebellum concepts. The hospitality and manners that southerners of all walks traditionally valued in their daily social contacts proved to be natural assets in the generally receptive treatment accorded tourists.

Some local residents found the wealth and styles of the vacationing tourists glamorous; others found their different manners unbecoming. Nan Hough Forester recalled, "At first, the relationship between the locals and the tourists was not very cordial, especially after it got around that some of the tourists called the residents 'natives' in a condescending manner. We went out with hats and usually gloves; they were always bareheaded. Camden women and girls rode horses with sidesaddles; the tourists rode astride!" Overall most "natives" found it more lucrative to exercise decorum than disdain with tourists. Some locals even wryly joked in private conversations about profits to be made from dealing with tourists, concluding, "It's easier to pick them than to pick cotton."

By 1916 the *Camden Chronicle* was printing lengthy social columns focusing on the winter tourists—identifying them by names along with the places they were staying. Appreciation grew as tourists and townspeople grew better acquainted on return visits and as some tourists bought local homes to become residents at least part of the year.

A tip to locals from one in the tourist business appeared in the November 24, 1916, newspaper. The winter resident Paul Rhenborg, the proprietor of Craft's Shop "dealing in souvenirs," had arrived to open his seasonal business among Camden tourists. He commented that on his visits to summer resorts in the North and the East he had found literature describing a number of southern towns; however, he had found nothing printed and available about Camden. He suggested that it would benefit Camden "to issue a booklet and have them [booklets] placed in the public places of interest in the north." Some picture postcards from the early 1900s focus on the tourist interests and hotels of early Camden and are the objects of present-day collectors.[18] Clearly tourism grew as a local business, seasonal but profitable.

Three Winter-Season Hotels

In 1900 Caleb Ticknor refurbished the Uphton Court resort that had closed following Mrs. Perkins's death two years earlier and reopened it as the Court Inn.

By that later name, and with additions and embellishments over the years, it established a long and renowned reputation as a grand hotel. Frank Eldredge continued improvements to the now well-established Hobkirk Inn, the first of the grand hotels, and also continued to operate Goodie Castle nearby.

Camden's reputation as a tourist resort gained added luster in 1903 with the completion of the area's third grand hotel, the Kirkwood Hotel, on the ridge of Hobkirk Hill north of Greene Street. The nucleus was the former home of Major John Cantey, surmounted by extensive wings of rooms, porches, and pleasant accommodations. The April 8, 1904, *Chronicle* reported, "The grounds of the Kirkwood have been placed in the artistic care of Elliott, the landscape gardener of Philadelphia, who will make them rival the gardens of California." The article also mentioned that the capacity of the stables would be doubled from the previous year.

In 1916 the Kirkwood added fifty-three rooms to accommodate the growing number of visitors yearly. T. Edmund Krumbholz managed the facility until his death in 1923. As it developed, the hotel's two hundred rooms had capacity for 350 guests, who could stroll the grounds, ride horseback, or play golf, tennis, or polo. The Kirkwood stables held twenty-five rental horses that guests could ride more than two hundred miles of trails. The hotel had two golf courses and two polo fields. Trains curved around the hill, delivering travelers directly to the rear of the Kirkwood.

The oldest of the grand hotels, having been in operation during the past century, the Hobkirk Inn was described in the May 2, 1913, *Camden Chronicle* as "the smallest of the tourist hotels." The still-sizable inn served a special niche, however. The Hobkirk regularly remained open "longer than the others . . . to care for the leftovers from the Kirkwood and Court Inn." All the grand hotels operated only during the "winter season"—roughly late fall through early spring.

Tourism in the County

Local citizens often became tourists themselves in summer months, traveling to escape the heat. Special vacation rates attracted many to board trains. In the summer of 1916, for example, a traveler could depart Camden aboard the Seaboard for a weekend excursion north to Wilmington, North Carolina, for $5.50 or south to the Isle of Palms or Sullivan's Island for $4.60. Summertime was the main season for at least one tourist site within Kershaw County, and trains delivered tourists to some sites year-round.

Near the Southern Railway station in Kershaw stood the year-round Benton Hotel, where visitors could stay overnight or just dine in a restaurant noted up and down the track for ample, good home cooking. Meals were coordinated with the train schedule so that a stopover provided just enough time for passengers to disembark, walk up to the hotel dining room for a filling repast perhaps sprinkled with conversation, and make it back to the train in time to continue their travel. Old-timers recounted stories that former Confederate captain Samuel Benton, the proprietor and entertaining raconteur, could sometimes be seen following a departing group to hand out second servings of pie. Haile Gold Mine executives, traveling salesmen (drummers), and tourists heading either north or south were commonly among the overnight guests. Political speakers used the upper floor of the Benton Hotel as a podium from which to address potential voters.

A second well-known hotel in Kershaw was the Whitfield, owned and managed by an enterprising mulatto woman, Roxie Belk. Born in North Carolina, Roxanna Starnes married a man named Whitfield, and the couple moved first to the Haile Gold Mine. After her husband died, the widow moved to Kershaw and established a mercantile business. Through frugality she acquired property, built the two-story brick hotel she named the Whitfield, and then married the widower William Belk. Roxie maintained a popular, separate dining room for whites in the front of the hotel. She drew her regular clientele from both the black and white segments of the community and from both locals and transients stopping in the town between trains.[19]

The increased customer base in Kershaw prompted some Camden merchants to expand to the town. Harry L. Schlosburg, for example, established a branch store in Kershaw in 1914. His dry goods business opened in a new store built by J. C. Cook. Sam Karesh, who was in the jewelry business in Macon, Georgia, moved to Kershaw to manage Schlosburg's store.

The Seaboard railroad gave tourists access to a popular summer spot in another part of the county, Big Springs. Twenty miles northeast of Camden and lying on both sides of the border with Chesterfield County, the mineral springs on the Lynches River near Bethune had been patronized by locals for many years. Twentieth-century roads and the railroad made it an inviting destination for tourists from afar also. In 1914 the Maynard family of Cheraw founded Big Springs Resort Company and built a railway station and a hotel. The hotel had landscaped grounds and covered bathing pools. Water from the mineral springs was also bottled and shipped nationwide.[20] The Seaboard established a stop at the Lynches River bridge, and from there gasoline-powered launches met Big Springs guests and transported them downriver to the hotel. There was also a road one and one-half miles long from the bridge to the resort for those preferring land transport. The special weekend train excursion rate to Big Springs was seventy-five cents round trip, June to September, from Columbia and Hamlet, North Carolina, "and intermediate points" such as Camden. When the "Miami-Quebec highway" (U.S. 1) was built, its route by Big Springs brought in additional auto travelers.

Historical Activities

With many changes coming to the old sections of Camden and Kershaw County, and with curious visitors asking questions about the sites, the time was ripe for activities related to the collecting, writing, and commemorating of local history. Apparently the suggestion for the writing of a history came around 1900 from Caleb Ticknor, Court Inn manager and friend of the two men to whom he made the suggestion—Thomas J. Kirkland and Robert M. Kennedy. Their work was under way by 1901, when they were collecting papers, information, and artifacts from local residents. In 1905 they published the scholarly and substantial *Historic Camden: Colonial and Revolutionary.*

Historical Society

Work in progress toward that publication inspired, as a support group, the 1904 organization of the Camden Historical Society. At the second meeting, held at Camden High School, where Kennedy was superintendent, new members joined, a constitution was adopted, and officers were elected. Kirkland was chosen as the first president and Kennedy was made secretary. Other officers were W. D. Trantham, vice president, and Dr. I. H. Alexander, second vice president, with Mrs. M. M. Young as treasurer and Mrs. M. A. Shannon as "Custodian of Relics." The early group apparently held regular quarterly meetings for programs and papers, such as one delivered in December by E. C. von Tresckow on the history of Lafayette Hall, which had burned a few months past. They also held business meetings, such as one to decide on "the nature of the tablet to be placed in the new court house [then being planned] to commemorate Lafayette Hall" and also to take steps toward mounting Revolutionary War cannon in front of the new building. At another program E. P. Mills read a paper on historical places in and around Camden, reflecting historical interest in the county area as well.

Hobkirk Hill DAR

The April 24, 1908, *Camden Chronicle* gave notice of an application to charter a chapter of the Daughters of the American Revolution (DAR) to be called the Hobkirk Hill Chapter. The notice was signed by Mary Ancrum Shannon and Frederika Alexander Kirkland. The May 1 issue reported that Mrs. E. C. (Sadie Kennedy) von Tresckow was a delegate to the national DAR.

The September 20, 1912, *Camden Chronicle* reported that the Camden Historical Society had lent its collection of relics to the Hobkirk Hill Chapter of the DAR. The receiving organization removed the collection from "the rooms of the Historical Society at the High School" to "their Chapter house," the old (Robert Mills) courthouse.[21] The DAR chapter requested anyone owning similar artifacts to consider lending them to add to the chapter's collection. The Historical

Society's relics included "Indian pottery, and implements of warfare, together with Revolutionary and colonial relics" that had been "washed up by freshets, or unearthed by excavations."

Confederate Memorials

As the county moved forward, segments of its past became part of activities typical of Progressivism at the time, specifically humanitarianism and education. Parts of the Confederate past became object lessons in the educational experiences of young people relative to the erection of two memorials in 1911, the year observing the passage of fifty years since the commencement of the Civil War.

Impressive reminders to children on the kind treatment of fellow human beings and animals emerged in a campaign conducted among local schoolchildren to raise money for a memorial to Kershaw County's Sergeant Richard Kirkland, who had carried water to wounded enemy soldiers during the Battle of Fredericksburg, Virginia. A watering fountain for horses and small animals was donated to the community by the National Humane Society, and the pennies that were collected by the children, with other local donations, paid for its installation. Originally the fountain stood in the midstreet intersection of Broad and DeKalb in Camden. From all directions horses drank from the surrounding upper bowl, and dogs and other small animals from the smaller pockets below.

The second memorial was a six-columned ornamental fountain pool, which became known as the Pantheon, in the park on Chesnut Street between Lyttleton and Fair, then called Kershaw Square and now Rectory Square or Rectory Park. Each individual column was inscribed to the memory of an individual Confederate general from Kershaw County. The schoolchildren were told of the six men, then treated as heroes, who had once been youngsters from their own community and who grew up and acted patriotically to defend their homes and families in time of need. The county was also held up for the children's admiration when they were told that no other community of its size in the South had contributed so many generals to its defense. In a half-dozen years the schoolchildren who first heard these lessons before the two memorials were tested as they faced the patriotic defense of their country in a world war.

The April 14, 1911, *Chronicle* reminded readers that "fifty years ago tomorrow soldiers left Kershaw County for the Confederate War." The newspaper of May 11 reported on the many Memorial Day activities in Camden. The line of march formed at 10:15 A.M. at the graded school and moved to Kershaw Square for the dedication of the fountain memorializing the six generals. The marchers then proceeded to the intersection of Broad and DeKalb streets for the unveiling of the Richard Kirkland fountain. The crowd continued to the opera house for addresses on the six generals and on Richard Kirkland. After the speeches the veterans were served dinner "in the Opera House store." The day's festivities culminated at 6:00 P.M. with an address in the cemetery by former lieutenant governor T. G. McLeod.

The fiftieth anniversary year, which was observed on Memorial Day 1911, fell during the time that the authors Kirkland and Kennedy were researching and writing *Historic Camden: The Nineteenth Century.* By 1911 Kennedy had served eighteen years as superintendent of the Camden Graded School system, then including the grammar and high schools, the Factory School, Malvern Hill School, and Jackson School for Negroes. Kirkland, an attorney, took office in 1912 as a member of the S.C. House of Representatives from Kershaw County. Their second history was published in 1926, twenty-one years after their *Historic Camden: Colonial and Revolutionary.*

Fraternal Groups

Many fraternal, social, and educational organizations existed in Kershaw County in addition to the historical organizations. Some hint of the fraternal scope is suggested by the August 10, 1910, *Wateree Messenger,* which listed the following schedule of regular night meetings in Camden: Fraternal Union of America no. 429 (the last Wednesday of each month); Kershaw Lodge Independent Order of Odd Fellows, or I.O.O.F., no. 119 (every second and fourth Tuesday "in the hall corner Broad and DeKalb Streets, 2nd story"); Knights of Pythias, DeKalb Lodge no. 41 (every second and fourth Thursday); Kershaw Lodge no. 29, Ancient Free Masons, or A.F.M. (first Tuesday); Live Oak Camp no. 49, Woodmen of the World, or W.O.W. (first and third Thursday); and Pine Creek Council Independent Order Junior American Mechanics, or I.O.J.A.M., no. 20 (first and third Friday "in the hall in the Opera House").

Sports and Entertainment

Some of the leisure activities of the period were developed as part of the tourist business. Some were simply outgrowths of the activities that local people, naturally acclimated to the outdoors, had long enjoyed; some were new interests. Brass bands were popular for performers and audiences alike and were indicative of public spirit. In 1912 Bethune had formed a brass band, and other communities were challenged to do so since neighboring Jefferson just across the county line had two bands. The May 24 newspaper reported that "colored people of Camden" under "Cornice, a colored carpenter," had organized a brass band with eight members that they expected to expand to twelve.

Baseball

"During 1906, Camden was a member of the Palmetto baseball league," recalled Thomas Ancrum, "and won the pen[n]ant. This little league produced many well known big league players, and the enthusiasm at the games was fever-heat, especially when Camden and Sumter played. This rivalry was carried over from the old fireman's tournament, several years earlier." Friendly physical competitions between various volunteer firemen's units, in and out of the immediate community, had become popular diversions in the tradition of old militia musters. The concept of cheering on one's community or team developed naturally from such encounters and carried over into organized sports. With the approach of summer in 1912 the *Chronicle* posted a notice that H. L. Watkins, "who has for several seasons managed the Camden base ball team," was starting another team.

In 1907 the South Carolina State League of Baseball Clubs had been formed with the help of a former Kershaw County representative and speaker of the house who served the first three years as president of the sports league. Mendel Lafayette Smith, a native of Smithville, had moved to Camden with his family at age thirteen. The area remained his home throughout his life. In college Smith was regarded across the nation as one of the best student athletes of the time. Although recruited by major baseball leagues, he began a long career as a lawyer and judge. His enthusiasm for sports as well as for sensible laws and societal improvements was notable in the local community and beyond.

Swimming

Colorful details of hot weather escapes to the water emerge from Thomas Ancrum's descriptions: "Swimming was the big sport during the hot months and part of the Camden crowd went to Red Hill point of the Wateree Lake and the other part to 'Clarks,' a swimming hole on the far end of the lake." The "Wateree Lake" to which he refers was not the present one of that name, for the dam was yet to be built and the waters were yet to be impounded for that body. Wateree Lake was then the name used for the old Factory Pond, now Kendall Lake, when the Wateree Cotton Mill operated there.

At the turn of the century public swimming was strictly for men only. Ancrum recalled, "No one wore a bathing suit and women were not supposed to go anywhere near the lake in summer months." Some years later swimming became more sociable, especially after the Saddle and Paddle Club was formed at the mill lake and bathing suits became fashionable. Ancrum recalled that women came there "with bathing suits to their ankles and all wore stockings." In fact, he said, "it was about 1912 before the first form fit[t]ing suit was worn by one of Camden's fair young ladies, home from college, and it created a sensation." The June 7, 1912, *Chronicle* described Saddle and Paddle as an "attractive little club house on the banks of the blue lake" with a club room upstairs and grounds made attractive by "rustic seats and swings."

Swimming-hole activities and customs were similarly followed in the early 1900s in millponds, springs, creeks, and rivers throughout the county. Smyrl Alvin Creed, born in 1912, told the writers of this history that his grandfather throughout his life followed the old-time custom of men-only swimming, wearing nothing in the river water but a brimmed hat to protect his head from the sun. Creed as a boy swam bare with him and other men of the family. Dorothy McLeod Anderson, born in 1914, described to the writers a spring-fed pool that her grandfather Zachery Barfield had dug out in a grove on their property in the southeastern part of the county to give his children a swimming place. Like her mother, she swam there as a child. In 1916 Nannie S. Campbell wrote a letter from a summer vacation in Lugoff describing pools there that had been cemented for bathing.

Equestrian Sports

Thomas Ancrum recalled the popularity of horse-related activities, both spontaneous ones and organized ones. Of the first type, he said:

> Nearly every one owned horses then and occasionally someone claimed to have the best horse. To settle a dispute, a half-mile course was laid out on Fair street, which started up near the Kendall residence [near the Greene Street intersection] and finished near the present home of Reeves Rutledge, near Rectory Park. Two horses, one owned by Evans Collins, a well known Negro livery stableman[,] and Gus Sanders of Hagood were raced over that street track. It was nip and tuck, until the saddle girth of the Collins horse broke near the finish line, throwing the rider and knocking him out for a few minutes. Hundreds of Camden people assembled for the race.

Regarding organized sports, Ancrum spoke about the continued development of polo: "After the erection of the Kirkwood hotel, a polo field was laid out back of the hotel. . . . Many polo matches were [in time] held with teams from Miami, Orlando, New Orleans and from Northern cities playing the Camden team." John H. Daniels says that the Camden Polo Club was elected to the United States Polo Association on April 17, 1900, making it the fourth-oldest club in the country. In that year the local team played its first exhibition game in Columbia.[22]

In 1914 a polo tournament for "the Southern circuit cup" took place in Camden from March 14 to March 28. The local team of Duncan Edwards, Newton C. Boykin, C. M. Taintor, Charles L. Little, and W. C. Salmond was managed by K. G. Whistler. The following week the *Camden Chronicle* advertised an exciting new attraction. The Camden Horse Show on the Carolina Horse Show circuit featured exhibition flying when Edwin A. Robbins, a manufacturer of airplanes, brought one of his crafts to Camden for three days, taking off and landing on the polo grounds each morning.

Movies and Entertainments

In addition to sports local audiences enjoyed carnivals, traveling entertainments, and minstrel shows, and they readily took to a new medium—the flickering black-and-white silent film. The author of "Our Town" recalled a traveling show that caused quite a stir, especially among the younger folk. Pawnee Bill's Wild West Circus, similar to the more well-known Buffalo Bill's, brought an entourage of cowboys and Indians. The writer remarked, "Children ran from the Indians, having visions of a scalping party."

The Camden Opera House, a traditional site for public entertainment, introduced local audiences to the new medium of film. The first movie seen locally arrived in Camden about 1900 as part of a road show. More people viewed another film, "Mount Pelee," scenes of a volcano eruption, as part of a 1902 carnival in a tent pitched in the middle of Broad Street. In the first decade of the new entertainment industry, movies were novelty acts, part of an evening's entertainment. In 1912, for example, a capacity crowd gathered at the opera house to view motion pictures, to see who would win five dollars in gold, and to learn who would get to wear a chain and pendant as the winner of a popularity contest; Miss Rhetta Wilson took the latter honor. The fanfare of showmanship was part of the early "movie shows."

Early movies were not sent individually for projection on locally owned equipment. Instead they were brought in, set up, and presented by traveling companies. The April 17, 1914, *Chronicle* announced that the Edison Talking Picture show would return to Camden on April 27 and 28. The opera house also continued to book traditional stage plays, such as the romantic melodrama *Dora Thorne* in 1914, a year before it was made into a popular silent film. The local newspaper asserted that the vaudeville between the acts was in itself worth the admission price—twenty-five, thirty-five, or fifty cents. For many in its day such entertainment was not inexpensive.

Competition quickly faced the aging opera house, however, as movie technology improved and costs decreased. In 1907 C. E. Boynton set up a former store building to show movies, with chairs lined on one side for white patrons and on the other side for black patrons. Two other operations were set up shortly afterward, one in the old Camden Baptist Church building that afterward served as the Kershaw armory. By 1914 audiences could also view moving pictures at the Air Dome, an open-air operation set up on DeKalb Street during hot weather, or the Victoria Theatre in a Broad Street building during cold weather. David L. Shatenstein, the owner of the theater, soon modernized it with "an orchestra consisting of a piano player and drummer," with doors and windows to improve air circulation, and with a rear exit in case of fire.[23]

In 1915 T. Lee Little entered the movie-theater business in Camden and dominated the local industry past midcentury. Little first became noted as a showman in 1910. As secretary of the Kershaw County Fair, he arranged for "the first aeroplane ever to visit South Carolina to come here for daily flights from the fair grounds." The grounds, at the ball field near the Seaboard freight depot off East DeKalb Street, grew so crowded the last day of the fair that when the little pusher plane landed, it "went into the crowd, bowling them over like ten-pins," but miraculously it caused no serious injuries. Parachute jumps from balloon ascensions at the fair were said to be another first in the state. Little later became secretary of the Horse Show Association and arranged shows that attracted exhibitors and audiences from across the state and beyond to view three- , four- , and six-gaited horses with saddles and with buggies.

In the spring of 1915 the builder R. W. Mitcham completed Little's new venture, the three-hundred-seat Majestic Theatre on East DeKalb Street. "Modern in every way," it had a "cool air ventilating system" for summer and a hot air system for winter. An experienced projectionist operated two machines to run film continuously without unnecessary waits between reels. A large crowd attended the opening. Ushers sported uniforms, and a local orchestra provided live music to accompany the silent films. Within fourteen months Little remodeled his theater, enlarging the screen and extending the building thirty feet to space existing seats and add one hundred more.

Filmmakers kept audiences returning to theaters with exciting weekly serials that ended in cliff-hangers. Pearl White, star of the series *Perils of Pauline,* was one of the country's most popular actresses when she came to Camden with costars Creighton Hale and Shelton Lewis to film scenes for the beginning of a new series, *The Iron Claw.* Filming on location was so new in the industry that film histories fail to credit this early outdoor filming, which took place in 1915

Officers displaying "blind tiger" wagons in Camden, early 1900s, after they were seized while transporting contraband liquor. Courtesy of the Camden Archives

on the grounds of the Court Inn and the front porch of what is now the George Washington House. Contemporary local accounts verify that when the episode played in early 1916, Kershaw County citizens returned again and again to see familiar scenes and extras as the pretty blond heroine repeatedly eluded the clutching hand of the villain with the iron claw.

The community got its first onstage view of form-fitting swimsuits when bathing beauties from the Mac Sennett comedies appeared live at the Majestic in an advertising campaign. *The Keystone Cops* was a local Sennett favorite.

Crime

Despite the signs of change in Kershaw County, the persistence of violence and lawbreaking continued to hamper progress. The January 25, 1901, *Camden Chronicle* reported the capture of twenty-five gallons of blind-tiger whiskey and gave an account of a mule stolen from J. E. Creed by a "gang of gypsies." Some crimes were of more dangerous nature.

As public gathering places, train stops sometimes became scenes of crime. In 1904 two homicides occurred in one week at train stops. At Boykin station on the Southern line, two men quarreled with deadly results about a fire set on a plantation managed by one of them. At Shepard station on the Seaboard line, a railroad foreman shot a man who complained about chickens trespassing on his property.

A Kershaw Lynching

On October 1, 1904, the town of Kershaw was the site of two acts of violence—a murder and the lynching of the victim's assailant—within the space of some four hours. The drama of the events increased as law enforcers futilely attempted to rush to the site by two separate trains to prevent mob violence.

John T. Morrison, a man of violent reputation, reportedly had accosted William Thomas Floyd, one of the area's leading citizens and grandson of Kershaw's first intendant. Supposedly without provocation Morrison shot and killed the unarmed Floyd near the Kershaw Mercantile and Banking Company on the corner of Marion and Hampton streets. When Morrison's revolver jammed, he was arrested and placed in the jail, a twenty-four by thirty foot granite structure that was the oldest building in Kershaw. Police Chief Ernest Bateman and Dr. L. T. Gregory remained in the jail with the prisoner.

News of Floyd's murder circulated rapidly in the community, stirring talk of immediate rope justice against a man who had killed before and been acquitted by the courts. Two telegrams alerted Governor Duncan Clinch Heyward of the Kershaw situation—one from Kershaw mayor James V. Welsh and the other from Morrison's wife. When Governor Heyward was unable to reach Lancaster County sheriff John P. Hunter by phone, he telephoned Captain S. C. Zemp in

Camden to bring the Kershaw Guards immediately to the trouble spot. Zemp agreed to comply as soon as the railroad could get a head of steam. Zemp informed the governor that Sheriff Hunter too was rushing en route from Lancaster to Kershaw on a special train, rail travel being quicker than an automobile on poor roads.

Meanwhile what had begun as a quiet night quickly erupted into a fever pitch. The electric lights went out, and Police Chief Bateman was overpowered. His assailants took away the keys to the cell and removed Morrison. As the mob hurried the prisoner out of town, the train steamed in with Sheriff Hunter and his deputies. Although met by a crowd of about one thousand men, the sheriff was unable to learn the whereabouts of the lynch mob.

The vigilantes had taken Morrison to a wooded area about a mile northeast of town, the site of present Stevens Park. The mob hanged Morrison in a tree by a pair of buggy reins and then shot him several times. The train with the Kershaw Guards arrived in town at 8:40 P.M., twenty minutes after Sheriff Hunter; both were too late to prevent the hanging.

The Floyd-Morrison situation has been seen as symbolic of its age. The barbarity of both acts reflected the violence that had persisted in the post–Civil War decades. The lynching—as brutal as it was—was also indicative of public desire for restoration of law and order. Morrison had previously verbally assailed and physically beaten a number of people and had killed three men without penalty. He reputedly had bragged that he "could commit any crime" in South Carolina and "get out of it at a trial."

An editorial titled "The Kershaw Lynching" in the October 7, 1904, *Camden Chronicle* asserted that the situation had resulted because the courts had failed. A respected citizen, Will Floyd, had been killed because "a red handed murderer [Morrison] had for the third time been allowed to go 'scot free.'" The paper stated that it deplored mob violence, "but if the courts will not [mete] out justice the people will rise up and demand it." The editorial concluded, "Let it not again be said that a guilty man goes free." Even some Progressives so despised what many called "a rotten court system" that they accepted Morrison's end as justified.

The lynchers were never brought to justice, although several suspects were arrested. Among nebulous issues was the question of jurisdiction. Sheriff Hunter pointed out that it appeared that Morrison had been killed prior to being hanged, and since Kershaw was divided between two counties, it was unclear whether the death had occurred when the mob was in Kershaw or Lancaster County.[24]

Hampton Park Murder

In Camden one year later the robbery and murder of a popular local merchant was the headline topic of the October 5, 1905, newspaper. R. A. McDowell had closed his downtown store and was walking home when an unknown assailant emerged from "behind one of the large pines near the sidewalk at Hampton Park." Another man, R. W. Porter, walking with McDowell was also injured with severe cuts on his head. The October 20 newspaper, referring to the crime, urged authorities to install "electric lights in all the squares in Camden."

Bloody Holiday

The upper county was the scene of four violent deaths just before Christmas 1907, all on Saturday, December 22, at three separate locations in or near Kershaw. Two incidents took place on different sides of the same bridge. On one side a constable shot a man whom he was attempting to serve with a warrant. On the other side of the bridge two inebriated companions argued, one pulled a knife, and the other shot him. The third situation was a barrage of gunfire in a downtown barbershop resulting in two men slain and a third wounded.[25]

Arson

Citizens dreaded arson, which was difficult to detect from fires of natural or accidental causes. For example, two 1913 fires in Blaney only ten days apart caused arson to be suspected. The first blaze destroyed two stores and their contents, and the second burned the Seaboard passenger and freight depots and their contents. In 1914 a fire caused twenty-five thousand dollars in damage to the Camden Brick Company. The plant, with one million bricks estimated on the premises, had been shut down for three weeks, but several employees were in the office and quickly discovered the blaze. Since there was no water nearby, however, flames spread quickly, consuming dry kilns. Manager Hough at first surmised that sparks from the engine of a train picking up a load of bricks was responsible for the fire. However, the cause seemed more suspicious soon afterward when another fire seriously damaged the nearby plantation of the brickyard's owner, G. A. Guignard. There a large building previously used as Smyrl's distillery and at the time filled with baled hay on one end and oats on the other was burned. Guignard's large grain house, filled with thirty-five hundred bushels of threshed oats, was nearly a total loss.

Blind-Tiger Woes

Persistent violations of liquor laws backlogged justice in cases of all types. When liquor could be legally purchased, the blind tiger operated to bypass the taxation. When liquor sales were outlawed by local, state, or national prohibition, the blind tiger provided a black-market product not otherwise available.

Some citizens praised the efficiency of the July 1916 session of criminal court, with Judge Mendel L. Smith of Camden presiding. The entire docket was cleared, including cases carried over from the previous year. As a result of a large number of convictions, the July 14 *Chronicle* reported, "a four horse wagon load of chain gang recruits" created quite an attraction as it "passed down DeKalb street . . . enroute to the public works near Bethune."

Many of the cases involved liquor-law violations. A sting operation by law enforcers had taken place, and the special officer G. E. Bateman, commissioned by the governor, was the state's chief witness in every blind-tiger case. Defense attorneys made Bateman the subject of derision throughout the court term, and in the last case he was denounced as "a spy." As a consequence Bateman and the attorney G. G. Alexander came to blows in a fistfight in front of the Camden Motor Company. Both men were served warrants. In the years following Reconstruction, the public was ambivalent in attitudes toward law enforcement.

Natural Disasters

As the twentieth century began, destructive floods continued to plague the county. For example, in 1901 the Wateree River reached a record 32.5 feet on May 24, threatening the iron bridge built in 1883. Heavy rains in July 1904 caused destruction in the Abney community by washing away J. M. Kirkley's gristmill, gin, and cotton press.

Wateree Bridge Loss of 1908

On August 25, 1908, a freshet brought the Wateree River even higher than the record set seven years earlier. Rushing waters swirled around the iron bridge that in 1902 had been raised five feet higher to protect it from such damage. Again, however, bridge piers were jeopardized by trees and other flotsam brought down by the flood. One of the bridge company officials, Henry Savage, was standing on the bridge directing men who were working frantically to dislodge a raft (a logjam) of debris piled against it by the rushing waters. The bridge abruptly tumbled, and the raft broke free, hurling the workmen and other people on the bridge into the water. Four were drowned, and ten others "were swept into trees on the bank and were saved." Savage was rescued ten miles downstream, having "floated on driftwood." The dramatic incident and remarkable rescue led citizens to refer to this bridge as the "Savage" bridge and to the freshet as the "Savage freshet." The next day the river stood at thirty-nine feet, seven inches. Few witnesses thought that level would again be equaled in their lifetimes.

Other Flood Damage

While the ferry operated again, the county moved quickly to secure state approval and to assume the debt of rebuilding a bridge. In 1909 county supervisor M. C. West offered bonds for sale, forty thousand dollars at 5 percent, due in twenty-five years. The bridge was to consist of two concrete abutments, one concrete pier, and two spans of steel bridge, one 375 feet, the other 130 feet.

Consulting engineers Wilson, Sompayrac, and Urquhart of Columbia were chosen.[26] By August 10, 1910, the *Wateree Messenger* predicted early completion of the magnificent steel bridge over the Wateree River. The bridge opened on September 15, 1910, free to traffic, and was inaugurated by a celebration complete with barbecue.

The bridge stood, but damage in other parts of the county was widespread in March 1912 when a freshet brought the river's waters within a few feet of the flood of four years earlier. Roads leading south and east from Camden were impassable. Forty feet of the road to Columbia was washed away. The bridge over Town Creek was lost, thus closing the Charleston road as well. The road east to Bishopville was closed, and the spur track and bridge leading to Hermitage were submerged. The Camden Brick Company shut down because of several feet of water in its offices and the flooding of its clay pits.

In September heavy rains caused a breach in the millpond of Pine Creek Mill, formerly known as the old Factory Pond. The released waters washed away the bridge below the dam on the Cheraw road. Rain torrents that washed out a Seaboard railway culvert in Lugoff derailed a freight train, overturning some dozen boxcars. The county chain gang was moved in to repair various damages.

Wateree Free Bridge, the steel bridge completed by the county in 1910 to replace the private toll bridge washed away in 1908. This steel bridge was destroyed by flooding in 1916. Courtesy of the Camden Archives

Tornadoes

Tornadoes struck the county in the spring of 1915. At Kershaw destructive winds destroyed almost everything in a path two hundred yards wide. John R. Baker lost nearly every building on his plantation. At Tiller's Ferry tornadoes cut a "path 2 or 300 yards wide," striking in spots and destroying buildings, crops, and timber. One barn was lifted into the air "leaving the horses standing in their stalls."

Wateree Bridge Loss of 1916

Unknown to local people in summer 1916, a hurricane spawned in the Gulf of Mexico dumped torrential rains on the mountain source of the Catawba-Wateree system. Floods were rushing toward Kershaw County even before local people began to experience rain in this section. On July 18, 1916, following two days of heavy rain, floodwaters on the Wateree River reached a record 40.4 feet, damaging crops and washing away yet another bridge over the river, this one still unpaid for.

The July 21 *Camden Chronicle* stated, "The county bridge is nearly a total loss—the two piers on the western bank of the river gave way and precipitated the immense steel structure overhead into the water." The raging waters also swept away the Seaboard Railway trestle. When the trestle began shaking, a number of coal-filled gondolas were moved onto the bridge to weigh it down in hopes that the procedure would stabilize the structure. Instead, when the bridge gave way, the gondolas plunged into the river as well, making the railroad's loss even greater.

The newspaper reported that the "old Southern Railway depot south of Camden was several feet deep in water," and only the roofs of a residence and A. M. Christmas's grocery store "near the depot creek" were visible above the water. There were many reports of flooded croplands and loss of livestock and timber as well as accounts of people stranded in houses and even in trees.

Damages had been heavy above Camden as well. An entire $250,000 five-story brick cotton mill in North Carolina had totally vanished from its site. A number of the mill workers' houses and a warehouse with an estimated one thousand bales of cotton were also swept away. A dozen or more cotton bales were spotted in the river near Camden.[27] A body was reported floating downstream. The Southern Railway reported that some black persons had disappeared into the river when a train trestle near Charlotte gave way; a reward was offered for the recovery of their bodies. Communications by telegraph and telephone were practically nonexistent for some time, with only one wire working between Camden and Richmond.

Immediately following the disaster the Seaboard employed crews night and day to replace its trestle across the Wateree River at Camden in order to get rail service moving again. More deaths followed. Raging river currents swept away and drowned three workers after "a lighter on which they were engaged in placing heavy piling in the river capsized."[28]

Concerned local citizens met at the Camden Opera House on July 18 to begin plans for establishing a temporary ferry, for gathering information on replacing the bridge, and for investigating federal funds that might assist in the rebuilding efforts. E. D. Blakeney of Kershaw spoke for citizens of Buffalo Township, requesting the group to make no definite decisions before people from that section could meet with them. The assembly agreed to meet again and to invite citizens of all areas of the county to join them.

Citizens from Bethune, Kershaw, and Camden who assembled were of one mind that the bridge needed replacement as quickly as possible. Thomas Kirkland, responding to questions about the county's financial state, asserted that it was in better condition than when the previous bridge had gone down in 1908. He recommended that the replacement bridge be a toll bridge located "at least a mile higher up river than the present site." So widespread was the damage from the hurricane that Congress appropriated eight hundred thousand dollars "for the relief of storm and flood sufferers" in five southeastern states, allotting three hundred thousand dollars to North Carolina and one hundred thousand dollars to South Carolina.

As a result of local rain and flood damages, merchants of Camden began operating a free ferry service for foot passengers across the river. S. H. Twitty and David Perry managed two boats for this purpose near the downed bridge site. Besides the Wateree River bridge and the Seaboard trestle, a total of seventeen county bridges—many of them in Buffalo Township—had been destroyed or partially damaged. D. J. Guy of Bethune was awarded a contract to build a twenty-five-ton flatboat to serve as a ferry until a new bridge could be built. The county furnished materials and paid him $150 for the fifteen by sixty- foot craft. The cable-operated flatboat could balance six or eight teams per a load.[29]

A mysterious incident at the bridge site aroused suspicion. On the night of September 20, while the ferryman and his helper slept "in the little house on the ferry," the damaged pier on the western side of the river was blown up. A lawsuit alleging faulty construction had been filed by the attorney Thomas J. Kirkland on behalf of Kershaw County against the Pennsylvania company that had constructed the lost bridge, and the pending suit soon included an investigation of the collapsed pier.[30]

By the end of 1916 a government engineer and a Seaboard Railway bridge inspector had surveyed the riverbanks for a suitable location for a new bridge to span the Wateree. Three locations were suggested, according to the newspaper: "the old site, another just above the Seaboard bridge and still another about two miles above the Seaboard bridge at the mouth of Twenty Creek [contemporary name of Twenty-five Mile Creek]." Despite the plans and hopes of anxious and eager citizens, they were forced instead to make do with ferry crossings for four long years. The war in Europe and in 1917 America's entry into it made money and materials—especially metals—scarce or even impossible to obtain for some time.

The Wateree River has never again reached the level seen in 1916. Within a few years construction of dams at various points on the Catawba-Wateree River system allowed the power companies to regulate the waters, thus minimizing damages along its channel. In the interim Kershaw County labored under difficulty to overcome the handicaps of isolation.

A Search for Political Solutions

For help with natural or societal problems, many citizens favored a government that would take a hand in finding a solution. Other citizens preferred a government that would let them solve their own problems. In the early twentieth century a divided electorate debated this question.

Campaign Views

Electioneering of the day was taken directly to the people and went on in both large and small communities. In 1910 Coleman L. (Cole) Blease, self-styled champion of the people and especially of textile workers, began the first of two consecutive terms as state governor. That year Kershaw County candidates held their final out-of-town campaign meeting about twelve miles above Camden at "Smyrl's park at Shaylor's Hill." In this small, tightly knit community candidates for state legislature, for county positions, and for township commissioners spoke. A Columbia newspaper reported the speeches, pointing out that most of them favored prohibition. In conclusion the Honorable Mendel L. Smith invited the crowd to Camden on September 15 "to celebrate the opening of traffic over the Wateree river steel bridge and to welcome back all of our old West Wateree friends."[31] (The new bridge washed away in 1916.)

A September 1912 political discussion in Blaney turned violent. What began as a debate concerning "how their fathers had voted in '76," turned into a melee between Lon Bowen and Thomas Sessions and his son Louis. The *Columbia Record* described the scene: "Bowens [*sic*] picked up a brick and one of the Sessions drew a knife. Bowens retreated to a store where one of the other men assaulted him with a knife inflicting several painful gashes about the head, back and arms." At this point Charles Hall "ran up and promptly knocked down the man who was using the knife," and other bystanders helped prevent further violence. The newspaper concluded, "While blood has again been spilled and blows were given and taken the battle of '76 remains as unsettled as ever."

In 1914 there was active campaigning, with much of the debate regarding controversial Cole Blease, who was not a candidate.[32] The campaign opened in

Bethune on a Monday and moved to Kershaw the following day. Since the latter town was divided, candidates from both Lancaster and Kershaw counties campaigned. On Wednesday at Westville candidates were asked to declare whether they were pro-Blease or anti-Blease.

Statewide prohibition was the hot question of 1915 to be settled at the polls. The "Local Option League" placed a large notice in the September 3, 1915, *Camden Chronicle* that presented logical arguments against voting in favor of prohibition, although they professed, "We are not presenting an anti-prohibition argument." The league warned that if prohibitionists had their way in September but at the same time failed to elect a law-enforcing administration, "the responsibility for a period of disorder, corruption and crime, with open if unlawful barrooms, will be on them." Having just gone through the Blease era when hundreds of convicted offenders were annually pardoned by the governor, a number of citizens questioned whether the restrictive law that was proposed could be enforced. Prohibition was voted in almost two to one in Kershaw County. A letter from W. B. deLoach in the September 17, 1915, *Camden Chronicle* said, "It is now up to each and every citizen of this county to see that this law is enforced."[33]

Campaigning in 1916 included a backlash against the factionalism that had permeated elections two years earlier. The Farmers Secret Association of Kershaw County adopted several resolutions, the first of which stated "that no candidate be requested to state his preference for governor" and "that all candidates be given respectful hearings." Those resolutions were presented at a major political rally at Pine Grove schoolhouse in West Wateree. According to the May 12 newspaper, "There were only twelve candidates for sheriff present—the others being detained by sickness or other permissible excuse."

End of Neutrality

The conflict in Europe served as a backdrop to the 1916 political campaigns. U.S. Senator Ben Tillman, in his farewell address, alluded to both state and world conditions with conflict between "privilege and freedom, between equality and favoritism" and said that this conflict was "world-wide and ages old." Tillman added, "It has brought the cataclysm which we are witnessing in Europe today. The people of that continent are struggling to free themselves from the shackles of autocracy and the divine right of kings."[34]

The September 25, 1914, *Camden Chronicle* printed a letter from Tressa Block, a niece of L. L. Block, a Camden merchant who had emigrated from Germany. Miss Block had left Camden several months earlier to visit her old home, where her three brothers were serving in the German army. Her letter to "the German colony in Camden" asserted that Germany was in great order and its people enthusiastic. She opined, "Germany can't lose" and added that the idea that

Americans there were in danger was "paper talk" since Germans were "too cultured to offend strangers." Apparently some others in the local winter colony thought the same during the early part of the war, for references in some printed letters compare German spirit and gallantry to that of the Confederates of the Old South.

Other opinions, however, were quickly sympathetic with victims of the war. Among other European war news that became well known to the American people was the plight of the Belgian people following the German army's invasion of their country. Camden resident Charles J. Shannon chaired a local Belgian Relief Committee of prominent citizens, and a "nice shipment" of foodstuffs left Camden for Belgium.

Mexican Border War

In 1916 news that President Wilson had called out troops for patrol duty on America's southwestern border temporarily disrupted concern about matters in Europe. Political unrest in Mexico led to raids into the United States by Mexican guerrillas. According to the May 12, 1916, *Chronicle,* this marked "the first time since the Spanish-American War, [that] a President has called out state militia to assist regulars in an international crisis." Militias from Arizona, New Mexico, and Texas joined with four regiments of regular infantry brought to forty-five thousand the number of troops on duty.

The border problems and war in Europe heightened preparedness by and interest in the local military. In May 1916 the Kershaw Guards hiked six miles to Vaughan's Mill north of Camden, where they pitched their tents for weekend training. This activity was consistent with national preparedness efforts. Although the local militia had also gathered a number of recent recruits, a notice in the May 26 newspaper indicated that the Kershaw Guards needed seventy-five men.

Company M left the morning of June 23 for Mexico.[35] The ladies of the Civic League had given the troops a farewell reception and dance at their armory several days earlier. To show support and appreciation, local merchants closed their shops from 8:15 to 9:30 A.M. to see the militia off at the Seaboard station. The August 11 newspaper reported that Major E. C. von Tresckow's unit was on its way to Texas for border patrol duty. The local militia remained there just under four months, returning home in December.

Controversies in 1916

County citizens carefully followed political races in the summer and fall of 1916 as incumbent governor Richard I. Manning and former governor Cole Blease squared off for nomination to the state's top office. It was an interesting contest, for both candidates had previously run afoul of various interests in Kershaw

County. During his time as governor Blease had pardoned a convicted local blind tiger who had previously been arrested several times. The act still rankled Kershaw County residents, especially because Blease had also ordered that the chronic offender's fine be refunded.

Governor Manning too had created a local storm the previous year when he charged Sheriff W. W. Huckabee of Kershaw County with neglect of duty, alleging that he had "permitted a 'blind tiger' to operate unmolested" and had "refused to enforce the law against the unlawful sale of intoxicating liquor generally in Kershaw County." Huckabee had been removed from office and temporarily replaced by Coroner G. L. Dixon. Afterward, Governor Manning had appointed Isaac C. Hough of Camden to fill out Huckabee's term. Hough stated that he had not sought that office and was surprised at his appointment. The state supreme court in December 1915 ruled that the governor did not have the authority either to remove Huckabee or to appoint his successor. Huckabee returned to office. When Manning received the gubernatorial nomination over Blease, the local newspaper expressed pleasure.

Effects of City Improvements

Many improvements in the city of Camden affected not only the residents in the municipal area but persons in the county as well. In 1910 the Camden–Kershaw County Chamber of Commerce was founded and soon proved to be beneficial. Male and female members of the Civic League in Camden, a volunteer organization, promoted activities that improved the community and welcomed visitors. The new hospital organized in Camden accepted county patients, and a new post office enhanced service for all. In addition improved communications systems and economic activities located in the city benefited area residents.

More Health and Safety

Reminiscent of muckraking exposés that garnered national attention, a letter from Laurens T. Mills in the February 21, 1913, *Camden Chronicle* described "entrails . . . decaying meat . . . blow flies . . . [and] roaming dogs" in and around the Parlor Meat Market in Camden. Mills also wrote of an individual who "butchers and feeds hogs" and who had in the past six weeks lost forty hogs to cholera. This individual's lots drained into a little pond dammed to supply water for washing the meat, and the stream fed into Pine Creek Mill (Factory Pond). This, the writer pointed out, presented a real danger of spreading infection.

Another potentially dangerous situation came to light in 1913. A contractor discovered an open well thirty feet deep hidden under the sidewalk near the Episcopal rectory in Camden. The newspaper commented that "pedestrians had for no telling how long been walking over [it]." Wells created many problems. In June 1915 the community was alarmed by several cases of typhoid fever and one death, all within one week. The board of health sought out the source, condemning two wells that proved to be contaminated. The board analyzed city water twice a month and tested samples of ice manufactured by Carolina Public Service Company.

The Civic League actively worked to improve Camden's health as well as its appearance. In 1916 the group requested the police to put a stop to tree and shrub damage by cows that residents of "Team row" pastured in Seaboard Park and to notify Monument Park tennis court owners to remove the rubbish left from their construction. Concern over mosquito control resulted in town ditches being cleaned and covered with petroleum. Many Camden women were leaders in Civic League activities, which also included male members.

Attention was frequently paid to fire-alarm maintenance and to public response in emergencies. In 1916 Camden fire chief W. M. Young published the numbers and locations of fire-alarm boxes: 64, Main and Kirkwood; 62, Main and Chesnut; 55, Fair Street opposite the hospital; 53, Lyttleton Street opposite the new Catholic church; 45, Fair Street opposite L. A. Kirkland's; 42, Lyttleton Street opposite Mrs. P. T. Villepigue; 34, Broad and Lafayette; 32, Main and Laurens near the monument; 31, Lyttleton and Laurens at Schlosburg's corner; 27, Main and DeKalb; 25, Lyttleton and DeKalb; 23, Fair and DeKalb; 21, Campbell and DeKalb; 16, lower Main Street near McGirt's store; and 14, Lyttleton Street near John W. Wilson's residence. The old boxes and locations were in use for many years. In 1916 city aldermen W. R. DeLoache, W. R. Hough, W. L. Jackson, and fire chief W. M. Young drove to Greenwood to examine a motorized fire truck being considered to replace the current horse-drawn hose wagon.

Water and Lights

In May 1902 the power house of the privately owned Camden Water, Light and Ice Company burned, and for a long summer the town was not only in darkness but, more seriously, also without water resources to fight the fires that regularly threatened. Discontent ruled when company owners hesitated to rebuild, and the city had to renegotiate contracts to restore power. By 1912 the water supplied by the company was so insufficient and expensive that officials at times cut off the city fountains installed the previous year. That year voters elected W. Bratton deLoach, Dr. W. J. Dunn, and Henry Savage to a three-man utility commission to develop a water and light system to be owned by the city of Camden.

To establish its own utilities system, the city took options on a tract at the mouth of Dicey's Creek near the entrance to Factory Pond, estimating that the creek could furnish water for a city of one hundred thousand.[36] A city-owned power plant, it was said, could also provide adequate electricity at a lower price.

The 1912 *Chronicle* approved it as a progressive step for Camden and pointed out that nearly all progressive cities owned their water and light plants.

With four hundred acres purchased as a watershed surrounding Dicey's Creek, in January 1914 the city awarded the construction contract for a modern waterworks and electric light plant. Work that began in March was delayed while the Seaboard built a spur line at nearby Spalding Junction to lessen the cost of hauling materials by wagon from the depot. The pumping station on Dicey's Creek was designed to pump water through three separate filters to a cement basin at the main plant on present Dicey's Ford Road. Water was pumped to a standpipe, a holding tank for pressure, on the crest of Jumelle Hill in Kirkwood. From here the pipe also provided excellent water pressure to fight fires.

Pipelines and related construction were added to provide water service, and poles for electrical wiring went up along city streets. A group of citizens complained to the Civic League when utility workers cut down trees to wire the streets. Disruptions from pipeline digging provoked other complaints. Citizens worried that attractive features of their neighborhoods were being adversely affected by the changes.

Lighting the Camden business district with 215 nitrogen tungsten lamps would make the city one of the first in the nation to be so illuminated. "Leading from Lafayette Avenue to York street, and from Market to Church on Dekalb street, the city will have a white way, the equal of any city in this section," the newspaper stated. Ornamental stands, each with five lights, were to be placed at two-hundred-foot intervals on both sides of the streets. After business hours an automatic timer would switch these lights over to arc lights.[37]

In the July 3, 1914, newspaper Camden fire chief H. L. Watkins warned that construction of the city's new streetlights and the changing of the fire alarm wires on Main Street were disrupting the Gamewell Fire Alarm System. He advised citizens to use the telephone to report fires. Watkins also requested that people having any type of explosives stored on their property notify him immediately of the exact locations since electrical sparks could ignite them.

The electricity from the public power plant was turned on for the first time on August 18, 1914. The August 21 *Camden Chronicle* stated that with a dependable lighting system having been for twenty years only "a proposition," it was a relief for it finally to be a reality. When the electric pumps that moved water from Dicey's Creek through the new system were turned on for the initial time, they functioned well. However, the existing water mains that the city had agreed to purchase, provided they could withstand 150 pounds per square inch of pressure continuously for two hours, failed to meet standards and had to be replaced.

For some customers the new power system necessitated adjustments. For example, Isaac English, proprietor of the Eureka Barber Shop, replaced two oscillating fans in his shop since, he said, "the old fans could not be used with the new current from the new power house." English remarked that the new fans were much better, however, and were "providing a treat" for his customers. Citizens fortunate enough to afford the power to their homes enjoyed it once they made necessary adjustments to their wiring and appliances.

Communications

When the installation of Camden's new streetlights necessitated the removal of telegraph utility poles from Main Street, the postal telegraph office determined that it was less expensive to move from their West Rutledge Street location than to bury new wires underground. The telegraph office in 1914 thus moved to the Murchison Wholesale Company's building on the corner of Broad and DeKalb. The Southern Bell Company operated from the First National Bank building at Broad Street in Camden until 1916. The company then undertook a three-hundred-thousand-dollar project to improve local operations by installing a new plant in the Savage-Crocker building, at the northwest corner of Broad and DeKalb. New switchboards, wiring, electrical machinery, and a large current-generating motor in the office updated and expanded telephone services.

Another modern development had brought free city mail delivery to Camden by late June 1912. Preparations had begun two years earlier with the numbering of streets and individual houses. Three carriers were assigned to home delivery.[38]

New Hospital

In March 1912 native Camdenite Bernard Baruch, then a wealthy Wall Street financier, made an unexpected trip to Camden to meet with a Chamber of Commerce committee on the progress of the proposed local hospital for which he had recently promised a contribution of twenty thousand dollars. A year earlier citizens interested in developing a modern hospital at Camden had read of Baruch's contributions to a New York hospital and had approached him by letter and with a personal visit from a kinsman, a Camden merchant.

Baruch was the son of the Civil War surgeon Dr. Simon Baruch, who for fifteen years after the war practiced medicine in Camden, where Bernard was born and had spent his boyhood before the family moved to New York in 1880. On the visit to his hometown Baruch said that he desired to honor his father's work and to follow his mother's admonition to remember her people, the people of the South. He expressed pleasure in the fund-raising under way and examined the proposed site—the old Presbyterian manse and property at the corner of Fair and Union streets. Learning that the cost would be five thousand dollars for the land and thirty-five thousand dollars for the building, Baruch told the planning committee to purchase the site and proceed with construction. He would double his offer and pay for the land and the building.

Local citizens rallied to provide ten thousand dollars to equip the facility. Appeals were made to tourists and winter residents, who would also benefit from a local hospital. Reverend J. W. Boykin led the drive among the black citizens, whose first fund-raiser was a musical program at Jackson School. The Hospital Auxiliary organized in early February and in three months raised nearly one thousand dollars. One successful fund-raiser was a mock court trial. During summer months the Hospital Auxiliary made and sold ice cream on Tuesday afternoons on the square, where townspeople gathered to watch drills of the Kershaw Guards. From its beginning the hospital was intended to serve all citizens of Kershaw County.

Meanwhile efforts in public health continued. The Kershaw County Medical Society in 1913 elected officers: S. C. Zemp, president; S. F. Brasington, vice president; and W. J. Burdell, secretary-treasurer. The society appealed to the county board of commissioners to support a project to eradicate hookworm. The Rockefeller Commission sent a physician to conduct a free hookworm dispensary, and the county paid for the medicine. Nutritional problems resulting from hookworm infestation were widespread among the county's poor.

On April 16, 1913, Camden Hospital was incorporated with a board of directors that included Mannes Baruch, W. J. Burdell, H. G. Carrison, J. W. Corbett, W. R. Hough, Jesse Rowan, William Shannon, L. A. Wittkowsky, and S. C. Zemp. That same month Richland Construction Company of Columbia won the building contract for the long-awaited facility. New construction was designed and modifications planned for the standing structure, the former manse, which would serve as an administration building. Work on the twenty-bed facility began in May. The two wings standing separate from the remodeled building each constituted a ward; one was for white patients and the other for black patients. Each ward also had separate sections for males and females. Operating rooms were located between the two wings. In addition the administration building had "reserved space for several private rooms for pay patients."

On December 1, 1913, Camden's new hospital opened. Its chief benefactor, Bernard Baruch, with his father, Dr. Simon Baruch, arrived from New York to participate in the dedication. During its first year of operation the patient cost per hospital day was $2.64. A local fund, the annual proceeds of a $100,000 estate, was rolled over to provide medical care for free patients at the hospital. Captain John Burdell, a former Columbia police chief who had moved to West Wateree and acquired extensive farm and timber lands, had died in December 1911 and designated the annual income of his estate to "the alleviation of the suffering of the poor, white and colored, of Kershaw County." In spring 1915 the hospital lost its experienced head nurse when Miss Kathleen Crawford left for a new position as superintendent of the State Tubercular Hospital in Columbia.

New Post Office

Construction of another important public building, the new Camden post office, was begun in 1914. An Alabama firm, with a bid of $34,924, received the contract in May. The new structure was built on the old hotel site at the northeast corner of Broad and DeKalb. Brick for the new seventy-five by forty-six–foot building was obtained at the Camden Brick Company, and sandstone, limestone, and stucco provided finishing elements. The trowel used by Lafayette to lay the cornerstone of the De Kalb monument in 1825, now in the possession of the Grand Lodge of South Carolina Masons, was used to lay the cornerstone of the post office.

The public entrance to the post office was on DeKalb Street, and a driveway and hitching posts were at a rear entrance for rural carriers. J. B. Zemp had the contract to prepare the site for the foundation, which included a ten-foot basement housing "the steam heating plant, toilet rooms and carriers rest room." The contract allowed fifteen months for completion, but the building was finished in May 1915, four months ahead of schedule.

Carnegie Library

The Camden Library Association organized in 1900 and utilized a room above a store on the southeast corner of Broad and DeKalb streets as a subscription library. A 1912 fire destroyed some three thousand volumes. Camden's Civic League and other groups and individuals worked to secure a new library. In December 1914 the Andrew Carnegie Foundation agreed to donate five thousand dollars for the construction of a separate library building. Tentative plans were drawn for the colonial-style building, and a site was chosen on the "square between the two schools directly to the north of the 'Hughes house.'"

Shortly after the library site facing Main (Broad) Street was announced, the newspaper printed a letter from C. D. Kershaw, who took issue with the proposed location. The writer, a descendant of Joseph Kershaw, the man who had donated the public squares to the town, stated that there had not been any doubt until recently "for what purpose the squares were given." She was concerned that placing a building on space the donor had designated for a park would set a dangerous precedent. Although the decision of the library location was not changed, a point was made that influenced future decision making restricting the use of public green spaces within the city.

In 1915 construction began on the Camden City Library building. One of fourteen South Carolina recipients of Carnegie funds, Camden's new library opened in 1916 and eventually became part of the later organization of the Kershaw County Library.[39]

Around the City

The commercial convenience of Camden's railroad location increased as spur tracks were added in various parts of the town. In 1912, for example, the Seaboard ran one line to the Camden Brick Company at the lower edge of town and another to the rear of the Main Street business section. The latter benefited buyers at the lower Main Street cotton platforms, who no longer had to transport purchases by wagon to the freight depots nearly a mile distant. The platforms marketed more than twenty thousand bales of cotton annually.

However, throughout the city and county railroad operations also posed dangers for pedestrians, mounted riders, vehicles, wagons, and livestock. In 1912 the city council ordered southbound Southern trains to stop at the crossing near the Court Inn or to place a watchman there to signal pedestrians. The newspaper warned about the crossing because one man had already been killed there, and recently a wagon driver had been severely injured and his two mules killed.

Housing Expansion

Fanfare and advertising attracted public attendance to the May 1912 sale of the Monroe Boykin tract in Kirkwood. Near Spalding Junction, the intersection of the Seaboard Air Line and Southern railroads, the tract had been subdivided into lots to provide attractive and healthful homesites for black citizens. A sales manager of Columbia's Winona Realty Company spent a week in Camden making preparations for a big auction, complete with refreshments and a brass band. In a large promotion of the sale two lots were given away, one for school purposes and the other to a lucky ticket holder. The section of property, which had been deeded during Reconstruction to Reverend Boykin for antebellum services, expanded development of a black suburb called Kirkwood, which retains that name.

In 1914 the efforts of Baron Egmont von Tresckow's Lafayette Hall property were replicated with the development of the A. A. Moore property (in the vicinity of the Baruch home) on North Broad Street. Dr. F. M. Zemp purchased the tract through the Kennedy and Shaw agency and planned to build a street (Walnut Street) between the Moore and Hirsch homes from Broad to Campbell streets. Zemp proposed to divide the property along the new street into building lots, much like those on Lafayette Avenue.

Safety and Order

The July 1914 grand jury reported that the jail was in good condition but recommended again that lights be put in the building. The courthouse was also found in good repair, but the panel thought that the gallery might not be safe when crowded and suggested that two columns be installed as supports. The county home for the poor was in good condition, and the inmates were well cared for. The telephone poles on Liberty Hill Road were said to be too close to the highway and needed to be moved, and the crossing over the Seaboard Air Line Railway on the Ridgeway road needed to be raised. Surprisingly the grand jury found the county's roads in good repair.

A letter signed "Citizen" in the April 16, 1915, *Camden Chronicle* commented on Camden's need to improve its status as a tourist resort. The writer commended the installation of the "much needed fire escapes on our opera house" and the city guard house repairs. He suggested having the clock illuminated at night. The writer stated that Camden had "too much law, and too little need for [it]." Urging Camden to "be progressive," he suggested the removal of the signs reading "All Automobiles Must Stop Here" at Broad and DeKalb.

The mayor promised that the city would provide a light as well as water for "the generals' fountain," the Pantheon on Kershaw Square, and made the same offer for the other city squares. The June 18, 1915, newspaper also revealed that there had been "depredations on the fountain to the generals," the culprits being "nurses with little children and older boys using the fountain as a play ground and bicycle speedway." A petition to the city council proposed to warn parents of a five-dollar trespass fine for anyone convicted of playing on the fountain.

Downtown Renewal

In 1912 improvements energized downtown Camden, while plans were under way for the new hospital. Eugene Dibble renovated his building at the southwest corner of Broad and DeKalb streets and erected three other stores. A Chinese laundry operated in new quarters on lower Main Street. Spero Beleos made extensive repairs to the Candy Kitchen. Residents moved into two new houses on Lafayette Avenue.

A citizen wrote to the March 13, 1914, *Camden Chronicle* pointing out the need for a new theater. He stated, "The lower part of Main is lined with the most uncouth, dilapidated, and untidy buildings to be found anywhere." He lamented the mud during rainy spells and the dust otherwise. In remarking on the possibilities for downtown renewal, he referred to the new post office having recently replaced the dilapidated old hotel.

The writer contended, however, that the opera house and city hall should be in the center of Camden, "the best part of town, not in the lower part." He cited health conditions in the upper part being better "than down by the river and lower Main." He added, "Let lower Main die in a good cause and become a rich cotton field like the block where the old Cornwallis house was. Are we working for the interest of the few people 'hanging on' there, or are we working for the city as a whole?" The writer stated that "the city now includes Kirkwood" and that section's interests should be of no less importance than those of lower Main.

In 1915 Henry Savage purchased the property at the northwest corner of Broad and DeKalb streets for ten thousand dollars, which was three thousand dollars more than it had been sold for the previous year. Here Savage and his associate Joseph B. Crocker, a Bostonian and a winter visitor to Camden for several years, constructed a forty-thousand-dollar multistory office building, the first in town. The structure built of brick from the Camden Brick Company opened with a bank taking up the first floor, the Masonic Temple occupying the third floor, and nineteen offices on the second floor, which the realtor L. C. Shaw was in charge of renting.

By October 1916 Savage was involved in two city projects. He was opening a new street "between the old Truesdell residence and that of Mrs. C. R. Lewis." In addition Savage and his associate Crocker were remodeling "the old Smyrl house" on Lyttleton Street for conversion to a tourist hotel. A Mr. and Mrs. Chandler, from Danville, Virginia, were to manage the twenty-five-room facility, to be known as the Park View Hotel, overlooking Hampton Park.

New and Revived Enterprises

In September 1912 Thomas J. Kirkland, W. H. Dawes, J. T. Burdell, and W. E. deLoache obtained a charter for the Camden Ice and Fuel Company, a business welcomed by area citizens, who had endured "an ice famine during the past two summers," according to the local newspaper. The fifteen-thousand-dollar corporation manufactured ice and sold wood and coal near the main line of the Seaboard Air Line Railway.

The January 9, 1914, *Camden Chronicle* described W. O. Hay's new welding machine, an oxo-acetylene outfit from a German manufacturer, being used in his auto repair shop on South Main Street. It was a type of machine then unknown "in these parts." It generated such extreme heat that it could cut through hard steel as though it were soft metal, and it was capable of mending broken machinery in a fraction of the time previously required. The machine was put to use a week later when an accident to the linotype machine delayed production of the *Chronicle*. The newspaper was effusive with praise for Hay and his new welding machine for his repair of the broken equipment in about six hours. Again in 1916 at the newspaper plant a "delicate part of the machinery broke," shutting down the whole operation. Once again Hay brought his welding machine, and he and his assistant Ernest Frietag made the repair, saving the newspaper from having to order a new part from Rhode Island. The demand for welding increased in proportion to the new machinery added in the community.

In 1914 J. W. McCormick, one of Columbia's prominent undertakers, leased the new Dibble building at the corner of Broad and DeKalb and began his Camden business on November 15. He constructed stables in the rear for his "hearse, ambulance and horses." In 1916 he purchased the Sullivan Building on North Broad and moved the funeral home there, where he and his family occupied the top two floors of the building. The first floor was reserved for the undertaking parlor. By 1916 Collins Brothers at 714 West DeKalb Street advertised as "Undertakers for Colored People." C. W. Evans of the Camden Undertaking Company was another mortician.

In later years the author of "Our Town" recalled new industries in the early 1900s, including a large coffin and woodworking plant that operated along the Southern railway siding and a large lumber company on West DeKalb Street that was later replaced by a veneer plant. The writer also recalled, "The little brick-making plant below the fairgrounds was enlarged to a modern plant."

In 1916 the North State Veneer Company of Statesville, North Carolina, began operation in Camden on the A. D. Kennedy property. Shipping by the side track of the Southern Railway, the company used between two thousand and five thousand feet of lumber daily, employing thirty workers at the start. Kershaw County was an ideal location, the company said, because of the abundance of gum and poplar in the area, the "excellent railway facilities and natural advantages," and the fact that manufacturing firms locating in Camden were exempted from taxes for five years.

In March 1915 R. L. Moseley "fitted up two of the vacant stores in the old Clyburn block on lower Main Street . . . as a milling house." The Camden Milling Company ground thirty thousand bushels of corn into meal and hominy each year and made all kinds of feeds. Moseley said that he could grind the cob with corn seed, which yielded good chicken feed. The 1915 newspaper also advertised the "Three T's Milling Company," the initials standing for Team, Tiller, and Thurmond, in West Wateree. The establishment advertised flour processed at its mill on the old Jordan place.

The Camden Steam Bakery and the Camden Candy Kitchen advertised their wares in the 1914 papers. "McLeod & Kelly, Proprietors" and "First Class Bakers" offered "Prompt Delivery" and the city's "Most Efficient Bread Service." The Candy Kitchen, in addition to its soda fountain, advertised, "We Deliver Ice Cream to All Parts of the City." In 1916 the owner Spero Beleos advertised fruits and vegetables at the establishment.

An advertisement in 1914 by "Scip, the Barber," whose shop was just north of the Chero-Cola Plant, explained his longtime discounting system. Scip said that he began "about '88 or '89," when a shave in Kershaw County was fifteen cents, to charge a nickel less: "if you shaved once a week, I have saved you $2.60 [yearly]; twice a week, $5.20; three times a week, $7.80; and so on."

In 1916 Dr. F. M. Zemp signed a ten-year lease on the southwest corner store at Broad and DeKalb then "owned and operated by E. H. Dibble, the colored merchant[,] as a grocery store." Zemp added a fifteen-foot storeroom on the rear and made significant modifications to the structure. Dibble built a new brick building on West DeKalb Street, where he resumed his grocery trade.

A sampling of advertisements for automobiles and related products in the April 1916 *Camden Chronicle* revealed the following: D. T. Yarborough was the agent for Maxwell automobiles in Bethune; the Camden Motor Company sold Dodge automobiles; and the Kershaw Motor Company was the Ford dealer in

Camden.[40] W. O. Hay of Camden was the dealer for Fisk nonskid tires. H. E. Beard in Camden sold tires and offered repair services, including welding. In Bethune tires were sold at the Bethune Drug Company. (The Bethune Drug Company and Pearce-Young in Camden hosted the United States Tire Show.)

Camden's third soft-drink plant opened in 1914 when T. J. Lipscomb began bottling Chero-Cola, along with Acme ginger ale and other flavored drinks. Specialized equipment was installed to clean and sterilize bottles. To run deliveries locally and to small surrounding towns—Hagood, Jefferson, Kershaw, McBee, and Rembert—Lipscomb first used wagons and the railroad and then added a twenty-horsepower Chase truck from Syracuse. As warm weather approached that year, the soft-drink business was especially active. Every week H. W. Pace of Kershaw sent two wagons, each with the capacity of forty-four crates, down to the Coca-Cola plant in Camden. By the spring of 1915 the plant had opened a branch of its bottling company in Kershaw. The equipment was installed in the building recently vacated by City Pressing Club, on the corner of Hampton and Richland streets. Cuthbert Clark of Camden managed the Kershaw establishment.

A group of Sumter investors established the Southern Clay Company, a kaolin plant, by buying out "the holding at Blaney . . . and at James Crossing, near Horrell's Hill . . . of parties who have been operating kaolin plants at those places." According to the June 16, 1916, *Camden Chronicle,* the new owners expected to operate more efficiently in mining kaolin and dealing in crude and refined clay to sell their products to manufacturers on a national level.

Facing Gloomy Prospects

A real obstacle to indications that Kershaw County was progressing economically was termed by the *Camden Chronicle* in 1914 as the "demoralized cotton market." Yet many local citizens were joining a movement that was spreading across the cotton belt. The "Buy-a-Bale" plan requested individuals to purchase one bale of cotton each and keep it off the market "until the world will buy it at a fair price." The subscriber would pay ten cents per pound, or fifty dollars for a standard five-hundred-pound bale, and purchase it directly from the planter.

The September 18, 1914, *Camden Chronicle* reported that the Camden Chamber of Commerce had joined the movement and formed a committee to encourage everyone who could to purchase a bale of cotton. A week later the newspaper reported that county merchants had agreed to take 2,185 cotton bales off the market under the ten-cents-per-pound program. Some participating merchants traded merchandise or accounts receivable in exchange for the cotton.

The following month a group of West Wateree farmers of the Trinity School community met to discuss the demoralized market. The October 16, 1914, *Camden Chronicle* reported that the group reached a consensus that selling their cotton at the prevailing price of six or seven cents "meant ruination to the farmers from which it would take five or six years to recover." Those assembled passed a resolution to sell no cotton until they met again on October 31, when they would assess the actions of the state legislature and other surrounding states before determining a further course of action. The group discussed the possibility of crop reduction in the future and determined to attempt to get all the county's farmers to organize in a similar manner.

One of the problems affecting cotton was the multinational struggle ongoing across the Atlantic. The September 25, 1914, newspaper declared, "European war has temporarily cut off a market for between six and eight million bales." The farmers' struggles with weather and markets, with underproduction and overproduction, would linger to become submerged without solution in the larger world struggle that would soon entangle America. On April 2, 1917, President Wilson asked Congress to recognize that a state of war existed between the United States and Germany. The country had entered the Great War, and Kershaw County soldiers—farmers, factory operatives, store clerks, and professional men—headed for its trenches. The achievements since 1900 were to be severely tried.

13

Bridging Isolation

The Great War

When the United States was drawn into the epic struggle of the Great War (later called World War I), Kershaw County citizens expressed little surprise. National defense and the drive for victory became priorities during the relatively brief but significant American combat period from spring 1917 through fall 1918. For a time in the latter years of the decade, the local economy expanded.

Facing the War

From 1914, because of dangers abroad, some wealthy winter tourists canceled voyages to Europe and instead boarded trains to the sunny South. The Camden resorts emphasized the sporting and cultural attractions favored by the leisure class and promoted local history to visitors accustomed to antiquities. Camden tourism swelled.

On the eve of war more immediate concerns in Kershaw County were part of other regional and national situations. By 1916 local cotton farmers had been shown specimens of boll weevil damage from Georgia, but few growers were able to prepare for the destruction advancing toward them. Those with means converted to wheat and livestock, which were impervious to the weevil. Anticipating wartime demands for bread and meat, investors began buying land to revitalize for food production. Small, debt-ridden farmers who could not diversify or expand their holdings had few options.

Isolation was another serious concern. In early 1917 officials were scrambling to replace the Wateree Bridge that had been swept away by floodwaters the previous year. The railway company had already raised a wooden structure to replace its lost trestle, but a bridge for public use came slowly since a large debt was still owed on the old one. War-related shortages of materials and money further hampered efforts. In 1920 a wooden toll bridge was opened to the public in place of the steel bridge that had operated free of charge. For nearly four years until that time, only a slow and tedious ferry had transported the general public across the river divide. During those years mammoth construction upriver ensued at a persistent pace, shifting acres of earth and rock to raise the Southern Power Company's huge Wateree Dam and to construct its generating plant for electricity. The industries that the operation was intended to power were as yet largely undeveloped, and some were even unimagined.

Fighting the War

In early 1917, before becoming involved in Europe, America had to withdraw from a military distraction on its Mexican border. There the National Guard had been engaged for several months in "the Punitive Expedition," pursuing Pancho Villa for launching renegade raids onto American soil. The *Camden Chronicle* on February 2 summed up the situation: "The futile attempt of the United States government to 'get Villa alive or dead' has cost the American people a number of lives and a sum of money estimated at close to $70,000,000. . . . Although Villa is far more alive today than when [U.S. brigadier general John J.] Pershing went into Mexico, it is expected that the American forces will be withdrawn in the near future. Military men and civilians agree that the troops are doing no good where they are and that they are only causing irritation to the Mexican people." The Kershaw Guards under Major E. C. von Tresckow, Company M in the First Infantry Regiment of the South Carolina National Guard, had been part of the first state troops to entrain for the border. Thus they were some of the first troops brought home. Company M returned to Camden aboard the Seaboard in December 1916 and were greeted by cheering crowds. The men continued training in the following months, energized by their adventure. In the spring of 1917 they immediately rallied in support of President Woodrow Wilson's call to arms against Germany.

National Guard

Just ten days after the congressional declaration of war on April 6, 1917, the Kershaw County National Guard left home in the nation's defense. Large crowds at the departure of Company M made local headlines. Sunday night attendance overflowed the Lyttleton Street Methodist Church in Camden when community ministers united in a service for the departing "soldier boys." The next afternoon "the entire population" was at the train station to say goodbye. Almost 40 percent of the embarking guards were new recruits. All were white.

Draftees

Local support was strong for President Wilson, who had lived part of his youth in Columbia. When the president called for all males ages twenty-one to thirty-one, whites and blacks, to register for the draft, Kershaw County men of both races readily responded. The June 8 *Chronicle* reported that all who were supposed to register did so and that "negroes contrary to what was at one time expected, were not only willing, but in all cases, seemed to be anxious to serve their country . . . ready to go anywhere that the government wanted them."

Many places of draft registration covered the county in May 1917; all were familiar community gathering spots. These included thirteen schools, ten stores, two churches, two railroad depots, two private homes, two gristmills, a textile

Company M, First Infantry Regiment, of the South Carolina National Guard in front of their armory at 1111 Broad Street, before their deployment to the Mexican border in 1916. Courtesy of the Camden Archives

mill office, a private office, a bank, a post office, a barbershop, and a place of entertainment. Men registered at seven schoolhouses named for communities—Buffalo, Ned's Creek, Oakland, Shamrock, Stockton, Stoneboro, and Three C's. In other communities too men registered at schoolhouses—in Antioch at Gumberry Schoolhouse; in Beulah at Cleveland; in Harmony at Blythdale; in Hermitage at Mill; in Pine Tree at Beaver Dam; and in Shaylor's Hill at Piedmont. Men also registered at stores, all named for their owners: in Abney at Kirkley's; in Beaver Dam at J. A. Rabon's; in Belk Hill at T. B. Blyther's; in Cantey Hill at J. E. Creed's; in Doby's Mill at Campbell's; in Liberty Hill at N. S. Richards's; in Lugoff at Team's; in Shepard at Hall's; in Swift Creek at B. H. Boykin's; and in Twenty Creek at Hinson's.

Men registered in Enterprise at Mt. Zion Church and in Sandy Grove at Sandy Grove Church. In DeKalb and in Westville they signed up at Southern railway depots, and they registered in Roland at W. E. West's Mill and in Salt Pond at Dinkins's Mill. Men signed up in Lockhart at L. J. Jordan's residence and in Raley's Mill at M. L. Raley's place. Other sites included Bethune at the Bank of Bethune, Blaney at the U.S. Post Office; Camden at the opera house; Cassatt at the barbershop; and Kershaw at McCaskill's office.

By June 8 Kershaw County had registered 2,400 men, 395 of them from Camden. An "extra" edition of the *Camden Chronicle* on July 23 listed 494 names that had been drawn for enlistment, and the July 27 issue printed the rest of the list.[1] The first name drawn was that of Eugene Joy of Camden. The initial draft was for the first 350 men. The newspaper reported that five sons of J. C. Jones of Kershaw had been drawn in the selective draft, two of them in Minnesota; and B. W. Ogburn of Westville had four sons drawn. Recruiters for the army and the navy competed in offering choices to volunteers.

African American Soldiers

Although men of different races were organized into segregated units consistent with custom, for the first time locally both black and white recruits were accepted for national defense. The October 12 *Chronicle* reported the community send-off for black soldiers, who left separately for segregated training at Camp Jackson:

> A large crowd of unusually happy colored folks gathered at the Seaboard station last Saturday to say goodbye to the large number of selective draft soldiers. There were also quite a good number of white friends of these negroes at the station.
>
> The men all formed in line at the court house and marched to the station where they were placed in charge of William Randolph Williams. They left here with banners flying and with the knowledge that they had the best wishes of all as to their welfare and hopes for their safe return.

A few days earlier both black and white citizens attended a farewell service at the Mt. Moriah Baptist Church led by Pastor J. W. Boykin. The audience sang "America," the Jackson Graded School sang "Mother Land," and Nathaniel Boykin recited "The Negro Soldier." Mayor C. H. Yates, Professor C. C. Lowery of Jackson School, the Reverend J. H. Graves, the Reverend E. W. Stratton, *Wateree Messenger* editor C. W. Birchmore, the Reverend J. H. Toatley, the Honorable L. T. Mills, Dr. John W. Corbett, and Senator A. J. Beattie spoke, followed by solos by Dr. J. P. Pickett and Mrs. Theodosia Frierson. Jackson students sang "USA Forever" to the tune of "Dixie" and presented each soldier with a copy of the song, tied with patriotic ribbons. "God Be with You till We Meet Again" was sung before Reverend T. J. Williams's benediction and the serving of cake and ice cream.

Home Guard and Others

In the absence of the regular guard, a home guard was organized, and it in some cases accepted youths as young as sixteen. Boy Scouts, under the leadership of Scoutmaster T. K. Trotter, studied military tactics, undertook patriotic activities, and drilled at times with the home guard. Other qualified individuals—both males and females—responded to the national call for "stenographers and typewriters" and took civilian work at army posts. Dr. W. J. Burdell, a West Wateree practitioner for twenty-two years, departed as a medical volunteer in 1917. By

September 1918 older men, ages forty-five to fifty-six, were being recruited for service in France with medical, ordnance, and quartermaster corps.

Location

Newspapers emphasized the crucial role of the South—and especially of the local area—in the war effort. In 1917 the *Columbia Record* stated, "Not only will more than half of the army be trained in the South, and a large portion of it within 125 miles of Columbia, but . . . the purchasing of supplies for the armies is to be put into the hands of a Southern man, Bernard Baruch, a native of Camden" (quoted in the June 1 *Chronicle*). The *Record* referred to critics of President Wilson as "disloyal" and to complaints of the Wall Street background of Baruch as "sniveling." Local newspapers backed Wilson and expressed pride in Baruch's career and in the area's service in the war effort.

Education

Since illiterate persons were not accepted into the armed services, one patriotic response was to organize community night schools, "lay by" schools (during the lull of fieldwork), and reading clubs to improve adult literacy.[2] Volunteer teachers and adult students were encouraged on the basis of patriotic duty. Self-improvement became a national defense weapon.

For schoolboys, football was promoted as patriotic since it built strong bodies and teamwork. It was in the spirit of "public good" that fans were urged to cheer on the Camden High School football team. In August 1917 Mrs. E. L. Zemp's "open air" school in Camden featured instruction out-of-doors to invigorate the health of anemic children. The war inspired energy and innovation in the physical and mental education of youths and adults alike.

Winning the War

National Guard units awaiting deployment were given immediate duties to protect vital bridges and railway trestles. The May 4, 1917, *Chronicle* described local efforts "for the comfort and pleasure" of the Anderson (S.C.) Company guarding the Wateree River trestle near Camden. According to the press, "There are 16 men guarding . . . at all times, who come in reliefs from the headquarters at Cheraw. They are encamped on the opposite banks of the river in two tents." Citizens contributed quarters for ice cream, tobacco, and other treats. Boy Scouts canvassed door to door, collecting magazines and fishing tackle and seeking a Victrola to help guardsmen pass the time. At their posts too local guardsmen were reported receiving "royal treatment" and "every possible courtesy."

Despite the holiday-like air, a week later the May 11 newspaper revealed that duties were not risk free. Private Gilliam Hall of the Kershaw Guards, a veteran of the Mexican border, was reported killed in a train accident while guarding a

Black River bridge. Another incident, overblown but reflective of wartime anxiety, was quoted from the *Columbia State:* "National Guardsmen doing patrol duty in South Carolina captured their first German Saturday, when a squad . . . took into custody at Bethune a man who gave his name as John Bowen." Captured in the woods with several area maps, the middle-aged hobo suspected of spying was simply a recent immigrant with a poor command of English, a discharged railroad worker in search of a new job.

In the same issue the U.S. Navy announced that two German commerce raiders, seized by the government, were being renamed for German generals who had fought for liberty under General Washington in 1776. The ship *Prinz Eitel Frederich* was renamed the USS *DeKalb* in honor of the Revolutionary War leader buried in Camden and was subsequently placed in American naval service.

As the war proceeded, patriotic memories of the Confederate past blended with contemporary feelings for America. The June 1, 1917, *Chronicle* noted that seventy-seven-year-old Mrs. Sarah J. Brown, a former county resident now living in Lee County, paid "her first visit to this city since 1861 when she accompanied her brothers here to enlist in the War Between the States." In July timbermen cutting a poplar in the Swift Creek swamp cut into a grapeshot ball imbedded nearly twenty feet high and eight inches deep: "It is supposed to have been fired into the tree during Potter's raid in that section." On January 11, 1918, the reminiscing *Chronicle* columnist from Flat Rock, Henry L. Fletcher, compared present engagements to the battlefields of Virginia. In May 1918 the annual dinner for Confederate veterans on Memorial Day was served to thirty-four survivors. The memories evoked by the Confederate past reflected on defense of home and loved ones, the same concerns held by citizens in the modern cause.

Increased Food Production

With the declaration of war came immediate appeals for increased production of food. The educational roles of the Cooperative Extension agents and the nation's land-grant colleges became even more important. Kershaw County farm agent Dr. Walter Sowell everywhere described the "seriousness of the food shortage that faces the American people today." Miss Selma Parrish, the county home-demonstration agent, emphasized the message with women and young people.

In April 1917 the Bank of Bethune, the Bank of Camden, the First National Bank, and the Loan and Savings Bank joined in running a large ad: "CHILDREN CRYING FOR FOOD. This Will Happen in Kershaw County Unless We Grow Foodstuffs for Use Within 3 months." The banks jointly promised farmers: "Depend On Us To Help Any Way We Can." The Bank of Camden offered farmers prizes of gold in a corn-growing competition.

A shortage of agricultural workers was a concern since able-bodied men were being called to battle duty and better-paying jobs were available in the North. Spring 1917 issues of the *Camden Chronicle* reported on a campaign to retain and inspire farmworkers: "The colored people have enlisted under the leadership of prominent colored men throughout the state in preparation for more food," said the April 20 newspaper. As the campaign chairman, Reverend J. W. Boykin called immediately for a meeting in Camden at Mt. Moriah Baptist Church and for similar meetings afterward throughout the county. On May 18 C. C. Lowery, secretary of the Central Committee on Civic Preparedness, described an "enthusiastic" meeting at Zion Hill Church led by I. J. Johnson, chairman of the Antioch precinct. At Kershaw in the Unity (black) Baptist Church, Reverend Richard Carroll of Columbia addressed what the May 25 paper described as "a large audience of both white and colored on the subject of food preparedness and in opposition to the migration of the negro from the South."[3]

The success of increased wheat crops was reported on August 3: "Numbers of wagon loads of wheat have been hauled through Camden the past week to [E. E.] Holland's Mill north of Camden, formerly known as Vaughn's mill[,] for ginning into flour." The Lenoir mill near Hagood and the Buffalo Milling Company in the upper section of the county were also successfully operating. The quality of these mills' products was reported to be "excellent," and "there will be many people who this year will eat home grown flour instead of having it shipped." The Buffalo Milling Company also modernized the old Raley Mill as a roller mill and a gristmill, adding a ginnery the following year.

A serious business setback dismayed the residents of Kershaw during the first year of the war. On the night of November 14, 1917, the wooden store buildings in a four-block area were consumed by flames. The next day three-fourths of the county's second-largest town lay in ruins. Replacing the lost buildings was especially difficult because of wartime shortages of labor and materials.

Wateree Bridge Construction

In June 1917 bids to replace the washed-out Wateree Bridge were two to four times the one hundred thousand dollars that the state had approved for a bond issue. Yet national security required transportation of men and materials, and work was urged forward. In July the county board of commissioners empowered Supervisor M. C. West to build a pontoon bridge for temporary relief to the long lines at the ferry. However, extremely variable and unpredictable water levels made the plan impractical. Pontoon bridges across the Wateree were erected by the military from time to time for specialized and temporary purposes.

The only consistently feasible public method of river crossing utilized existing roadways to access the traditional, heavy flatboat ferry at the site of the downed bridge. The system was clumsy and slow. Traffic volume, especially of motorized vehicles, had increased since the last period of ferry operations. In January 1917, when Supervisor West was en route to West Wateree with two businessmen, his automobile plunged off the ferry into the river about midway across. When his vehicle struck the bottom, West escaped through the side window curtains, and a companion tore out through the back. The third man jumped out as the car reached the water and grabbed hold of the old steel bridge lying in the water. A number of similar dunkings took place while the ferry was in use.

In early May the river fell so low that the ferry flatboat was stranded. Some Camden motorists returning from the National Guard base at Camp Styx, Lexington County, were forced to pass the night camping on the opposite bank of the Wateree while waiting to get home. In July the large truck that transported the county chain gang plummeted into shallow water on the west side of the river when one of the ropes fastening the flatboat to the landing gave way.[4]

Engineers for the new bridge had problems to overcome related to materials, location, and threats of flooding. By August 1917 the site for the new bridge, a mile and a quarter north of the old site, had been determined—"just below the confluence of Twenty Five Mile Creek," reported the August 10 *Chronicle*—and the building contract had been let.[5] To minimize water resistance, a tall bridge

Wagons exiting the Camden to Lugoff ferry on the west side of the Wateree River within site of concrete remains (left) of the steel bridge destroyed in 1916. Courtesy of the Camden Archives

of wooden spans on concrete piers was designed to curve linearly across the river channel and to reach high above the flood-prone waters. Lengthy stretches of wooden approaches on tall pilings above the floodplains were planned for access roads to the bridge.

One month after the site was chosen, the engineer C. S. Foster for the Austin Company began work on coffer dams to place the concrete piers. Camps were erected nearby for the thirty or forty laborers initially hired. The work was exacting and dangerous. S. L. Spangler, for example, fell from scaffolding on the bridge and was severely injured.

In the more than two years that work was under way on the bridge, mishaps also continued with river crossings. In early January 1918 an exceptional winter freeze locked up the ferry for several days as ice three inches thick caked on its sides. Ferryman S. H. Twitty reported that it was possible to walk far out into the river on the jam of large blocks of ice that floated downstream. Lengthy lines of automobiles were stranded on both sides of the river. Later that month the January 25 *Chronicle* reported that a fifteen-year-old Columbia youth stole a touring car from the front of the Richland County courthouse, sped down the road to Camden, and, "thinking he was crossing a bridge," went the old route and landed in the river with the purloined auto.

At long last, on February 3, 1920, the new Wateree Bridge opened for traffic, with levied tolls of fifty cents per automobile and five cents per head for mule teams.[6] Now the ease of crossing had been restored, but for many years more, public pressure would resound to end the toll and "free the bridge."

The Wateree Dam

Even more expansive than the work on the bridge was the work upriver on the dam for the Southern Power Company. In early March 1917 Camden merchants solicited funds to build a road on the west side of the Wateree to the site of Hardaway Construction, the major contractor. In April supplies arrived in Kershaw for H. W. Pace to string electrical cables between the construction site and the Great Falls power plant. H. F. Haile of Liberty Hill, representing the power company, met in Kershaw with other attorneys and Judge W. B. deLoach of Camden on rights-of-way for transmission lines. In May a jury convened on the Liberty Hill property of W. Z. Hilton and granted him $750 for fifteen acres condemned for a transmission tower. On July 27 the Camden newspaper reported a "crowd of workmen" camping at Cantey to work on the power lines. Several cases of smallpox were active in the area. Communicable outbreaks added to the problems of the various work camps throughout the building of the dam.

Several hundred Hardaway Construction workers were constantly employed in the heavy labor at the dam site. Because of a concern that the war would drain prime laborers, salary incentives were increased. The work was dangerous, exhausting, and carried on in areas isolated from roads and community habitation. It was reported that able-bodied men who found their way to the construction site were given work as long as they stayed, without exceptional concern for age, background, race, training, or military status. Accidents and illnesses bore serious consequences, however. Through heat and cold work moved steadily forward despite occasional outbreaks of disease, strained tempers, personal violence, or mechanical malfunctioning.

Accidents could be sudden and deadly. In November 1917 a huge derrick lifting a load of heavy rock turned over and upset the steam engine that powered it. A "horribly scalded" nineteen-year-old engineer died within a few hours. In March 1918 a swinging bridge crossing the river from the east to the Hardaway site broke during a sudden windstorm and injured four persons, who were plunged into the water.[7] Robert Stover, the father of five children, died from pneumonia. Far longer than the nation's soldiers fought in the Great War, the Wateree Dam workers struggled with nature. Eventually they harnessed the power that forever changed the region and its people.

A view from Eagle's Nest on the east side of the Wateree River of construction on the Wateree Dam. Collection of Kershaw County Historical Society

Industrial Activity

When maritime hostilities interrupted international shipping, the Kershaw Mining Company of Lancaster County in 1915 reopened the old Haile Gold Mine, three miles from Kershaw, to extract the mineral pyrite. More commonly known as "fool's gold," it was urgently needed to produce sulfuric acid for making explosives. One of the operations making use of the extract was a munitions plant of E. I. du Pont de Nemours on the coast of South Carolina at Georgetown. Although the mines operated on the other side of the Lancaster County line, workers included Kershaw County residents, and improved economic conditions influenced the upper part of the county.

By the time America entered the war, the Kershaw Cotton Mill, as part of Lancaster Mills under Leroy Springs, had been operating three years. Just across the line in Lancaster County it employed a number of Kershaw County residents.

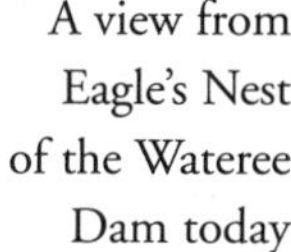

A view from Eagle's Nest of the Wateree Dam today

The 1916 *Columbia Record* commented about the plant that "employees come from right around Kershaw and are good citizens." The Kershaw mill operated profitably with the wartime demand for goods. It was one of five mills that Springs ran as separate companies at war's end, the others being at Chester, Fort Mill, and Lancaster.

Wartime orders for bandages and hospital supplies increased production at the two cotton mills at Camden, although government regulations mandated seasonal shutdowns in national efforts to conserve fuel. Shortages of coal and weather-induced problems of drought and freezing temperatures menaced all water- and steam-powered manufactories.[8] Operatives received partial pay during shutdowns, and improvements were made to the plants and the villages. In September 1917, besides constructing a large new warehouse and new cottages, Wateree Mill added a huge tank and well with electrical equipment to provide running water in each home in its mill village. A "nice new furnace" was installed to replace the old heaters in the mill church. In the spring all cottages were screened, and the bathhouse and recreational equipment at the swimming area were freshly painted. Modern, sanitary, and pleasant living conditions for workers were clearly a competitive edge to keep employees. Both Camden mills operated with relative profit during the war period.

Local textile mills hired white operatives only, so jobs in integrated northern "war plants" were enticing to black persons who lacked similar opportunities at home. Many from Kershaw County boarded trains—where separate sections were reserved for "coloreds"—and within a few hours began new lives in northern cities, often among other southern transplants. The national Colored Citizens' Patriotic League painted discouraging pictures of discriminatory conditions in the North and urged southern blacks to remain at home and "grow Southern plants." Some transplants to the North thrived; some were relieved to return home.

The Red Cross

Even before America committed to the war, volunteer fund-raising to aid European victims was under way in Kershaw County. Local churches and civic groups collected money and supplies for "Belgian relief" and "Armenian sufferers." At times tourists joined in these activities. During the 1917 winter season at the Kirkwood Hotel, local and tourist women made and shipped more than four thousand articles for relief. In March an entertainment benefit, the Moving Picture for the American Ambulance in the French Field, raised more than fifteen hundred dollars in one evening. One guest alone donated an entire ambulance and outfit, and others raised enough for two more.

Tremendous civilian effort poured into Red Cross work once war was declared. Those who gathered at a May 1917 public meeting agreed to organize a chapter of the Red Cross, "the only organization authorized by the government to render war relief service." Leaders were the health officer Dr. A. W. Burnet, Mrs. E. C. von Tresckow of the Civic League, Mrs. N. R. Goodale of the Federation of Women's Clubs, and Miss Jim Eldredge of the Hobkirk Inn. The founding meeting on May 21 at the courthouse featured red, white, and blue bunting; Old Glory; and patriotic music sung by town choirs and schoolchildren. Dr. Burnett was elected president; Mrs. Kate C. Wallace, vice president; Mrs. Margaret C. Miller, secretary; and L. T. Mills, treasurer.

Red Cross chapters were forming in other parts of the county by July. At Bethune, Reverend J. M. Forbis, Reverend A. M. Gardner, Dr. A. W. Humphries, Dr. E. Z. Truesdale, and D. T. Yarborough organized the first meeting. At Lugoff thirty-seven members enrolled when Reverend J. C. Rowan and Red Cross officers from Camden assisted the organization.

The public welcomed personal contacts with military units in training. In March 1917 a Camp Jackson machine gun battalion under Captain H. H. Hall of Kershaw County hiked to Blaney, camped overnight, marched to Camden for "a delightful lunch" served in Monument Square by local ladies, and headed on to camp near the Kirkwood Hotel. Keeping public spirits enthusiastic were events such as the giant Liberty Day Patriotic Rally in Kershaw on April 27. A large parade concluding at the Main Street park featured a speech by a British officer.

Fund-raisers in the mill villages and in black and white churches across the county regularly collected generous sums for war bonds and for the Red Cross. Schoolchildren countywide bought war stamps instead of more expensive bonds and did odd jobs to earn pennies for the Red Cross. Tourists contributed the proceeds of polo games, teas, concerts, and other benefits.

One highly successful Red Cross drive, chaired by Mrs. Belton Boykin, was described in the May 24, 1918, *Camden Chronicle.* It kicked off with a large rally at Camden Baptist Church. Uniformed Red Cross members filed in singing patriotic hymns. A "Flying Squadron" of speakers and uniformed nurses canvassed the county in the following days—first rallying at Bethune, the Westville schoolhouse, Cassatt, Beulah Church, Boykin, and the Three C's school. After crossing the river they addressed an all-black audience at a Lugoff church, visited Blaney, and then returned to rally at the Lugoff schoolhouse. Back in Camden they met at the mill village schoolhouse and then at the Beaver Dam church.

The single most productive rally was at the Hardaway Company's dam construction site on the upper Wateree River. About a dozen borrowed cars transported the Red Cross workers and nurses, including "the colored auxiliary." Visitors expressed awe at the sight of the enormous construction. When the meeting chairman, S. A. Burrier, asked the more than four hundred employees to "give a day's work" to the Red Cross, every single person consented to donate his Monday pay.

The Red Cross also raised money from recreational activities in 1918. Admission fees at Camden's opening polo game were donated to a Washington's birthday benefit fund. A ceremony unfurling a flag on a new pole at the Kirkwood Hotel entrance garden sparked "spontaneous and enthusiastic celebration" and donations from nearby golfers. At Factory Pond the Red Cross operated as a benefit the old Saddle and Paddle Club, which had lately been the Millbank Swimming Club. Season tickets for supervised swimming ranged from a quarter to a dollar, and ice cream and soft drink sales rounded out profits. At Big Springs, Dr. J. E. McLure turned summer operations over to the Red Cross. In Camden the organization maintained a workroom to prepare bandages and other supplies and also ran a Broad Street canteen where volunteers served hot biscuits, salad, tea cakes, and "ice tea." A committee at the train station saw drafted men off with the best wishes of the community.

War Bonds

Although the county consistently met or exceeded assigned quotas for sales of war bonds and savings stamps, there was some grumbling that government quotas were based on high contributions during the tourist season and worked hardships on less-affluent residents when tourists left. In June 1918 C. J. Shannon Jr. was chairman when the county was given the goal of raising $280,000 in "loans" to Uncle Sam during the last two weeks of the same month. Black citizens, under appeals from Isaac B. English and Thomas J. Boykin, had just recently pledged their day's cash receipts on May 28 to purchase thrift and war savings stamps. Wateree Mill workers likewise had subscribed $600 to the Red Cross war fund in May. Yet with continued effort the additional hefty new goal was met as well. Kershaw County again in October oversubscribed its quota in the fourth Liberty Loan drive, which was likewise completed by local effort before the arrival of tourists.

Public Morality

War tensions increased measures to combat immorality, viewed as a threat to public security. The same issue of the *Camden Chronicle,* April 20, 1917, that in one article lauded the huge public send-off for the county's first group of war-bound soldiers also bore an uglier headline: "Negro Is Shot to Death by Man in U.S. Uniform." One of the Kershaw Guards scheduled to leave had killed a black man at "a disreputable negro house" the night of the send-off. Instead of attending the religious service at the Methodist church on Sunday night, the soldier "invaded the red light district and tragedy followed." Captain W. M. Young "went to the jail and stripped him of his uniform leaving him for the courts to deal with." Another unflattering article described illegal liquor sales and incidents of intoxication among the crowd at the train station farewell.[9]

Consistent with similar actions nationally, local efforts for security supported closing brothels and enacting national Prohibition. In December 1917 the Eighteenth Amendment—which took effect in 1920—was passed to ban the manufacture and sale of intoxicating liquors.[10] Locally preachers supported such moves from their pulpits, assuring congregations that God would favor a nation morally worth saving. Individuals and groups also advocated "clean pictures," and local theaters agreed to censor their movie showings. Regular prayer meetings on behalf of local soldiers were held by all denominations in all communities, a war effort consistently mentioned in letters to and from the front. The editor of the *Wateree Messenger* printed a "Letter from Colored Soldier in France" written on October 28, 1918, by the mechanic Edward McKain, who acknowledged: "I know you good Christians are praying for us."

The End of War

Intensification of the war was obvious by the end of December 1917 when the government took over the operation of the nation's railroads. Residents of Kershaw County, which was no great distance from Camp Jackson and along major railroads and roads, saw much of the movement of men and equipment. In August 1918 a motorized convoy of fifty-four huge army tanks from New York passed through Camden on the way to Camp Jackson. Many citizens watched with interest as the tanks were laboriously ferried across the Wateree River. In the same month Henry Savage Sr., returning to Camden from a visit to his old home at Cape Cod, reported hearing a German sub shelling coastal travelers in that area.

Many times citizens publicly acknowledged their feelings. In July 1918 bells tolled in Camden and business stopped for five minutes in memory of Massenburg Trotter, the first Kershaw County man to fall in battle. In October, Camden city lights were turned off for one minute each night for citizens to bow in silent prayer "for ceasing of hostilities in the war."

The Flu Pandemic

By October 1918, however, Kershaw County citizens, like those in the rest of America, were gripped at home with suffering and death from causes other than the battlefield. The pandemic, or global epidemic, of what was then known as "Spanish influenza" reached its height in this country. People of all ages were affected. In that month, considered the deadliest in the country's history, 195,000 Americans fell victim to the flu—numbers dying in wild delirium and in a matter of hours from the onset of the highly contagious illness, which was marked by high fever and prostration.

Schools and churches in Kershaw County were ordered closed because of flu, and the November court, like other public gatherings, was called off. Work at the mills ceased. A circus scheduled to open in October was barred from entering the county, and the state fair in November was cancelled. All ages and all communities were afflicted. The October 31 *Bethune Observer* reported that Dr. E. Z. Truesdale in that section claimed that he had treated more than three hundred patients with the flu, and Dr. A. W. Humphries had treated a like number. Public health warnings urgently tried to spread hygienic messages—to wash hands, to cover coughs with handkerchiefs, and to avoid spitting in public. Persons who had to be in public during the epidemic's height often wore face masks.

While many more people died from the flu than from the Great War, even with its dreaded gassing, the end of warfare brought relief to the spirits of those bereaved by both causes. The December 20, 1918, *Chronicle* reported that Captain A. L. Humphries of Camden had written home that he was "on the firing line as the last shot was fired" and was "unharmed and feeling good."

The Return Home

Almost immediately after the November 11 armistice, the return of troops to everyday life was being anticipated. In December 1918 Henry Savage Sr. put up for sale his Lugoff-area Westerham Plantation, which was cut into smaller tracts in preparation for auction. By January 1919 news reports were filled with details of the soldiers and their wartime exploits and with announcements of medals and awards. Local victory parties included fund-raising for religious and ethnic groups afflicted by the war. Grover C. Welsh, the new county sheriff, moved his home from Kershaw to Camden, and the press reported that his men were active with law enforcement against the prostitutes and bootleggers who, it was presumed, were ready to prey on returning servicemen. By mid-April "the largest crowd ever seen in Camden" welcomed Company M home, and reports were frequent of other soldiers rejoining their families as well.

Nationally and locally some veterans returned home to enjoy the status of heroes; others had more trouble fitting back in. Among the latter group were black veterans—men who had served their country but who returned home still politically voiceless and not embraced in its voting process. "They went when called," said the nephew of two such Kershaw County soldiers, one of whom died in service. "When the war was over, they did not feel welcome at home."[11]

Local newspapers throughout 1919 attempted simultaneously to maintain patriotic enthusiasm for returning men and to address various societal disorders. Grumbling was vocal from the first of the year over the sluggish operation of the Wateree Ferry. Implications were leveled that the county was profiting by delayed completion of the bridge. Strong language, fisticuffs, and scuffling were reported among impatient and frustrated occupants of the long lines of vehicles waiting to cross.

Acts of violence intensified attention to crimes in 1919, some of them sensational in nature. In February the local policeman Robert Latta was shot to death by Peter Hudson, whom the press at one pointed labeled a "negro desperado." Hudson, in an attempt to escape, was at first thought to have been "fatally shot by citizens while he was barricaded in a house," but he later recovered from his wounds.[12] In July, in an exchange of gunfire during a raid on an illegal liquor operation near Cassatt, Constable J. P. Bateman was mortally wounded. The still owner likewise died. Another man, also shot, was later tried for Bateman's murder but was not convicted after pleading that the exchange of gunfire had taken place while he was passed out from intoxication.

Signs of Progress

Along with old problems came signs of progress. In July 1919 heavy rains and a freshet flooded roadways and suspended the operation of the Wateree Ferry for several days, much to the public's frustration. The increased precipitation was also feared to be inviting boll weevil infestation. However, waters continued rising behind the massive concrete impoundment of the Wateree Dam, and by fall the level was high enough to begin turning turbines to power a new generation of industries. The station went into operation on September 14, 1919, transmitting a maximum of a hundred thousand horsepower into a general power circuit. "It was," said the historian Rachel Montgomery, "a fantastic achievement of that day."[13]

Signs of progress were seen too as some deficiencies of education were addressed. Public school trustees and representatives from various sections of the county were described as "enthusiastic" when they met in August 1919 to target adult illiteracy, an issue sometimes seen as beyond their traditional role of educating youngsters. Treated as an emergency in wartime, adult illiteracy required continued peace-time combat. At the meeting, which had been requested by Miss Nelle Wilkes, Kershaw County organizer of lay-by schools, two school trustees, L. O. Funderburk and P. I. McNaughton, spoke. Afterward the boards formed an association to promote adult education, electing Funderburk as president and W. T. Holley as secretary.

Wartime also brought attention to the sore need for improvement in education for southern black people. Some assistance in this direction was given Kershaw County public schools by a private foundation, the Negro Rural School Fund. This foundation was financed by a legacy from a wealthy Quaker woman from Philadelphia, Anna T. Jeanes, and was strongly influenced by the ideas of Booker T. Washington.[14] In 1919 Elise F. (Mrs. Thomas) McLester, with her husband and children, moved from their rural home in the Bethune area so that she could accept an appointment in Camden as Jeanes Fund industrial supervisor.

Here, in a way that other educated black persons and other women of the time operated, Elise McLester began her work quietly and in the background.

Her job was to help improve teaching, including vocational skills, in rural black schools. Serving as a liaison to speak for the needs of the students and teachers, she cooperated with white school supervisors to raise funds and to organize activities to improve the schools. She served effectively in this position into the 1930s.

Also following the war a strong community influence emerged as veterans nationally and locally drew together in mutual support. In 1919 Congress chartered the American Legion to represent veterans' claims before the federal government and authorized the formation of local groups called posts. The organization of county veterans began with what was first called Kershaw Post 17, headquartered at Camden. One of this group's earliest tasks was to organize the distribution of war medals, and the post planned ceremonies at various locations to honor both white and black recipients.

Final Effects

In the months and years immediately following the war's end, personal wartime tragedies lingered even as the society moved forward. The county's war dead numbered forty-nine and were almost equally divided by race: twenty-four blacks and twenty-five whites. Slow, tedious transport delayed communication and the long-distance return home of the bodies of the war dead, some of whom still remain buried in distant fields. One by one caskets arrived from afar and were laid to final rest in quiet corners of the county.

Lieutenant James Leroy Belk died in October 1918, but it was "many months after [he] was killed [be]fore the family was notified, and then he was reported being among the missing." It was June 1920 before his father learned from one of his son's comrades the firsthand details of his death.[15] By the following year a Young Men's Christian Association (YMCA) worker in Europe, William M. Young, formerly of Camden, had located Belk's grave in the American cemetery in France and notified the lieutenant's father, who visited it in spring 1921. In the fall Belk's body was shipped home for burial at Kershaw. The county's first American Legion post changed its name in the lieutenant's honor and was chartered on October 1, 1920, as James Leroy Belk Post 17.[16]

Others among the county's war dead included six buried in Camden and sixteen laid to rest in rural areas of the county, according to information compiled from records of the Catawba-Wateree Genealogical Society.[17] In Camden, David L. Gamble lies in Cedars Cemetery, and five others lie in Quaker Cemetery: Malcolm A. Bateman, Henry T. Brown, William Bratton deLoach Jr., Willie K. Humphries, and Eben J. McLeod. In addition a memorial stands in Quaker Cemetery to Augustus Massenburg Trotter, buried in France.

Sixteen gravestones indicate rural burials. Four in West Wateree include Ben D. Abbott at Harmony Baptist Church in Elgin and three in Lugoff: Mendel L.

Gladden at Pine Grove Baptist Church; James Bailey at Smyrna Methodist Church; and Moses Shannon at St. Matthew Baptist Church. Three gravestones stand in the northern part of the county, one of them at Bethany Baptist Church, Westville, for Walter Haile Johnson, for whom American Legion Post 63 at Kershaw was named. At DeKalb Baptist Church lies Henry B. Cook, and at Liberty Hill Presbyterian Church lies Lieutenant Stephen Malone Richards, the only son of a postwar South Carolina governor.

Nine of the war dead are buried in eastward areas of the county. Two are buried at Antioch—Swillie H. Hinson and James M. McLain. Three are buried in the Sandy Grove community: at Cantey Hill Baptist Church, Furman Peebles; and at Sandy Grove Methodist Church, Gilliam A. Hall and Harrison H. Stokes. In the area of Bethune lie three: at Mills Creek Baptist Church, Henry Williams; at Pleasant Hill Baptist Church, Cleveland Outlaw; and at Red Oak Cemetery, John D. McClester. At Timrod lies Pat W. Davis, who was also memorialized with Walter M. Loyd on a plaque at the entrance of the Wateree (Kendall) Mill in Camden: "Employees of This Company Who Died in the Service of Their Country."

More than half of the forty-nine war dead from the county lie elsewhere, many presumably in battlefield cemeteries. Additional deaths accrued from lingering effects of the war. For example, Robert Powell, buried at Wesley Chapel Methodist Episcopal Church, south of Camden was disabled by effects of poisonous gas. He was sent in 1919 to the Casualty Hospital at Washington, D.C., where he died in 1920.[18]

Line of Traditions

Annual services to honor the veterans and casualties of the Great War joined the traditional ceremonies recalling past sacrifices. In 1921 a two-day reunion of the United Confederate Veterans of South Carolina met at Camden. More than five hundred people were housed in homes throughout the area to attend the reunion. The May 27 *Camden Chronicle* described the "enthusiasm" attending the event: "a monster parade which was composed of veterans, sponsors, maids, matrons of honor, the American Legion, Kershaw Guards . . . followed by an open air reception, the feature of which was community singing, more than 1,000 school children taking part."

One resolution that passed at the reunion provided pensions for "the negro servants of soldiers of the field," several of whom were present and "wearing their medals." The resolution recognized that "it is known to the surviving soldiers of the Confederate States of America, from personal observation and experience, that the negro servants of soldiers in the field were, with few exceptions, faithful to their masters or employers . . . and . . . shared in all the hardships incident to the life of the soldier, notwithstanding the many temptations and opportunities to desert their employment, and . . . readily encountered peril of their lives in caring for their masters or employers." Kershaw County's last surviving slave-soldier, the pensioner Washington Drakeford of Company E, Second South Carolina Regiment, lived until 1929 and is buried at Parker Baptist Church on Flat Rock Road.[19]

Area residents were reminded of past and recent wars when the March 16, 1923, *Chronicle* reported that Mary McGraw of Lugoff, the widow of a soldier in the War of 1812, was South Carolina's last such survivor. At Hardshell Cemetery in Lugoff her gravestone, beside her much older husband, Reverend Marshall McGraw (McGrath), dates her death in 1928. In 1925 the paper recognized another death that brought reminders of times past: Rena Bracey was believed to have been 112 years old and a former slave of L. W. R. Blair. Lives such as these had witnessed great changes.

14

Inns, Farms, and Mill Whistles

The 1920s

After the Great War the much-fabled decade of the Roaring Twenties in some ways unfolded in Kershaw County as flamboyantly as it did in the rest of America—with high style and youthful energy, with big spenders and big losers. Yet the economy, elsewhere expanding, failed to stabilize the cotton-growing South. Thus in some ways much of Kershaw County passed through the decade more somberly and conservatively. The Great Depression spread over the country after the 1929 stock market crash, but its looming shadow had darkened southern prospects long before that date.

Historians often view the 1920s as the beginning of modern society. In Kershaw County the description is appropriate in a number of ways. Agriculture declined as an ideal way of life. Industrialization, though sometimes scorned, increased in significance. Mechanical alteration of the environment accelerated. Cultural and social changes highlighted differences among people of varied social, economic, and racial backgrounds and increased the need for resolving inequities. Both those who looked to the past and those who looked to the future exerted influence as Kershaw County remolded into a closer resemblance of its present characteristics.

In 1920 the Nineteenth Amendment extended voting rights to American women. The change, of course, reached each voting precinct in Kershaw County at the time: Abney, Antioch, Belk Hill, Bethune, Beulah, Blaney, Buffalo, Camden, Cantey Hill, Cassatt, DeKalb, Doby's Mill, Enterprise, Harmony, Hermitage, Indian Ford, Kershaw, Liberty Hill, Lockhart, Lugoff, Ned's Creek, Oakland, Pine Tree, Rabon's Cross Roads, Raley's Mill, Roland, Salt Pond, Shamrock, Shaylor's Hill, Shepard, Stockton, Stoneboro, Swift Creek, Three C's, Twenty Creek, Wateree Mill, and Westville. In all these areas since the end of Reconstruction, political power had been firmly held by Democrats and firmly controlled by white males.

In the first week they could register, more than sixty Kershaw County women "called at the court house" for their voting certificates. Their given names, printed in the local newspaper, reveal that the first registrants were mostly town women of above-average education and standing within church, social, civic, or business circles. Courtesy titles of "Miss" or "Mrs." were attached to each name;

apparently all were white. Among them were wives or daughters of lawyers, doctors, bankers, and merchants as well as women who were teachers, bookkeepers, or stenographers.[1] For some time longer, county women continued acting behind the scenes in public influence rather than speaking from platforms at political rallies, although the public presence of women—especially educated women—gradually grew stronger. In 1920 one of the first female voting registrants, Lena Lineberger, became the first woman named as a notary in Kershaw County.[2] It would be the end of the decade, however, before a woman was elected to public office.[3]

Of the distinctions that divided the society of the 1920s, the most inescapable was racial. Boundaries of the separate worlds in which black and white citizens held influence had been defined by custom and by law, both subject to challenge and negotiation. As part of a national drive to improve relations between the races, in January 1921 national and state spokesmen of the YMCA led an interracial conference at the Kershaw County Courthouse. To organize local efforts as a follow-up, YMCA leader Laurens T. Mills, a Camden attorney, was named as chairman of a group of community leaders that included a "colored committee" as well as some rural representation.

Employment and Agriculture

The surge of economic improvement that had been bolstered by wartime subsidies, jobs, and contracts had waned in peacetime. Mining jobs in the Kershaw area ended with the lessened demand for munitions. Textile production in local mills slowed following cancellation of government orders. The end of jobs created by wartime need left spasmodic employment opportunities, and veterans were sometimes among those looking for work.

As construction ended on the Wateree River bridge and dam projects, numbers of manual workers were let go. Some afterward were employed in road improvements at various periods of the decade and in Camden's street-paving program that began in 1922. In 1924 work resumed on the Wateree Dam to raise it six feet higher for increased hydroelectric capacity. In 1926 labor began on Highway 97 to access the eastern area behind the dams, Liberty Hill, and the upper parts of the state. Also in 1926 paving of the Camden-to-Columbia road completed the first continuous hard-surface link between the two cities, and by the end of the following year paving began on the Camden-to-Charlotte road, thus connecting three cities. In 1929 plans were announced for Federal Route no. 1 (U.S. Highway 1) to be built through Camden. This more than two-million-dollar project within the county promised jobs for locals and continuous access for tourists from New York to Miami.

Employment and economic fluctuations at times created community tensions. Higher pay and varied opportunities decreased interest in seasonal farm labor or other low-paying and subordinate jobs. Along the upper boundary of the county in 1920, during the labor-intensive cotton-picking season, an exceptional outbreak of Reconstruction-like response was reported. The October 29 *Camden Chronicle* reported "Night Riders at Kershaw Warn Unemployed to Go to Work," stating: "On last Thursday a band of night riders visited the various quarters and posted notices in several places, ordering all unemployed among the colored to find work . . . and also warned those who were more or less disrespectful and defiant in their manner to tone down and become more respectful." The next day one man with "inflammatory and threatening language" quit his job at the depot, and as a precaution the Kershaw police chief locked him up. Later he made a public apology and returned to his job. That night "a negro . . . west of town was given a whipping . . . for inflammatory utterances." Regarding the incident afterward, it was reported, "no undue excitement or feeling [was] apparent among either white or colored."

In the preelectricity days when large families were typical, many town and country households of whites, even those of ordinary means, customarily employed domestic help. Resentments sometimes chafed toward textile mills, where whites found more profitable employment. A Camden woman on November 22, 1920, reported in a family letter: "The low price of cotton continues and has completely demoralized business. People are turning off help in every department of work, even the Wateree Mills are closed part of the time, and the wages of laborers are reduced in many places. It may result in good finally and enable people to hire cooks etc at moderate wages."[4] By the end of the decade some households were building smaller, more efficient homes and adding modern labor-saving appliances. However, much more time would lapse before low-paying household employment was no longer commonplace.

Farming Conditions

The economic problems of agriculture affected the majority of county citizens. Farmers who had grown more food for defense were at war's end producing surpluses that were no longer profitable. Some growers carried extra debt as a result, and their soils required expensive fertilizers for cash crops such as cotton. Quantities of warehoused cotton remained on hand since textile manufacturing had slowed. In 1920 falling cotton prices, as always controlled by the futures market and not by production costs, created alarm.

The Boll Weevil

Compounding cotton farmers' problems in 1920 was the arrival of the long-dreaded boll weevil, the sharp-snouted insect that deposited consuming larvae in emerging cotton forms. The county farm agent warned that various contraptions being commercially marketed as "weevil catchers" would prove useless. In

July the weevil appeared in Kershaw County and spread rapidly. Evidence of damage both around and within the county was shown to employees of the *Camden Chronicle,* who reported it in the July 16 issue: "We were shown several specimens of boll weevil on Tuesday gathered from the farm of Mr. T. M. McCaskill in West Wateree. County Agent J. W. Sanders has them in his possession at his office over the Evans undertaking parlor and those who have never seen the noted pests can get a look at them in several stages by calling on Mr. Sanders. He also brought along many squares and small bolls that had been punctured and had fallen to the ground." Quickly the pest was "well represented in practically every cotton field in Kershaw county." Farmers were advised to pick up dead plant parts and burn them to limit the rapid spread of emerging insects. However, by the first frost the boll weevil had covered all sections of South Carolina.

In 1920, with the weevil reducing crop yields, cotton demand was down, and prices fell to less than half those of the previous year. In September state textile mills reported orders in recent months "off fully one half," and most began laying off workers. At the beginning of low prices the Clemson College Extension Service had estimated that, "with cotton selling around the 20 cent level, at least 60 per cent of the crop must go to pay for the fertilizers used and the expense of picking and ginning." Prices actually fell about five cents lower, so that the percentage required for repaying expenses rose even higher.

Organizing of Farmers

About the time area farmers began picking up weevil-damaged squares and bolls from their fields, a statewide campaign to improve marketing conditions kicked off. Meeting in July in the town of Kershaw, the state convention of the American Cotton Association reported four hundred to five hundred growers present from Lancaster and Kershaw counties. L. I. Guion of West Wateree, a platform speaker, encouraged "organization and co-operation" to demand gin inspections, cotton graders, and state warehouses for storage. L. W. Boykin of Boykin outlined a plan to fund a cotton grader at Camden.[5] County-level meetings followed at Bethune and Camden, climaxing on July 20 at Lugoff with a family barbecue and visitors from around the state.

In fall 1920 the governor declared September 20 "Cotton Day" across the state with a meeting in each county. In Camden 175 farmers and businessmen heard L. W. Boykin, chairman of the county cotton association, and W. B. deLoach, L. I. Guion, and C. J. Shannon Jr. speak on plans to reduce cotton acreage, to increase food and feed production, and to form an export corporation for marketing cotton abroad.[6] Farmers were asked to "steer clear of attempts to make 1921 a bumper cotton crop."

Improvements were not expected immediately. A West Wateree correspondent reported, "The boll weevil has nipped some of our prospects for making a flourishing little town out of Blaney. We feel that it will take several years for our farmers to adapt themselves to new modes of living and a more diversified crop adjustment."

Pressure and Advice

Farmers who could afford to do so held their cotton, but many had to sell, even at a loss, to repay expenses. It is unclear the extent to which Kershaw County was affected, as were some other parts of the state, the following year by masked or robed "gin posters" or "gin burners" who put up signs or destroyed gins in warning or outrage.[7] There were various efforts to encourage farmers to act together responsibly, but there was a lack of agreement about what to do or how to influence change.

In the cotton-marketing center of Camden, for example, a number of businesses advertised advice in November 1920. "Take Your Cotton Around to F. M. Wooten and Get Top of Market," encouraged a longtime buyer whose office was behind the Loan and Savings Bank, an institution that promised "to relieve you of vexatious details and to co-operate with you in the discharging of financial worries." J. L. Mosely invited farmers to "See Me" as he offered "Money Advanced on Cotton."

"Hold Your Cotton and Insure It," urged Williams Insurance Agency, headed by President R. M. Kennedy and Manager J. K. Shannon. "This Agency Stands Ready to Insure Your Cotton," said C. P. DuBose and Co. "A Wise Man Insures his cotton, cotton seed, dwellings, barns and outbuildings before he has a fire," cautioned Camden Loan & Realty Company, managed by Miss Ethel C. Rodgers. "Face This Fact Squarely," admonished New York Life Insurance agent L. C. Shaw, explaining that "in a period of depression when the business world is unsettled," what the farmer really needed was life insurance.

Rise and Fall of Prices

The smaller yield of 1921 resulted partly from volunteer acreage reduction and partly from the boll weevil. Plummeting prices were called a "disaster" for farmers. Government warehouse commissioners advised them to be patient and to hold their cotton as long as possible. At all financial levels prices were of concern. The cotton firm Hutson & Co. advertised that it had taken a room on the first floor of Camden's Kirkwood Hotel, where a "wire" received daily market reports. Other companies reported there by wire as well. Investors among the tourists kept an eye on stock and commodity prices between hunts and golf rounds. Their concerns with cotton prices were from a different perspective. Most of them were expecting to make money. Some were buying on speculation and considered low cotton prices good news.

In early 1922 county agent John W. Sanders held individual meetings for cooperative marketing with farmers at Bethune, Blaney, Boykin's Mill, Camden,

Cassatt, Cleveland School, Kershaw, Liberty Hill, Lugoff, and Westville. Over time long-term strategies to improve efficiency and to rely on supply and demand seemed to be working. In September 1923 Kershaw County farmers were urging one another to "be slow to sell cotton." By the following month the *Camden Chronicle* reported that money in the community was more plentiful and that farmers were paying off loans. There was cheerful talk about thirty-cent cotton and a bull market. The situation brightened other business prospects. Speculators who had bought cheap cotton earlier were jubilant.

Although various strategies to increase cotton prices prolonged hopes for a season or two, weevil infestation also simultaneously increased. The difficulties and expenses of production were compounded—handpicking weevils, gathering and burning infected foliage, and making and applying poisons. Arsenic mixed with molasses and mopped by hand onto leaves of cotton plants proved relatively effective in some conditions, but it was a labor-intensive remedy.[8] Some farmers simply dusted the cotton with arsenic timed to adhere to evening dew on the leaves. Sometimes rains washed away a poisonous application at a critical point. Arsenic carelessly handled could prove deadly to beneficial insects, animals, and humans.[9] Many farmers found the labor, uncertainty, and risks too difficult and gave up the struggle. Abandoned fields that nurtured infestations threatened others' land, so that deserted farms were sometimes believed to have been burned by neighbors desperate to prevent such problems.

By spring 1925 the cotton situation was so bleak that the Camden-born financier and philanthropist Bernard Baruch was targeting aid and loans to areas of South Carolina damaged by the boll weevil. A prolonged summer drought stunted growth and intensified insect problems, and in December, despite yield shortages, cotton prices again went down. As prices fell, some buyers locally and elsewhere continued to purchase and store cotton, believing that current low prices could not continue and that another bull market would come again. Some buyers were local businessmen who relied on farm customers to keep their own related businesses operating. In 1926 cotton prices declined even further. The situation was declared an "emergency." Home Furnishings of Camden, faced with customers without money or credit, widely advertised that the company would accept cotton in exchange for furniture.

Amid the epidemic "cotton hysteria," there were other worries. Cautious persons viewed land exhaustion with concern and noted swirlings of dust rising from sterile fields. Deepening gullies marred eroding hillsides. Along with weevils, the leafhoppers, worms, and other insects increased on deserted farmlands. A newspaper columnist in November 1926 recognized that an economic disaster was coming but glossed it over with the assurance that "Depression will be a blessing" since it would discourage dependence on cotton. An "old-timer" declared, "There Are No Hard Times" compared to wartimes or to conditions in other countries. Elsewhere, when a son of the late Confederate major Zack Leitner of Camden committed suicide in December 1927, the local press reported that recent cotton quotes were found stuffed in his pocket. Scenes more typically associated with the Great Depression of the 1930s were already rising on southern landscapes.

At Camden the public cotton weigher R. A. Bruce described weevil infestation in 1927 as "alarming." The fall crop was only two-thirds that of the previous year. In Flat Rock, for example, some fields yielded only two bolls per five stalks. In the southern part of the county farmers tried cutting off the tops of plant growth to admit sunlight to lower branches in hopes of harboring fewer insects. In 1929, when the area faced the heaviest infestation yet, the Bank of Camden ordered a huge supply of calcium arsenate and molasses to distribute at cost to its customers. The economy of the community was tied to the farmers' struggle.

A Community Market

Improvement of agricultural incomes involved the participation of all members of farm families. In early 1920 the farm demonstration agent set up Pig Clubs for boys and girls across the county for hands-on experience in raising livestock. The Bank of Camden advertised that it would lend money to any county youngster who purchased a pig as part of that program. Livestock shows, parades, and prizes rewarded successful competitors who raised and marketed pigs. Like earlier Corn Clubs for boys and Tomato Clubs for girls, the Pig Clubs provided valuable education in diversified farming.

In late 1920 Kershaw County farm women became leaders in marketing food surpluses to improve family incomes. Through Home Demonstration Clubs, organized under the home-demonstration agent Blanche G. Tarrant, farm women sought the cooperation of the Camden Civic League and the Camden Chamber of Commerce to set up a community market in the city. Here they sold "products raised in the county and needed in every home." In the beginning market day opened a few hours every Friday in Agent Tarrant's office, upstairs over Thomas's ice cream parlor on DeKalb Street. Sometime later the business day was changed to Saturday.[10] Before the market opened in the morning, farm women brought in their surplus produce—advertised in 1920 as including chickens, turkeys, eggs, sausage, pure cream, butter, homemade syrup, home ground meal, turnips and other vegetables, and canned goods.

In 1921 the women elected Mrs. Kathleen Watts as their first secretary, her salary to be paid from market profits. Before long the market expanded to various larger locations, and by the end of the decade it was operating at the rear of the post office. Over time enterprising farm women grew more sophisticated in marketing. Fruit, watermelons, pumpkins, grapes, nuts, and honey were among other seasonal offerings. Some women added to their butter-and-egg money by producing specialties—jellies, jams, baked goods, and other home produce as well as holiday greenery and flowers. The market that county farm women began at Camden thrived for years and was recognized as a model for similar operations set up through agricultural extension agents across the state and in other parts of the nation.[11]

Cattle

While a weekly community market could supplement income, it alone could not support a family. County agents continued to promote beef and dairy cattle as the most profitable contender with cotton. In 1920 several local herds were improved when prize cattle belonging to the late J. A. Shanklin were auctioned in Camden. Cattlemen from across the state eagerly purchased at high prices the results of his lifetime cattle-breeding efforts. One prize bull considered too valuable to sell was deeded to Clemson College. A little over a year earlier Shanklin had moved from Columbia to operate the new Camden Dairy and Livestock Company on the Guignard property between the city limits and the river. Names of local buyers were reported in the press: from Blaney, H. A. Martin; from Camden, J. H. Burns, Fred Cooley, L. M. Hall, Rose Kinard, J. E. Pearce, Wiley Sheorn, W. H. Tiller, and G. C. Welsh; and from Lugoff, W. L. Kinard, L. P. Rabon, and W. H. Tiller. In 1922 a small flurry of cattle rustling, especially targeting purebreds, challenged West Wateree herd owners.

In the mid-1920s the site of an early Camden-area dairy gave way to urban expansion. In 1925 the Belle-Shaw Dairy farm of the widow Rebekah Workman (Mrs. Albertus S.) White was subdivided and sold for suburban homes east of Camden. The section along the highway was subsequently called White's Gardens, and the section of larger hillside properties farther eastward was named Pine Haven.

West of the Wateree, however, the dairy business flourished. In 1924 N. P. Gettys's Rock Springs Creamery, founded two decades earlier to make butter, began delivering fresh milk daily to Camden. Only purebred Guernsey stock was raised on the seventeen-hundred-acre farm and dairy operation. Proclaimed "unexcelled for pure certified milk," the Rock Springs Creamery was widely described as "one of the most sanitary and modern dairies in South Carolina." Both individual households and wholesale markets were served in Camden, and an outlet of the Rock Springs Creamery operated on Rutledge Street.

L. I. Guion of West Wateree, a leader in the local cotton association, was widely diversified and another dairy leader. In 1925 the *Chronicle* stated that his Lugoff Dairy was delivering fresh milk, poultry, and eggs to Camden daily. Guion's operations had expanded significantly over the past two years. In August 1925 Lugoff Dairy milked fifty head of Guernsey and Jersey cows, and in winter that number was doubled to serve the tourist hotels. The operation touted the sanitation of its vacuum milkers, stalls, and bottling and cooling plant. A flock of six thousand white leghorns furnished fresh eggs and fryers, and a large flock of fancy pigeons provided squabs in the fall. In addition Guion grew grapes and peaches, shipping them in large quantities, and marketed young pecan trees for nursery stock.

Technical Improvements

Diversification, to be successful, required complex and technical operations. By November 1929, when two train car loads of purebred Hereford cattle were shipped to Mulberry Plantation from Tulsa, Oklahoma, for David R. Williams, the local market was also primed for beef cattle. A cold food storage ice plant in Camden had recently made the following possible: beef raised in Kershaw County by local farmers was butchered and dressed here, refrigerated in the cold storage plant, handled by a local meat market, bought in a local grocery, and prepared and eaten by county citizens. Every dollar spent stayed within the county.

Mechanical improvements modernized ginning equipment. In 1929 the county farm agent, along with the Chamber of Commerce, campaigned "to save Kershaw County the estimated loss of more than $50,000 due to defective gins." Sponsoring inspections, the program advertised cotton gins that met upgraded standards resulting in high-quality bales. Gins in all sections of the county were approved.

In the late 1920s cutover forestlands, often badly eroded, marred many areas of the county. Most of the virgin timber was gone, and turpentine chop boxes or chevron scars on trunk faces marked many longleaf pine stands. Briars and blackjack oaks of little value dominated the new growth. The South Carolina Forestry Commission was established in 1927 to address the problem. The April 26, 1929, *Chronicle* announced the selection of a five-acre site two miles from Camden on George T. Little's property by Federal Highway 1, near the present river bridge, for the state's first forest tree nursery.

Manufacturing Conditions

Textile manufacturers in the 1920s sought to regain wartime production profits and to avoid the strikes that were making news elsewhere. In recent years living conditions had improved in the county's mill villages. Both the Hermitage and Wateree mills had installed running water in all their homes by 1920, and electrical power followed. These utility installations came in advance of those throughout the city of Camden.

Mills provided noncash benefits, such as low-cost housing, to maintain work-force loyalty. "Just as mills have had to compete in welfare work to hold their operatives," contemporary economist Broadus Mitchell contended, "it is clear that these extra concessions were simply a convenient avoidance of cash payments."[12] Some workers grew restless under paternalistic management, preferring increased wages and a voice in decision making.

To strengthen work-force loyalty, local mill company publicists supplied the public with copious optimistic reports and with folksy community columns in the local newspapers. Hermitage Cotton Mill in 1920 also began its own newspaper, *Hermitage Citizen,* and in 1922 Wateree Cotton Mill began issuing *Wateree Gauzette,* its name a play on the local *Wateree Gazette.* The Hermitage paper was introduced under Mary Gist Fleming, who headed community work at the local mill and also at the Osage Manufacturing Company in Bessemer City, North Carolina. Reuben B. Pitts of Camden, "Big Boss," as Hermitage workers came to call him, was president and treasurer of the two plants.

In 1920 Pitts had been associated with Hermitage a dozen or more years, and he would maintain that authority another twenty-eight years.[13] The son of a Baptist minister, in his youth he had worked in Greenville cotton mills. His working experiences, unusual for a mill owner, encouraged his hands-on management: "Mr. Pitts was sometimes blamed for the hard circumstances of the people, but he was constantly borrowing money to meet the payroll. His own sons were shown no favors—they shoveled coal, cleaned humidifiers, and worked at other menial tasks."[14] The local family association with the Hermitage Mill differed from the more distant corporate operation of Wateree Mill.

In 1916 the Wateree Cotton Mill was purchased by Lockwood, Green & Co. of Boston as the first cotton mill owned by Henry P. Kendall, head of a company manufacturing surgical dressings. His business boomed in wartime, but as Kendall later related, "At the close of the war, the Government and Red Cross threw on the market tremendous quantities of surplus surgical dressings, the bottom dropped out of prices and earnings, and our business entered one of its most critical periods."[15] In the struggle to survive, Kendall said: "I couldn't build a large business by trying to do everything myself or know everything myself. I delegated responsibility to our young executives and gave them authority to act."

At Wateree decision making was shared further. "Men of the mill" were described as "enthusiastic" at a mass meeting at the Wateree Clubhouse on March 5, 1920.[16] Here they established a village government and began to make many decisions affecting their daily lives. Lying outside the city limits of Camden, the mill communities were technically under the authority of the county government, although as private property they were generally controlled by decisions made by designees of mill executives.

To operate their new government, the Wateree men elected their first mayor (manager H. K. Hallet) and an alderman to represent each block of homes in their village. The action suggests cooperative agreement between labor and management. The first aldermen included both mill supervisors and operatives. They

Wateree Cotton Mill on what is now Kendall Lake. The adjoining mill village established its own government with a mayor and aldermen in the 1920s. Courtesy of the Camden Archives

were Lewis P. Anderson, J. Clyde Baker, B. T. (Till) Davis, Gilliam (Gib) DeBruhl, Ike DeBruhl, W. R. (Rand) Dority, Ben Gardner, John Morris, Benjamin F. Robinson, John J. Sanders, John D. Shaw, John C. Shirley, and Yancey Threatt. The recorder was personnel manager A. Stanley Llewellyn, likely the newspaper publicist for the new organization.[17]

Immediately the newly elected men began to conduct their business, which was "to discuss, suggest and institute laws which pertain to the betterment of the village in general." In their first month the Wateree village government set up baseball teams, insurance benefits for sickness, garden spots, a fire alarm system, and a system of condolences for bereavements. By the following month 110 employees had signed up for the Employees Mutual Sick Benefit Association. At a meeting shortly afterward with operatives and executives, Alderman Anderson—who had first worked in the mills as a boy and was now a supervisor—was quoted in the March 26 *Chronicle* as stating, "A brighter day is dawning, that a government of the people, by the people, and for the people in the mill village will solve many problems heretofore unnoticed."

In other early actions the village board addressed issues of safety, health, and good order. They appealed to law enforcement authorities to deal with the problems of outsiders speeding through their neighborhood. Three pedestrians had been struck and a child killed in recent incidents. The governing board oversaw the erection of street signs, ran cleanliness campaigns to eliminate flies and mosquitoes, and organized recreation and entertainments. They heard appeals on day-to-day problems—for example, cautioning boys about random damage when playing with stray golf balls from the nearby Sarsfield course.

May Day and Fourth of July celebrations at Wateree Mill in 1920 were planned in elaborate detail. On the Fourth a dramatic presentation was staged between the midday barbecue and the afternoon baseball game. A large cast of mill employees, directed by Alderman Lewis P. Anderson, enacted a pageant "vividly" depicting mill conditions of the past. The July 9 *Chronicle* correspondent reported: "In every detail Mr. Anderson's reproduction was true and exacting. The cruelty of the overseers, the unsanitary condition of the mill, the child labor and the unfairness of everything . . . showed the marked improvement which has come about in recent years." The correspondent asserted, "Those of us who remember the old days . . . pray God [they] will never return."

Plant managers, supervisors, and representatives of operatives met together for banquets at local inns and in Columbia. Manager Hallet and President Kendall arranged trips to Boston for various supervisors and aldermen to meet company executives. All lauded the fact that management and labor were meeting face-to-face and working together, by implication unlike places where strikes and violence were reported.

By October 1920, however, both the Camden textile mills were running only four days a week. The December 3 *Chronicle* reported that Wateree had closed Wednesday, and its several hundred employees had no word when it would reopen: "Market conditions is [*sic*] given as the cause of the shutdown." However, "Hermitage Cotton Mills is operating full time," the paper stated on December 17, adding that "employees are very grateful that they have their jobs." Despite the shutdown, which continued through the winter, the Wateree village government appeared to have held the people together. Christmas services at the church and holiday sings continued. Those who in later years recalled difficult times in either of the mill communities cited close-knit experiences of neighbor helping neighbor.

In spring 1921 Wateree Mill was modernized, including the installation of new Draper machines, and by April it was again running at full capacity. A new "piece rate" system tied operatives' pay to their production, and throughout May mill officials met with workers, "explaining the costs that enter into operating a cotton mill." In July the plant began day and night operation and soon doubled the number of employees. In December, with the plant still running full time, day and night, it was reported that "every home in the village is occupied and others are waiting to come."

Work had resumed at Wateree despite the loss of some employee benefits—especially the sick leave plan. The negotiations of labor and management that were part of the village government were believed to have spared the mill the public threats of "strike" or "union" that affected other plants. Paradoxically, even as southern political voices urged cotton farmers to join agricultural organizations and to stand together, the same voices adamantly decried cotton textile workers joining unions to stand together. A prevailing public attitude regarded union organizers as "outsiders," as threatening and dangerous as the "outsiders" who controlled cotton prices. In 1921 the mill owner "Colonel" Leroy Springs was depicted heroically in area newspapers when he "refused to be dictated to" by striking workers at Lancaster and closed that mill for three months until an agreeable workforce returned. Springs also owned the textile mill at Kershaw, where a number of Kershaw County citizens were employed. The Kershaw workers endured economic slowdowns, shutdowns, cutbacks, and policy enforcements made throughout the Springs chain, and here workers too were reported to be "grateful that they have their jobs."

The Wateree village government was a model when Hermitage Mill in fall 1923 formed the Hermitage Community Association. With each employee and adult resident a voting member, the group drew up bylaws and regulations and elected officers and directors, none of them mill managers or superintendents. The mill contributed a monthly sum to the association for athletic, recreational, and social activities and for sickness and financial emergencies. It was stated, "Under this plan the Hermitage Cotton Mills village is an independent, self-governing, self-supporting community in which the living conditions, the health and the happiness depend upon the individual members themselves and their own elected leaders."

While local family ownership of the Hermitage Mill linked its management to the community, the area ties of the Wateree Mill also strengthened when the owner Henry P. Kendall joined the Camden winter colony. In 1924 Kendall acquired an old Fair Street home, the Sycamores. From that year the chain of which the Wateree plant was a part operated under the name Kendall Mills, Inc., until 1928, when it became Kendall Company.

During the 1920s opportunities for workers at the Camden textile mills generally exceeded those available to them outside of the mill community. Here illiterate adults as well as children could acquire basic literacy and computation skills. Untrained individuals could be apprenticed to acquire job skills. An experienced mill hand earned more per month than a college-trained schoolteacher and also built up life insurance benefits the longer he worked. In the village each working family had a sanitary home with screened windows, running water, electrical power, and sometimes by the end of the decade an indoor toilet. Each household was allotted garden space and could graze a cow and raise a hog and chickens. The mill store allowed a worker to charge against his salary. There was a first-aid clinic with a nurse on duty, and a doctor was called when needed. There were health campaigns for all and tonsil clinics for children. Each mill village had a church building, predominantly Baptist but shared with other denominations. Each mill had a community house where various clubs and organizations met—men's clubs, mothers' clubs, and young people's clubs. At Wateree a kindergarten operated for preschoolers, and at both villages a Boy Scout troop was organized.

Factory work, it was agreed, was less physically taxing than most manual labor. If it was also more repetitious and boring, as many also agreed, the companionship of fellow workers and the pleasure of group recreation during off-hours helped to compensate. Baseball was the favorite team sport, and with avid attendance mill teams played one another as well as town and military teams. In the 1920s both mills also had tennis courts and equipment for volleyball and basketball. There were organized picnics, barbecues, hikes, fish stews, oyster suppers, cakewalks, and community sings. May Day, Fourth of July, and Christmas celebrations were the most important holiday events and involved much group planning.

Both mills utilized their lakes for fishing and other recreation, although swimming was most popular with the mill and town people at the historic old Factory Pond (now Kendall Lake), which for some years was called Wateree Lake before that name was given to the impoundment behind the Southern Power dam in the upper part of the county. The swimming area at the Wateree village lake included a large float, a diving board, and a bathhouse with dressing rooms. Swimming tournaments and lifesaving instruction were organized. Camping was especially popular around Hermitage Lake. Both millpond areas were utilized for fishing. Beyond these areas other outings were organized, and groups from the mill visited places such as the Precipice at Paint Hill and the Terraces, the home of Miss Charlotte Thompson, south of Camden. Through a hunting club, mill men visited rural areas to engage in that sport.

In 1923, inspired by the enthusiasm of the Wateree village supporters, a brass band was organized, made up of men and boys who had never before played an instrument. The first instruments were donated, and fund-raising secured more instruments as well as uniforms. Early music instructors included H. F. Cobb, L. S. Helton, and Ted Jacobson. The band played at ball games, marched in parades, performed in churches, gave Sunday afternoon concerts, and became the pride of the mill people. Soon a female glee club was organized, and instruction began with stringed instruments for accompaniment. For many of the activities engaged in by townspeople or tourists, to some extent there were related counterparts in the mill villages.

Business Growth in Camden

The area economy, though dominated by the cotton market uncertainties, was profitably infused through the 1920s by the steadier, more predictable year-round dollars of salaried mill workers and industrial expansions. Especially in Camden, which was close to the mills and crisscrossed by railroads that were likewise growing busier, businesses grew and residential sections of the town were subsequently extended. The availability of electrical power to city homes and businesses through the Camden Power and Light Company was a vitalizing factor in the area's growth. The building trades were kept busy in raising new structures as well as in modernizing old ones.

The traditional periodic infusion of dollars from winter tourists continued to be important to the area economy, although tourism began to change. The paving of streets and highways through the city and county brought more travelers into the area, but the same "good roads" that led them here also easily led them elsewhere. Kershaw County businesses had to cater to an increasing number of temporary customers, many of them passing through en route to Florida, America's newest real estate and vacation boom.

Automotive Businesses

The automobile was the darling of the decade and the bane of the railroad. In 1920, when the best roads were still only sand and clay, businesses selling vehicles actively advertised in Camden, offering a great variety of models and prices. A. K. Blakeney sold Hudson Super Six and Essex Four models for the Chicago factory to which he personally carried orders from buyers at the downtown Men's Shop, a fashionable clothing store. The price for the Essex Touring or Roadster was $1,680, and the Hudson Speedster or Touring cost $2,600. Blakeney advised, "Cars are scarce and will continue to be." Alexander-Boykin Motor Company on Market Street advertised Samson vehicles, a "Line of Motors . . . to Revolutionize Farming." Tractors sold at $840, trucks at $655, and the Samson Touring Car at $750. Camden Motor Company sold Cleveland autos, and Carolina Motor Company offered Chandler, Cleveland, Maxwell, and Paige autos. One line ranged from the Chandler Six limousine at $3,395 to the seven-passenger touring car at $1,895. W. R. DeLoache, a Carolina Motor salesman, also handled the Traffic Truck, which cost $1,390.

Also in Camden, George T. Little, a former liveryman, sold Chalmers, Chevrolet, and Hupmobile autos as well as used cars (Chevrolet, Ford, Oakland, Overland, and Studebaker). Kershaw Motor Company sold Fords, Liberty Motor Sales Company sold Liberty Sixes, and Moseley-Taylor Motor Company sold Haynes vehicles. Springs & Shannon sold Titan Tractors, which operated on "low priced, low grade fuels—kerosene, distillate, etc." West Motor Company in Camden sold Transport Trucks.

For the county area in 1920 Alex G. Clarkson Jr. of Boykin was the dealer for Columbia Tractor and Truck Company, which advertised that farmers could, for

$1,395, "Beat the Boll Weevil with Cletrac Tank-Type Tractor." Customers were urged: "Wire, telephone, or write at once. Tractors are hard to get." Threat-Plyler in Kershaw advertised secondhand Ford autos.

Other advertisements in 1920 reveal a sampling of the garages operating in the county area to sell gas and to service the various vehicles: in Bethune, Mays' Garage; in Camden, Beard Brothers Garage and W. O. Hay's Garage; in Cassatt, Walters and McGuirt; in Rembert, Rembert Garage. Tires and oil were sold everywhere—groceries and pharmacies included. Because breakdowns and accidents were frequent, C. P. DuBose reminded the public to buy auto insurance. Furthermore, for those who preferred to travel and farm traditionally, in Camden, Rhame Brothers advertised the sale of Thornhill wagons, and Shannon and Springs promoted sales of "*Mules!* Slick—Fat—Young. Come and see them. Just received a carload of fine young mules—not rough haired Western stock but Kentucky and Tennessee mules of high quality."

In 1922 W. T. Redfearn constructed a new brick garage at the corner of Hampton and Richland streets in Kershaw and later took charge of Redfearn Motor Company at Lancaster. In 1926 he moved to Camden to take over the operation of Kershaw Motor Company from D. S. Trapp. As a Ford dealer, Redfearn welcomed the public to dramatic exhibits of stylish new models, for Ford was stopping its eighteen-year production of the standard, popular, economical Model T. In November 1927 Redfearn advertised for sale in Camden new pleasure cars for $385 to $570 and trucks for $460 to $610.

Grocers and Merchandisers

Changes modernized the marketing style of some downtown businesses. In 1920 McCaskill's Grocery on Broad Street changed its name to Cash Grocery and offered "new and up-to-date ideas": "They have arranged the store with shelves on each side and shelves in the center. All goods are marked in plain figures and the buyer can wait upon him or herself without the aid of a salesman."

In 1920 the opening of a cold storage plant improved the regular availability of fresh meat downtown, although for several more years the fresh meat vendor W. A. Anderson continued to drive a meat wagon daily through the mill villages and nearby residential areas. Fresh bread and baked goods went into large production on DeKalb Street with A. C. Drawdy's Electrik Maid Bake Shop. Bread went out regularly not only to town and county communities but on the train as well.

The grocer B. H. Baum added the operation of Winter Green Cannery to his business enterprise. In 1925 he advertised "canned vegetables of every variety" with the slogan "Live in Camden and eat Camden products." In the late 1920s South Carolina advertised nationally the health benefits of iodine in the fruits and vegetables grown in the state. By fall 1929 the Seaboard representative and

J. Team Gettys, Kershaw County head of the Iodine Products Resource Commission, began a promotion to build a large canning operation in Camden that would employ two hundred persons during canning season.

Changes to other merchant styles were also made during the decade. Individual local stores began to give way to larger chains. In spring 1929 Baruch Nettles, a Camden clothier for more than twenty years, sold out to J. C. Penney. In the fall L. Schenk and Company closed and rented its store to J. J. Newberry.

Floral Industry

In 1920 Camden Floral Company greenhouses near the Seaboard railroad tracks on the western end of Laurens Street in Camden were growing plants for local gardens and for shipments by train. By the end of the decade the company had fifteen greenhouses in the area covering "60,000 feet of land under glass" and keeping fourteen regular employees busy. Steam heat made possible year-round cultivation of a wide variety of flowers, which were shipped to the North as well as to Florida. In April 1929, for example, thousands of Easter lilies were shipped in bloom for the season. For a time flowers were also shipped by train to market from the Guion farm in West Wateree, according to Nellie (Mrs. Alvin) Creed, whose family farm was nearby. As a schoolgirl her elder sister Anna Kate Watts was employed by Mrs. Louie Guion to help in the growing process and in picking the flowers for shipment.

Furniture Manufacturing

In 1921 "Made in Camden" office furniture was being built, labeled, and sold at the J. L. Guy Lumber Company, which had a complete woodworking plant that included James F. Gardner, "well known cabinet maker of Camden." A large filing cabinet he had built and which was displayed at Camden Furniture Company was "a fine piece of workmanship . . . all hand made," with small and large drawers, of painted mahogany.

Other furniture was being made in the county by individual craftsmen, such as the cabinetmaker Julian B. Rush. James Harrell, who was described at his death in 1929 as a "recluse around whom many tales of mystery centered," worked as "a weaver and rebuilder of early American furniture." From the Antioch community individual craftsmen surnamed Sutton were so well known and admired that local people sometimes referred to shuck-bottomed furniture as "Sutton chairs."

In 1929 a group of Camden businessmen chartered the Wateree Wood Shop, which began in March manufacturing and marketing "Beautiful Native Furniture." A news article stated, "For many years furniture of the type . . . has been made by the negro artisans of the neighborhood. However, the demand for the product has exceeded the readily available supply so the new shop has decided to make a specialty of it." Described as "attractive in designs, unique and durable," the furniture was built mostly of oak and poplar, all with hand finishing. Twisted corn shuck or woven split oak bottoms were typical for chair, stool, or settee bottoms. Tables, benches, and swings were also manufactured.

Metalwork

More numerous and complex machinery, with needs for old and new systems to work together, created a demand for metal craftsmen. While individual blacksmiths remained useful, other metalworkers went into business also. In spring 1921 an experienced foundry man, C. C. Shaw of Columbia, opened Camden Iron and Brass Works and began casting parts in his shop off DeKalb Street by the Southern railroad tracks. In 1926, next door to the foundry, Lewis P. Anderson, a former machine shop operator at Wateree Mill, began Camden Machine Works for welding and metal construction.

Black-Owned Enterprises in Camden

A diverse number of businesses operated south of Rutledge Street in Camden, sometimes called "Colored Town" for the dominance there of establishments owned by African Americans.[18] In other parts of town, too, black enterprises were part of the business community. Twenty-six grocers were identified in the 1925 Camden city directory as "colored." Personally grown produce was often part of the sales. Some grocery merchandisers, such as the Dibbles, operated stand-alone stores, and others conducted grocery sales at home or in combination with another businesses. Mary J. Peoples, for example, operated as both a dressmaker and a grocer at her Gordon Street residence. In the specialty line, several in the McGirt family were butchers or meat or fish dealers in the downtown area; Edward C. McGirt, for example, owned the Palace Meat Market on Rutledge Street. Robert S. Boykin had a bakery adjoining his home on Market Street.

In 1925 three black-owned restaurants operated on Broad Street: the Blue Mouse Cafe of Robert Williams, the Gem Cafe of Wesley Alexander, and McGirt's Cafe. In addition a number of black-owned "eating houses" served the community. D. H. Hunter's residence on Broad Street doubled as a grocery as well as a place to eat. On the same street Josephine Benson, Postell T. Brown, and Frances J. Hart ran eating houses separate from their homes. A similar place was operated by Carey Ballard on York Street, while Juliet Benson on Campbell Street and William Nelson in the Kirkwood section had eating places in their homes.

Five filling and service stations were owned and operated by blacks in 1925, and some auto repairs were made there. In the Kirkwood section the Kirkwood Filling Station was in operation. On Broad Street, Tobe Kirkland owned one station and T. S. Levy was proprietor of the Square Deal Service Station. On DeKalb Street, David N. Collins owned the Camden Service Station and William Kelly the Red Light Filling Station. Except for Collins, who also sold fancy groceries at his station, these concerns rarely advertised in print, but according to reports they remained competitive with white-owned stations by charging a little less for gas and services.

Thomas McLester owned and operated a taxi, sometimes driving as far as New York. W. S. Collins, who offered auto livery and baggage transfer, also sold and delivered wood to local homes. The funeral director Ammons R. Collins, an undertaker and embalmer on DeKalb Street—the counterpart to C. W. Evans, also on DeKalb, in the white community—advertised motorized ambulance and hearse services.

In 1925 the city directory identified only one Camden barber as white, Luther Yates at Hermitage Mills. Otherwise the profession that local men relied on for shaves, haircuts, and shoe shines was dominated by African Americans as owners and operators. On Rutledge Street there was Gene's Barber Shop (Eugene H. Davis). Three shops on Broad Street included the Eureka Barber Shop (Isaac B. English), the McGirt Brothers (Paul and W. C.), and McLain's Barber Shop (then owned by Walter Wright). Other barbers with their own places were Benjamin T. Spaulding on DeKalb and the following on Broad: James M. Belton, Robert Blanding, and James C. Reynolds. Most places employed additional barbers. Female hairdressers included Phyllis McGirt at her home on Church Street and Lula McLain at her home on Lyttleton.

Law

In November 1922 Kershaw County's first black lawyer was admitted to the bar. The son of Camden butcher Eli McGirt, Herbert F. McGirt was a Camden native and a graduate of Mather Academy and of Claflin University. Decorated by the French for bravery during the Great War, McGirt returned to graduate from Howard Law School in Washington, D.C. On Broad Street in March 1923 McGirt opened an upstairs law office over a downstairs pool hall that he also operated, next to the McGirt Family Diner. The January 4, 1924, *Chronicle* named him as chairman of the committee for the Emancipation Celebration observing anniversaries of the end of slavery. Other committee members were also black leaders: James Alexander, Reverend J. W. Boykin, R. H. Haile, Dr. J. P. Pickett, and Reverend A. G. Vaughan. Clearly McGirt's presence was conspicuous in the community. He was listed at the same office in 1925.

The following year unclear circumstances show McGirt entangled in charges against him and appealing his innocence to the state supreme court. In spring 1927 McGirt and his wife, Vera, moved to Gary, Indiana, where he expected to open a law practice. On July 4, while leaving a movie theater, McGirt was shot to death in a random holdup, the victim of "a maniac or amateur negro bandit," according to his wife, a witness. McGirt's funeral in Camden attracted a large attendance and was accompanied by fraternal honors.[19]

Medicine

The Kershaw County Colored Medical Association in the mid-1920s included two physicians, Dr. Jonathan P. Pickett and Dr. Jesse Horace Thomas, and one dentist, Dr. Christopher C. Brevard, all practicing on Broad Street in Camden. The city directory of 1925 identified one midwife, Rebecca Deas, "colored," but by all reports, midwives were far more numerous. Dr. Pickett was also proprietor of the Peoples Pharmacy on Broad Street, and just a few doors away Dr. Thomas Williams Jr. was a second druggist.

Entertainment

In New York in the early 1920s the Harlem Renaissance was stirring national interest in black expression through the arts. In Camden just a few doors below the opera house and nearly opposite his Broad Street tailor shop, Isaac B. Alexander managed a movie house, the Lincoln Theatre. Rarely advertised in local print, it was likely affiliated with other Lincoln Theatres across the nation that featured vaudeville acts and silent films oriented toward a black audience. It was probably through a Lincoln Theatre booking in March 1922 that a live touring production of *The Dixie Girls,* a "colored musical comedy," played to black audiences in Camden. For such a special show, the entire Camden Opera House with its more spacious seating was "reserved for colored people and colored society was out in full dress attire," the newspaper reported. So well received was the "exceptionally clean" show and so "well behaved" were the audience members that a return engagement followed at the same location the next week.

Tourism

In the winter months the three resort hotels in Camden remained the cornerstone of area tourism. The Hobkirk Inn, the Court Inn, and the Kirkwood Hotel were owned by outside concerns and managed by professional hotel personnel who spent their summers at northern resorts and came south for the winter. Activities at the hotels were the focal point for all winter visitors, including those who stayed in guest homes or smaller hotels and those who purchased their own homes or rented places for the season. The Camden Real Estate Exchange, under B. G. Sanders and T. K. Trotter, was one local business that made "Rental of Cottages for Winter Season a Specialty."

"The 'roaring twenties,'" according to John H. Daniels in his history of local polo, "will always be remembered as Camden's finest, busiest, and most successful years in the winter resort game."[20] A New York public relations firm, hired by the local resorts along with the Camden and Kershaw County Chamber of Commerce, kept national and local publications supplied with lively descriptions of the hotels, activities, and winter visitors. Balls, banquets, concerts, bridge games, and sporting activities were constant. Orchestras, dancing instructors, performers, artists, photographers, and even academic teachers were regularly engaged by the hotels. Mrs. E. L. Zemp, a local educator, organized a private winter school in which visiting children could continue individual lessons without interruption. Families of the day were typically large, and children and nannies often accompanied parents on extended vacations.

For much of the decade the writer who was employed to cover the social news of tourists and their whirl of activities was a Camden native whose home, except for the winter season, was then in New York. She was Mrs. Sarah K. Winkler, a daughter of Confederate general John Doby Kennedy, the widow of county legislator Cornelius L. Winkler, and the mother of the prolific contemporary biographer John K. Winkler. Some seasons Mrs. Winkler also presented "informal talks on literary topics of current interest." Local writers too helped with publicity. For example, Ellen Nettles's guide to the Camden scene, "In the Heart of the Pines," appeared in the 1920 New York newspapers, and Louise Salmond Nettles covered tourist events for years as the local society editor.

A polo match on the field behind the Kirkwood Hotel.
Courtesy of the Camden Archives

Negative situations were screened from contemporary newspapers, such as an outbreak of typhoid from contaminated milk at the Kirkwood Hotel in the 1920–21 season. It was recalled in later years by Minnie Tewell (Mrs. Bernard Harry) Baum, who first came to Camden by train from New York as a registered nurse to care for one of the patients. "Miss Minnie" married here and continued in the medical field as a permanent resident.[21] Daniels's polo history reveals another fact that was little publicized:

> The secret shared by the northern resort owners—Krumbholz, Ticknor, and Ellerbe—was that they all ran "restricted" resorts which unabashedly did not allow Jews to register or stay in their facilities. . . . Camden had a long history of Jewish families interwoven into the community and there were many distinguished Jewish families living in Camden. The attitude of discrimination seems to have arrived with the New England innkeepers. . . . They were simply doing what was expected of them by their gentile customers and were operating under the standard procedures of their times. Almost every city in the north followed the same practices.

Daniels points out that to play polo in a March 1922 tournament at the Kirkwood, the prominent Jewish player Julius Fleischmann arrived and stayed in his private railroad car, parked on a spur behind the hotel. Fleischmann had been mayor of Cincinnati twice and was the former president of Fleischmann Yeast Company, the fortunes of which helped found the *New Yorker* magazine. Fleischmann's team "swept up *all* the trophies in the 1922 March tournaments."[22]

Circumstances too excluded most local people from participating in resort life. In later years, when he was being interviewed about the Kirkwood Hotel, former Camden mayor Henry Savage Jr. recalled, "Not many Camden people went to the hotel. It was all too formal for us country boys. You had to put on a tuxedo for dinner every night. They had footmen in uniform and all that, and you just didn't go there unless you had a tuxedo, and not many Camden boys had tuxedos. . . . they couldn't go. It wasn't a part of the community life at all." Regarding those who were involved in activities at the club in the Kirkwood basement, Savage said, "There were very, very few Camden people. It was a completely segregated society. If they were admitted to the club it was because they were leading families, or part northerner like I was, so there was no social intercourse between the local people and the young people who stayed there."[23]

In the summer of 1923, having operated the Kirkwood Hotel since it opened twenty years earlier, T. Edmund Krumbholz died in Camden. The new owner, another experienced hotelier, Karl P. Abbott, started the next season without interruption. Abbott's Camden experiences are recounted in his autobiographical *Open for the Season.* The annual opening he describes at the Kirkwood was similar at Camden's other resorts: "We brought many of our staff down from the North but also employed a large number of colored people, who lived in

Camden, as bellboys, chambermaids, kitchen help, yardmen, and caddies. Many of these people had been employed as butlers, maids, and cooks in southern homes and were especially well trained." Abbott mentions, for example, Willie Gamble, "a Christian colored gentleman" who was bell captain at the Kirkwood and served also at other Abbott resorts.[24]

Traditions of the professional wait staff were maintained with pride and dignity, and some local families consider it a point of prestige to have had a family member employed thusly in the resort business. In later years Edna Gamble Bates recalled the Kirkwood when her father, Edward Gamble, was caretaker and gardener. Before their father died in 1924, the family would move from their Gordon Street home to live at the hotel during the off-season: "not only the family but also their horses, pigs, and chickens went up the hill to the hotel." Mrs. Gamble was a dressmaker and "made all of the uniforms for the maids . . . complete with whalebone, like a corset around the waist, so they would stand up straight."[25]

Priscilla Ann Trantham Oliver's memoir *Living in Camden* states: "Many local persons, particularly among the black community, found employment at the hotels; some of these alliances were so successful that many of them moved with the season with their employees." Oliver also points out the economic impact on the community at large: "In addition to the patronage enjoyed by the stores and businesses, the hotels provided a steady market for eggs, butter, chickens, vegetables, and firewood, sometimes sending scouts into the countryside to obtain their needs."[26] Others recall during the era that kitchen refuge from the hotels was eagerly carried off by local farmers to fatten their hogs. Coli Branham, an old-time weaver of split white-oak baskets, stated in later years that he had learned the craft from his father, a farmer who in winter months made the baskets for sale to tourists.[27] Other crafters, including women skillful with needlework, likewise found seasonal markets for their work in various local and resort shops.

Smaller Hotels and Inns

Kershaw County's commercial hotels that served the traveling public were affected by changing travel patterns in the 1920s. The town of Kershaw saw the waning years of the Benton and the Whitfield hotels, which had operated successfully in the heyday of railroad travel. The growth of the trucking industry and the increased use of automobiles decreased reliance on the railroads that had earlier made Kershaw a major stop. The volume of motorized traffic passing the way of Kershaw was not large enough to support the aging old hotels in their former style.

Bethune, however, was on the main highway route from New York to Florida. In the 1920s the town experienced a large volume of road traffic on "the Jefferson Davis Highway," and before it was paved as part of national Highway 1 at the close of the decade, slow travel along sandy roadbeds made overnight stops welcome. In 1920 George Sedley King sold the King Hotel on Main Street to H. E. Hyatt and moved to Florida for his health. Thereafter the establishment continued as the King-Davis Hotel. At one point having three stories, thirty-two rooms, a lobby, and a balcony, it was sizable for the community. However, in the 1920s the hotel was often filled by road trade and by visitors to the recreation area of Big Springs, a few miles away.

In 1920 Dr. J. E. (Eugene) McClure bought out other interests in the Big Springs Resort Company, with which he had been associated, and renovated the nearly forty-room hotel built by the Maynard family at the popular old watering hole near Bethune. He accommodated the traditional health-conscious customers and recreational summer business, continued prescribing and bottling the famous mineral water, and also expanded services to year-round travelers on the increasingly busy highway. The rural location of Big Springs made its hotel a convenient lodging place for winter hunting parties and often attracted such groups from the Camden resort community. One of the young guides that Dr. McClure employed was Bill Tolbert, who in later decades became owner of the Big Springs property. Tolbert recalled the old hotel with its huge ballroom as "the scene of many lavish parties, staged by the hotel's rich northern guests."

In 1924 Dr. McClure added steam heat for the comfort of winter guests, but during a mild spell in February 1925, when the hotel operators Mr. and Mrs. Robinson were using a small oil heater instead, a fire erupted and burned the large building to the ground. Despite the loss estimated at thirty thousand dollars, Big Springs opened again that summer and by 1927 was again advertising to host hunting parties. A much smaller hotel replaced the older one, however, and furnished cottages were also rented. Improved roads and auto travel replaced the Lynches River motor launch that had carried railroad guests part of the way to the hotel.

Camden had two commercial hotels that likewise operated on the main New York-to-Florida travel route through town, along DeKalb Street. While these establishments were open year-round for the traveling public, during the winter they were filled to overflowing with guests who lingered to enjoy the attractions of the resort season. The right wing of the Commercial Hotel at the Market Street corner, across from Bethesda Presbyterian Church, was badly burned in February 1921 when a guest built a fire in his room and left it while he attended a moving picture show. George T. Little was then hotel proprietor, and Mrs. Herbert and family were operators. In 1925 Mrs. Mary Clark, wife of the livestock dealer John H. Clark, was proprietor. West of the Commercial Hotel the modern three-story brick Camden Hotel (also Hotel Camden) offered guests both American and European plans, and its dining hall was widely patronized for business and civic dinners. In 1925 the proprietor and manager was Ellis M. Wilson. An annex built in 1927 added additional rooms and renovated dining space.

Other commercial ventures in Camden also housed and entertained visitors, although on a smaller scale. Owned and operated by local people and not tied to resort chains, some remained open year-round, although all were especially busy in the winter season. These places accommodated both tourists and locals for business or social meals and entertainments as well. In 1917 former sheriff Ross Brooks Williams and his wife, the former Marietta Isbell, sold their home on Broad Street, the south-facing Williams Hotel (also Hotel Williams), and moved a block eastward to the former Smyrl home on Lyttleton Street. Here, after changes such as a two-story wing added to accommodate a dining hall with extra rooms and including grounds that extended to present Little Street, "Miss Etta" for many years operated the Park View Inn, overlooking Hampton Park. Throughout the 1920s social columns described bridge parties and dinners at the Park View.

Also on Broad Street, north of the business district, two large historic old homes associated with the Baruch and Baum families advertised year-round for guests. The home of the former family, the birthplace of Bernard Baruch, was operated by J. W. T. Lesure as the Ivy Lodge Inn. Through most of the decade Mr. and Mrs. Bernard Harry ("Miss Minnie") Baum kept boarders and lodgers at the other home, a distinctive one known simply as "the Baum place." After it was sold to the New York decorator Ruth Richards in 1927, it was operated as the Greenleaf Villa, an antique shop and tearoom, and two years later it advertised for guests again. Both homes faced south, had side entrances to the street, and featured lovely landscaped gardens. The architectural features often described as "Charleston style" were typical of the homes constructed in that part of town.

In 1926 the local proprietor Wheeler P. Thomas traded downtown property for "the magnificent Savage property" near the Court Inn to operate the King Haiglar Inn at Laurens and Mill streets that season. The following season Miss E. Mayo, a New Yorker, was its operator. The newspaper called the inn a "very exclusive" operation, and overflow customers from the Court Inn were often housed there. Variant spellings, such as Haigla and Haighler, were sometimes used for the name, apparently to help guests pronounce it.

Other boarding and lodging houses listed in the 1925 city directory operated year-round. These included places run by Mrs. F. C. Jones and Mrs. C. R. Lewis on Broad Street, Mrs. Sallie Beasley and Mrs. Alice Owens on DeKalb Street, Mrs. Rebecca White on Fair Street, Mrs. Susanna E. Welch at Hermitage Mills, and Ola Wright, identified as "colored," on Campbell Street. In banner tourist years the Chamber of Commerce asserted that all rentable spaces in the town were occupied.

Guest Homes

In addition to resorts, smaller hotels, cottage rentals, and commercial establishments, there were a number of local homes that accepted "paying guests" for the season. Oliver states, "Outstanding among the Camden women whose homes were thus put to gracious use were Mrs. Edward DuBose, known to Camden as 'Miss Lou,' of Fair Street; 'Miss Freddie' Kirkland (Mrs. Thomas J. Kirkland) at the corner of Lyttleton and Chesnut; Mrs. Julia Knapp at her Mill Street residence Deare Place (presently known as George Washington House); and Mrs. David R. Williams at Bloomsbury."[28] On Broad Street, Mrs. William ("Miss Emma") Hough took guests at her home, advertised as the Hedges. Dr. Shannon DuBose, a granddaughter of "Miss Lou" and later owner of the Fair Street home, recalled being told that most Camdenites then could not afford the expense of painting old houses, but because tourists would not stay at places that looked rundown, "if you 'had Yankees,' you had to paint; if you didn't have Yankees, you didn't paint."[29]

Mrs. DuBose's reputation as a cultured hostess extended beyond the local scene. In the summers for fifteen years she assisted at the MacDowell Colony in Peterborough, New Hampshire, the nation's first endowed artists' colony and still in operation today. It was begun by a cousin of Mrs. DuBose's late husband, the pianist Marian Nevins MacDowell, and her husband, the late composer Edward MacDowell, to provide a quiet environment for artists of all genres to work. In his lifetime Edward MacDowell, the first American composer internationally admired, was in Camden two winters. For many years afterward a grand piano on which he had worked remained in a local home. Various passages of MacDowell's opus *Woodland Sketches* were locally said to have been inspired or composed here. "To a Wild Rose" and "The Old Trysting Place" were particularly popular in local music lessons and recitals. For many years a MacDowell Music Club met in Camden, presenting concerts and recitals to benefit the colony and to encourage musical training for young people.[30] Similar clubs were formed across the country, encouraged by Mrs. MacDowell, who was several times a Camden visitor and a benefit concert performer here.

Literary Scenes

A number of visitors to Camden preferred the quiet, genteel setting of a guest home to the busier stirrings of the fashionable resorts. In 1923 an aspiring young female playwright, recovering from ill health, spent three months in Camden, mostly at Mrs. DuBose's. Ten surviving letters that the young woman sent her mother in New York reveal pleasant, leisurely activities as well as cultivated tastes she found among the guests.[31]

On February 18 she wrote: "I've just finished [reading] a book of charming poems called 'Carolina Chansons: Legends of the Low Country' by two young men, DuBose Heyward & Hervey Allen—The former is a cousin of Mrs. DuBose & a friend & ardent admirer of Dorothy Kuhns—The little book is really poetry." The writers of *Carolina Chansons,* published in 1922, extolled writing about local scenes: "It has been said, perhaps wisely, that the immediate future of American Poetry lies rather in the intimate feeling of local poets who can interpret their own sections to the rest of the country as Robinson and Frost have done so nobly for New England, rather than in the effort to 'yawp' universally. Hence there is no attempt here to say, 'O New York, O Pennsylvania,' but simply, 'O Carolina.'" The young playwright at Mrs. DuBose's home was pleased when her Camden hostess helped her arrange a side trip to Charleston, with an invitation to a meeting there of the Poetry Society of South Carolina. The society was America's first regional poetry circle, and DuBose Heyward was a cofounder.

The letter writer was correct in her knowledge of Heyward's admiration for the aspiring playwright Dorothy Kuhns, for in March the pair were married. They had met two years earlier at the MacDowell Colony, where they also spent the summer after their marriage. In 1924 Heyward published *Porgy,* a landmark novel of black characters set in Charleston, and his wife collaborated on its dramatization, first staged in 1927. Another MacDowell Colony artist, George Gershwin, joined with them to compose music for the opera *Porgy and Bess* in the following decade. At times during these years the Heywards visited the DuBose home in Camden, where DuBose Heyward's name is signed in an old guest book. They also stayed at the Hobkirk Inn, where they gave literary talks. In 1925 the various resort hotels, with Goodie Castle, rotated as meeting places for current fiction and poetry courses led by area college professors.

Another literary personality at the Hobkirk a number of years was the colorful Oscar Laighton, then in his eighties. Most of his life he was proprietor of a family inn on the Isles of Shoals, ten miles off the New England coast and a haven for Boston artists and writers. The brother of the poet-artist Celia Thaxter, "Uncle Oscar" also wrote poetry. At least two works he composed at the Hobkirk were published in the *Camden Chronicle:* in 1921 "Agnes of Glasgow," based on the familiar local legend; and in 1922 "Uncle Billy," respecting an elderly black man who had seen Lafayette here. Harry G. Marvin, manager of the Hobkirk Inn, had been Laighton's manager at Isles of Shoals. Ella Adams, the housekeeper there for years, was housekeeper at the Hobkirk Inn in the winters.[32]

In the early 1920s the British author John Galsworthy, later winner of the Nobel Prize for Literature, was a guest at the Kirkwood Hotel.[33] In 1927 he published *A Silent Wooing,* an interlude in the *Forsyte Saga.* The fictional narrative begins: "The first of February, 1924, Jon Forsyte, convalescing from the 'flu, was sitting in the lounge of an hotel at Camden, South Carolina, with his bright hair slowly rising on his scalp. He was reading about a lynching."[34] Forsyte's reading is interrupted with an invitation to ride horseback to nearby Indian mounds for a picnic with other guests, some of whom traveled there by auto and left afterward to watch a polo match. A brief, restrained romance ensues with a friend's sister, who rides with Forsyte to see another mound. In fact in the 1920s Camden brochures said that there were "several" Indian mounds in "easy walking distance" of the town, and outings similar to that described by Galsworthy were often undertaken by visitors.

Sports Scenes

Outdoor recreation for tourists and winter residents focused on sports such as tennis, golf, hunting, and equestrian activities. All the resorts and several other locations kept up tennis courts, where tournament play and individual matches were active. The annual horse show, begun years earlier by the Camden Polo Club, remained a major event. The Camden Riding and Driving Club was incorporated to build a riding track and polo fields, and a Camden Hunt Club was begun with beagles imported from England. In the postwar years all these sports continued and, in fact, developed further.

In 1920 the new sport of trap shooting, under the guidance of professional coach "Buffalo" Smith, was featured on the inner circle of the Riding and Driving Club's half-mile track. The Country Club of the Kirkwood Hotel hosted an invitational turkey shoot, while the Boykin Cantey Club offered wild turkey hunts in the Wateree Swamp. Some winter residents purchased or leased old fields and forests as hunting preserves. In the early part of the decade, for example, winter resident W. H. Kirkbride hosted hunts in upland pine forests and open sandhill fields at his country home, historic Cool Spring, and in additional fields, forests, and bottomland swamps at Fairview, his farm at Knight's Hill.[35] In 1926 a tourist column described winter hunting activities, citing the Lausanne Field and Stream Club, six miles east of Camden: "The shooting around Camden always attracts large numbers of hunters, the various preserves being unusually well stocked with game of all sort. Covies of quail and doves abound in the upland, and in the low-lying regions about the Wateree river may be seen numbers of wild ducks, turkeys and geese." Even night-time raccoon and possum hunts "on the full of the moon" were diversions.

Over the past decade hunters in Boykin had been developing a new breed of hunting dog from a special, agreeable little stray that had been sent to L. Whitaker Boykin by a hunting partner, Alexander White of Spartanburg. From "Dumpy" descended the breed now known as the Boykin spaniel, presently the official state dog of South Carolina. The right size to fit in the small boats that maneuvered the Wateree Swamp, the intelligent and companionable little dogs were trained as turkey dogs and waterfowl retrievers.

Tourists who wished to hunt often hired guides, and Bolivar D. Boykin of Boykin was one who advertised "hunting parties taken out by appointment from Camden hotels." However, many times hunting guides or partners were secured just by word-of-mouth references and were simply local men, black or white, who hunted and knew the area woods. Quail hunting and dove hunting were especially popular among tourists, men and women alike being among the shooters. Local caterers were sometimes employed to deliver hot beverages and sandwiches to the hunting field, and help was also employed to dress the game of successful hunters and often to prepare and serve tasty meals with it later.

Golfing improved as courses expanded and professionals helped advance the game. In late January 1920, when ice and snow blanketed rival resorts at Pinehurst and Southern Pines in North Carolina, Camden publicists gloated that "there has not been a day when golfers failed to appear on the links of both the Sarsfield and Camden Country Club [Kirkwood Hotel]. Truly Camden's winter climate is hard to equal." In early 1922 the Court Inn put into play an additional eighteen-hole golf course of its own between its hotel building and the Sarsfield links. In 1924 the Kirkwood Hotel installed to its north an eighteen-hole golf course and to its south across Greene Street another, nine-hole course, both designed by the acclaimed champion and golf course architect Walter J. Travis. As was typical for their time, the greens of the local courses were sand, but Travis had them laid over beds of peat four feet deep to maintain pitch and reliability.

Regular polo games had a strong following throughout the decade, with teams representing the local resorts playing teams from other resort communities and the military. Typical in the early part of the decade were professional coaches from England and seasonal visitors, rather than local residents, as players. The 1920 schedule, according to John Daniels, was typical of the rest of the decade: "polo matches on two fields on every Saturday afternoon, weather permitting, from December, 1919, to the end of March, 1920."[36] In 1920 women, for the first time locally, staged a game of polo. One of the players was Martha Ticknor, the granddaughter and daughter respectively of Court Inn owners Caleb and Benjamin Ticknor. In 1922 she led briefly successful efforts to field women's polo for a few games.

In 1926 the same skillful horsewoman, by then Mrs. Dwight Partridge and still associated with Court Inn management, became the first Master of Fox Hounds for the newly organized Camden Hunt. According to Jeff McMahan's history of the club, "The hunt country was located in the Peck Woods (now Lloyd Woods), Weeks Woods (between Springdale Drive and the Wateree River), and occasionally at Mulberry Plantation. Horses for hire were available at Bramlett's Stables located by the Polo Field."[37]

Abbott humorously contrasts the style of the local night-time foxhunt, as "pursued for generations" in the Carolinas, with the new club's formal English

The golf course in front of the Kirkwood Hotel. Courtesy of the Camden Archives

day-time hunt. Abbott was familiar with the former style: "We took our dogs back in the hills of a moonlight night and turned them loose, then we'd build up a fire, make a few side bets, and await developments." The new hunt club, riding horseback and attired in full regalia, "made a very fine showing . . . in black coats with orange collars and cuffs and with their horses groomed until they flashed in the sun." At the club's first live hunt, Abbott said that he and stable-owner Luce Bramlett, "knowing nothing about the etiquette of crying 'Tallyho' and riding behind the master and the whippers-in and staying with the hunt," set off with excitement when they heard the dogs bark. Knowing the lay of the land, they headed swiftly cross-country and caught up with the fox at Sanders Creek. Heading triumphantly back to town flourishing the foxtail trophy, they were surprised to encounter outrage from the formally suited hunters they met, who were still riding together in pursuit.[38]

In 1927 three changes of residence influenced the equestrian community. David R. Williams, who had restored Mulberry, his family plantation, as a dwelling, sold it to his similarly named nephew, David R. Williams Sr. Thus a family of sportsmen and sportswomen took up residence in the historic home and joined in local activities. Also, Ernest Woodward and Harry Kirkover bought residences in Camden. Woodward, heir of the Jell-O fortune, purchased historic Holly Hedge, and Kirkover purchased Bohemia (the Villa Roseland), opposite Holly Hedge. The two friends were influential in the founding of the Camden Hunt, and Kirkover persuaded Woodward to buy the four hundred acres that eventually became the Springdale Racetrack. In 1929 on that course the Camden Hunt sponsored the first Washington's Birthday Race, the first major event before the next year's Carolina Cup Steeplechase, which would inaugurate a lasting tradition.

Lazy Days of Summer

Winter tourists had long left the area when year-round Kershaw County residents sought their own vacations, desiring to escape summer heat. A few retreated for spells to seaside cottages at traditional lowcountry spots such as Pawleys Island, and some helped swell newer coastal developments at Myrtle Beach. At the latter, for example, the H. G. Carrison family put out a sign that duplicated Camden's trademark Indian weather vane and gave their cottage the name "King Haiglar."

Most citizens, however, remained near home. The inaccessible shores and vast waters newly impounded behind the Wateree Dam, today Lake Wateree, were generally avoided in the early 1920s. The pink-hued water, colored by the red clay fields it had covered, and the floating debris from sunken woodlands were described as "unnatural" looking for a number of years.[39] Sportsmen questioned whether healthy fish could live in the environment of "the Big Pond," as some called it, although fishing was popular at the foot of the dam, where fish swam upriver and were unable to go farther. In the early 1920s sturgeon eight feet long occasionally made their way upriver this far to their ancient spawning grounds, and a few were taken by startled fishermen, although fish and game authorities quickly publicized such catches as illegal.

Despite initial lack of interest in the present Lake Wateree area, at almost every other millpond, large spring, or creek side around the county, "tent colonies" of families, friends, and chaperoned young people were set up. Special rates were advertised at Big Springs for "Sunday School picnics, Boy Scouts or Camp Fire Girls." Some Camden families lived for weeks in tents at Hermitage Lake, the father daily traveling back and forth to his work in town or simply joining his family on weekends. Clever names were popularly given to tent colonies, such as "here today, gone tomorrow, fondly remembered." Fishermen sometimes put up tents or shacks at the end of walkways extending over the water to reach favorite fishing holes or to make seining or setting fish traps easier. Ladies' nights were often featured at men-only fishing camps, with fried fish dinners served to visiting wives and children. Laurens T. Mills established one such annual camp on the western bank of the Hermitage for businessmen who worked in Camden during the day and returned to camp nightly. A radio and other conveniences enlivened "Camp Mills," where Jim Smith, "a well known negro cook," served "excellent meals." The businessman "Uncle Jimmy" DeLoache was another favorite campfire and outdoor cook often mentioned.

West of the Wateree there were picnics, swimming, and fish fries reported at Jordan's Mill, at Heath's Pond, and at Rose's Pond. Fishing parties at "Twenty Creek," the colloquial name of Twenty-five Mile Creek, cooked their catch on the banks. Swimming parties below the dam at Boykin's Mill Pond sometimes concluded with informal picnics on the wooded bank. Fishing and fish fries were popular also at Vaughan's Mill on Sanders Creek. At Liberty Hill swimmers favored Singleton Creek, and flatbed truck rides careening and swerving to and from picnicking areas on the steep hillsides of the area made the trip as much fun for young people as the destination. Between Camden and Liberty Hill, E. E. Holland's millpond on Sanders Creek, "famous for picnics in by gone days," was enjoying popularity for camping parties when it was described in the July 1, 1921, *Chronicle:* "It is a beautiful, picturesque spot with a lake of clear water suitable for fishing, boating and swimming—its banks fern-fringed and shaded by giant oaks that have no doubt been standing for ages past. On the pine clad hill side is a tented village entirely under feminine control, and so it has been named 'Camp No Man's Land.'" Numbers of visitors, the paper stated, were traveling back and forth.

Enterprising folk developed some camping areas more elaborately and charged small fees for participation. At the lighted pavilion at Holland's Pond in 1926, when orchestra music for dancing was provided by the local band George Coleman and his Saucy Seven, popular jazz tunes were no doubt in the repertoire. Holland's was closed to the public at the end of the decade when Walton Ferguson purchased the site as part of the Chancefield and Sunny Hill plantations he acquired for a private estate and new homesite.

In the mid-1920s Robert M. Kennedy gave the name "Colonial Lake" to a fish pond he developed behind another old mill farther up on Sanders Creek. This was the location of the campsite that Gates had been attempting to reach when colonials encountered the British at the Battle of Camden. In 1927 Kennedy leased his pond property to Herman Baruch and the band leader George Coleman. There they improved for public entertainment a swimming area that included bathhouses with forty stalls, a lighted pavilion, campsites, and fire pits for fish fries. Fourth of July celebrations included music, fireworks, swimming competitions, and motorboat rides.

Swimming—or bathing, for the less active—was the favorite sport of the season, though it was not without controversy. Form-fitting swimsuits raised eyebrows earlier in the decade but gradually replaced "Mother Hubbards," although the looser, more modest outfits continued to be rented to bathers at Big Springs. Church groups from time to time wrestled with questions of whether swimming was a violation of the Sabbath and whether it was decent for men and women to swim in the same area. In 1925, when complaints came from downtown shoppers that "quite a few young people have been seen driving up to soda founts in automobiles attired only in their bathing togs," the Camden City Council banned swimsuit attire on Broad and DeKalb streets.

At the Old Factory Pond joining Kirkwood and the Wateree Mill, various Camden mothers and service organizations in different years took on responsibilities to chaperone the safety of popularly patronized swimming holes by organizing "clubs"—the East Lake Swimming Club, the Kirkwood Swimming Club, and Saddle 'n Paddle, to name a few. Rough shelters and primitive bathhouses were erected from time to time, and rules were set up as needed. When the American Legion operated the Saddle 'n Paddle in 1925, they asked children to leave their dogs at home since a neighbor kept rabbits.

The coldest summertime water in the county was at Big Springs, where the artesian water in the twenty by forty foot spring never varied year-round from sixty degrees, flowing at a rate of three hundred gallons a minute just a few feet from the Lynches River. A swinging bridge crossed the spring, and two swimming areas—sometimes women at one and men at the other—were also developed along the river, one of which happened to fall on each side of the county line. In later years T. K. "Kirk" Watts recalled that some visitors swam in the spring, "although the water was a bit on the cold side."[40]

Adaptations to Tourism

In addition to recreation, tourists enjoyed shopping, but the greater affluence of winter visitors made that season the profitable one. The Kirkwood Hotel included on its premises exclusive shops selling clothing, sports equipment, gifts, and souvenirs. Similar places operated nearby, such as the winter branch of New York's Larrabee Shop at 1818 Broad and Rounswell, Inc., at the Villepigue House at 1811 Lyttleton. The Torii Shop at 1216 Broad was also widely advertised. At the local resorts Mrs. Grace P. T. Knudson's gift business was so successful that in 1929 she marketed her own book advising others how to conduct similar resort operations. One of her popular displays sold books autographed by southern writers. Locally owned, the Studio Shop of Catherine Harris Goodale offered an intriguing and changing variety of luxury items, for example "Imported Goods, French lingerie, art linens, Persian rugs" and the like. Mrs. Henry E. Beard's Camden Antique Shop catered to the tastes of those who liked what they saw in the old southern homes of the area.

Several specialty shops operated year-round in the downtown Camden business area and were patronized by tourists as well as locals in the 1920s. On Broad Street, Edward B. Buddin's Book Store and Willis Sheorn's cigar store and pool room, the Wigwam, carried some souvenir novelties with their regular merchandise. Miss M. E. Gerald's Millinery and Notions, a clothing store, included a gift shop as well. A competitor, the Fashion Shop, owned by Sam Karesh at the corner of Broad and DeKalb, advertised clothing and millinery appealing to upper-scale shoppers. In 1922 Franklin D. Goodale, a jeweler and watchmaker, opened for business, advertising diamonds and silverware.

For sweet treats a trip to the Beleos family's Camden Candy Kitchen was an established tradition. Thomas's Confectionary, a DeKalb Street ice cream parlor owned by Wheeler P. Thomas, included a gift shop operated by Mrs. Florence Boykin. Thomas's wife, Elizabeth, expanded their hospitality ventures with the Betty Thomas Coffee Shop, offering a different edge to the tearooms that reigned widely.[41] Nearby on DeKalb, E. L. Moseley managed the Rest Shop, a year-round tearoom. In 1927 Miss Carrie Wooten opened Wooten Tea Room, which became long established in the community. Several ventures, such as the Cozy Celler Tea Room, the Studio Tea Room, and the Palmetto Tea Room, were widely advertised during the winter season.

Several tearoom ventures were conducted by women from their homes or in residential areas during the winter tourist season. Guests attired for winter outings by horseback, buggy, or touring car enjoyed breaks for sandwiches, cookies, and steaming hot tea on the gracious, sheltered porches or sunrooms that were popular tearoom settings. Persons away from their own homes found tearooms to be, as advertised, "a pleasant and convenient way to discharge social duties" by arranging entertainments there. A formal tea poured from a gleaming silver service by a gracious hostess was intimate enough for a small group and elegant enough for a large one.

The Woman's Exchange, operating under the auspices of Grace Episcopal Church to sell handiwork and crafts, opened a tearoom on the sunny south porch of the remodeled parish house. Later the tearoom operated on the porch and sunroom of the separate exchange building "nestled under the pines" on Laurens Street. For several seasons Miss Ethel Yates managed the Woman's Exchange, while Mrs. Jack Whitaker Jr. for a while had charge of the tearoom.

On Broad Street opposite the Camden Baptist Church on the corner of Lafayette, the Martha Washington advertised "delicacies" in its tearoom and fruit shop. In 1925 it featured waitresses, such as Misses Catherine DeLoache and Lucile Smith, in colonial costumes. Later in the decade a Mrs. McMahan assisted in the tearoom and gift shop at the Green Leaf Villa.

Eastward from the business area and overlooking the town, the House on the Precipice, owned by the landscaper K. G. Whistler, was the location of the Precipice Tea Room. It was managed by Miss Louise Mickle, who also catered dinners there. In 1929 improvements to that establishment included a Tom Thumb (miniature) golf course, with greens the bright-colored clay of its Paint Hill setting.

Several seasonal tearooms on plantations south of Camden were popular with tourists for their Old South atmosphere. Mrs. Willis Cantey, in charge of the Holly Tree Tea Room, sometimes added musical entertainment for her guests—for example, a 1925 holiday program by the Good Hope Negro Choir. The sisters

Bland and Babs Williams opened the renovated slave house and kitchen behind the main house at Mulberry Plantation and operated a gift shop and tearoom, Hannah's Cabin, where fees benefited Camden Hospital. Seven miles southeast of Camden, Mrs. Burwell Boykin and Miss Minette Boykin supervised a tea-room at Mt. Pleasant, where the plantation setting attracted many visitors.

Tourists venturing northward on "the Liberty Hill Drive" (today Highway 97) could stop three miles above Camden at the Poppy Garden tearoom, operated in the hilltop home of Mrs. Ella S. Hough with Mrs. E. F. Miller. A few miles farther brought travelers to another hilltop tearoom, the Pines, the home of Mrs. B. R. Truesdale. Both tearooms catered luncheons and dinner parties, and the Pines developed into a long-patronized establishment that also offered music and evening dancing.

Farther beyond these homes, on a lovely wooded peak seven miles from town, a "picturesque cabin" was outfitted by two female and two male members of the winter colony to serve as a comfort station. At Liberty Hill, a favorite destination, the sisters Clara and Louise Johnston operated the Hill Top Tea Room in their home, the Henry Brown House, a site noted for its extensive views of the surrounding rugged countryside. Travelers from Camden to Kershaw could dine in the latter town at the Rose Tea Room, operated by Mrs. W. W. Horton and Mrs. A. B. Whitaker.

The in-home tearoom business had become so popular and acceptable by the end of the decade that in 1929 three enterprising Camden schoolteachers took the concept a step further. Miss Margaret Burnet, Mrs. J. M. Dempster, and Mrs. G. E. Taylor bought a summer cottage at Myrtle Beach and invited the patronage of vacationing friends at their Myrtle Green Tea Room.

Age of Prohibition

Many of the varied facets of life in Kershaw County in the 1920s were affected by consequences of the reform-minded Eighteenth Amendment to the Constitution. From 1920 until 1933, the year when the amendment was repealed, the manufacture, transportation, and sale of beverage alcohol anywhere in the United States were illegal. Locally as well as nationally, however, an outlaw community rose to quench the thirsts of the unreformed. Public sympathies waffled for more than thirteen rocky years before national Prohibition finally ended.

Before the amendment went into effect, some persons purchased still-legal supplies and stockpiled private cellars to wait out the latest dry period in ever-changing liquor regulations. Later, however, when less prudent people desired alcoholic beverages or when private stock ran out, there were many directions in which to turn.

In South Carolina the earlier dispensary years and the various periods of local prohibition since then had already given some lawbreakers practice in secretive alcohol operations and evasion. The old "blind tiger" slang was outdated during the 1920s, but "moonshining," "rum-running," and "bootlegging" became common lingo and lucrative enterprises. The illicit manufacture, transportation, and sale of beverage alcohol grew in scale and in technical sophistication, far beyond

a simple cottage industry down on the farm.

"At his old tricks," said the local press about a familiar violator brought before the Kershaw County court on February 1920, its first seating since Prohibition had gone into effect the previous month. Sheriff Grover C. Welsh and his deputies were active within the county at a variety of locations, indicating patterns to follow. A hidden still was located and destroyed in the Wateree Swamp on Betty Neck. A Liberty Hill white man riding in a buggy driven by a black man was apprehended with whiskey and wine. In May, black runners with a keg of whiskey were arrested in a Cadillac on the overhead bridge near the Kirkwood Hotel, and more kegs associated with them were found hidden on the roadway to the old ferry crossing. That operation was termed "the largest liquor seizure ever known in the county," a phrase that would repeatedly describe even larger, more-daring deliveries and more-complex operations uncovered in succeeding raids.

The struggle to apprehend lawbreakers took curious twists. In December 1921 the sheriffs of Kershaw and Lancaster counties jointly raided along their shared boundary, where they located on the Kershaw County side an underground still covered with leaves. One of the moonshiners taken prisoner to Camden was a one-legged man, his location revealed by the tell-tale trail of his wooden stump. In that same month a local judge put two white men on the chain gang—then a sentence generally reserved for black offenders—to express outrage at their audacious scam selling jars of water for booze.

In July 1922 officers apprehended a "mountaineer" who had moved from northern Georgia to ply the old trade of his region. When deputies located his still on Black Creek in the Sandy Grove section, it was set up but not operating. They tracked the old man's bare feet to a nearby peach orchard, where he was gathering more fruit for his mash. The old-timer, officers said, had been selling liquor in the Buffalo area for several years.

Supporters of Reform

From the first there were opponents to Prohibition, but there were also supporters who wanted to see a real reform work. In August 1921 eastern Kershaw County citizens held a meeting at Beaver Dam to discuss enforcement of law and order. The next month "the Law and Order League of Kershaw County," a temperance group, announced that its monthly meeting would be held at Bethany Church, Westville. J. S. Sturgis reported in the September 23, 1921, *Chronicle* on the meeting, which had been attended by "determined men from various sections of the county": "The making of monkey rum in tin can stills is only one of the many evils and the good people have been silent so long that we have, to a large extent, lost our public conscience. The people violate the law with impunity and hardly realize that they have committed any wrong. The fight will be long and hard and will require leaders who are willing to stand abuse and criticism and make many sacrifices, but happily Kershaw county has plenty of men of this type." The Wateree Mill's columnist in the January 20, 1922, *Chronicle* described a meeting of "the Law Observance League" with the Wateree Baptist Church: "The wave of crime that is sweeping over our land is proof of a growing disregard for law and order, and is also a challenge to all real men and women to rise up and demand a change." The church had already held a mass meeting, "resolved to stamp out lawlessness in our midst," and raised a one-hundred-dollar reward for the capture and conviction of anyone caught selling whiskey in the mill village.

In that same year three hundred women of Camden, "practically unanimous in their stand," signed their names to a petition that they circulated door-to-door; they were "fully convinced that the prohibition laws are very flagrantly violated in and around our city." The petition suggested observance of a day of prayer on June 11 "that the demon of drink may be cast out of our country." Complaints on behalf of rural citizens in Buffalo District were presented to the court by the grand jury regarding illegal liquor sales in their community. In the fall Governor-elect Thomas McLeod, speaking at Wateree Baptist Church at a meeting of the Law Enforcement League, pledged that his office would oppose violators.

In spring 1923 the nationally noted evangelist Billy Sunday (William Ashley Sunday) drew huge crowds to the Camden Baptist Church. His reputation from a quarter of a century's preaching preceded him. One of the nation's most celebrated supporters of Prohibition, the evangelist was preaching salvation at the local meeting but minced no words on social reforms. He was noted for rapid-fire delivery of stinging, catchy phrases, summarizing his points with oft-repeated zingers such as, "Whiskey and beer are all right in their place, but their place is in hell."

The March 23 *Camden Chronicle* stated about the Camden meeting, "The church has a seating capacity said to be around 700 and it is estimated that fully 1200 or more people were crowded into the aisles and standing room was at a premium—many being unable to get in." The *Columbia State* reported that the evangelist spoke in an overflowing building, while an estimated five hundred persons outside "crowded around the doors and windows" and "as many more could not get close enough to hear his voice. Besides the citizens of Camden, people were present from Bishopville, Kershaw, Bethune, Westville, Blaney and a large number of tourists from the nearby hotels." Crowds of Kershaw County citizens also drove to hear him preach in Columbia.[42]

The association of sin, amusements, and alcohol was frequently made in many pulpits—the extremes of which were openly ridiculed by some and sincerely taken to heart by others. These attitudes would be significant in the political arena.

The belief that social issues must be addressed by church and school was underscored by leaders such as the influential Camden attorney and legislator Mendel L. Smith, former Fifth Circuit judge. The May 1925 *South Carolina Gazette* quoted his remarks on the current crime wave: "Education would be far more effective in building up the right sort of citizenship if lessons in the value of good character and good morals and the necessity of religion were more directly and thoroughly stressed in all our schools. However the problem cannot be solved by the schools alone. There must indeed be a moral and religious revival throughout the state if the present deterioration and decay are to be stopped and if immorality and crime are to be checked."

The Lawbreakers

Despite such efforts there were many citizens who opposed Prohibition and defied it by making illicit liquor purchases. In all parts of the county many stills were set into operation. Many were discovered by lawmen and destroyed, but wily operators frequently escaped, and those who were captured often paid only light penalties and then promptly started up their illegal businesses again. Escapades of both lawmen and lawbreakers made colorful newspaper copy and captivated public attention. Even tragic effects of alcohol abuse gained status from prose that both shocked and entertained.

"White Men Fight," announced the August 7, 1925, *Camden Chronicle,* describing the arrest of four men: "The use of mean liquor in all too generous quantities seems to have been the notable factor in developing a free for all fight and human carving demonstration on the river bridge highway a half mile from Camden early last Saturday afternoon." Another article in the same issue, "Bystander Gets the Bullet," described a fight at the Fountain Filling Station on South Broad, "a falling out over a fruit jar filled with ice water." The shot that injured a youth nearby was fired by the operator, who was being given "a sound beating" by his helper, "a cripple." The owner had on many occasions been before the courts "charged with selling other than gas."

With a growing segment of otherwise respectable citizens thumbing their noses at Prohibition, public sentiment sometimes elevated flamboyant lawbreakers to the status of folk heroes. One adventure vividly illustrates the type of press coverage avidly followed by readers with whom stories of speed and daring were popular. The Camden paper reprinted from the June 25, 1926, *Columbia State* the account of a "desperate" nineteen-mile chase "in which life and limb were often risked." The wild ride began in Pontiac in Richland County with rural police officers in pursuit. It ended dramatically in downtown Camden, in front of several hundred people, with the arrest of the twenty-three-year-old driver and his mother, who were in possession of thirty-one gallons of whiskey in half-gallon fruit jars:

> Over the hills and around the curves, with a zigzag motion at 50 to 60 miles an hour, the light . . . car . . . often swerved close to the heavy car of the pursuing officers. . . . On a curve just this side of the Wateree river bridge, the lighter car swerved slightly to the left and apparently allowed enough room . . . to go around. Just as the officer's car was even with the fleeing automobile . . . [the fleeing driver] swung his car . . . , pushed him into a bank, yanked the left front door off the officer's machine, smashed the left rear fender and narrowly escaped turning the heavy car over. . . . Soon the chase was on again.
>
> At the toll gate on the [Wateree] river bridge [the fleeing driver] went flying through, hurling his toll fare from his car as he went. So close upon him were [the officers] that before the gate could be dropped, they were through and skidding to prevent smashing into the rear of [his] car.
>
> Over the river bridge at 50 and 60 miles an hour went the two cars and approaching Camden held the same high speed. After getting into the city limits . . . so close were the two cars that the bumper of [the officers'] car caught under the left front fender of the [other] car. . . . For several blocks the two cars went, hooked together. As they were about to cross Main [Broad] street, which was heavy with traffic, the officer's chance came and he cautiously began edging in. Seeing a crash imminent, [the driver being pursued] slammed on his brakes and skidded for 33 paces before stopping.

The officers stated that a third passenger had been injured while escaping during the high-speed chase in Camden: "The man attempted once to jump from the speeding machine . . . but picked an unfortunate spot since as he leaped he crashed into a post and was hurled back into the car. Almost immediately, though, he repeated the attempt and was successful." The officer driving in pursuit said that the chase took so long because, "seeing there was a woman in the car, he did not take chances that he might otherwise have taken."

Behind the runners, the dealers, and the still workers across the nation lay an increasingly complex network of masterminds, many of whom were never brought to justice. Such was likely true locally as well. Kershaw County court dockets swelled with liquor violations and convictions, mostly of persons caught in action. In 1923 local, state, and federal law enforcement—along with the office of Governor Thomas G. McLeod—combined in the prosecution of an alleged "big man." As a result the October court sentenced Keith S. Villepigue, "a wealthy white man 77 years of age," to serve a year in prison. It was his third conviction, according to the press, and he made headlines again in February 1924 when he was reported sent off "to the pen" to begin serving his sentence, with federal charges, it was said, pending at its completion.

Villepigue reportedly owned a residence and several stores north of the city limits in the area known as "Dusty Bend." The community had acquired its name based on its reputation as a place noted for bootleg sales. By traditional account the stretch of shacks and small stores north of the Seaboard railroad tracks was often visibly obscured by an overhanging cloud of dust stirred up by the frequent auto traffic of buyers hurrying to and from the area along its curving dirt road. A decade earlier Villepigue—then "bailiff and court crier at the Kershaw county courthouse . . . better known in his way than any other citizen of the county"—had been convicted of liquor law violations. He was subsequently pardoned by Governor Cole Blease. At the time of his earlier arrest, Villepigue was described in the August 22, 1913, *Chronicle* as "the 'king bee' among the tigers of the county," having grown wealthy as the result of "plying his trade in different parts of the county for many years" and "so bold with the sale that it was common talk among his patrons as to where they secured their liquor."[43]

Lying beyond the regular authority of Camden police (and, some said, neglected in other ways also), Dusty Bend had an established reputation of operating independently by its own law. In general liquor sales by various operators there were not openly transacted face-to-face. Instead some version of the following would occur: A prospective buyer would enter an empty house, place money on the table, and leave by way of a back door, passing through another empty room in which a bottle sat unattended. Or, if there was no bottle in sight, he simply left, and outside some nondescript person, perhaps an elderly woman at work in a garden, would casually mention a location where he might want to walk. There, with no one around, the buyer would find a "package." Thus seller, buyer, money, and contraband could rarely be proved to be connected. Within the casual flow of the ordinary activities of the community's mostly black populace, it was rarely possible to detect who among them were the "watchers" or to determine who owned the "empty" houses.[44]

Almost every country-store area of the county at some time or other was mentioned in police reports as a site of illegal activities, such as a "rum row" near Galloway's place on the Bishopville highway. The traveling public bought and sold in motion—from wagon beds, rumble seats, or even saddlebags. The streets and highways that were being improved and paved in the 1920s opened access and sped along the transportation of contraband beverages.

Still Busting

Since so many otherwise law-abiding citizens participated in liquor law abuse by making casual purchases, the primary strategy of limited-funded and undermanned law enforcement was directed at stemming the flow of alcohol at its source. Hidden stills were located in various parts of the county. From the beginning, swamp locations were most frequent choices, providing isolation, access to water, and natural camouflage. Officers often followed tips or relied on observation and their knowledge of local terrain to seek out still sites, but on occasion they were aided in unusual ways. Drunken bees flying in an irregular swarm might indicate a nearby source of fermenting mash, officers learned. In one incident officers located a still after coming upon a pair of cows staggering down the river road.

Especially in early years, all across the county stills were constructed of varied and even dangerous materials. Near the site of the Battle of Camden officers located "a gasoline can arrangement" that was so well concealed by a blind that even within a few yards of its operation it could not be detected. In Cassatt they found "a crude outfit" manufactured from an automotive gasoline tank; at Lockhart, an operation made from a vegetable canning outfit; and in Shepard, a "booze mill" with a worm made of twisted pipe.

The April 8, 1927, *Camden Chronicle* reported that rural police officers had been "quite active the past week capturing nearly a still a day," most of them in West Wateree. Barrels of mash and other parts of still operations were destroyed in the Cherry Creek section, in the Spears Creek section, and on a Branham property. Two more stills were destroyed in the Doby's Mill area, and one in the eastern part of the county near Hall's Mill.

Two weeks later the newspaper reported on a number of additional seizures of equipment and violators, many in eastern sections of the county. Seizures took place in areas near Raley's Mill, near a Buffalo church, close to Kershaw, and at a Bethune home. Another arrest was made at a rural home south of Camden. Additionally two white men in a Packard touring car were apprehended delivering whiskey in a predominantly black section of south Camden.

Returning in the same period to West Wateree, Kershaw County officers destroyed a still deep in the Gum Swamp of the Betty Neck section. Also in April a state constable and Richland County officers raided the Wateree Swamp just on their side of the border and destroyed two huge stills so remote that wagons were required to transport confiscated equipment for six miles before reaching a point that trucks could penetrate. The *State* was quoted: "Thousands of gallons of beer were poured out. Hogs running in the swamp, officers said, imbibed so heavily in the beer, that they were intoxicated to staggering proportion. After partaking of a quantity of the stuff the wild swine became bold and swaggered around the officers without the least fear."

A few months later the August 5 *Chronicle* reported that a successful raid had smashed a sophisticated liquor operation in a dense area of the Wateree Swamp eighteen miles southwest of Camden and close to Richland County. At the distinctive but remote landmark of Dunn's Mount, "operators had dug a well at the foot of the Mount in order to get a supply of water." Two seventy-five-gallon copper stills, "described as 'double-headers'—one being fired while the other was being made ready," were in operation when officers arrived. The same day a small copper still with a barrel of peach mash was located near Twenty Creek operating in the smokehouse of a tenant on the Burdell lands that had been deeded to Camden Hospital.

Within two more weeks further action took place. Two whiskey-laden automobiles, driven by black "denizens of the 'Dusty Bend' north of Camden," were pursued in the early morning hours from near Antioch schoolhouse until one was captured near Camden Oil Mill and other near Hermitage Mill. Also in the early morning hours officers happened upon a white man and woman near the Springdale clubhouse with thirty gallons of booze in their vehicle. In other separate activities dealers at "a notorious joint north of Camden near Childers Mill" were arrested selling moonshine, an auto chase ended on York Street with the arrest of another liquor seller, and a Dusty Bend "pocket dealer" was apprehended with booze on his person. Raids on stills were successful in three separate operations in West Wateree, all in areas along the old wire road near the Richland County boundary. One of the stills was a "60 gallon gasoline drum outfit," the type most likely to yield a potentially fatal brew.

Aggressive enforcement sparked changes in moonshiners' tactics. By the end of the decade Kershaw County officers frequently encountered vehicles equipped with smoke-screen devices to confound the vision of those in pursuit. In another tactic "extremely young men," boys who knew little or nothing that could be divulged about the illicit operations, were enlisted to drive liquor-loaded vehicles. By the instruction of those who hired them, youthful drivers gave up easily if stopped and, officers complained, could get off lightly.

Governor John G. Richards

Especially active enforcement was encouraged when a new man became governor of the state. From 1927 to 1931 John Gardiner Richards of Liberty Hill, a native son of Kershaw County, stood as a strong proponent of law as a means of correcting the ills of society. He had been born into a community that took pride in conservatism. The local historian Louise Johnston refers to the "character, courage and piety of citizens of this small village" as well as a "high degree of human nature that became cantankerous at times": "In those days a Square was a person of high Christian character, whose word was as good as his bond. The expressions 'Four square and all wool a yard wide' were often used in referring to citizens of Liberty Hill. Present-day Liberty Hillians continue to claim honor with the title of being 'Squares.'"[45] Governor Richards took the ideals of his home to the State House.

The July 22, 1927, *Chronicle* stated: "Governor Richards means business. He is trying to stamp out liquor. There are no half-way or half-hearted measures with him. There is no compromise. It is a battle to the finish." The strength of the lawbreakers was powerful, as liquor was so plentiful in Columbia that it was selling for fifty cents a half pint or under six dollars a gallon. "It is not my purpose to single out any special law for more rigid enforcement than another," Governor Richards wrote to the state's sheriffs, encouraging enforcement "with uniformity and earnestness" of all laws on South Carolina's books. Thus began enforcement in several areas that some applauded and others considered excessive.

In December 1927 a tourist protested to the *Camden Chronicle* about "the Blaney speed trap, where motorists have been held up and made to pay fines for alleged violation of the speed laws." He disagreed with the justification "that the lives of school children are in jeopardy" since the school was fenced, and he said of Blaney, "I don't think there were fifty people in the place, in fact you wouldn't know it was a town."

In March 1928, the same week that deputies rounded up "a bunch of wily crap shooters" at Dusty Bend, the *Chronicle* reported a raid about fifty miles distant that included state and federal agents: "About 15 local sports from Camden and vicinity, including several northern tourists, were caught in the cock pit . . . when officers rudely stopped one of the biggest cocking mains ever pulled off in this state near Florence. . . . The fight was staged on an island in a swamp, and when officers came up many took to the swamp through mud and water. . . . It is said one Camden man was refereeing the [cock]fight." Karl Abbott, who treats the illegality lightheartedly, attributes much of the local cockfighting activity to the stable owner Luce Bramlett, "who came down out the North Carolina mountains every fall" with a string of horses, grooms, and gamecocks.[46] In 1929 the governor carried antigambling enforcement forward against "slot machines, punch boards and other gaming devices," including those at the state fair.

The governor's most controversial campaign began shortly after his inauguration when he wrote the state's sheriffs: "We have all grown more or less careless about Sabbath observance. . . . I am urging that you use the same diligence in the enforcement of our Sabbath observance laws that you give to the other laws of the state." A highly publicized case involved the arrest of eight Camden men playing golf on the country club (Kirkwood Hotel) links on Sunday, March 6, 1927: James DeLoache Jr., Fred L. Harlow, J. F. McDowell, W. T. Redfearn, Ralph N. Shannon, Mendel L. Smith Jr., Hughey Tindal, and John Whitaker. Although the prosecution was headed by the attorney general of the state and the trial lasted four hours, a verdict of "not guilty" was decided by a jury of local businessmen in four minutes and upheld by the supreme court. It was determined that the old blue laws that banned many Sunday activities did not specifically mention golf and therefore did not apply to the sport. In later years those involved openly admitted that the game and the arrest had been locally "arranged" to be able to argue the merits of excluding golf from blue-law enforcement.

Addressing Problems

Inequitable accessibility to educational, social, and economic opportunities widened gaps between diverse groups during the 1920s. Schools, churches, and community-service entities attempted to address various conditions and negative effects of the times, although they did not seriously confront or attack core problems of race, segregation, disenfranchisement, agricultural overproduction, or low wages and prices.

Schools

The county was divided into many school districts, and in each district white trustees managed the schools of both races in their jurisdiction. Taxes, services, quality of teaching, curricula, and even length of the school year varied greatly among the schools and districts and were largely dependant on the economic status of the citizens there. Though inequities continued, reports of the state superintendent of education reveal increased opportunities during the decade.[47] For example, the number of high schools for white students increased from only one in 1919–20—Camden—to seven by 1929–30—Antioch, Bethune, Blaney, Camden, Charlotte Thompson, Midway, and Mt. Pisgah. J. G. Richards Jr., a principal in the earlier period, became superintendent of the Camden schools and a leading influence in education in the county.[48]

Jackson High was the county's only high school for black students, but in 1923 a new brick building was built to enhance its facilities. Principal Petros B. M'dodana (Mdodana), a tall, well-spoken man, was influential with both races in the local community. Born a full-blooded African of the Zulu tribe at Cape Idutywa, Transkei, South Africa, during British colonial conflicts, he immigrated to America as a youth in 1903. Sponsored by Baptist missionaries and educators, he completed his education in this country, and while serving weekdays as Jackson's principal, he was also pastor at a Bennettsville church in Marlboro County throughout the 1920s and beyond.[49]

Jeanes supervisor Elise F. McLester continued serving throughout the decade and into the next as "rural supervisor of colored schools" and worked with the Kershaw County Colored Teachers Association. Part of a report she filed was printed in the February 13, 1925, *Camden Chronicle:* "The negro schools of Kershaw county have improved greatly since 1919, the year the writer was put on the work as Jeanes industrial supervisor for at that time most of our schools were taught in poorly built churches and halls, with a few log cabins in places to serve as school houses." Since then, she said, "we have been able to erect eight modern Rosenwald buildings," and she anticipated the day that "shabby one teacher schools will cease" and instead "consolidate into two, three, four and five teacher schools."

The American clothier Julius Rosenwald, part-owner of Sears, Roebuck and Company, in 1917 began the Rosenwald Fund for philanthropic purposes. In part the organization provided matching funds that helped build more than five thousand schools, shops, and dormitories for teachers to improve African Americans' education. Records at Tuskegee Institute in Alabama identify the eight Kershaw County schools that had received grants by 1925: Jackson High, Knights Hill, Mickle, Prince Edward (a joint school with Lancaster County), St. Matthew(s), Shepard, Swift Creek, and Wood schools. Later in the decade Lugoff, Mt. Joshua, Mt. Zion, and Red Hill schools also received grants, as did another joint school, Lancaster County's Kershaw. In 1930–31 the last local Rosenwald grant went to Kirkland School.

Overall the Rosenwald Fund granted onetime amounts of $500 to $1,500 per site. The top amount went to just two schools, Jackson and Kershaw, both six-teacher facilities. The next-highest amount of $1,100 went to the four-teacher schools of Lugoff, St. Matthews, and Swift Creek. Local fund-raising by black citizens totaled $10,189, with an additional $1,300 donated by whites to match the $12,250 from Rosenwald and $44,939 coming from public funds.

Several private schools operated for white students, and the private Mather Academy continued to serve black students. Sometimes called Browning Home School, Mather was the only educational institution in the county to have teachers of both races, although it too had a white administration. Browning Home was the "model home" residence of the school's white female missionary teachers, most of them single and the others widowed, who taught and mothered the female students who also lived there.[50] Russell Memorial Library began in 1922 as a memorial to a late missionary teacher.

In 1928 a boys' dormitory was constructed at Mather, and Lula Belle Bryan, the new principal, whose service lasted to midcentury, raised academic standards. Agriculture was also added to the curriculum but did not prove to be a popular course. When Mather added grade twelve in 1928, it was one of only three high schools in the state, white included, to go beyond the then-standard eleven grades.

Despite inequities in the schools, as in society, a number of serious efforts were made to address important educational issues. Compulsory education began in Kershaw County in November 1920, but enforcement faltered when the state and then the county declined to hire a truant officer. In 1921 mill president R. B. Pitts voiced public concern that the county was spending less per capita on education than were the more economically successful counties it wished to emulate. Night schools at the mills helped decrease adult illiteracy, as did summer schools for adult farmworkers. In 1922 George Wittkowsky, a Camden student at the University of South Carolina, published a study identifying problems in the county's education system affected by overall inequities and economic inadequacies. In 1925 Superintendent John G. Richards appealed directly to parents, giving specific advice about ways they could help students to do better in school. Parent-teacher organizations formed in following years in black and white schools. Also in 1925 Judge Mendel Smith linked problems of "the current crime wave" to situations that could be improved through better education. Reviewing schools in fall 1928 under the duress of "almost complete crop failure," county superintendent J. Team Gettys advocated consolidations of schools to save money and to improve education for a better future. Curriculum experiments brought government films to rural classrooms by mid-decade and radios for music classes by the end of the decade.

It was not until 1929 that a woman was elected to a public office in Kershaw County. In July, Kathleen B. Watts, who had been principal of the Lugoff school and head of Antioch High School, began her first four-year term as county superintendent of education. The press noted too that she was "one of the few women in South Carolina to represent the voters officially." Mrs. Watts was a tireless advocate promoting close ties between schools and communities for mutual benefit.

One popular educational activity, the school pageant, was brought to an exceptional pinnacle in May 1925 when eight hundred costumed schoolchildren, with some community members, performed in a three-hour, locally written outdoor production, *Camden: Yesterday and Today.* Staged on the golf links of the Kirkwood Hotel after the close of the tourist season and filmed for national newsreel coverage, the production marked the one hundredth anniversary of Lafayette's visit to Camden.

The writer and director of the production was the Camden High teacher Mary Frances Blackwell of Kershaw, soon afterward Mrs. Donald Morrison. She had studied theater in New York and acted in community theater productions in Kershaw and Camden. The script used material from Kirkland and Kennedy's *Historic Camden,* the second volume of which had recently been published. Music and dance as well as elaborate costumes and props enhanced the pageantry. Dancing styles included the symbolic, such as representing freedom or nature; the representational, such as those of Indians; and the historic, such as the minuet or the Virginia reel.

When possible, local historical figures were portrayed by student-descendants and costumes included authentic antique garments. An antiquated coach, pulled by a team of horses, dramatically enhanced the scene of Lafayette's arrival. Other episodes presented King Hagler, Joseph Kershaw, Agnes of Glasgow, Cornwallis, George Washington, and Richard Kirkland, and these concluded with a rousing horseback ride by high-school boys as Hampton's Red Shirts. Community participants included Great War veterans, a fifty-member black choir singing

Participants in the 1925 local-history pageant presented by townspeople, including eight hundred schoolchildren, on the grounds of the Kirkwood Hotel. Courtesy of the Camden Archives

spirituals, and small black boys clogging to "Turkey in the Straw." Viewed by an audience said to number three thousand and with scenes shown in movie theaters in many locations, the production was discussed for many years.

For reasons of enormous tragedy, an event at a country school eight miles southeast of Camden attracted nationwide attention and is still annually memorialized. On the evening of May 17, 1923, some three hundred adults and children who were attending a traditional graduation play on the second floor of the Cleveland School were caught in a horrific fire that left seventy-seven dead, countless injured, and a community traumatized. Because of close ties, almost every family for miles around lost at least one relative, many lost several, and some entire families were lost. The audience was especially large that night.

Because the well-respected school was to be consolidated, it was supposed to be closed for good after this night, and students were to attend other schools the following year. The last act of the play *Topsy Turvy* had just begun when an overhead oil lamp fell to the stage floor, catching the dried greenery of stage decorations afire. Flames spread. The audience, at first calm, panicked at the only exit to the first floor, a narrow, unlighted stairway between two walls. The press of bodies soon became a logjam of crushed and struggling humanity that could not be extricated.

Upstairs some persons jumped from windows into the darkness below and some were thrown; various injuries and additional deaths resulted. All those left inside were consumed by the flames that leveled the building to smoking ruins by morning light. Tales of terror and tales of heroism have been repeated for generations.[51]

Most of the victims, largely unidentifiable, were buried together in a huge forty by seventy foot mass grave at Beulah Methodist Church, one mile from the school. At the school site a large marker bears the names of those who died.[52] An annual memorial service is observed at Beulah Church.

After the fire, sympathy and offers of assistance were immediate from many directions. Funds were set up to help survivors and the families of victims. The American Red Cross assisted under its new plan for disaster relief. Charlotte Thompson, benefactoress of St. Mary's (Our Lady) Catholic Church in Camden, sold school trustees her historic home, the Terraces, at a nominal fee to serve as the new consolidated school, which was afterward named for her.[53] Benefiting future generations, the South Carolina legislature mandated fire exits

Memorial monument on the site of the 1923 Cleveland School fire

and other safety measures for public buildings and required fire drills and fire-safety training in schools.

Churches

In seeking to deal with problems in the 1920s, many people sought spiritual guidance through long-established denominations and churches. Others found inspiration in the preachings of other religious bodies, such as Seventh-Day Adventist, Holiness, and Pentecostal, that had begun to attract followers in Kershaw County.

For various denominations, revival meetings, which were often held in tents, drew large crowds. Music and singing were almost always major features. At the Camden mill villages one of the most popular preachers was "the Indian Evangelist" whom the press described as a full-blooded Cherokee. Between services the Reverend A. S. Lockee captivated the attention of children with Indian stories and bow-and-arrow-making demonstrations. In 1921 Wateree Baptist Church added 104 members following a revival he had led.

Enthusiastic revivals near Blaney led Columbia newspapermen to refer to participants as "holy rollers." When the Camden newspaper used the term in a local obituary, the editor was politely reprimanded by the wife of the late preacher, who had stitched together cotton sacks to make the first tent in which he preached. The eastern part of the county was in an area especially influenced from the mid-1920s by meetings of the High Hills True Light Church. One True Light revival attracted wide attention in 1927 when it continued unabated for ninety-five days. Among black congregations, revivals with "boy" preachers had special appeal. While evangelists came and went, a number of county churches were established from roots set down in revival meetings.

In times of trouble, different congregations often pulled together. When a 1925 fire almost totally destroyed Trinity United Methodist Church, Mt. Moriah Baptist Church shared meeting space with them, and black and white citizens alike contributed funds for rebuilding. Black churches also contributed aid to victims of the Cleveland fire, all but one of whom were white. In addition Jewish citizens contributed to campaigns that provided supplies to build Christian churches.

Health Agencies

In 1920 efforts were renewed to organize charitable work in the community under the umbrella group Associated Charities, which had formed earlier but lapsed. Shortly silver teas, popular fund-raisers appealing to winter tourists, were under way to benefit the efforts. Organized support was critical early in 1921 when the main building of Camden Hospital was consumed by fire and required forty thousand dollars to rebuild. When Bernard Baruch visited the site to offer some assistance, the Hospital Auxiliary already had a bridge benefit under way.

The Camden Hospital, which served Kershaw County from 1922 through 1958. Courtesy of the Camden Archives

The Civic League went to work securing volunteers to lend cars or give rides to people needing transportation to distant hospitals while repair work was under way. With community fund-raising directed to black and white businessmen and churches as well as to the winter colony, the new building was completed in early 1922. Within a few years the hospital qualified for funding from the Duke Endowment, a continuous annual contribution. An especially successful benefit for tourists at the Court Inn in 1928 raised two thousand dollars for the hospital in one evening. The hospital continued to rely also on the proceeds of its original endowment from the Burdell Fund, which consisted of profits from the crop production and rental of agricultural acreage in Lugoff.

Several strides forward in public health began in 1920. When the public health nurse Annie O'Dell conducted a survey of the county's children that year, she found "defective teeth" to be the most common health problem. She initiated a campaign to fatten up underweight children with foods such as collard greens and milk in order to prevent influenza and tuberculosis. Nutrition education was directed to adults as well. Pellagra, which had been discovered to be preventable by the addition of vegetables and dairy products to the daily diet, was widespread in the county. It caused suffering, dementia, and death, especially among the county's poor and elderly, whose diets were often limited to fatback and cornbread. Furthermore a lack of rural medical services prompted many persons to rely on home remedies or to seek folk cures from "root doctors." Cassatt's "Doc Sheorn" gained a reputation for prescribing castor oil for a wide range of ailments. Another root doctor was found guilty of Prohibition violations.

In spring 1921 the Red Cross sponsored a dance at the DAR Hall, the historic old courthouse, to benefit public health nursing, and later in the year the Public Health Nursing Association was organized under Dr. John W. Corbett. The following year the Red Cross sent a county youngster suffering from infantile paralysis to a Georgia hospital and published before-and-after photos to prove the effectiveness of treatment.

By mid-decade baby parades and baby contests were popular among society matrons and mill mothers alike. Doctors and public health nurses served as judges and encouraged such competitions to educate parents in child care. Prizes went to chubby, active babies, as contests were won based on weights and measurements taken by health officials, who also discussed immunizations and hygiene with parents.

Associated Charities was busy in the decade organizing society mothers as the Junior Welfare Workers (League) to aid public health officials in improving the health of area children. Free help was sought for individual children from medical personnel such as Dr. D. C. Hinson of Kershaw, a dentist who moved to Camden in 1929, and Jerome Hoffer Sr., a jeweler-optometrist who fitted glasses for the Hoffer Company.

With economic conditions bearing down on needy families late in the decade, Associated Charities looked to many needs. One of the Red Cross members, Margaret Carrison (Mrs. W. J.) Mayfield, took special interest in the children and was part of the Goodfellows club that organized specifically to provide Christmas cheer and small treats for children usually deprived of them. The proceeds of Junior Welfare League fund-raising for this purpose were placed in Mrs. Mayfield's hands.

The Camden Airport

Of all the changes in the 1920s, the one that moved Camden and the county forward most dramatically into a new era was the building of the Camden Airport, Woodward Field, which officially opened in November 1929. The event was timed to coincide with the usual fanfare opening the annual county fair. The new field was named for the airport benefactor Ernest Woodward, who had donated the property north of Camden along U.S. Highway 1. Until Camden had an airport, pilots in the infancy of aviation made landings where they could visually see open spaces on the ground. Reportedly too often to suit the sportsman Woodward, they were landing on the local polo field or race track, to the dismay of horses and riders alike.

Celebrating the safe landing of a biplane in the grassy fields that preceded later runways at Woodward Field. Courtesy of the Camden Archives

Almost as soon as construction began, the airport was in use and prompting other changes. By spring 1929 Camden Building and Supply was selling "over 100 lots priced low to sell quick." The airport subdivision opened on a new, paved road. Even before the first hangar was built, Mabel Cody's Woco-Pep Flying Circus was taking off and landing at the airfield and entertaining the public with daredevil stunts. Billed as the niece of Buffalo Bill, she was advertising Woco-Pep gas and offering rides to "see beautiful Camden from the air." Passengers paid according to their weight, a penny a pound. By December the aviator N. N. Prentiss was permanently stationed at the field to give rides to sightseers or to take them on trips.

Many people dreamed of the positive impact that the new flying machines would have on the future. Yet that impact, as well as the effects of the electrical power that was beginning to flow from the Wateree Dam on the opposite side of the county, would have to wait for a time. The October 1929 stock market crash, which was more keenly felt elsewhere at first, would combine with southern agricultural woes to depress for some time the flowering of technology, industrialization, and communications.

15

Empty Pockets

The Great Depression

The decade of the 1930s was shadowed by the local, national, and international hard times that became known as the Great Depression. When 1930 rolled in, it followed not only the tumultuous national crisis of the 1929 stock market crash but also what had been locally the wettest year on record, a period with three damaging tornadoes in the area. In the new decade the summer of 1930 was sweltering, with temperatures of more than one hundred degrees for several weeks. The extended drought pattern, while not as intense as in the infamous western Dust Bowl, nevertheless parched fields and raised dust storms that further robbed soil of its fertility.[1] The weather extremes added personal misery to lives already troubled with economic woes. The January 17, 1930, *Camden Chronicle* reported the urgent appeal of the Associated Charities of Camden and Kershaw County on behalf of the needy: "The failure of the cotton crop for three years and the lack of employment makes [*sic*] real distress and suffering. These people do not want charity—they want employment."

At the beginning of the hard times, the concept of "rugged individualism" prevailed, a belief that people were better off working out their own problems without governmental interference. The concept "helping people help themselves" was advocated locally as well as nationally. As the Depression deepened, however, realization set in that more than local help was essential, and gradually federal money was sought to relieve suffering. President Herbert Hoover, whose name was often associated with the lean years, had set up a small public works program by the time he left office. In March 1933 President Franklin D. Roosevelt, elected on the general promise of "a new deal," was inaugurated. Roosevelt's tackling of the problems of the Depression brought both change and controversy but overall was locally welcomed. Over the rest of the decade substantial changes—some temporary, some long-lasting—took effect in Kershaw County.

The Hoover Years

In the early years of the decade the county struggled largely on its own to deal with the growing difficulties of the times. An area that had long prided itself on possessing special qualities, Kershaw County more and more frequently accepted public acknowledgment as one of the state's smallest and poorest counties. There was little to spare in the public coffers, and volunteer efforts had to be relied on to aid the poor and needy.

Local Economy

During the worsening financial crisis that gripped the nation, in January 1930 the Bank of Bethune closed its doors and elected its former cashier G. E. Parrott as receiver. The following month all the banks of Kershaw County met at Bethune and joined hands to support a new agricultural program. However, public nervousness was fueled by bank runs and closings nationwide. In January 1931 the Loan and Savings Bank in Camden closed its doors. Later in the year Dr. R. E. Stevenson, receiver, began mailing installments for partial payments while the bank reorganized. All banks struggled with heavy withdrawals during the continued uncertainties.

Faltering businesses also caused concern, and failures were common. In March 1930 the decade-old Camden Clothing Company was sold at a sheriff's sale. Perhaps even more than closings, sluggish sales marred the general atmosphere in which "money was hard to get." The county farm agent warned in late 1930 that many farmers would find it practically impossible to get credit the next year.

Railroad profits sank. The railroads had always depended on travelers, farmers, mills, and businesses—all of which were suffering. Highway motor transports competed for the dwindling commerce at less expense. By 1930 the Seaboard, having expanded to Miami, Florida, was financially overextended and was in receivership. Meanwhile, as local governments faced reduced railroad tax revenues, debts that had been undertaken to entice railroads to build in earlier years fell due. In 1932 Kershaw County had insufficient funds to pay maturing refunded bonds that had originally been issued in 1887 to construct the local section of the Three C's Railroad. The county avoided default by making installment payments at 5 percent interest.[2]

In September 1931 S.C. comptroller general A. J. Beattie, a former Kershaw County legislator, instructed county sheriffs to force the collection of back taxes. The newspaper called what lay ahead "a winter of distress." Local governments were warned to expect the burden of care for the unemployed. Yet few persons encouraged a direct dole. A number suggested a program of public works, although a plan was not yet significantly organized.

A shifting number of transients added to the hard times for the population within the county's borders. Individuals and families searching for work or improved conditions became familiar sights. Likewise numbers of county natives also took to the roadways or railways, leaving home and family to find work to feed those staying behind. The November 1, 1935, *Chronicle* summarized distinctions among the classes of vagrants who had become familiar since the early part of the decade. The "hobo" was a hard worker whose migrations were important to the economy of seasonal employment. He traveled on wheels, though "not necessarily by ticket." The "tramp" walked, migrating "by whim or chance," working off and on but "not by sense of responsibility." Both types were said to despise the "bum," who traveled nowhere and did nothing, living by "begging, borrowing, stealing, loafing." Some transients traded odd jobs for food at homes and farms in the county.

The Depression conditions grew more extreme in 1932. Economic difficulties were increasing with more bank failures looming. South Carolina had no money to pay schoolteachers, and Kershaw County teachers were receiving vouchers for salaries. Local officials urged teachers not to sell their vouchers below face value and promised that they would be redeemed. Area merchants and businessmen accepted the vouchers like regular currency, and some papers exchanged hands several times. Concerns were widespread about whether schools could open another session under such conditions.

Also in the same month unemployed Great War veterans from across the country assembled in Washington, D.C., to request early payment of the bonuses that had been promised them for their military service. On June 13, 1932, S.C. Supreme Court judge Mendel L. Smith addressed sympathetic listeners at American Legion Post 17 in his Camden hometown. Referring to those "unemployed half-starved comrades of yours and mine, many of whom have left behind wives and children, broken in spirit and hope for the ordinary necessities of this life," Judge Smith stated: "Sixteen years ago the men who are camped now in . . . Washington were received there and elsewhere with flying banners, [martial] music and the vociferous applause and greetings of the American people. . . . Today they are cuffed about under police vigilance, treated as common thugs and anarchists—the men who dared all to save our institutions and to perpetuate to our generations the blessings of freedom and democracy." He expounded that "no right is more sacred or more essential to free government than the right of the people peaceably to assemble to petition any department of the government for a redress of their grievances."[3] In July 28, in the sweltering summer, a violent confrontation erupted in Washington between the "bonus marchers" and the U.S. troops sent by President Hoover to break up their encampment.

That same month Kershaw County's widely admired Congressional Medal of Honor recipient Hobson Hilton was elected as commander of the South Carolina American Legion. A Westville native and former sergeant, Hilton had lost an arm in France during the war when he rushed a machine gun nest, killing six and capturing ten enemy soldiers before being struck by an exploding shell. In the public eye afterward, he was outspoken on veterans' issues.[4] In September

1932 the Kershaw County American Legion was on record in support of immediate payment of the bonuses. The local group maintained unanimous support until the issue was at long last resolved in the veterans' favor three years later.

Meanwhile in 1932 L. B. Ogburn, a Wateree River bridge keeper, was the first farmer of the season to get a new bale of cotton picked out and ginned on the Camden market. The traditional 1¢ above the regular market price for the first bale—6½¢ per pound—was only one-third the price of cotton three years earlier. At local farmers' meetings debate continued about ways to improve prices, including the suggestion being advanced throughout southern states to "outlaw" the growing of cotton for a season.

In September 1932, when Midway School opened late because of funding problems, parents were told to anticipate a short session for the same reason. They were urged to help their children concentrate to get work done in the short time. For the first time, rather than the traditional annual change of faculty thought healthy for a school, the same teachers were returning. Across the county other schools coped in similar fashion. In individual cases some children stopped attending school when families could no longer afford clothing or books for them or when their labor was needed to help the family survive. However, children in some of the poorest families actually attended school more since there were fewer paying jobs for their labor.

One school district in 1930 improved educational opportunities for several hundred children by addressing school operating costs. In the hilly upper part of Kershaw County, where recent highway improvements were enhancing access, a large new brick school, Baron DeKalb, consolidated more than a half dozen smaller rural schools in what the July 25, 1930, *Camden Chronicle* called "a wide and populous territory." Located near the site of the Battle of Camden, the school took its name from that battle's hero, who was also memorialized by the name of the nearby railroad's DeKalb Station, the surrounding DeKalb community, and the area's post office, at times alternately called Kalb.

Schools that were consolidated included the white schools of Cantey, DeKalb, Flat Rock, Lockhart, Piedmont, Truesdale, Westville, Whitty, and "possibly other smaller schools," according to a list at the time. The consolidation was a cost-cutting initiative in order to make a high school education accessible in the area. The first diplomas were given in 1934.

Baron DeKalb, for first graders through high schoolers, was one of the state's "most modern school buildings in the rural districts." In its opening months, with a student population of around three hundred and a building that was not quite complete, some of the classes met temporarily in the converted home of the late Capt. L. L. Clyburn at DeKalb Station. The completed new school was dedicated on November 26. Pride in the new facility quickly unified a widespread area and symbolized hope during hard times.

Baron DeKalb pupils who lived at long distances were transported to school aboard open-bed trucks hand-fitted with simple wooden benches. As they had done before, a number of students still walked or rode farm wagons, horses, or mules to school. Rarely a student came by auto.[5] Occasionally the transportation was a "wheel," as the motorcycle was called. At least one of the school's early female teachers rode to Baron DeKalb each day by horseback. Like almost all who attended the county's other rural schools, the children rose at daylight to complete chores on the family farms before proceeding to school. The board set opening time, at least in the fall harvest season, at 9:00 A.M., "in order that the children may get out earlier and have the afternoon to assist in gathering the crops."

Community Spirit

On a day-to-day basis people in various parts of Kershaw County survived economic ups and downs in their traditional way, pulling together and keeping up the spirit of community. Not all was Depression gloom, for community activities emphasized the positive and filled unemployed hours with music, worship, sports, and entertainments as well as education and other meaningful tasks. As did schools and churches, local organizations led by farm and home-extension agents from the state's land-grant colleges did much to assist the holding together of communities. Such organizations were formed separately and at different times among white and black citizens, as the colleges carried out missions to disseminate the findings of agricultural and home-living research to the public.

By 1930 each rural community had a Home Demonstration Club and a community house. Even where it was little more than a shelter, the community house was a gathering point for meetings and informal get-togethers, and it was used by various groups. In summer 1930 the Kershaw County Council of Farm Women, unifying the clubs, raised a camp house five miles north of Camden at Childers Mill, near DeKalb.[6] The millpond, owned by J. B. (Blake) Zemp of Camden, was most often called Lake Shamokin after the following year, when Zemp began milling flour there and with other local men developed a summer swimming and playground area.[7] The modern building of the Camden Shrine Club stands at the location of the old camp house.

The recreational site was ready by August 1930 in time for the first of many 4-H camps in coming years and for the beginning of weekly benefit square dances hosted by the farm women. For the early dances, W. T. Dempster and his fiddlers furnished the music, and the farm women sold cold drinks. Proceeds supported a scholarship for a 4-H club girl to attend Winthrop College. The campsite was described as in "a beautiful pine grove," and the building where the dances were held was "spacious enough for [dancers] and . . . onlookers too." The site quickly became a popular location for other area events as well.

Community Exhibits and Activities

Also in the fall of 1930 farm and home agents organized individual community fairs to encourage the development of exhibits for an improved county fair in October. They challenged each community to tout its best to awaken the spirit of its residents. Such events were educational for persons of all ages; there they received information and ideas for improvements on farms and in homes. Schools and their exhibits were a major part of each fair, so that the public could examine the products of the local education system.

There were fairs at Antioch, Bethune, Blaney, Cassatt, Charlotte Thompson, Liberty Hill, Mt. Pisgah, and Pine Grove, with a Clemson judge at each. The Blaney fair was filled to capacity, with even more exhibits than expected. The Liberty Hill fair bragged, "No sign of hard times," displaying with pride that the local schoolchildren had started their first newspaper, the "Liberty Hill School News." At the Mt. Pisgah fair, besides exhibits of community products and a lunch served by the ladies, there was good country fun—horse racing, mule walking, a cow-judging contest, and an afternoon basketball game. It was reported that "Mrs. [Kathleen] Watts, county superintendent of education, showed unusual skill in hitching and unhitching a horse from a buggy in the horse-hitching contest for the ladies." In 1931 Bethune expanded its fair to two days. The Blaney fair displayed more than fifteen kinds of fresh vegetables, canned fruits and vegetables, fancy work (needlework), and flowers. One exhibit alone included eleven different fresh vegetables.

Other community activities grew out of the spirit of cooperation and friendly competition. In spring 1932 the Midway Home Demonstration Club divided into sides to make quilts, with the side making the most having to host a party for the other. At the home of Mrs. Henry McCoy, losers dressed in "tacky" costumes to entertain the winners with a bountiful supper, games, and old-time country music provided by "the Ray boys."

Bethune in 1932 organized a library association to establish a community library. The group freshened an available building with paint and kalsomine (whitewash) and started collecting books. A friend in Philadelphia donated one hundred volumes. About the same time a young men's club also organized in Bethune.

A large crowd at the 1932 Blaney community fair viewed new competitions for cut flowers and potted plants along with twenty-five different varieties of fresh vegetables; other exhibits included jellies, pickles, cakes, breads, and needlework. Special attention was paid to J. M. Martin's exhibit of ribbon cane and sorghum, and to H. A. Hawkins's huge pumpkin.

Community enthusiasm spilled over to the county fair at the end of October. White students on Friday and black students on Saturday lined up by schools for their traditional annual parades down Camden's Broad Street to enter the midway gates free of charge. Fair exhibits were admired, such as the presentation from Lugoff that displayed "everything from flowers to a model little farm." Blaney citizens showed, besides farm products, other ways that cash was being earned in that community, with homemade furniture and a handmade violin on exhibit. Residents of Bethune and Gates Ford displayed honey, cream, candles, and even shrubs as samples of their household and farm products.

The largest exhibitor of cattle at the county fair was N. P. Gettys, while John L. Weeks's Hereford bull was the grand beef champion. The *Camden Chronicle* reported: "The midway, especially at night, with all its gala lights is attracting the crowds daily. The riding devices, ever-popular with the youngsters[,] are kept busy with their passengers. 'Bingo,' that old and young like to play, draws its share of patrons. The fat man, the old plantation show, the house of freaks, all the side shows are well patronized." The newspaper summarized the main benefit of the county fair: "the carnival spirit prevails, drawing closer urban and rural population, thus forming friendships and good feeling for one another in discussing the problems to be met every day."

Causes

Community spirit carried over to worthy causes. Notable examples were those that helped provide life-saving food, clothing, and shelter in hard times. In other situations communities sometimes helped individuals achieve their dreams. For example, Camden rallied behind fund-raising to help send the local high school football team to its annual summer camp at French Broad River in North Carolina. Elmer Nolan three decades later recalled the trips to football camp in the 1930s:

> The 185 mile journey in those days was made in an open truck loaned to the football team by the late Blake Zemp, who also gave Camden High the present football field [Zemp Stadium] that bears his name. Half-filled with straw to cushion the hard floors, the truck was without seats on top. We always wondered what would happen if it started to rain. . . . Boys who attended football camp during those years had to work during the summer months and pay their own fare. I recall that eight varsity members of the state championship club [1936] of my senior year shoveled coal 10 hours a day for three weeks to pay their way to football camp. Little wonder they dubbed the line as the days of the hungry athlete . . . during my four years of football at Camden High, not one boy quit the team.[8]

Recreation

Like community functions, club activities and outdoor recreation often drew people together. In 1932 the Camden Shrine Club entertained west of the Wateree at Wildwood Manor, the property of Karl T. Roseborough. More than forty members and guests pitched horseshoes and ate fried chicken with trimmings prepared by Gus Ward of the Lugoff area. Fish fries and picnics were common club and community functions.

That same year, when the Kirkwood Hotel closed for the summer and turned over its small links to the city of Camden, prices for summer golf were reduced. Membership fees for the whole summer were five dollars per person, with caddy fees at twenty-five cents for eighteen holes. The clubhouse opened to the public in the afternoons, and some locals were able to gather regularly in an elegant setting.

However, most families had to keep recreational expenses minimal, choosing instead swimming and sometimes camping as means of escaping the summer heat. Traditional swimming holes as well as organized areas such as Big Springs and Colonial Lake continued to draw patrons. A drowning tragedy reported in the September 2, 1932, *Chronicle* verified that some families had also begun taking recreational advantage of the impoundment behind the Wateree Dam. In reporting the accidental death of four-year-old Tommy, the son of Mr. and Mrs. Dewey J. Creed, the paper stated: "Mr. Creed and several associates have a nice cottage on a pretty island in the lake. Many motor boats are at a beach near the lake and many townspeople have been guests for the week-end on the island." A remnant of Creed Island, in present Clearwater Cove, is still known to some by its early name.

The Winter Season

In some circles during the Hoover years, life continued much as before. Although the winter tourist season was slow to open during the months following the stock market crash, the visiting colony had gathered in force by the first of the following year. For the equestrian-minded, on January 1, 1930, the New Year's Day races opened in Camden on a "fine new day at Springdale," where H. D. Kirkover and E. L. Woodward were joint owners of a new course they had developed on an old cotton field, near an earlier racing field. The inaugural running of the Carolina Cup steeplechase drew a large and excited crowd to the Springdale Race Course in spring 1930. No admission was charged in the early years, the race over timber hurdles being "for sport, not profit" and for "gentlemanly" competition, not "base diversion."

The 1930 tourist season was a busy one. The many bridle trails winding through area pine woods in and out of town were described as constantly in use by many recreational riders. Polo matches and field sports attracted many people. One of the pioneer winter residents, Mrs. Julie Warden (William N.) Kerr of New York, carried on without interruption her tradition since the late 1890s of presenting informal Sunday afternoon receptions for her friends at her Greene Street home Mostly Hall, which was near the Kirkwood Hotel.[9] Mrs. Sarah K.

Winkler resumed her publicity work, busily supplying columns of social news to local and northern papers.[10] The photographer E. T. Start, who had by that time worked in Camden for nearly three decades of tourist seasons, actively captured images of local scenes and individuals.[11]

Kershaw County's seasonal tearooms opened in 1930 as usual. Tourist columns referred to the Green Leaf Villa, the Precipice, and the Woman's Exchange in the Camden area; to Mt. Pleasant south of town; to the Pines north of town; and to the Hill Top Tea Room in Liberty Hill. Also in operation were Mrs. Catherine H. Goodale's Studio Shop, the Torii Shop, and exclusive hotel lobby shops, complete with displays of luxury goods, art, and books.

There were new additions to the old places. About 1930 J. A. Sterne and his family took over management of the Hotel Camden on DeKalb Street. At Boykin in January 1930 Miss Frances Boykin and Richard Blackwell "Dixie" Boykin opened the Old Mill Tea Room, a place "rustic in appearance with cheerful fires." In February 1930 another new tearoom, Thickety (also Thickety Place), opened

A Carolina Cup steeplechasing photograph that inspired Jak Smyrl's design for the weather vane at the Springdale course, where the event was first held in 1930. Courtesy of the Camden Archives

at the home of Mrs. W. D. Trantham II, not far from the Sarsfield golf links. Here, as the artist Jane Bauskett Trantham, she soon became noted for cutting silhouettes, those of children and of grandparents being in special demand.

In early 1931 K. G. Whistler's Precipice tearoom, where miniature golf was still a popular feature, expanded under new management, and a night club opened on the premises. In the fall of 1931 Mrs. H. L. Schlosburg opened an additional tourist housing establishment, the Marion-Frances Inn, in her remodeled home at the corner of Laurens and Lyttleton streets. In December 1931 Ruth Richards added Sunday and Thursday buffet suppers to the Green Leaf Villa's operations.

Highway 1

An important influence on tourism was completed in 1931 when the final section of U.S. Highway 1 was paved at its approximate midpoint, near Cheraw, about sixty miles from Camden.[12] The first national highway now stretched in a continuous hard surface from Canada to Miami, linking all state capitals along the way. U.S. Highway 1 ran through Kershaw County along the old Sandhills route, paralleling and crisscrossing the Seaboard railway. In South Carolina it threaded together the main street sections from northernmost Cheraw, Patrick, and McBee with Kershaw County's Bethune, Cassatt, Camden, Lugoff, and Blaney and southward to Columbia. South Carolina's U.S. Highway 1 Association, of which Henry G. Carrison of Camden was one of four board members, went right to work advertising the use of the highway for business and travel to reach points in the state and in other states north and south. One of the highway's effects was to improve motor-travel access for northern visitors to Kershaw County's resort areas.

Estate Sales

Tourist society news columns in 1931 referred to the "prevailing low price of land in all sections" around Camden. Because of deflation, visitors were finding this an "opportune time to buy." For example, the Chicago contractor Clifford M. Leonard purchased thousands of acres north of Camden, including the old Mickle place known as Sunny Hill, and another tract, Chancefield, where he built a large new home.[13] In the meantime Leonard was leasing another Camden estate adjoining the Sarsfield golf course. With the increased popularity of field sports and more land being devoted to hunting, interest in conservation likewise grew among serious outdoorsmen.[14]

In addition to land for sale, labor and supplies were available. Unemployed workmen were anxious to be hired, and businessmen were eager to sell supplies. Antiques and furnishings from old homes were being sold by families short on cash. Persons of means who owned or acquired local estates began a significant period of restoration and building. Both social columns and the grapevine of the leisure class passed the word that fine materials, locally made or acquired from old dwellings to be pulled down, were available for building and improvements. Recognizing opportunity, K. G. Whistler in 1931 hired an experienced brick man at his Precipice property at Paint Hill and began manufacturing bricks, said to have been especially "beautiful in color." In the same year R. A. Carpenter opened Wateree Lumber Company near the Seaboard freight station to manufacture rough and dressed native pine lumber.[15]

Landscapers and yard men too were available for hire to improve the grounds of grand homes. Some of the gardens noted for their beauty had been laid out in earlier years by K. G. Whistler or by Samuel Russell. To maintain these estates and to improve others, landscape architects were often brought in from out of town. One was Thomas W. Miller of Lexington, North Carolina, head of the southern branch of America's largest landscape company, Lewis and Valentine of Pennsylvania. Miller and his wife, Margaret, also a horticulturist, established a company of their own in Camden, the Colonial Boxwood Company, advertised as "Big Tree Movers." They also specialized in shrubbery, including "rare evergreens," some of which Miller brought from the North Carolina mountains where he spent his summers collecting plants. The Camden landscaper J. W. "Woodie" Trotter, owner of Evergreen Nurseries, countered out-of-town competition by advising, "Get Fresh Plants: Out of ground only a few hours—not for several days."

In spring 1932 a Camden Garden Club "pilgrimage" toured landscaped showplaces that were "unusually lovely just now"—Cedar Knoll (Mr. and Mrs. Robert W. Pomeroy), Goodie Castle (Mr. and Mrs. Carroll K. Bassett), Holly Hedge (Mr. and Mrs. Ernest Woodward), Millbank (Mr. and Mrs. Samuel Russell), and Mulberry (Mr. and Mrs. David R. Williams)—and ended at Miss Fannie B. Fletcher's Little Hedges at Brevard Place. In the same year Ward Belcher purchased Horse Branch Hall, the old homestead originally built by the McRaes, and announced his intention to renovate it to a showplace. Garden Club interest was especially keen on the cultivation of azaleas. A slide-lecture in the school auditorium was well attended when the noted Charlotte, North Carolina, landscape architect E. S. Draper featured Kershaw County estates among the illustrations of his talk on historic southern gardens.[16]

In September 1932 two local men, M. L. Smith Jr. and G. T. Little Jr., organized a new business, Smith & Little Co., with J. H. Watkins as manager, to deal with insurance, real estate, rentals, and hunting preserves. "Farm property is now a real investment," they advised. "Never before have our choicest lands been so cheap. Vacant property in our City can be developed at unheard of prices." Such enticements to the affluent were spread through society news and travel articles produced by the publicists hired by the hotels and local business community. Both the highway and railroad associations also joined in publicity.

Real estate, in contrast to the failing banks and businesses, seemed to some people with money a safer investment for the times. A number of property transfers in Kershaw County resulted in the ownership of large holdings shifting from local to northern hands.

Polo

An opposite type of transfer, from northern to local hands, describes participation in the sport of polo during the 1930s. Although publicity columns spoke of polo games in glowing terms, its local historian, John H. Daniels, says that the early years of the Depression left the sport languishing because of the absence of the northern players who had once been regulars here.[17] Another blow to the sport occurred in February 1932 during the running of the Carolina Cup when the polo stables near the Kirkwood Hotel burned to the ground, destroying valuable ponies as well.

That same month Camden Polo Club president Samuel Russell publicly expressed regrets "that more southern boys do not go in for the sport." He was, in fact, inviting their participation. Southerners, after all, were widely admired for fine horsemanship. However, the expensive demands of leisure time and the required equipment and string of polo ponies needed had previously put the sport as played at the tourist hotels generally beyond the means of local equestrians. The rejuvenation of the sport by horsemen with local ties and local ponies was recalled by one of its participants, Henry Savage Jr., who described 1932 summertime cow-pasture practices at Mulberry Plantation in an article two years later in *Polo* magazine. By September 1932 the state's first polo game between all-local teams with local mounts was played in Camden. By the time the winter season opened, polo games were being played three times a week, and a women's team was attempted again with occasional practice games.

Deflation Benefits

The deflated economic conditions of the Depression sometimes proved favorable in other ways to local interests. For a long time the Ladies Aid Society of Grace Episcopal Church had been working to construct a parish house. Church fund-raising, begun in previous years and much of it through the Woman's Exchange, benefited from the lower costs of materials and labor. In early 1932 a one-story brick parish house was completed. Connected to the main church building, it included a rector's study, a kitchen, six classrooms, a kindergarten, choir rooms, and an auditorium seating three hundred. Silver teas continued to benefit its furnishing and maintenance.

Women of Bethesda Presbyterian Church too raised donations for their church needs and improvements by hosting silver teas, typically serving sandwiches, cakes, mints, tea, and coffee. At Bethune during the Thanksgiving season of 1932, Methodist women served a widely patronized turkey supper at the King-Davis Hotel to benefit their nearly completed new parsonage. The DAR sponsored silver teas, card parties, and dances for restorations to their aging headquarters in Camden, the historic old county courthouse. Teas, dinners, and other benefit entertainments, from small bridge parties to large balls, were most profitably timed to take place during the winter tourist season, and the money raised during the Depression sometimes went further when spent.

Charitable Help

At the beginning of the decade Associated Charities of Camden and Kershaw County had been in operation for ten years. Linking several different charity efforts, the association had never before faced as many needs as during the early years of the Depression. In January 1930 the newspaper said of the beneficial work of current president Margaret C. Mayfield of Camden: "She began her work in the war and became so interested that at its close she continued with the Home Service Bureau of the Red Cross and gradually has worked with the sick and needy until she might almost be said to be 'The Charities' itself." An educated woman of the local Carrison family, Mrs. Mayfield was an effective liaison who appealed to both the year-round community and the winter colony in support of charitable goals. Among both groups significant contributions were made to alleviate suffering.

The Children's Home

In June 1930 Associated Charities purchased the Hinson property, the old James L. Brasington home at 814 Fair Street, to set up a children's home, which it had chartered in April. By September it housed fourteen children from two to twelve years of age. On two and three-fourths acres, the home had four large and two small rooms, along with a "large roomy chicken yard and large vegetable garden with cow barn." Property for its use was soon expanded and other rooms added, and the Children's Home and other charity work were dovetailed. Beggars requesting food were referred to the home, where they were provided appropriate work in exchange for food and other necessities. Chores included gardening and food preservation, which fed children at the home as well as other charity cases. Carpentry, painting, cleaning, laundry, and other services for the Children's Home and for care of sick and needy persons also provided work for the otherwise unemployed.

The Duke Endowment, the legacy of Duke Power Company founder James Buchanan Duke, contributed annually to the Children's Home, as well as to Camden Hospital. The fund that aided children's homes and hospitals throughout the Carolinas praised the operation of the local establishment, where the expense for keeping a child was $145.20 a year, compared to $322.26 at similar places elsewhere. The operation of the local home in coordination with relief work was both unusual and cost effective.

In mid-1931 a field worker, a Mrs. Gettys, was hired to drive the Associated Charities truck daily throughout the county soliciting foodstuffs. The contributions of country folk were loaded into the truck to swell the food that fed the hungry. That summer Associated Charities volunteers and clients put up more than thirteen thousand cans of vegetables and fruits, especially peaches. In addition to feeding children at the home or being given to general charity cases, canned foods were sometimes sold or exchanged for other foodstuffs and supplies. Associated Charities operated an office at the rear of the county courthouse where food and clothing were dispensed to the needy on Saturdays. On one such Saturday in February 1932, more than two hundred persons were given food, including fourteen bushels of cornmeal, several bushels of dried peas, and dozens of collards, in addition to other food having been given out during the week at the Children's Home.

Intended for emergency cases, the Children's Home served families in distress. In one of its frequent public reports in October 1931, Associated Charities described its purpose as "a children's placing home and not a home commonly known as an orphanage which takes children and keeps them until they are grown and able to care for themselves . . . we take children in that have no homes or have such homes as are entirely unsuitable and keep them only until such time as we can turn them back to their parents or guardians under proper conditions or until we can get them placed with some of the various orphanages of this state." Mrs. Mayfield was the investigator for cases of child placement.

During the Depression, South Carolina orphanages were filled to the limit and had long waiting lists, and many families could not afford to adopt extra mouths to feed. Of thirty-five children served by the local home in its first year and a half, sixteen were placed or sent back to their families or guardians under improved circumstances. Some children accepted at the home were "ill or undernourished or in bad physical condition." After receiving food and medical and dental care, most were restored to health. Children old enough to help with their care were given instruction and assigned tasks. Girls were taught sewing and useful housework; boys worked set hours in the garden. In later years some children who had been cared for in the home remembered the time with sorrow because of difficult life changes; others remembered their time there with gratitude. Circumstances were often desperate, and the Children's Home was the only chance for many.

In February 1932 Associated Charities appealed to the public for aid, describing itself as the "only institution taking care of the general charity situation." In addition to operating the Children's Home, the association dispensed medical and dental aid, clothing, food, and general welfare services. Health services were generally donated by local medical practitioners. Associated Charities pointed out: "We are the only help and refuge to hundreds of people in the county." Furthermore, the group said, "We help both black and white alike. It makes no difference . . . what a person's color is if they need help."[18]

Government Donations

In May 1932 charity workers were pleased when word came that the federal government would donate flour to the Kershaw County government for distribution by the Red Cross to the needy. Before long six hundred barrels—a three-month supply—arrived on boxcars, and forty-eight hundred sacks were given out. A similar shipment was promised at the end of three months. Some people, however, were frustrated when government red tape slowed the process of delivering aid to those most in need. To receive flour, an applicant had to submit a written application verified by a reliable citizen who personally vouched for the applicant's needy circumstances. The applicant also had to call in person to pick up the flour from the point of distribution. Pride, inability to complete paperwork, or lack of transportation hampered relief in a number of cases.

In fall 1932 the federal government, "helping people help themselves," donated 13,500 yards of cotton fabric to the community with the strict requirement that it had to be made into garments before it could be distributed to the needy. By October, Associated Charities was operating a sewing room in the Broad Street business district. Averaging use of three yards to the item, local volunteers went to work cutting and stitching to make 4,500 garments. Each day of the week, Monday through Saturday, a different church or social organization was in charge of the sewing room headquarters, where a number of machines were collected. Pleas were sent throughout the community for help on the project in many ways, from providing sandwiches and coffee for workers, to cutting cloth, to hand-sewing buttons and buttonholes. Associated Charities urged, "This coming winter promises to bear down on a great many people in Kershaw county and this Government cloth will be a God-send to large numbers."

Health Care

Health problems, such as pellagra from malnutrition, increased along with the climbing rate of poverty in the county. Education in the past decade about balanced-diet choices was lost among people who lacked enough to eat. Dr. A. W. Humphries, county health director, preached the necessity of improved sanitation to prevent the common illnesses of typhoid fever, hookworm, diarrhea, and insect-borne diseases. Large numbers of families, however, had no financial resources to afford sanitary toilets, disinfecting procedures, or screening for houses. Such families continued to rely on open wells or springs for drinking water as they were unable to afford the recommended closed pump. They also often lacked the means to give milk vessels the special care needed to prevent the spread of infection.

By 1932 the number of charity patients being treated at Camden Hospital was outnumbering the paying patients, according to the administrator Dr. John W. Corbett. Furthermore, he said, the Burdell Fund for indigent patients, based on the rental of West Wateree farmland deeded for that purpose, was now bringing in negligible income. A giant countywide fund-raising effort kicked off in the fall to meet the hospital crisis. The general chairman was A. Stanley Llewellyn. The Reverend J. W. Boykin organized "the six colored churches" that led the efforts in the black communities. W. T. Redfearn chaired work in the rural areas and was assisted by others, such as W. A. Boykin Sr. at Boykin, W. T. Holley at Mt. Pisgah, and Pat Thompson at Liberty Hill. Mrs. Harry G. Marvin, chair of the Hospital Auxiliary, organized the women, and Reverend J. B. Caston organized the churches.

Thanksgiving was set aside as a countywide "Pounding Day" for the hospital. Farmers donated produce rather than cash to the fund drive. "White and colored" schools were asked to serve as receiving depots, with teachers collecting and forwarding food contributions. A variety of benefits raised cash. There was a square dance at the Lugoff community house and an entertainment at Trinity Club at West Wateree, a mile beyond the N. P. Gettys plantation. The Camden Business Women's Club gave a card party at St. Mary's Hall. The Camden football team shared its gate proceeds from games with Barnwell and Bishopville. Henry Savage Sr. arranged three polo games, during which nurses from the hospital collected funds from the crowd. A wrestling match also raised money. Hot suppers among the black citizens were part of entertainment benefits in the Boykin area. Schoolchildren throughout the county were asked to earn and donate ten cents each, without asking their families or others for donations, and teachers were asked to give fifty cents apiece. All groups were asked to avoid house-to-house canvassing, the fund-raising approach relied on for general charity relief in the county. Volunteer efforts of all types reached throughout the county, and still the need was great.

Cultural Adjustments

People coped with the difficulties of the times in many ways. Styles and popular activities reflected a general toughening of attitudes, an admiration of strength more than polish. Heroes tended to be daredevils, challengers, and sometimes a bit rough around the edges. Those hoping for a better future took great interest in what was new, although others preferred to look back to a past they visualized as gentler and more romantic. A variety of attitudes spilled over into styles of religious worship.

Entertainments took timely twists. The Junior Welfare Workers in past years had hosted many elegant benefits. A January 1930 *Chronicle* article described their "Bowery Ball" at the Precipice Tea House to benefit the tonsil clinic. The Country Club orchestra played, but instead of formal attire, guests wore theme-related costumes: "The men were well armed, each carrying pistols in their hip pockets and several shots . . . were heard during the evening." Small tables with red-checked tablecloths and beer bottles holding candles lined the side walls. Where refreshments were sold, a large sign reading "Bar Room" amused Prohibition-era guests.

Among private and church entertainments, one of the most popular was the "tacky" party, to which guests wore ridiculously clashing and unattractive garments. A partygoer needed only imagination to be in style. The whimsical trend carried over to a 1932 bridal shower given at the C. P. DuBose shack outside town, where guests were served mulligan stew and toasted marshmallows.

Instead of favoring the fancy, delicate foods of the past decade, many appetites during the Depression longed for simpler, heartier fare. Across from the Kershaw County Courthouse in 1931 DeWhite Walters opened the Broad Street Lunch, which, typical of the decade's trend toward acronyms, became known as BSL. Its featured sandwich—a beef patty on hand-sliced loaf bread—introduced the hamburger to many. Gradually coffee shops attracted increased patronage over tearooms, and taverns with beer on tap quickly became popular after Prohibition was repealed in 1933. That same year in Lugoff, Gus Ward's Restaurant opened on the Camden-Columbia Highway and served hearty meals featuring beef and barbecue.

Competitions

Avidly followed sports pitted competitors in tests of spirit as well as tests of brawn. Local football entered a new era in the 1930s with Camden High coach John M. Villepigue's innovative offensive strategy that made the Bulldogs a state powerhouse team of the decade. His strategy, similar to but in advance of the later developed T-formation, was described in later years by Fred Mullen: "The Villepigue book of plays was diverse, using springs into the line, ball carrying ends, rapier-like straight forward thrusts, hand offs, reverses, double reverses, trap plays, and powerful end sweeps." As a result, "The play was rhythmical, fast, wide-open, deceptive, explosive, and downright breath taking! The Camden fans just loved it!"[19]

The community went wild when the Bulldogs, "the old gold and black," garnered the school's first state championship—played in Chester at dinnertime on Christmas Day 1931. At the time *Columbia State* reporter John Montgomery cited the contest as "the most sportsmanlike act of 1931 in South Carolina sports."

He explained that Camden refused the state championship on a forfeit: "John G. Richards, Jr., superintendent of Camden schools, made a statement in behalf of Camden . . . offering to play Chester, upper state champion, for it. In story-book fashion, Camden captured the state Class B championship by a decisive margin, breaking the reign of Chester that had lasted three years."

The following fall Mather Academy played the first football game in the school's history. The Mather Grey Eagles lost 7–0 to the Mayo High Black Bears, but the local newspaper on November 18, 1932, called the game "one of the best seen on the local gridirons this season" and praised the coaching given the team in the past month by J. W. Martin of Johnson C. Smith University. The paper stated, "It has been possible for Mather Academy to have a football team and equipment . . . through the cooperation of the kind-hearted people of Camden, both white and colored, with I. B. English and other business and professional graduates of Mather." By traditional history the Jackson High Tigers, "the black and gold," entered gridiron play in the 1930s also. Their record in 1933 was 8-1-1, their only loss said to have been Mather, which remained their staunchest rival.

An underground sport with a stubborn following resurfaced in the public eye in April 1931. A United Press correspondent widely reported: "The cockfighting laurels of two South Carolina cities were trailed in the dust today when gamecocks representing Camden and Rock Hill fought five minutes to a double knockout, fatal in both cases, in an illegal tournament near Camden." The contest was followed by "an extended argument if bets should be paid when both the winner and the vanquished were dead." The event was not a small one, for "breeders from more than 20 towns in at least three different states entered candidates. Some bouts were over in a few seconds. The historic battle between Camden and Rock Hill lasted longest."

Boxing attracted large and enthusiastic audiences at two venues—the Rutledge Street armory and the opera house. Occasionally wrestling matches were also offered. The fight promoter Carl Schlosburg and the "colored boxing promoter" Joe Harrison arranged matches at both places, where fighters faced opponents of their own race. In October 1932 Schlosburg opened the season at the opera house with local amateurs, hoping to build interest in a training program. In the first bout Archie Reeves, Wateree Mill's "Ace," won over J. C. Tunstall, Hermitage Mill's "Pride." A bout with Beck Russell was stopped almost immediately as he outmatched his opponent. Three bouts ended in draws—Joe McNinch versus "Wall Street" Wooten, "Galloping" Gettys versus "Duke" Dunlap, and W. L. Jackson Jr. versus J. T. Kelley. Real excitement came in the fifth bout when Red Jennings knocked out his opponent, Ed Robinson. A wrestling match in the following days featured "Bear Cat" Jones versus Leo Jeffords, and soon afterward six events and a free-for-all pitted black boxers in an elimination contest to select challengers for the state's "colored championship titles."

Sounds

In January 1930 Majestic Theatre owner T. Lee Little had in place the newest film innovation, a sound system, and the old silent film showings were completely outdated. Sound was in demand everywhere. While radios had been a coveted novelty in much of the 1920s, by end of the 1930s most families—despite hard times—had radios, although they did not have electricity. Over the air waves, received in homes by antennae attached to quartz crystal sets, came sounds that enticed throughout the decade. Even remote rural families gathered at night around bulky, static-prone machines to laugh at comedy routines and listen to classical, old-time, or up-to-date jazzy swing music.

Music everywhere enlightened the spirits of the Depression-era population. In 1931 a concert of the Benedict College Quartet was especially anticipated at Mt. Moriah Baptist Church because the group had lately sung over the radio. In early 1932 performances of the local Kirkwood Orchestra were broadcast in half-hour specials over WIS Radio in Columbia.[20] Young musicians too performed on WIS, such as the pianist Aileen Belk of the MacDowell Music Club of Camden, who presented two numbers with the Mozart Music Club of Columbia. The media's popularity continued with the national radio appearances of Benjamin DeLoache of Camden, a baritone with the Philadelphia Grand Opera, who was also a local favorite when he returned home for live performances. Camden musician Mrs. Ernest C. Zemp in 1932 opened a studio at her home to teach voice culture.

An interest in southern music of varied types was prominent. In early 1930 the Glee Clubs of Mather Academy presented a public program of spirituals at the Browning Home Chapel. The following month the ladies' auxiliary of Bethesda Presbyterian Church sponsored a silver tea featuring a lowcountry folklorist reading spirituals. In 1931 the Dixie Jubilee Minstrels performed at Charlotte Thompson. At Bethune the Methodist women's mission group studied Booker T. Washington and heard a performance of spirituals by "Hattie Aiken and her daughters (colored)."

Southern music styles later called "country" were popular under the designations "hillbilly," "mountain," or "old-time" music. "Fiddlers' conventions" brought musicians together for fun and competitions, sometimes as fundraisers, and were especially popular as benefit entertainments at rural schools. Homemade instruments were sometimes among those used, and dancing or clogging was often part of the music making.

Dance music also varied. One dance at the Rutledge Street armory in 1930 featured the Original Cotton Pickers of Tennessee, and area country-music bands frequently performed locally. In 1932 a benefit dance at the armory to defray the expenses of the Camden High summer football camp featured Joe Burke and his seven Dixie Jolly Boys, "a local colored orchestra." At the Pines, another popular dance location, dressy affairs with orchestra music were separately presented in spring 1932 by the Junior Welfare League and the Camden Cotillion Club. Throughout the summer, for 50¢ a person, the Pines featured weekly square dances "with music by a good orchestra" at each. During the winter holidays, for $1.10 a person, the Pines held "a round dance" with the Dixie Serenaders performing currently popular music.

Minstrel shows and vaudeville performances with related music and tunes retained popularity. In October 1930 a huge American Legion carnival attracted large audiences. It featured a variety vaudeville show with singing, dancing, musicians, a magician, black-face skits, a prizefight, and horse races with a half dozen Camden girls riding as jockeys. There were bingo stands with prizes and games of chance with ham and bacon wheels and candy wheels, as well as balloons, crickets, walking canes, and confetti as prizes. However, the biggest draw was probably the Ford coupe given to the holder of the lucky ticket. Just one month later the American Legion and the Kershaw Guards joined to present their annual cabaret at the armory, which was described as "snappy entertainment"—that is, jazz style—with dances, singing, and good music, most notably featuring a blues singer.

Perhaps the broadest effort to bring music into the community came through many "singing conventions" held throughout the county, often involving various church congregations. The People's Chorus, developed across America and other countries as well, was a concept in which the musical performers and the audience were one and the same. The February 19, 1932, *Chronicle* announced that Mrs. Helen J. Snyder would direct the People's Chorus for Camden and that instruction was free, dues were small, and only "rudimentary knowledge of music and desire to sing" were needed to participate. All choirs of the city were invited to join.

Religion

Religious worship reflected the concerns and styles of the time. Many people sought answers to troubles through faith, and religious messages were often spread through the public media as well as churches. In February 1930 headlines announced a round of services to be preached in Camden by "Pugilist Gangster" Joe Percente, "once light-weight champion of the world and physical trainer to Theodore Roosevelt and former gangster of Chicago underworld, bootlegger and convict." The same month a theologian's services spilled over from Bethesda Presbyterian's church pews into the Majestic Theatre's movie seats.

Local preachers exerted extensive influence. In fall 1930 the Reverend B. R. Frith died. He was literally a giant of a man, and his handmade coffin measured seven feet long. Several years earlier he had founded Free Will Baptist Holiness Church between the two mill villages. It was said to be the city's first Holiness congregation. Reverend Frith's obituary stated: "His activities created quite a sensation on the mill hill where he erected a tent of sacks and curious crowds from town and country lined the National highway at his nightly meetings." Many holiness and pentecostal congregations were established throughout the county, many of them outgrowths of early revivals.

Some preachers led a number of churches and held wide influence. In February 1931, when the Reverend A. H. Hayes died, he was called "one of the best known colored ministers of our county," one who "labored faithfully with his race trying to uplift them both mentally and spiritually and was a power for good with both races." He was preaching at Wesley Chapel and Good Hope churches and teaching at Mt. Zion school. His funeral was held in Trinity Church in Camden, and he was buried in the cemetery at Mt. Joshua in Longtown, where he had once been pastor.

Revivals—or "protracted meetings" or simply "big meetings," as they were also called—were especially widespread as the Depression lengthened in the summer of 1932. For ten days or two weeks or more, congregations according to individual practice variously sang, prayed, wept, praised, sometimes shouted, and sometimes spoke in tongues. Worshippers sought understanding, forgiveness, salvation, and a better way of life. Two remaining campgrounds, at Bethune and at Blaney, are reminders of days when the presence of religious meeting grounds was more common.

The Jewish community in Camden drew together even more closely as difficult times increased in the 1930s. Their local numbers are suggested by the list of stores closing for Rosh Hashanah in 1931: the Fashion Shop, M. H. Heyman, Hirsch Brothers & Co., the Leader, L. Lomansky Shoe Store, the Outlook Shoppe, Schlosburg, I. Wolfe, and Wolfe-Eichel Co. The Hebrew Benevolent Society was active, supported by Hebrew Men and by Women of the Camden Temple Sisterhood.

In January 1933, the same month that Adolf Hitler became chancellor of Germany, the "second inter-county meeting of Jewish people within a radius of fifty miles" was held at the American Legion Hall in Camden. The program, chaired by L. A. Wittkowsky of Camden, focused on "religious education and the problem of the Jewish people in the small communities where there is no temple." A symposium for youth was headed by Julian Eichel of Camden.

As the Nazi regime expanded in Germany, the tendency grew from some local pulpits to interpret world events apocalyptically. Overflow crowds in February 1933 attended Lyttleton Street Methodist Church's Reverend C. F. Wimberly's popularly repeated sermon "Radio in Prophecy." When space was insufficient to accommodate all the African Americans he had invited to sit in the balcony, Reverend Wimberly delivered the same sermon in Trinity Methodist Church.

Throughout other churches in the county and other parts of the nation, he also presented the message of the "second coming," one of several sermons in which he correlated contemporary times with biblical prophesies of the future. Also in early 1933 the evangelist Reverend Jacob Gartenhaus, calling himself "a completed Jew," appealed at the Camden Baptist Church "for fellowship and brotherhood . . . not for Jews and Gentiles in America alone but all peoples everywhere."

The Advance of Aviation

Perhaps no location in the county inspired public imagination more about the potential of technology than the recently built airport at Camden, to which more and more flying machines were attracted. It was still the age of the barnstormer and, as a local airplane mechanic, James L. Anderson, later described it, "the days when the wind was hitting you in the face."[21] Colorful reports of Woodward Field activities focused more on thrills of danger and daredevilry than on practical applications.

In January 1930 airport manager Nathan N. Prentiss invited the public to Woodward Field to watch a young man make his first parachute jump, apparently also the first jump from a plane seen at the field. Such demonstrations were sometimes intended to reassure potential passengers about the safety of flying. Later that summer Prentiss, with whom some adventurous local folk had taken their first airplane rides, died when his plane crashed on a visit to one of Camden's winter residents at Woodstock, New York.

The next Woodward Field leasee, Weeks Aircraft Corporation of Milwaukee, staged a giant air show in the fall to inaugurate the opening of its operations. A daredevil stunt pilot and a delayed parachute jump thrilled the crowd. A three-day air show there in January 1931 filled the skies with many wonders, including airships, parachute jumps, and a full display of Weeks aircraft. The Goodyear zeppelin astounded downtown Camden shoppers as it skimmed overhead along Broad Street.

In June more than fifty airplanes believed to be returning from military maneuvers were seen and heard passing over the town, most of them following the path of the Seaboard railroad tracks through the county. In the early days of flight, unreliable equipment and lack of information often made it difficult for pilots to find their way, so following railroad tracks was a common navigational device. In November anticipation was great for the Camden arrival of the famous round-the-world flyers Wiley Post and Harold Gatty, who in their Vega airplane *Winnie Mae* had circumnavigated the globe in just eight and one-half days, faster than anyone before. Tickets benefiting the Chamber of Commerce had been sold to those wishing to hear the aviators speak in the Camden school auditorium, but the plane failed to arrive. Perhaps on the assumption that the pilots had been unable to recognize their destination, huge letters spelling the name of the city were soon afterward painted on the flat roof of city hall, positioned for visibility from the air.

The following month, December 1931, Ford pilot Howard Crawford in a large trimotor plane flew to Woodward Field to offer rides to citizens. Later in the month the celebrated rigid dirigible *Akron* circled low over Camden at an early morning hour. The giant military airship, built by Goodyear, was on a southern tour exhibiting the new pride of the navy. At 785 feet long, buoyed by nonflammable helium, and powered by eight engines, the airship had an unusual huge-bellied platform that could launch and retrieve five airplanes in flight. "Lights were burning on the vessel," said the *Chronicle,* "and many were thrilled at the sight of the big air traveler." Two years later the dirigible crashed at sea, killing most of its crew.[22]

In spring 1932 Woodward Field was leased to the longtime airman Clyde W. White and Dr. Boldridge of Charlotte, North Carolina. In November, Camden was ceremoniously added to the U.S. Postal Service's airmail route, contracted to Eastern Airways. A special cachet was issued to commemorate the occasion. At a celebratory luncheon at the Camden Hotel, an Eastern Airways executive praised the connection of cities on the Charlotte-Camden-Columbia-Augusta route: "One can leave Camden at 10:40 in the morning and go via Charlotte to New York, arriving in New York at 6:10 that afternoon. At Charlotte the Camden plane will connect with the New York–New Orleans air line, and Camden will then be within a day's travel of New York or New Orleans. . . . The tourists will be able to stay in touch with their Northern homes in a manner that they did not dream of a few years ago. They can join their families here for weekends, and get their New York papers each day. . . . The business men of Camden can have letters delivered at long distances each day by planes or receive mail the same way."

Other technical advances were soon in evidence. In January 1933 the sighting of an airplane traveling at night stirred attention. Later that month crowds at Woodward Field marveled at the movements of "a phantom auto," a driverless vehicle operated on the ground by remote control from an airplane flying overhead. Along with other air stunts and parachute jumps, a tire from Camden's DeKalb Service Station was tossed out of an airplane with a Tavannes wristwatch from Hoffer's Jewelry in its hub. The test was an advertising gimmick to prove the quality of both products.

Across the county wonder was sparked when citizens lifted their eyes from views of isolated cotton fields, dusty roads, or weathering storefronts to catch sight of a giant airship or to follow the sound of a small engine making its way through the sky. Most people lived in homes that had no electricity, no indoor plumbing, and no telephone. Times were hard. Yet overhead there was visible evidence of potential change and of human beings making change possible.

Election of President Roosevelt

In the fall of 1932 most Kershaw County voters were either fired by the hope of "a new deal" to end the Depression, as promised by Democratic candidate Franklin Delano Roosevelt, or at least cheered by prospects of a Republican defeat. A huge and enthusiastic election rally on October 28 in Camden received wide publicity throughout the Carolinas and elsewhere. Its chairman was Camden mayor R. M. Kennedy Jr. Shrewdly the rally was timed to coincide with the county fair, on the Friday of the traditional march of white schoolchildren through town to the fairgrounds. The fair was well attended by families and in itself one of the county's biggest and most popular annual events.

A host of invited guests was entertained and displayed, including Governor Ibra C. Blackwood and former governor John G. Richards, as well as generals, congressmen, professors, and editors of state newspapers, along with American Legion state commander Hobson Hilton and two other local Congressional Medal of Honor recipients, Cantey Villepigue and Roy Truesdale.[23] In the morning an estimated four thousand persons in the parade march, pepped up with various bands, began at the courthouse at the upper end of Broad Street and proceeded southward along flag-draped streets. At the lead were motorcycle officers followed by fifty mounted Red Shirts under Chief Marshall Henry G. Carrison. The Red Shirts, a reminder of Hampton's Reconstruction overthrow of Republicans, were recruited for the occasion from polo players and county horsemen. Free of charge, DesChamps dry cleaning shop had dyed shirts that were turned in ahead of time, and some red shirts were also seen among spectators.

The mounted men were followed by Confederate veterans and Red Shirts of 1876 riding in decorated cars. Then came cars bearing city and county officials, followed by members of the United Daughters of the Confederacy, the Daughters of the American Revolution, and the American Legion Auxiliary, with veterans of the Spanish American War. Marching behind were the American Legion; Company M, under Captain Brevard Boykin; the Boy Scouts; the fire department; the Shrine Club; and members of the Camden and Sumter high school football teams, who were playing that afternoon. The carnival band next led forward fifteen hundred to two thousand schoolchildren.

The crowd eagerly awaited the finale, a parade of "Hoover buggies" competing for cash prizes, including five dollars for the most unusual. The contest, attracting entries throughout Kershaw and neighboring counties, had been announced with a political twist: "Instead of two cars to every garage, as promised by the great Republican party, many farmers feel lucky to have a Hoover buggy, which everyone knows is nothing but the rear axle of a Ford mounted on automobile tires, and a seat on the same. Shafts are attached and a mule pulls it instead of a high-powered motor."

The finale of the parade was, however, only the beginning of the rally. A viewing stand, with pictures of FDR and George Washington, had been erected at the old courthouse on south Broad Street. When the parade reached that point, the distinguished guests, Confederate veterans, and Red Shirts mounted to seats of honor. From this stand speech making followed the parade, with each guest allowed two or three minutes followed by unlimited time given the chief orator, the "silver-tongued" Honorable Roach Stewart of Lancaster, a popular area speaker. After the rally both the governor and the former governor posed for photographs seated in an ox-drawn "depression cart." Governor Blackwood asserted, "If present troubles are to be corrected, we cannot look for correction to those who have had control of the country during the past two administrations." Governor Richards urged "the same unity of effort as in 1876."

At the ongoing fair crowds were entertained by a company of acrobats sponsored by the American Legion and the Shrine Club. "Death defying" high aerial and platform stunts sent chills through the audience. In the afternoon football game, Camden won 13–7 over Sumter before "the largest crowd ever to see a football game here." It was followed by a horse show, which was managed by George T. Little and Clarkson Rhame and included entries from across the two Carolinas. Then came a dog show, managed by Samuel Russell and M. L. Smith Jr., with statewide participation. The night ended with boxing and wrestling matches on the football field. Furthermore, if county sports fans needed any more excitement, they could attend the football game the next day on Negro Fair Day. Jackson High School and Avery Institute faced off as crowds admired the speed of Waddy Rudolph, Murray James, and Richard Dow, local players coached by Charles Watterman, formerly of State College at Orangeburg.

The melding of politics, entertainment, and excitement with popular history and hometown heroes was a cheerful episode for children and old folk alike. Enthusiasm was at a high pitch when Roosevelt's election followed in November, although five months stretched out before his inauguration, when the New Deal began to take shape. During those intervening months volunteer and local relief efforts continued, and some began to merge into broader though weakly funded federal programs.

The New Deal—Early Years

Immediately upon taking office at the beginning of March 1933, Roosevelt called Congress into a special one-hundred-day session. During this short period every program he requested was enacted, a record amount of major legislation. In his campaign the new president had supported the repeal of Prohibition as a practical step. The Twenty-first Amendment, ratified in his first month in office, brought an end to Prohibition. Immediately taxes were levied on newly legalized alcohol sales to raise badly needed government revenues. Beer, the first available beverage, was for sale in downtown Camden by mid-April.[24] The Kershaw County Ministerial Union took a relatively mild step, making immediate appeals to stores to close by 11:00 P.M. on Saturday nights so that Sunday services would not be adversely affected.

Banking Holiday

One of Roosevelt's first actions tackled banking problems. Bank runs and failures had become epidemic across the nation, and in the climate of distrust and uncertainty Kershaw County banks had fared variously. The Bank of Kershaw had actually earned praise in January 1933 when the *Calhoun Times* called it the "most remarkable small town bank record that has come to our notice in a long time." The article, reprinted in the *Camden Chronicle,* stated that Kershaw was "only a village in a rather poor county" but that the bank was "not to be sneezed at. . . . It has rediscounted no paper, borrowed nothing, and owes nothing."

On March 6, 1933, all the nation's banks closed for a federally mandated banking holiday while inspectors carefully examined books and allowed only sound banks to reopen. Since new deposits were secured with government insurance, some citizens "brought out of hiding" money that they had previously

A well-attended young people's temperance rally at Trinity Methodist Church in Camden, 1930. Courtesy of the Camden Archives

withdrawn and put it back into sound banks. The First National Bank in Camden was able to reopen without restriction. The county's oldest bank, the Bank of Camden, was under restrictions to reorganize. The *Chronicle* editorial adopted an overly optimistic tone: "The renewed confidence of the people generally has been well shown by the deposits in the banks here since their reopening. . . . There is a general feeling that conditions are improving and will continue to improve. The clouds are lifting. Faces are brighter and everyone has new hope." Adjustment, in fact, came gradually. The Bank of Camden remained closed, with its president Henry G. Carrison, one of the original organizers from 1888, serving as conservator. The Commercial Bank, with Carrison at its head, opened instead. In 1934 the First Federal Savings and Loan opened in Camden and began making progress. Efforts were under way to stabilize local and national banking.

Camden's Bicentennial

During the banking holiday Camden's mayor R. M. Kennedy announced a decision "in view of the unusual situation prevailing over the entire country." The much-anticipated, weeklong celebration of the two hundredth birthday of Camden would begin as scheduled on March 19, but its centerpiece, the planned reenactment of the historical pageant *Camden, Yesterday and Today,* was cancelled. First produced nine years earlier, the lengthy pageant was in preparation under its original director, Mary Blackwell, now Mrs. Donald Morrison, and many committees, teachers, schoolchildren, and other local citizens.[25] Organizers had been counting on pageant ticket sales to defray production expenses but feared that the current banking situation would jeopardize their sales. It was likely too that they considered the hardships of families whose children were expected to appear in the pageant.

Other activities continued as planned, however, and the "Bi-Centennial" was recalled in later years as "a splendid success."[26] The cover of the keepsake program, drawn by Samuel Russell, artistically featured its advertising emblems—the effigy of King Hagler at the center and with longleaf pines on each side. Activities included polo games; a two-day horse show; a gymkhana; tours of Camden battlefields and estates; several dances, including a Hunt Club ball at Mulberry and a Cotillion Club event; and the running of the Carolina Cup. Thursday the events of the celebration were "turned over to colored citizens of the town," who planned "an elaborate program" including a parade, tree planting ceremonies, and a "pageant to depict the development of the negro from the time of the Civil War to the present day," along with the singing of folk songs and spirituals.[27] A *Sportsman's Map of Camden and Vicinity,* privately printed and sold by the artists L. W. Boykin II and Ken Millard and "Celebrating the Bicentennial," depicted historical and present locales of interest in sporting circles.[28]

Bicentennial events, widely advertised, drew many affluent visitors into the community and sought to entice them back again. The entertainments were favorite activities of the cottage colony and the resort tourists, who preferred these over events in which the local public at large could easily participate. However, the events were widely photographed and reported, and they resulted in outstanding publicity at a critical time. While the divide was great between those who participated in such events and those who were struggling at the other end of the economic ladder, community leaders hoped that bringing in outside dollars would benefit all.

The Relief Council

In the waning months of the Hoover administration, some of the local relief work that had been handled through charities and volunteer efforts was merged into broader government programs. In early 1933, before Roosevelt took office, the Kershaw County Relief Council was headquartered in a Camden city office adjoining the old opera house. Council chairman W. T. Redfearn was also head of the Kershaw County Board of Directors, through which the Reconstruction Finance Corporation (RFC) distributed the funding that the council dispersed. The federal money was intended to stabilize banking by stimulating the local economy with works projects.[29]

The Relief Council was authorized to pay labor-only costs, at "necessarily small" rates, on a small number of jobs programs. The main work in January was cutting firewood to furnish Camden's poor, but agreements were also made for laying water mains in the northern part of town and for improving school grounds and buildings throughout the county. Work probably included the grounds of the Charlotte Thompson School, the old Terraces plantation, for in February the landscape architect E. S. Draper stated that restoration was under way there when he discussed the site as a historic local garden. For several months after Roosevelt took office in March 1933, the Relief Council continued to administer ongoing work programs while new regulations were phased in.

In the springtime relief workers cleaned out ditches in the county to improve drainage and thereby public health. By summer a sewing room was under way on the second floor of the opera house to make clothing and bedding for the needy. Unlike the earlier sewing room, which had operated with volunteers, this one employed sixteen women to sew until ten thousand yards of government-donated fabric was used. Under the director, Miss Thelma Flowers, the sewing room made garments of all sizes for adults and children and fashioned quilts from the scraps, all for distribution to the needy.

As the number of government programs increased and likewise the number of workers, relief administration grew more demanding. Because of time and responsibility conflicts, Redfearn resigned from relief positions. By October, according to one historian, Kershaw was among the state's seventeen neediest counties, where "30 percent or more of the population was on relief."[30]

New Deal Work Projects

Oscar J. Smyrl, a Camden businessman and county farmer, was appointed in October to head Kershaw County's Emergency Relief Administration (ERA). For three years he continued to administer county relief work at the head of various government programs. In November 1933 the Relief Council was merged into the Civil Works Administration (CWA), a jobs project organized within the Public Works Administration (PWA). Smyrl also headed the CWA until it was phased out in 1934. He continued to administer ongoing relief programs as county head of the Federal Emergency Relief Administration (FERA) through 1936.

During the transition of the agencies bringing in federal dollars, the January 18, 1935, *Chronicle* quoted Smyrl: "It has been our aim throughout Emergency Relief work to not only give relief but at the same time to accomplish something worthwhile." The statement is part of a report that describes ten months' work, from November 1933 through September 1934. It not only documents a large number of accomplishments but also shows extensive involvement of county citizens as workers and volunteers.

During those ten months relief workers made repairs and additions to public buildings, constructing a five-room addition to Camden Hospital and painting the Camden Water Works. The old Camden Opera House, lately a city hall, was renovated into a modern auditorium with a seating capacity of seven hundred. For city offices 110 desks and filing cabinets were built. In Bethune a fire-ravaged city warehouse was rebuilt.

In addition five county schools were repaired or renovated, with materials being salvaged to build new ones. A new brick school, later named Pine Tree Hill, was constructed for three hundred to four hundred children east of Camden. It replaced the old school serving the mill villages. Within Camden three playgrounds, five city parks, and ten miles of streets and sidewalks were improved, and three miles of sewer and water pipes were laid. Elsewhere in the county fifteen miles of new roads were built, five hundred miles of roads were repaired, and sixty right-of-way miles were improved.

For use as community buildings throughout the county, ten small huts were constructed, as well as a forty by one hundred foot dining room at Lake Shamokin. Two swimming pools were built, one of them in Liberty Hill. For health improvements, about seven miles of two creeks were drained for malarial control, and 750 sanitary toilets were constructed in the county.

Most important to many, products of relief work also provided direct aid to the hungry, helpless, and needy. Wood was cut and hauled to more than nine

The Camden Library, built with Carnegie assistance in 1916, now the Camden Archives and Museum. Courtesy of the Camden Archives

hundred relief cases, and a community garden furnished free vegetables to all, with more than fifty thousand cans of surplus vegetables being canned from the garden. Some one thousand children across the county received hot lunches at school. A two-week camp at Lake Shamokin fed fifty undernourished children. In addition in more than three thousand cases free commodities were distributed. A mattress factory, operated on the upper floor of the old courthouse, made five hundred mattresses, and sewing rooms made more than seventy thousand items of clothing and bedcovers, all for distribution.

In a different but significantly important program, old wills in the county courthouse were copied and bound, and all books in the Camden Library and the libraries of three schools were repaired.[31] Also seven adult schools, with a goal of teaching basic literacy, were conducted in various parts of the county.

Details of the individual activities provide a fuller picture of the scope of local activities under the CWA and FERA. In many cases volunteer citizen initiative and community goodwill supplemented the assistance of the government relief work programs.

Adult Literacy

The adult school literacy program was announced with the words "This has been the dream of Miss Wil Lou Gray for years." South Carolina's noted activist for adult education was in the forefront to unite federal funding with the state's education department, then struggling even to provide minimal education for children. Mrs. Kathleen Watts, county school superintendent, and the county board of education actively cooperated in getting the adult program running in Kershaw County. FERA paid the teachers; the state education department and local volunteers supplied the rest.

In October 1933 public meetings in schoolhouses across the county sought the participation of "adults who have never been privileged to receive an education." At Beaver Dam the teacher Mrs. J. R. West led the program, and at Lockhart two teachers, Miss Sallie Young and Mrs. G. C. Rush, were in charge. At Midway the Reverend J. B. Caston and R. M. Stevenson were speakers. The teacher O. R. S. Pool invited all West Wateree to meet at Smyrna Church, where the program included music and remarks by Superintendent Watts. Musical selections and citizens' remarks introduced the adult school to people of the Wateree Mill, Hermitage Mill, and DuBose Park communities. This group met in the auditorium of their new school, which was soon named Pine Tree after the original name of Camden and later was known as Pine Tree Hill School.

Across the county individuals donated magazines, books, and secondhand elementary textbooks to supplement the night-school program. Boy Scouts, under their leader William Nettles, collected the donations door-to-door.

Camden Library

At the Camden Library relief workers painted walls, floors, and inside and outside woodwork. They repaired the roof and washed the windows; they cleaned the basement and installed a furnace and light fixtures. CWA library assistants cataloged and accessioned books, added pockets and date-due slips, rebound books, and even collected book donations throughout town. They also started a picture collection and clippings for a vertical file. A CWA cabinetmaker, a Mr. Rush (probably Hoyt Rush of Rush Cabinet Works) built bookshelves, a dictionary stand, a book display rack, a bulletin board, a newspaper file, and a table and chairs sized for children. Some of the work is still evidenced in the library building, which is presently the Camden Archives.

School Lunches

The lunch program at schools came together through the cooperation of many, with Mrs. Leon Schlosburg as head of Women's Work of the CWA. She was assisted by Dr. A. W. Humphries and Miss Christie Hay of the county health department, as well as school personnel. In March 1934 more than two thousand children were being served hot food to supplement their lunches brought from home and were also being given lessons in nutrition, mannerly eating habits, and mealtime socializing.

Opera House

The Camden Opera House remodeling in 1934 kept a large force of CWA workmen busy for some time. Plans were drawn by the architectural firm Lafaye and Lafaye of Columbia and supervised by the local architect R. W. Mitcham, with work done under the local contractor George A. Creed. The old town tower, topped by King Hagler, was left intact, but the winding stairway inside it was altered to open into the auditorium gallery. On each side of the building the walls were reduced to lower the building height by eighteen feet. Inside the front entrance a lobby measuring eight by twenty feet featured two restrooms on each side and an entrance to the gallery on each end. The auditorium held a twenty by forty foot stage with two dressing rooms at the rear. Movable seating was planned so that the auditorium could also be used for dances. The building was extended twenty-one feet in the rear to accommodate a heating plant. When timber was torn out of the old building, workmen declared it "as good today as it was when put in" in 1885.

By October the city announced that it would profit from the building, having leased it to Majestic Theatre owner T. Lee Little for the location of a second motion picture operation, the Haiglar Theatre. At the Haiglar, where the gallery was "reserved for colored" audiences, the first showing was *City Slicker,* starring Robert Montgomery and Maureen O'Sullivan. Little, who paid the expense of the six hundred seats he placed in the building, also scheduled seasonal stage shows there, including musical comedies and vaudeville.

In response to a few local grumbles that taxpayers' money was inappropriately benefiting an individual business, city officials pointed out that the city had paid only $6,692.13 for materials to renovate a deteriorating building that for half a century had served as a public gathering place and that would continue to do so while also earning the city rental income. They called it "one of the most worthwhile projects" undertaken in the county, having preserved the architecture of a local landmark while restoring it to good use.

Hermitage Lake Restoration

Perhaps the most enthusiasm given a single works project was expressed by the Camden Merchants Association, headed by John T. Mackey, for the extensive work in 1934 on "the big dam project" three miles east of Camden. At the Hermitage millpond the CWA project restored the ruined dam, which had been blown out in a flood several years earlier. At times as many as one hundred or more laborers were at work on the dam, within easy view of the townspeople who flocked to watch the progress. Pilings were driven to build a coffer dam across the main stream while the greatest number of workers with shovels and wheelbarrows moved earth to replace a gap in the former dam. It was the largest project the CWA had undertaken in the county.

A sawmill was rented, and operators sawed timber for the project, also cutting down trees and stumps in the pond bed. Citizens lent boats for workmen to use while sawing timber that was standing in water. Additional timber for construction was solicited free from landowners, especially those on whose property government workers cut firebreaks. Cooperative citizens were repaid with promises of a period of free fishing rights in the finished lake.

The new dam, with floodgate and spillway, was erected slightly east of the old floodgates and raised the water eight and one-half feet higher than it was standing when work began. The new lake flooded approximately 825 acres, as compared to 936 acres originally. The thousand-acre tract on which the lake stood was intended as a recreational center for fishing, boating, swimming, and other water sports. A commission was appointed to oversee the lake and the sale of permits for use of the premises.

Local merchants, supported by the local Game and Fish Association, campaigned for the new area to be approved as a government park representing the sandhills of Kershaw County. A bathing pavilion, dressing rooms, and a dance hall were built on the eastern side of the lake. At its upper end, fed by several sandhill springs, a nursery fish pond was constructed on the J. H. Sinclair place to supply fish to the lake. As the fish matured, the gates of the pond were opened to drain into the larger lake and then were closed so that the nursery could be restocked for the future. The sale of fishing rights was intended to pay for maintenance.

Use of Hermitage Lake began on a high note in summer 1935, topped with a festive Fourth of July celebration. The water had risen just right for boat races, rides, and aquatic stunts provided by privately owned speed boats gathered from Camden and Columbia. Tickets were sold in advance for a big fish supper, which was enjoyed on tables erected for picnicking parties and families. Walter A. Rhame, a Red Cross instructor and lifeguard, supervised the swimming area, and a fireworks display with aerial bombs lit up the night sky.

Only a week after the big celebration, however, the excitement of the new recreation area was marred by tragedy when two young men lost their lives in a boating accident. On what was to be the last motorboat ride after a number of other people had safely enjoyed trips on the lake, a horrifying event occurred before a crowd of witnesses helpless to intervene. On a sharp turn, three men were thrown out of a speeding boat, which "kept circling at them throwing great waves."

Aside from the tragic event, the new lake proved to be a popular draw to families and sportsmen. The following season permits for fishing, swimming, and boating were selling well. Some persons, however, especially area residents who had used the old Hermitage millpond at no cost, held that the lake had been "fixed up" at taxpayers' cost, and they eschewed the formality of acquiring a slip of paper before returning to fish by way of their old-time trails.

Lots acquired at Hermitage Lake began to draw families. In 1936 Henry Beard built for summer occupancy a two-story log cabin of six rooms, designed to provide a lake view from all sides. Summer shacks began to dot the shoreline.

WPA Projects

In addition to CWA and FERA, other New Deal agencies carried out work projects, including the larger PWA and the later WPA (Works Progress Administration). Sometimes the work begun under one agency was continued under another, and at other times a large project was handled in different phases by different agencies. Over time the alphabetical distinctions blurred so that in later years many projects were remembered by the name of the much larger and better-funded agency that supplanted some of the others and hung on longer—the WPA, which continued some of its programs into the early 1940s. Under the broader WPA, relief projects in Kershaw County were administered by district executives who had responsibility for work in several counties at a time.

Several WPA projects involved new school buildings in the county. In March 1934 while extensive repairs were under way to the grammar school at Kershaw, a night-time fire broke out and, fanned by high winds, gutted the building. Firemen concentrated on saving the nearby high school. In 1936 a new school and gym were built at Kershaw with WPA assistance.

Likewise at Camden in 1936 two new schools, later with gyms, were built as work projects—Camden High School on Laurens Street and Jackson High School on Campbell Street. Both were brick, two-story buildings constructed under the architectural firm Lafaye and Lafaye, with the local contractors George A. Creed and R. E. Chewning. Large trees removed from the sites were cut into firewood and distributed to the needy. Lumber salvaged from old buildings pulled down at the Jackson site were recycled for other school building projects.

Other WPA projects at mid-decade included the operation of day nurseries for underprivileged and relief children. Some of the youngsters were cared for so that parents could work; some, so that the little ones could receive nutrition, health benefits, and instruction. The Camden Emergency Nursery School operated on Lafayette Avenue next to the courthouse. Another nursery, under Miss Gertrude Zemp, was operated in the renovated basement of Wimberly Hall of the Lyttleton Street Methodist Church.

Nurseries and sewing rooms operated at various locations in the county under the WPA. In 1936 the women of the Pine Tree sewing room were treated to an outing at the Happy Hour playground of the Pine Grove community in West Wateree. Kershaw County Recreation Project supervisor Mrs. Roland Nettles planned the activity with Miss Sophie Richards, supervisor of women's work: "The ten-minute auto ride from the sewing room to the playground was a rare treat to many of the workers." Nearly seventy-five people were present.

Guests were welcomed by Mrs. Hugh McCullum, community recreation leader and planner of the playground, on a pine-clad hilltop. Cleared enough for games, the site had "rustic seats, see-saws, and a great outdoor fireplace for cooking." The group participated in a baseball game, a relay race, a peanut contest, and similar diversions and supped on chicken salad, crackers, pickles, cake, and iced tea. Miss Mary Williams, WPA supervisor, was also present.

The continued participation of civic groups and volunteers in cooperation with government programs was illustrated in the summer 1936 nutrition camp held at the Kershaw County Community House at Lake Shamokin. More than seventy-five undernourished boys and girls ages ten to thirteen gained weight on healthy food provided them through community and government contributions, and they slept on regulation army cots in a well-ventilated dormitory and cabins. Campers swam in the Shamokin millpond belonging to Blake Zemp, who donated "hominy (grits)" from the mill. The children's clothes were furnished from the sewing rooms, and laundry was done free by City Laundry. John M. Villepigue provided an icebox, ice, and other assistance, and Benjamin P. DeLoache of the Rehabilitation Department gave a fish fry.

Black Community Programs

Some assistance programs had special focus in the black community, which was eligible for all the other emergency government programs, although participation was generally segregated from white participation. Private support continued to aid Mather Academy and the Browning Home. The Jeanes Fund also continued funding for the Jeanes teacher Miss James Dibble, a Camden native and former Mather teacher, to guide and supervise black public-school teachers throughout the county.

Other significant guidance was added with the hiring of black assistants to carry out other government programs. In November 1933 Jennie Carter, a graduate of State College at Orangeburg and for some time a teacher in the county schools, took the position of emergency assistant worker, under the Emergency Relief Administration and the Extension Service. Within two months she had organized women into clubs in the black communities of Boykin, Cedar Rock, Ebenezer, Hickman, Kirkland, Liberty Hill, Long Branch, Mickle, Mt. Zion, Parker, St. Matthew, and Westville. In January 1934 she was giving demonstrations on making laundry and toilet soaps, teaching women to make hot beds to start spring gardens, and assisting the other agents in a meat-canning campaign.

By March, Carter had been able to secure the use of "an empty store in the busy section" of downtown Camden to begin a market for "the colored home demonstration clubwomen." In one of her reports printed in the *Chronicle,* she explained, "Quite a number of them had been and were selling their products up and down the streets taking whatever they could get for them, which was very little."

In her work Carter focused attention on nutrition, health, infant care, and home improvement. Summer lessons included teaching women to fashion durable window screens from onion sacks for fly protection and to soften fabrics for baby clothing. She attempted to amend a custom of the time: "In visiting the churches and homes in the country I found babies not more than three months old dressed in gay colors made of stiff materials. Their napkins were of flesh towels or other coarse materials, all of which was very uncomfortable for the child. Almost all of them wore no shoes. Some of them wore wraps made of gay striped outing."

Four other emergency workers, all white women, were added at various points to aid the home-demonstration agent Sadie Craig within various sections of the county, and they too assisted Craig and Carter at times with black families. Workers in fall 1934 were Mrs. E. B. Buddin, eastern section; Mary Hayes, southeastern section; Sadie McRae, Liberty Hill; and Mrs. B. C. Zemp, West Wateree. Before the end of the year Craig left the county, and in her place Margaret Fewell began a long and influential career in the Extension Service.

Civilian Conservation Corps

By far the most popularly received program of the New Deal was that of the Emergency Conservation Program, more commonly known as the Civilian Conservation Corps (CCC). Originally intended to serve national forests, the CCC almost immediately added state-forest and private-land programs for states, such as South Carolina, that had no national forests. In 1933 unemployed young men, unmarried and between the ages of eighteen and twenty-five (later seventeen to twenty-three), were enrolled for six-month (later renewable) stints in a work program that offered many personal benefits beyond unemployment relief. For cash-strapped or relief families, the impact was immediate. Each CCC worker earned thirty dollars a month, of which twenty-five dollars (later twenty-two to twenty-five dollars) was sent directly to his family at home. The impact on the community was also significant. Families had cash to spend, and areas near camps benefited both from the workers' labor and from camp-related spending.

In April 1933 the first group of sixty CCC recruits from Kershaw County left home to train and work in forestry conservation. Several hundred more county men—perhaps in all as many as a thousand men—were hired through the rest of the decade.[32] Gradually, CCC enrollments were adjusted by quotas to aid relief families, minorities, and unemployed war veterans.

In its first summer CCC enlistees from across the country were sent directly to army camps for "reconditioning," as most of the recruits reported to duty poorly clothed, malnourished, or in need of medical attention. Guardsmen of

Kershaw County's Company M were called up to help with organizing the first camps, which, while they did not give military training, introduced recruits to the general routine and discipline of camp life.[33]

Throughout CCC employment each worker was provided appropriate clothing (shoes, underwear, and denim fatigues), fed amply three times daily, given medical care, housed in tents or barracks with running water and electricity, assigned meaningful physical labor for eight hours daily, and given opportunities for education, recreation, entertainment, and spiritual expression. A general spirit of camaraderie prevailed in many camps, and experiences there were often recalled with nostalgia for friendships formed and with pride for the significant work accomplished in "soil erosion, forest improvement, fire protection, construction of trails, building of lookout towers and reforestation."

In June 1933 Kershaw County's first CCC recruits completed their reconditioning at Fort Benning, Georgia, and left for their assigned work camp in Horry County at Conway, South Carolina.[34] Two of the group, Arthur DeLoache and Beckham Russell, were among those who detoured by Camden for a quick visit home on the way. Another local member, Harold McNinch, began writing a camp newsletter from Conway that was periodically published in the *Camden Chronicle* and no doubt elsewhere.

Local forest landowners were pleased in 1933 when approval came for one of South Carolina's sixteen initial CCC camps to be situated within Kershaw County. The forester Charles Nuite was credited with having worked "day and night" to secure a 250-man reforestation camp for the county. Besides being available to work on public property, the CCC was allowed to clear and replant sections of private property when landowners joined programs to reclaim eroded land and to prevent forest fires. Nuite began immediately to sign up landowners interested in CCC services.

Kershaw County, site of the state's first forest nursery, was also the site of the South Carolina Forestry Commission's first fire observation tower, erected at the expense of private landowners.[35] The Kershaw County Forestry Association, organized in 1930, assembled the one-hundred-foot steel structure on the property of Horatio G. Lloyd, north of Camden.[36] Another fire tower was begun in 1932 at Liberty Hill when twenty-four landowners in that community organized a forest association branch. Proved interest and leadership in forestry conservation helped qualify Kershaw County for CCC services. Now, without expense to local landowners, state and federal officials agreed to erect additional steel, one-hundred-foot public fire towers and to connect all the county's towers with telephone lines for fire-fighting communications. Officially coming to an end were the ancient days of unrestricted cutting and unplanned forest growth controlled only by the whims of nature and by randomly set or accidental burnings.[37]

The Blaney CCC Camp

The county's first CCC camp, a "private land" camp, was set up by July 1933 in West Wateree Township near Blaney. Located on an old eight-hundred-acre estate known as Wildwood Manor, the property of Karl T. Roseborough of Lugoff, the camp was situated a couple of miles off U.S. Highway 1. In preparation to receive the young men, RFC forces erected a dining hall, a recreation hall, tent floors, incidental buildings, and pumps. In their first month the young men at the camp began recording their activities in a camp newspaper, at first written by Edwin C. Kennedy, with portions published periodically in the *Camden Chronicle.* They also dug a well at the camp, put up a water tank, set up telephone poles to Camden, and ran electrical lines. At no other place in the county was rural electricity or telephone service available. At the center of their new camp the CCC boys erected a flagpole and ceremoniously raised the American flag. The young men attentively gathered to hear radio addresses made directly to them by President Roosevelt and cabinet members. The camp reporter described the words as "inspirational."

Community welcoming of the CCC camp was strong. A "Homecoming Week" was celebrated in early August, with gala activities both at camp and in Camden. Although torrential rains washed out an intended Friday night street dance in front of the public library, the nine-piece orchestra instead played to a large crowd at the Camden armory.[38] Some 240 guests went to the camp on Saturday to enjoy a tour and boxing matches, swimming events, and a baseball game with a team from CCC Camp Pearson at Parr Shoals. A number of campers were in Camden on Sunday for Sunday school and church.

Shortly afterward the tragic death of a Kershaw County war hero inspired the name chosen by the CCC boys for the site—Camp Hilton. The one-armed veteran Hobson Hilton drowned in Lake Murray attempting to help victims of a boating accident. On August 25 at Blaney, in the presence of a large crowd of Legionnaires gathered in honor of their recently departed commander, General James C. Dozier, a fellow Congressional Medalist, unveiled a memorial tablet to Hilton.[39] Judge I. F. Holland, the county's oldest living Confederate veteran, was a special guest. Following a barbecue, 150 couples danced at Guion Hall, the camp's recreation center, named for West Wateree's Louie I. Guion, a state leader in forestry conservation.

In the following months teams of CCC workers labored throughout the county. Some of their work included clearing unproductive and eroded land, digging ditches to drain swampland, planting trees, building roads, opening firebreaks, and also fighting fires. Their work was publicly praised, and positive effects on the workers themselves were also recognized. In the fall Camp Hilton supervisor Mr. Conrad spoke to the Camden Rotary Club. He described young men "who come to the camp soft and tender . . . many of whom had never done manual labor before, and today have developed into fine specimens of manhood and can work now stripped to their waist and are brown as berries."

In fall 1934 there was local regret when the workers at Camp Hilton were removed to Wedgefield in Sumter County to join other units on the massive project to shape Manchester State Forest. Kershaw County began immediate efforts to secure another camp within its boundaries.

The Veterans CCC Camp

By spring 1935 the Camp Hilton site was again populated, this time as a work camp designated as S.C. Veterans Camp no. 4. In response to the demonstrations in Washington, D.C., two years earlier, the New Deal had set up separate CCC units to employ war veterans regardless of age or marital status, but annually bonus marchers returned to the capital, still seeking their original goal. To discourage unemployed veterans from camping in Washington, several work camps were set up for them, seven in Florida and four in South Carolina.

Tablet dedicated in 1933 at the Civilian Conservation Corps camp in Blaney. The camp was named for World War I hero Richmond Hobson Hilton.

The Kershaw County site was one of these camps, today indicated in the Elgin (formerly Blaney) area by the nearby highway place name Veterans Row. Near the campsite Veterans Row intersects with Wildwood Lane, which likewise recalls the original name of the estate on which the camp stood. In August 265 veterans were reported at the Blaney camp, with the unsympathetic *Time* magazine reporter Charles McLean asserting that 15 of them were on the chain gang.

In the fall of 1935 Camp Hilton was grief-stricken by a tragic disaster that struck one of the veterans camps in Florida. On Labor Day a devastating hurricane—still the strongest ever recorded hitting the United States—struck the Florida Keys. Here 259 veterans, trapped at a work camp, lost their lives. Soon afterward the *Camden Chronicle* described dismay at the Blaney camp, where the flag now flew at half-staff. Israel Grostein, a camp reporter, explained that "brothers are longing for brothers, whose fate is still in doubt." He stated, "Many of the men in this camp have been on the very ground where disaster now stalks, working there alongside of most of the hurricane embattled veterans."

In the face of national criticism for having neglected to protect the Florida workers, the federal administration moved quickly. There were 910 men in the South Carolina veterans camps, "many of them former bonus marchers," according to the *Chronicle.* By the end of the month these camps had been ordered abandoned, and work was under way dismantling them.[40] Eligible men were immediately enrolled in various CCC camps. Others were sent home or dispersed to other transient camps. The *Chronicle* for September 27 stated that about 104 of the men at the Blaney camp had signed with the CCC.

The Cassatt CCC Camp

Also by spring 1935 a CCC camp was in operation about three miles west of Cassatt on a high sandhill location on Providence Church Road, one-half mile from Porter Road. Here the CCC helped build a fire observation tower the following year. The *Hill Top* was the name of the camp newspaper, which was at least part of the time edited by Blevin Horres, who taught literacy classes to the campers. Surviving issues from November and December 1935 provide a number of camp details.[41]

Additional references to the Cassatt camp, including those to white and to black campers, are found in local newspapers from the following year. Federal regulations at the time stipulated policies of racial segregation in the nation's CCC camps. The researcher Harvey Teal stated that, while the campsite at Cassatt housed both races, "due to customs and conditions at the time, they would have been segregated for eating, sleeping, and recreational activities such as ball games."[42] Likely the relationships were cordial and familiar, for the camp newspaper brags about having "the best negro basketball team in the area."

The local newspaper reported that the Presbyterian church in Bethune had at their sanctuary enjoyed the singing of spirituals by the "negro glee club" from the CCC camp. In a separate and exceptional episode, when one of the black campers was imprisoned in October for the knifing death of a black man from Camden, the result of a fight downtown near the Haiglar Theatre, the campers contributed to his defense fund. Presumably both blacks and whites donated. State newspapers reported on the violence, and the camp newspaper reminded campers of the importance of being law-abiding. In May 1936 the CCC camp invited Camden folk to a barn dance, at which all the musicians and callers would be camp members. It was reported that relations between camp and community were generally peaceful and supportive.

The extent of CCC activity continuing in Kershaw County is suggested by the March 20, 1936, *Chronicle* report that in the past three weeks, under the supervision of state foresters, two hundred thousand pines had been planted in Kershaw County with labor supplied from the CCC camps at Cassatt and Pontiac. Indications are that after the closing of Camp Hilton at Blaney, a good deal of forestry work in West Wateree was carried out by the CCC "Camp Pontiac," just across the line in neighboring Richland County at U.S. Highway 1 and present Clemson Road. That camp was still in operation in the early part of the following decade.

Liberty Hill CCC Campers

Some Liberty Hill citizens recall CCC workers in their area also. Here tented "transient" work camps were sent out from the other camps, which had more permanently established facilities, being more accessible to highway and railway supplies. One Liberty Hill camp was located west of Highway 97, about a half mile past the Thompson house, on the property of Mrs. James (Eva Perry) McCoy.

The high-hill altitude of Liberty Hill made the area especially important in forest fire management, as it overlooked parts of three counties and two sides of the Wateree River. Working with the cooperation of the state forestry commission and local voluntary fire district associations, CCC labor helped complete a telephone-linked system of steel fire towers, firebreaks, and roads for firefighting. An observer in each strategically placed tower kept watch over the surrounding area.

The county's third fire tower, constructed at Blaney in 1933, was linked to the Camden and Liberty Hill towers, and in 1936 two more towers were constructed—at Westville and Cassatt. In 1946 the Buffalo fire tower was completed, the last of six towers that covered the entire county. At first wardens served as tower keepers, reporting fires and then joining ground crews to fight the blazes. Later separate tower men were hired.

The Liberty Hill historian Mary Ellen Cunningham, whose father was the first warden in that community, became its tower watchman in the later 1930s. Beyond their fire-fighting importance, the towers intrigued county citizens.

Cunningham describes the appeal at Liberty Hill: "The panoramic view was magnificent! During the summer months it was often the gathering place for young people who came from near and far to enjoy the view. They came at night to view the lights far away and to enjoy the moonlight and cool breezes."[43]

Supreme Court Interventions

Two New Deal programs were struck down by U.S. Supreme Court rulings less than three years later. One decision affected the National Recovery Administration (NRA) and the other, the Agricultural Adjustment Administration (AAA), both of which were initially undertaken with general acceptance in Kershaw County. In both cases the court ruled unconstitutional some of the assumption of executive powers.

By late 1933 Henry Savage Jr., a Camden lawyer, had written a political treatise, published in Philadelphia and copyrighted the following year. *America Goes Socialistic: An Interpretation of Our Governmental Drift* received serious legal and scholarly attention. Over time much debate has waged over political philosophies and implications of increased national government, a process of change under way during the New Deal.

AAA

The Agricultural Adjustment Administration aimed to accomplish what had been attempted many times before—to counter the market glut of cotton and tobacco and thereby improve prices. In March 1933, at the beginning of the AAA's acreage reduction program, cotton and tobacco were already growing in the fields. Landowners were paid to sign agreements to "lease" a portion of their cropland to the government and to plow under the crop growing on that portion. Farmers in South Carolina were expected to plow up 30 percent of their estimated production. They were free to use the plowed-up plants in any way, such as hay or manure, and they were allowed to plant and harvest other crops on the leased land.

County farm agents, who were called upon to examine and estimate crop yields, were responsible for explaining the reduction program to farmers and for encouraging their cooperation in accepting payments to plow under the requested portion. Compensation in the county began at six dollars an acre. Local compliance was quick and willing, according to the farm agent Henry D. Green. In fact Kershaw County was reported to be the first in the state to complete the contract process. Farmers who destroyed crops were resentful of those who did not, asking why the latter should profit from the former's sacrifices.

In 1934 crop reduction was made mandatory by a heavy tax placed on any cotton sold outside government contract. Most county farmers complied by signing the agreements to limit their crops. William M. Teal, a Cassatt farmer, did not object to voluntary controls but had refused to sign this contract since he was opposed on principle to the government telling him what he could do on his own land. As a result Teal had to tag and sell all his cotton at a lower price in the fall. With a family to feed, he felt compelled to accept a contract the next year.[44] In January 1936 the U.S. Supreme Court voided the tax, ending mandatory enforcement. Later in the decade crop control was restored more successfully as part of soil conservation. Farmers received payments as incentives to reduce crops, such as cotton and tobacco, that wore out the soil and to plant instead crops that restored nitrogen in the soil, such as lespedeza and crotalaria.

NRA

With patriotic energy Kershaw County citizens, businesses, and industries in August 1933 signed up to display the distinctive "blue eagle" representing compliance with the National Recovery Administration. Hardly any more encouragement was needed than that their president had asked them to do so. With economic recovery as the goal, many people were willing to accept emergency wage, hour, and price controls just as they had done in wartime. The county campaign to encourage compliance with controls was organized to include all citizens. The Camden merchants organized and agreed to accept uniform hours—8:00 A.M. to 5:00 P.M. on weekdays and 8:00 A.M. to 9:00 P.M. on Saturdays, with half days off on Thursdays in August.

The owner of one local enterprise expressed immediate doubt that the company could carry on business restricted to the standard hourly controls, although he agreed to try. The Electrik Maid Bake Shop had to bake a perishable commodity in time to sell it in their DeKalb Street store and to ship it to other markets, dependant on train schedules. Dairies likewise had similar objections. Even as hour adjustments were made industry by industry, many local concerns had problems paying higher, standardized wages. Businesses that struggled to comply with government regulations resented those that ignored or flouted them.

The Strike of 1934

During negotiations establishing industrial codes, complex problems in southern textile mills came to a head along with those of other mills across the nation. The major ongoing complaint of South Carolina workers was the employee workload. Some mills, they said, gave workers too few hours' work to earn a living wage. Other mills, they said, let some workers go while requiring the remainder to complete more work in the same time. Mill owners asserted that they had to increase efficiency in order to operate profitably.

Southern textile workers, hoping an industrial code would amend "speed-up" and "stretch-out" conditions, relied on the NRA to protect their promised right to bargain collectively. By February 1934 Local Union no. 1913 had organized in

Camden and was raising funds with a benefit at Pine Tree School, featuring hillbilly and Hawaiian music by two groups of radio artists. Information on whether the union engaged in negotiations with local mills or if there were local grievances was not made part of published accounts.

Also in February 1934, coincidentally, the *Chronicle* published a guest list of Henry P. Kendall, owner of the Wateree Mill, at his Camden winter home, the Sycamores. Kendall, who had been an adviser to President Hoover, was now an adviser to President Roosevelt and a committee member of the NRA. Other powerful national leaders visited him in Camden: Dr. M. L. Wilson, director of the Division of Subsistence Homesteads; F. A. Silcox, chief U.S. forester; Walter Lowdermilk, head of the Soil Erosion Department; and Rexford Tugwell, undersecretary of agriculture and original member of the "Brain Trust" that aided FDR's economic plan in his first one hundred days.

Later in 1934 American labor groups, frustrated that boards negotiating industrial codes were overweighted with representatives of management, combined efforts to invoke government enforcement of NRA promises of fairness. Beginning on Labor Day 1934 Kershaw County textile workers joined other mill employees across the nation in a strike called by the United Textile Workers (UTW). It was the second-largest strike to date in the country and the first general strike in South Carolina. Kershaw County mills were closed throughout its three-week duration.

Some local attitudes toward the strike were revealed in a September 7 *Camden Chronicle* editorial and in the exchange it prompted. "We are happy to number many of the workers in the two mills here among our best friends and we sympathize with them all greatly at this time," the editorial began. However, a familiar claim followed: "We cannot help but feel that they are being made tools of for the benefit of others." The *Chronicle* continued, "We know that the men and women who are striking here are doing so honestly, but we are just as sure that the strike will result in no good to them; on the other hand, that it is going to do them untold harm and that they and their neighbors will suffer." The editorial further stated:

> If the strike continues our friends at the mills will have to spend any money they have saved against a rainy day and will then be compelled to join the relief rolls. Conditions may not have been altogether ideal, but everyone has been up against it for the past several years and the average mill worker has gotten along just as well, if not better than his fellows in other walks of life.
>
> The strike coming just at this time is bound to seriously injure the farmer, who will not be able to sell his cotton if it cannot be manufactured and if it continues for any appreciable length of time it will paralyze business throughout the South . . . we do not think that the workers of South

> Carolina should be called upon to jeopardize themselves and their families and to injure their friends and neighbors at the whim of the big dogs in the organization who, to tell the truth, know nothing about them and care less. . . . We want to say to our friends at the Wateree and Hermitage Mills that we hope they will give this matter further and more serious consideration, and question among themselves, if they are helping our President in trying to bring prosperity back.

In response, two weeks later the newspaper printed a letter to the editor, "What the Public Should Know," signed by "A Southern Worker," stating that "the textile workers of the community wish to disagree with some of the statements" in the editorial. The writer denied that the strikers were "tools" of union leaders and pointed out the following:

> When the local unions of South Carolina and other southern states were organized, there was no thought of a strike being called as long as all the code was complied with. Therefore the workers were not organized under stress.
>
> We people of the south claim at least a little common sense and like to be considered as human beings: not as a bunch of slaves, serfs or convicts; and under the existing conditions in some of the southern mills we are regarded by our employer as little more.

The writer gave several examples of overwork: "Can our criticizing public imagine a woman or young girl with her clothes wringing wet with perspiration, pausing for a moment at a window to get a breath of air only to be whistled at by a section man or overseer and ordered back to their work? Some of the workers are even forbidden to go and get a drink of water unless their job is caught up, which is very seldom." The writer also referred to "a man with a family of five or six trying to feed and clothe them all on from $9.00 to 12.00 per week at the present commodity prices" and asked:

> Can he be expected to enjoy any of the luxuries of life that mean so much to his employers and others of their class, who go to the mountains and beaches and take their vacations for weeks, while the men and women who make this possible for them work and toil their life away and reap only a bare existence.
>
> We workers don't expect to get an equal share of the profits of our employers but we do feel that we are entitled to a wage that will enable us to clothe and feed our families and perhaps give us a few of the luxuries that our employers have all of.

South Carolina strikers picketed with signs supporting the New Deal and claimed to be upholding the government. Mill owners too claimed government protection. When "flying squadrons" of workers picketed individual mills in large numbers to shut them down, Governor Blackwood responded under state law to quell disturbances, calling out the National Guard to enforce the peace and protect property. Blackwood ordered guardsmen to "shoot to kill" any striker illegally entering mill property, which was also being protected by local deputies and other men privately hired by mill owners.

The Kershaw Guards, under Captain Brevard Boykin, were ordered out to Laurens County to keep order at the Joanna Mills at Goldville (today Joanna), near Clinton. There were no shootings here, as there were in the neighboring county at Honea Path, where private guards killed seven picketers and wounded a number more. However, in a nonviolent confrontation in front of the Joanna Mills, the Kershaw Guards faced a squadron of seven hundred strikers. The strikers withdrew peaceably after a discussion with Captain Boykin. When the Kershaw Guards returned home, W. A. Moorhead of Joanna Mills published a grateful letter to Governor Blackwood praising them as "all fine fellows" and asserting that the governor's quick action had prevented bloodshed in "one of the most serious situations this state has ever faced."

Three weeks after it began, the strike ended with an agreement that a workload code would be considered, giving rise to immediate UTW claims of victory. In fact the outcome was decidedly different. Newspaper headlines stated flatly, "Strikers Have Gained Nothing by Walkout," not even union recognition. Many mills delayed opening back up, first selling inventory on hand and then reportedly taking back only the workers they chose. Most strikers had exhausted their financial reserves, and many lost jobs in the end. There were plenty of unemployed people ready to take the places of those who had lost favor with mill bosses. No workload code was ever passed. The NRA had no means to enforce the codes that had been proposed.

In Camden the Wateree Mill was opened immediately at strike's end, operating "full blast, both day and night shifts," and the Hermitage Mill opened a few days later. The October 5 *Chronicle* editorial rejoiced: "The entire community is glad that we again hear the whistles and the hum of the machinery at the Kendall and Hermitage Mills here. The operatives have gone back to work; we have not been advised just what the terms of settlement were, but it is our understanding that all differences will be ironed out by a commission or board, chosen under a plan agreed upon."

The writer of the editorial lamented that the strike had occurred at the market time of cotton, "about our only money crop," producing "a most disheartening effect on the people of the South." Elsewhere, Governor Blackwood called the strike's effect "calamitous," having "paralyzed ordinary business." The *Chronicle* editorial writer attempted a cheery tone in closing: "The folks at the mills here are to be complimented. . . . They conducted themselves in a most orderly manner and the friendliest feeling between those in authority and the workers prevailed." In fact the undisputed aftermath of the experience was a common distaste for union activity that lingered for decades.[45]

Continuing Tourism

In the first days of New Deal administration, the local newspaper reporter and tourist publicist John W. Lyman brought attention to the continuing pattern of life in Camden's winter colony: "Closing of banks and all this talk of depression which now seems paramount in conversational art has in no manner dampened the ardor and enthusiasm of such keen and optimistic sportsmen as Harry D. Kirkover and Ernest L. Woodward, who are going right ahead to make the annual running of The Carolina Cup steeplechase meet on March 25th [1933] the biggest and best ever run over the famous Springdale track." Lyman quoted Kirkover: "Every mail is bringing in entries which have to be listed and, in spite of what some folks may call depression, we are finding it rather difficult to attend to anything else."

Backing winners cheered those with equestrian interests. During the Depression it seemed, in fact, that everyone loved a winner, especially long-shot winners. Although fans still followed the sport of polo, public fancy was captivated by a number of racing champions among local riders, trainers, and owners. Some stories have been told over and over. Excitement reigned in 1933 as Ray Woolfe rode Hotspur, an "aged chestnut gelding," to a second-time win in the Washington's Birthday Race. "Gentleman jockey" Carroll Bassett, also an accomplished equestrian sculptor and Camden winter resident, rode the locally trained Battleship to three national victories, including the U.S. Grand National, in 1933–34.[46]

Kershaw County natives followed with special interest the riding career of Jimmy Clyburn, a native-born jockey successfully garnering accolades. Governor Blackwood was said to miss a steeplechase seldom and was often in Camden, where his supporters included a number of the winter colony.[47] Even Bernard Baruch was racing in the steeplechase field. Although located out of state, he recalled his roots by using the name Kershaw Stables.

In 1935, the first year admission was charged to attend the Carolina Cup, Joe Williams wrote from Camden to the *New York Evening World-Telegram* describing the excitement of the Springdale course: "There is no grandstand or club house. You drive into the rolling grounds, park your car against a rail, getting as close to the finish line as possible, and see the race that way. . . . There is a delightful informality about Cup Day down here . . . there are no stands at all, but railed land, studded with timber, fences, and hedge. If you were a Club member, you see the Show from the infield. This puts the race practically in your lap. You are close enough to see the wild stare in the horses' eyes, the drawn faces of the riders, feel clods of flying dirt fly past your ears, and hear the ominous orchestra of pounding hoofs."

Older equestrian facilities were expanded after Marion duPont Scott (wife of the movie star Randolph Scott and formerly Mrs. Tommy Somerville) purchased land near a former skeet field and the old "Cherokee [driving club] race track" for a residence and stables in 1935. In the following year, with her brother William duPont, Mrs. Scott consulted with track engineers to find property for a mile-long flat course and a schooling track. Near the western end of Chesnut Street they chose a seventy-seven-acre tract that included the old "Race Track Place," where spirited racing had attracted the owners of fine area horses in past generations. Work extended throughout the next two years to complete what was considered one of the South's top mile tracks.

In addition to equestrian reports, plugs for other resort activities and for related shops and entertainment spots were worked into columns of social news. Golf was active at the Kirkwood and Sarsfield courses. At the Camden Hotel the Boston Shop sold upscale clothing, and the Hoffer Company marketed optometry and jewelry. Near the Hobkirk, Mrs. Catherine H. Goodale's Studio Shop maintained sales of luxury items. At the Court Inn the Resort Shop of Rhoda Burke of Detroit advertised "Hand-Knitted Suits, Afternoon and Sport Dresses, Fine Underwear, and Hand-Made Table Linen." In the lower lobby of the Kirkwood, Razook of Lake Placid, New York, featured "silk and woolen sportswear suitable for resorts and evening wear." The Southern Garden Grille at the Kirkwood attracted fashionable diners.

In May 1935 in-state liquor sales were made legal again through state licensing. The first local license was issued to Elihu Schlosburg, owner of Rex Billiard Parlor. He promptly opened the S & S Package Shop at 1028 Broad Street. In early June the city passed regulations requiring Camden liquor stores to close from 3:00 P.M. on Saturday until sunrise on Monday. Society columns treated as glamorous the Court Inn's opening of its Cocktail Lounge, renamed the Bang Bang Club two years later, and reported a rage of fashionable cocktail parties in elegant homes. However, the local newspaper reported as scandalous the incidents of liquor consumption in the houses at "the lower end of town."

As fashionable settings for entertainments, nightclubs drew increased patronage. The month before liquor sales were legalized, a raid had seized contraband at the Sunset Club near the Precipice, but later in the year the club reopened "under new management" for dining and dancing with an orchestra and a Thanksgiving floor show. About the same time Dixie Boykin's new place, the Supper Club, was promoted in social columns. Meanwhile an illegal liquor sale at the Log Cabin on the Camden-Columbia road resulted in its owner being the first Camden dealer to lose his license. In the following months other *Chronicle* articles referred negatively to "roadhouses," tourist camps, and "loose living."

Effects of Travelers

Some county businessmen were pleased to see tourism expand beyond the resorts. Increased automobile traffic on U.S. Highway 1 stirred investment in at least seven new service stations in Camden in 1936. Most of them were directly on that route, and others were nearby. The area's first Amoco station opened on DeKalb near the Southern Railway. Near the Seaboard Air Line Railway a Sinclair station opened. U. N. Myers opened a Gulf station at the corner of DeKalb and Fair, and another Gulf station opened opposite the Baptist church on Broad. John T. Nettles erected two Texaco stations, one on DeKalb and the other at the corner of Rutledge and Market. Henry Beard opened a Standard station on lower Broad. In addition W. R. Bowden opened a new Western Auto Associates store on Broad. Also in 1936 the Seaboard, steadily losing passengers to highway travel, entered freight competition by seeking contracts with local truckers to deliver goods directly to stores.

Tourist advertising took forms other than traditional written ones. Camden was one of the resort communities in which South Carolina erected signs reading "Motorists, Give Horsemen Every Consideration." The signs called attention to equestrian activities for both safety and publicity reasons.[48] Three handsome billboards advertising Camden "in gay colors, framed in wrought iron lattice work" were painted here by George Franklin in 1934 and erected by the city at three key points along U.S. Highway 1—at Cheraw; at Raleigh, North Carolina; and at Stormburg, Virginia. The Chamber of Commerce reported that the advertising was essential because "last season persons had been hired to stay at filling stations and crossroads to direct tourists over the Coastal highway" and away from the route through Kershaw County.

One of the enticements away from U.S. Highway 1 was an old thorn in the side—the tolls over the Wateree River bridge. Serious objections were being raised that it was the only such charge on all Highway 1 and that because federal money had been used on the road, such charges were not legal. The county argued that the toll was not on the roadway but on the bridge, which had been built solely at county expense and on which the county still owed money. The Highway 1 Association was concerned because multiple areas were affected by any discouragement to traffic along the route, and the group widened the appeal to the state legislature to end the toll.

In April 1934, acting on a bill arguing that tolls should have been lifted three years earlier when the state highway put a hard surface on the bridge, the General Assembly agreed to purchase four bridges in the state, one of them the Wateree. Kershaw County was compensated $147,500, paid in nine annual installments. The toll house was immediately razed, the bridge was resurfaced, and the tolls were lifted on April 30. The *Chronicle* praised the event: "County motorists, as well as out-of-county motorists, hail with delight the freeing of the bridge, and the glad news will no doubt spread rapidly."

Other advertisements induced tourists not to pass through the area but to linger. In the 1920s resort hotels had bragged about their direct wires to the stock market, but in the 1930s they touted their relaxing baths. The Kirkwood Hotel, for example, had an eye-catching header for an ad: "I feel like a Thousand Dollars but only pay 2.00." The Kirkwood had "Medical Baths . . . Electric Cabinet, Massage and Medical Gymnastics, Reducing Massage and Exercise. Oil and Salt Rubs, Hot Fomentations, Etc.," and all were "Scientifically done by Swedish Masseuse and Medical Gymnast." The worries of the time or stresses of travel were relaxed away.

Along with the tourist-related guest homes, tearooms, and gift shops typically operated by females, several larger establishments catering to winter residents were taken over by female management during the Depression. In 1935 Mrs. Margaret E. Miller moved to Camden to continue the landscaping business she had operated with her husband, Thomas W. Miller, lately deceased. On Broad Street she opened the Colonial Boxwood Company in a remodeled portion of the old Gerald family home, which had been ravaged by fire the previous year, and set about beautifying the grounds of the old estate. In 1936 she married the rival nurseryman J. Withers Trotter, and for years afterward the couple operated the Evergreen Nursery near Quaker Cemetery.

When J. A. Sterne died in spring 1936, his widow took over the operation of the commercial Hotel Camden, which her husband had managed. In fall 1936, after Harry Greenwood Marvin died at their home on the Hobkirk Inn grounds, his widow continued the management of that resort for years. That same season, after Banyan R. Truesdell died, his widow continued operation of the Pines, a dining and social hall, at their home between Camden and Liberty Hill.

The Arts

Various facets of life in Kershaw County were interpreted through the arts. A brief flurry attended a premature announcement in November 1933 that a Hollywood studio was planning to film "the first motion picture to be produced in South Carolina" on location in Boykin. The movie, never made, was to be based on the 1932 novel *Dark Surrender* by former Camden winter resident Ronald Kirkbride, a published young poet, novelist, and editor of *Story* magazine. To the extent that it exploits the black culture that is its subject, the book may offend; yet it may also record information not elsewhere available. A lengthy dedication expresses gratitude to Dixie Boykin, the model for a white character named "The Boss," for "the truthful and extraordinary material which he has so generously made available to me, . . . impossible to obtain if he had not lived his entire life upon the self-same plantation." Through him the author claimed to have met "individually, each of the characters who appear in this book."[49]

In Kirkbride's younger years his family members were prominent winter residents at their plantation, Cool Springs. In preparation for writing his novel, Kirkbride and his wife lived in Boykin for a month on "Miss May Boykin's plantation," the setting of the novel. This suggests an effort to represent with familiarity the daily lives of people who were rarely presented in print. The extent to which Kirkbride informs, entertains, or offends with his portrayals will be judged by his readers. Conversation is rendered with dialectical spelling, and a number of characters are developed stereotypically. The novel was illustrated by pen sketches of rural scenes and black characters by Adele Savage of Camden, a young art student at the Boston Museum School of the Arts.

Crime

Widely advertised area attractions, the presence of wealthy persons, and easy in-out access to the community drew in criminal activity as well. Some involved familiar lawbreaking that the county had long been dealing with, such as bootlegging and periodic episodes in town and country among transient people labeled "gypsies." There was occasional variety. In late 1934 two young men from "prominent white families" were apprehended after a nightclub robbery four miles east of Camden. Officers learned that one of the youths over recent times had stolen and robbed at least fifteen slot machines in the county. Since all such machines were illegal, the owners had "so far been afraid to make an outcry."

The county's most daring escapade of robbery was a far different crime, however, and was believed to be the work of "nationally known jewel thieves." The Carolinas' largest theft of jewelry to date was deftly executed while home owners were attending the 1936 Carolina Cup. At that time "clever crooks invaded Holly Hedge, the spacious winter estate of Mrs. Ernest L. Woodward, socialite and sportswoman, and escaped with valuables worth approximately a quarter of a million dollars," a fabulous fortune for the time. Only one caretaker was at the home when the jewelry box was taken from a second-floor dresser drawer.

Not a word about the crime was published for a month, as the local press cooperated with the "absolute secrecy" of the police investigation that enlisted "crack detectives from New York, Miami, and elsewhere." Camden residents were reported to have "positively identified the pictures of several nationally known jewelry thieves" seen there the day of the race, but the crime went unsolved. Press attention was discouraged, no doubt from fears of its negative impact on tourism.

A Tragic Accident

What was probably the most shocking local accident of the decade occurred on August 3, 1935, north of Camden. Nine persons, all passengers in a single truck, were fatally injured in a collision with a southbound Seaboard train at the Dusty Bend crossing. The victims, en route to town for a routine day's shopping, were residents of the county's Lockhart section, also known as Boonetown.[50] Eyewitnesses reported that the driver of the truck, Murdock Baker, twenty-one years old, "swerved to the right to try to avoid" the train, which loomed in front of him, but the truck was thrown against the train at the embankment. The gruesome scene of mangled body parts stretched for more than one hundred yards, prompting warnings about the notorious curve for years to come. Seven of the victims, all surnamed Baker, were buried at Bethany Baptist Church in Westville. Newspapers estimated funeral attendance at four thousand. Likewise an exceptional crowd attended the funeral of the other two victims, surnamed Jordan, at Providence Baptist Church in Cassatt. The accident reminded many of the sudden, intense community losses from the Cleveland School fire the previous decade.

Effects of Aviation

Practical people were concerned in July 1933 when federal budget cuts threatened airmail services and thereby jeopardized the survival of the local airport business; Camden was, after all, the smallest city in the United States on a regular airline route. However, Kershaw County quickly joined the Charlotte, North Carolina, Chamber of Commerce to petition to keep the Charlotte-Camden air delivery route to Augusta.

There were more-flamboyant activities at Woodward Field that kept up public interest, however. In March 1934 the *Voice of the Sky,* a triplane, entertained from overhead with "amplified snatches of music, hearty human laughter, crisp sentences . . . plainly heard." It was part of an advertising campaign by Pure Oil Company for Purol Pep gasoline, distributed locally by Carolina Motor Company. In October 1934, when the air stunts of Russell Holderman were garnering local headlines, the *Chronicle* stated: "The young men of Camden are getting more and more air-minded, three having planes at the airport and others taking lessons. Those who have already made solo flights are Seldon Hunns, Clarkson Rhame, Johnnie Rickard, Capers Zemp, Arthur Harris DeLoache and Christopher Vaughan."

Several of these young leaders within a few years became casualties of the early years of aviation. In May 1935 Vaughan had a narrow escape when his engine went dead over Lake Shamokin and his plane after a forced landing stood on its nose and turned over.[51] DeLoache was killed in July at Sumter airport piloting a plane owned by Hunns, who died three years later stunt flying in North Carolina.

Meanwhile aviation continued to progress in a culture that admired thrills and spills and sought out the extraordinary. In July 1933 the Camden merchants' Mammoth Trade Day sponsored an "old-time balloon ascension" and parachute jump. "Daredevil Diavalo" rose upward by "the world's largest balloon" to leap out at 3,000 feet. The October 1934 county fair featured the nightly high dive of Captain "Daredevil" Leo Simon from a 105-foot ladder, with Simon "rocketing through space with his body enveloped in flames making 1½ turns backwards and landing on the flat of his back in a roaring furnace of fire." Other exotic attractions arrived via the Southern Railway later that month for a two-day show on a side rail. A special 120-foot car held "the mighty monster," a captive fin whale 55 feet long, as described to audiences by the veteran whaler Captain Mike Dolan. Appearing also were Professor W. E. Alexander's London Trained Fleas, all live, while outside audiences viewed "the world's largest cow," Lone Star, more than six feet tall and weighing more than seven ordinary cows put together. For a while longer aviation would continue to be regarded by many as primarily a sideshow entertainment.

Yet serious applications of aviation also were under way, and important discoveries were made as a result. More than four decades later Henry Savage Jr., in the preface to his study *The Mysterious Carolina Bays,* described his first commercial flight. The Camden lawyer flew to Washington, D.C., in "a futile attempt to reopen one of our local banks, following the March 1933 'banking holiday.'" On his return trip, when the plane was flying low over the Pee Dee, he "first became aware of the spectacular and mysterious topographical phenomenon of the Carolina bays."[52] The elliptical depressions pockmarking the surface below were also recorded by New Deal photographers assigned to document farmland conditions. The accidental revelation of the Carolina bays on aerial photographs opened new areas of scientific inquiry that are still under way.

The New Deal—Later Years

In 1937, the first year of Roosevelt's second administration, a recession slowed the progress of national recovery. Locally, however, many individuals felt the effects of what the *Chronicle* called "a new mark in banking history." In September the family of the octogenarian Henry G. Carrison Sr., who died shortly afterward, organized the Carrison Holding Company to discharge speedily the final obligations against the closed Bank of Camden, which he had headed for more than forty-four years as founder, organizer, and president. Unpaid deposits of $208,000, "the savings of 1,900 depositors, white and colored, in the old Bank of Camden, which closed in March 1933," were liquidated in the following two months. An editorial calling the action "business ethics" and "*Noblesse Oblige*" predicted a significant local impact since almost every depositor was a county resident.

In Kershaw County public and private construction pushed forward changes in several areas in 1937. At new locations a National Guard armory and a Seaboard railway passenger station were constructed. The facilities were erected a short distance from one another on a relatively undeveloped stretch of U.S.

Highway 1, west of the city limits of Camden, today West DeKalb Street. That same year, just within the western city limits, a new athletic field was developed on the Mather Academy campus.

The new armory that replaced the old, outdated armory on Rutledge Street was essential to meet the revised standards to retain a guard unit in the community. A federal grant of fifteen thousand dollars was added to ten thousand dollars raised by local and state funding, and yet corners had to be cut. Although the building was large and met the standards of its time, it was constructed without any heating system.

The site for the new train station was a tract of eighty acres donated by Ernest L. Woodward to the city of Camden. The station was in a "natural park," adjoining what was expected to become a premier polo field. Service was inaugurated in November with a great ceremony featuring local dignitaries acting as honorary crew members. Fred Ogburn, American Legion commander, had the fun he had dreamed of since boyhood—blowing the whistle coming into the station.

Increased traffic in the area justified state approval to widen the bituminous paving onto the shoulders of the stretch of U.S. Highway 1 between the Seaboard overpass and the "western gate" of the city. At each side of DeKalb Street's Gordon Street crossing, the highway's two-lane western entrance to Camden, a distinguished brick column was erected for a gateway, planned as a "Monumental Memorial" to veterans of the First World War.[53] The completion of the new paving was the first movement in the county toward a four-lane highway.

A Wateree River Focus

Westward progress continued as the U.S. Highway 1 Association supported local efforts to construct a new state bridge over the Wateree River. The necessity was made obvious in April 1938 when a two-ton truck skidded on the frosty surface of the antiquated wooden bridge and plunged into the swamp thirty to forty feet below its western end. Flames from exploding fuel tanks consumed seven spans of the bridge and necessitated several days of hard work to repair the damage. All traffic needing to cross the river had to be diverted miles out of the county. It was recognized that a lengthy interruption would "paralyze" the local economy.

By May 1939 the design had been determined for a new concrete and steel bridge to be constructed two thousand feet downstream from the old bridge, which would remain in use during construction. The stronger materials in the new design called for a straight bridge with straight approaches, unlike the old curved bridge and curved approaches.

Santee Cooper

The largest New Deal project in South Carolina, the Santee Cooper project, was approved in 1935, but its construction was delayed by legal challenges for four years. Private power companies and northern leisure sportsmen were alarmed by the General Assembly act creating the South Carolina Public Service Authority to produce and sell electricity and to manage the navigation and wetlands of the Santee, Cooper, and Congaree rivers. Although these voices sounded protests in local newspapers, many local citizens awaited the job opportunities and power benefits later realized through Santee Cooper.

Since the Wateree River flows into the Santee River system, Kershaw County in various ways was affected by Santee Cooper decisions. In fall 1938 arguments in Washington supported the improvement of Wateree River navigation as far north as Camden since it was "one of the largest pulp wood concentration points in the state and also offers other commodities that could be carried [south] on river barges." By December companies were being solicited to ship building materials southward by the Wateree River for the Santee Cooper project. Work clearing the river soon began moving northward. At a public meeting in Camden in February 1939, the city promised to build a public dock and terminal here once navigation was improved to this point.

By spring 1939 the historic role of the Wateree River must have seemed potentially revivable. In March the tugboat *Helen* steamed up the river to a gravel company at Wateree in Richland County carrying fertilizer and crude oil and then returned to Charleston carrying gravel. It was noted as the first such craft to make that trip since 1916. Federal engineers surveyed as far north as the U.S. Highway 1 bridge at Camden and in August approved a river snagging plan on the Wateree and a new bridge over the Lynches River.

However, by August, when Becker County Sand and Gravel Company of Crosby, Minnesota, established a super gravel and sand production plant near Lugoff, the company laid a two-mile spur track to the Seaboard. The company's plans for supplying the Santee Cooper project did not refer to shipping on the Wateree. The plant, employing eighty workers, most of them local men, opened with a daily capacity of twenty-five carloads of washed gravel and washed sand for concrete construction.

Meanwhile in October 1937 Santee Cooper representatives met at Liberty Hill to investigate land and prices negotiated by the old Southern Power Company for the building of the Wateree Dam. Their study would "aid in the adjustment of values on lands that must be bought for the big Santee-Cooper project." Duke Power Company, which had absorbed the old company, was the largest corporate taxpayer in Kershaw County, followed by the Southern Railway Company, Kendall Mills, Hermitage Mills, and the Southern Bell Telephone and Telegraph Company.

By the end of 1937 Duke Power Company, described tongue-in-cheek by the *Chronicle*'s Liberty Hill correspondent as the owner of "much land adjacent to the Big Pond near here, on which many people lived," stopped renting land and began to tear down and remove all houses on its property. Thus ended settlements at old construction camp sites as well as scattered homesteading by renters and squatters.

Economic Climate

By 1937 production was under way in various parts of the county. A number of citizens had taken work at Haile Gold Mine near Kershaw after a cyanide process was installed two years earlier, and the operations continued to expand. The Camden Floral Company under N. R. Goodale shipped many varieties of plants by railroad to points all along the Eastern Seaboard. The company still held the distinction of being the nation's largest grower of Easter lilies and one of the largest shippers of poinsettias. In the fall the Powe and McLeod Veneer Company started operation west of Camden, beginning with twenty-five men and soon doubling its employees. "Giant" logs were rolled onto "monster" lathes, which peeled "long thin ribbons of wood" cut to dimension and then stacked, dried, and shipped by train to furniture manufacturers across the South and the East.

Wage and price scales continued to be troublesome, especially in traditionally low-paying jobs. In spring 1937 a gang of fourteen black woodcutters went on strike protesting their wage scale. When their employer, Dewey Creed, refused to negotiate with their spokesman, four men returned to work and ten remained on strike, but logging resumed as the men were easily replaced by newly hired workers. In October 1938 the *Chronicle* denied as "wild rumors" the reports sweeping through downtown Camden that area industrial plants were closing because of wage and hours laws. To the contrary the newspaper reported that the management of Guy Lumber Company, the Wateree Lumber Company, and the Powe veneer plant had no intention of shutting down.

Charitable Aid

Charity and government assistance continued to help those in need. Often help was individually provided. For example in 1937, when the Westville native Dr. William Richard Clyburn died after forty-eight years as a physician and surgeon, his obituary spoke appreciatively of him as "an old-time family doctor—who responded to every call—white or black—many a time—with no hope of reward—other than duty well done. It has been known of him to buy for, and carry, necessary drugs—and in many instances where it was a poor family—he would carry groceries to sustain the family." All the businesses in Camden closed for the hour of his funeral.

Both Camden Hospital and the Children's Home received benefits from the Duke endowment as well as from local fund-raising. In 1937 the Junior Welfare League presented a portrait of Mrs. Margaret C. Mayfield to hang in the Children's Home in honor of her charitable work. Many saw the home as a way of saving lives and sparing children from want and suffering. In 1938 the home, looking for expanded quarters, took in 30 babies and successfully placed all in homes for adoption. Since the home was opened in 1930, 195 children had been adopted by 1939.

The annual tonsil clinics and dental clinics of the Junior League continued aid to county children, and the Goodfellows Club carried on its traditional Christmas gift giving to the underprivileged. Volunteers raised funds and provided services for the local Red Cross and increasingly for the Kershaw County Tuberculosis Association. Extensive campaigns to sell Christmas Seals in the fight against TB reached countywide into both white and black communities.

Government Assistance

In 1937 and 1938 a number of government projects provided jobs to improve education, health, and general well-being in the community. Across the county schools for blacks and whites were built, enlarged, or repaired with the assistance of WPA construction workers. New buildings included an auditorium at Blaney High School, a gymnasium at Camden High School, an auditorium and gymnasium at Charlotte Thompson High School, and teacherages (dormitories for teachers) at Antioch and DeKalb. In addition frame schoolhouses of two to eight rooms were erected at Blaney, Camden, Liberty Hill, Mt. Pisgah, Pleasant Hill, and Stoneboro.

Across the county a dozen library centers were operated. A Library on Wheels program that had been inaugurated the year before grew from a circulation of four hundred to more than thirty-three thousand books by spring 1937. Jessie Johnson Baker with the assistance of Daisy Carroll headed a staff that included four binding helpers and eleven junior librarians, with one placed in the Camden school system and one in the Wateree school system. The county book truck ran nine routes that made fifty-two stops at rural locations. The mending library also repaired books used in county schools.

Assistance to demonstration service programs, to sanitation projects, and to hot lunch programs at schools was widespread across the county. Nursery school programs and nutrition camps strengthened needy children. Ditch drainage and highway landscaping improved health and safety conditions, while curbing and sidewalk improvements at Quaker Cemetery stabilized its landscaping.

At Liberty Hill a community recreational building was constructed with a small stage and a large stone fireplace. At Camden an outdoor concrete skating rink, with benches along the sides, was built at the corner of Laurens and Broad streets. Recreational programs encouraged well-being. At Camden work began to develop a recreational park on the eighty-eight acres that Ernest L. Woodward had donated to the city for that purpose.

In mid-1938 funds were approved for a long-sought goal, the building of a new county jail to replace the outmoded one that grand juries had complained about year after year. Assistance from both PWA and WPA was needed for the major project. Later in the year a new jail was also approved as a WPA project at Bethune.

However, government employment changed in the closing months of 1938 as some seven hundred to eight hundred of the WPA workers in Kershaw County lost their jobs, part of the national reduction of employees now eligible for recently available Social Security and of farmers eligible for other aid. No new assignments filled vacated positions. Some people considered the ending of government jobs to be an indication of an improving economy.

Among projects continuing in 1939 were sewing and recycling activities, such as one at Bethune, where "the thrift-room in the old bank building adjoining the drug store presents an active scene these days approaching the Christmas holiday season." Fourteen women were making and dressing dolls for the commodity office in Camden to distribute during the holidays to the county's needy children. The women were busy too with their regular work, piecing and quilting bedcovers and weaving scatter rugs and seat bottoms. It was pointed out that "the splendid training received here is of great value to the workers in their homes as they carry out the useful practice of thrift."

At the beginning of the New Deal, training programs such as the CCC focused on young men, but later in the decade the National Youth Administration (NYA) had programs that also included opportunities for young women. In 1939 a *Chronicle* reporter visited the NYA Home on Laurens Court in Camden "to observe the work being done with girls from the rural districts of Kershaw County." In the old Blackwell home thirty-six girls ages eighteen to twenty-four, divided into two groups, lived for alternating weeks to receive "training in cooking, sewing, home and table manners, hear current news events discussed and analyzed and in general fit themselves to be dependable, economic and cultured young women."

NYA center supervisor Anna McCullum was an instructor and a housemother; Rachel O'Daniel (later McGrew) taught night classes in home economics; and Ralph McCaskill instructed in current events. The young women cooked their own meals, made tablecloths and napkins, and quilted bedcovers for the Children's Home. The county provided rent for the home, and the city donated water and lights. Activities were financed by the Red Cross, the TB Association, the Junior Welfare League, and other civic organizations. In a workshop near the courthouse William Rast in 1939 supervised an NYA project training a similar number of young men in building construction.

Building Boom

In spring 1938 construction was under way on a new Camden residential development between Broad and Lyttleton, and Chesnut and Hampton streets. Carrison Avenue was opened, serviced by water mains and a sanitary and storm

Young women at the National Youth Administration stop of the county bookmobile in 1937. Courtesy of the Camden Archives

sewage system. Dr. R. E. Stevenson, a project initiator, and W. T. Redfearn each had several homes, priced from thirty-five hundred dollars to five thousand dollars, under way. Federal financing incentives provided purchasers with terms "cheaper than rent": a down payment of four hundred dollars and monthly payments of around twenty-four dollars.

Aggregate construction prompted the *Chronicle* to claim on April 15, "Never before in the history of the city has there been such a pronounced revival of building activity." The most impressive business structure under way was Kornegay Funeral Home at ten thousand dollars. A new Kershaw County agricultural building of brick and stone was under way at a cost of twenty-five thousand to thirty thousand dollars to house thirty-two separate office units. Developers promised brick apartment buildings with exceptional innovations of central heating and air-conditioning equipment and electrical cooking and refrigeration appliances. The claim was made, perhaps for the first time, that "the fact that Camden is within easy commuting distance from Columbia, has resulted in the request from Columbia people for home accommodations here."

By fall the Camden boom continued for both bungalows and large homes and had expanded further. At both Bethesda Presbyterian and Grace Episcopal churches renovations were under way. Grace refinished its interior, installing new choir stalls, raising the windows at the back of the altar, and adding several new memorial art glass windows. The previous year Bethesda's sanctuary had been closed from April to December for extensive work to restore the interior of the historic church to its original appearance, which had been altered by 1890s remodeling. Langston Motors built a new garage and service station on Broad Street near the post office, and a new Sinclair station opened at Market and DeKalb streets. The energy of new construction was viewed positively in several areas. The veneer plant enlarged, the Commercial Bank underwent renovation, and the fire department modernized.

Sports Spinoff

Recreational facilities expanded, including a baseball park with new bleachers and a grandstand added at the football field in Camden, with a clubhouse to be shared by teams of both sports. Organized sports participation and enthusiasm had been encouraged throughout the county by WPA recreation programs that were promoted for health reasons and in various facets reached all parts of the county, all ages, both races, and both genders.

So excited were football fans about the Camden High Bulldogs' state championship wins in 1931 an 1936, that they pooled resources to buy their coach, John Villepigue, a new car. It was a grand gesture, given the times, and representative of high personal regard as well as sports fever.

Interest in baseball was high when the Syracuse Chiefs of the International League wintered at the new park for a couple of seasons, and locals in response formed a new amateur baseball club, the Camden Chiefs, in 1939. Their shirts, compliments of the professional team, each bore the image of an Indian head, which was considered appropriate as a reference to King Hagler.

Softball leagues for all ages and both genders also played throughout the county. The American Legion junior baseball club formed in 1937 under Coach Hulan Small, better known as "Pop" to teams and fans who followed his leadership in several sports. Donald Morrison, who had become the city health officer, was player-manager of the Camden Municipal Softball League in 1939.

Two years earlier Morrison had taken charge of a nine-hole municipal golf course established by the city on the south portion of the old Sarsfield course. Like golf, tennis also expanded as a public sport with the addition of courts widely. In 1939 the third annual Kershaw-Lancaster County tennis tournament was played on courts at Kershaw, headed by tennis coach R. E. Edwards. Backboards for practice were opened to the public at a small fee in 1939.

Tourism

Changes that had been taking place in the tourist industry presented a challenge to those who hoped to see the resorts hold their longtime prominence in the local economy. Aging structures with their ambiance of charm were costly to maintain, especially when they stood empty and made no money most of the year. They were also difficult to convert for the modern conveniences of heating, cooling, plumbing, and electricity that attracted wealthy patrons to newer facilities. For a few seasons from 1936 Ruth Richards converted the use of her Green Leaf Villa to a boarding school for girls. The school opened under Mrs. J. B. Zemp, who for many years kept in her home and at the Kirkwood a private school for children of the winter colony.

In 1937 Ivy Lodge, nearly a century and a half or more in age, was given a sound renovation by its new owner A. R. Moseley, a Camden native, who had spent more than a dozen recent years in the hotel business in Florida and eastern North Carolina. His ambition to maintain the birthplace of Bernard Baruch as a fine tourist inn was frustrated in 1939 by repeated fires of undetermined origin that caused thousands of dollars of damage. Outside of town the Sunset Club, recently remodeled as a nightclub, burned to the ground the same year. The heart pine of which most buildings were constructed burned easily.

In 1937 when the Court Inn was sold to a group of Camden men, the aged facilities included a three-story main building with basement and eighty-eight rooms, one six-room cottage and one nine-room cottage, and fifty acres with pines, a landscaped maze, and an arched shrubbery walkway known as Lovers' Lane. Redecorated and with modernized plumbing and a central switchboard, the Court Inn reopened in October, leased for new operation as a commercial-tourist hotel. Its major competition was the Camden Hotel, which advertised as "the city's year-round commercial hostelry."

By offering both European and American plans, the Court Inn proposed to stay open year-round to become "the center of Camden social activities." Among its first guests were the thirty-three members of the University of South Carolina football team and Coach Don McAllister the night before the biggest game of the year, the Carolina-Clemson game. Each succeeding year, however, there was a different manager at the Court Inn, and at the end of the decade the dining room was often closed. In the spring the Court Inn sought the business of northbound tourists who had wintered in Florida, and in the summer it was advertised for boarders at commercial rates.

Both the Hobkirk Inn and the Kirkwood Hotel were sold in 1938 and underwent renovations. The Hobkirk could accommodate 100 guests on 11 acres with its main house, seven cottages, a group of tennis courts, and landscaped gardens. The Kirkwood covered 132 acres with 170 guest rooms, several cottages, riding stables, and a golf course. Both establishments in 1939 offered free concerts on Sundays, and townspeople with appropriate dress and manners were welcome to attend. That season proved to be the closing one for the Hobkirk, however, as Camden's original tourist home the following year was sold to a private owner and, with property divided and guest wings removed, later reverted to a stately residence.

The golf course at the Kirkwood Hotel had also been sold in 1939 and underwent major redesign to incorporate modern grass greens in place of the old sand greens and to eliminate fairways that crossed the railroad track. The course was formally reopened in December 1939.

More sensational headlines followed a robbery attempt that year at the Kirkwood that evoked memories of the still-unsolved Woodward theft two years earlier. Kirkwood bell captain William Gamble and manager Milton C. Smith chased two accused high-profile jewel thieves through the hotel corridors and scuffled with them in the front court until a woman roared up in a high-powered automobile, the men jumped in, and the trio raced off in high gear. The incident was colorful but not the type of publicity that the resort community liked.

Community Spirit

In 1937 a "rejuvenated" Camden and Kershaw County Chamber of Commerce, under its executive secretary Frank H. Heath, adopted a goal to "knit the people of the county and city more closely together." One of its enthusiastic promotions in April was a trade exposition in Monument Park, opposite the public library, where the sloping ground allowed a large crowd to view the judging and coronation of Miss Kershaw County. Communities had voted representatives: Antioch, Alice Peebles; Bethune, Ava Shaw; Blaney, Mattie Rabon; Camden, Susan Team; Charlotte Thompson, Wanzalee Truesdale; DeKalb, Mary Lorick; Kershaw, Cornelia Truesdale; Midway, Ruby Gay West; and Mt. Pisgah, Ruby Hornsby.

Yet another Miss Kershaw County competition was held at the county fair in October when girls vied for the popularity title by selling votes that entered buyers into a drawing for a twenty-five-dollar prize. The fair also featured a fairgrounds wedding of an "undisclosed young couple" whose identity was kept secret until the last moment. The minister, ring, and bridesmaids were all provided by the Kershaw County Fair Association. Bridesmaids were representatives of local business firms, which also provided gifts for the couple.[54]

In October 1938 the Chamber of Commerce inaugurated a new countywide event to coincide with fair week, the "first annual" Cotton Festival. A goal was fun for all. Features included both a hog-calling contest and a husband-calling contest, a pavement dance to "hill billy music," and a water fight between two fire department teams, as well as races, a parade, and the crowning of the carnival queen. The evening highlight on Laurens Street was an outdoor Mardi Gras ball at which Mr. and Mrs. Beckham Russell took the prize for the best waltz. The ball, which lasted until after midnight, was attended by twenty-five hundred to thirty-five hundred persons, while parked autos lined all streets for blocks.

So successful was the Cotton Festival that in 1939 it was expanded to a three-day event. Queen Emily Zemp was crowned wearing a mantle made by the NYA. Farmer-Mayor N. P. Gettys and other rural farmers took over city offices. With floats, parades, contests, entertainments, dignitaries, displays, a dinner, a ball, and airplanes dropping confetti, goodwill seemed to reign. However, there were sobering moments. At the last minute *Life* magazine sent regrets that war in Europe prevented the magazine from keeping a promise to send journalists to the Cotton Festival. Concern over international events also entered the remarks of General Dozier, Congressional Medal of Honor recipient, at the Cotton Festival luncheon. "In the United States we can keep on raising cotton," he told his audience, and added, "Let's not jump at conclusions; we are 3,000 miles away from the European war and we can stay neutral."

International Concerns

The county was not isolated from world events reported in newspapers and by radio. For example, in 1937 the local press described military actions of Hitler and Mussolini, the explosion of the airship *Hindenburg,* and the search for the missing aviatrix Amelia Earhart. The local military past was also recognized that year as the U.S. Navy launched a new war vessel named *Camden* in honor of the Revolutionary War battle, and the deaths of two of the county's last three Confederate war veterans were reported, leaving Gilliam B. King of Bethune as the last Kershaw County surviving veteran of the Civil War.

One of the county's most familiar observers of both the local and international scenes was Camden native Mrs. Sadie Kennedy von Tresckow, whose husband, Edmont Charles von Tresckow, was consulate to Yugoslavia in the 1930s. On her return at the end of the decade she resumed active leadership at home. Her letters to the local newspaper broadened understanding of events of the time. In 1939 Kershaw County farm women stretched their presence afar when their home-demonstration agent Margaret Fewell represented them abroad at the international convention of the World Council of Farm Women and then gave many talks on her return.

Those in Camden's Jewish community kept in contact with family members in Europe and worried over growing political pressures. William Reasonover in later decades recalled the distress of "Miss Minnie" Baum, then his neighbor on Lyttleton Street, when she received letters from Europe. Tearing her hair and clutching her mail, she often walked up and down the street while weeping. Later a refugee child of relatives lived for a time with the Baums and, without yet knowing English, attended the Camden school.

In September 1939 members of the Camden Bulldogs football team and chaperones were sightseeing at the top of Mt. Pisgah at Pisgah National Park near their North Carolina summer camp, "on top of the world," when a radio picked up the newscast that Britain and France had declared war on Germany.

"It was," said the sports reporter accompanying them, "an interested crowd of young and old as the news of the world came in."

In the following months Kershaw County–area scenes reflected war anticipation. Haile Gold Mine opened a new ore strip on its Red Hill property, expecting renewed demand for pyrites "if the European war continues." Camden Iron and Metal, recalling the shortages of the last war, began advertising top prices for scrap metal. The Red Cross began a drive for eleven hundred county members, realizing that the organization may be called upon to "shoulder a responsibility never before dreamed of."

Curious juxtapositions of past, present, and future military images mingled in the closing weeks of 1939. At the Court Inn in Camden, members of the DAR heard a plea from the Rock Hill DAR on behalf of historic allies, the Catawba Indians, who were now in dire economic straits. Residents of Camden, having King Hagler as their "patron saint," were urged to support "early Federal action to change their status from wards of the state to wards of the U.S. Government" so that they could qualify for much-needed government aid. In December at the site of the Battle of Camden, the National Guard conducted weekend maneuvers while observation planes circled over the old Revolutionary War battleground to practice target spotting. In December, President Roosevelt passed through Camden aboard a Seaboard train bound for his treatment resort at Warm Springs, Georgia. At the Dusty Bend crossing FDR was most clearly seen slowly waving as the train passed without stopping. The leader of the New Deal would soon become the leader of a nation at war.

16

Wings of War

The 1940s

Long before the December 7, 1941, bombing of Pearl Harbor brought America into World War II, the probability of the nation's eventual role affected Kershaw County. In late 1939, across the Richland County line, the U.S. Army activated Camp Jackson, a former Great War training site that was then a S.C. National Guard training camp. Renamed Fort Jackson, the facility became a permanent military post in 1940 and underwent an extensive, multimillion-dollar expansion. A mass land condemnation doubled its size to nearly fifty-three thousand acres. The economic impact was significant in neighboring Kershaw County. The Chamber of Commerce solicited local rental properties to meet housing shortages for officers' families. Farm agent W. C. McCarley coordinated area truck farmers to serve Fort Jackson's food needs. A number of Kershaw County citizens found civilian jobs in construction, services, or offices at the fort.

In mid-1940 when Hitler besieged Paris and Mussolini declared war on England and France, the Camden City Council wired President Roosevelt to support the defense of those two nations. Fifth District congressman J. P. Richards of Liberty Hill urged Congress to their aid. A *Camden Chronicle* editorial advocated "every possible assistance . . . short of war." Hopes that America could remain at peace were still present.

Prelude to War

Along with improvements to the military infrastructure came the nation's first peace-time conscription, enacted in September 1940. The law established local draft boards to oversee the compulsory registration of eligible men.[1] The headquarters for the county draft board was in Camden's Legion Hall, 537 East DeKalb Street.

Registration day on October 16 was declared a state holiday in South Carolina, and schoolhouses were used to enroll white and black men ages twenty-one to thirty-five, one-fourth of the state's population. Schoolteachers assisted with the registration process. In Kershaw County 3,375 men registered. A lottery followed to draft individuals for twelve months of duty, although President Roosevelt later extended their time of service. In February 1941 veterans of "the World War," as World War I was still being called, were registered for emergencies in "strenuous times ahead."

Many military activations called citizens to duty in the prewar defensive buildup before what would become World War II. In September 1940 the local South Carolina National Guard unit, Company M, 118th Infantry, was ordered to Fort Jackson for a year of active duty. A large send-off honored Captain Brevard Boykin, his three officers, and ninety-six other men as they boarded a Seaboard transport train on Chesnut Street, where they had encamped in the park near the old station. A full-page newspaper ad announced the going-out-of-business sale for Arthur stores in Camden. Lieutenant Colonel H. M. Arthur, president, and Lieutenant A. A. Arthur, general manager, had both been ordered for duty with the National Guard.

Among other activations Commander Shannon Heath, chairman of the local Red Cross chapter, was recalled for duty at the U.S. Naval Academy at Annapolis. Midway School lost Superintendent Ford B. Stanton. From Baron DeKalb High School the agriculture teacher F. N. Culler was called into service and the commercial teacher Beatrice Lockerman took a job with the Federal Bureau of Investigation (FBI) in Washington, D.C.

The Reverend C. P. Cowherd of Timrod Baptist Church left to become a chaplain at Fort Jackson. Also ordered to that fort was F. N. Wimberly, who for five years had been a CCC camp officer before going to Camden High, where he had organized the school's first marching band. Wimberly was allowed to return to Camden twice weekly from the fort to continue directing the high school band.

At least one local youth had a brief moment of fame during prewar military service. Bethune's William R. Myers was one of the eleven South Carolinians in Fort Benning's 501st Battalion who appeared in the film *Parachute Battalion.* The recruitment-oriented drama played at Camden's Haiglar Theatre in October 1941. Recruitments for all branches were active during the prewar period. The governor even offered to pardon any former state prisoner who enlisted in the army, navy, or marine corps.

Near the end of 1940 Kershaw County organized a civilian Council of Defense, naming as its chairman John K. deLoach, commander of the home guards, Company E, South Carolina Defense Force, which served locally in the absence of the National Guard. The council compiled a local list of crisis volunteers and urged families to protect themselves from food shortages by planting home gardens. In January 1941 citizens collected arms, steel helmets, and binoculars for the American Committee for the Defense of British Homes. American Legion Post 17 donated more than two dozen rifles and steel helmets from its World War relic room. To strengthen home defense, the various WPA branches met to coordinate the health, nutrition, hospital, social, welfare, recreational, and library services of the county.

Local schools and the federal government paired to support programs that hired vocational specialists to teach defense-essential job skills to youths ages seventeen to twenty-five. In 1941 at Camden High School, James L. Anderson taught night classes in welding and machine work to train young men and women for ship-building jobs at Charleston. At Baron DeKalb the local garage owner Claude Truesdale taught classes in auto and tractor mechanics, woodwork, and electricity. Supervised by the agriculture teacher Francis Culler, the classes used both school equipment and "extensive tools and machines provided by the federal government." Other young men from Kershaw and Richland counties joined an NYA-supervised resident program at Columbia's Maxcy Gregg Park to train in a modern machine and sheet-metal shop.

The National Youth Administration continued support of the resident program on Laurens Court in Camden, where young white women were trained in homemaking skills. In January 1941 an NYA center for blacks opened at 804 Chesnut Street, supervised by Hettie Frazier and Edna Gamble Bates, a Mather Academy home economics teacher, to serve forty town and rural residents in a similar program. Healthy families were considered basic to national security.

During the nearly two years before America went to war, Kershaw County experienced much growth and change, although nothing matched the impact of two developments directly related to the nation's military buildup. These were the establishment of the Southern Aviation School (SAS) at Woodward Airport and the vast staging of army maneuvers across the county. Each development brought area towns and communities national and world attention, and created financial windfalls that helped jolt the laggard economy from its Depression hangover.

Southern Aviation School

By late 1938 President Roosevelt, recognizing the growing importance of air power and the potential of being drawn into the war in Europe, supported the development of a national air force. In 1940 Camden's Woodward Field, favored by pilots stopping between Florida and northern destinations, added clay runways and made other improvements with local, state, and federal funds. Meanwhile during the prewar buildup, the War Department created three centers across the nation to be responsible for military pilot training. The Southeast Air Corps Training Center in Alabama was assigned to oversee thirty-three training schools, four of them in South Carolina, including one at Camden. By the end of 1940 work had begun at Woodward Field to establish the Southern Aviation School, a civilian corporation under government contract to prepare about one hundred primary pilots every ten weeks for advanced military training in other states. Soon the frequent sights and sounds of training planes filled Kershaw

Southern Aviation School at Woodward Field, created to train pilots for World War II. Courtesy of the Camden Archives

County skies, and pilots practiced landings and takeoffs at various remote auxiliary fields across the county.[2]

Initial staffing at the Camden school included some 70 officers, mechanics, and department heads. The U.S. Army provided up to 30 representatives, and 23 flight instructors directed the opening quota of 112 cadets. Sixteen mechanics maintained thirty-two new Stearman training planes. School officials were Frank W. Hulse, president; Ike F. Jones, vice president; and the Camden lawyer Henry Savage Jr., secretary-treasurer. Other local employees included Jack Nettles, airport manager, and Gertrude M. Zemp, dietician. Jones became SAS director in August 1941. Among the first instructors was a local pilot, Sam Boykin.

The economic impact of the aviation school was tremendous. At Woodward Field a hangar was constructed first, and an administration building, a mess and recreation hall, a classroom unit, and a barracks followed. The WPA employed scores of men for filling and grading, and paid other workers to extend city water lines along U.S. Highway 1 to the airfield. During construction the SAS administrative office operated temporarily at the Sanders Building just west of City Drug on DeKalb Street. For officers' quarters the school leased historic Deare Place and the Sarsfield Club, both near the Court Inn. The antebellum DeSaussure home Green Haven, on the corner of Mill and Haile streets, became a social club for cadets and enlisted men at SAS, and later another antebellum home in Kirkwood Heights became a club for instructors.[3]

By the first open house to show off the new school in March 1941, expenditures had run into the millions and facilities were reported "taxed to capacity." The school almost immediately expanded further to serve nearly twice as many cadets. The city water extension to the school benefited other area residents along the way. Private investors moved quickly to build apartments and small cottages to meet the area's rising demand for midpriced housing in the range of thirty-five to forty dollars per month. Local businesses made additional changes to serve the school. For example, the Wolfe Building, 1024 Broad Street, was refitted to modernize the Camden Dairies' pasteurization plant, under contract for milk.

To demonstrate the local effect of the Southern Aviation School's payroll, the company made its first fifteen-thousand-dollar semi-monthly payoff in two-dollar bills, which flooded local businesses. The flying school also attracted widespread publicity for the local area. The May 1941 *Dixie Air News,* one of America's largest aviation magazines, featured sixteen pages of text and photos on the school and on Camden as a winter sports center.

In June 1941 the community warmly welcomed sixty-five Royal Air Force (RAF) cadets from London, Manchester, Bristol, and other English cities. They were the first group of three hundred British airmen who would train in Camden. Since four dozen of the first arrivals were Anglican, numbers of them attended Grace Episcopal Church. One dozen even sang in the choir on their first Sunday there. Rector Dr. Maurice Clark regularly offered a prayer for England in his services. Bethesda Presbyterian Church furnished recreational space for aviation cadets, other members of the armed forces, and their friends. Decades later one of the RAF cadets, George H. Foster, recalled his arrival in Camden: "It was 2 o'clock in the morning yet half the population was at the station with headlights blazing and grabbing us to offer hospitality at their homes."[4]

Sympathy for the struggles of England inclined the local community to extend extra hospitalities to the British fliers, including invitations into homes and encouragement with friendly overtures. Public sadness was genuine in October 1941 when one of the young Englishmen, George James Pritchard, died at Camden Hospital from burns and injuries sustained in a training crash. The local United Daughters of the Confederacy donated a burial plot in the "Little Arlington" section of Quaker Cemetery near the grave of Richard Kirkland. Crowds of citizens and all the Southern Aviation School attended the military funeral at Grace Episcopal Church and Quaker Cemetery. Services included an honor guard, a band, a gun salute, and a flyover of five planes.[5]

Carolina Maneuvers

In 1941 Kershaw County was at the center of action in the largest battle maneuvers in U.S. peacetime. During two months of winter-time war games, called the Carolina Maneuvers, two complete armored divisions along with aviation units tested a hypothesis that would ultimately be of major national consequence—that "mobile antitank gun units, offensively employed, could defeat armor." The maneuvers were planned at the direction of U.S. Army chief of staff General George C. Marshall, who in the middle of that year also established a new command, the U.S. Army Air Force.

General Marshall supported maneuvers to give troops realistic combat training and to test equipment and methods for defeating tanks. Elsewhere in the world at the time, Moscow was under siege by the feared German panzers. The mock exercises in the Carolinas helped the U.S. military reveal deficiencies in American equipment, training, and leadership to counter such attackers. The exercises also brought to the forefront leaders such as General George S. Patton Jr., who was active in the maneuvers in Kershaw County at the time.[6] Publicity resulting from the maneuvers advanced public support for rearmament, an issue that many had shied away from after the end of the last war.

In January 1941 the enormity of the maneuvers planned for October and November became apparent locally when the U.S. Army requested trespass rights to eighty thousand acres in Kershaw County. The area lay between the two maneuvering "armies," one at Fort Bragg, North Carolina, and the other at Fort Jackson. U.S. Highway 1, which bisected the county, was the major connecting route for nearly seventy thousand military vehicles. Nearly a year of planning went into the fifty-seven days of war games that engaged four hundred thousand troops of the First Army in mock battles over ten thousand square miles in North and South Carolina.

South Carolina's governor, Burnet R. Maybank, appointed Ernest C. Zemp of Camden as Kershaw County maneuvers director, and the army named Fort Jackson's Lieutenant J. D. Dial as their contact man in Camden. Both had offices in the Chamber of Commerce suite in the Crocker Building. To secure the trespass rights, the Kershaw County delegation appointed a citizen-contact committee of J. H. Clyburn, Fred Ogburn, M. M. Reasonover, Oscar J. Smyrl, and Dr. Carl West. They reported overwhelming cooperation. Kershaw County Chamber of Commerce secretary Frank Heath pointed out that the military would spend $67 million on the maneuvers, and the mock war would attract journalists and both U.S. and foreign observers. Publicity would prove greatly advantageous for the state and for local communities. Mayor Francis N. McCorkle urged Camden to "put on its best face." Bethune and Kershaw likewise began planning for visitors.

Small previews punctuated the months prior to the winter maneuvers. In March 1941 some sixteen hundred North Carolina soldiers of the 120th Infantry of the Thirtieth Division bivouacked at the Kershaw County fairgrounds in Camden. Hundreds of civilians toured the camp of the "Old Hickory Division," impressed by new gas kitchens, Garand rifles, trench mortars, walkie-talkies, and antitank weapons. Both the Camden High School marching band and the army's regimental band performed spirited numbers. In April the Liberty Hill newspaper correspondent reported several hours of traffic passing through that community, "a continuous line of big army trucks" heading south.

For several months 165 army engineers camped at the fairgrounds in Camden. From that base they made war surveys and mapped fourteen thousand acres to be included in the war games. A military spokesman promised that the army would "spend money on roads, tighten bridges, and fix things that need fixing afterwards," especially with regard to tanks using local roads.[7]

Meanwhile a number of meetings outlined further needs during the maneuvers. Staples such as flour were to be shipped in to feed the troops, but vast amounts of fresh vegetables, eggs, butter, milk, and other perishables would be purchased locally. The First Army would consume more than 265 refrigerator cars of beef, requiring the slaughter of 14,000 cattle. Some local businesses acquired profitable government contracts. For example, Newkirk Industries of Camden, which roasted, ground, blended, and packaged coffee under various labels, including Hobkirk and Polo, contracted to supply several army posts, including Fort Bragg and Fort Jackson. Newkirk remodeled the Burns Building, off East DeKalb and Mill streets, for a 228,000-square-foot plant to process four million pounds of coffee beans. An increase in the contract to supply the fall maneuvers added another six million pounds, requiring the plant to operate three shifts twenty-four hours a day. The smell of freshly roasted coffee beans drifted pleasantly over the town at all hours.

In statewide conferences with mayors, health and law enforcement officers, and Chamber of Commerce officials, the military addressed issues from water and food safety and sewage disposal to restriction of liquor and control of prostitution and venereal disease. Mayor McCorkle announced his determination to work with law enforcement to keep Camden free of camp followers. Since maneuver activities took place on weekdays, Kershaw County citizens were expected to provide wholesome recreation for soldiers' weekend leave times. The Chamber of Commerce appealed to citizens to register available rooms, apartments, or houses for rent.[8]

Those who attended a community meeting in Camden decided to set up recreational equipment in Legion Hall, and by May a service club there was "open for all men in uniform," including those at the Southern Aviation School. Later, in the old armory on Rutledge Street, the WPA built tables, benches, and recreational equipment such as Ping-Pong tables to establish a nightly community center with weekend refreshments, games, and dances for soldiers and visitors. Eventually the service club, operating under the United Services Organization (USO), expanded into donated space in the Sanders Building on DeKalb Street, across the street from the Camden Theatre and Legion Hall.

The Camden Merchants Association agreed to allow movies on Sundays during the maneuvers, excluding morning and evening church hours, and approved the playing of baseball and similar healthy sports for the soldiers' entertainment. Ministers did not object. Anticipating highway congestion, the merchants postponed the annual October Cotton Festival to combine it with the December Christmas Festival. The city of Camden had twenty-four benches built and placed in the parks and on the sidewalks along DeKalb Street between Broad and Market "where the post office, theater, service club, restaurants, and soft drink establishments are located." Since the city planned the benches for the use of visiting soldiers and, after the maneuvers, winter tourists, local loiterers were discouraged from sitting there.

In May the War Department made permanent the assignment to Camden of the Company D, Thirtieth Engineers Battalion, which was camping at the fairgrounds. Electric lights had already been rigged in tents, and the troops were using the fair's main exhibit building and showering at the football and baseball facilities. Although water pipes were added to service the camp, it soon afterward moved to a site near the new armory on West DeKalb Street. Here the men had better offices and showers and escaped some problems of the old location, primarily insects from the swamp and smoke and odors from the nearby city dump. The old armory on Rutledge Street was also modified, with thirteen showers added to its single one. A welcome winter-time announcement gave approval for the new armory to install a heating system, which Depression-era construction had completely omitted.

In June the War Department selected Camden as the publicity center for the Carolina Maneuvers and leased the entire Kirkwood Hotel for headquarters. On Greene Street in front of the Kirkwood, the normally dusty roads were improved with crushed rock and additives of calcium chloride and oil. Other parts of Greene and Campbell streets were also surface-treated for dust, and the roadways and paths through the hotel area were graveled.

The thirty-eight-year-old hotel also underwent many changes. One room was adapted as a communications center for twenty Western Union operators. Radio broadcasting equipment was enhanced to send out fifteen-minute programs over Charlotte and Raleigh radio stations. The 161st Signal Photographic Company arrived with movie cameras, specially equipped movie trucks with sound equipment, and additional photographic technology. On the hotel grounds a unit of 165 men from Fort Benning, Georgia, set up tents, where 200 officers and enlisted men of Battery E, Tenth Coast Artillery, from Fort Adams, Rhode Island, also quartered.

By the beginning of July a cavalry unit set up camp in West Wateree. To the awe of area residents, the 107th motorized cavalry bivouacked with fifteen hundred men, one hundred officers, five hundred horses, and large numbers of motor vans at the fork of the Camden and Ridgeway highways. In September five hundred men of the Twelfth Engineers Battalion of the Eighth Division set up camp near the new armory in Camden and arranged recreation at the Hermitage Lake public beach.

Continuing preparations in Camden, the First Army public relations headquarters opened Unit Dispensary no. 7, adding a dental clinic, at the old Clyburn residence on 1707 Broad Street. The largest community gathering in years heard the state sanitary engineer and a military spokesman explain army regulations. The speakers made plain that noncompliant eating places and roadhouses would be placed off-limits with military police posted to keep soldiers out. Furthermore local law enforcement would allow no trailers to stop in the county during the maneuver period, giving any such arriving vehicle only twelve hours to leave. The required policy was quite a change for an area accustomed to frequent tourist travel. Camden police chief Alva Rush stationed policemen at town limits on all highways, and county deputies patrolled to keep out prostitutes and other "undesirables" attempting to move in advance of the troops. Officials urged parents to take extreme care with their daughters since girls out at night "just out of curiosity" might be "picked up by error" by law officers. Taxi drivers were informed of federal punishments for carrying a prostitute or soldier to a place of assignation.

With opening ceremonies at Hampton Square in Camden on October 6, 1941, the Carolina Maneuvers officially began. Mayor McCorkle welcomed First Army commander Lieutenant General Hugh Drum and the governors of South Carolina and North Carolina. The dignitaries then proceeded to the headquarters at the Kirkwood for a nineteen-gun salute and lunchtime remarks. Public relations officers hosted an evening reception and buffet dinner at the Kirkwood for four hundred or more local citizens.

Army maintenance crews were busy afterward at the old hotel. The battery of 75 mm howitzers that saluted dignitaries also shattered windows and lightbulbs, cracked plaster, and loosened the heating system's pipes. A pleasant surprise was that the vibrations likewise cleared sluggish drainage in the Kirkwood's aged plumbing.

Despite advanced planning, some glitches appeared in arrangements for entertainments during maneuvers. Camden citizens had been told far ahead of time that they would need to prepare for one thousand to fifteen hundred soldiers to be in town on three major weekends in November. In fact the town entertained large numbers for months in advance. However, Camden was caught off guard the first weekend in October when one thousand soldiers arrived unexpectedly, and community resources were strained in accommodating them. The USO promised that no more than five hundred would arrive the next weekend. Camden's merchants stocked their stores, and various committees planned entertainments, including a Hampton Park band concert and a dance at the old armory. To local residents' dismay, only fifty-seven men showed up that weekend. Later in the month nearly six hundred soldiers attended a WPA-hosted dance at the old armory, but only eighty girls were present to dance with them. Mrs. Leon Schlosburg, American Legion Auxiliary president, appealed to the area's young ladies to "show their patriotism" and ensure successful future dances for the soldiers. Chaperones and transportation were promised.

The first weekend in November three thousand soldiers showed up in Camden on Friday evening and twenty-five hundred on Saturday. The new armory housed four hundred men. Many slept in church Sunday-school rooms throughout the county, as well as in private homes. Crowds continued the following weekend, attracted to entertainments that included on Friday a football game between Camden and Hartsville high schools, on Saturday horse racing for the first time at Millway track near Boykin, and on Sunday polo matches in Camden. At the half-mile flat track that Bolivar D. Boykin built in a peanut patch at his Boykin Pond plantation Millway, some fifteen hundred people paid a one-dollar admission fee for the first running there of the Generals' Races, named in honor of the six Confederate generals from Kershaw County. The press reported that spectators included "attaches and officers of many South American nations, Canadian and British governments, and scores of big ranking officers of the United States."

Other communities also entertained soldiers in various ways. Bethune hosted some in local homes on several weekends and served ice cream and sandwiches at D. M. Mays's Friendly Cabin. An annual community picnic became a custom after the successful entertainment of maneuvering soldiers in 1941. In Kershaw, T. M. Little, manager of the Kershaw Theatre, ran several movie shorts free of charge. These included films that the U.S. Signal Corps and 20th Century-Fox shot of troops in Camden during a river-crossing exercise on the Wateree River. Kershaw's longtime police chief W. F. Mothershed expressed amazement at the manner in which military policy (MPs) handled the huge traffic volume in his town. Kershaw, with its population of two thousand, was encircled by camps of fifty thousand soldiers. Chief Mothershed said, "Everything from motorcycles and those little bantams, on up to those big ten-ton trucks hauling all the big guns, is rolling through here all the time."

Liberty Hill home owners had arranged to entertain visiting soldiers one weekend, but only one, a New Yorker, arrived to stay. The Fifty-sixth Signal Battalion unexpectedly converged on the Baron DeKalb school grounds and pitched tents for a two-day bivouac. The five hundred officers and men were given use of the school's athletic equipment, restrooms, and showers in the afternoon and were also allowed to use the library with its books and writing materials. The battalion thanked the community by presenting an impromptu evening talent program in the school auditorium. At Stoneboro another group of soldiers entertained area residents with a Sunday evening band concert.

Additional entertainments for visiting military evoked tourist-style elegance, including a service club dance at the Court Inn, a tea at the Sarsfield Club hosted by Camden bridge clubs for officers' wives, entertainments for visiting Russian diplomats, an officers' ball at the Court Inn honoring sixty Fort Jackson nurses, and frequent dining and dancing at the Sarsfield Club. At one point the intermingling of distinguished visitors at the Kirkwood Hotel headquarters was described as including twenty-two members of the Military Affairs and Appropriation Committee of the U.S. House of Representatives, nine U.S. generals, fifty-six other officers with ranks from captain to colonel, and twenty-three high-ranking officers from ten foreign countries.

The 1941 Armistice Day program in Hampton Park was especially meaningful during the maneuvers. The concert by the 109th Field Artillery band and the address by Commander Drum were broadcast over stations in Columbia, Charlotte, and Raleigh to all men in the maneuver area. The American Legion's honor roll had two additions, SAS's Cadet Pritchard and Private Edward Lorick, a local soldier who had recently died in Tennessee maneuvers. In November a fatal collision on Galloway's Hill east of Camden took the life of a soldier on maneuvers in Kershaw County.

Most area citizens viewed the visiting troops and their equipment with great interest but also found them noisy, sometimes even from a considerable distance. From Liberty Hill came reports of the "roaring and rumbling" of trucks and airplanes west of the river in Fairfield and Chester counties. Residents of Camden and Lugoff sections were abruptly awakened early on a Sunday morning by the pounding sounds of vehicles, guns, and planes staging an "attack" on the Wateree River bridge. When a soldier proudly exclaimed that the bridge had been "blown to hell," a Camden police officer quipped that it was "too bad it didn't happen ten years ago."

In a colorful newspaper article, an inquisitive *Camden Chronicle* reporter, Frank Heath, guided by the local sportsmen Dewey Creed and Charles Shannon IV, described winding along secluded riverbanks to view uniformed men swarming over the terrain to stretch pontoon bridges across the river. Huge bulldozers were ripping out trees and stumps to open a road, and more than one hundred soldiers were "splashing about in the red colored water of the old Wateree" to put pontoons in place. Three bridges were installed, one hefty enough for the twenty-ton tanks that were driven across it. Bridges were then taken up for future use.

On Saturday, November 29, 1941, the maneuvers officially ended in central South Carolina with a final review and retreat in front of the Kirkwood Hotel. The war games had impacted the area significantly. In several cases repairs had to be made. The superstructure of the Wateree River bridge had been damaged when an army truck and a log truck sideswiped the narrow, curving structure, and traffic-jamming load limits were imposed until repairs were made. Across the two-state area military authorities reported the deaths of ninety-three soldiers during the maneuvers, mostly motor vehicle accidents. The county profited in a number of ways from the maneuvers—in financial boosts, in publicity, and in early preparations for wartime conditions. For example, traffic snarls resulting from the maneuvers gave public demonstration that a long-sought change on U.S. Highway 1 west of Camden was essential for security. In September 1941 construction began on a new and safer Wateree River bridge, which was important for daily and emergency use.

Humanitarian Efforts

In the prewar 1940s local humanitarian efforts strongly favored the Allies in their struggles, even as prayers were frequently offered for peace. Local Red Cross publicity chairman Mrs. Sadie K. von Tresckow, with firsthand experience living abroad as a diplomat's wife, served as an international conscience in her native community. In talks and newspaper articles she continually informed the public about the plight of Allied refugees and refuted rumors that relief supplies intended for the Allies were going to Germany instead.

By June 1940 Red Cross workers had collected more than thirteen hundred dollars, and volunteers at the chapter workroom in Camden were sewing and knitting garments to be sent to war victims. During intense summer heat, volunteers took work home. Women across the county stuck to their production promises. At Liberty Hill women sewed at the community center. In Bethune, Mrs. D. M. Mays promised that she would make 120 girls' woolen dresses, a chapter's full quota. The Temple Beth-El Sisterhood under Mrs. Stanley Babin completed a full quota each month. A September 1941 newspaper reported a five-year-old girl making doll dresses for little English girls, and Mrs. Elizabeth Owens, nearly ninety-five years of age, was making blankets and quilts from scraps.

For some time the Camden Red Cross moved about as it struggled to find a suitable chapter building, relying on patrons' donations of space. For a time Moultrie Burns lent the old Hughes house at 1310 Broad Street, beside the library, and then a large room over Belk's store. Arthur Smith lent a room next to his furniture store, and Mrs. Warren Harris secured the Gerald house, previously the Colonial Boxwood Company. In Bethune, with Miss Mabel Todd Campbell in charge, the Red Cross and Civilian Defense Office operated in the building adjoining Loring Davis's store.

Some activities aided specific European groups oppressed by war. A local Finnish relief organization, chaired by Henry G. Carrison, requested a nickel donation from each schoolchild throughout the county, "white and colored." A

Finnish Night ball at the Kirkwood Hotel in March 1940 netted eight hundred dollars. Collecting donations from a cross section of the county, Camden's Greek businessmen Chris and Gus Beleos raised more than one thousand dollars for war relief in their native land. In their front glass windows large glass pickle jars remained to collect coins to aid the suffering in Greece. A "Bundles for Britain" chapter, headquartered at a tourist-related business at 1807 Fair Street, "Miss Spark's shop," collected and sent clothing to Great Britain. On learning that British children might be evacuated to escape the German siege of their country, the Kershaw County Chamber of Commerce offered homes for refugees. However, none of the children could be transported since all ships were needed to combat the Nazi thrust.

Community Concerns

Amid growing concern over world events, county citizens also focused on community matters. Local newspapers frequently printed chatty columns from Antioch, Bethune, Blaney, DeKalb, Flat Rock, Flint Hill, Gates Ford, Kershaw, Liberty Hill, Lugoff, Malvern Hill, Midway, Mt. Pisgah, Pine Grove, Three C's, and Timrod. Most of the items focused on faith, family, and friendship. Church gatherings, community meetings, and social visits were meticulously reported. Home Demonstration Clubs were active throughout rural Kershaw County, providing farm women with up-to-date information and opportunities for service in improving their homes and communities. The Antioch, DeKalb, Flat Rock, Gates Ford, Lugoff, Malvern Hill, Midway, Mt. Pisgah, Three C's, and Timrod clubs met regularly with well-planned programs. A number of these, such as Gates Ford and Three C's, met in their own clubhouses. By 1940 home-demonstration agent Miss Margaret Fewell had been serving the county for half a dozen years and was a trusted home and community influence. When home-demonstration women turned toward home-front preparedness, Mrs. Oscar J. Smyrl joined Miss Fewell as Kershaw County's emergency war food production and conservation assistant. The clubs were an important link between the government and individual citizens.

A flurry of assistance followed an early morning blaze that destroyed the Children's Home at Camden in September 1942. Swift actions by matrons Miss Louise Scott and Mrs. Ida Scott rescued the nine children then living there. Various neighbors boarded the little ones until later that month an eight-room home at the corner of Fair and Laurens streets was purchased from the Blackmon estate and thereafter became the Children's Home.

Health

A shortage of doctors, nurses, and medical facilities was a concern in prewar years. In 1940 Dr. George S. Rhame moved into his new office building on Fair

Street facing Hampton Park. Dr. A. W. Humphries and one of the area's newest physicians, Dr. F. Grayson Shaw, taught first-aid classes to Red Cross members. By 1940 Dr. John W. Corbett had been serving Camden for fifty-five years, even before Camden Hospital was organized. President of the hospital board since 1921, he continued to serve in that capacity until 1946.

Two of the county's oldest physicians were its only two black doctors, Dr. J. P. Pickett and Dr. J. H. Thomas, practicing since 1904 and 1910, respectively. One of the busiest health practitioners was the longtime nurse at Wateree Mill, Mrs. S. M. (Docia) McCaskill, who also examined each mill preschool child. Area dentists aided the Junior Welfare League's dental clinic for underprivileged elementary children, where Doctors Clyburn, Hinson, Sowell, and Williford of Camden and Kershaw's Dr. Gunter were assisted by Mrs. Minnie J. Ingram of the county health department in performing cleanings, fillings, and extractions. Dr. A. W. Humphries, practicing since 1912, headed the health department.

Despite WPA drainage of mosquito-ridden swamps, malaria remained a threat, and local drugstores advertised remedies. Polio was feared, but outbreaks of influenza were far more common. A flu epidemic in early 1941 cancelled community gatherings and closed a number of schools, from West Wateree and Kershaw city schools in January to Bethune schools in February. Camden Hospital manager Mannes Baruch reported that admissions of flu victims had filled the hospital, and many more were on a waiting list.

The most dangerous health problem, however, was tuberculosis, or TB, the leading killer of its day. Kershaw County had no treatment facilities, and serious cases had to wait for state sanatorium vacancies. In 1940 the county placed twenty-two citizens there for treatment. In December alone five persons within the county died with the disease. In 1941 the Kershaw County Tuberculosis Association tested more than one thousand schoolteachers and students and found 20 percent of them positive, with living tuberculosis germs in their bodies. With no vaccine for prevention or drug for cure, the only weapon against the disease was knowledge of its characteristics. The Tuberculosis Association worked actively with fund-raising through its Christmas Seal sales to support X-ray clinics and distribution of information. In 1940 Petros B. Mdodana, chairing the Kershaw County Colored Citizens Christmas Seal drive, pointed out the especially deadly effects of the disease in that population.

Safety

In the early 1940s extended drought and record temperatures increased age-old, ever-present dangers of fire in forests, fields, and developed areas. At the Wateree Dam settlement in West Wateree, a fifteen-room, twenty-four-year-old rooming house burned so brightly in March 1940 that its red glow was reported visible as far as Columbia. In Camden that year the Electrik Maid bakery was gutted by fire in January, rebuilt, and burned again in December. Once even the mail caught fire on a delivery route, and scorched letters and packages were delivered throughout the county.

Safety and law enforcement techniques advanced. Camden mayor Francis N. McCorkle was reelected in 1940 on a campaign promoting installation of traffic lights and modernization of fire and police departments. Firemen acquired a new pumper and a hose truck. The police department added a high-speed police car and new .38 revolvers. For the first time, Chief Alva Rush said, the city owned enough guns to arm each of his men. A traffic light was added at Lyttleton and DeKalb, "the most dangerous corner next to that of the postoffice." Widespread problems of drivers double-parking on busy city streets led to suggestions of municipal parking lots behind store buildings.

After Sheriff J. H. McLeod Sr.'s son, Deputy J. H. McLeod Jr., attended the national FBI academy, he helped incorporate new fingerprinting methods in the county. The sheriff and his family lived in the new jail, a seventy-thousand-dollar structure built with WPA labor on Lafayette Avenue to house up to fifty prisoners. The old jail at the rear of the agricultural building was remodeled as an office building, and in 1942 it housed the new Kershaw County Health Department.

Moonshiners, blacks and whites, were persistent offenders. As the nation edged closer to war, federal executives sought the support of local law officers to enforce the new Espionage Act. Sheriff McLeod appealed to citizens to notify his office concerning actions or conversations that might be construed as "un-American."

Labor and Agriculture

Disagreements among the Kershaw County legislative delegation and the county administration over budget appropriations stirred controversy in the local press in 1940. When Senator Murdoch M. Johnson, Representatives J. Clator Arrants and James M. Thornton, and Chairman of the Board of Directors W. T. Redfearn failed to agree on a county budget, WPA projects were reported as jeopardized since they were not assured of matching local funding. Had the controversy not been settled, according to the press, the loss would have brought hardships to from five hundred to six hundred WPA workers with a monthly payroll of nearly forty thousand dollars, as well as to recipients of the seventy-five to one hundred tons of commodities and fifteen hundred to two thousand garments distributed monthly in the county.

Ongoing WPA projects involved roads and bridges, offices, the airport, school lunches, housekeepers' aid, the library, the sewing room, the nursery school, and mattress manufacture. When the WPA in Washington moved to discontinue many of these small projects in South Carolina, Fifth District congressman J. P.

Richards of Liberty Hill visited national headquarters to protest. Local pressure was strong to keep federal dollars coming into the county, but the WPA presence was winding down in the face of other concerns.

Agricultural Kershaw County continued to struggle with old problems. Farming was yet little affected by mechanization. Local businesses advertised mules more frequently than tractors. Ads for potash reminded farmers that shortages had occurred in the last war, but the mineral was still available for the time being. Agricultural supplies were for sale all over the county, from the Westville Feed and Seed Store to Blaney's S. H. Ross and Bailey Distributing and Milling Company. In Camden many businesses advertised guano and fertilizers and seeds and feeds. Some of these were Camden Feed and Implement Company, J. T. Hay Cotton Company, McLeod and McLauchlin, S. N. Nicholson, Southern Cotton Oil Company, B. E. Sparrow, S. P. West, and Whitaker and Company, and even J. J. Newberry Company sold live baby chicks.

A large ad "For the Year 1941" reveals what was expected of farm employees. The ad sought an overseer with "experience raising cattle, hogs, peanuts and potatoes" for a large farm, and a "share farmer who can supervise some five or six other share farmers and exert casual supervision over about sixteen renters, enforce shooting rights, etc." The ad also sought "a tenant who owns two mules, has plenty of feed and is willing to work, and will move on a farm some ten miles North of Camden."

In 1941 the boll weevil infestation increased during an extended drought, cutting cotton production to about a third of the previous year's and yielding the smallest cotton crop since Reconstruction years. The government sought to aid farmers by paying them to convert eroding land to the cultivation of soil-protecting crops, one of which was the rapidly growing perennial vine kudzu. County agent W. C. McCarley encouraged kudzu as a sound investment for high-quality grazing and for hay. In September 1941 the Chamber of Commerce protested federal action that would bar imports from Japan since that would create a scarcity of kudzu plants. When regularly grazed and cut, kudzu was successfully grown in Kershaw County and enriched deficient soils; later notorious overgrowth resulted when crops were neglected or abandoned.

A bemusing agricultural experiment entertained the public in the early 1940s. Matt Ferguson and Dixie Boykin purchased Alice, an eighteen-year-old India elephant, from Clyde Beatty's circus in Florida and brought her to Chancefield Plantation, north of Camden. Boykin managed the seven-thousand-acre estate for Matt's mother, Mrs. Walton Ferguson Jr. Soon Fox Movietone News visited Chancefield to film Alice at work and play, and theatergoers and magazine readers across the nation learned her story. Ferguson and Boykin said that Alice exceeded expectations, pulling the plows and other implements, and excelled at clearing new land. She could pile brush, push over or pull up stumps, load logs onto a trailer, and then pull the trailer.

After several months Alice, it was reported, was discovered to be pregnant and was sent to the Atlanta Zoo to live. When Ferguson went into the military, newsreel cameras publicized scenes of Alice accompanying his unit on maneuvers in order to demonstrate how elephants could assist American military equipment. Local citizens who had watched Alice at Chancefield, or some who said they had visited her and her offspring at the Atlanta zoo, retold the stories often.[9]

Rural Electrification

The single advancement of the decade with the widest impact on thousands of county residents began to take effect in the 1940s with the providing of electricity to individual homes in rural areas. In August 1940 the Rural Electrification Administration (REA) approved a project of the Black River Electric Cooperative to run electrical lines into Sumter, Lee, Clarendon, and Kershaw counties. A month later the REA approved two additional projects. One permitted Fairfield Electric Cooperative to provide service to customers in Chester, Fairfield, and Kershaw counties. The other allowed Lynches River Electric Cooperative to extend lines into Chesterfield, Lancaster, and Kershaw counties. The Black River project turned on lights by February 1941, and the others followed shortly afterward, although the decade would end before all parts of the county were within reach of power. Besides providing lighting, electrical power allowed home owners to install pumps for indoor plumbing. As a result the convenience, comfort, and hygiene of rural dwellers began to improve—as did their safety and health.

Memorial Gateway

Concerns of a new war awakened memories of recent sacrifices. A popular subscription had raised funds to honor veterans of "the first world war" with bronze plaques, which were to be mounted on the tall brick columns of the memorial gateway at the entrance to Camden from the Wateree Bridge along U.S. Highway 1.[10] Dedication ceremonies sponsored by the American Legion and Legion Auxiliary on May 30, 1941, were described in the press as "inspiring." School bands, singers, prayers of various denominations, and several speakers were part of the program. Mayor McCorkle stated that the structure symbolized that the nation was united "under the Starry Banner of Freedom . . . and that no madman, or his hirelings, will ever control America."

World War II

News of the Japanese attack on Pearl Harbor that precipitated America's entry into World War II reached local citizens by radio and by word of mouth on Sunday, December 7, 1941. As long as they lived, citizens of the day retold stories of where they were and what they did when they heard the news that day.[11]

In the following hours and days young men solemnly asked their friends, "Are you ready?" In steady streams they joined lines of volunteers signing up to go "wherever needed" in the military service of their country. Many of them reported to training camps and were in uniform within days or weeks, ahead of the draft notices that soon called many more to active duty. Volunteer enlistments also soon included women, for whom service opportunities expanded. Weddings and "war brides" added romance to the emotionally charged wartimes, as many young couples sealed commitments before being separated.[12]

Barely a week after Pearl Harbor, in neighboring Sumter County the first group of cadets began basic pilot training on December 15 at the new army airfield, Shaw Field, where construction had begun in mid-April 1941. Less than twenty-five miles from Camden, Shaw Field impacted Kershaw County much as Fort Jackson had in creating civilian jobs and demand for supplies and housing. With America's entry into war, the Southern Aviation School at Camden intensified flight training for increased numbers of cadets. Link trainers, the first flight simulators, were added at the aviation school to give realistic cockpit training in instrument-only piloting in preparation for actual flying.

In Kershaw County in-progress construction of the new Wateree Bridge pushed forward with urgency. Its completion in spring 1942 was applauded far and wide. Built 1,000 yards south of the old narrow, curving wooden bridge, the straight 1,950-foot structure of reinforced concrete, with ¾-mile approaches, had a roadway 26 feet wide edged with 2½-foot sidewalks.[13]

On May 1, 1942, the $350,000 bridge opened to traffic following a formal dedication service. A motorcade of Kershaw County officials approached a ribbon barrier from the east to meet a similar motorcade of dignitaries from Richland County. Twelve large planes from Shaw Field roared an overhead salute. Speaking for Governor Richard Manning Jefferies, Adjutant General James Dozier stressed the value of the new bridge for civilian needs and as a war measure, significant in connecting Fort Jackson and Fort Bragg. Work began the next week to dismantle the old bridge and its approaches and to recycle its materials. Creosoted timbers and bolts repaired other county timber bridges, and metal spans were sold to the government for war use.

Home Front

Following the Japanese attack, American citizens felt personally vulnerable. The day after Pearl Harbor, Kershaw County law enforcement agencies went on alert at the report that three Japanese men had been spotted speeding through Cheraw in an automobile. Two days later, at the request of Camden police, Fort Jackson soldiers arrived to guard the city water plant and supply lines.

As initial alarm settled, the Kershaw County Council of Defense, the emergency agency already in operation, began earnest work. The women's division registered volunteers for civilian defense. Black and white citizens cooperated through similar activities set up in their separate neighborhoods. The Civilian Service Corps organized the activities of the community's war volunteers. They conducted clothing and hosiery collections, waged salvage and conservation campaigns, and pushed war bond drives. The goal was to find a war task or responsibility for every man, woman, and child.

Scrap Collections

With the nation's supplies diverted to the war effort after Pearl Harbor, shortages quickly struck the home front. Scarcity increased through four years of war, but cooperation was widespread for scrap drives to collect essential materials for defense. The first actions of the local Council of Defense set up bins to collect paper for recycling into cardboard for ammunition boxes. The council also urged farmers to sell old tools and machinery as scrap metal for tanks, ships, and planes. In a wire bin at the corner of the Camden post office, housewives deposited aluminum pots and pans for recycling into airplane parts. For similar purposes old keys were tossed into a century-old iron pot placed nearby. Used table fats were left at various other collection points for recycling into medicines and ammunition. Donations of silk hosiery were converted into ammunition packing.

Natural Resources

Wartime needs created demands for natural resources in the area. Mineral gold being held nonessential to the war, commercial mining stopped at nearby Haile Mine when the workforce dwindled. Reportedly, the government quietly mined some areas for vital minerals and patrolled sections such as Liberty Hill to prevent valuable quartz from falling into enemy hands. New technology that the military turned to in radio communications relied on quartz oscillators, but much of the development was done in secret for fear of enemy spies.

However, landowners everywhere were openly urged to "send . . . trees of fighting size to war." Pulpwood was needed for many uses—explosives, packing containers, parachutes, smokeless power, shell casings, blood plasma containers. In 1941 Dewey Creed employed five hundred men in his timber-cutting business, many of whom were draft-eligible in wartime. So critical was the need for pulpwood, however, that men working to cut trees received draft deferments.

Growth in the timber industry also renewed consideration of improvements to the Wateree River to provide shallow-draft transport by water between Camden and Charleston, a position long lobbied in Kershaw County. In mid-1943 a report of the Army Corps of Engineers nixed improvements to the Catawba-Wateree for flood control or navigation. The decision, citing excessive costs, did not totally quash interest in the possibility of renewing the ancient transportation route.

In 1944 the Cooper Motor Lines applied to the Interstate Commerce Commission for authority to establish a barge line "between Charleston and Camden, Charleston and Columbia and between Georgetown and Cheraw." The Ports Authority encouraged the service as "a much needed addition to the already overcrowded transportation facilities" and said that it would "lend considerable impetus to industrialization of the state." Wartime needs made industrialization critical, and the natural resources were scrutinized for potential use in advancing industry.

Rationing

As the war lengthened, government-imposed rationing affected more and more goods. Immediately following Pearl Harbor, Japanese possession of most of the world's commercial rubber trees halted American manufacture of all civilian rubber goods, including auto tires. The month after the attack, Detroit auto factories had switched to war production and stopped making civilian cars. Camden city officials seriously discussed putting up downtown hitching posts to encourage a return to equine travel, but the shortage of horseshoes made the suggestion impractical. Instead more than one hundred bicycle stands were installed downtown.

People who had lived through the Depression of the previous decade knew what must be done to survive—conserve, recycle, substitute, do without. Most also knew to share and cooperate, although law enforcement officers also dealt with increased thievery of scarce supplies such as auto parts. In Washington, President Roosevelt appointed Camden native Bernard Baruch as head of the committee to deal with the rubber shortage. In the summer of 1942 Kershaw County led the nation in a scrap-rubber campaign, collecting twenty-three tons in six days. Home-demonstration agent Miss Fewell taught women to extend the life of household rubber articles, from gaskets to foundation garments. Agricultural agent McCarley advised preservation of farm fruits and vegetables by home drying, which did not require canning equipment using rubber, steel, and tin and which conserved the scarcest food commodity, sugar.

Items in short supply were reserved for demonstrated essential use for the war effort. Anyone wishing to purchase one of the few available automobiles or tires—even used ones—had to prove "essential necessity" to a county board. M. G. King of Bethune and B. D. McDonald of Kershaw served on the auto and tire board with John M. Villepigue of Camden, the county rationing supervisor. Farmers also answered to a farm implement board chaired by King with Gordon Bell and C. P. DuBose Jr. Ration boards could, when necessary, seize previously acquired items such as extra tires or even vehicles if owners were not entitled to them under wartime guidelines. The Chamber of Commerce organized carpools. From Council of Defense headquarters in the post office basement, the new chairman Ralph Shannon urged motorists to form "Share-Your-Car" clubs with neighbors. For about thirty dollars hardware stores sold "victory bikes," which any gainfully employed person or schoolchild working on a farm and commuting to school was allowed to purchase.

The ration-board headquarters was located on the second floor of Legion Hall, where three clerks assisted Supervisor Villepigue as well as the chairman of the sugar unit, Reverend A. D. McArn, and the chairman of the gasoline unit, Dr. T. B. Bruce Sr. Gas was rationed to encourage conservation of tires and auto parts. For three days in May 1942 county schoolteachers worked to issue 3,826 ration cards to individuals and businesses. In November coffee and butter joined the list of scarce commodities, and rationing of meat began in January 1943. As the war wore on, items such as shoes, kerosene, and coal joined rationing lists.

On the bottom floor of Legion Hall, the Boykin Liquor Store shared space with the headquarters of the Selective Service Board.[14] In September 1942 a new federal draft law lowered the age of eligibility for military service from twenty to eighteen. In April 1943 eligibility was extended from age forty-five to sixty-five. Schoolhouses used for registration included Antioch, Baron DeKalb, Bethune, Blaney, Camden, Charlotte Thompson, Hopewell, Jackson, Kershaw, Kirkwood, Liberty Hill, Lugoff, Mickle, Midway, Mt. Pisgah, Pine Grove, Pine Tree, and Red Hill. Again schoolteachers assisted with registration.

Young Contributors

Schoolchildren also performed important patriotic services. Boy Scouts added new members and organized new troops throughout the county to assist in home defense. A "Negro troop" was formed at Mather Academy. Scouts helped the Red Cross gather books for service men, collected scrap iron, and aided the theaters in selling war bonds. Scouts also learned to perform first-aid, signaling, and messenger services, offering their aid in civilian defense activities.

To improve the physical conditioning of male students, schools implemented recently mandated physical education requirements and encouraged sports participation. Students of all ages were encouraged to help with defense efforts, and many classes formed citizenship clubs. In a 1942 drive Blaney schoolchildren collected 5,552 pounds of waste paper. Baron DeKalb students collected more than 20 tons of scrap metal and rubber in their community. Nine-year-old Eloise Gettys of Lugoff won the scrap metal drive in the Camden schools by bringing in 49,620 pounds, and runner-up Marion Boykin brought 32,550. Kershaw pupils collected a total of 87,275 pounds of scrap metal, led by Joe Copeland with 6,330 pounds and Carlyle Baxley with 5,817 pounds. Midway students voted to forgo the annual awarding of medals for scholarship.

At Camden High the machine shop, woodworking classes, and home economics students built stretchers for emergency use. Vocational agriculture students under their teacher M. I. Cline helped local farmers with equipment repairs when steel shortages increased maintenance problems. In another program CHS students trained to work in local retail establishments in place of employees entering the military.

One of the most interesting projects at Camden High was building model airplanes to precise standards for government use in aircraft recognition training and gunnery sighting practice. The local models were among the ten thousand constructed for each of fifty different types of fighting planes. The Camden Kiwanis Club gave support and assistance to H. A. Small and G. E. McGrew, supervisors of the local project.

At Lugoff School, Mrs. L. F. Keistler, Mrs. John Team, and forty-one students knit afghans for the Red Cross. They also purchased defense stamps, collected scrap, and planted a defense garden of onions, spinach, greens, carrots, and radishes for the school lunchroom. At Jackson School, Dr. J. P. Pickett taught Red Cross first-aid classes, and students helped to roll bandages. Camden High School students called off the 1942 junior-senior banquet and gave the money they had raised for it to the Red Cross.

Food Production

The call for "food for freedom" rallied persons of all ages, as adequate nutrition was the first line of defense for individuals at home and on the battlefront. The Camden Garden Club advised town residents in planting victory gardens. In countywide meetings at Jackson School, black farmers and farm women studied ways to increase production. The Kershaw County Council of Farm Women held many canning clinics in schoolhouses, where families could use government equipment to preserve surplus food. S. B. Boykin, a black home-demonstration agent, taught canning to black families.

A family who produced 75 percent or more of their food and feed crops on their own farm was eligible for a "Better Farm Living" certificate. A ceremony at the county courthouse in 1943 recognized families who had received the award for three years in a row, including Mr. and Mrs. F. R. Hall, Mr. and Mrs. W. T. Holley, Mr. and Mrs. E. C. Pearce, and Mrs. Mattie R. West. For the previous year thirty-seven white families and fifty-one black families were recognized. The numbers earning the award continued to increase throughout the war.

Fred A. Thompson, a county member of the U.S. Department of Agriculture war board, told farmers that "idle land is like an idle factory." A Lynches River conservationist, V. T. Mullen, said that farmers could "take a personal crack at Hitler and the Japs" by planting beans early enough to harvest a double crop. Farm agent McCarley and AAA administrator J. D. Crawford urged equipment maintenance, comparing a broken implement to a battlefield gun that would not shoot. Agents also rallied farmers to fight the boll weevil as a "patriotic duty" since cotton produced necessary war materials. When the Southern Cotton Oil Company began making oil from peanuts as well as cotton, county farmers quickly added peanut crops to their production.

With coffee rationing and loss of government contracts, Newkirk Industries in Camden closed, but a new food-processing business moved into its former building space on West DeKalb Street. Fresh-Dry Foods, Inc., operated in three shifts twenty-four hours daily, dehydrating and shipping sweet potatoes, cabbages, onions, and other crops, many purchased from local farmers. Although the odors of run-off water from the drying food and its refuse, especially from onions, were not always pleasant, the income generated by the industry was welcomed.

Petticoat Regime

Women were already a part of the labor force in many ways, but their numbers increased in countywide elective leadership positions. "The Petticoat Regime" was one light title given to the simultaneous service of the following women in offices usually held by men: Lena (Mrs. James H.) Clyburn, clerk of court; Etta (Mrs. Clarence M.) Hough, game warden; Maggie (Mrs. J. H. Sr.) McLeod, sheriff; and Kathleen (Mrs. C. E.) Watts, superintendent of education.

Civilian Defense

Across the county citizens joined civilian defense activities. Both military and civilian beliefs were widespread that Kershaw County's associated airfields and its location between and proximity to military forts on the national highway—the very reasons it was a key location during prewar maneuvers—made it vulnerable should enemy air raids or saboteurs strike inland. In Bethune, Mayor B. W. Brannon held precautionary meetings in the school auditorium. To improve security in Camden the city built a six-sided, windowed police lookout station with a telephone at the southeast corner of Broad and DeKalb streets.

Dr. A. W. Humphries and Donald Morrison headed a countywide decontamination squad; Perry Langston, a bomb squad; and Mannie Fort, a demolition squad. Trains, with miles of rural tracks, were considered vulnerable to sabotage. At one point verbal reports circulated that a troop-carrying train had been deliberately derailed near Lugoff, but security kept the situation quiet. Local newspapers cooperated also by not publicizing details of military movements in the area at the time they were going on.

At the Camden Airport civilian flyers formed a chapter of a newly organized volunteer service group, the Civil Air Patrol (CAP). Instructor Sam Boykin was an early flight commander. Members of the local CAP flew surveillance in the county area, served as spotters for suspicious aircraft, and cooperated with the U.S. Forest Service to prevent fires. Because of timber's importance to the military, saboteurs were feared, and county ranger L. E. Smith warned, "Careless Matches Aid the Axis."

Fire-tower operators also spotted for airplanes, and local newspapers printed charts of markings so that citizens could aid in identification as well. Air-raid drills and blackouts were practiced seriously. When some of Camden's winter visitors attempted to have exceptions made because cutting off lights "imposed a hardship upon the travelers in that they cannot locate the tourist homes late in the evening," the complaints received no sympathy. Daylight savings time, begun in 1942, helped many workers get home before dark when lights had to be extinguished.

The county's first air raid, involving three hundred volunteer workers, was made to seem realistic with a simulated bombing attack by a squad of Shaw Field army planes flying over Bethune, Blaney, Camden, and Kershaw. Mill whistles and church bells in Camden synchronized to join the pulsating blasts of the air-raid siren so that the sounds of an alarm could reach all townspeople. Fire Chief William R. "Buddy" Denton instructed Camden citizens on protection of their homes. At the sound of an emergency signal, parents were to see to their own safety and not to attempt to reach their schoolchildren, who were trained by their teachers to follow safety procedures at school. In 1943, when W. Roscoe Bonsal was chairman of the Kershaw County Council of Defense, the corps commanders for various areas were J. E. Bailey, Blaney; J. R. Brown, Kershaw; C. P. DuBose Jr., Camden; and J. L. King, Bethune. Nine emergency observation posts were maintained in Kershaw County, sometimes on twenty-four-hour duty.

In 1942 the Red Cross moved to larger quarters in Camden at the Clyburn house, 1707 Broad Street, the site of an army clinic during prewar maneuvers. Several local Red Cross patrons together purchased the property and donated the space for the organization's use. First-aid stations for public emergency were set up at Wateree Mill under Mrs. S. M. McCaskill and at Hermitage Mill under Mrs. Abbott Goodale. At the former Hobkirk Inn, now privately owned by Edith H. (Mrs. E. L.) Woodward, an auxiliary base hospital and first-aid unit were established under Olive Whittredge in the former reception area. Additional first-aid stations operated at 1818 Fair Street under Mrs. Thelma Moody and at the old Rutledge Street armory under Dr. J. P. Pickett.[15] Scores of county women became certified as drivers for the Red Cross Motor Corps after completing at least thirty hours of first-aid training, thirty hours of motor training, and sixty hours of volunteer service. These drivers further aided by transporting donations collected during scrap drives. Trixie (Mrs. Leon) Schlosburg headed the Red Cross War Fund drive as overall chairperson, and Jennie Carter served as chair of the "colored unit."

Also in 1942 Bernard Baruch made another donation to the Camden Hospital and Nurses Home to allow for an additional expansion, adding a second floor to a section of the facility. Newspapers pointed out that with Baruch's latest contribution, he had given a total of $107,000 to the hospital. The present gift had come when the local area and the county were in need of increased medical facilities.

Community Changes

Power shortages and blackouts ended night-time sports events, and fuel rationing kept athletic teams from traveling away from home. Neon signs advertising downtown businesses stayed off. County and community fairs were halted. The Carolina Cup steeplechase event was not run in 1943, 1944, or 1945. Horse shows, foxhunting, and polo likewise were suspended. Boarding students at Mather Academy did not go home for holidays. Tourists who ventured to local areas by car could be rationed enough gas to return home but not to travel about while here. Military priorities for trains made travel on them uncertain and time-consuming.

The amenities and leisurely entertainments that had once attracted tourists to Camden were clearly altered by war conditions, which had inevitably altered travel and leisure overall. Kershaw County faced instead the housing needs of another type of fluctuating population. With the advent of war, Camden was named a defense rental area, where rents had to be lowered to "proper levels" or face government intervention. Resorts, already financially strapped, struggled to continue traditional operations.

In the tourist season of early 1943 the Kirkwood Hotel, the Court Inn, the Camden Hotel, and the smaller tourist homes such as Magnolia Inn and the Park View were reported to be filled to "overflowing," but many of those guests were war-related, not free-spending persons of leisure. Karl Abbot, a former Kirkwood owner whose chain took over the old hotel again in fall 1942 after a trustees' sale, had predicted that fuel shortages in the North would send many visitors southward for the season. In winter 1943, however, well-to-do tourists who were able to seek out pleasure spots went instead in overwhelming numbers to newer resorts in Florida. In Camden the national ban on "pleasure driving" stymied many social events, for example, postponing the annual winter-time hospital ball at the Kirkwood. In April two hundred to three hundred couples waltzed and jitterbugged at the rescheduled ball, some of the guests having walked or bicycled there in formal finery. The ball proved to be the last great event of the grand hotel, which was sold off in various stages in the following months.

Sold again in September 1943, the two-hundred-room Kirkwood went to a Columbia real estate man, Simon Faust, who two decades earlier had been a Camden grocer. Faust arranged a widely attended December auction of the hotel fixtures and furnishings. Many of the items were said to have been purchased for sentimental reasons, which brought prices wildly higher than market worth. A newspaperman visiting the empty, dilapidated building described it as

a "veritable fire trap" with cracked plaster and damage still evident from its use during army maneuvers. Faust then stripped and sold off its salvageable metal, stating that he hoped to see a remaining portion of the former hotel safely restored and expanded as a modern resort.

Left standing was part of the original core, the old Cantey home around which the hotel had extended, and a two-story annex that had stood behind the hotel. Parts of the Kirkwood property had been disposed of separately.[16] Lem Bramlett, a longtime stable operator, bought the stables. A group of sports-minded citizens purchased 117 acres of the Kirkwood golf course for the Camden Country Club, which was organized in 1942 to begin year-round operation of the Kirkwood links and tennis courts.[17]

In December 1943, the same month as the auction at the Kirkwood, the Court Inn suffered a disastrous fire, requiring extensive restoration to its roof, lobby, and first floor rooms. The last of the resorts, scaled back in size and amenities, the Court Inn struggled to remain afloat. Also in December 1943 the once-popular old tourist home Deare Place was sold to the local businessman and banker John Whitaker Jr. to be remodeled as a residence. Some homes that had once opened rooms to winter residents converted to wartime apartments.

In contrast to declining tourist establishments, residential housing was differently affected by war conditions. Because of the Southern Aviation School's expansion in wartime, Camden was one of three South Carolina cities that President Roosevelt certified as a critical war area.[18] It was thus qualified to issue government-backed mortgage insurance to builders of new homes for war workers. Some of those homes were built between the Court Inn and Kendall Mill on lots subdivided from the old Sarsfield golf course. One of the first areas sold off for home lots was Upton Court, part of the Court Inn property, in 1941. In many areas trailer courts also mushroomed, and communities of trailers grew seemingly overnight.

Other government mortgage aid supported the building of rural homes to replace deficient ones. Thus, despite shortages of materials, rapid construction of small but efficient housing surged in Kershaw County. This was especially true in areas in the eastern part of Camden, near the airport, and along rural routes toward Shaw Field in Sumter and Fort Jackson in Columbia. Often the dismantling of large old homes, hotels, and other buildings provided materials for the smaller, newer constructions.

A new business that opened with fanfare in early 1943 began a long life in Camden. According to the *Chronicle,* "They walked, they came by bicycles and officers of the flying field with their wives, came in cars—but they came to be present at the formal opening of Camden's new and swank tea room, introduced to the public Saturday night under the name of 'Thomas' Tavern.'" Mrs. Elizabeth Thomas had returned home after seven years of restaurant management in Hollywood to cater local parties and club meetings, and to serve chicken and steak dinners daily. Praised as "a model of modernity," the tavern featured fashionable colors of red and aqua with waxed woodwork, a "swanky bar" for beer and soft drinks, and gas heating and cooking with "no odor of kerosene or coal smoke." Living and looking "modern" had become appealing in Kershaw County.

Military Connections

Maneuvers before the war had introduced Kershaw County citizens to some aspects of military action. In spring and fall 1942 army maneuvers encompassing Kershaw County continued. Even though smaller in scope, they were said to exceed the earlier ones in intensity since the participants expected soon to be in real battles. Maneuvers continued in the county throughout the war. Fewer weekend leaves were given, although the community continued to entertain off-duty soldiers.

At least one military exercise during mock fighting on the Wateree River gave the county a practical benefit. Officials were concerned that standing remains of the old Wateree Bridge would wash downriver in a freshet and damage the new bridge just south of it. As demolition practice, military divers attached explosives to the piers of the old bridge and safely brought down its remnants. Some flattened concrete remains can still be viewed at the river's edge north of the present bridge.

In a significant operation in Kershaw County on March 29, 1943, the 505th Parachute Infantry Regiment from Fort Bragg made the first regimental mass parachute jump in U.S. Army history. The exercise was staged as an assault on the Wateree River bridgehead. Troop-carrying gliders, flying engineless on silent wings, flew along with roaring transport planes. In the Lugoff area of the former major landing zone near the bridge, a monument on U.S. Highway 1 explains that the success of this exercise "established the feasibility of and conduct of large scale parachute operations in World War II." Only a little over three months later the 505th made the first U.S. Army regimental combat jump on July 9 in the invasion of Sicily. This marked the beginning of a decisive role played by American airborne troops in World War II.

The site of thousands of white silk parachutes dropping through the sky in three waves of a mock attack awed local observers. Several reported deaths were a sobering part of the maneuvers, which overall included Camden, Kershaw, and Lancaster. There was interest, though, in the fact that the first paratrooper to make the jump at Lugoff was a Camden youth, Ivey K. Connell, whose relatives

The Lugoff monument to the 505th Parachute Infantry Regiment, commemorating the first large-scale parachute jump in American history

excitedly greeted him at the Wateree Bridge with a basket of sandwiches and soft drinks. A few months later Connell died in a combat jump in Italy.

Service Families

Kershaw County citizens felt the realities of war most keenly in reports of deaths and casualties. The first combat death of an area resident was reported in June 1942. John Furman Jenkins Jr. of Camden died of burns suffered when the ship he was on was torpedoed in the Gulf of Mexico. By December 1943 twenty men from Kershaw County had been reported among the war dead. However, any accounting of numbers could hardly reflect the contacts that citizens had with the fluctuating numbers of soldiers in and out of the county, and with the kinfolk of its many citizens here and elsewhere.

Many families supplied multiple members to the military. Often homes displayed with public pride the emblem of a star, typically placed in a front window, to honor a relative in service. Churches too displayed service flags with stars honoring individual members in service. Special recognition was often given families with many stars. A few samples can only hint at the widespread number of recognitions given at the time. Perhaps the first woman locally reported eligible for honor as a "Four Star Mother" was Mrs. Bertha Catoe on Flat Rock

Road near Kershaw. In December 1941 she already had four sons as well as a son-in-law in service, and her two daughters held jobs at Fort Bragg. At Wateree Mill Village on Mother's Day 1942 emblems of honor were presented to Mrs. J. B. Riggins for four sons in service, and to Miss Bessie Tidwell as surrogate mother to four orphaned brothers in uniform. The Kershaw County Chamber of Commerce later that year appealed for four-star recognition of a Lugoff widower, Otis Hinson, the father of four sons. In 1943 it was reported that Alice (Mrs. John) Hinson of Camden was proud of her ten-star service flag honoring nine grandsons and one grandson-in-law. Two years later she had fourteen grandsons in service.

In early 1946 American Legion service officer M. M. Reasonover summarized information, reporting that thirty families in Kershaw County had contributed four or more immediate family members to World War II. The family with the highest number was that of Mr. and Mrs. W. L. Stokes of Camden, who had six sons and one daughter in service. Two families contributing six sons each were identified as "colored": Boykin and Charity Belton of Blaney; and Lemuel and Fannie Belton of Camden. Other families contributing six sons were headed by K. C. Etters, Camden; Smiley Johnson, Kershaw; and I. O. McKenzie, Camden.

The 2008 rededication of the Blue Star Highway marker honoring World War II veterans in Camden's Hampton Park, beside U.S. Highway 1

Families contributing five offspring were headed by Charlie Catoe, Kershaw; Craig Clyburn, Camden; B. R. Connell, Camden; John D. Crolley, Camden; George D. Elkins, Wateree Mill; T. E. Goodale, Camden; Mrs. Florence Gregory, Camden; Bertus Rabon, Lugoff; John Rabon, Lugoff; W. T. Roberts, Hermitage Mill; and Mrs. Maud Williams, Camden.

Communications

News from the front was received with varied reactions. Lewis Newkirk, struggling with his emotions, left the Camden Theatre during a newsreel when he recognized his late brother Jack, a Flying Tiger squadron leader, in footage taken shortly before he was shot down in a bombing mission in China. Families eagerly tuned in radio newscasts to hear general events of the war—torpedoed ships, bombing missions, landings, and invasions—and waited anxious weeks longer to learn by mail of the fate of individuals. In 1944 in three separate communications, Mr. and Mrs. William T. Roberts of Hermitage Mill Village learned of the deaths of three of their five sons in different combat missions. The community grieved with each family that received hard news, delivered in person or by telegram. "Everyone dreaded a knock at the door," recalled Helen M. Anderson. A family whose loved one had died abroad had to wait until war's end to arrange the return of the body if burial at home was desired.[19]

Reassurance that loved ones were well brought great relief. After the invasion of the Solomon Islands in the Pacific, a 1944 news article, "Soldiers Abroad Enjoy Shave-Haircut," identified Private First Class Wade C. Humphrey of Bethune as a "self-made barber" on Bougainville Island. The Camden war bride of a former Southern Aviation School cadet, Rosa Lee Marturano was notified by the military that her husband, Victor, was missing in action after his plane was shot down over Austria. Refusing to believe that he was dead, she learned with joy from newspaper accounts that he was one of ten flyers rescued "from the icy fields of the eastern Alps . . . just as they were about to die from exposure." Mr. and Mrs. L. R. Vincent of Kershaw were reassured by a letter in 1944 from their missing son Leonard confirming that he was a prisoner of the Germans. Captured during the Sicilian campaign, he was working six days a week on a farm. He said that the Red Cross was a "Life Saver," providing food, clothing, and even a Christmas package. In early 1945 the newspaper reported sad news delivered to a Blaney family, that Captain Arthur T. Simpson, previously listed as missing in action, was confirmed killed.

A column in the March 30, 1945, *Camden Chronicle* serves as just one sample of the broad scope of experience reported from local servicemen in the last year of the war. Second Lieutenant Douglas M. Kennedy, wounded on the western front, was in a French hospital. Private Ellie McManus, wounded in Belgium, was in the United States in an Augusta, Georgia, hospital. Private First Class

Dan Banks of Camden had served in Iceland, Scotland, southern England, and France. Sergeant John R. Teal of Cassatt was convalescing from combat wounds at the Camp Butler, North Carolina, hospital. His brother, William, was a staff sergeant in the Pacific. Private First Class Jack L. Lyles of Hermitage Village was fighting the Japanese in Burma. Sergeant Dillard Elliott was wounded on Iwo Jima after serving twenty-seven months. Corporal Harold Ray Boykin of Camden had been killed at Iwo Jima after twenty-six months' overseas duty, and a brother, Marion, was on duty in Europe. Corporal Glover Lee of Bethune was in Italy, where his unit, the 387th Engineering Battalion, operated a sawmill and rock quarry and repaired military highways "feeding the Fifth Army front." As time passed, more was learned of prisoners of war (POWs) and those reported missing in action.

Women served away from home in a number of positions. The local Red Cross recruited for nurses, hospital aides, and field workers. The Women's Army Auxiliary Corps included the first women besides nurses to serve in the U.S. military, although not with equal status as men. Local women served in the field as WAACS (Women's Auxiliary Army Corps), or WACS (Women's Army Corps), and WAVES (Women Accepted for Volunteer Emergency Service), a similar navy branch, as well as in the Red Cross. Second Lieutenant Helen L. Vereen served with a nursing unit on the staff of a former World War I hospital in France. The Camden cosmetologist Everlynne Kyzer became a WAC assigned to duty in New Guinea, where she was able to meet her brother assigned in the same country. Virginia Yarborough was another Camden WAC, as was Virginia L. Joyner, who managed and directed a band and dance orchestra in Belgium. Mather Academy graduate Betty Ellison, who had been teaching in Kershaw County schools, also served in the WACS. Locally recruiting for the WAVES were women with navy relatives, Mrs. Rhetta Heath McDowell at the Corner Book Store and Mrs. Catoe Glover. Martha Rutledge (Dolly) Singleton was promoted to lieutenant commander in the WAVES. Other Camden WAVES included Thelma Frances Stokes and Margaret Clarke, who served for forty-two months.

POW Camp

News of the D-day invasions in June 1944 was closely followed by local citizens, who rejoiced in Allied victories and anxiously awaited information about loved ones. In August, the same month that the Allies entered occupied France and liberated Paris, the Southern Aviation School at Camden closed, its training role having been assumed at military bases.[20] Meanwhile, as the Allies continued to gain ground in Europe, German prisoners of war were being shipped away from battle zones to various locations in America by the tens of thousands each month. Here a prisoner's only chance to reconnect with his native land and family was to cooperate peacefully with his captors as he awaited the end of the war.

In April 1945 several hundred German prisoners of war were assigned to Camden, where they were housed in two barracks and the mess hall at the former Southern Aviation School. Confined at night within barbed wire enclosures, the prisoners were put to work during the daytime harvesting crops or cutting timber in the county.

Some local citizens resented what they perceived as too much freedom and privilege for the Germans, who were not seen as under heavy guard and who at times were put to work alongside American farmhands and timber crews. Although rumors were disproved that the prisoners dined on fried chicken and ice cream and were allowed to visit the pool hall and theater, resentment was influenced by conditions that the Allies had found when liberating German work and concentration camps. Scenes of some of these locations appeared in newsreels in the local theaters.

In the nine months the POW camp operated locally, only a few prisoners attempted escapes by walking away from work gangs. However, clothing and language barriers readily identified the prisoners, and each escapee was said shortly to have turned himself in when he found that no one would give him food or protection. Reports said that prisoners were ostracized by the local community, and all were accounted for and sent back to Germany after the end of the war. During the time that the POW camp was in operation, its location adjoining the still-working Camden airport was not treated as a serious security risk. Clearly, Germany was in retreat, and there was confidence that America was winning the war.

Preparing for Peace

Partly because of government censorship and partly from intent to "keep up spirits," radios and the print media throughout the war focused on news that reassured rather than discouraged. Mail and details from the front were censored and sometimes arrived slowly, not immediately available to the press or the public. Especially early in the war warnings were stern to prevent information from reaching the enemy: "Loose lips sink ships." However, all information that could pass the censor was eagerly received by those in service. At various points throughout the war, Kershaw County home folk put together newsletters, typically mimeographed, to send to local men and women in service. In 1945 Bethesda Presbyterian Church mailed a lengthy Easter newsletter that included a group photograph of the church membership taken on March 4. Camden Baptist Church sent a detail-rich Father's Day newsletter that included a picture of the interior of the sanctuary with its service flag bearing 108 stars and the caption "How proud we are of every star!"

The latter newsletter also shared the community's mourning with a description of "unbelievable" news on May 12:

> Little knots of people drew together—in stores and outside of stores. . . . Voices were very quiet—eyes were serious or bright with unshed tears. He had been our leader, our President. We had talked about him, often against him. We had never seen him nearer than the movies. But, now, it seemed as if someone much nearer—one whose personality (if not his person) had been in and out of our homes, even as a neighbor comes in and out—was gone. A very personal loss. . . .
>
> Friday and Saturday were quiet days, even though business went on as usual. For the hearts of all Camden—all Kershaw county coming in for Saturday shopping—all strangers passing through—all were quiet with the deep thoughts which attended that sense of personal loss, and national loss. When the town clock gave the signal at four o'clock for the closing of the stores during the hour of the funeral, the hush of a Sabbath morning fell upon the streets. Now and then the sound of a radio voice—turned down unusually low—telling of what was happening in Washington, would come out to passersby. On Saturday morning every church had a memorial service.
>
> Thus did Camden mourn the passing of Franklin D. Roosevelt.

In 1945 a wartime Kershaw County newspaper that was begun for service men and women showed the changing focus to peace-time concerns. Planned under the title the *Camden News* but changed by the third issue to the *Kershaw County News,* the paper announced its staff: Thomas Ancrum, business manager; editors, Mrs. Dion (Peggy Wing) Kerr, Miss Jane Trantham, and Mrs. R. E. Montgomery; staff, Mrs. Whit Boykin, Miss Margaret Fewell, Mrs. John Mullen, Mrs. George Stuart Jr., and Frank H. Heath. Miss Emma Villepigue soon was a general editor, and others also informally assisted. There were no advertisements or solicitations, although sponsors—local businesses that paid for printing—were named. For news of interest and for names and addresses for mailing, the staff called upon volunteers, especially churches, the American Legion, service clubs, and families and friends of those in service.

In April 1945 the publication gave a positive spin to community progress, pointing out that in recent years more houses had been built in Camden than at any other time in its history, and that local banks had on deposit nearly three times as much money as at the end of World War I. The recent cotton crop was a little under 15,000 bales, compared to 42,215 bales in 1920, but was the best since 1940, and "in 1920 many farms were heavily mortgaged, but now the farmers are either free from mortgages or have them in satisfactory shape with long term payments." Compared to the end of the last war, there were now triple the number of cattle and pigs, and planting was diversified to include "good money crops" such as tobacco, peanuts, and lespedeza.

The publication added that the county was now well paved and that additional secondary roads were scheduled for postwar paving. Indeed farmworkers, drawn by high wages in war industries, had "flocked North by hundreds," so that most farmers had only one or two tenants instead of ten or twelve, but since tractors and farm machinery could compensate, the migration could be "a blessing in disguise" to modernize agriculture. In the county timber was bringing top prices, adding to the farmers' incomes and providing good steady pay to pulpwood laborers. Overall, "Labor is working shorter hours and getting more money and it is doubtful if labor will ever go back to the long hours of a few years ago."

The fourth issue of the *Kershaw County News* was a stapled newsletter printed in June 1945, not long after the German surrender and the joyful May 8 V-E Day celebrating "Victory in Europe." The opening article, "Looking to Your Future," quoted a letter that was "being handed each Kershaw County man along with his discharge." Signed by Henry Savage Jr., county chairman of the state Veterans' Advisory Assistance, the letter began: "Dear Veteran: Welcome Home! And in the same breath let us tell you that we hope you are going to stay here in Kershaw County."

The letter's welcome was several months premature, however, for the many service personnel in the Pacific or on their way there. The Japanese, who had first involved America in the war, were still fighting. Atomic bombs on Hiroshima and Nagasaki on August 6 and 9 hastened the end, however, and word came on August 14 that the Japanese had agreed to surrender.

That evening, as the news reached Camden, fire and air-raid sirens shrilled, and bells rang in celebration. Citizens rushed from their homes, swarming the downtown streets. In black neighborhoods singers spontaneously raised their voices in traditional hymns of praise. Throughout the county and up and down the streets of town, cheering citizens happily drove the cars they had been conserving and honked their horns merrily. "Overhead planes darted through the air, discharging paper streamers and confetti," reported the *Camden Chronicle* the next day. "After the excitement had subsided [the] downtown district looked like a section of New Orleans after the Mardi Gras." Partying continued through midnight, mixed with thankful prayer meetings in area churches and homes.[21]

Postwar Changes

The county's death toll from World War II totaled ninety-nine, about twice that of the previous war, and mourning mixed with rejoicing.[22] The Kershaw County to which veterans returned was not the Kershaw County they had left, and it was also far different from the place it would become only a few years later. Men returning from war came home with many ambitions, some discontents, and promises of benefits for education, job training, and housing loans. The

Servicemembers' Readjustment Act, "the GI Bill of Rights," had been signed in 1944, before the war's end, to address the types of problems encountered after the last war. The act's benefits did not extend to women, and opportunities in the South for blacks to access advanced education were still limited. However, GI benefits effected many changes on many levels.

By January 1946 more than fifteen hundred Kershaw County men and women had been released from service in World War II, according to the local American Legion service officer.[23] Besides physical wounds, psychological effects of "combat fatigue" and sheer exhaustion accompanied many veterans home.[24] For some, these issues complicated their return to civilian life, as did a restrictive economy still enduring price controls that held down production and chaffed the nation with material shortages and labor strikes. Habits of self-defense that had meant survival in wartime promoted postwar suspicion of actions perceived as antagonistic to public well-being. On one hand, a national fear of growing "Communist infiltration" reinforced traditional southern distaste for "outside influence." On the other hand, wartime experiences and postwar education altered perspectives and led to questioned traditional views. Societal questioning and adjustment brought change over time.

Veteran William Miller and his wife in the American Legion Post 17 Memorial Room, viewing photographs of local military personnel who died in action

Returning veterans had a significant voice in events of the day. In addition to the American Legion posts at Camden and Kershaw, which rapidly enlarged with new members, in 1946 a Veterans of Foreign Wars unit organized. At an organizational meeting at the Kershaw County Courthouse in February, fifty veterans enrolled in what became VFW Post 5928, with H. E. "Buddy" Beard Jr. as first commander. In 1947 a party at the National Guard armory in Camden thanked the retiring Company E, South Carolina State Guards, under Captain S. C. Clyburn. The time-honored title of "Kershaw Guards" was then transferred to a newly commissioned National Guard unit, Battery B, 713th AAA Gun Battalion, under Captain Robert E. David ("Captain Jack"). In late 1949 Lieutenant Colonel William G. Major Jr. became the new commander of Battery B. In February 1949 Company D, 122nd Battalion of Engineers, organized with thirty-five members under Captain W. L. Jackson as commander, and it soon more than doubled in number.

Membership in civic groups also swelled with veterans ready to join in hometown improvements. The Camden Junior Chamber of Commerce, known as the Jaycees (or JayCees), formed in fall 1946 with 34 business and professional men as charter members and Frank Montgomery as the first president. By mid-November the group had 142 members ready for work on community projects.

Other service organizations, such as the Kiwanis, Lions, and Rotary clubs, also increased in membership. The Eastern Star and the Lions Club sponsored the formation of a Salvation Army service unit. The Temperance and Law Enforcement League revived, especially as many church revivals motivated citizens to curb excesses of wartime influences. Working women maintained an active community voice by chartering the Business and Professional Women's Club in 1949 with fifty-four members and Miss Margaret Fewell as its first president.

Interest in conditions at home did not block concern for war sufferers abroad. In 1946 M. H. Heyman, A. Sam Karesh, and Mrs. Leon Schlosburg headed a Camden committee for the United Jewish Appeal for Refugees, Overseas Needs and Palestine. In soliciting their quota of twenty-five hundred dollars, the committee stated that the refugees' situation was "not exclusively a Jewish problem but one of general human concern. The Jews were the first and primary victims of . . . a planned conspiracy against world civilization." In 1947 Mrs. O. J. Smyrl of Camden, president of the South Carolina Council of Farm Women, represented the state at an international conference of Associated County Women of the World at Amsterdam, Holland. After touring as a goodwill ambassador in Belgium, England, France, and Germany, on her return she described to many state and local groups the conditions among people rebuilding war-torn lives.

In Kershaw County housing was the immediate practical concern for returning veterans. Every spare room in the county, it was said, was converted for dwelling space at the war's end. Abandoned tenant houses were hastily restored. Some large older homes were remodeled into apartments. In Camden the Yates home on Broad Street and the Lenoir home on Fair Street were sold for conversion to apartments. The Red Cross moved to smaller quarters, the former Sara Wolfe kindergarten building at the rear of the Wolfe home on Lyttleton Street. In Bethune, Loring Davis sold the King-Davis Hotel to D. M. Mays, and it was divided into apartments. Often recycled materials were used in conversions since a shortage of building materials was delaying more ambitious projects. In Camden the standing central portion of the Kirkwood Hotel was sold to Thomas Hair, owner of the Kirkwood annex, who set about plans to remodel it into a modern resort.[25] In January 1946 Dr. R. E. Stevenson offered building lots between Broad and Gordon streets, south of the old Kirkwood Hotel, adding a street named Kirkwood Circle.

Employment was another major concern for veterans. Women who had taken jobs to replace men during the war generally gave up their positions. Wartime industries such as Fresh-Dry Foods in Camden closed down, with resulting unemployment. Some locals who had worked afar returned home when war jobs ended. New jobs were needed, especially jobs to fit mechanical and technical skills and interests that had been acquired in service or defense jobs and that seemed destined to be part of a modern society.

New Businesses

In the two years after the war, Kershaw County gained from seventy to one hundred new businesses. A number focused on modern needs, used updated equipment or methods, or enlarged smaller efforts into larger ones. Into that climate entered the initial probing of a major new industry that by the end of the decade had a new plant under construction near Lugoff. E. I. du Pont de Nemours and Company (DuPont) brought new jobs, new people, and new opportunities to a county already experiencing postwar change.

Aviation

Some of the changes resulted over several years as aviation-related property that the federal government had acquired in the county for the war effort shifted to ownership by local government and private hands. On May 30, 1947, Camden and Kershaw County took over control of Woodward Airport, with W. R. Gettys as chairman of the newly formed Airport Commission and Jim Darby as airport manager. On July 18 the War Assets Administration (WAA), in charge of disposing of government surplus, deeded former Southern Aviation School properties to its related town and county governments. Thus facilities at Woodward Field and auxiliary Bateman Field, valued at five hundred thousand dollars, were conveyed to Camden and Kershaw County, and Stevens Field, another auxiliary landing site, was conveyed to the town of Kershaw. A third auxiliary strip, Trotter Field, was sold in a government surplus sale.

At Woodward the WAA conveyed control of the airfield, three hangars, equipment, the control tower, the mess hall, and the administration building. The transfer also included the barracks and classrooms, but the WAA stipulated that those structures must be removed within sixty days, a provision that the local governments successfully lobbied to waive. In December 1949 the county ceded its interest in the aviation properties to the city of Camden. The city in turn agreed to assume control of airport activities and to permit the barracks and classrooms to be used by a newly formed private military prep school, the Camden Academy. The role of aviation remained significant in the postwar economy.

Several new businesses developed at the Camden Airport and capitalized on increased interest in aviation. In January 1946 at Woodward Field's Hanger no. 2, J. M. (Jerry) Hoffer opened Hoffer's Flying Service, which offered commercial flying, flight instruction, airplane and engine repairs, and passenger rides. A flight over Camden cost one dollar. By fall 1947 Hoffer employed four people and was operating five planes and providing instruction to twenty-five veterans under the GI Bill and to four other students. He also had a sales department for parts and planes. To provide required night training, Hoffer added portable runway lighting.

Former SAS instructor M. E. Moody, owner of the Camden Flying Service, attracted attention with his offer of a free solo flying course to the first eligible grandmother to register for training. He especially wanted to sign up young male students, whom he believed "should learn to fly as casually as they learn to drive." Henry J. Bagley Jr., a C-45 pilot in China during the war, started another flying school for GI's at Woodward Field with four Aeronca Champion planes and one Aeronca Chief.

Bill Grant, also formerly connected with SAS, opened Grant Hangar Service in Woodward's Hangar no. 1 with three employees. The business engaged in crop dusting, aerial applications of fertilizers and pesticides on agricultural crops, throughout the county. Others who soon went into that line of work were J. G. David of Dixie Dusting Company and Bill Clyburn of Clyburn Dusters, Inc.

Automotives

Since civilian autos had been in scarce supply during the war, one of the largest fields of new businesses was auto sales and repairs. There was considerable excitement in the county when new automobiles were again available. Drakeford's Garage in Camden advertised in February 1946: "The new Hudsons are here" with "a new Hudson dealer to serve you." Making the first of the newly manufactured automobiles, the Hudson company was back into production using a prewar body style. In June fanfare surrounded Myers Motor Company's premier showing of the first restyled postwar automobile, the 1947 Studebaker.

Transportation being essential to employment, the demand for cars made even old rattletraps valuable. E. C. and W. C. Elliott opened Camden Body Works, including among their four employees a veteran taking On-the-Job Training (OJT) under the GI Bill. W. T. Redfearn modernized his garage for body repair and painting, adding as service manager W. H. Clyburn, former chief of maintenance at Southern Aviation School. D. M. Davis and Whit Boykin opened Boykin Pontiac and AMC, specializing in radiator work and service on a desirable new option for new vehicles, the automatic transmission. Camden Motor Company and Bethune Motor Company advertised Buick's automatic transmission, Dynaflow. Clarkson Rhame and Whit Boykin opened Camden Motor Sales, offering sales and service for Willys Overland vehicles, Jeeps, and trucks—military look-alikes for civilians. John T. Nettles Sr. opened a Kaiser-Frazier dealership with a used car lot and employed a man well known to returning veterans—retired policeman Dallas Mahoney, operator of the Mahoney Soda Shop on DeKalb Street, a popular teenage hangout.

The automotive business continued growing in 1949. Smoak Motor Company, an Oldsmobile dealer, formally opened, and Myers Motor Company added Mack Truck distribution. Service Motor Company moved into a new facility, with three veterans on OJT. Perry Langston constructed a modern garage and gleaming salesroom at Broad and Walnut streets, advertising a new service: "We own and operate our own airplane for the fastest possible pickup and delivery service on Chevrolet parts."

There seemed to be a filling station on every block in downtown Camden. Six of them carried the green dinosaur symbol of Sinclair Oil Corporation. E. B. (Ned) Beard, who had previously worked with his father, the local franchise owner, returned from service to rejoin the family business, Camden Petroleum Oil Company. Stations operated also in other areas of the county, expanding services beyond filling tanks. At Liberty Hill, R. J. Wardlaw updated his station, moving into the post office building he purchased from C. D. Cunningham. Skipper's Auto Service in Blaney advertised auto and truck parts, tires, batteries, and electrical appliances, along with repairs and wrecker service. E. F. Dabney opened a garage on U.S. 521 near Black River Road, employing three workers and offering twenty-four-hour wrecker service. In Lewisville, a new suburb east of Camden past DuBose Park, the Pure Oil distributor Carolina Motor Company renovated C. S. Blackwell's station. On Highway 34 seven miles from Camden, Ben R. Galloway built a large combination store and Esso filling station on the site of the old turpentine still. Galloway's wife and his brother Winford J. Galloway assisted in the new operation, which included fluorescent lights and modern gas pumps.

Town & Country, a "super service station" and snack bar, opened on April 12, 1948, on U.S. Highway 1 beyond the Camden city limits, with New Yorker Robert J. Kunzler as owner and manager. Described as a "service center with gleaming white porcelain enamel finish," its modern appearance featured a "clock tower and hundreds of feet of gleaming plate glass," illuminated by powerful floodlights. Open twenty-four hours a day, seven days a week, the station dispensed Esso gasoline from six pumps.

Radios and Refrigeration

Besides auto repairs, another large field of new businesses in the postwar years was radio and refrigerator repairs. Such appliances, in demand for modern living, were sold in furniture stores, where repair businesses frequently operated. On Broad Street in Camden, J. B. (Joby) Gaskin, a former Link instructor at the Southern Aviation School, operated Marjoe Radio Service in Carolina Furniture. I. A. (Bert) Rush ran the radio repair department of Camden Furniture. G. A. Gaskin Radio Service operated on South Broad, and brothers Ned and Paul McDowell opened a service in the backyard of their home at 1813 North Mill.

Camden's Western Auto Store expanded rapidly under owners W. R. and H. S. Bowden, who added two repair shops—one for radios and the other for bicycles. W. R., who had been an inspector of radio installations in B-29 bombers, was assisted by Harvey Hall, a former navy aviation radio operator. Former paratrooper Eddie LaTouf was in charge of the bicycle and small electrical appliance repair shop.

Announcement of a charter application for a local radio station came in June 1946 from Henry Savage Jr., one of the incorporators of the Camden Radio Company. Two years later Radio Station WACA went on the air on July 22, 1948. The one-thousand-watt station broadcast entertainment, news, and advertising from a building and tower in Lugoff off Highway 34 north of U.S. Highway 1. R. O. Darby was general manager, M. E. Morris was chief engineer, and Dowd Sullivan was the announcer.

Partnerships

Several other businesses expanded as war workers and veterans returned. Brothers often made natural business partners. James L. Anderson, welding instructor at the Charleston shipyard, and his brother Lewis F. Anderson, an army glider pilot veteran, bought from their father the family business, Camden Machine Works, which had moved to larger quarters at the old state highway shop on South Mill Street. Two of their other brothers, Jack and Mac, also veterans, assisted them for a time.

On U.S. Highway 1 brothers C. C. and W. L. Jackson opened Jackson's Nursery and Garden Shop, offering garden supplies and ornaments in addition to several acres of nursery plants and shrubs, including roses and fruit trees, that they grew on the family farm. To specialize in building kitchen cabinets, brothers Ed and Harold Segars, who had outgrown their home shop at Segars Mill, opened Segars' Cabinet Shop in the rear of Boykin Pontiac. Later they opened the Open-Air Curb Market on Market Street, selling fresh country vegetables.

Three brothers—Ernest, Francis J., and Fred Sheheen—took over and modernized their father's South Broad Street business, the forty-six-year-old A. Sheheen Grocery. Francis had worked with his father during the war and chaired the city salvage committee, and the other brothers had recently been discharged from service. Sheheen Grocery and Meat Market soon advertised the "latest in vegetable display cabinets and racks."

Agribusiness

Other businesses went into operation to update agricultural practices. Camden Tractor & Implement Company, Ford-Ferguson dealers, opened in March 1946 under Frank Caston. Percy Mays, manager and owner of a Ford tractor dealership on East DeKalb Street in Camden, conducted tractor schools at Antioch and Midway in cooperation with school officials, covering basic tractor operation and maintenance.

In Camden in the former Springs and Shannon cotton warehouse on the north side of East DeKalb Street near the railroad, Joseph M. Upchurch opened a manufacturing plant, Southern Tractor Manufacturing Corporation, to make Gardenaid tractors and implements that could be shipped to fifteen southern states. An engine-powered, two-wheeled, walk-behind tractor, the Gardenaid was an early development in modern yard and garden equipment. After ninety days of operation, the plant was producing fifty tractors a week. Generally it employed about twelve to fifteen workers.[26]

Agricultural improvements were being encouraged by progressive farmers who joined the Farm Bureau chartered in South Carolina in 1944 to "organize, advance and improve" the state's agricultural interests by unifying its farmers. The first local president was L. O. Funderburk, who defended the concept of the organization when detractors questioned the wisdom of forming a "farmers' union" that could potentially control food production and prices. The bureau, he said, was not "that kind" of union. In 1946, however, he paradoxically opined, regarding the mineworkers' and steelworkers' strikes blamed for shortages of materials in the South: "Let the farmers get organized and refuse to sell any farm products and see how long these strikes last."

James R. West of DeKalb Township was Farm Bureau president in 1947 when at year's end the county membership stood at 700. Kershaw County also had the distinction of having the first black county Farm Bureau organization in the state. With a membership of 160, it was said to be growing rapidly. In early 1948 Usher Myers, chairman of the county board of commissioners, announced bids opened for construction of the Kershaw County Farmers Market. Located west of the agricultural building, the market opened in June. President West in August 1948 reported negotiations for government loans to secure a cotton storage warehouse at the former location of Fresh-Dry Foods. Farmers seemed to be reaching some long-standing goals.

One new business welcomed by farmers and cattle raisers was a large packing house, Supreme Products Meat Packing, which in 1947 modernized the century-old Southern railway freight depot in Camden to process meats under the trade name "Supreco" and the slogan "Quality that is supreme." Also on Rutledge Street in the old armory building, John DeMars opened Frozen Foods, Inc., a "high class meat market" supervised by Tally Rabon. Open daily from 6:00 A.M. to 6:00 P.M., the business that became known as "the freezer locker" sold meats, fresh poultry, and frozen seafood, and also allowed patrons to rent freezer space for storage.

In July 1948 the first mechanical cotton picker in Kershaw County drew curious viewers to Whitaker and Company on Rutledge Street. Ancrum Boykin, Whit Boykin, Charlie DuBose, and James Sweet had ordered the International Harvester machine, which the company claimed was capable of picking eight to ten bales a day at about ten dollars per bale. Costs and limited availability of machines, however, prevented widespread use for quite a while.

Some farmers instead were encouraged by prospects of a new crop to replace cotton growing—shatter-proof soybeans.[27] Some farmers shifted to other agricultural pursuits. At Liberty Hill, the Virginian J. W. Sublett in 1946 was so successful with tobacco cultivation that the Camden Jaycees encouraged the city to consider building a tobacco warehouse. In May 1949 Al Kiester established Kershaw County's first turkey farm on 102 acres on U.S. Highway 521 eight miles north of Camden. Cassatt was one of several areas of the county that shipped large numbers of watermelons by rail in summer 1949. In July, Blaney shipped fifteen train cars of watermelons per week. In a significantly different approach, Louie I. Guion Jr. of Lugoff diversified his family's agricultural interests into six new firms—trucking, construction, equipment supply, a flour and feed business, a garage, and a filling station.

Industrialization

Just after World War II substantial changes in industrialization were variously delayed by government restrictions, shortages of materials, and adjustments in the climate of labor relations. However, once new industries got established in Kershaw County, they were seen as a wave of the future. It was a recognition that some citizens lamented but many welcomed.

Jaclyn Hosiery Mill

In 1945 negotiations began to locate a new industry, Jaclyn Hosiery Mill, in Kershaw County. It was the first large outside industry to come to the county in some time. Plans were made public in January 1946, but several more months of delay followed before construction began on the modern, windowless building on U.S. Highway 1 just west of the Camden city limits. Glass brick provided natural lighting, and the area's first industrial air-conditioning cooled the building. Headed by James C. Stewart, the company expected to attract skilled laborers to serve a luxury-starved public by manufacturing ladies' nylon hosiery, which was still being rationed. To accommodate the plant the city extended water, sewer, and power lines and installed streetlights and fire hydrants westward from the business district. The county built the connecting roads, and the state constructed a sidewalk along U.S. Highway 1 for the safety of employees walking between work and town. Mayor McCorkle, Chamber of Commerce executive secretary Sam Boykin, and the industrial department of the Seaboard Air Line Railroad (formerly Railway) had all cooperated in securing the plant's location within the county. By its August 1947 open house, Jaclyn Hosiery was operating with forty-five employees and anticipating expansion. When the company refused an election to organize a union of the American Federation of Hosiery Workers, the National Labor Relations Board investigated unfair labor charges. In a November 1948 election ordered and conducted by the board, the union was voted in 36–24. In March 1949 thirty of fifty-two eligible employees petitioned to oust the union, and hearings continued in the fall.

DuPont

In April 1946, while the hosiery mill was trying to get construction under way, local officials were also quietly responding to inquiries from another group that had its eye on the Kershaw County area. Again the city, the Chamber of Commerce, and the Seaboard were part of the negotiations, often corresponding through the Camden lawyer Henry Savage Jr., who became mayor in 1948.[28] The December 10, 1951, issue of *Time* magazine explained that "in 1946, Camden's townspeople grew curious when small groups of tight-lipped engineers, labor specialists, tax experts, lawyers and power analysts began dropping in from 'the North.' The visitors would take samplings through the length and breadth of Kershaw County, then fly mysteriously back whence they came."

Hush-hush negotiations proceeded for some months, amid local rumors. Inquiries from Frank Heath of the *Camden Chronicle* brought a confidential letter from the Seaboard Air Line Railroad's industrial agent saying that options had been taken on land near Lugoff for a large company that also held options in two other states. He cautioned that the company would not make a decision for six months and that a premature announcement could cause Camden to be dropped from consideration. Requesting Heath not to release information yet, the agent promised to help him get the story later.

Meanwhile, Savage exchanged many letters with agents of the railroad and "the large company," E. I. du Pont de Nemours and Company (DuPont) of

Wilmington, Delaware. The letters covered a wide range of topics, including transportation, power, housing, education, and community attitudes. A November 11, 1946, letter to a DuPont engineer shows that transportation by way of the Wateree River was also considered. Savage suggested that if "large quantities of bunker oil" were required, "tankers could come through the Santee-Cooper waterway and reservoirs to within twenty-five miles of the Lugoff site" to a point easily accessed by highway.

Negotiations instead were under way for electrical power, with Savage assuring DuPont officials that "the local people are willing to expend a substantial sum to attract your plant." DuPont was also concerned about adequate housing and a pleasing community environment for employees. Opposed to constructing or owning employee housing, the company in 1948 suggested that local contractors be encouraged to build houses of five thousand to twenty thousand dollars value for sale or rent. DuPont was also concerned with discussions to consolidate school districts since the Lugoff district at the time had no schools for white students.

Influential help to secure DuPont's location came from many sources. Savage in December 1947 wrote thanking Governor and Mrs. Strom Thurmond for hospitality to company officials and for "going out of your way to show them that we really want them in South Carolina." The governor, pleased that DuPont seemed to be "leaning in favor of Camden," offered to do anything else that he could. Later that month Savage invited U.S. senator Burnet R. Maybank to a January 1948 luncheon with DuPont executives and the governor, suggesting that the Washington delegation "come down by private [railroad] car, at least from Richmond, along with the DuPont executives." Referring to the possibility of DuPont's locating here, Savage stated that "although this is supposed to be a secret, it is generally known around here."

Time magazine in 1951 wrote breezily that "only one leading citizen of Camden" openly opposed the coming of DuPont, fearing that it "would ruin the town's winter-resort business." When word of the opposition got out, "three carloads of young bloods roared over to the man's house and—in a variation of a waning Southern custom—burned an oil-soaked cross on his front lawn." The situation was more complex. DuPont executive G. W. Filson wrote to Savage on March 12, 1948, that a Camden citizen had visited the Wilmington, Delaware, headquarters and offered three concerns: problems absorbing large numbers of new persons, objectionable odors, and competition for labor with other local employers. Few citizens, however, joined the protest.

An April 9, 1948, *Chronicle* extra announced that E. I. du Pont de Nemours and Company had exercised its option to purchase some 800 acres on the Wateree River. Presumably they intended to proceed with plans to build a manufacturing plant on the site. The South Carolina General Assembly passed a resolution by Senator R. M. Kennedy welcoming DuPont to the state. In May the company acquired title to the plant site, 550 acres about three miles west of Camden, on the opposite bank of the Wateree River and between the Seaboard railroad and U.S. Highway 1. The approximate purchase price was seventy-five thousand dollars.

In June 1948 a DuPont public relations agent answered an inquiry from the South Carolina Wildlife Federation by stating that the company would take steps to protect the fish in the Wateree River. The product of the new plant, the agent stated, was a new one "still in the test tube stage." Plans were not yet finalized for DuPont's operation in Kershaw County, but the company had chosen a name for the product it was considering for manufacture—Orlon. A synthetic textile product previously identified as "Fiber A," Orlon was identified as a polyacrylonitrile fiber ideal for awnings, automobile tops, and other outdoor uses because of its superior resistance to sunlight-caused decomposition. Among other uses it was also suited for household curtains.

In October 1948 DuPont's finance committee approved the Camden plant. Approximately eighteen months and eight hundred workers would be required to construct the multi-million-dollar Orlon plant, which upon completion would employ five hundred men and women. The $17 million plant for processing Orlon was the first and largest commercial manufacturing facility to come to South Carolina after World War II. That winter the 100 by 250 foot brick building that the old Kirkwood Hotel had used as a garage was rented by its owner Thomas Hair to the DuPont Company for a warehouse to store gathered building supplies. Meanwhile, Seaboard engineers laid spur lines to the DuPont site. Construction began in Lugoff in February 1949 with Governor Strom Thurmond digging the first shovel of soil. James D. Wilson arrived in Camden to head the construction, which was expected to last eighteen to twenty-four months.

As other employees arrived, their first priority was finding places to live. The Chamber of Commerce requested local citizens who had vacancies to register with its office. In June, DuPont chose Leland M. Jones, a sixteen-year veteran with its rayon division, as manager of the Orlon plant, which was to be named the "May Plant" for Benjamin M. May, retiring head of the rayon division.

Labor strife at the Lugoff site practically halted construction several days in July 1949. DuPont's refusal to recognize a Common Laborers Union, an affiliate of the American Federation of Labor, led to picket lines at the site.[29] The union represented about two hundred of the eight hundred skilled workers at the construction site. Some six hundred of the workforce refused to cross the picket line. DuPont and the union settled their dispute, and workers returned to the job on August 3. The settlement pledged DuPont to bargain collectively with the union "but did not involve complete union recognition." Construction was completed, and the plant was ready to operate by spring 1950.

Textile Mills

Meanwhile long-standing textile mills in Camden expanded; both of them were manufacturers of cotton gauze. By June 1948 construction was under way at Hermitage Mill to nearly double its capacity and to employ 225 additional workers. Most of that year the Wateree Mill of Kendall Company operated at full capacity, employing more than 225 people with an annual payroll more than six hundred thousand dollars. Breaking with paternalistic tradition, in spring 1948 the company sold 99 of its 104 mill village homes to individuals, often the former renters, and donated its streets and public utilities—valued at eighty thousand dollars—to the city of Camden. Making the step from renter to property owner was a major one for many a mill employee, but a number of home owners were soon busy sprucing up their private dwellings. Later in the year the former mill village was annexed into the city of Camden.

By October 1949 both mills were running three shifts, six days a week, and together they had 760 full-time employees. C. L. Taggart managed the Wateree Mill, owned by Kendall, Inc. The officers of locally owned Hermitage Mill were C. H. Zemp, president; R. B. Pitts Jr., vice president; W. B. Pitts, secretary; and Isaac P. Pitts, treasurer.

Horse Industry

In May 1947 Ben Heath, formerly a local equestrian publicist, wrote a letter to the *Chronicle* urging Camden people to support development of its "*horse* industry." Heath used the term in response to a complaint heard that "Camden needs to stop worrying about horses and get some *real* industry." Heath was supported by a letter the following month from Mrs. Emma Brunson, who gave several reasons that horses were needed in the community. Publicity about the successes of Camden-trained horses in the postwar years was quite persuasive in showing that there was money at the top, which meant profits to employees and associates along the way.

In April 1946 Camden-trained Elkridge had reached career earnings of eighty-four thousand dollars and was voted the outstanding steeplechaser of the year. The horse's owner-trainer, Kent Miller, purchased Cool Springs plantation in Camden and for the 1947 winter training season brought in Elkridge and other winners that year—War Battle, Battle Cruiser, and Cooper Beach. A "larger than ever" number of horses arrived at Mrs. Marion duPont Scott's Camden training grounds, which was managed by her trainer-rider Ray Woolfe. Mrs. Scott was owner of Battleship, the only American-trained horse to win the Grand National in England. In fact the top three money horses in summer 1946 had been Camden-trained.

Five trainers alone brought a total of more than 130 horses to the Scott training grounds in 1947, and others brought more in smaller numbers. Winning continued that summer. C. V. Whitney's Phalanx captured the forty-thousand-dollar Wood Memorial, and at Aqueduct Park, New York, the top three winners were Camden-trained, the first two belonging to Kent Miller. In Camden polo also revived under Fred Tejan, and Harry Kirkover's enthusiastic promotion continued to spread the reputation of the Carolina Cup.

Community Developments

Transportation improvements, essential to the growth of commerce and industry, had important influences in the economic and community developments of the postwar years. Blacktop paving projects in 1946 included West Wateree's Route 217 (present Highway 34) from Lugoff to the Fairfield County line and the Black River Road from Camden to Pisgah. U.S. Highway 1 between Lugoff and Columbia was straightened and resurfaced. Camden added a new street to its business district, Commerce Alley, at the rear of busy Broad Street stores. Haile Street, from Mill Street through the Wateree village and along "the old National Highway," was paved to connect with U.S. Highway 1. In fall 1947 new steel spans and modern piers, required by heavier and faster modern trains, replaced the Seaboard railroad trestle over the Wateree River.[30]

In 1948 paving was approved for McRae Road and for Campbell Street from Chesnut to DeKalb in Camden. Senator R. M. Kennedy pressured for increased federal funding to improve county farm-to-market roads, described as in nearly "impassable condition" sometimes for weeks at a time. The state highway system in 1948 included 403 miles of roads in Kershaw County, of which 230 were unimproved earth.

Protests were heard from some citizens in Camden when the Confederate monument that stood in the middle of Broad Street at Laurens, with the islands north and south of it, was removed for traffic safety as part of the widening of Broad Street in winter 1949.[31] Other citizens deemed the move wise, just as the fountain to Richard Kirkland had been removed to Hampton Park from its midstreet repositioning on lower Broad, where the memorial was several times struck by negligent or intoxicated drivers. The Confederate monument was moved to Monument Square, across from the library.

Accessing the improved transportation routes, competition was keen among Roberts, Hudson, and Hinson taxi services. Camden's first motor-bus line began operation in 1945. The blue and white buses of the City Transit Company, begun by T. W. Hughey Jr. and T. W. Hughey Sr. of Rock Hill, opened with three routes in Camden. One route ran between Quaker Cemetery and Dusty Bend; the second was between Woodward Airport and the Seaboard passenger depot; and the third route ran between the downtown and mill areas. Later a route would extend to industrial areas as far as DuPont. In 1947 Horace Crimminger became manager, and in 1949 Jake Smith held that title. Long-distance bus service improved with the construction of Atlantic Greyhound's new DeKalb Street terminal, begun in 1949. Highway and transportation improvements overall aided connections between the various communities of the county.

Blaney

The year 1949 was one of progress in Blaney, a community that hoped to reap benefits from the building of DuPont in neighboring Lugoff but was also banking on successful cotton agriculture. A "great crowd" gathered in February to dedicate the new Blaney High School gymnasium with a WIS Radio personality as master of ceremonies. Postmaster J. D. (Donnie) Watson, chairman of the board of trustees, crowned Ollie May Branham as Queen of Love and Beauty.

The April 8 *Camden Chronicle* reported a Blaney building boom: "Neon signs are more numerous. Dwellings are being erected, and the general atmosphere is one of progressiveness." The Blaney Grill of Mrs. Thelma Kelly and her father, Glen Dowey, served meals to tourists and locals. I. W. Bagnal bought and remodeled Miles Cabins, and a North Carolina developer built another cabin court. W. Lamar Rush opened the new Midway Colony Furniture Company. E. T. Bowen constructed a drugstore with a registered pharmacist, a soda fountain, and office space for a medical doctor. He also built a house for the pharmacist Fred Ogburn Jr., who was a stockholder and the business manager, and a house for Dr. R. A. Cochran.

A large new cotton warehouse had been built, and there farmers could store their bales awaiting good market prices. There were also new cotton platforms to process some seven thousand bales, double the previous year's output. The facilities in 1949 presented "an optimistic outlook for the financial future of Blaney." However, further growth—especially in housing construction—was being hampered by "the lack of an adequate water supply." Postmaster Watson believed that without additional water the town had reached "the peak of its growth"; Blaney needed the construction of at least a four-inch pipe to benefit housing, industry, and business.

Meanwhile a number of Blaney businessmen promoted themselves in April by sponsoring a bargain day. Participating companies included Blaney Esso, Blaney Grill, T. E. Campbell's Grocery and Shell Gas, J. M. Carn's Parts & Garage, B. B. Cooper's Corner Grocery, W. H. Graddick's Dry Goods, Midway Colony Furniture, Moak's Grocery, A. B. Nelson's Station, and Mrs. Mattie Watson's Grocery. In spring 1949 T. W. Hackel of Georgia set up a "mobile theater tent," and "good crowds nightly " attended the motion pictures. A short time later Ross Burr of Chesterfield gave a free movie preview in an open lot prior to opening a drive-in movie next to the new drugstore.

In 1949 four hundred persons feasted at Blaney's seventh annual Fourth of July barbecue, hosted by Thurston Goff at the home of Otis Goff, with cooking by J. R. Hornsby, Joe Hornsby, Lexie Moak, and G. P. Monroe. The menu consisted of two barbecued cows (four hundred to seven hundred pounds), four dressed hogs (one hundred pounds each), coleslaw, tomatoes, iced tea, lemonade, and cake. Mr. Goff, who annually supplied nearly all the food except for "baskets brought voluntarily," was planning for "well over 1,000 next year."

Bethune

In 1948 prospects were looking up in Bethune, still a close-knit agricultural community, where the citizens hoped to progress industrially. The area had been working for better telephone service but was then without any service at all for its population of seven hundred to eight hundred people until midyear, when Southern Bell agreed to put up posts and serve the town. In spring 1948 Bethune Pottery owner Guy Daugherty extended his business into an additional part of the county. With Jim Clarkson Jr., Daugherty opened Camden Pottery on U.S. Highway 1 five miles from Camden at the intersection of Highway 26 (presently 601), moving into the fast-growing Lugoff area.

Veterans had a voice in the new energy of Bethune. Approximately twenty-five veterans of the vicinity in July 1948 applied for a charter for an American Legion post. Bethune Memorial Post no. 155 was organized in October, electing Neil Ratcliff commander, with John Don McLaurin as adjutant.

By fall 1948 the Seaboard Air Line Railroad had built a new depot in Bethune to replace one that had burned the previous year. Construction also began on a new plant to produce Sacony-label garments for the Egmont Manufacturing Company, then operating a sewing room in an old warehouse near the Bethune railroad tracks. In February 1949 the new factory was in operation and there were plans to put in more machines and hire more workers.

The year 1949 also saw the construction of a new Presbyterian manse, a new grocery store, a new coffee shop, and a new venture called the Pix Movie Theatre. Joe Baker, a Bethune native who had recently moved back to town with his family from Flint, Michigan, ran the theater—the community's first—and the coffee shop. From 1948 to 1949 citizens lobbied to keep a liquor store from opening, declaring that its influence would be negative to community aspirations.

Congressman J. P. Richards was the principal speaker at the 1949 July Fourth picnic and barbecue, which was served at D. M. Mays's open-air garage. An afternoon gymkhana at the baseball diamond followed the morning parade of twenty-eight floats. The event also featured a baseball game between the Camden Midgets and the Bethune Midgets, swimming at Big Springs, and the crowning of Rita Davis as Miss Bethune.

In September a crowd of 250 attended the dedication of Bethune's town hall. The recreation center of the hall included an up-to-date kitchen, tables and chairs to seat 100, and swings and sand piles for preschool children. The Shirley

Clemens Library moved to a portion of the building, and Miss Mary Arthur became librarian. In winter 1949 the Scotch Cemetery Association was organized to maintain the historic community cemetery. The following served as officers: Mrs. A. B. McLaurin, president; Mrs. Frank Lee, vice president; and Stella Bethune, secretary-treasurer.

Camden

At the end of the war, in 1945 a group of Camden businessmen purchased the Court Inn, hoping that the community's tourist industry would revive in peacetime. The new owners—Moultrie B. Burns, John M. Villepigue, C. C. Whitaker, John Whitaker Jr., and W. Robin Zemp—renovated the interior and advertised an "air of quietness and comfort."

A week after the 1948 public announcement that DuPont would locate in the county, Clyde Massebeau began an asbestos-sided, four-unit apartment complex on Fair Street just south of East DeKalb. It was the first of many building projects responding to the demand for housing. Construction of modern brick and steel apartment complexes had begun only a year earlier with Park Court Apartments on the southeastern side of Monument Square.

In 1949 George A. Creed, Mattie S. Creed, and S. Alvin Creed constructed the thirty-unit King Haiglar Apartments at the corner of Laurens and Mill across from the Court Inn, and Joseph M. Upchurch began construction of the thirty-unit Kirkwood Apartments on North Broad Street.[32] Mrs. B. H. Baum developed a portion of her Highland Avenue property with rental houses and sold a section to a Bishopville developer, who added more homes on Highland Avenue and opened Lee Court "up to Greenleaf Villa" for additional homes. North of the Kirkwood Hotel property in late 1949 Ralph Little was selling lots in Cantey Acres, opened along a new street, Cantey Parkway.

East Camden was now being referred to as a "suburb," a new word in local usage for the developments that stretched in that direction outside the city limits.[33] City water and electricity served the areas east of the city limits, which stopped at Pine Tree Creek, and notice was made that they "would eventually need sewerage, police and fire protection."[34] In 1947 a large section of the old Rhame farm beyond the mill villages was cut into building lots by J. P. Lewis and C. C. Whitaker Sr. In 1948 Henry E. Beard and J. B. Cantey subdivided lots on the old Hermitage Farm property, opening Paint Hill Road in the area. Also east of Camden, on U.S. Highway 1 Charles Barrett of Camden offered Sky-Vu subdivision homes, which qualified for 100 percent financing to veterans. The homes were near Little's Sky-Vu Drive-in Theatre, constructed in 1949 by George Little.

In spring 1948 the longtime movie owner T. Lee Little opened the modern, one-thousand-seat, air-conditioned Little Theatre on the DeKalb Street site of his old family home. The Camden downtown was made festive in December 1949 when four city utilities workers led by line foreman Neal Parker shinnied to the top of the town tower and hung hundreds of colored lights, which cascaded down from King Hagler's perch. A long-standing annual holiday tradition was born.

Kershaw

In the postwar years a major area employer, Springs Cotton Mills, which had dedicated its Kershaw plant to manufacturing combed broadcloth for shirting, made many improvements. By 1947 a modern cafeteria served Kershaw workers on all shifts, and by 1948 air-conditioning was being added section by section. New rental homes in the mill village were five-room brick structures with bathroom and garage. According to the mill, the majority of workers still owned their old farms in the area, so they preferred renting to acquiring ownership of these homes. In 1948 the company provided both life and hospital insurance and by then had increased salaries to cover vacation time. That year too the company acquired ocean-front property at Myrtle Beach, and by 1949 it had completed Springmaid Beach, with cottages, clubhouse, and cafeteria, where employees could "take their vacations with friends and with economy."

At Kershaw in February 1949 Governor Strom Thurmond was the keynote speaker and the Walter Johnson American Legion post formally raised the flags at the dedication ceremonies of the new Kershaw Memorial Library. The free public library, "Kershaw's living memorial to its service men and women of World Wars I and II," was a joint unit of the Kershaw and Lancaster County Library systems. Mrs. Mamie S. Rice was librarian of the fireproof facility, built opposite the public schools on property donated by John T. Stevens.[35] At the memorial service, Governor Thurmond praised the "sacrifices and service rendered by those who fought to preserve our way of life," but he warned of encroaching communism, from which, he said, "the American way of life is again being threatened."

Liberty Hill

Still counting on a revival of agriculture to spur its community forward, Liberty Hill sought to attract farm laborers. The developer W. B. Fort advertised farm property for sale—"to colored only"—in the nearby development of Sublett's Heights. In winter 1949 C. D. Cunningham sold W. C. Wardlaw the property on which stood the historic building being used for the Liberty Hill Library. The library books and furniture were moved to the Community House, and some of the books of use to schoolchildren were given "to the negro school." A great deal of farmland was being converted, however, to timber growing. In this most isolated part of the county, the lack of a labor force discouraged the potential interests of industrial developers, who were seeking out other areas for development.

Lugoff

The area closest to the actual site of DuPont became home, at least temporarily, to many laborers building the new plant. By 1949 construction was beginning to boom in Lugoff. At F. M. Watts's trailer court, a separate building housed showers, restrooms, and a laundry for sixty trailers parked along three streets in the camp, with telephone service and electrical outlets at each space. Artesian water supplied the camp, which was expected to double in size. Nearby the Watts grocery store and filling station added a modern meat market.

H. F. Branham, H. D. Boulware, and C. S. Caskey built another sixty-unit court in the area, the Riverside Trailer camp. With a stone building housing six showers, six washrooms, and washing machines, this camp too expected to expand. Additionally several private homes were under construction by 1949, and a number more were planned. In response to residents' requests for a convenient place of worship, in spring 1949 Springvale Baptist Church sponsored the dedication of a new church, Lugoff Baptist Church, on a knoll near U.S. Highway 1. Roseborough Acres, offering lots for sale, advertised their convenient proximity to the Lugoff church, radio station, stores, and bus lines. Residents of the growing Conifer Acres subdivision began working on a new recreational area, which became Drakeford Park.

Gus Ward's Tavern, popular for steaks and fried chicken, served a growing number of customers. In December 1948 Ben Emerson, with his wife supervising the kitchen, opened Emerson's Drive-In Restaurant across the highway from the DuPont site. In spring 1949 George Koumas of Camden and a partner leased the east end of the Riverside Mercantile Company, a grocery store that had opened in late 1947 at the Highway 34 (present Highway 5) junction with U.S. Highway 1 near the bridge. Here the men operated the Arcadia Grill with modern kitchen, tables, and bar. Near the intersection of then Highway 26 (present U.S. 601), the drive-in Wayside Theatre, built by Charles Blyther in spring 1948 and operated by G. B. Blyther, entertained with movies. Within a few short miles along U.S. Highway 1, energized by industrial prospects, the former agricultural rhythms of Lugoff were being transformed.

Conflicts of Interest

Postwar Kershaw County, caught in a tide of change, confronted not only practical situations such as housing and employment but also major social issues. At the heart lay civil rights—basic issues of citizenship itself. In peacetime many white citizens longed to return to a familiar old world in which racial separation and white leadership were established parts. In peacetime many black citizens expected the old social order to move forward and allow them full participation in democratic citizenship. In February 1945 the Camden Community Civic League held a countywide mass meeting at Trinity Methodist Church on the topic "The Negro and Postwar Planning," but little is published about the content of that event.

When President Truman in 1946 desegregated the nation's military, there were varied local responses. Many people anticipated that similar federal actions would follow in civilian life. As a whole, older citizens of both races tended to feel more comfortable with traditional ways, while younger people were more willing or eager to adopt changing ways. Furthermore citizens who looked to politics, to science, or to faith for answers sometimes encountered additional conflicts in changing times.

The postwar climate in which social issues came to the forefront was emotionally charged for a number of reasons. From 1945 to 1949 the international Nuremberg Trials examined Nazi war crimes, revealing atrocities under an all-controlling government. Winston Churchill in 1946 warned that an "iron curtain" was descending between free and communist nations in Europe.[36] In 1947 in America the House Un-American Activities Committee investigated the loyalties of Hollywood filmmakers and other artists. In 1948 Russia imposed the Berlin blockade, which was countered by humanitarian airlifts from America, England, and France. There was speculation, even in the local press, of a possible World War III.

In late 1947 Kershaw County's first body to be returned from World War II arrived home for burial, and a number more followed in 1948. Widely attended funeral ceremonies solemnly evoked both patriotism and sadness for individual sacrifices. The following year President Truman announced that Russia had the atomic bomb. The cold war was under way.[37]

Communism

Anticommunist warnings became part of local language and politics. Local distaste for unions and strikes included suspicion that they were "communist tactics." Harold Booker, *Camden Chronicle* editor since November 1947, wrote frequently on the subversive dangers of communism and spoke often at area civic clubs and gatherings. He warned of "infiltration of communists into the factories, schools, churches and even the government."

Groups such as the Hobkirk Hill Daughters of the American Revolution acted on the messages. In 1949 the DAR requested Camden and Kershaw County superintendents to exclude a textbook that asked students to imagine living in a communist society. The chapter urged local theater owners to beware subversive content in films. In July the DAR and other visitors, encountering rain on a memorial visit to the Battle of Camden monument site, returned to the Lake Shamokin shelter for speeches by Senator R. M. Kennedy and Harold Funderburk. Recalling local patriotic heritage, the speakers inveighed against modern "subversive thinking" and "un-American ways."

When the nation's first "flying saucer" reports were publicized in 1947, the local newspaper soon afterward stated that no such flying objects had been seen "yet" in Kershaw County skies. However, in January 1948 a Camden man reported seeing a flaming plane go down, and since no evidence was found, the media speculated that he may have seen a flying saucer. While many persons scoffed, some individuals turned wary eyes to the skies, alert for signs of foreign espionage or alien invasion.

Public Health

Closer to home in the late 1940s there were real worries about "mad" dogs, and several people took "the Pasteur treatment" to avoid hydrophobia following contact with cases of rabies. After three dogs bit children and were confirmed with rabies in spring 1949, all dogs in Camden were ordered inoculated, and strays were rounded up for disposal.

Polio was an even more fearful public health concern. The Camden Lions Club raised more than two thousand dollars in 1946 to purchase an iron lung for Camden Hospital during a campaign displaying one of the bulky breathing machines in a downtown store window. In the last three months of 1947, five new cases of "infantile paralysis" developed in the county, one of them a fifty-year-old woman. The local March of Dimes appealed for additional national foundation aid, and county fund-raising increased. However, in January 1948 a Camden-Aiken polo benefit, "Polo vs. Polio," attracted fewer than one hundred spectators because of people's instinctive avoidance of public gatherings.

On the prevailing theory that polio was spread by flies, in July 1948 the entire city of Camden was "fogged" with sprayings of DDT. The *Chronicle* reported official requests: "People of the city are asked to keep their doors and windows open so that the fog may penetrate the homes." The Jaycees purchased additional DDT for the city to spray garbage cans when trash was collected.[38] Post-war Camden also tackled sewage problems, closing open ditches that drained many parts of town and banning the raising of hogs within the city limits. Also in 1948 the city began burying refuse in a landfill and stopped burning trash at Magazine Hill.[39]

Public health monitoring increased for polio, tuberculosis, and hygiene-related illnesses, and treatment became more accessible for the needy.[40] Families with children moving to Camden from polio-prevalent areas were required immediately to contact city health officer Donald Morrison. County health officer Dr. A. W. Humphries, with the Kershaw County Tuberculosis Association, set up "out-centers" in Bethune, Blaney, Boykin, and Kershaw where a mobile X-ray unit examined "white and negro patients" of all ages. Camden held periodic testing at the County Health Department behind the agricultural building. A series of free clinics in 1948 identified a dozen definite cases of tuberculosis in the county. The TB Association sponsored "health demonstrations" by nurses who visited schools and community meetings. In 1948 Jennie McMaster resigned as TBA executive secretary to become the first full-time school nurse in the Camden city schools.

Camden Hospital, with ninety-three beds and eighteen bassinets in 1946, operated with good reputation and was accredited by the American College of Surgeons. That year the hospital was among the first in the nation to receive for civilian use the first TB "miracle" drug, streptomycin. The following year the facility was approved as a Blue Cross hospital under a new plan to help families meet medical expenses through insurance. The Camden Hospital Women's Auxiliary, which in 1947 held its first annual white-elephant sale, provided volunteer service. Yearly the Camden Hospital School of Nursing graduated eight or nine registered nurses.[41] The main problem of Camden Hospital, at its original site on the corner of Fair and Union streets, was its small size for serving Kershaw County's expanding population.

Strongly favoring a living memorial over other types of monuments, the public supported plans to construct additional wings to Camden Hospital in commemoration of local residents who died in World Wars I and II. To undertake the increased responsibilities of fund-raising for such an expansion, in August 1948 the Camden Hospital board enlarged to thirteen members.[42] The Kershaw County delegation in winter 1949 agreed to provide $100,000 toward the $450,000 cost of the planned expansion.

In a move toward efficiency and better services, city and county officials consolidated all public health responsibilities in the Kershaw County Health Department, headed by Dr. A. W. Humphries. One of the concerns Dr. Humphries frequently expressed was the need for a community home for care of the elderly. Others agreed, but resources were unavailable. Associated Charities continued to coordinate the charitable work of various groups and to assist with problems not covered by others.

Delinquency

In addition to health concerns, postwar families worried about young people falling prey to juvenile delinquency. Increasing crimes of vandalism and theft by local youths, as well as inappropriate social behavior, were blamed on "wrong influences." Civic clubs actively united behind a highly touted concept—the teen canteen, a supervised recreation and social hall for teenagers' leisure hours. The county's first canteen, serving white youths, opened in January 1947 in an old Lyttleton Street Boy Scout hut owned by the Masons. That building, revamped by the Jaycees, was soon outgrown, and by fall 1948 a building had been constructed for the canteen and other community meetings on the southeast corner of the Camden Grammar School property. A black youth canteen too opened in early 1947, in a remodeled building on the Jackson School grounds. A supervised place for games, music, dancing, and hanging out with friends, the teenage-canteen concept had general community approval for several years, although such facilities served only a small percentage of the county's youths.

Countywide efforts addressed concerns for youths through a newly funded recreation program. In spring 1948 Senator R. M. Kennedy made appointments to a committee that included three members each from Bethune, Blaney, Camden, and Kershaw.[43] Citizens of Lugoff quickly appealed for a voice and a share of funding for their community, urging that youngsters in rural areas such as theirs not be overlooked. Throughout the county playgrounds and sports equipment were placed at various schools and community centers.

Religion

From the end of the war through the following years, religious revivals were frequent and heartfelt events throughout the county. They were especially publicized among Baptist, Methodist, and Pentecostal congregations. Preachers typically focused on bringing those exposed to excesses of wartime behavior and modern temptations back to paths of moral rectitude. Abstinence from alcohol, or at least temperance, was widely encouraged. Gambling, sex outside of marriage, and sometimes card playing and dancing were discouraged. Sunday diversions, makeup, immodest dress, and suggestive music, movies, and books were targets on occasion. The Bible was widely approved for use in the schools. Traditional family roles—mothers at home, faithful fathers, obedient children, regular church attendance—were upheld as models.

In fall 1948 Camden civic clubs sponsored the Church Loyalty Drive, an intensive three-month campaign promoting church attendance. At Christmastime that year black churches in Camden, under the Reverend J. C. Wright, organized a seventy-member community choir to sing carols at the old courthouse, the post office steps, the Sarsfield Hotel, the Court Inn, Camden Hospital, and various city parks. Contributions solicited in advance paid for presents that the choir distributed to the poor and needy in the black community.

Religious activities abounded the following year in black and white churches throughout the county. In early 1949 Shamrock Baptist Church in Bethune replaced its old building with a new brick sanctuary. In April, Hermitage Baptist Church held a temperance crusade, and the Pentecostal Holiness Highway Church of Blaney held a two-week revival and sponsored a singing convention. At midyear, under the slogan "Camden for Christ," black churches united to make a religious survey of traditional black neighborhoods in the city and in subdivisions of Cartersville, Kirkwood Heights, and Smyrl Hill.[44] In late 1949 an extended, three-week revival at the Camden First Baptist Church, led by the temperance-evangelist Reverend John Haggai, brought four hundred responders forward for conversion or repentance. The meetings also energized plans for constructing a modern educational building beside the First Baptist sanctuary on the site of the old Baruch home.[45]

Statewide a conservative climate was supported by South Carolina law. Strom Thurmond, governor from 1947 to 1951, sided politically with strict enforcement. In postwar Kershaw County those seeking to revive the tourist industry and its related activities felt its effects. Enforcement of alcohol restrictions against "bring-your-own-bottle clubs" that had operated during the war curtailed nightclubs and restaurants operating in the style of social clubs. Anticipating a quieter postwar climate, the Schlosburg brothers sold the Sarsfield Club and transferred their business energies to modernizing the Camden Hotel on DeKalb Street and operating it as the Sarsfield Hotel.[46] When enforcement of blue laws jeopardized Sunday movies, swimming, ball games, golf, and polo, the Kershaw County delegation sought special legislation so as not to "hurt the tourist trade" in Camden.

With the postwar return of equine sports in Camden, bookmakers returned also. The April 4, 1947, *Camden Chronicle* stated the following of the recent Carolina Cup: "Bookmakers, who operated here in past years despite their illegal status in South Carolina, were stopped by state constables after they had taken bets on the first race. The bookies were not allowed to pay off and were required to return all money placed to the betters. . . . The bookies work all the spring hunt meets and this was the first time in 15 years they have been halted here. Their absence disappointed many fans." Clearly opinions varied among citizens of Kershaw County over lifestyle choices and over which traditions should be changed to improve the community.

Politics

Amid postwar changes and other tensions, the civil rights movement stirred the politics of Kershaw County. Efforts to end legalized racial segregation and white supremacy engendered support as well as actions to oppose those efforts. On a national level civil rights decisions were hammered out through legislation and court rulings. Locally decisions had to be worked out face-to-face, neighbor-to-neighbor.

Political resistance was the first reaction of opponents to integration. Kershaw County Democrats, represented by their executive committee, approached the 1948 presidential primary disaffected with the national party and eager to unseat President Truman. *Chronicle* editor Booker, who fervently agreed with the local committee, was chided by retired minister John Knox Tibbits in a letter to the editor, which the newspaper printed on April 16:

> Your editorial of March 5, advocating a new political party "Dedicated to state's rights, segregation of races, and the preservation of principles which have made this great country what it is today[,]" calls for comment both by

> Christians and by true Americans. The great story of America is that any man, of whatever race or color, has an opportunity here to make good and to enjoy the full rights of citizenship. The basic principles for community living are the Golden Rule and justice, or, in common parlance, kindliness and fair-play. We all believe in state's rights, but we deny the right of any man, or community, to do wrong by interfering with the rights of others. It is plain to most of us that to condemn a race as a race to an inferior position involves great wrong to many individuals, and is as un-American as it is un-Christian.

In July, despite strong southern opposition and a walkout at the national convention, the national Democratic Party renominated Truman. The next week representatives from Kershaw County were among those who went to Birmingham to form the "Dixiecrat" Party and put forward a "states' rights" platform and a third-party nomination—Governor Strom Thurmond for president. At home, in a called meeting, the Kershaw County Democratic Executive Committee unanimously endorsed Thurmond.

For three months there was a flurry of campaigning and a concurrent flurry of voter registration. Lugoff folk sponsored a states' rights fund-raising dinner at Gus Ward's; Camden residents sponsored a later one at the Sarsfield Hotel. With personal recollection of the Reconstruction politics of 1876, the Camden octogenarian George S. Barnes wore a red shirt to the White House, intending to ask President Truman to "respect the traditions of South Carolina." He was admitted to the White House but not to Truman's presence. Editor Booker asserted that the South had two enemies: "the Russians and the crowd in Washington."

Voter registration took place under new terms. A ruling of U.S. Circuit Court judge J. Waties Waring of Charleston abolished the loyalty oath by which the only party with a real voice in South Carolina—the Democrats—had controlled elections since Reconstruction. The possibility was now opened that "the Negro vote," maybe Republican, could sway an election—if not this one, then ones in the future. Leaders of the local black community, especially preachers and teachers, assumed educational roles to prepare the unregistered to meet voting requirements. Their actions were quiet and nonconfrontational.

Kershaw County Democrats, as ordered, opened registration books to enroll other voters, but the process was not easy. The South Carolina Constitution required a voter to certify that he could "read and write any section of the constitution submitted to him by the registration officer, or can show that he owns, and has paid taxes . . . on property . . . assessed at $300 or more." The efforts to increase numbers of black voters also encouraged the enrolling of more white voters.

In November, Truman was reelected in what the press called a "remarkable upset." The *Chronicle* headlines described local voters as "dazed" at results. Most had expected a Republican victory; states' righters had hoped for a runoff; few had expected a Truman victory. Thurmond had swept Kershaw County and had taken four southern states, including South Carolina, but without success elsewhere the Dixiecrats faded as a third party. However, 1948 voter registration changes and election events opened a window for two-party politics in the future.

The election over, politics took a quieter path the following year. On April 27, 1949, Camden hosted Baruch Day, honoring native son Bernard Baruch, whose statesmanship and influence had lasted through six presidential administrations. Baruch attended with his son B. M. Baruch Jr., of the United States Navy, and daughter Belle Baruch. All the schoolchildren of Camden, black and white, were present at the unveiling of a marker at Baruch's Broad Street birthplace. In Hampton Park a number of dignitaries, including Baruch, made remarks. Seated with honor was a ninety-five-year-old black woman, Georgiana Blount, who had been his childhood nursemaid.

Baruch addressed young listeners and spoke of changes in his lifetime: "Our country, like this state and this city, has moved forward a great distance since my childhood. Many things have not moved forward as far as we would like them to, but they are moving forward." He encouraged personal effort: "In my day we had to depend on ourselves; we had only our will to work. We had no friendly government to befriend us and do for us many things which we did and can do better for ourselves."

Public Schools

For a number of reasons changing school situations added to tensions in the postwar years. Since the beginning of the century, well over one hundred differently named public schools had operated at various times in the county.[47] Consolidations gradually eliminated many small facilities, so that by 1940 about two dozen different names identified larger schools or school systems in the county. By 1949 further consolidations reduced these to about half as many names: Antioch, Baron DeKalb, Bethune, Blaney, Camden, Jackson, Kirkwood, Midway, Mt. Pisgah, Pine Grove, Pine Tree Hill, and St. Matthew.

In the 1940s the county continued consolidating what had lately been 36 different school districts, each operating under some self-administration. In 1949 General Assembly legislation mandated that counties work toward combining South Carolina's 1,630 districts into 46 districts, one per county.[48] Each local school or district consolidation involved controversy since changes not only expanded opportunities but also threatened community identity and determination. Parents worried about their children's reception and success in a distant school with diverse educational and home influences.

A heated issue in 1949 was a proposal to consolidate the schools in West Wateree while building to accommodate the growth expected with DuPont families. One of DuPont's hesitations about building in the area had been lack of adequate schools. The small number of white students in Lugoff, considered too few for a separate school, had been riding by bus to school in Camden.

Lugoff black students, numbering three times as many as white students, had grade schools, but there was no black high school in West Wateree and no bus to one. Blaney residents, who had more schools in their area, were agreeable to consolidate in West Wateree, but only if their community was the site for the new school construction. Lugoff residents disagreed with that rural location, preferring for their children to continue traveling to Camden until facilities could be built in their own area. Educational improvement became an important issue in emerging industrial development.[49]

Postwar scrutiny of segregated schools governed by the law mandating "separate but equal" encouraged some repairs and additions to make inadequacies less glaring. Several improvements upgraded facilities at Jackson, Kirkwood, and St. Matthew black schools as well as at rural schools. Playground equipment was added to a number of county schools. Surplus government food was distributed at all schools, but modern lunchrooms appeared first at white schools and later at black schools.[50]

St. Matthew, with Leon Bennett as principal, became the county's second black high school in the 1944–45 term. A probable impetus to expand the St. Matthew school to upper grades was the need for increased space to educate returning black veterans. Many young men had had basic education interrupted by the war, and afterward those under age twenty were allowed to return to high school to finish diplomas and sometimes to do postgraduate work. An occasional reference calls the new school St. Matthew "trade" or "training" school.

High schools could offer veterans any course for which there was enough demand. Agricultural and industrial training classes were popular, in addition to needed academic courses.[51] Kershaw High taught a Bible course. At Blaney High "on-the-farm" training, under Adolphus Dowey and the agriculture teacher R. M. Richbourg, included hands-on practice and field trips. Veterans at Baron DeKalb High organized a Young Farmers of America chapter, with Sam Truesdale Jr. as president, and extended membership to others interested in "scientific farming." Drivers' training classes began at Antioch with a purchased Studebaker with dual controls and then were added at Midway and Baron DeKalb with autos provided by local dealers.

Kershaw County had many high schools in the late 1940s—Antioch, Bethune, Blaney, Camden, Jackson, Midway, Mt. Pisgah, and St. Matthew—and also shared expenses with Lancaster County at Kershaw High School. Until the 1948–49 term, when the twelfth grade was added statewide, public-school students in Kershaw County graduated at the end of the eleventh grade. No graduation ceremonies were held in spring 1948, although some students took

"11th grade diplomas" and did not return in the fall. The 1949 graduating class, the first one to meet the new requirement, was relatively small as a consequence of those who had taken the older option.

Expanding school programs coincided with rapid school population growth. In Camden schools enrollment in 1948 increased 10 percent over the previous year and in 1949 increased another 20 percent. Furthermore the postwar baby boomers had yet to reach school age.

The rezoning of some Camden schoolchildren to Pine Tree Hill in 1948 for a time alleviated some overcrowding in lower grades. Construction began the following year on the county's first junior high, a new concept in school organization. Camden Junior High School, built next to the elementary school, was occupied with nine classrooms for 360 students and with J. Clyde Walton as principal, followed by Mary B. DuVal. Lottie Anderson started the library.

One feature that in recent years had distinguished Camden High School was its marching band. In 1946 new director Hal Middleton had to begin the fall term without instruments, so band members for a time marched solely to the cadence of its drum corps. In February 1947 the band gave its first concert, and the following term it launched a successful campaign to raise one thousand dollars for uniforms and equipment for a bigger, better band in 1949. That year a new director of music was hired for the Camden city schools, Spartanburg native Guy Hutchins.

Private Schools

The changes of the times also included stirrings in private education in Camden. Mrs. J. B. Zemp's private school, begun more than two decades earlier to serve the tourist colony, had closed briefly during the war but reopened. In this period it was generally referred to as the Calvert School, so called for the parent school in Baltimore with which its program was affiliated. As before, a flexible, individualized curriculum had appeal for families in transition.

At the war's end, various plans promoted educational use for the former Southern Aviation School campus at the Camden airport. With an eye to acquiring the property when it was released by the War Assets Department, in late 1946 Thomas E. Hair, who had purchased part of the former Kirkwood Hotel, and Major Charles T. Smith of Columbia took out a charter to incorporate Kirkwood Military Academy as a junior college and prep school for males. They anticipated serving veterans who preferred not to attend a school with younger students in order to catch up with their education. However, in 1949 the SAS facilities became home for eight years to Camden Academy, a military prep school for secondary day and boarding students.

Camden's oldest private school, Mather Academy, under Principal Lula B. Bryan, continued operation as an oasis of opportunity for black students in grades seven to twelve.[52] In 1945 war-related teacher shortages resulted in loss of the school's rare A rating by the state. A dissertation completed in 1950 describes educational conditions at Mather in the late 1940s as it made efforts to regain credentials and overcome postwar financial difficulties.[53] The ambitions of students were strong and reflective of changing times. Although about 60 percent of the student body came from rural areas, the fifty-two graduates in 1949 had almost no interest in agriculture. Not one boy and just one girl planned on returning to the farm, and only a few were going to return to their home communities. A follow-up of these fifty-two graduates the following year found thirty-four of them attending college, an impressive percentage. Large numbers of the graduates each year went north because of the lack of opportunities at home.

Other sources reveal additional information. Browning Home / Mather Academy celebrated its sixtieth anniversary in February 1947. Amelia Boykin, the first graduate of the Model Home, as it was then called, gave the kick-off address for the weeklong celebration recognizing past and present student achievement. The following February, during the 1948 observation of National Negro History Week, the Columbia attorney Harold R. Boulware spoke to Mather faculty and students on the topic of civil rights. Boulware, also president of the state chapter of the National Association for the Advancement of Colored People (NAACP), was involved in voting-rights legislation. With future Supreme Court justice Thurgood Marshall, he was among the plaintiff's attorneys in the *Briggs v. Elliott* case, which became part of the landmark *Brown v. Board of Education* case decided in the U.S. Supreme Court in 1954.

Growing up on the Mather campus during these years was John Roy Harper II, later a civil rights and NAACP advocate in 1990 legislation to have district boundaries drawn so that blacks could win both state and U.S. legislative seats. Harper's parents were the longtime Mather teachers John Roy Harper and Mary Frances Smith Harper. A number of other Mather students as well were influenced by exposure to leaders in contemporary efforts to improve social conditions, and many became leaders in other efforts.

One former Mather student who attracted national attention after World War II was the baseball player Larry Doby, who helped to break the color line in sports. In 1946, after serving two years in the U.S. Navy, Doby returned to his former position on the Newark Eagles and helped lead his team to the Negro National League pennant and World Series championship. In 1947 he joined the Cleveland Indians to become the second black player, after Jackie Robinson, to play in the modern major leagues and the first in the American League. Doby's home run won the Indians the fourth game of the 1948 World Series. In 1949 one of his home-run balls traveled an astounding five hundred feet. Doby's quiet persistence in the face of opposition made him a role model. In 1949 the Mather student Roosevelt Jackson won first place in a Palmetto Scholastic Press Association contest for his article "Larry Doby Was a Matherite."

Libraries

Access to books, always important to continuous learning, varied among Kershaw County citizens. Those who recognized the importance of print materials sought to expand library services. The WPA-originated Kershaw County Public Library system, organized the previous decade for bookmobile services, was replaced by an appointed Kershaw County Library Commission to continue transporting and lending books countywide. Regular borrowers at the Camden Public Library on Broad Street, which owned 10,240 books in 1945, came from three different groups roughly equal in size: city residents, schools, and county residents. Small community libraries functioned independently in Bethune and Liberty Hill, though none stood south of Camden or west of the Wateree.

At all these locations patrons who were allowed to check out books were white. Any circulating book lent to a black citizen was quietly borrowed and returned on his behalf by a white person. Books donated from various libraries to black schools were sometimes also circulated among community readers. Informational government publications, distributed through farm and county agents, were available to black and white readers. Until 1947 the private Russell Memorial Library at Mather Academy, with about 2,500 books, was the only library facility for black patrons and was generally limited to those at the school.

Among postwar movements for change, the Kershaw County Library Commission suggested that the Camden Library be converted to a museum as the fireproof Carnegie building would make an excellent repository for the area's relics. A new building was needed to consolidate the city and county libraries, the commission decided. Under Chairman Mrs. O. J. Smyrl of Camden, the commission had representation from Bethune, Blaney, Boykin, Kershaw, Liberty Hill, and Lugoff.[54] One of its early projects was to open a "Negro unit" for library services, set up in a section of the teen canteen at the Jackson School campus. When the repository opened on May 1, 1947, there were 700 registered borrowers and 631 books in circulation. Before long the unit's patrons were planning expanded services.

In summer 1947 the city and county libraries consolidated into one operation named the Kershaw County Library. It was planned that until a suitable large facility could be built, the "county unit," under Mrs. J. B. Baker, would continue in the agricultural building, and the "city unit," under Mrs. Douglas Boykin, in the Carnegie building. Miss Marie Sparrow was in charge of the bookmobile, and Mrs. Joe Thomas headed the children's department. Each Saturday morning the county library featured a story hour, which was generally attended by two-score or more rural children whose parents had dropped them off before shopping downtown.

The dream of the time, a consolidated building, was placed on hold for many years more, in part because of uncertainties in the changing conditions of racial integration. The city-county operation would again be separated before finally coming together in the present museum (archives) and library system, which exists much as the facilities were visualized in the postwar years. In the interim, libraries of the county continued to evolve in various ways. In 1949 the community library at Bethune moved into the new town hall, the library at Liberty Hill moved into the Community House, and Kershaw dedicated its fine new Kershaw Memorial Library building. The county library acquired its own building, though an aged one, and a new bookmobile went into operation, making more than 125 scheduled stops in the county every two weeks. At Camden planning got under way on a new building to house the library for African American patrons.

17

Cultural Crossroads

From Midcentury

At the middle of the twentieth century Kershaw County stood at a cultural crossroads. Despite modernization in some areas, in 1950 most rural roads had yet to be paved, and households in some sections still lacked electrical services and indoor plumbing. Within the following quarter of a century, however, as industrialization toppled agricultural dominance, technology minimized some of the isolation of remote corners of the county. An interstate highway system, radio, movies, and especially television created a more homogeneous youth culture, which was tuned in to music, styles, and ideas that raised eyebrows of many elders. Within that quarter of a century a number of World War II–era babies grew of age to serve or to question U.S. military involvement in Vietnam, and youngsters who had been born into a segregated society of Jim Crow laws attended local schools that were fully desegregated by 1970.

Kershaw County's shift from an agricultural economy to an industrial one took place during a relatively short span of time. DuPont's May Plant, which opened in Lugoff in 1950, was the most dramatic herald of that shift. The mammoth plant physically altered the agrarian landscape along the west bank of the Wateree River, and its operation influenced political, economic, educational, and social changes throughout a large area. The impact of industrialization was most immediately evident in areas that were already most comfortably settled, but it gradually spread to influence rural and outlying sections. In West Wateree, DuPont's presence began the conversion of farmland, dairies, and idle lands to housing and commercial tracts. These changes created the demand for urban services and infrastructure.

In spring 1950, when DuPont began accepting applications for several hundred jobs to commence at the time of the plant's opening, the corporation announced plans for an additional plant in Kershaw County. It projected employing one thousand workers, even more than the first plant still under construction. The second plant, to manufacture Orlon acrylic fiber in staple form, was to be built beside the one nearly completed, which would manufacture Orlon as continuous filament yarn. Although the news of immediate expansion met with considerable excitement, it intensified the area's problem of providing adequate housing to meet the already heavy demand.

An aerial view of the new DuPont plant in then-rural West Wateree.
Courtesy of the Camden Archives

Much publicity promoted products of the new synthetic fiber market. In one campaign Camden's Walter Wright was publicized as the first barber in the nation to use DuPont Orlon sheets, given to him by May Plant project manager J. D. Wilson. Wright inaugurated their use when cutting the hair of eight-month-old William Michael Clyburn, a member of the fifth generation of that family to use Wright's services. Mary Rice, a fashionable Camden clothing shop for women, attracted public interest downtown with a front-window display of the prototype eye-catching Orlon suits.

The Opening of DuPont

DuPont's May Plant gradually started up operation, producing its first Orlon on July 1, 1950. After eighteen months of construction and finishing work, DuPont formally dedicated the plant on October 6. Because of work under way on the adjoining expansion, there was no space on-site for the public for the dedication. However, the corporate president and a large entourage welcomed representative city, county, and state guests.

Afterward the public attended the plant's dedication activities at the National Guard Armory, where Governor Strom Thurmond introduced the DuPont president as the keynote speaker. Other guests included an array of dignitaries representing political and economic interests—for example, Senator Olin D. Johnston, Congressman J. P. Richards, and the presidents of the Carolina Power and Light Company and the Seaboard Air Line Railroad. Between events local Jaycees took those dignitaries on an afternoon driving tour of Camden and historic sites, followed by dinner at the Court Inn.

On the day of the dedication the October 6 *Camden Chronicle* was a record-breaking fifty-six pages long and consumed two tons of newsprint. The special edition, financed by "progressive merchants and business men of Camden" to highlight DuPont, was said to be the largest edition ever for a Camden newspaper. The plant put its own periodical, *May Times,* into production, and in mid-October its second issue reported that there were then 801 employees working at the May Plant.

The first area of the county to begin filling with new DuPont residents was the city of Camden, the closest community where facilities, infrastructure, and organizations for family living were already established. Both King Haiglar and Kirkwood Apartments filled immediately upon opening, and construction began in 1950 just off Chesnut Street on Pinewood Apartments for black families. A weekly newspaper section listing present and previous addresses of newcomers reveals that many moved first to apartments or tourist courts. The Airport Tourist Court added extra trailer spaces with electricity and city water and advertised access to the city bus line.

"New homes are springing up in every section of the city," stated a September 1950 editorial, "but still there has not been a dent made in the needs of the city along that line." Kennedy Insurance & Realty advertised the convenience of lots along Highland Avenue in Highland Heights, three and a half blocks from downtown and near schools, churches, and the library. By the end of the decade the overcrowded city population had declined as families moved into suburban developments that opened outside the edges of the city and in Lugoff areas nearer the May Plant. To improve area eligibility for government housing loans, Camden mayor Henry Savage Jr. made several trips to Washington, D.C., to secure a "critical needs" designation, which was granted in mid-1951. In 1953 Kershaw County hired its first county administrator, James R. West Jr.

In the early subdivisions simple designs were typical of the modern homes and featured two or sometimes three bedrooms and one or occasionally two baths. Though smaller than traditional designs in the Camden area and lacking the typical high ceilings, fireplaces, and front porches of those designs, the new homes had strong appeal for their efficiency and ease of upkeep with modern plumbing, wiring, insulation, and heating systems. Popular floor furnaces used fuel oil delivered by gravity feed from fifty-five-gallon drums outside. Asbestos siding was promoted as fireproof, weather-tight, and having the appearance of "fine old cedar shingles." DuPont nylon shutters were extras for some houses.

Smaller yards were praised for reduced landscaping demands on working home owners. Designed to provide comfortable and pleasant living conditions for families, most homes also had a carport to protect the jobholder's all-important vehicle that got him to work. Local businesses advertised labor-saving furniture for the inside of homes also. Plastic dinette sets and plastic covers for sofas and chairs were promoted for practicality.

Time-saving construction of prefabricated housing appealed to some property owners. Gunnison Homes sold well in the community. Each house consisted of uniform-sized plywood panels, variously arranged. The factory-built units were shipped on a single trailer truck and quickly assembled on the customer's foundation, often a concrete slab.

Real estate agents such as McCorkle and Woodrum, J. B. McGuirt, and Elbert L. Moseley advertised several new suburban developments near Camden. W. B. Fort subdivided seventy-five lots on Knights Hill Road three miles west of the city for Fort Ellene Heights, "exclusively for Negroes." Three miles north of the city on U.S. Highway 1, Norris Heights opened with thirty-four lots.

Just beyond Camden's eastern limits, Moultrie Burns and Pine Tree Building & Supply opened Burndale Avenue and got construction under way on the first of seventy-five homes for Burndale subdivision. Also just east of the city limits, Grainger Kornegay began construction in Camden Heights for twenty-five homes on three new streets: Kornegay Circle, Crestmont Drive, and Hazelhurst Street.

The area east of Camden had steadily expanded since World War II airport development. In 1950 the area included eighteen hundred residents, 329 homes, thirty-eight businesses, and four churches. In June that year citizens held an election to determine whether to incorporate. In case the issue carried, they also voted on a name for the town, a mayor, and six aldermen. Incorporation was rejected by nineteen votes, however, so the mayoral winner, H. A. Elliott, had no office to fill. The area continued to be known by the name that voters selected—East Camden, chosen four to one over other choices, Dixie and Lewiston.

Growth expanded also west of Camden and near DuPont in West Wateree. Just outside city limits, W. B. Boyle Construction of Sumter began the first of fifty homes at Cherokee Place, along the new Laurens Street extension. Also, on U.S. Highway 1 and divided by Chesnut Ferry Road, Lyndale subdivision offered fifty homesites. In West Wateree on the Ridgeway Road just off U.S. Highway 1, Woodrum & Switzer opened the first model home in Sherwood subdivision, and Dr. R. E. Stevenson purchased twenty acres from the M. E. Truesdale estate for thirty-five Lugoff homes off U.S. 1 and S.C. 231.

Homes for executives inspired subdivisions with more-elaborate details. Just across U.S. Highway 1 from the DuPont plant, L. P. Claytor of Virginia laid out a fifty-home development featuring a wide street, DuPont Boulevard, intersected by a street named for himself. The six- to twelve-room homes were planned with fashionable "colonial" designs. As West Wateree subdivisions increased, the need for a recreational community gathering place was recognized. In 1951 the Lugoff Community Center was begun on land donated by E. D. Drakeford, a site that became known as Drakeford Park. The center was dedicated the following February. A small pond with a swimming and picnic area enhanced the recreational facilities.

Of all the midcentury developments, the most extensive was built north of Camden on 212 acres that the Springdale Land Company purchased from Harry D. Kirkover, part of the McKee Graham estate. Kirkover Hills, laid out in a rolling, wooded landscape, featured larger lots and homes than most other subdivisions offered. It was developed within sight of the Carolina Cup's Springdale Race Course, a quarter of a mile from the Camden Country Club's golf course, and one-eighth of a mile from Springdale Hall, a private social club. Opened in 1950, Springdale Hall offered "winter season" hospitality in the style of the old tourist inns. On January 1, 1951, ground for the first home in Kirkover Hills was broken at 1907 Brook Drive. Four years later the one hundredth home was built.

The proximity of Kirkover Hills to traditional community appeals—later summarized as "history, horses, and hospitality"—attracted less general interest at the time than did the modern designs and features of the new homes. Paved streets, city water, fire protection with hydrants, streetlights, and bus service to schools gradually converted the formerly rural area into one with urban amenities. The fronts of many homes featured large picture windows revealing glimpses of modern living rooms inside. Some of the homes accommodated the climate with screened side or back porches. Efforts were made to retain various native trees, many of them pines.

Those who filled the new homes had come to work and to raise families. Most were well educated or well trained, and they were often well paid. They were loyal to the company, which offered health and security benefits. The workers and their families expected to take part in those aspects of the local community that they liked, and what they did not like, they expected to find a way to change. The people wanted to re-create here the lives they had experienced elsewhere. Their concerns and focus sometimes conflicted with those of longtime residents who saw the benefit of ways already established. Icebreakers and discussion groups helped ease adjustments between old and new residents. Associations with churches and community groups helped form new relationships.

Changing Views
Camden, Old and New

A number of public changes in 1950 marked transitions to a new age even as some of them maintained ties with tradition. When deterioration threatened Camden's most familiar old symbol, the tower of the former Camden Opera

House, then the city-hall building, topped by the King Hagler weather vane, citizens voted on one of three designs by the architect Ralph Little for repair of the tower. Eighty-six percent of voters favored the costliest plan, to retain the tower's original appearance.

Restoration that began on the city tower in spring 1950 revealed an additional need for a new roof. King Hagler was taken down from his perch. Clyburn and E. C. Elliott, auto body shop men, placed the effigy in a chemical bath for several days to remove the rust and old paint. They "plugged up the bullet hole in his tummy" and repaired his broken arrow and then applied several coats of primer before spraying a finish coat of gold. By the end of April the "venerable chief" once again watched over Camden from atop the repaired and repainted tower. The town clock was converted to electrical operation because of the potential danger from the two tons of weights that operated the old clock, a temperamental mechanism that required trial and error to fix and weekly cranking by its keeper, the jeweler F. D. Goodale.

Communication services improved when Western Union modernized in spring 1950 so that messages from Camden could be flashed directly to a high-speed switching center in Atlanta, where a single operation sped them to their destination. That year too the Southern Bell Telephone Company in Camden moved from its office in the Crocker Building, where it had been located for forty-two years, into a separate new office building on North Broad Street. Four years later the utility was changed over to a dial system, and after a few months workers installed Camden's four thousandth telephone. Since the war's end, telephone ownership had quadrupled.

In spring 1950 the city of Camden began using a new two-way radio system, which was installed in two police cars, a fire department rescue truck, and three utility trucks. The twenty-four-hour radio monitoring made obsolete the policeman's booth at the corner of Broad and DeKalb streets, and it was removed.

Early in the year the city installed a new 186-foot, 250,000-gallon water tank near Lafayette and Church streets to serve increased demands and to meet insurance requirements. During the final stage of construction, heavy winds hit while workers were painting the surface and blew "aluminum rain drops" over the city, peppering vehicles with "measles and chicken pox of a silvery shade."

By mid-December a new city jail was ready for occupation at the rear of the city police department on Rutledge Street behind city hall. The ten cells, which held two inmates each, included two for women. By fall 1950 a new white way doubled the illumination of downtown Camden's Broad Street with modern mercury vapor lights. Awaiting state approval to widen DeKalb Street, the city widened Broad Street from Chesnut north, adding sidewalks. The Kershaw County DAR urged contractors to watch for "skeletons, belt buckles, buttons," and such from soldiers buried after the Battle of Hobkirk's Hill. To the disappointment of many, no notable discoveries were uncovered.

When a storm of protests rose in 1950 about the cutting of tree branches on upper Lyttleton Street to make way for electric lines, the Camden city manager referred concerns to a state park arborist, who reported that the pruning was properly carried out. The Parks and Streets Commission, not consulted in advance of the trimming, did not concur. They enlisted two tree surgeons and "a storm of criticism from many citizens" to convince the city council to make changes. The commission asserted that Camden's trees were the city's "greatest natural asset and . . . must be preserved and protected at all times." Similar concerns had been voiced before and would be repeated in other decades as well.

In May 1950 the city formally assumed ownership of the Camden Airport, with Jim Darby continuing as manager. Work had continued on Camden Academy for a fall opening; buildings were leased and property interests assumed at the former Southern Aviation site. In September the new military prep school began with forty-two students from five states. Their first weekend the cadets were measured for uniforms and bused to a Camden High football game and then to the Episcopal parish house for a dance given by Tri Gamma, a local social club for girls of high school age. Other groups also welcomed the cadets. The Kiwanis Club, for example, took them to Dewey Creed's summerhouse at Lake Wateree for fishing, boating, and a local specialty many had never tasted before—catfish stew.

Efforts continued locally to promote interest in the arts. Camden in 1950 was the smallest town in the two Carolinas supporting a community concert series. The Camden Choral Society raised funds to bring in well-known artists and orchestras and to encourage local talent. Highlighting the Christmas season was a concert by a twenty-five-piece orchestra of visiting musicians who accompanied a chorus of local musicians, joined by three guest soloists. Directing the visiting orchestra was Camden High School band director Guy Hutchins, whose students opened the concert performing seasonal music. Interests created by the quality and scope of such performances continued to sustain a long community tradition in performing arts.

Lugoff, Old and New

With population and housing growing in Lugoff, business interests expanded along U.S. Highway 1. Blaney, at a greater distance from DuPont, stirred with anticipation in 1950 but as yet exhibited few outward alterations. Some area residents, for instance Blaney's E. T. (Earl Talmadge "Tal") Bowen, were active in county affairs and took part in the process of overall change.

In Lugoff, C. S. Caskey bought out family interests and modernized the Riverside Mercantile Company at the S.C. 34 junction. At that time the highways met at the location of present Highway 5, opposite the DuPont entrance. Charles Poss opened Lugoff Motor Sales, a used car business, between the plant entrance and the Wateree Motor Court. Nearby, Ben Emerson's Drive-In

Restaurant and Esso Service Center advertised Sunday dinners for $1.25 each; diners could choose from six meats and eleven vegetables, along with dessert and a beverage.

Established agricultural operations continued in 1950. Jordan's Dairy Farm advertised Guernsey milk and fresh brown eggs. Rock Springs Creamery distributed Golden Guernsey milk for Edisto Farms. Changes to agricultural lands began taking place, however.

In 1954 Robert Lee of Manning purchased the old Funderburk place and the former Guion Farm from the estate of Frank H. Brown, who had purchased the 4,500-acre tract from Edwin Boyle. In 1956 Williams Furniture Corporation of Sumter purchased from E. T. Bowen a tract of 3,460 acres along the Wateree River three miles below the DuPont plant. Long known as the Jordan River Place, it was expected to produce timber for the Sumter furniture factory. River property ownership also shifted on the opposite bank. In announcing the 1956 sale, the newspaper pointed out the DuPont family's purchase two years earlier of Red Bank and Hopewell plantations in Boykin.

Hospital Facilities

The expanding county population strained facilities at the seventy-six-year-old Camden Hospital at Fair and Union streets, where workers tried to keep abreast of modern medical changes. Blue Cross Hospital insurance and, from 1950, Blue Shield Medical insurance were advantages that many families realized for the first time with industrial employment.

In a space-saving move adjacent to its nursing school, the hospital board approved the erection of a Gunnison home to house hospital superintendent George R. Darden and his family. At the affiliated Camden Nursing School, headed by Elizabeth Barfield, student nurses were trained and graduated annually. Hospital dietician Mrs. W. C. McCarley and her staff fed 100 to 125 people daily by using two kitchens. In 1950, when A. Sam Karesh became the fourth president of the hospital, replacing H. G. Carrison, the hospital was operating at a cost slightly below average for similar area hospitals, but it faced urgent needs. The hospital treated twice as many charity patients as those facilities did.

Besides lacking modern equipment, the hospital had a shortage of operating rooms and bed space. The lack of isolation wards made it dangerous to treat persons with contagious illnesses. With polio fears rampant, children with whooping cough, pneumonia, meningitis, or diphtheria had to be treated elsewhere. The segregated facilities had no private rooms for black patients. In the private space for white patients there were only two bathrooms (one male, one female) to serve twenty-three persons. With only two maternity rooms available, women in delivery at times lay in hallways in view of hospital visitors. There were additional concerns about fire safety in the old buildings.

Differences of opinion began to arise about whether another expansion and update at the existing site would solve the situation at reasonable expense, or whether investment in new facilities on a larger site would be more cost-effective in the long run. Some opinions were firm that complete modernization was essential to public health. Occasionally nostalgic points were raised regarding Bernard Baruch's gifts to the hospital honoring his father, the Confederate surgeon—points that other people thought were irrelevant to its current needs.

Churches and Religion

Changes of industrialization also affected local church practices and congregations. In 1950 the South Carolina General Assembly passed a new labor law prompted by the arrival of DuPont. Company officials asserted that their industry could not be shut down on Sundays because its chemical processes had to continue without interruption. "Natural law" could not be altered, and for the industry to operate at all, work customs had to be adjusted. The new law exempted "continuous chemical process industrial plants with rotating work shifts" from time-and-a-half Sunday pay and from prohibitions against Sunday employment of women.

Some people of faith were disturbed by what appeared to them to be a scriptural break to allow Sunday labor at all. Other people, some of them also people of faith, viewed Sunday blue laws as legal rather than spiritual concerns. Some practical businessmen eyed changes as precedents to ease blue-law restrictions for other enterprises as well. Churches increased weeknight activities to retain members who worked alternating weekend shifts. Overall churches were most influenced by an increasing population of potential new members moving into the community. The numbers of churches and their size rapidly increased.

In mid-March 1950 a thirty-one-year-old evangelist named Billy Graham dined at Gus Ward's restaurant in Lugoff. A number of county residents attended meetings of Graham's ongoing revival in Columbia. On Sunday afternoon, March 12, more than ten thousand people were turned away as he preached to a capacity crowd of forty thousand in Carolina Stadium, the football field of the University of South Carolina in Columbia. Effects of the revival spilled over into different local denominations, coinciding with increasing interests in churchgoing.

At the Kershaw County Courthouse in April 1950, a number of citizens of various denominations, including thirty Lutherans, attended the area's first Lutheran service since colonial times and made the first steps to establish what became St. Timothy's in Camden. The group held Sunday night meetings for a time at the courthouse, then at the Bethesda Presbyterian education building, and later at the Lyttleton Street Methodist chapel. By September they were meeting at the former tourist-era Sarsfield Club on the northern corner of Mill and Hampton streets, where they installed an altar and renovated rooms for Sunday-school meetings.

Soon the Lutherans were sharing their new space twice weekly with a Baptist mission group, which shortly organized with fourteen members as Lakeview Baptist Church. When the Lutherans found a Mill Street site (between present Christmas and Mackey streets) on which to build a sanctuary, the Baptists purchased the Sarsfield Club property. They sold it to build a new sanctuary in 1962 on the opposite corner of Mill and Hampton streets.[1]

In White's Gardens east of Camden, construction began on a Presbyterian chapel, later Morningside Presbyterian Church, in August 1950. The men of the congregation did most of the work themselves, gathering daily after finishing their regular jobs. A former filling station provided Sunday-school space. Reverend A. Douglas McArn, pastor of historic Bethesda Church, held the first regular services in the chapel. The downtown Bethesda congregation began construction of its own in September, adding an addition to its Sunday-school building because of the "tremendous influx of new families into the community."

In October 1950 Church of God members broke ground for a new church adjoining Pine Tree Hill School. Anticipating growth, the congregation of 76 built to accommodate more than 250 people and added ten Sunday-school rooms and a pastor's study. In November a Lugoff congregation that had begun as a mission of the Springvale Baptist Church organized a new church, the First Baptist Church of Lugoff, with 35 charter members. It likewise began rapid growth. Also by that fall Lugoff's Rowan Presbyterian Church had grown enough to call its first full-time minister and to break ground for a church manse.

The Worldview

The avalanche of economic, technological, landscape, and population changes that transformed Kershaw County in the early 1950s took place against a background of international affairs that also affected the local state of mind. Tensions grew following North Korea's June 1950 invasion of South Korea, which established public belief in the potential for another world war between communist and democratic ideologies. Also of interest and of some concern was the announcement late in the year that the Atomic Energy Commission had selected the DuPont Corporation to build a nuclear "bomb plant" in Aiken and Barnwell counties.

Nearly two weeks before the North Korean invasion, a *Camden Chronicle* headline revealed that anticipation of war was already present: "Deepest Hole Is Safest Place in Event of an Atomic Bomb Blast." An assistant to the surgeon general gave civilians instructions from the Armed Forces in case of atomic attack: "Take cover in basements or underground shelters, if possible, and stay there for about 90 seconds." He cautioned against eating, drinking, chewing, or smoking until food, water, and such were checked since "a small amount of radiation outside the body is harmless," but "inside the body it may cause much trouble." According to the report, the blast itself caused most of the casualties, primarily from flying debris and secondary fires, and the "lingering Alpha and Beta radiation is so small it is not a hazard. Disregard it."

In December a *Chronicle* editorial described survival practices in the event of nuclear attack, stating that "one must recognize the fact that we are facing an atomic war and . . . we never know where the enemy may strike." The advice on preparing shelters quoted an Associated Press science editor, who asserted, "Radioactivity does not strike any one dead. It shrivels nothing. It is the least painful of all A-bomb injuries."

Such mistaken information from official sources was widely spread in the decade of the 1950s, even as much of the uneasy public grew convinced of the possibility of pending nuclear attack. Mayor Savage put into action the civilian defense plan of the National Security Board in accordance with the General Assembly's South Carolina Defense Act of 1950. Governor Thurmond's endorsement stated, "Civil defense is one of the most pressing needs of all our people at this time." The plan covered "emergencies . . . and enemy attack against the civilian population." The Camden City Council asked American Legion Post 17 to spearhead the organization of local defense activities.

Kershaw County schools directed children to practice "duck and cover" drills, during which they took shelter from an imagined atomic bomb by crouching under their desks. Many families dug primitive bomb shelters or holes for protection in their backyards. Some families kept extra canned food, containers of water, and first-aid kits on hand for survival after an attack.

The Defense Department and the air force, however, were convinced that the southeastern states were invulnerable to bombing since even the most advanced communist aircraft, those of the Soviet Union, lacked the capacity to reach this far from any communist base. In fact, administration officials cited this as a reason for locating large military operations in the area, including the Savannah River "bomb plant" near Aiken.

Against other dangers the state's civil defense director called for industrial plants to "protect against sabotage, espionage and subversiveness." The November 17, 1950, *May Times* reported on steps that DuPont had taken to comply with FBI requests to increase industrial protection. Visitors to the Lugoff plant had to wear special badges and remain under escort. No group tours were permitted, and vehicles were restricted. Fingerprints of all plant employees were filed for checks "to determine their loyalty to the United States government in an effort to weed out Communists and fellow travelers." Potential employees were closely scrutinized to exclude anyone with a "shady background."

The Korean War had an immediate impact on the county's organized military units. On August 13, 1950, the 92-man Company D, 122nd Battalion of Engineers, commanded by Captain W. L. Jackson, left for two weeks' encampment at Fort Jackson. Battery B of the 713th AAA Battalion, under Commander First Lieutenant William G. Major Jr., received alert orders shortly after returning from a two-week encampment and was federalized on August 14 with 4 officers and 137 enlisted men reporting for active duty. Until departure the battery encamped at the local armory, and the men were allowed to go home in the evenings. In Korea men of the battery filled vacancies in combat units.

Under a new draft law, the Kershaw County Selective Service Board was reactivated in summer 1950 and began calling men in August for preinduction physicals at Fort Jackson.[2] The board's published lists included each man's name, address, and a designation "white" or "negro." The first local men to be inducted were Dalton Lavern Ford Jr., Robert Napper, Francis Sheheen, and Bobby Love Smyrl. By the end of the year the board had sent more than four hundred for examinations, and about fifty of them were inducted in the first six months of the war. Hot conflict continued another long year, and engagements dragged past the middle of 1953 before coming to an uneasy armistice. Twelve Kershaw County servicemen lost their lives in the Korean War.

Community Concerns

Communities at a physical distance from the DuPont developments were less obviously affected by immediate local change, but they too were influenced by conditions of the time. Of all longtime settlements, Liberty Hill was the most remote, and aging citizens in the steep-hilled area continued life from day to day in much the same way they had long known. Those concerned about the community's future lamented that few opportunities were available to entice young families to locate there.

Town of Kershaw

In spring 1950 a group of Kershaw merchants organized the Kershaw Retail Merchants Association with W. D. Cathcart as president and began contacting the seventy-three businesses in the vicinity that were eligible for membership. A new energy was at work in the town, half of which lay in Kershaw County and the other half in Lancaster County, and Mayor Arthur L. Jones was pleased about the forward movements. Change was obvious with the addition of Belk's new store and the absence of an old landmark, the Kershaw Mercantile Company, which had been destroyed by fire but was to reopen in a new location. The Hayes corner had been renovated, and both Hayes Pharmacy and Dodds had remodeled facades and a new tower at the rear. Baxley's store had been repainted, and the Kershaw Jewelry and Gift Shop hung out a new sign.

Shaw Motor Company boasted a new showroom, and the Kershaw Auto and Electric Company, the Western Auto, and the Byers Building updated their building fronts. Foster's Theater extensively remodeled, as did the bus station,

Taylor's store, and Juanita's. Baker's Florist opened next to the drugstore. New homes were completed, and others were remodeled or enlarged.

Besides the established Springs industry, another textile facility was on the scene. By June 1950 the Sacony garment plant moved from the converted warehouse where it had begun into a large, modern, well- lighted, and heated brick and concrete block building. There its 175 employees produced women's ready-to-wear clothing. Mayor Jones was also pleased about the new health center under construction at the corner of Hart and Richland streets, financed by state and federal appropriations.

Once again an old issue arose: would not the town function more smoothly if it were all in one county, rather than divided between two counties, and if so, which county would benefit it best? Mayor Jones conducted an unofficial poll and declared the townspeople "about evenly divided" in their preferences. A September *Camden Chronicle* editorial declared that Kershaw County had much to offer and would be delighted to have the whole town.

Instead of choosing between two counties, some townspeople were strongly inclined to create a new county. Neighboring communities in Chesterfield, Kershaw, and Lancaster counties considered the issue. Mayors, councilmen, and other representatives from Bethune, Buffalo, Flat Creek, Hanging Rock, Heath Springs, Jefferson, Kershaw, Liberty Hill, Three C's, Westville, and "the river section" met that fall to discuss the formation of a new county. Jefferson's mayor declared that his council was "100 per cent in favor." The Heath Springs mayor expressed preference for Kershaw to move entirely within Lancaster County. Attitudes differed overall, and questions simmered a while longer.

Bethune

In 1950 Bethune citizens continued to celebrate small-town closeness. In March the Bethune Community Center held a party to highlight its various facilities. On weekdays a branch of the Kershaw County Library operated there. The center also had swings and other age-appropriate toys for youngsters, as well as cooking and dining facilities for one hundred people. A nursery opened each morning, and an afternoon program offered adolescents croquet, Ping-Pong, and table games.

In July a record crowd of nearly two thousand attended the annual Bethune picnic and, as was the tradition, honored servicemen, heard guest speakers, and ate barbecue. The special honoree was Dr. E. Z. Truesdell for his long service to the community. Camden physicians A. W. Humphries and Carl A. West made laudatory remarks, and community members presented Dr. Truesdell with a book filled with messages of appreciation. Organizers gave gifts to the youngest and oldest persons present whose births Dr. Truesdell had attended: Tommy McKinnon, born that fall; and Mrs. John Cato, born in 1908.

Dr. Truesdell's career had begun in the horse-and-buggy days. Like other old-time country doctors, he had treated his patients in their homes when they could not come to his office, and his pay had been received in produce from those without cash. Finding replacements and adjusting to modern practices were challenges facing Bethune and other, similar rural communities.

Change came faster to Bethune after Kendall Corporation broke ground for a new eight-million-dollar finishing plant in spring 1955 and began operations in June of the following year. More than fifteen hundred people showed up the first day Kendall accepted job applications. The area's longtime efforts for telephone service were satisfied in spring 1956 when the Sand-hill Telephone Co-op began operation of a Bethune exchange, Edgewood, with 125 dial phones.

Agriculture

Traditional agricultural interests continued to occupy many persons throughout the county. Although jobs in industrial and textile plants were luring away many farmworkers and owners, others continued in familiar patterns. In 1950 the county reported "the best corn crop . . . it has ever had." Tobacco did well also. Eighteen farmers planted Turkish tobacco, marking the first time the variety was grown locally. Antioch was the community exhibit winner at the 1950 Kershaw County Fair, with Blaney, Baron DeKalb, and Mt. Pisgah finishing second, third, and fourth respectively.

A record boll weevil emergence troubled cotton interests in 1950. Eight pages of the June 2 *Camden Chronicle* focused on the message above the masthead: "Determined fight to be made on boll weevil in Kershaw County." L. O. Funderburk chaired the countywide cotton committee, coordinating farmers, businessmen, and agricultural officials with state efforts to combat the menace.

Advertisements divulge much about the era. Kershaw Mercantile Company in Kershaw offered "a good supply of Black Strap molasses, calcium arsenic, and B.H.C. [DDT] for dusting." In Camden all tractor and equipment dealers advertised dusting and spraying equipment. Local dealers included Camden Feed & Seed (Case), Camden Tractor & Implement (Ford), Shiver Implement (John Deere), and Whitaker (Farmall). They recommended tractor-operated equipment for large acreages, although "a two-row mule-drawn duster" was adequate for a twenty- to thirty-acre crop, and a "rotary hand duster" would do for five acres. For eighty cents an acre the crop duster Warren Roland of Boykin provided guaranteed coverage of dust or liquid spray by airplane.

Four department stores—Belk's, Eichel's, J. C. Penney, and J. J. Newberry—sponsored a full page of recommendations for weevil control. The Commercial National Bank's half page advised farmers to "follow recommended practices." The First National Bank's half page asserted, "Early weevil control pays dividends." In mid-July the cotton committee reported that sixteen thousand of the county's twenty-five thousand acres had been treated, with weevil infestation in the poisoned area down to 12 percent, compared to 70 percent infestation in the untreated area.

As was traditional, the signal events of the 1950 cotton season were duly noted by the press—who brought in the first open cotton boll, which farm produced it, the date the cotton was planted, which gin produced the first bale, who purchased it, and at what price. In August 1950 the Blaney ginner E. T. Bowen bought the first bale, 514 pounds, from the producer L. P. Rose for forty cents per pound. John L. Shiver & Son, Inc., with more than three decades of experience as cotton ginners, installed a modern ginnery in 1950 at their old place, Pisgah Crossroads, and drew farmers from Kershaw, Lee, and Sumter counties. The gin offered night and day truck service.

County youths actively participated in projects of agricultural clubs. Bethune's Young Farmers captured first place in 1950 competitions between high school veterans. The Chamber of Commerce sponsored the annual Fat Stock Show for 4-H competitors. Future Farmers of America (FFA) chapters brought high honors home on their projects. The Camden High livestock judging team—Edward Barfield, Edward Jones, Lester Branham, and Ralph Jordan—were state winners and earned a trip to the national convention in Kansas City. Their agriculture teacher, Hulan A. Small, and *Camden Chronicle* editor Harold Booker also received state recognition. At the national convention Small received the highest award, the Honorary American Farmer degree. The Camden FFA was the first South Carolina chapter to earn a gold award and won seven national plaques and six honorable mentions—more honors than any other high school team in the United States.

Amid efforts to keep young people interested in agriculture, shifts to livestock and timber also continued on county lands. By the mid-1950s county agent W. C. McCarley reported that Coastal Bermuda Grass for pasturage was becoming widely favored by county farmers for its ability to thrive on poor and sandy soils. By 1954 John H. McLeod's Liberty Hill operation Cunningham Quarters, a six-thousand-acre former cotton plantation that once boasted one tenant per one hundred acres, was growing two million pine trees with only one tenant per one thousand acres.[3]

The Environment

Among persons less enthusiastic about industrial development were some who were concerned about environmental effects, especially from chemical discharges. It was a public issue about which DuPont took an active defense. Before opening the May Plant, in spring 1950 DuPont sponsored an Academy of National Sciences study to measure the "number, variety and health of the aquatic population in the Wateree River near Camden." Officials of the May

Plant assured the public that they periodically studied the effects of chemical discharges by examining aquatic life in the adjoining Wateree, where the plant's treated wastewater was disposed. The company did not, however, publish the results of these studies. There were no requirements to do so.

When air emissions were visible and at times whiffs of a somewhat "fishy" odor were detected in the community, May Plant spokesmen assured the public that the company was working to alleviate the problem since any escape of chemical by air or water discharge meant that the company was "losing money." Such an explanation seemed logical to citizens who felt assured about practical motivations. Some county residents chose not to be bothered by an occasional plant emission or odor, borrowing the attitude that coastal residents held regarding the paper mills that brought them profits in hard times: "Smells like *money* to me!"

When DuPont was negotiating its move to Kershaw County, an old proposal was in the air again to straighten the Wateree River channel below Camden for use in industrial transportation. Any interest that DuPont or others may have had in such an idea came to an end after an April 1950 public hearing and a final negative report by the Army Corps of Engineers. Mayor Henry Savage Jr., appearing as a private citizen, was the only speaker at the hearing to favor straightening the channel. The owner of land along the river at Lugoff, Savage cited the advantages of cropland flood control and said that public expenditures now would dissuade any future project in the area such as the Santee dam, which flooded miles of private land behind it. Other landowners, especially those along the meandering swampland channels, believed that straightening was impossible and worried about the effects on croplands, grazing, and hunting and fishing. The Corps of Engineers simply cited prohibitive costs in rejecting the idea. The values of wetlands protection were not then public issues.

County Government

Rapid growth in the county prompted movements to manage that growth beneficially, but those movements also involved controversy as they sometimes provoked resistance to perceived interference and controls. Under General Assembly legislation, Kershaw County in 1950 began requiring building permits for all new construction in excess of one thousand dollars outside the corporate limits of cities and towns. Mayor Savage of Camden urged legislation establishing county planning and zoning boards. He pointed out to the Municipal Association of South Carolina that problems in fringe areas were often greater than those in the city, and undesirable businesses could reduce values of nearby residential property.

The Kershaw County delegation also passed a special act creating a county board of tax assessors to assure equalization of assessments. When the five-member board reported finding "quite a bit of property not on the tax books" as well as lands inequitably assessed, controversy stirred. There were charges of unfairness to allow "a privileged few to ride the tax gravy train," as well as claims that the board was misreading the tax books out of unfamiliarity with the system. One calculation to explain thousands of untaxed acres pointed out that river channels, county roads, state highways, state farms, city streets and parks, as well as churches, schools, hospitals, and related lots were untaxed properties that were counted in the county's overall acreage.

Kershaw County voters joined those across the state in voting by secret ballot for the first time in the November 1950 elections. A male voter had to present a registration certificate and a poll tax receipt; a female, only the registration certificate. Three statewide constitutional amendment issues passed with large majorities: to eliminate the poll tax as a voting requirement but retain it as revenue; to require only one voting registration certificate instead of multiple credentials; and to propose school redistricting on a statewide basis.

Members of the new county delegation took office. J. Clator Arrants as senator and John E. Baker and Donald Holland as representatives replaced, respectively, R. M. Kennedy Jr., Ezell Kelly, and W. R. Gettys. In the run-off primary, Clator Arrants of Camden had defeated, by just ten votes, Arthur L. Jones of Kershaw. When the General Assembly convened its next session, twenty-one-year-old Cassatt native Don Holland, a senior law student, was the youngest member of the South Carolina House of Representatives.[4]

Library Branch

Early in 1950 racial cooperation accomplished the building of a "colored memorial library" to honor war veterans and to serve literacy needs. Support was widespread for the DeKalb Street building, which was erected on the southwest corner of the Jackson High School block in place of the library depository that had operated in temporary quarters for three years. At biracial meetings Mrs. O. J. Smyrl, president of the library board, and Mrs. J. B. Baker, county librarian, pledged their support, as did school superintendent J. G. Richards Jr.

The city donated the property and pledged five thousand dollars, with the black community pledging a matching five thousand dollars "in cash, labor, or building materials." The county delegation also approved five thousand dollars for the project. Fund-raising committees and leaders included the following: churches, Reverend W. R. Gregg; lodges, Reverend J. C. Levy and Jimmy Alexander; clubs, Mac Wolst Sr.; letters, A. H. Boykin; publicity, Mrs. A. M. Devore; businesses, A. R. Collins Sr.; veterans, B. F. Pickett; teachers, Miss J. L. Dibble; pledges, Mrs. L. B. Sasportas; labor and building, J. R. Harper and A. H. Boykin; carpenters, J. Harrell; brick masons, I. B. Boykin; plasterers, Joe Brown; plumbers, Gus Hayes; electricians, Amon Levy; and painters, Jimmie Brown. Mather Academy's shop teacher John Roy Harper designed the modern brick building, and his students were among workmen who contributed labor to raise and complete it.

Approximately two hundred persons of both races were present for the library's June 1950 groundbreaking ceremonies, led by Senator R. M. Kennedy, City Manager Lott T. Rogers, and Reverend W. R. Gregg. Senator Kennedy called the project "a symbol of unity, of kindliness and of good feeling in the community and city." Estellene P. Walker of the state library board pointed out that thirty-six of the state's forty-six counties offered library services, but Kershaw County was only "the second to extend its facilities to all the citizens." City commissioner J. E. McKain commented that "education is the only way to beat Communism." In order to make the library eligible for state aid, the Kershaw County delegation in 1954 put through legislation to make it a branch of the Kershaw County Public Library.[5]

Hospital Issues

Hospital issues attracted divisive concerns in Kershaw County in the 1950s. Principles, practicality, and politics all became involved during the decade. In a November 1952 referendum, voters approved a bond issue of $2 million for a new hospital, but in the same election they voted against amending the constitution to permit the bonds to be issued. The matter continued to be a heated topic. In January 1954 another referendum failed to settle the impasse.

A *Camden Citizen* editorial compared the situation to another dispute that had divided the town three decades earlier. The younger group wanted to float bonds and pave the streets. The older faction said that "good clay streets were good enough for anyone." They were concerned that beautiful trees lining the streets would be cut and feared that the project would "bankrupt the town." The newspaper continued, "Thirty years from now, we're convinced that our children will feel that the building of a new hospital was just as wise and as progressive a step as was the paving [of] Camden's streets thirty years ago."

Public finances concerned taxpayers who worried that the hospital was another example of too much expense being taken on too fast. The county delegation had lately allocated seventy-five thousand dollars to the recreation commission, headed by Roland Goodale, to develop a county park on the two-thousand-acre Adams Mill Pond property on Pine Tree Creek east of Camden. A delegation-sponsored bill authorized the county to borrow one hundred thousand dollars for improvements. In 1954 the pond was filling, bathhouses were being built, and visitors were using picnic tables. Some voters, especially those who lived at some distance from the park site, considered such expenditures extravagant.

Issues concerning the hospital intensified in 1954 when a Charleston bond attorney notified Kershaw County Hospital Board chairman John C. West that the board might not be legally constituted to authorize spending. The board's eleven members included two representatives of the Medical Society and one person chosen by each of the following: the Farm Bureau, the Hospital Auxiliary, the Ministerial Association, the county board of directors, the county delegation, and the town councils of Bethune, Blaney, Camden, and Kershaw. In other words, it was argued, board members lacked elective or appointive authority to commit tax money.

Political wrangling relating to decision making and taxation issues in the hospital controversy also included debate over whether Camden Hospital was a private or public institution. Robin Zemp, president of the hospital, asserted that it was a "non-profit, charitable institution and for about 35 years has, I think, creditably, cared for the needs of the sick of Kershaw County, without discrimination as to race, creed or color; which is as provided for in its charter." He added that the hospital's directors were from all over the county and no section, profession, or business predominated.

Disagreements between "regular" and "independent" Democrats in 1954 overlapped the hospital issue, tying up funding for county supplies as well as hospital operating expenses. The General Assembly passed a Kershaw County bond bill, Governor James F. Byrnes on request vetoed it, and the General Assembly overrode the veto 97–2, all on the basis of different party influences in the county. A compromise that was intended to send the hospital issue back to the voters became snarled when the county Democratic Committee requested the governor to open an investigation of local registration rolls. After continued wrangling and compromise, plans evolved in late 1954 for a new eighty-bed, $1,250,000 hospital. Four years later the modern facilities of the newly constructed Kershaw County Memorial Hospital opened on a rolling hill site on Roberts Street.

Civil Rights at the Center

Controversies in 1954 politics were also tinged by reactions to impending civil rights changes. The May 28 *Chronicle* reported large crowds at county campaign meetings, the first of which came only one week after the landmark Supreme Court decision *Brown v. Board of Education* ruled that racially segregated schools were unconstitutional. The newspaper stated, "The Kershaw County Hospital, higher teachers' pay, segregation, a constitutional convention, and ring rule seemed to be the issues to be fought out on the stump as the 1954 county campaign tour got underway this week at Blaney. Charges, counter-charges and denials and rebuttals filled the air Monday night at Blaney, Tuesday night at Pine Grove [Lugoff], and Wednesday afternoon at Kershaw."

At Blaney, John Carl West made what he called from the podium his "maiden political speech."[6] Although his interest in the hospital issue had initiated what turned into a long career in public service, West was immediately thrust into the limelight of civil rights controversies. His first political speech, with reference to the recent court decision, was quoted in the *Chronicle:* "Seven days ago a group of men in Washington put upon the South the greatest problem we have been faced with since 1876. By an edict of a court sitting at Washington, it has been determined that our children cannot go to segregated schools. The solution to that problem will rest on the shoulders of the men you send to the legislature. I cannot offer you a wrapped up solution to this problem. But I can tell you that I will work with all the talents at my command to see that the races are not mixed in our schools." In the decades ahead, however, West evolved as a civil rights moderate and an influential leader in the progress of desegregation.

The 1954 election year made history when former governor Strom Thurmond ran as a write-in candidate against the veteran politician and regular Democratic nominee Edgar Brown to fill the U.S. Senate seat vacated by the death of Burnet Maybank.[7] Following an intense campaign, Kershaw County voters favored Thurmond 2-1. He became the first person in U.S. history elected to a major national office by means of a write-in ballot.

At the time of the announcement of the Supreme Court decision, construction was under way on the building of a modern new Jackson High School on Chesnut Ferry Road, a more spacious location a few blocks southwest of the old campus. In May 1954 uncertainties in the changing school situations prompted Governor Byrnes to halt the letting of all new school contracts in South Carolina. The order postponed the start of six schools planned for blacks in Kershaw County—Blaney, Bethune, Hickman, Kirkland, Kirkwood, and St. Matthew. Jackson High, already under construction, was not affected by the order and opened for its first classes in the fall. It was the county's most modern school at the time.

The other six schools intended for black students were also shortly afterward constructed. In the following decade the "separate-but-equal" school buildings were presented as evidence that some facilities for black students were in fact superior to those for white students. Many in the white community hoped that the black community would be "content" with the good faith of the improvements and not push for other changes. The expense of the schools added to the tax burden that was affecting other issues in the county.

Adjustment to changing racial relations challenged both white and black citizens. The *Brown* decision in itself did not mandate change, set deadlines, or extend the interpretation of "equal protection of the laws" beyond the schools. Implications and applications were hammered out at local, state, and national levels through a variety of actions and mandates based on the decision's interpretation. Through two more decades racial unease tinged community changes.

In spring 1956 a Kershaw County citizens' council organized, stating that it intended to offer a more moderate voice of dissent than emergent Ku Klux Klan rallies seeking members at various gathering points throughout the county.[8] Open to membership of all white citizens, the new group expressed belief in the "protection of . . . rights reserved to the . . . states and the people" under the U.S. Constitution, and announced intent to "exert every legal means and effort necessary for the permanent segregation of the white and negro races" in the schools.[9] Some persons who attended such meetings in the beginning said that soon individuals began conferring one-on-one with people they knew in the black community to seek common-ground agreements about how they could work together to minimize the impact of national pressures that they foresaw affecting the children, black and white, in the local community.

Aside from similar concerns, many black citizens supported changes mandated by the Supreme Court decision. In later years they recalled local group meetings of the NAACP, including planning sessions for voter registration, in order to continue moving legal actions forward. Meetings, sometimes more openly announced than in the past, were held in churches, homes, schoolrooms, storerooms, and the new library. The following appeared in the *Chronicle:* "NOTICE! All registered Negro voters of Camden & Kershaw County and all persons wanting information on voting in the coming election requested to meet at the 'Recreation Center' on Clyburn St. on Mon. May 31, 1954; posted by the 'Executive Committee of the Community Civic League.'"

In the flurry of political interests, additional newspapers were organized in Camden. The *Camden Citizen* operated from 1953 to 1955, and the *Camden News,* edited and published by Harold C. Booker, operated from 1956 to 1962. In general the local newspapers favorably quoted black citizens only in support of segregation, such as the Camden mortician E. J. Brown's outburst on integration: "It won't work!" The Reverend P. B. Mdodana, former Jackson High principal, criticized the Palmetto Education Association, of which he was a founder, for denying him the right to present a resolution favoring segregation, and he resigned from the NAACP because of their "agitation on the segregation issue." Favorable publicity was accorded, however, to notable black figures from the local area who remained out of the public eye on racial issues—such as the baseball star Larry Doby or the popular singer Brook Benton.[10]

In the summer of 1956, sponsored by a national board of the Methodist Church, a biracial group of teenage boys and girls arrived for a stay at Mather Academy, intending to demonstrate the benefits of interracial cooperation while helping to paint a dormitory. Rumors that a Ku Klux Klan unit had organized in the county were seemingly confirmed when a cross was burned on the Mather campus and an anonymous phone call threatened to blow up the school unless the interracial sessions were discontinued.

Mayor Savage met with the youths and their leaders.[11] He remarked that project organizers had "overestimated the advance of racial tolerance in the Deep

South." If threats were carried out, the intent to demonstrate successful interracial relations would instead demonstrate the opposite. Savage requested that the group avoid that possibility by taking the project to "a more tolerant environment." At the time he also called the governor's office to request troops to protect the group if they chose to remain. The group instead moved to another work site in Kentucky.

A few nights later a cross was burned on Savage's lawn in disapproval of his decision to protect the group had they stayed. Anonymous telephone threats followed his public criticism of the Klan.[12] Ironically, Savage also drew criticism from a large group of Columbia University students, who attacked him in a nationally published letter for "intolerance" in suggesting that the group leave. The mayor said that the situation dramatized the difficult position of a racial moderate, being branded by some groups as an "integrationist" and by others as a "bigoted racist."

One victim of moderate racial views was Camden High band director Guy Hutchins, who in 1950 began working with the Mather Academy music program as well. On December 27, 1956, on the way home alone at night from a Charlotte concert, Hutchins had a flat tire near Westville. When he had almost finished changing the tire, another car drove up, and five men got out and covered his head with a hood. The men forced Hutchins into their car, placing a pistol under his chin. They drove to a wooded spot, tied him to a tree, and beat him. The men said that the attack was retaliation for remarks Hutchins had made on integration. Community residents were stunned. Indictments, trials, and convictions of perpetrators did much to discourage Klan sympathy afterward and to encourage a common desire for harmony.

Unified Schools

As legal processes were worked through, an understanding grew that schools would eventually no longer be segregated. Clearer heads began to plan for adjustment. As school situations adjusted, racial tensions grew less confrontational in other areas.

For a time schools moved forward still segregated. Improved salaries for teachers were an attempt to hold veteran educators and attract others. Significant pressures to increase student performance followed the Soviet Union's successful launching of the space satellite *Sputnik* in 1957. Almost immediately school curricula entered the "space race," and "accelerated" programs were initiated in local schools, particularly in districts where parents were well educated. IQ tests and achievement data were carefully studied as bases for advancement. The merits of skipping grades and graduating early were debated. Foreign language classes were added, especially Spanish, and oral proficiency was stressed, particularly for young children.

Parents became more involved in school activities, both to encourage program enrichment and to assure student safety. In 1959 Camden High students moved into a new building on Laurens Streets across from their old building, which then became the junior high. Also in 1959 a parents' booster club was organized to support the school band under Director William Basden; four years later the group voted to call themselves the Camband Club. They helped Basden found the Southern States Band Festival in 1970.

New technology entered some county classrooms. Advanced subjects that faced teacher shortages, such as high school chemistry, and subjects taught to many students, such as South Carolina history, were offered by 1960 over classroom televisions via the pioneer South Carolina Educational Television (SCETV). Added to Camden High School in 1964 was an auditorium named to honor the sisters Ada and Helen Phelps, veteran educators in Camden schools. Phelps Auditorium became a significant site for community meetings, performances, and concerts.

Landmark legislation, the Civil Rights Act of 1964, was signed into law following a tumultuous year in national history that witnessed the assassination of President John F. Kennedy. There was now no question about authority to

At Zemp Stadium, Mayor Clarkson Rhame presenting the 1964 state band trophy to Camden High drum major Elizabeth Goodale and band director William Basden. Courtesy of the Camden Archives

enforce desegregation. In 1965 Kershaw County superintendent of education Arthur Stokes announced the first steps to integrate Kershaw County schools: "All students in the county public schools will have freedom of choice to attend any school in the county, regardless of race, color, or national origin." By May the school board had assigned twenty-nine black students who had applied to previously all-white county schools for the fall. No white students applied to black schools.

Independent of the public schools, in July a study committee of area white parents concluded that the formation of a new private school in the community was "not only feasible, but practical and desirable." In 1957 Camden Academy became Camden Military Academy, and the institution reported an increased number of applicants. Mather Academy, having merged with the Boylan-Haven School of Jacksonville, Florida, in 1959 and now operating as Boylan-Haven-Mather Academy, was dealing with declining enrollment.

Public Schools

The first desegregation of the public system began in summer 1965 with Project Head Start, an eight-week, biracial kindergarten program for disadvantaged children. In the fall the freedom-of-choice plan desegregated three schools: Bethune, Blaney, and Camden. For six years black students in small numbers crossed color lines by choice. Part of the time white teachers were hired specifically to cross lines and teach in black schools.

Construction of additional up-to-date schools continued. Lieutenant Governor John C. West was present in August 1967 at the dedication of Jackson Junior High School, opposite Jackson High School on Chesnut Ferry Road. The following week Lugoff Elementary School, with an initial enrollment of four hundred, was dedicated. Some Lugoff parents regretted that upper-grade students in their area continued to be bused to Camden schools.

In 1968 another innovation, the Kershaw County Vocational Center, opened near the airport property to serve students bused part of the day from high schools in the county. The following September, E. Ross Beard of the Kershaw County Chamber of Commerce announced "Operation: Job Impact," in cooperation with the school district, to encourage local businesses to "retain and employ" graduates of county schools.

In August 1967 the commissioner of education notified Superintendent Arthur Stokes that Kershaw County's freedom-of-choice plan had not resulted in "significant progress" in desegregating its schools. Thus the district was not in compliance with the Civil Rights Act, and federal funds would be withheld until it complied. Kershaw County, receiving about seven hundred thousand dollars annually in federal funds, began negotiations with the Department of Health, Education, and Welfare (HEW) on a plan to desegregate completely all Kershaw County schools.

By May 1969 plans had been hammered out for the operation of the unitary school system that began in fall 1970. All white and black students in each attendance area attended the same school. Building uses shifted to accommodate the doubling population at each grade level, and all school names were simplified to represent the attendance area of the school. For example, the former Camden High and Camden Junior High buildings that faced one another on Laurens Street became instead the new Camden High School and accommodated all former CHS and Jackson High School students. Likewise the former Jackson High and facing Jackson Junior High buildings at Chesnut Ferry Road accommodated the former JJHS and Camden Junior High students and became the new Camden Junior High School. Upper-grade students from Antioch and Midway also were assigned to attend the unitary Camden schools.

Similar adjustments across the county resulted in area consolidations and the closing, renaming, or restructuring of individual buildings. A new building uniting Blaney School and Lugoff students became Lugoff-Elgin High, and the former Wateree School in Lugoff became Luggof-Elgin Middle. St. Matthew Elementary was closed, and Jackson Elementary became simply Jackson School, a districtwide special services school. Grades 1–5 in the Camden areas, according to attendance lines, attended Camden Elementary or Pine Tree Hill. Those grades in other areas were likewise assigned to Antioch, Blaney Lugoff, or Midway Elementary schools.

Grades were divided differently at Bethune and Baron DeKalb to utilize building space. In each area one school housed grades 1–3; another, grades 4–6; and a third, grades 7–12. The "middle" group in the Bethune area attended the former Carver Elementary; in the Baron DeKalb area, Kirkland Elementary. Because of space, most students in the Kershaw area were allowed to continue attending Lancaster County schools. The Kershaw County Vocational Center continued as before to serve students from all county high schools.

Another regulation of HEW required the elimination of all vestiges of a dual transportation system in favor of a single bus system. Also the numbers of black and white teachers in each school had to approximate the ratio of black to white teachers in the entire district. A student was allowed to transfer from a school where he was in a racial majority in order to attend one where he was a racial minority. In the early 1970s regulations also required dual elections of student officers and representatives—for example, black and white student council presidents served together; black and white queens reigned together at homecoming.

A Private School

Amid questions about the effects of change on the quality of education, in July 1965 a new private school—Joseph Kershaw Academy (JKA)—incorporated at Camden. The academy began the fall school term with 121 white students in grades 1–8, eight teachers, and tuition of three hundred dollars a year. The school, also operating a kindergarten, opened in the YMCA-converted building that was the remaining vestige of the old Kirkwood Hotel, a remodeled servants' wing. Books, transportation, and lunches were parental responsibilities.

An active parents' group assisted the school to set high standards for achievement and enrichment and aided in community fund-raising. Meeting expenses remained a challenge. With 1970–71 enrollment expected to peak at 250, JKA officials undertook an ambitious project to erect a new building on property donated to the school by Raymond C. Firestone off present Springdale Drive. By school year 1976 the school had four separate buildings on the campus.

Blended Patterns

Community changes from midcentury into following decades blended patterns of modern ways of life with those of the past. Results proved most successful when the new patterns represented the most positive and beneficial aspects of present and past.

In 1954 J. A. Langwiesce of *Reader's Digest* visited the county while gathering research to write "The Changing South from the Air." As he flew into the area, the writer observed a graphic image of the past, represented by Mulberry Plantation, on one side of the Wateree River and an image of the modern industrial South, represented by DuPont's May Plant, on the other side. Langwiesce, also studying water issues, recognized that the river was a critical link to both past and future, and he observed that both the plantation and the industry depended on water. While in Camden he met with Mayor Savage, with whom he shared similar interests since Savage was writing a book on the Santee River.

In 1954 a group of history-minded friends met at the home of Allison and Belle DuBose in Camden to discuss reviving a historical organization for the local community. A second meeting followed and resulted in the name Kershaw County Historical Society. Harold Funderburk was elected president, and other officers were Allison DuBose, Mrs. George Stuart, Mrs. Sumner Waite, and C. T. Baldwin. At the well-attended charter meeting at Grace Episcopal Church in March, the native archaeologist George Stuart III discussed and displayed local artifacts, including Indian arrowheads, pots, and sherds. He also showed films of the 1952 excavation at Mulberry Plantation, during which he had gathered some of the artifacts. The enthusiasm of the new group grew with each program that encouraged members to preserve important aspects of the area's history.

The construction of a new $410,000 Camden City Hall in the mid-1950s symbolized the blending of community interest in the past and the present. The removal of an antebellum dwelling between Lyttleton and Fair streets at the end of Rutledge Street provided the building site for the new city hall, begun in 1955 only a couple of blocks from former offices at the old opera house. The handsome colonial design, by the Camden architect Ralph Little, combined classic elements with modern features. A cupola, echoing the old town tower, was topped with a replica of King Hagler fashioned by the local metal artisan Ken Daniels. The cornerstone was laid with the Lafayette trowel associated with other significant area edifices. Miss Bessie Young, granddaughter of the Camden silversmith Alexander Young, who had fashioned the trowel, was seated on the ceremonial platform.

The modern features of Camden City Hall attracted attention at the 1956 open house. In addition to comfortable quarters for firefighters, features included the nation's first drive-in jail, which provided security for law-enforcement officers, and a drive-in window for utility payments. A photo at the time depicted an elderly customer in a mule-driven buggy pausing at the new window to pay his light bill.

Public Improvements

During the 1960s there were improvements to other public buildings, and new services were necessitated by county changes. The 1963 Kershaw County Fair operated for the first time at a new location a half mile beyond the airport. Fair buildings at the former site in Camden on Broad and Bull streets had been razed to build the city arena. At the December open house for the new facility, South Carolina governor Donald Russell told a crowd of 900 that the arena was an "investment in the future of Camden." The sizable structure, named to honor Mayor E. C. Rhame, could seat 1,860 for concerts or 1,500 for sports, using telescoping bleachers and folding chairs.

Also in 1963 direct long-distance dialing improved telephone service in midlands communities. Camden had seven thousand telephones by October 1962, eight thousand by February 1965, and nine thousand by April 1966. Southern Bell installed Camden's ten thousandth telephone on May 1, 1967. Meanwhile postal costs increased to six cents for a first-class stamp and ten cents for an airmail stamp. In 1965 the Camden post office moved back into its newly renovated building at Broad and DeKalb streets after having operated for a time in an old Colonial Store building to its rear. Workman soon razed the temporary quarters.

From 1963 to 1968 work was under way to raze and rebuild a new Kershaw County courthouse on its former site at Broad and Lafayette streets. The new building, at a cost of $1 million, was constructed as a less expensive and more efficient alternative to remodeling the older one. A linear, modern design with a soaring glass entrance presented a new look to community architecture. The facade featured a large metal seal in the motif of the newly adopted county flag, designed by the architect Henry Boykin to illustrate the area's early history. The disk, bearing the date 1791, depicted the winding Wateree River in the background, a lone pine tree, and the symbol of King Hagler in the foreground.

In front of the new courthouse, the carefully preserved Lafayette Cedar still maintained its sentinel beside the entrance walk. Formal services dedicated the courthouse on May 18, 1968. A significant change had recently taken place within the court system in February when twenty-five women were selected for grand and petit juries, the first time female names were drawn.

A number of public health issues were significant in the 1960s. After the U.S. Public Health Service endorsed Albert Sabin's oral polio vaccine, Kershaw County health officials established a "Polio Sunday" in October 1963. During this time 23,500 citizens—that is, 70 percent of the population—ate Sabin vaccine sugar cubes at fifteen clinics in the county. The following month 1,200 more took the vaccine at the county hospital, and another 220 obtained it at the health department. In December more than 20,000 citizens "braved cold, rainy weather" to take their second vaccine doses at county schools. Meanwhile the local newspaper warned citizens of the continued threat of tuberculosis as fifty-six cases were then active in the county.

In 1964 the nursing school at the Kershaw County Memorial Hospital graduated its last class of nurses. The school's educational program had been outmoded by costly new state standards for instructors that required medical instruction to shift to larger facilities. Five years later the nursing school facility beside the hospital was given as an administration building to the Kershaw County schools, now organized into a single school district.

In 1968 the hospital approved an important new facility for the county, the building of a long-term care wing at the hospital to serve a longer-living, aging population. A nursing home that had been operating at the old Camden Hospital closed when the A. Sam Karesh Long Term Care Center opened at the Kershaw County Memorial Hospital in 1971. With eighty-eight beds for seniors needing skilled nursing, the Karesh Wing was dedicated in 1972.

Emergency services were also of public concern. By 1967 owners and operators of funeral homes, which had operated the county's ambulance services, announced that they would stop because of financial losses. An ambulance service was set up for part of the county through the hospital, for the Bethune area through the Bethune Rescue Squad, and for the Kershaw area through a Kershaw-Lancaster service.

Fire protection was a major issue for steadily growing areas of the county. Lugoff in 1968 voted to organize a fire district within a three-mile radius of Radio Station WACA. The Lugoff Sertoma Club headed fund-raising for a fire truck; Clyde Branham and Ben Newman donated land for a fire station; and a ten-mill tax was levied on citizens in the district. The Lugoff Fire Department began operation on January 1, 1969, with thirty volunteer firemen trained by the Camden Fire Department.

The future water needs of the city of Camden appeared to have been secured in 1970 when Mr. and Mrs. Richard Lloyd donated the city watershed rights in Peck Woods. In 1972 the city remodeled its water treatment plant on Dicey Creek Road and built a modern wastewater treatment plant off Ehrenclou Drive on the banks of the Wateree River. The city also added water lines as well as storm drainage and sewer lines in various outlying areas. County development moved ahead with impetus from the organization of the Cassatt Water Company, serving rural areas previously out of reach of water lines. In addition the city built the Walter M. Crowe Animal Shelter on Fair Street to serve the county.

Housing Swell

The demand for public services and varied community activities had grown along with the swell in new housing. Following the initial impact of midcentury changes, steady population growth continued in Kershaw County. In 1963 the U.S. Department of Commerce reported that one-third of the county's 9,737 homes had been built since 1950.

Inside the Camden city limits, Clyde Branham advertised homes on Perkins Lane, and National Builders developed Memorial Heights near Zemp Stadium. Palmetto Arms opened with "luxury apartments." Several miles east of Camden, Robert Hall offered lots in three developments—Lake Elliott, Pickett-Thomas Acres, and Valley Park. Don Campbell Agency advertised homes east of Camden in Arrowwood and north of Camden in Lafayette Village. Also north of Camden two subdivisions named for historic plantations were promoted—Cool Springs, by J. B. McGuirt and Sons, and Sunnyhill, by Tetterton and Riddick. One home in the latter area attracted special attention for it featured a "fallout shelter." In Lugoff a Columbia firm developed Stratton Hall opposite DuPont, Clyde G. Branham developed Lakewood, and Charlie E. Nash and Donald F. Dabney developed Starcliffe Estates. At the end of the decade Camden's Trinity Methodist Church filled a special community need by opening a five-hundred-thousand-dollar, fifty-unit, low-income apartment complex at Bull Street between Campbell and Church streets. Reverend Granville A. Hicks served as one of the five incorporators applying for an eleemosynary charter for the complex.

One victim to the demand for modern housing space and facilities was the landmark Court Inn, which various local groups and individuals had hoped would somehow be preserved. In November 1963 the Camden businessmen Guy Hutchins Jr. and Jack Karesh purchased the old tourist inn and its remaining 5.7 acres from its last owners, who had operated it since December 1960. Fire Chief Carl Hammond expressed relief that the new owners intended to raze the inn and subdivide the property into about a dozen lots. The chief stated that

A postcard promoting the Court Inn's historic past, still distributed during the inn's waning days in the early 1960s. Courtesy of the Camden Archives

he had seriously considered the condemnation of the rambling, outdated old inn as a fire hazard.

Transportation

Increasing development both affected and was affected by transportation changes of the period. Public transportation systems retained patronage for a time, although both train and bus riders declined in numbers as highway improvements encouraged private drivers. In 1950 a new Greyhound bus station opened in Camden at 407 DeKalb Street, with Anne Young as manager of the station and cafeteria, which at the old location had been managed for twenty-three years by Mr. and Mrs. V. H. Sinclair.

A local bus service, City Transit Line, attracted many who had been riding since 1950, when twelve metal tokens cost only one dollar and daily routes ran regularly to mills, hospitals, shopping areas, and even DuPont. Gradually demand and profits fell off. The owner of the line, J. W. Outlaw, ended his service in 1963, and other efforts stopped in 1966. The following year the Camden Greyhound–Continental Trailways Company moved to a new terminal at 907 South Broad Street to continue distance-travel service. Several local cabs were in business in the 1960s, offering "courteous and sober service" among advertised enticements.

In 1966 Woodward Field improved airport lighting, added a new waiting room, and extended one runway to forty-five hundred feet, which made possible the first jet landing in February 1967. Within months jets belonging to DuPont and other corporations were making regular use of the new facilities.

Highway changes at midcentury involved significant paving and straightening projects. To facilitate workers' travel to and from industrial plants, several main roads were paved in 1955. Cobblestones on South Broad Street in Camden, "believed to have been brought over as ballasts on ships from France 150 years earlier" and "part of the first paving done" in the town, were removed from the city street and relaid as a walkway in Hampton Park.

In April 1968 a dedication ceremony opened a dual lane to and from DuPont over the newly named Howard F. Speaks Bridge on U.S. Highway 1 over the Wateree River. Feeder highways were likewise widened. Local traffic was 75–80 percent of the 10,800 vehicles crossing the river each day.

Construction began in the mid-1960s on the county's portion of a major national superhighway system, Interstate 20. Completion of I-20 required an additional crossing site over the Wateree River. Twin bridges were constructed just south and within sight of the major pre–Revolutionary War river crossing for the Camden area and the first bridge over the Wateree. The Kershaw County section of I-20 was completed in 1974, although sections of it were operational as early as 1967. Completion of the interstate eventually connected the county with I-95 near Florence and I-26 and I-77 near Columbia. Almost immediately persons with a traditional interest in tourism recognized the gateway value of the interstate to bring visitors to the community.

Kershaw County native John C. West, who served as governor of South Carolina from 1971 to 1975, recalled that the opening of I-20 made Camden "almost a bedroom community for Columbia." Not only did many urban employees outside Kershaw County begin to seek new homes within its less hectic neighborhoods, but also more local residents began commuting to jobs outside the county. New transportation patterns diverted some of the traffic from the U.S. Highway route, with resulting effect on businesses along the way, and areas along interstate exchange routes gradually built up.

Automotive Adventurers

Advancing technological developments and local automotive interests combined with interesting effects in the 1960s, when fast cars and daring drivers attracted faithful followers. A number of Kershaw County citizens were part of stock-car racing and drag racing at local and national levels.

C. C. Canada of Camden was a frequent participant in races across the Southeast. The builders Ralph Boykin and Elliott Dority and pit-crew chief Lee

Vincent got Canada ready for events. The Camden garage owner Leland Colvin was also well known on the racing circuits.

A twenty-five-year-old Camden upstart named Bondy Long impacted the stock-car world in the mid-1960s. Long's team, led by the driver Ned Jarrett, won the National Association for Stock Car Auto Racing (NASCAR) championship. The team consisted of crew chief John Erwin, Allen Wooten, Tommy Granger, John Henry Reynolds, Walt Foley, Mark Howard, Ray Hill, and Bruce Jackson. In May 1966 Dick Hutcherson came to Camden to drive for Bondy Long. He started forty Grand National races, won four, and finished in the top five twenty-five times. Lee Roy Yarborough drove Long's Ford to victory at Daytona in 1969. J. P. Berthlette of Camden prepared the car.

Bruce Williams, owner of Williams' American Station on Camden's Broad Street, won forty-three first-place trophies in sanctioned drag races and won every race he entered from April 1966 to February 1967. In summer 1967 Junior Rodgers opened a drag strip five miles north of Camden on U.S. Highway 1, where regular drag races were held every Saturday night.

Kershaw County attracted the biggest drag-racing names when Ed and Sandra Smith opened the Blaney Drag Strip in spring 1968. Smith had used equipment

Local citizens and officials at the unveiling of a marker honoring Camden native Larry Doby near the intersection of Highway 521 and Interstate 20

from his road-construction business to build an earlier strip in 1961. As cars got faster and required more space beyond the finish line, he closed the first tract at the end of the 1965 season. The Smiths purchased a three-hundred-acre tract between White Pond and Green Hill roads and began planning what was to become one of the top five drag strips in the Southeast. The facility was sanctioned by the National Hot Rod Association (NHRA) and hosted national meets.

Two weeks after the Blaney Drag Strip opened for its second season, the track record of 173 mph was shattered. Time and speed records continued to fall. National champ T. V. Tommy Ivo drove his Dodge-powered rail 205 mph in 7.03 seconds, and "Big Daddy" Don Garlits ran a 7.05-second quarter mile, setting a new track speed of 214.28 mph. Although the noise and traffic annoyed some area residents, the drag strip "brought a lot of attention and money to the community," according to Sandra Smith.[13]

Continued Expansion

For some time industrial growth proceeded in Kershaw County. In 1954 a new factory offered to locate in the Camden area if a building were erected for it. Camden agreed to pay $105,000 of the $140,000 construction cost, and Skyline Manufacturing Company of Kingston, New York, agreed to purchase twenty-five acres on Dicey's Ford Road for a new garment assembly plant, Tic Tac, to employ mostly women. Operation began in December 1954, and by the following spring the plant had nearly three hundred workers.

The undisputed leader of county industry continued to be DuPont. With 1,457 employees in 1958, the May Plant employed more than the combined total of all the county's other leading manufacturers: Hermitage Cotton Mill (423), Tic Tac (291), Bethune-Kendall Mills (249), Wateree Cotton Mill (196), and Jaclyn Hosiery Mill (116). In addition the May Plant's more than $9 million payroll was about three times the sum of those five other manufacturers combined.

Blaney to Elgin

Industrial impact continued to be especially strong in the West Wateree area and gradually spread along U.S. Highway 1 into the Blaney area. Three years of negotiations were finalized in 1958 when Whitehead Brothers Sand Company, with Lester Tomlin as manager, began operations at a three-hundred-thousand-dollar sand foundry between Lugoff and Blaney. Soon another change stirred Blaney folk with even greater enthusiasm.

In October 1962, by a vote of 61–16, the small town's name was changed from Blaney to Elgin in honor of the Elgin National Watch Company, which built a $1 million assembly plant on its outskirts. The *Camden Chronicle* issue of September 5, 1962, officially confirmed the plans of the watch company to build east of the Seaboard railroad crossing on U.S. Highway 1. Two days later the entire newspaper was devoted to the new company and included a letter from South Carolina governor Ernest F. Hollings. When applications opened for the initial 240 jobs, more than 1,000 persons applied.

Blaney leaders had long maintained that the absence of an adequate water system stymied the town's growth. The watch company's decision to locate there necessitated such an investment. By January 1963 the newly named town of Elgin was drilling wells as part of a new $150,000 water system. In February 1963 the Elgin watch plant began production, and 5,000–7,000 people attended its dedication the following month. Corporate president Henry M. Margolis presented Senator John C. West with the first watch assembled in the new plant, lauding his "numerous contributions" in assisting the company's move.

However, to the disappointment of many, officials of the Elgin National Watch Company announced in fall 1967 that the plant would be sold to B. F. Goodrich, a manufacturer of tennis shoes, which was expected to offer former Elgin employees comparably paying jobs. Elgin officials cited an inability to compete with imported watches from Switzerland, the Virgin Islands, and Japan. Meanwhile in September 1967 Hardwicke Chemical Company broke ground at a fifteen-acre site near Elgin for "large scale custom manufacturing of Organic chemicals for the chemical industry."

Other Growth

Expansion continued in other parts of the county as well. In May 1967 a well-attended, three-day Kershaw County industrial fair in Camden gave citizens a look at locally produced products, with an emphasis on contributions of industry to the county's economy. In Camden in the early 1960s Productions Unlimited specialized in the manufacture of a new product, fiberglass. Described as "one of the new wonder creations of modern chemistry," fiberglass was said to be "four times as strong as steel." At Bethune, Kendall energized with a $1.5 million expansion in 1962. That year too DuPont's May Plant announced a one-year, $3 million improvement to meet increased demand for Orlon. In 1968 the plant expanded to a two-fiber operation to produce bulked continuous filament (BCF) nylon fibers for automotive and residential carpets and for upholstery. In 1971 the plant added a third operation to produce Dacron polyester fiber.

In June 1969 Linde Division of Union Carbide Corporation announced plans to build an air separation plant in Lugoff to produce oxygen and nitrogen for DuPont and other industries. Investment funds were pumped in from international sources in 1973 when Shinme Kasuskiki, a Japanese textile firm, announced plans to build a $5 million weaving plant in Kershaw County. Wateree Textiles, located near I-20, was attracted to the area's abundant water supply, which was necessary to operate the Nissan water-jet loom producing polyester fabric.

Camden banking expanded as a result of investment growth. First Federal Savings and Loan opened a Lugoff branch in 1969. Wateree Savings and Loan of Camden opened a Kershaw branch in 1968 and later opened one in Lancaster. In 1975 Wateree Savings and Loan changed its name to Palmetto State Savings and Loan Association to reflect its wider base.

Agricultural Survivors

The countywide shift away from agricultural dominance intensified under a federal program designed to fight erosion and to increase prices of farm products by reducing the amount of farmland under cultivation. From 1956 to 1964 the Soil Bank offered farmers three- to ten-year contracts during which the government paid them a per-acre stipend for "banking" the land instead of cultivating it. A number of landowners improved their property because of cost-share assistance to plant seed grasses, legumes, or trees. In South Carolina, Georgia, and Alabama farmers in the program put 1,255,531 acres into pine trees. Farmers also established wildlife cover, managed water and marsh for wildlife, and constructed dams and ponds for livestock, irrigation water, and fish. Under the Soil Bank and subsequent programs that followed, vast acreages in Kershaw County, in small and large plots, were transformed for new use, some for the timber industry and some for other environmental improvements.

In 1957 Hettie Rickett of Cassatt began raising turkeys, the first agribusiness that would eventually bring the poultry industry to prominence in Kershaw County in future decades. For eleven years, however, she had the only turkey farm in the county, shipping forty thousand turkeys annually to the Armour Packing Company in North Carolina. The Ralston Purina Feed Company owned the turkeys and feed.

Cotton interests in Kershaw County in early 1963 protested what they called "two price cotton." On a cotton bale displayed in the Camden C&S Bank, information stated that the bale that cost a local mill $182.50 could be bought by a foreign mill for $140.00. "You the American Taxpayer pay that difference of $42.50," warned the display.

At President Lyndon B. Johnson's request in 1964, Congress made permanent a pilot food stamp program instituted three years earlier. Officially promoted to strengthen the agricultural economy and to improve nutrition among low-income households, the legislation effectively gave Congress control over the pilot program by enacting its regulations into law. Food stamps had far-reaching local effects.

Kershaw County livestock buyers and sellers gained a competitive advantage in January 1969 when the sixteen-acre Central Carolina Livestock Market, owned by John Conder, opened just off U.S. 601 in Lugoff. The "newest and most modern market in the Southeast" could accommodate three thousand head of cattle at a time and to a lesser extent also dealt with horses.

Area Disasters

In late 1952 a startling explosion "shook windows throughout the community," and smoke boiled on the horizon, alarming citizens when fire broke out in a storage area at DuPont's May Plant. A quick response brought the blaze under control in an hour. However, the event temporarily stirred some local concerns about potential dangers from the increasing industrial and chemical exposures in the area.

One of the county's worst fires in history broke out in August 1955 at Speaks Oil Company in a main business district of Camden. The fire claimed two lives and sent twenty-six other persons to the hospital for treatment of burns. Glenn Speaks, brother of the company owner, Howard Speaks, was transferring gasoline from a tanker truck to a storage tank at the oil company on DeKalb Street, near Mill. When the tank began to overflow, Glenn Speaks pulled an electrical switch to cut off the pump motor. A spark ignited the fuel on the ground and enveloped him in flames. He died about ten hours later.

Meanwhile the Camden Fire Department, a team from DuPont's firefighting unit, and the Columbia Fire Department arrived on the scene to fight a long battle with flames spreading to other buildings and threatening to ignite nearby storage tanks. Camden assistant fire chief J. T. Haynes and his son Tommy, a volunteer firefighter, were standing side by side shooting water on the fire when one tank exploded, covering them with flames. The elder Haynes died at the hospital, and the son at first was given little hope of surviving. In addition to damage to the oil company, a tire warehouse was also badly burned, and an adjacent business, Boykin Supply Company, was completely destroyed. Wooten's cotton warehouse was extensively damaged, and Thomas and Howard wholesale distributors suffered damage as well.

In June 1956 the town of Blaney was threatened by the night-time fury of a five-hundred-thousand-dollar fire that completely destroyed Blaney High School, including all records. Following an investigation of arson, the Blaney school superintendent was convicted for breach of trust and misappropriation of funds. The community was deeply aggrieved.[14] Other damaging school fires of the period were attributed to accident, including the loss of an eighty-eight-resident barracks at Camden Military Academy in 1962 and the complete destruction of Pine Grove Elementary School in West Wateree on Christmas morning in 1966.

"The stench of burning horsemeat—from the dressed carcasses of 22 horses" drifted over Camden as a result of the April 1963 fire that destroyed Hill Packing Company. Two highly explosive dangers faced the firemen battling the Hill Packing blaze—volatile ammonia used in the refrigeration process and stored .22 caliber ammunition used in slaughtering. The pet food company, employing more than forty people, had opened in 1955 in the former Supreme Products packing company at the foot of King Street, in the area of the old Southern railway depot, and did not rebuild after the fire.

Divisive Times

In late summer 1962 Kershaw County was at the center of a 3.5 million-acre "war zone" as part of Operation Swift Strike II. A July newspaper reported that 850 soldiers were stationed at Woodward Field, some of the 70,000 soldiers and airmen who portrayed invaders and defenders in the "biggest U.S. peacetime maneuvers" in the Carolinas since 1941. Based on a concept of Defense Secretary Robert S. McNamara, the operations were a test of the effectiveness of a new U.S. Strike Command. McNamara had melded the fighter and transport units of the air force's Tactical Air Command with the army's ground forces to create "a force that could instantly be deployed anywhere around the world." Kershaw County was part of the aggressor nation "Gutasu," which extended from the Lynches River to Columbia.

A year later army engineers as part of Swift Strike III obtained maneuver rights on 385,400 acres in the county. At the beginning of the activities, local children helped hand out leaflets on the street while planes dropped them from the sky. The flyers urged citizens to resist the takeover and to "go underground." The various military and civilian techniques practiced in maneuvers also became part of the nation's unpopular war in Vietnam.

In Kershaw County, as across the nation, involvement in Vietnam evoked a variety of responses—most of them troubling and conflicting. Here as elsewhere veterans of the late 1960s and early 1970s, both volunteers and draftees, returned home to general silence and a sense of isolation. There were no local parades or public celebrations. Soldiers returned as they left—one by one, not in the company of local comrades. Kershaw County counted fifteen war dead. Numbers of veterans experienced psychological or physical postwar effects, some of them returning with alcohol or drug problems mirroring those increasing in society at the time. GI benefits assisted many veterans in making adjustments to civilian life, but the controversies over Vietnam added to the other tensions and uncertainties of the era.

Community Balance

Amid times of change and moves to modernize, conscious efforts also continued locally to preserve positive community heritage and to balance the practicality of work and science with an appreciation of recreation and the arts. Several accomplishments that worked toward these goals benefited the community economically as well.

Equestrian Interests

Near new housing developments and altered schools, and not far from glimpses of an industrial skyline, a circle of persons with equestrian interests continued to pursue their traditional patterns. In 1950 at the Springdale track the Camden Hunt renewed the first hunter trials since that event had been suspended in wartime fourteen years earlier. The Camden Junior Hunt opened its fifth season with a large number of young riders. In the following decade Camden hosted annual conventions of the national Fox Hunter Association with field trials and bench shows that drew sporting enthusiasts to several venues in the county.

The Carolina Cup, drawing annual crowds, remained a focus of public attraction. The 1950 event inaugurated a public address system and used starting tape, the latter for the first time in America. Marion duPont Scott purchased the Springdale Track in 1954. That year the Carolina Cup purse increased to forty-five hundred dollars, and in 1961 the race was telecast live by WIS-TV. Dangers of the steeplechase were highlighted in the 1963 event when three falls killed two horses and injured a third horse and four jockeys. Cup manager Ray Woolfe stated that this was the first time a horse had been killed in the timber feature.

U.S. equestrian teams training in Camden in the 1950s and 1960s for Olympics and Pan-Am events attracted a number of international connections to local stables. Camden-trained horses also continued to do well at national events. Kent Miller's locally trained Elkridge, the first steeplechase horse anywhere to win two hundred thousand dollars, continued his winning ways. Elkridge Drive in Kirkover Hills subdivision was named for him. Nearby, Battleship Drive commemorated another famous local racehorse. Both were inducted into the National Thoroughbred Hall of Fame in the 1960s.

Camden's reputation as a quality training center and, especially, its growing appeal to foreign stables were enhanced by the addition of a new equestrian event in 1970. The inaugural running of the Colonial Cup international steeplechase race in November added a major fall event to the Springdale Course and attracted fat purses that exceeded those of the older Carolina Cup. Furthermore awareness grew that horses represented more than merely sport, and the concept of "equine industry" evolved.

Historic Camden

In May 1967 the Kershaw County Historical Society announced the formation of a foundation "for the purpose of preserving property of historical interest in South Carolina and especially in Kershaw County." The land on which the Revolutionary War powder magazine once stood was donated to the new entity, the Camden District Heritage Foundation. The foundation announced that it would consider restoring the powder magazine and publishing "an addenda volume" to update Kirkland and Kennedy's *Historic Camden: Colonial and Revolutionary* and *Historic Camden: Nineteenth Century.*

In September the foundation authorized the University of South Carolina archaeologist Alan Calmes to gather documentary and archaeological evidence. Goals were "to build a military museum on the site, reconstruct a part of the old British stockade, and perhaps create some dramatization of events that took place during the Revolution." In July 1968 the project workers discovered the palisade trenches of old Camden, and the following June excavations began at the site of the northeast redoubt, at the south end of Lyttleton Street. The location of the foundations of Joseph Kershaw's house that had been used by Cornwallis as British headquarters created special excitement.

In 1970 enthusiasm was high when the re-created site at the southern edge of Camden—aptly named Historic Camden—opened to the public. Costumed guides and reenactments of battle scenes and colonial life were soon adding to the sense of reality created by restored palisade walls and by the authentic log cabin and early home structures that had been moved onto the site. Exposures of preserved archaeological foundations along with diorama and museum displays added further education about colonial and Revolutionary War days. Federal grants and local contributions helped develop Historic Camden as an outstanding and authentic tourist attraction and an affiliated area of the National Park Service.

Recreation and Arts

Additional community improvements followed to enhance the area's attraction for residents and tourists alike. In 1973 the Kershaw County Council, appropriating twenty-five thousand dollars for a countywide recreational program, offered 740 acres of the current county park to be developed by the South Carolina Department of Parks, Recreation and Tourism into the N. R. Goodale State Park.

In 1973 the long-anticipated merging of county and city libraries was finally accomplished when the newly constructed Kershaw County Library opened at 1304 Broad Street in Camden. In 1974 the Fine Arts Center of Kershaw County was established, taking its first steps forward in the restored historic Douglas-Witherspoon home at Lyttleton and York streets. Furthermore in 1975 the newly developed Camden Archives occupied the renovated old Camden City (Carnegie) Library building to begin its work preserving documents and evidence of the Old Camden District, from which Kershaw County was born. The educational and cultural benefits of all these organizations blended appreciation of past and present with a vision for the future.

18

Landmarks and Interstate

Into the Twenty-first Century

In the last quarter of the twentieth century, the Kershaw County population expanded significantly. Areas where people lived and worked underwent change, a process that continued into the new century. The Interstate 20 corridor that sped traffic in and out of the area linked local interests to those far beyond county boundaries. Chain stores, expanding in size and numbers, clustered in suburban shopping centers and competed with traditional downtown merchants. In the 1980s Wal-Mart opened in Camden's Dusty Bend and then moved to a "superstore" near the Wateree River bridge, where three shopping centers developed at the U.S. Highway 1 intersection with Springdale Drive. Fast-food franchises, large grocery chains, and discount superstores, part of a trend nationally dubbed "walmartization," took effect.

Other national and international concerns—wars, economic upheavals, energy crises, and new technology—also influenced local changes. In the post-Vietnam years ideas that had once seemed unorthodox entered the mainstream here as elsewhere. The terrorist attacks in America on September 11, 2001, and military actions in the Persian Gulf, in Afghanistan, and in Iraq brought tensions of warfare. Uniformed women as well as men were sent into combat situations.

Young people, growing up in climate-controlled buildings, tuned in to individualized audiovisual electronics more often than to the summertime front-porch talks and winter-time fireside chats with which the older generations had grown up. Societal tensions that had peaked divisively around midcentury shifted to other concerns—double-digit inflation, unemployment, education, fuel shortages, pollution, drug abuse, health care, immigration, gangs, terrorism, militarism, and the rights of multiple groups whose voices had gone underrepresented in the past. Family values, spiritual beliefs, and confidence in government all were questioned in the final quarter of the twentieth century and the beginning of the twenty-first century.

A Bicentennial Reappraisal

In 1976, just a year after the United States withdrew in disorder from Vietnam, the national bicentennial prompted many local activities that drew together citizens of various points of view to celebrate their common heritage of the past two hundred years in America. To some extent the historical perspective promoted a healing reconciliation. Churches, schools, and civic groups aided in hosting parades, homecomings, and pageants. The public responded with enthusiasm for donning historical costumes for bicentennial events. Beards and long hair, homemade bonnets and long dresses, as well as horse-drawn wagons and old automobiles became common sights. Period music and dancing were part of entertainments. Interests increased in old-time crafts and skills that were common in early home life and agriculture. One project was the research and publication of *Kershaw County Legacy: A Commemorative History,* which includes articles and oral interviews by adults and students.

Public enthusiasm for history during the bicentennial was revived locally in 1983 when Camden celebrated the 250th birthday of its founding. For the occasion the Camden City Council commissioned a downtown mural by the artist Blue Sky. Painted on an alleyway wall east of the post office, the painting depicts a foxhunting scene in front of the old Kirkwood Hotel, with guests arriving to enjoy the hospitality for which the community has traditionally been noted. *Legacy II* was published to include additional articles and interviews with county citizens by students and teachers from all the county's public middle and high schools as well as its private academies—Camden Military, Joseph Kershaw, and Boylan-Haven-Mather. With younger people interviewing older citizens, personal contacts across generations were especially valuable. Historical perspectives bridged gaps with different experiences and points of view.

Emerging Patterns

Within just the last decade of the century, the population of Kershaw County increased 21 percent. In West Wateree, within the sprawling reach of urban Columbia, the number of residents nearly doubled. The 2000 census for the county counted 52,647 persons, proportionally identified as 72 percent white and 26 percent black. The total included 886 Hispanic persons, the county's most rapidly expanding ethno-cultural group, although officials acknowledged that an undetermined number of transients may not have been counted.

Within a national pattern of increased migration, immigrant workers were quickly filling local positions, especially in heavy labor and service fields, construction, stables, and forestry. Often resident workers, because of improved education and increased opportunities, had gravitated away from such employment in recent years. Churches, social agencies, and schools made adjustments to changing cultural needs, and ethnic restaurants and groceries opened with community acceptance. In the new century economic downfalls brought hardships and job losses to workers at all levels and increased competition for jobs. Challenges continue.

Though at times controversial, Kershaw County zoning ordinances since 1969 have sought to limit and manage development in order to achieve stability of growth and better manage the delivery of services to citizens and business. In Elgin planned housing developments became dominant in the growth spurred by Columbia's urban sprawl. In the 1980s Duke Power began selling the lots it had formerly leased on Lake Wateree, and home building on Lake Wateree changed from simple shacks to million-dollar mansions.

Although all real estate markets declined in the later economic downturns, persons with an eye toward the future anticipated an eventual return to some growth patterns that had been under way. Liberty Hill residents expected luxury homes in lake communities to increase interest in their historic homes. Development in the upper county was predicted as Charlotte-Mecklenburg residents sought rural getaways there, choosing larger tracts for country homes than the housing developments of job-oriented West Wateree. Camden citizens, recognizing their limited space for development, often voiced opinions in city planning and zoning. County and municipal areas worked together for the orderly development of the new areas they service.

The Rural Way

In recent years the pattern of rural land use in the county continued to deemphasize crop cultivation in favor of livestock, poultry, and timber growth. In 2002 the number of farms in Kershaw County increased from 426 to 479, while average acreage decreased, shrinking from 190 to 146 acres. Fewer than half of those farm operators listed farming as the principal occupation. In 2003 Kershaw County ranked seventh in the state in timber harvests at well over $27 million. In 2005 county crops brought in just over $2 million, while livestock brought in $54 million. Meanwhile county turkey production was the first and egg production was the second in the state. Just 600 acres of cotton were planted and harvested in the county in 2006.

In an effort to continue traditional family food farming, in 1982 the Robert and Polly Marsh family converted to a pick-your-own operation, HoField Farms, which became a draw for area residents, especially in strawberry season. Educational and recreational activities for families and children were featured, as was preservation of old farm buildings and equipment. Hofield operated until 2008, and the family was a part of encouraging others to find ways to keep local food production viable. In 2005 the Kershaw County Farmers Market opened in downtown Camden, where area growers weekly sold (and still sell) their seasonal produce of plants and specialties such as vegetables, fruits, herbs, honey, fresh milk, and free-range eggs.

In 1980, when only three counties in South Carolina produced more timber than Kershaw County, a million-dollar Department of Agriculture grant aided Camden Forest Products / New South in constructing a modern facility near Cassatt for dressed and treated lumber. In 2006 a Canadian company, Canfor

Corporation, purchased New South, although two years later it cut production because of the slump in home construction. Later in the century large timber companies began divesting sizable landholdings, although they continued buying and harvesting operations, which remained strong in the county. Smaller landholders continued tree farming, with forest diversification becoming a goal of some growers.

Bethune's Cal-Maine Foods, at one point touted as the world's largest producer of fresh eggs, continued to be a top producer in the state. Prestage Farms, operating a feed mill at Cassatt, spread its turkey operations throughout the county. In 2003 it had 123 turkey houses on 37 different farms. Broiler chickens were also produced. For sanitation and disease control, most of these operations were carried on at some distance from public exposure.

Livestock experimentation in the 1980s brought cutting horses and then buffalo to a Westville training center. Buffalo were also later imported to the Elgin area and east of Camden. To some observers such scenes evoked images of the American Old West, but historians pointed out that buffalo had been present in the Kershaw County area in its early days, as had been cowboys whose cattle-handling methods had later been taken west. When Westfall Arena (later the South Carolina Equine Park) was built south of Camden, western-style riding and rodeos were featured along with the area's more familiar English-style events.

Equestrian activities also benefited in 1983 when Marion duPont Scott donated the Springdale Race Course and $1 million to the state to ensure continuation of the race meets. Training centers, favored by the sandy loam soils and mild climate, attracted about fifteen hundred thoroughbreds each winter. Horse barns and stables became part of many new rural home properties, and more acres of hay were grown in the county than any other crop. The trainer Dale Thiel was a leader in the development of the Hunt Country residential area on Red Fox Road, where generously spaced homesites and stables back up to miles of riding trails and natural forestlands.

Sporting and recreational use of rural land continued to have economic and environmental impact in the county. Private hunt clubs owned or rented lands, which were often improved with plantings of food plots for wildlife. Deer, duck, quail, and wild turkey were the primary game sought by most hunters, with wild hogs and raccoons being sought by some. Sporting clays and skeet and trap shooting attracted a following at commercial and private sites in the county. Competitive target shooting with prizes, privately organized as "turkey shoots," offered other diversion. Interest increased in offering fishing and hunting activities for a fee at private preserves.

Public fishing was popular at N. R. Goodale State Park and at Lake Wateree, where bass, bream, catfish, and crappie were most commonly caught. In 2007 access to the Wateree River was made easier. Public boat ramps were improved below the dam and beside the U.S. Highway 1 bridge, and efforts were renewed to remove from the riverbed the hazardous remains of early 1900s bridges downed by floodwaters. Negotiations during Duke Power's relicensing process resulted in plans for public recreational acreage to be developed in Kershaw County on Lake Wateree. The Lake Wateree State Park, in Fairfield County, attracted Kershaw County campers, fishermen, and picnickers.

The Catawba-Wateree basin continued under pressure from upstream environmental effects, however, especially from Charlotte-Mecklenburg County, North Carolina. Issues of water quantity and quality remained major concerns that affected the daily lives of Kershaw County citizens. To establish an environmental education center on the Wateree River, in 2006 Margaret (Peggy) Lloyd donated $2 million and an 853-acre tract west of Camden to Clemson University. Edging the eastern bank of the river for a mile above the U.S. Highway 1 bridge, the property for many years had been managed as a natural wildlife preserve.

Faced with increased development in the county, a number of private landholders set up land trusts to preserve or enhance natural areas on their properties and to protect them from encroaching commercialization. Efforts to enhance green spaces and wetlands also extended into urban neighborhoods, where community garden clubs undertook civic plantings as well as improved individual home landscapes. The Camden Tree Foundation assisted in the city. Margot Rochester of Lugoff, a newspaper columnist on gardening, developed a following among readers who admired her natural and enthusiastic methods of improving local soils and beautifying yards. Many landscaping companies operated in the county. The Clemson University Cooperative Extension Service continued to provide science-based informal education to residents regarding agriculture, natural resources, home life, and community development.

Industry

Northern and foreign-owned industries continued to be attracted to the Kershaw County area, in part because of active state recruiting since the middle of the twentieth century. About the time interest in foreign investment awakened, a former governor of South Carolina, Camden native John Carl West, was appointed by President Jimmy Carter as U.S. ambassador to Saudi Arabia and served from 1977 to 1981. West was lieutenant governor when the state began international recruiting efforts. Countries with significant investments in Kershaw County included Canada, China, Germany, Japan, Switzerland, and the United Kingdom. Incentives and vocational education programs proved appealing to industries.

Economic conditions and changing technologies—overall situations out of the control of local workers—affected directions of industries in Kershaw

County in the latter part of the century. Layoffs and changing work schedules signaled efforts to adjust to these situations. In the mid-1980s DuPont began downsizing, and there were community worries that the area's largest industry might leave completely. To counter effects of potential economic loss, local government undertook active industrial recruitment through the Kershaw County Economic Development Board. A number of citizens urged measures to maintain a balance of industrialization with environmental concerns.

In the latter years of the century the Kershaw County Economic Development Board led in the building of industrial parks near the I-20 interchanges with U.S. 601 (Lugoff) and U.S. 521 (Camden), and an office park in Elgin. The industrial parks attracted Yutaka Technologies (ATV steering) and a Target distribution center to the Lugoff area, and Howden Buffalo (fans) and Haier America (refrigerators) to Camden. The impact was viewed positively, although no single company had the individual impact that DuPont had on its arrival.

In 1998 DuPont made considerable improvements to the May Plant, but in 2003 the company ended its local presence by selling the plant to another chemical industry, Invista, Inc. (Koch Industries). Employing 800 in 2008, Invista remained the county's largest industry employer, followed by Target with 621. In 1987 Mack Trucks, the nation's second-largest heavy-truck manufacturer, opened a new operation at Winnsboro in neighboring Fairfield County. There was a spillover effect in Kershaw County in the need for related suppliers. In Lugoff, for example, Mancor, a machine shop, and Dana, a chassis assembly plant, opened in 1987. Although union troubles and economic conditions ended Mack Truck's presence in 2002, some of the Kershaw County businesses scaled back and adapted their operations to stay in business.

A number of firms were affected by industrial ups and downs. The trucking enterprise Builders Transport achieved success for a number of years. Cogsdill Tool opened in Lugoff in 1977 to manufacture precision metal-working products, and Oak-Mitsui opened at Camden in 1991 to manufacture copper foil. The county continued to advertise its favorable location on the interstate highway system.

In Kershaw County as elsewhere, the traditional strength of textiles and garments declined as world market conditions took these jobs abroad. Local sewing plants closed. The former Tic Tac property, after various changes, lingered in litigation. Local mills scaled back, retaining the manufacture of nonwovens and medical and surgical gauze. The oldest operating textile site at Camden, Hermitage, became DeRoyal Textiles; and the second oldest, Wateree, became Covidien. Kendall in Bethune changed to BBA and then to Ahlstrom Nonwovens. Kawashima Textiles opened in Lugoff to manufacture car-seat fabrics.

In the late 1970s, when prices of gold soared around eight hundred dollars an ounce, mining revived in the Carolina slate belt, which Kershaw County edges. Haile Gold Mine at Kershaw in Lancaster County was active from 1986 until the late 1990s, when gold prices declined and Haile turned to land reclamation. Kennecott Ridgeway Mining Company, acting on new discoveries of ore deposits, mined gold and silver near Ridgeway, Fairfield County, from December 1988 to November 1999, after which it too began extensive land reclamation. Economic benefits extended to Kershaw County while the mines were in operation. As gold prices rise, area mining operations are expected to resume.

Education

A major lesson brought home to workers in the latter part of the century was the importance of education, flexibility, and willingness to retrain. Kershaw County's public school vocational center, beside the Camden airport, changed its name to Applied Technology Education Campus (ATEC) to address a broader scope. In the private sector Reid Buckley in 1988 founded at Camden the Buckley School of Public Speaking to train executives and political leaders in communications skills.

In 1998 Kershaw County schools joined with SCETV to open a center at ATEC to deliver and originate educational programming for schools. Central Carolina Technical College for several years taught extension evening courses at the ATEC campus and in 2001 opened a branch campus in downtown Camden. In 2004 Kershaw County initiated a program to provide a laptop computer to each high school student.

Efforts to upgrade school curricula while equalizing opportunities and streamlining facility expenses resulted in various consolidations, closings, and building changes. West Wateree students, who had consolidated at newly formed Lugoff-Elgin High School on U.S. Highway 1 in 1971, required a new building in 1992. North Central High opened in 1976 on Lockhart Road to consolidate students from most of the upper county, although Bethune citizens kept their small high school open until 1997. Old buildings for Jackson School on Campbell Street and Camden Grammar on Lyttleton Street were razed in 1981 and 1982, respectively, and replaced with new ones. In 1992 Camden High moved to Ehrenclou Drive, where a new structure was built adjacent to the one that had originally housed Jackson Middle School on Chesnut Ferry Road. The original CHS building was razed and a memorial park established at its site.

Area private schools experienced decreasing enrollments and increasing operating costs in the latter part of the twentieth century. Boylan-Haven-Mather Academy closed in 1983, and its remaining buildings were razed in 1995 by new property owners. Joseph Kershaw Academy graduated its last class in 1985, and its buildings were sold for commercial purposes. The Montessori preschool program, which began in 1979 at JKA, continued to operate a private school on Battleship Road, serving students ages eighteen months to twelve years. Camden Military Academy merged with Carlisle Military School of Bamberg in 1977 and remained in operation.

The Kershaw County school system included eleven elementary, four middle, and three high schools, as well as the Continuous Learning Center, the Applied Technology Education Campus, and programs for adult education. In 2007 the district had major building projects totaling $102 million under way at thirteen different schools. More than 750 teachers served more than 10,000 students, and with other school employees the school district remained the largest employer in the county. In the latter part of the decade, economic cutbacks required South Carolina schools to reexamine all programs.

Public Services

Elected officials and appointees included a number of persons with long service records or who represented milestones. From 1986 to 1994 Representative Robert J. Sheheen served as Speaker of the House of Representatives. In a special election in June 2004, the county's first female representative, Laurie Slade Funderburk, was elected to the House to fill the unexpired term of Vincent Sheheen, who won a special election in February to fill the U.S. Senate seat vacated by the death of Senator Donald Holland, who had held that office for thirty-three years. In 2008 Reggie Lloyd was appointed chief of the State Law Enforcement Division, only the third SLED chief in the past fifty years and the first African American head.

As changing times and circumstances placed altered demands on public services and brought about new challenges and controversies, local governments made changes in structure. In 2010 Kershaw County is locally governed by a county council made up of seven members elected from single member districts with a chairperson elected at large. Steve Kelly Jr., who in 2010 announced plans to retire, had served as chairman since 1990. The city of Camden has the council-manager form of government, with councilpersons and mayor elected at large. Bethune and Elgin have similar municipal governments. Terms of office are four years. Camden's only female mayor, Mary V. Clark, who took office in 2000, was replaced in December 2008 by Camden's youngest mayor, Jeffrey Graham. In 2010 long-serving veteran mayors were in office in Bethune (Carlisle Davis) and Elgin (Pete James).

Water

The city of Camden municipal system and the Lugoff-Elgin Water and Sewer District provide water and sewer services to respective areas of the county. The Lugoff-Elgin Water Authority (L-EWA), created in 1974, was the first to draw water from Lake Wateree to supply its citizens. In 1999 the city of Camden abandoned its traditional water source and put in operation on Flint Hill Road seven miles north of the city a treatment plant, which began drawing three million gallons of water daily from Lake Wateree.

In other areas of the county Bethune, Cassatt, and Charlotte Thompson Water Districts also supply water, primarily from deep wells. Facilities to increase wastewater treatment in rural areas, especially West Wateree, remain a need. The city of Camden discharges wastewater into the Wateree River at its treatment facility south of the river's only bank-side housing area, on Wild Turkey Lane, near old bridge and ferry sites. Various industries that rely on the water source of the Wateree also treat and discharge wastewater into the river.

By the early twenty-first century, concerns about water quality expanded to include concerns about water quantity. On no other river system in South Carolina were so many demands being placed than on the Catawba-Wateree system. With Lake Wateree being the last impound in the watershed, all upstream stresses impact Kershaw County. Environmental alarms resulted when North Carolina cities were permitted to draw millions of gallons daily from the Catawba River basin and to discharge wastewater into other basins. Water transfers and extended drought in 2007 lowered Lake Wateree and Wateree River to levels that raised warnings about potential pollution increases and about damage to industries that depended on an ample water source.

Power

In 2010 water flow remains important to generate electrical power for the county. Three of South Carolina's twenty electric cooperatives—Black River, Lynches River, and Fairfield Electric Cooperatives—serve various sections of the county. In addition electric power is supplied to the county by Progress Energy, formerly Carolina Power & Light Company, and by the city of Camden municipal system. South Carolina Electric and Gas / SCANA supplies natural gas, and Carotane Propane Gas provides propane. Local phone services are provided by Bell South / ATT and Sand Hill Telephone Cooperative, with many long-distance carriers. Additional services arrived with cable television in the 1980s, Internet connections in the following decade, and cell-phone towers in the twenty-first century.

Hospital

The name Kershaw County Memorial Hospital was changed to Kershaw County Medical Center in 1994 and to KershawHealth in 2009. The main facility at Camden is an expanded modern building that includes beds for acute and long-term care as well as an agency for home health and hospice care. There are special centers for dialysis, oncology, cardiology, and sleep disorders. In addition

KershawHealth owns the educational Health Resource Center in Camden, health-care locations at Elgin and Bethune, and the West Wateree Medical Complex in Lugoff, which has primary health-care offices, a lab, X-ray facilities, and a therapy pool. Kershaw Health also operates the county's emergency medical services system. The county has more than five dozen medical doctors and nearly two dozen dentists.

Charitable Agencies

Major service and charitable agencies in Kershaw County have over the years joined in cooperative fund-raising as part of the United Way. In 2007 individuals and groups, including businesses and industries, joined a campaign to collect more than six hundred thousand dollars. In the 1980s changing social conditions and attitudes brought about the closing of the half-century-old Margaret C. Mayfield Children's Home, although many other agencies remained to serve families and individuals in crisis. From 1970 through 1988 Wateree Community Actions, Inc., brought together its present partnership joining Kershaw County with Clarendon, Lee, Richland, and Sumter counties to help the poor and disadvantaged achieve self-sufficiency.

Some of the groups addressing the difficulties of persons or situations include the following: the Alpha Center—alcohol, tobacco, and drugs; the Alston-Wilkes Society—offenders, homeless individuals, emotionally disturbed youths; the Board of Disabilities—disabled persons; the Council on Aging—senior citizens; the Family Resource Center—victims of sexual assault; the Family Service Center—financial counseling; the Foster Parent Association—foster children; the Literacy Council—the functionally illiterate and those speaking English as a second language; the Mental Health Association—the mentally ill; the Midlands Crisis Chaplaincy—emergency personnel; Sistercare—abused women and children; and the Teen Health Promotion Coalition—risky teen youths' behaviors.

Boy Scouts and Girl Scouts guide youths in many groups. The Kershaw County Community Medical Clinic provides health care and medicine to the needy, the underinsured, and the noninsured. The Kershaw County Habitat for Humanity assists participants in building affordable, decent housing for themselves. A Habitat Store opened for its benefit in 2008. In many ways community efforts help to improve the quality of life for all.

Arts

Within the last quarter of the twentieth century, the Kershaw County Fine Arts Center (FAC) became an established community entity. Manned at first by a single employee and then by a staff of several, it also involved twenty to thirty teachers and artists as well as hundreds of volunteers. The historic Douglas-Reed House on York Street, which was restored and donated for use as the original

FAC building, continues to be used. In 1982–83 a capital campaign provided for the adjacent Carroll K. Bassett Memorial Building, displaying inside the racing memorabilia and equestrian sculptures of the jockey-artist for whom the building was named. The stable-shaped building also included a performing arts theater with dressing rooms, a visual arts gallery, and office space.

In 1993 a capital campaign doubled the FAC endowment to $1 million, and in 1995 the Daniels Arts Education Building was completed to enhance instruction and studio practice, with spaces for music instruction, dance, visual art, and a clay studio. Programs of the FAC extend into the community and schools as well.

Recreation

Extensive programs of the Kershaw County Recreation Department cater to all age groups. In 2009 the department supervised twenty-two tennis courts, thirty-seven ball fields, twelve soccer fields, four volleyball courts, four walking trails, and a football stadium (Bethune), as well as an aquatic center on Battleship Road that was formerly a YMCA facility. Headquarters are on West DeKalb Street in a former teen canteen building. Recreation classes teach line dancing, the shag, ballroom dancing, square dancing, gymnastics, and yoga as well as sports such as Tae-Kwon-Do, Tai-Chi, golf, and tennis. The department offers summer camps and also organizes clubs with interests such as computers or model airplanes. The old armory on West DeKalb is frequently the location for some of these activities. The department serves physically and mentally disabled children through a variety of activities, including PAL Baseball.

Seasonal sports programs for various ages include the following: spring—baseball and softball; summer—swimming; fall—football, soccer, softball, and volleyball; winter—basketball. The main county parks for personal or competitive Recreation Department activities are Kendall, Seaboard, Scott, and Woodward parks in Camden as well as the Larry Doby Complex, Legion Field, the Kershaw County Aquatic Center, the West Wateree Park, and the Kershaw County West Complex. Other sites include Bethune Recreation Center, the Boyd Young Park, Rhame City Arena, Sandy Grove, the Science Park, and Washington Park.

Sports programs are also operated by some of the county's churches as well as country clubs. White Pines is a public eighteen-hole golf course, and other golf courses operate at Bethune Country Club, Camden Country Club, Green Hill in Lugoff, and Woodcreek Farms in Elgin.

Facing Difficulties

The number of personnel helping citizens face dangers and disasters has increased. The Kershaw County Sheriff's Department in 2008 operated with fifty-four officers and sixty-four patrol cars, and the Camden Police Department had twenty-eight officers and twenty-eight patrol cars. Rescue squads are coordinated through KershawHealth. In 2007 rural fire stations throughout the county were manned by more than fifty full-time and volunteer firemen, and the Camden Fire Department had twenty-five full-time and twenty volunteer firemen operating from two stations. The South Carolina Forestry Commission coordinated additional units for forest fires. The armory on Ehrenclou Drive in Camden has continued to be home to the 108th Signal Battalion of the South Carolina Army National Guard and, as needed, to the South Carolina State Guard. Church groups and community charitable agencies have also provided aid with daily problems as well as during unusual emergencies.

Ice Storms

Among the county's extended dangers and inconveniences, occasional ice storms brought transportation and communication to a halt for days at a time. In early 1979, for example, some areas of the county were without power for a week, and highway cleanup took even longer on back roads blocked by ice-broken trees. In January 1988 another significant snow and ice storm hampered activities for almost a week and claimed three lives. The following month a flu epidemic struck the community, hitting especially hard at schools, the largest of which had up to one hundred absences a day.

Red Fox Road Fire

In 1985 March winds blew across drought-parched soils during a record season of wildfires. On the morning of March 12 a dried branch fell onto a power line, creating sparks that fanned into spreading flames. A racing fire began in the Knights Hill section west of S.C. Highway 97 and swept eastward along the power line. The blaze jumped the highway, burning a path between Clay and Sycamore roads, and then jumped U.S. Highway 521 and continued along the power line corridor and adjoining woods. Attempts to plow firebreaks failed as wind-borne flames jumped from treetop to treetop through the tall pines.

When the conflagration paralleled the rear of Lafayette Village, a wind shift turned it to the southeast, away from the power line and toward Hunt Country and Red Fox Road. Before it was under control the following morning, the fire destroyed eight homes in the Red Fox Road area—most valued between one hundred thousand and three hundred thousand dollars—along with six barns, four vehicles, three horses, and five dogs. Extending to the east side of U.S. Highway 1, the flames burned a swath of several miles and destroyed some two thousand acres. Some 150 professional and volunteer firefighters and an undetermined number of citizens battled the fire, which caused damages in the millions of dollars. It was recognized as the state's worst rural-urban wildfire.

Hurricane Hugo

When television screens showed a massive category-4 hurricane named Hugo bearing down on the South Carolina coast in fall 1989, few Kershaw County residents imagined that it would also wreak unprecedented havoc in the midlands. After a storm surge pushed by winds of 139 mph devastated Charleston and coastal areas, Hugo swept into the midlands, hitting Kershaw County about 3:00 A.M. on September 22.

Darkness obscured damage until daybreak, when citizens were stunned to view the extent of the destruction. The Camden Water Plant had recorded only 2.23 inches of rainfall, but winds had been devastating. DuPont May Plant's wind gauge at least seven times registered winds more than one hundred miles per hour.

The whole city of Camden was without power Friday morning, only 10 percent of which was restored by Saturday. Fairfield Electric Cooperative lost almost its entire system but was able to restore power to most homes by midweek. Black River and Lynches River cooperatives were especially hard hit because the storm wrecked most of the transmission system of Santee-Cooper, their wholesale power supplier. Three-fourths of the Lynches system was down, but all twenty thousand people served by Black River were completely without power and facing lengthy repairs. Food spoiled in refrigerators and freezers, and commercial ice was in such demand that it was virtually unavailable.

Timber damage reached $29 million, and downed trees covered streets and roadways. Of the nearly one thousand miles of damaged roads, only two hundred miles were passable. In most places workers had only chainsaws to clear trees painstakingly one by one. In Camden cleanup crews worked for days from 7:00 A.M. to 7:00 P.M., at first able to clear only one lane of traffic. The enormity of debris required several weeks of removal efforts to clear streets and roadsides.

All Kershaw County's timber and most of its crops were uninsured. From 60 percent to 75 percent of its more than one thousand acres of cotton was ruined, and half of its forty-five hundred acres of soybeans were lost. Although nearly 70 percent of the county's two thousand acres of corn had already been harvested, the remainder had been destroyed.

County industries were hard hit with facility damages and production losses that ran into millions of dollars. Businesses, churches, and homes all suffered, with the most typical damages being to roofs and windows. Materials for repairs ran out and remained in short supply for several months. Some home owners drove hundreds of miles to find stores with tools and equipment for purchase.

The *State* newspaper's special issue "After Hugo: The Long Road Back" reported: "Kershaw County has been declared a disaster area. Estimates say 2,600 mobile homes were damaged, school buildings had $7.7 million in damages and government buildings suffered $40,000 in damages." Among injuries to historic buildings, the Robert Mills Courthouse roof was ravaged, and Liberty Hill's Presbyterian church was among buildings damaged in that area. Special fund-raising followed for repairs and improvements.

Kendall Dam Break

Despite the heavy property damage, advance warnings about Hurricane Hugo limited human loss to one fatality in Kershaw County. A sudden disaster in 1990 resulted in greater loss of life when the Kendall Mill Dam collapsed on October 10 in a deluge of heavy rain. From the broken dam, a wall of water swept down Little Pine Tree Creek, destroying property and bringing death. It took out the back wall of Haile Street Grill and damaged homes and businesses as far as East DeKalb Street. The torrent swept over U.S. Highway 1, carrying two vehicles downstream. Four people perished. Rescue workers were credited with saving other lives.

Other dams throughout the county also gave way in the same tremendous downpour. U.S. Highway 521 was closed temporarily when Colonial Lake dam gave way and Sanders Creek poured over the roadway. Many neighborhoods were flooded, and roads were impassable in several parts of the county.

Amtrak Derailment

When six cars of an eighteen-car Amtrak train derailed on July 31, 1991, near Lugoff in the swamps behind DuPont's May Plant, eight lives were lost and nearly 100 persons were injured. Carrying 426 passengers en route from Florida to Washington, D.C., the train had swiped two empty CSX cars on a side rail after its rear cars suddenly jumped track. The 5:00 A.M. accident, which authorities blamed on a defective switching device, was afterward cited as the worst rail accident in South Carolina history. Injured travelers were treated at Kershaw County Memorial Hospital and at Columbia hospitals. The uninjured were cared for at Camden High School, which was converted into a temporary shelter staffed by American Red Cross workers and school personnel. Local restaurants provided food and drink, and volunteers set up cots and attempted to meet the needs of emergency guests. Early morning darkness and the remoteness of the accident location complicated rescue and cleanup efforts.

Celebrations of Past and Present

Community closeness over the years proved to be a strength for dealing with crises as well as for preserving the quality of daily life. In addition to the continued draw of the Carolina Cup and Colonial Cup events, a number of other

Cub Scouts in the parade at the 1992 Elgin Catfish Stomp. Courtesy of the Camden Archives

activities have been undertaken to bring various residents together in celebration of the past and the present and to showcase Kershaw County's best features to visitors.

Festivals

Several community festivals and events have aided worthy causes while entertaining participants. Elgin in 1975 began the Catfish Stomp, held annually since then. In 1977 the Junior League of Camden began an annual Candlelight Tour of Homes. The following decade Camden's Hot Air Balloon Festival and Lugoff's River Rat Regatta added annual outdoor fun for several years. At the Kershaw County Fine Arts Center a festival held annually for several years attracted large and diverse crowds to enjoy music, art, and drama (MAD) events. A multicultural tea to celebrate African American culture evolved into the annual Heritage Tea in Camden. In 1989 Bethune instituted the annual Chicken Strut, and in most years since 1994 Boykin has held an annual one-of-a-kind Christmas parade that pokes affectionate fun at its country roots. Elgin's centennial in 2008 celebrated its origin, the founding of Blaney.

Heritage tourism expanded further, combining the arts at Historic Camden Revolutionary War Site with annual events beginning with market day and a crafts fair in 1995 and a colonial Christmas celebration in 1998. Musical venues spread from outdoor settings at Historic Camden and the Kershaw County Fine Arts Center to include local restaurants and bars. The lively outdoor music event Jammin in July began in 1996, followed two years later by two other annual events—Bluejeans, Bluegrass, BBQ & Oysters; and the Carolina Downhome Blues Festival. Traditional, popular, and original music were all part of the performances, which invited close contact with audiences.

Historical Ways

Time-honored traditions of community hospitality revived as several old homes in Camden were established as inns or bed-and-breakfast operations. Furnishing old and new homes with historic pieces, many antique businesses worked together to establish a business community with appeal to home folk and visitors alike. Three antique malls and several antique stores opened in Camden, and antique stores operated in other county areas as well.

An important resource in the changing times in Kershaw County has been the Camden Archives and Museum, which expanded in size and services in the

Planners for Wateree River improvement in 2009 examining the rusting, century-old remains of the 1916 flood-destroyed bridge—a sizeable obstacle in the riverbed near Camden. Courtesy of Peggy Ogburn

twenty-first century. A number of local publications, especially those of the Kershaw County Historical Society, encouraged preservation and study of historical places. In 1991, with the Catawba-Wateree Genealogical Society, the historical society published a three-volume survey compiling tombstone information from county cemeteries. The following year the society printed a guide to historic places in the county, supplementing a long-popular guide to Camden sites.[1]

Various groups sponsored historical markers to identify significant sites throughout the county. Most recently added in various areas were the battle monument at Boykin and signs identifying the following: in Camden, the store of E. H. Dibble and the campus of Mather Academy; at Cassatt, the birthplace of Senator Don Holland; at Charlotte-Thompson, the birthplace of Governor John C. West; and at Liberty Hill, Peay's Ferry. Several former school sites were also marked. The Kershaw County Historical Society with the South Carolina Archives sponsored a survey of county sites that was completed in 2002 to identify other rural locations of significance.

From the final quarter of the twentieth century, significant historical restorations and renovations for public purposes included the Bonds Conway House, the Price House, and the Robert Mills Courthouse. Their respective new uses

Horse Branch Hall in Camden, one of the many historic estates that have been restored

were as historical society headquarters, as a community building, and as headquarters for the Chamber of Commerce and Visitors Center. Community volunteers made improvements to Beth-El, Cedars, and Quaker cemeteries in Camden and to many church, community, and private buildings and burial places in the county. A handcrafted reproduction of the King Hagler weather vane was donated by the restorers, Lewis F. and Robert R. Anderson, to replace the fragile original on the repaired town tower in Camden.

Many tours included historic sites, homes, and natural areas. Restorative attention was paid also to the ancient Lafayette Cedar as well as aging oaks. Part of the Wateree River was designated as a Blue Trail, a nature trail on the water. The National Landmark site of the Battle of Camden became the object of renewed efforts to achieve National Park status for the battlefield in order to preserve and interpret it.

As preservation of history gained state and national support, identification of historic districts became significant to help home owners claim incentives for maintenance of their properties. To the National Register of Historic Places, which had already recognized the Camden Historic District, the following were added: in 1978, Liberty Hill; 1982, Kendall Mill; and 1992, Boykin Mill complex. An increased number of individual houses outside the historic areas were also added to the National Register during the period: three houses at Boykin, one outside Camden, and one each at Cassatt and Stoneboro. The Seaboard railroad station was added to the National Register because of its commercial significance, and additional Indian mounds were added to ones recognized earlier. In addition Mulberry was named a National Landmark, and Savage Bay was made a Heritage Preserve. A special initiative identified the county's existing Rosenwald schools, adding them to a multistate listing. The establishment of a National Steeplechase Museum at the Springdale course paid tribute to the area's equestrian history. A number of individuals placed conservation or preservation easements on private properties.

Recognition and preservation of historic places in Kershaw County during the last quarter of the twentieth century and into the twenty-first century included rural and urban sites and areas of multicultural significance. The natural environment and the built environment were recognized, as were private homes, public buildings, schools, churches, commercial places, and military sites. Such range demonstrates the degree to which Kershaw County has tried to preserve benefits of its past while planning for future growth and change.

APPENDIX Kershaw County Places and People

County Boundaries

1682—Area included within Craven County, one of four counties laid out in South Carolina for location of land grants, covering roughly the upper half of the state; lower part of area west of the Wateree River by some designations perhaps within old Berkley County; government centralized in Charleston

1734—Part of the area included in Fredericksburg Township

1769—Area included within the Camden District, one of seven judicial (circuit court) districts; courthouse designated at Camden

1778—Area divided by the Wateree River in the voting districts of new Whig government; the eastern part in the district eastward of Wateree River and the western in the district between Broad and Catawba rivers

1785—Area included in Lancaster County when judicial districts from 1769 divided into York, Chester, Fairfield, Lancaster, Richland, Claremont, and Clarendon counties; courthouse at Lancaster

1791—Kershaw County created from portions of Claremont, Fairfield, Lancaster, and Richland counties; named for patriot Joseph Kershaw; courthouse at Camden; area largely unchanged thereafter except for minor boundary adjustments

1902—Annexation of a southeastern section to newly created Lee County

1977—Annexation of a northeastern section, including the town of Kershaw, to Lancaster County, effective 1978

Township Divisions (from U.S. Census Designations)

1870—Buffalo, Flat Rock, DeKalb, Wateree

1900—Buffalo, Flat Rock, DeKalb, Camden, Wateree

1930—Bethune, Buffalo, Camden, DeKalb, Flat Rock, Wateree, Westville

2004—Buffalo, Flat Rock, DeKalb, Wateree

Cities, Towns, Communities

Municipalities

BETHUNE—Named about 1900 by Seaboard Air Line Railway for local land donor Daniel Murdock Bethune; area settlement earlier known as Lynchwood (1828) and Lyzenby or Lisenby; incorporated in 1901; Population in 2000: 352

CAMDEN—Named in 1768 for Lord Camden (Charles Pratt), who defended colonial interests in the British Parliament; area settlement earlier known as Fredericksburg (royal decree, 1733) or the Waterees; formerly called Pine Tree Hill; chartered in 1769; incorporated in 1791; county seat; population in 2000: 6,682

ELGIN—Named in 1962 special election when Elgin National Watch Company built a plant there; previously named Blaney about 1900 by Seaboard Air Line Railway for a company stockholder; area formerly Jeffers for a postmaster; incorporated about 1910; population in 2000: 2,426

Largest Unincorporated Communities

BOYKIN—Named for area family; mill site since 1780s; railroad siding established 1849

CASSATT—Named about 1900 by Seaboard Air Line Railway for a company executive, civil engineer Alexander Johnston Cassatt

LIBERTY HILL—Named for patriotic colonial spirit; summer-colony origin for planters' families from early 1800s

LUGOFF—Named about 1900 by Seaboard Air Line Railway for N. E. Lugoff, Russian or Prussian native, assistant chief engineer working on the line. Largest unincorporated entity. Population in 2000: 6,278

WESTVILLE—Name in use by about 1890 for an area family or for the "west section" of the sandhills; for a time also called West; a stop on the Charleston, Cincinnati, and Chicago (Three C's) Railroad

Town Formerly in County

KERSHAW—Named in 1888 for Confederate general Joseph Brevard Kershaw; formerly called Welsh's Station (1887) by Three C's Railroad for local land donor Captain James Vergil Welsh; earlier area settlements of Granny's Quarter and Flat Rock. Incorporated in 1888. Originally partly in Kershaw County and partly in Lancaster County; in the latter since 1977 annexation, effective 1978

Voting Places

Precincts and Managers

Selected lists with spellings as found in local newspapers. For antebellum years, an asterisk indicates location has been added or changed since previous list.

1824

Camden Court House—John Doby, Hugh M'Call, C. J. Shannon
Cureton's Mill—E. Cureton, A. Watkins, John Whitaker
Flat Rock—Isaac Knox, David G. Leigh, David Miller
Liberty Hill—John Bell, J. Cunningham, R. Goldsborough
John Lysenby's, Jun., Lynches Creek—M. DeBruhl, A. M'Caskill, B. Williams
Schrocks Mill, on Black River—Benj. M'Coy, Briton Nichol, D. Scarborough

1828

Camden Court House—Joseph Goodman, John G. McCaskill, William McKain
Cureton's Mill—John Motley, William Rabb, George D. Willie
*Dixon's old place—Hollis Horton, James Raily
Flat Rock—John Burgess, jun., Isaac Knox, David G. Leigh
*John Goodwyn's store, White Oak—John Barnes, William Dunlap, Samuel Smyrl
Liberty Hill—Jesse Giles, James McCorkle, Wyatt Patterson
John Lisenby's—Stephen DeBruhl, Allen McCaskill
Schrock's Mill—Benjamin McKoy, John Parker, Robert Turner

1829

*Boykin's Muster Ground—Joseph Belk, Joshua Davis, John Payne
Camden—Joseph Goodman, William M'Kain
Cureton's Mill—David Montgomery, John Motley, William Rabb
Dixon's—William Jones, Robert Kirkly, James Raley
Flat Rock—John Burgess, Isaac Knox, David G. Leigh
Goodwin's Store—John Barnes, William Dunlap, Thomas Smyrl
Liberty Hill—Jesse Giles, James M'Corkle, Wyatt Patterson
Lisenby's—Daniel Bethune, Alexander M'Caskill, Hubbard Tiller
Schrock's Mill—Benjamin M'Coy, John Parker, Robert Turner

1830

Polls—Boykin's Muster Ground, *Buffalo, Camden, Cureton's Mill, Flat Rock, Goodwyn's, Liberty Hill, Lisenby's, Schrock's Mill

1832

Polls—Boykin's Muster Field, Camden, Cureton's Mill, *Dickson's Old Place, Flat Rock, Goodwin's Store, Liberty Hill, Lizenby's, Schrock's Mill

1845

*Buffalo—Burrell Jones, Danl. Mahaffey, Jas. Pate
Camden—J. H. Anderson, C. Davis, William J. Gerald
Cureton's Mill—F. Bowen, D. Motley, John Motley

Flat Rock—Samuel Dunlap, William Fletcher, Joseph Kirkland
Goodwin's—R. Drakeford, James McDowell, J. L. Reid
Liberty Hill—John Brown, James B. Cureton, James Summerville
Lizenby's—Daniel Bethune, Rochelle Blair, Findlay McCaskill
Schrock's Mill—J. Lockhart, B. McCoy, R. Turner

1851
Buffalo—Laban Ferguson, William Mungo, James N. Sowell
Camden—Samuel E. Capers, James J. Villepigue, John J. Workman
Curetons Mills—Frederic Bowen, John Motley, J. P. Richbourg
Flat Rock—James Fletcher, W. G. Kirkland, Jesse Trusdel
Goodwyn Store—William Clyburn, Richard Drakeford, James Love
Liberty Hill—John Brown, Wiley Patterson, Hugh Summerville
Lizenby—James Bell, Daniel Bethune, L. W. R. Blair
Schrock's Mill—B. F. McCoy, Henry Ratcliff, Samuel Smith

1859
Buffalo—William Cato, William Mungo, Gilliam Sowell
Camden—Horatio Brown, John McDowall, John J. McKain
Cureton Mill—Frederick Bowen, Joseph J. Huckabee, Adam Team
Flat Rock—James Fletcher, James B. Hughes, Jesse Trusdel
Goodwyn Store—R. C. Drakeford, R. W. Dunlap, A. J. McDowall
Liberty Hill—A. D. Jones, Wm. C. Johnson, Robert C. Patterson
Lizenby—William King, Alex. McCaskill, Laughlin McPherson
Schrock's Mill—James Arrants, B. L. McCoy, Henry Ratcliff

1864
Buffalo—William Cato, William Mungo, Gilliam Sowell
Camden—John S. Meroney, C. A. McDonald, William McKain
Cureton's Mill—Frederick Bowen, Emanuel Parker, James Team
Flat Rock—James Fletcher, George R. Miller, Jesse Trusdel
Goodwin's Store—Benjamin Cook, John B. Mickle, James H. Vaughn
Liberty Hill—R. B. Cunningham, A. D. Jones Jr., R. C. Patterson
Lizenby's—Daniel McCaskill, Donald McDonald, John McGoughan
Schrock's Mill—B. L. McCoy, Alexander McLeod, Henry Radcliffe

1872
Supervisors of Elections
Appointments by the U.S. Court, naming parties: Democrat (Dem.), Republican (Rep.)

Buffalo—William Cato (Dem.)
Camden—John R. Goodale, John K. Witherspoon (Dem.); E. J. Conway, Frank Goss (Rep.)

Cureton's Mill—E. Parker (Dem.)
Flat Rock—L. B. Stephenson (Dem.); M. A. Wright (Rep.)
Liberty Hill—Daniel Harris (Rep.)
Lyzenby's—Murdoch Bethune (Dem.); S. D. Hough (Rep.)
Raley's Mill—J. M. Kirkley (Rep.)
Red Hill—W. K. Thompson (Dem.); S. D. Denton (Rep.)
Shrock's Mill—Henry Pate (Dem.); Elijah Hall (Rep.)

1876
Places for Tax Collections
Capitalized places were also traditional voting places.

East Wateree (upper county)—Z. Cantey's Plantation, Cedar Rock Place, Cureton's Old Field Place, Dr. Ford's, LIBERTY HILL, Burwell Muse's Place, Patterson's Summerville Place, Jno. Perry's Plantation, Red Hill, Round Top
Northeastern portion—Blair's Old Plantation, BUFFALO, Wm. Clyburn's Store, DuBose's Mill, FLAT ROCK, Shelton Hall's, Jas. Kirkley's Plantation, Knight's Hill, LYZENBY'S, Mungo's Store, Raley's Mill, Sandy Grove Church, SCHROCK'S MILL, Trapp's Mill, Zion Hill
Southern portion—Boykin's Mill [on] Swift Creek, Burrough's Place, Stockton Place
Western Wateree—Wylie Albert's Plantation, Baum's Plantation, Betty Neck, Brevard's Plantation, Cat Fish, Clark's Plantation, Clark's Red Hill Place, CURETON'S MILL, Doby's Mill, J. J. Huckabee's Plantation, Mobly Place, Rock Hill Place, Team's Plantation, Jno. Warren's Old Place

1900
Precincts and Managers of Elections
Capitalized places were traditional voting places for more than seventy-five years.

Antioch—J. J. Bradley, T. P. Brown, C. U. Myers
Brewer's Store—W. F. Brewer, C. A. Denton, John P. Twitty
Buffalo—R. L. Catoe, C. A. Johnson, J. M. Sowell
CAMDEN—J. B. Arrants, H. E. Beard, H. C. Singleton
CURETON'S MILL—C. A. Bowen, John T. Ross, J. M. Thornton
Hanging Rock—B. M. Jones, F. P. Truesdell, O. H. Watson
Kirkley's Store—Alex Brown, H. T. Horton, L. R. Kirkley
Lang's Mills—B. A. Bowen, R. W. Porter, D. E. Spencer
LIBERTY HILL—Edgar Cunningham, E. L. Jones, N. S. Richards
LYZENBY—R. F. Hough, E. B. King, L. W. West
McLean's Branch—J. T. B. Elliott, T. R. Thorne, B. Tidwell
Rabon's X Roads—J. F. Getty, R. T. Mickle, A. B. Rabon
Raleys Mill—E. L. Catoe, M. W. Hough, M. L. Raley

Schrock's Mill—I. F. Holland, Joseph Johnson, Henry Pate
Shaylor's Hill—S. W. Hornsby, J. O. Shaylor, R. L. Smyrl
Stockton Place—G. W. Ammonds, J. O. McCaskill, J. J. Rush

Turkey Creek School House—R. A. Baskins, G. B. King, B. J. Ratcliffe
Westville—T. A. Cauthen, J. A. McDowell, J. T. Young

1914

Voting Addresses of the "Democratic Clubs" and Primary Managers

Abney (Abney School House)—H. T. Horton, D. M. Kirkley, W. R. Outen
Antioch (Gumberry School House)—G. J. Baker, A. G. Bradley, H. C. McLendon
Beaver Dam (Old Hard Shell Baptist Church)—R. A. Jackson, E. W. Rabon, J. A. Rabon
Belk Hill (Trapp's Mill)—D. W. Joye, A. M. McCaskill, C. W. Shiver
Bethune (town hall)—L. W. West, D. T. Yarbrough
Beulah (Cleveland School House)—C. N. Humphries, J. O. Moseley, J. F. West
Blaney (post office)—G. E. Hinson, J. T. Ross, S. E. Ross
Buffalo (Lockhart and Kershaw crossroad)—M. A. Shaw, J. M. Sowell, W. P. Sowell
Camden (opera house)—C. W. Birchmore, Thos. J. Kirkland, L. T. Mills
Cantey (Creeds Store)—W. R. Barfield, J. C. Creed, Louis Hornsby
Cassatt (Seaboard Air Line Depot)—K. D. McCaskill, A. A. West
Doby's Mill (Cherry Bridge Shingle Mill)—B. A. Bowers, John Porter, J. W. Spires
Enterprise (Enterprise School house)—J. K. DeKay, W. L. Hunicutt, C. P. Spradley
Granny's Quarter (T. B. Clyburn's gin house)—J. W. Boone, W. F. Truesdell
Hanging Rock (council room, Kershaw)—B. N. Jones, L. D. Jones
Harmony (Harmony Church)—T. M. Mattox, T. M. McCaskill
Hermitage (office of the Cotton Mill)—W. A. Anderson, W. T. Hasty, W. T. Gardner
Liberty Hill (N. S. Richards's store)—G. R. Clements, H. F. Haile
Lugoff (Seaboard Air Line Depot)—W. J. Burdell, L. I. Guion, James Team
Oakland (Oakland School House)—I. F. Holland, C. L. Pate
Pine Creek Mill (office of the company)—J. D. McCaskill, J. E. Robinson
Pine Tree (Beaver Dam School House)—D. T. Blackmon, Ben Tidwell, J. A. West
Raley's Mill (Raley's Mill)—J. B. Munn, M. L. Raley, Amos West
Roland (West's Mill)—L. S. Spears, H. H. West, W. E. West
Russell Place (Stoneboro post office)—G. F. Hammond, J. R. Lyles

Salt Pond (J. R. Dinkins's gin house)—J. R. Dinkins, Levi Moore, George Watts
Sandy Grove (Sandy Grove Church)—P. B. Fields, Jim Watkins
Shamrock (Shamrock School House)—J. F. Baker, L. J. Baker, T. S. Williams
Shaylors Hill (Shaylors Hill School House)—R. L. Smyrl
Shepard (R. B. Elliott's gin house)—R. B. Elliott, W. E. Hall, W. L. Stokes
Stockton (gin house at Old Quarter)—G. W. Ammons, Belton Owens
Swift Creek (Boykin's Mill)—A. H. Boykin Jr., B. H. Boykin, J. Q. Godwin
Three C's (Three C's School House)—J. Robt Magill, W. J. Young
Twenty Creek (J. L. Hinson's store)—Ed. Barfield, W. E. Kelley, Dan Rabon
Westville (R. L. Bell's store)—T. A. Cauthen, J. C. Hilton, D. G. Fletcher

1916

Precincts and Managers of Elections

National election managers; state election managers
Beaver Dam School House—J. E. Brannon, H. J. Tidwell, W. N. West; J. S. Hyatt, R. C. Pitts, G. K. Price
Bethune—B. W. Brannon, S. T. Gardner, G. H. King; M. G. King, W. A. McDowell, D. T. Yarbrough
Blaney—J. W. Bradley, J. D. McLendon, W. H. Simpson; J. S. Ross, L. B. Sessions, W. H. Wood
Buffalo School House—J. B. Catoe, T. M. Hunnicutt, W. P. Sowell; D. L. Catoe, C. A. Johnson, J. M. Sowell
Camden—J. B. Arrants, W. C. Brown, H. Truesdel; J. R. DeLoache, W. A. Schrock, R. D. Williams
Cantey—R. A. Vaughan, E. C. Watts, A. F. Watts; Henry Barfield, J. E. Creed, S.C. Rose
Cassatt—Kenneth McCaskill, H. S. Thompson, Steve West; L. C. Fortner, L. O. Funderburk, William Thompson
Cleveland School House—E. A. Brown, Z. Z. Barfield, J. F. West; F. H. Arrants, R. A. Bruce, A. B. Shiver
Hermitage Mill—J. L. Campbell, W. T. Player, S. H. Shirley; C. B. Baker, J. J. Munn, P. L. West
Kershaw—James S. Elder, I. R. Hayes, F. L. Truesdel; Amos Cook, John A. McCaskill, G. C. Welsh
Kirkley's Store—W. T. Bowers, A. J. Gregory, R. B. Humphries; H. C. Horton, D. M. Kirkley, Frank Young
Liberty Hill—G. R. Clements, S. H. Cunningham, N. S. Richards; B. F. Floyd, S. M. Richards, L. P. Thompson
Lugoff—B. A. Bowen, B. T. Harrison, W. L. Jones; W. H. Branham, W. L. Kinard, James Team

Mt. Zion Church—Eugene Lee, J. B. McCoy, W. R. Moseley; L. H. Myers, C. U. Myers, J. M. Stokes
Pine Creek Mill—F. S. Shirley, Chas. Noland, Henry West; George Munn, A. E. Robinson, J. T. Truesdel
Rabon's Crossroads—R. A. Jackson, E. W. Rabon, J. M. Smith; English Branham, J. L. Hinson, Eddie Rabon
Raley's Mill—Luther Raley, Minor Raley, W. P. Rodgers; A. P. Gordon, W. T. McCaskill, S. J. West
Ratcliffe Mill—W. F. McCaskill, J. P. Ratcliffe, J. H. Williams; S. B. Hall, H. J. Ratcliffe, N. A. Watkins
Shaylor's Hill—S. W. Hornsby, R. L. Smyrl, L. L. Young; F. E. Holland, J. R. Hornsby, Henry Smyrl
Stockton Place—W. R. Gardner, Jesse Pearce, D. L. Sowell; G. W. Ammons, J. C. Humphries, E. M. Workman
Stokes' School House—P. B. Fields, Amos G. Hall, W. H. Watkins; R. W. Humphries, W. M. Outlaw, L. C. Pate
Stoneboro—J. G. Caston, G. F. Hammond, O. G. Hammond; T. E. Addison, C. V. Hammond, J. T. Moseley
Three C's—J. H. Barfield, J. M. Croxton, J. Robert Magill; Claude Faulkenberry, Boyd Magill, L. F. Robertson
Westville—W. L. Gaskins, W. F. Truesdel, Herbert Young; Foster Hilton, J. A. McDowell, W. C. Thomas

2004

Precincts and Poll Addresses

* = Precinct name for 90 years or more; ** = precinct name for more than 100 years; *** = precinct name for 180 years or more.

Airport (ATEC, Applied Technical Education Center)
**Antioch (Antioch Head Start)
*Bethune (Woman's Club House)
**Buffalo (Mt. Pisgah Elementary School)
***Camden (1. city arena, 2. First Baptist Church, 3. Phelps Auditorium, 4. Catholic church, 5. Fire Dept. substation, 5-A. Old Kirkwood School, 6. Kendall Clubhouse)
*Cassatt (Midway Elementary School)
Charlotte Thompson (Community Center)
*Doby's Mill (Doby's Mill Fire Dept.)
East Camden-Hermitage (Pine Tree Hill School cafeteria)
Elgin (1. Blaney Baptist Church, 2. Blaney Elementary School cafeteria)
Gates Ford (Gates Ford Community Center)
***Liberty Hill (Beaver Creek Fire Dept.)

*Lugoff (1. Lugoff Elementary School, 2. Lugoff-Elgin Middle School, 3. Wateree Elementary School)
Malvern Hill (Malvern Hill Baptist Church)
**Rabon's Crossroads (Pine Grove Fire Dept.)
Riverdale (American Legion Building)
*Salt Pond (Smyrna Methodist Church)
**Shaylor's Hill (Baron DeKalb Elementary School)
Springdale (Northgate Baptist Church)
**Westville (Westville Fire Dept.)
Whites Garden (Emanuel Baptist Church)

Post Offices

Synthesized from postal records in the National Archives and from Robert J. Stets and Harvey S. Teal, *South Carolina Postoffices and Postmasters 1860–65* (Columbia, 1995), and Robert J. Stets, *Post Offices of South Carolina 1865–1980 and Their First Postmasters* (Columbia, 1998). The date following each name is the year in which that postmaster took office. All postmasters are not included. Post offices still operating are capitalized.

Abney—James M. Kirkley (1882). Discontinued mail to Flat Rock, 1884. Reestablished, 1888. James M. Kirkley (1888), Daniel M. Kirkley (1895). To Kershaw, Lancaster County, 1904.

Anniedell—Charles Perkins (1857). Discontinued, 1859.

Antioch—Charles W. Alexander (1886), Charles M. Alexander (1886). Changed to Ionia, Sumter County, 1898. Reestablished, 1899. Charles M. Alexander (1889), Fletcher Sparrow (1901). To Lee County, 1908.

Azmon—Allen McCaskill (1898). To Cassatt, 1907.

Bee Tree—William L. Pickett (1850). Discontinued, 1860.

Bellfield—Formerly Smyrna. Henry E. Beard (1889), John B. Nelson (1894). Discontinued, 1903. To Longtown, Fairfield County.

BETHUNE—Formerly Lynchwood. John E. Copeland (1900), Laurence L. Copeland (1902), Louis W. West (1903), Lonnie K. Yarbrough (19—), Charlie E. Jones (1920), Benjamin R. Thompson (1920), Guy E. Parrott (1921), William R. Rozier (1921)

Blaney—Formerly named Jeffers. Jesse T. Ross (1900). Name changed to Elgin, 1962.

Boykin—Samuel Boykin (1886), Henry Deas (1887), Allen Deas (1894), Allumn M. Reese (1896), William A. Boykin Jr. (1905), Julius M. Green (1905), Mrs. Mattie P. Harling (1923), Mrs. Edna D. Clark (1925). Discontinued, 1973.

Boykin's Depot—Jacob Depass (1849), Thomas J. Jones (1852), Eugene L. Hogan (1853). Discontinued, 1855.

CAMDEN—(Originally as Camden Court House) Phineas Thornton (1820), John N. Gamewell (1843), John A. Gamewell (1852), Thomas W. Pegues (1856), W. D. Anderson (1865), Joseph M. Gayle (1866), John A. Boswell (1869), Edward Brooke (1875), Daniel C. Kirkley (1885), George G. Alexander (1889), Joseph B. Kershaw (1893), Charles J. Shannon (1894), George G. Alexander (1898), Charlie J. Shannon (1902), John R. Goodale (1919), William D. Trantham (1920), William T. Stewart (1924)

Cantey—Jasper A. Watts (1884), Nannie T. Watts (1910), James E. Creed (1911), Charles J. McKenzie (1919). Discontinued, 1921. Mail to Camden.

Carson—Murdock A. Shaw (1903). To Jefferson, Chesterfield County, 1906.

CASSATT—Jacob C. Price (1900), Kenneth D. McCaskill (1907), William J. Davis (1908), William E. Hall (1909), William T. Davis (1910), Mrs. Nannie E. Ballard (1922), William T. Davis (1926), Calvin L. McCaskill (1927), Lottie W. McCaskill (1928)

Cleveland—J. Frank West (1896). To Camden, 1898.

DeKalb—Oran L. Arrants (1889). Rescinded, 1893. [See Kalb.]

Dundee—Johnie M. Porter (1898). To Lugoff, 1905.

ELGIN—Formerly Blaney. James D. Watson (1962).

Elm Grove—James C. Haile (1853), Alison A. McDowell (1854). Discontinued, 1858.

Flat Rock—Jesse Trusdel (1823), James J. Dunlap (1837), Charles M. Breaker (1840), William B. Fletcher (1841), Francis M. Beckham, William G. Kirkland (1850). Discontinued, 1859. Reestablished, 1860. Lemuel B. Stephenson (1860). Discontinued, 1866. Reestablished, 1867. George B. C. Copeland (1867), Jesse Truesdale (1869), James Fletcher (1870), James H. Stephenson (1883), James E. W. Haile (1885), Thomas B. Truesdell (1891), Mattie O. Truesdell (1892), Thomas B. Truesdell (1891), Richard T. Blackmon (1900). Discontinued, 1903.

Grannies Quarter—James Love Sr. (1844). Discontinued, 1850.

Hanging Rock—John U. Ingram (1844), James M. Ingram (1845). Discontinued, 1866.

Jeffcoat—Hubert W. Jeffcoat (1889). Discontinued, 1890.

Jeffers—William T. Jeffers (1898), Jesse T. Ross (1900). Name changed to Blaney, 1900.

Kalb—Lewis W. West (1891), John G. Clark (1891), H. J. Munn (1903), William Gladden (1903), Bessie C. Munn (1903), Sadie V. Munn (1904), John F. Clark (1906), Bessie C. Munn (1908), Henry J. Munn (1910). Discontinued, 1918.

Kershaw—Henry F. Haile (1888). Moved to Lancaster County, 1890. Moved back to Kershaw County, 1930. Hobson B. Taylor (1930). Area annexed to Lancaster County, 1977.

Killgo—Lawrence S. Salmond (1892), James H. Shropshire (1902). To Cantey, 1904. Reestablished, 1908. William Atkins (1908). Discontinued, 1932.

LIBERTY HILL—Robert Goldberg (1830), Wyat Patterson (1838). Discontinued, 1867. Reestablished, 1867. James L. Brown (1867). Discontinued, 1868. Reestablished, 1876. Peter D. Gaither (1876), Darling J. George (1877), Stephen M. Richards (1877), Lily M. K. Richards (1892), Frederick J. Hay (1899), James B. Johnston (1903), William A. Cunningham (1907), Charles D. Cunningham (1918)

Lucknow—Charles B. Sineath (1892), W. A. Gardner (1894), Richard B. Rollins (1894), John D. Hyatt (1901). To Lee County, 1902.

LUGOFF—John N. Jones (1900), Nina J. Jones (1909), Sallie D. Truesdale (1919), Sallie T. Ward (19—)

Lynchwood—Lovick Young (1828), R. McKenzie, Alex Caskill (1833), Alexander McCaskill (1835). Discontinued, 1844. Reestablished, 1845. Samuel P. Murchison (1845), Alexander McDonald (1851), James B. Bell (1852). Discontinued, 1855. Reestablished, 1856. James B. Bell (1856), William A. Yarborough (1859), Daniel Bethune (1859). Discontinued, 1859. Reestablished, 1860. Samuel P. Murchinson (1860), J. P. Boswell (1866). Discontinued, 1866. Reestablished, 1867. Daniel McDonald (1871), Thomas Watts (1875), John A. McLaurin (1880), John E. Copeland (1900). Changed to Bethune, 1900.

Okolona—Jesse E. Pearce (1878), T. McCoy (1880), Wm. T. Hall (1880). Discontinued, 1883. Mail to Camden.

Palmetto—Columbus C. Haile (1853). Discontinued, 1858.

Red Hill—Jesse Kilgore, James R. Dye (1837), Daniel McMillian (1854), Hugh McDowell (1854), Jesse Kilgore (1855), S. Watt Wardlaw (1860). Discontinued, 1866.

Roland—John C. West (1886), William T. Hasty (1888), Willie E. Elliott (1891), John S. Brasington (1892), Samuel A. West (1894), Willie E. Elliott (1902), Henry N. West (1904). To Kershaw, Lancaster County, 1904.

Russell Place—David George (1829), William S. Stinson (1840), Darling George (1845), Nathan Mayblum (1851), Darling J. George (1854), James DeStanley (1856). Discontinued, 1867. Reestablished, 1871. James R. Magill (1871), John B. Magill (1886), James M. Beattie (1891). To Liberty Hill, 1894.

Sandton—John Fletcher, George Fletcher (1839). Discontinued, 1847.

Shamrock—Henry T. Johnson (1892). To Westville, 1895.

Shaylor's Hill—James J. Watkins (1877). Discontinued, 1880.

Smyrna—Lucy Sutton (1886). Changed to Bellfield, 1889.

Stoneboro—Formerly Lancaster County. George O. Hammond (1911), Clyburn B. Williams (1919), Carl V. Hammond (1921). To Heath Springs, Lancaster County, 1935.

Tiller's Ferry—James Tiller (1838), James W. Baskins (1854), Benjamin S. Lucas (1856). Discontinued, 1866. Reestablished, 1867. Joseph Stevens (1867), Elisha W. Hall (1867), Lewis F. Peebles (1877), Daniel W. Gardner (1880), William W. Hearon (1883), Daniel W. Gardner (1886). To Lynchwood, 1894. Reestablished, 1894. Benjamin Norwood (1894), George S. King (1898), Thornwell Thomas (1901), Daniel W. Gardner (1902). To Bethune, 1903.

Timrod—Moses Hough (1886). Discontinued. To Bethune, 1905.

Troy—A. A. McDowell (1869). Discontinued, 1871.

Tupelo—John W. Rose (1898). Rescinded, 1900.

Turkey Creek—Wiley Kelly (1834). Discontinued, 1858.

Welsh's Mill—James Welsh (1879), James E. Truesdell (1881), John Falkenberry (1881). Discontinued, 1890. Mail to Kershaw.

West—John C. West (1888), Henry F. Haile (1888), Thomas C. Stover (1890). Changed to Westville, 1890.

WESTVILLE—Formerly West. John C. West (1890), Reuben L. Bell (1891), Nannie A. Shannon (1897), Reuben L. Bell (1901)

Zemp—Thomas E. Sineath (1892). "Never in operation," rescinded, 1895.

Church Cemeteries

Locations of the following are in the Kershaw County, South Carolina, Cemetery Survey. If a church is no longer extant, its last vestige may be a cemetery, often near the site of an old congregation. Records of some of these churches, and some others as well, may be found in the Works Progress Administration (WPA) Inventory of Church Records.

Baptist

These church-cemetery names end in "Baptist Church"—Abney, Antioch, Beaver Creek, Beaverdam, Belmont, Bethany, Bethel Hill, Bethlehem, Bethune, Blaney, Broom Hill, Buffalo, Cantey/Canty Hill, Cassatt, Cedar Rock, Concord, Cooks, Cool Springs, Cooper Hill, DeKalb, Emmanuel, First Calvary, Flat Rock, Flint Hill, Fort Clark, Foxhill, Gaines, Good Aim, Green Hill, Gumspring, Hardshell, Harmony ("West," Elgin), Harmony ("East," Sandy Grove), Hermitage, High Hill, Hyco, Liberty Hill First, Lugoff First, Macedonia, Malvern Hill, Mills Creek, Mt. Hebron Freewill, Mt. Joshua, Mt. Olive, Mt. Olivet, Mt. Pilgrim, Mt. Pisgah, Mt. Prospect, Mt. Zion, Nazareth, New Grove, New Testament Mission, Oak Ridge, Oak Springs, Parker, Pine Grove (Lugoff), Pine Grove (Mt. Pisgah), Pleasant Hill, Providence, Red Hill, Refuge, Rock Hill (Liberty Hill), Rock Hill (Lugoff), St. John (Liberty Hill), St. John (Lee Co. line), St. Matthew, St. Stephens, Sand Hill Heights, Sanders Creek, Sandy Level, Scott Hill, Shamrock, Springvale, Sutton Branch, Sweet Home, Swift Creek.

Holiness
These church-cemetery names end in "Holiness Church"—Believers Temple, Bible Holiness Mission, El Bethel Pilgrim, Highway Pentecostal, New Jerusalem, (Deliverance) Tabernacle.

Methodist / A.M.E.
These church-cemetery names end in "Methodist Church"—Bethel, Beulah United, Damascus, Ebenezer United, Emmanuel United, Ephesus United, Mt. Joshua United, Mt. Prospect/ United, Rock Hill, Rock Springs United, St. John United, St. Matthew United, St. Paul/United, St. Peter United, Salem United, Sandy Grove United, Shiloh/United, Smyrna, United, Wesley Chapel United. These church names end in "A.M.E. Zion": Bingham Chapel, Ebenezer, Good Hope, James Chapel, Mt. Bethel, Mt. Sinai, Shady Grove, Zion Hill.

Presbyterian
The original Presbyterian church at Camden had a cemetery, and these church-cemetery names end in "Presbyterian Church"—Beaver Creek, Liberty Hill, Messiah (Liberty Hill Second).

Others
Also listed with cemeteries are Beth El (Jewish), Catoe Chapel Church of God, Community Bible Church, Faith Temple Church, Friendship Church, Long Branch Church, and McLeans Branch Church.

Public Schools

Sometimes the school was named for the community; sometimes the community, for the school.

1867–70
Compiled from research of Harvey S. Teal, *Public Schools, 1868–1870 (Education during Reconstruction in Kershaw County, S.C.)* Camden, S.C.: Harvey S. Teal, 2004). School name is followed by a location, if given.

Designated "Colored"
Dickerson (4 miles west of Camden), Dry Branch/Creek (Granny's Quarter Creek), Enterprising (8 miles southeast of Camden), Flat Rock, Marengo (present Goodale State Park), Pleasant Hill (present Cassatt area), Red Hill (south of Liberty Hill), Rock Hill (west of the Wateree), Rock Springs (Flat Rock Township), Sink Springs, Stephenson (6 miles below Camden), Well-Behave (Lugoff area), Whittemore (Boykin area at Rafton Creek)

Designated "White"
Beaver Dam (present Cassatt area), Bethel (Beaver Creek), Browns (Liberty Hill), Central (Sandy Grove), DeKalb (Camden), Flat Rock, Floras Branch

Seminary (Buffalo Township near Sandy Grove), Grannies Quarter (headwaters of Flat Rock and Grannies Quarter creeks), Hard Shell (Buffalo Township), Mackville (Flat Rock Township), McCoy (Stagecoach Road, near intersection from Cassatt), Mill Branch (Buffalo Township), Pear or Pea Ridge (Flat Rock Township), Ray/Roy Springs (10 miles east of Camden), Sandy Grove, Shiloh, Troy (Flat Rock Township), Turkey Creek (Camden to Darlington road)

Rural School Locations, circa 1938
Compiled from the 1938 S.C. highway map for Kershaw County

Lower West Wateree—black: Concord, Green Hill, Lugoff, Weeping Mary; white: Crescent
Upper West Wateree—black: Cooke, Hopewell, Johnson, Mickle, Mt. Joshua, Oak Grove, Parker, Wateree (abandoned), Wood; white: Pine Grove
Upper East Wateree—black: Bethel, Ebenezer, Flat Rock, Good Hope, Kirkland, Knight's Hill, Liberty Hill, Red Hill, Stonesboro, Truesdell (abandoned), Westville, Zion Hill; white: Pleasant Grove, Stonesboro, Thorn Hill
North—black: Buffalo, Hardshell, Lockhart, West Branch, Witty; white: Baron DeKalb, Gates Ford, Midway, Mill Creek, Mt. Pisgah, Ned's Creek, Oak Ridge, Pleasant Grove, Shamrock
South and east of Camden—black: Antioch, Black River, Cassatt, Mt. Zion, Nickmas, St. Matthews; white: Antioch, Boykin, Central, Charlotte Thompson

Public Schools 1900–1950
Various public records, newspapers, and/or other contemporary references document the existence of the following public schools, all racially segregated, during at least some of these years. Includes Harvey S. Teal's research from the annual reports of the state superintendent of education, school directories of the State Department of Education, and other sources (* = at least some of the time, a "joint school" with an adjoining county).

Designated "Colored"
Airport, Antioch, Bell Branch, Bethel, Bethune, Black River, Blaney, Blooming, Boykin/s, Buffalo, Cantey Hill, Cassatt, Cedar Rock*, Concord, Cook/Cooke/Cooks, Cool Spring, DeKalb, Dusty Bend, Ebenezer, Emmanuel, Ephesus, Flat Branch, Flat Rock, Fort Clark, Good Hope, Green Hill, Gumberrry, Hardshell, Hickman, Hopewell, Horton, Hyco, Jackson Graded & High, Johnson, Kershaw*, Killgo, Kirkland, Kirkwood, Knights Hill, Liberty Hill, Lockhart, Long Branch, Lugoff, McKnight, McLeod, Mickle, Mill Branch, Mill Creek, Mt. Joshua, Mt. Pisgah, Mt. Prospect, Mt. Zion, Ned's Creek, Nickmas, Oak Grove, Oak Ridge, Parker, Pine Ridge, Pine Tree, Pleasant Grove,

Pond/s, Prince Edward/s*, Red Hill, Rock Hill, Rock Spring/s, St. John*, St. Matthew/s Graded & High & Training, St. Paul's, Shepard, Smyrna, Stoneboro*, Stoney Hill, Sweet Home, Swift Creek, Truesdell, Wateree, Weeping Mary, Wesley Chapel, West Branch, Westville, White Oak, W(h)itty, Wood/s, Zion Hill

Designated "White"

Abney, Antioch Graded & High, Baron DeKalb Graded & High, Beaver Creek, Beaver Dam, Bethel, Bethune Graded & High, Blaney Graded & High, Bloomingdale, Blythedale, Boykin, Brannon, Buffalo, Camden Graded & High, Cantey/Hill, Cassatt, Cedar Creek, Cedar Rock*, Central, Chalk Hill, Charlotte Thompson Graded & High, Cleveland, Concord, Cook, Crescent, Cureton's Mill, DeKalb, Flat Rock, Gates Hill/ Ford, Gettys, Green Hill, Gum Spring/s, Gumberry, Hanging Rock, Hardshell, Harmony, Hickory Head, Highland/ Hyland, Indian Ford, Kershaw Graded & High*, Kirkley's Mill, Liberty Hill, Line Academy, Lockhart, Lugoff, Malvern Hill, McLeod, Midway Graded & High, Mill (Mill Village/Factory), Mill Creek, Mt. Pisgah Graded & High, Mt. Zion, Ned's Creek, Oak Grove, Oak Ridge, Oakland, Old Field, Piedmont, Pine Grove, Pine Tree, Pine Tree (Hill), Pleasant Grove, Providence, Ratcliff, Red Hill, Ridgeside/ville, Russell Place, Sand Hill, Savannah, Shamrock, Shannon Lane, Shaylor's Hill, Shepard, Stockton, Stoneboro*, Swift Creek, Team, Thorn/e Hill, Three C's, Timrod, Trinity, Truesdale/Truesdel/l, Turkey Creek*, Wateree, Westville, Whitty (Witte), Yarborough

High School Consolidations by Attendance Areas

1940, Charlotte Thompson to Camden. 1957, Antioch to Camden. 1966, Midway to Camden and St. Matthew to Jackson. 1970, Camden and Jackson combined as Camden. 1972, Blaney and Lugoff-area Camden students to new Lugoff-Elgin High. 1976 upper county students to new North Central High. 1997 Bethune to North Central and Camden.

Unified Schools Listed in Federal Desegregation Plan, 1970–71

Bethune, Blaney, Boykin, Camden, Cantey, Cassatt, Cedar Grove, Central, Charlotte Thompson, Concord, Crescent, DeKalb, Flat Rock, Gate's Ford, Hanging Rock, KC Vocational Center, Kershaw, Liberty Hill, Lockhart, Lugoff, Mt. Pisgah, Ned's Creek, Oak Ridge, Piedmont, Pleasant Grove, Providence, Rabon's Crossroads, Thorn Hill, Three C's, Trinity, Westville, Yarborough

Kershaw County Schools, 2010

ATEC (Applied Technology Education Campus), Baron DeKalb, Bethune, Blaney, Camden, Continuous Learning Center, Doby's Mill, Jackson, Leslie M. Stover, Lugoff-Elgin, Midway, Mt. Pisgah, North Central, Pine Tree Hill, Wateree

Twentieth-Century War Dead

From American Legion Rolls of Honor

World War I

Ben D. Abbott, John F. Arthur, James G. Bailey, Malcolm A. Bateman, James Leroy Belk, George Bolden, Bill Bonepart, Joseph J. Boone, George Boyd, Joseph Brooks, Henry T. Brown, J. Alfred Burdell, Julian Burrows, Luther Caldwell, George Clyburn, Henry T. Cook, Nathaniel Cunningham, Edward Davis, Pat W. Davis, William Bratton deLoach Jr., Lelan Dinkins, Robert Edgefield, David L. Gambell, Oscar Gardner, Ed Gee, Mendel L. Gladden, Gillam A. Hall, Furman B. Hilton, Swilley H. Hinson, Fred Hough, Willie K. Humphries, Walter Haile Johnson, Sidney N. King, Thomas G. Kirkland, Walter M. Lloyd, James M. McLain, Eben J. McLeod, John D. McLester, William McNeal, Cleveland Outlaw, Furman Peebles, Stephen M. Richards, Sam Sanders, Moses Shannon, John Smith, Harrington H. Stokes, A. Massenburg Trotter, Walter West, Henry Williams.

World War II

Pinkney Alexander, Calhoun Ancrum, Roscoe F. Baker, Ernest Z. Baskins, William D. Baxley, Fowler Boone, Harold R. Boykin, Henry S. Brown, William J. Brown, Milas C. Byrd, Thomas W. Byrd, Ivey K. Connell, Henry E. Cooper, Theodore R. Cooper, Wilber D. Copeland, William Aiken Croxton, James E. Cureton, George E. Dixon Jr., John C. Dixon, Henry Drakeford, Frank S. DuBose, Elmer Ellis, Edward L. Faulkenberry, Wesley E. Faulkenberry, Willie Banyan Ford, Robert L. Freitag, Hugh M. Gettys, Hugh P. Godwin, James Graham, Amos Gregory, Reese B. Hall, Vernon Hall, Grover A. Hawkins, Thomas S. Hendrix, Marvin P. Henry, Ernie L. Hinson, Robert Hinson, Henry B. Holland, Milton E. Horton, Joseph S. Hough, Conder Hunter, Albert H. Isbell, Henry Y. Jackson, John F. Jenkins Jr., Paul Jordan, William T. Lindenzweig, Otis Linton, Edward S. Lorick, William Clyburn Mackey, William R. Marsh, James Mickle, William T. McCoy, Havard McDonald, Harvie McKenzie, Purvis B. Morgan, James C. Munn, John Murphy, James Raymond Outlaw, Stewart C. Outlaw, Henry C. Rabon, Langford Rabon, Curtis R. Raley, David W. Reynolds, Edmand G. Roberts, Gilbert E. Roberts, Wilbert L. Roberts, Lemuel C. Robertson, Clifford Robinson, Jesse C. Rose Jr., Alva J. Rush Jr., Woodrow F. Sanders, Everett R. Shaw, James T. Shirley, Arthur T. Simpson, Thomas C. Snyder, Berkley Sowell, James N. Sowell, John G. Sowell, Boykin Stoney Jr., James C. Thorne, Mendel L. Threatt, Francis C. Truesdale, Raymond L. Truesdale, Robert E. Turner, Thomas J. Turner, Christopher C. Vaughn, John M. Villepigue Jr., Oliver Vincent, Abraham Wade, Robert L. Warr, Grover C. Watts, Thomas Racine West, Andrew G.

Whitaker Jr., Clyde I. Williams, Fred B. Williams, Edward Willis, Joseph B. Young.

Korean War

English W. Allen, Vernon C. Faulkenberry, Herbert H. Hornsby, Leroy S. Horton Jr., Lawrence Jones, Robert W. Littlejohn, Paul V. McDowell, Stanley McManus, Cecil G. Newman, William N. Player, Edward J. Taylor, F. Shannon Zeigler.

Vietnam War

Grover Coleman Bowers Jr., Dan Bradford Jr., Michael Christmas, Eddie Frazier, Terry Hearon, Leroy Hopkins Jr., Matthew Hough, Ruben Harold Humphries, Larry Jeffers, Eugene Nelson, Walter A. Samans Jr., Harry Lee Sowell, Jack Thomas Jr., Jerry Whitaker, Dan Williams Jr.

Designations of Historic Places

National Historic Landmarks

Bethesda Presbyterian Church, Camden Battlefield, Mulberry Plantation (James and Mary Boykin Chesnut House)

National Register Historic Sites and Districts

Adamson Mounds Site, Belmont Neck Site, Bethesda Presbyterian Church, Boykin Mill Complex, Camden Battlefield, Zachariah Cantey House, Carter Hill, City of Camden Historic District, Cool Springs, Thomas English House, Historic Camden Revolutionary War Restoration, Kendall Mill Historic District, Liberty Hill Historic District, Benjamin McCoy House, McDowell Site, Midfield Plantation, Mulberry Plantation, Russell-Heath House, Seaboard Air Line Railway Depot

Population Totals

1800	7,340	1910	27,094
1810	9,822	1920	29,398
1820	12,429	1930	32,070
1830	13,545	1940	32,913
1840	12,281	1950	32,287
1850	13,473	1960	33,585
1860	13,086	1970	34,727
1870	11,754	1980	38,887
1880	21,539	1990	43,599
1890	22,361	2000	52,647
1900	24,696	2010	58,861 (projected)

NOTES

Chapter 1. Landscapes

1. The South Carolina Geological Survey (Columbia, S.C.) and the Carolina Geological Society (Chapel Hill, N.C.) regularly publish guidebooks to field studies in the Carolinas, some directly relevant to Kershaw County. Studies of the area have related to topics such as the Carolina Terrane, an exotic volcanic arc, the slate belt, the Ridgeway-Camden gold belt, the Camden fault, the Liberty Hill pluton, mineral deposits, and water quality. L. R. Gardner and D. T. Secor, Department of Geological Sciences, University of South Carolina (USC), Columbia, led the Geological Tour of Richland and Kershaw Counties as part of the USC Bicentennial on October 27, 2001. The South Carolina Department of Health and Environmental Control and the South Carolina Department of Natural Resources provide valuable environmental information.

2. Ernst and Merrens, "Camden Turrets," 561. This study asserts that Camden was more oriented toward land travel and proposes that the geographic fall line position was relatively inconsequential. Our history, from a broader perspective, views the fall line position as significant to Native American habitation and trading paths, leading to establishment of the trading posts around which early Camden developed. Use of the river and contemporary belief in the economic importance of river travel are observed in the focus of postcolonial and later transportation improvements.

3. A number of large cities grew up along the Atlantic fall line, especially when waterpower could be harnessed to meet the needs of the immediate area. These include Columbia, S.C.; Philadelphia, Pa.; Baltimore, Md.; Washington, D.C.; Richmond, Va.; and Augusta, Ga. The relatively slower and smaller growth of Camden in comparison to these cities at the beginning of the age of electrical power may have been affected by the position of the Wateree Dam at a distance of nearly nine miles to the north rather than immediately accessible at Camden's boundaries.

4. The Lynches system is today identified as two *rivers:* the eastern fork as Big Lynches River at the border of the county, and the western as Little Lynches River. Over various times in the past, the two rivers, especially Little Lynches, have been called *creeks.* In addition some earlier maps reversed the labeling of the two forks, erroneously placing Big Lynches at the left and Little Lynches at the right.

5. The name of the preserve honors Henry Savage Jr., a Camden civic leader and naturalist author who urged preservation of such habitats. See Savage, *Mysterious Carolina Bays.*

6. This history undertakes to cover the area that eventually became and now remains Kershaw County, as well as sections once part of Kershaw County until they were separated into other counties.

7. *South Carolina: Resources and Population, Institutions and Industries* (Charleston, S.C.: Walker, Evans & Cogwell, 1883), 702. A few years later the trading settlements at Flat Rock and Welsh's were absorbed into the development of a new town, Kershaw, incorporated in 1888.

Chapter 2. Footpaths

1. Dr. Albert C. Goodyear, a research professor at the S.C. Institute of Archaeology and Anthropology at the University of South Carolina, has led excavations at the Topper Site in Allendale County since 1998, publishing and speaking on the work. The Allendale discoveries are reported not only to be pushing back dates of early man's habitation of America but also to be challenging accepted belief that all Native Americans descended from ancestors who crossed the once-exposed land bridge between Asia and America. Data from this period in Kershaw County have not been systematically isolated and studied.

2. Later chapters discuss contemporary discoveries of artifacts and remains. Chapter 8 and chapter 3, note 4, discuss a map by the nineteenth-century Camden medical doctor William Blanding that includes sites of remains. See Squier and Davis, "Ancient Works." The original copy of Blanding's circa 1845 map, slightly more detailed than the published version, is in the Library of Congress. Contemporary features such as the Wateree River bridge, boatyard, and ferry appear on the manuscript copy (c. 1845) but not on the print copy. George Erwin Stuart, "Some Archeological Sites in the Middle Wateree Valley, South Carolina" (M.A. thesis, George Washington University, June 1970), reprints the original map and revisits sites. Another study of the Smithsonian map and modern counterparts is Bierer, *Discovering South Carolina,* 41–49.

The Wateree Archaeological Research Project (WARP) of the University of South Carolina, first defined in 1984, conducts ongoing field study of "human-land relationships in the Wateree River Valley utilizing a wide range of approaches, including anthropology, archaeology, geography, history, folklore as well as the natural sciences."

3. Steen, *Stoneboro,* 2–8.

4. Individual discoveries of random fossil remains and fossilized exotic trees have been reported in the local press occasionally over various decades but not systematically uncovered or linked to a particular site.

5. Private collecting of local relics continues. See, for example, Amy Delpo, "Photo Essay," and Will Deane, "Indian Relics," in *Legacy II,* ed. Inabinet and Inabinet, 6–7; and Norman Myers Fohl, *Indian Relic Hunting in the Vicinity of Camden, South Carolina* (Camden, S.C., 1944). See also displays and collections in the Camden Archives, Camden, S.C. In 2010 some area collections were displayed in Camden in shows of the Piedmont Archaeological Society of North Carolina and South Carolina.

6. European settlers readily adapted to the advantages of the native dugout. In the late twentieth century such a cypress dugout, fashioned for eighteenth-century plantation use, was found submerged in the Pee Dee Swamp and was donated to the Historic Camden Revolutionary War Site in Camden, where it is displayed.

7. The interpretation of the Mississippian presence follows documentary and field research of the WARP of the University of South Carolina. Among archaeologists who have been working in the Camden area and who have published and lectured there on findings related to these people are Chester B. DePratter, Chris Judge, and Gail E.

Wagner. See, for example, Chester B. DePratter, "Cofitachequi: Ethnohistorical and Archaeological Evidence," in *Studies in South Carolina Archaeology: Essays in Honor of Robert L. Stephenson,* ed. Albert C. Goodyear III and Glen T. Hanson (Columbia: University of South Carolina Press, 1989), 133–50. Wagner, in continual fieldwork in the Mulberry area since 1990, has compiled evidence of the diets and lifestyles of the prehistoric and historic dwellers. Developing another perspective is Gene Wadell in *Carologue* 16 (Autumn 2000), 8–15, a publication of the South Carolina Historical Society. An archivist at the College of Charleston and a past director of the South Carolina Historical Society, Wadell uses largely documentary and linguistic evidence to propose that the Cofitachiqui assimilated as Catawba Indians and were Siouan speakers. Other researchers suggest that their language group was Muskogean.

8. Scarcer materials from the late Woodlands period suggest to some authorities that the Woodlands people declined or left the area for a time, although other theories suggest that they were physically driven away by the Mississippians. Other interpretations suggest that some Woodlands people remained in the area coexisting with Cofitachiqui people, over time mingling influences evidenced in local tribes known in historical time.

9. Because the written records related to these people were not produced by them and are limited in scope, the time may be referred to as "protohistoric."

10. In 1935 Congress created the U.S. De Soto Commission to map the route as an observation of the expedition's four hundredth anniversary. In 1939 the commission's study concluded that the main Cofitachiqui town was centered below Augusta on the South Carolina side of the Savannah River. However, later archaeological excavations indicated that the Mississippians had left that area before the Spanish arrived.

11. To identify specific locales, scholars are searching descriptions relayed by different scribes who accompanied Hernando de Soto or who wrote about the expedition later. In 2009 the archaeologist Val Green told the authors that his research leads him to agree that Mulberry was a part of the chiefdom at the time but that the principal town where De Soto met the Cofitachiqui was near Fort Watson in an area now mostly under Lake Marion.

12. Various legends are attached to this escape and to the fate of the chieftainess of Cofitachiqui.

13. John Lawson, *History of North Carolina* (Charlotte, N.C.: Observer Printing House, 1903). When originally printed in London in 1714, Lawson's writing carried the title *History of Carolina.* The 1903 work was published from a copy in the North Carolina Archives for the purpose of making public "the first real history of North Carolina." The publication, however, also includes travels in areas now in South Carolina.

14. Lawson was not the first contemporary Englishman to take this route inland and visit the Kershaw County area, according to the archaeologist Val Green, who in a January 19, 2003, lecture at Historic Camden described Lawson's route and the ongoing research of his journey. Green also referenced an unpublished journal of another traveler who took the same route two years earlier.

15. Here and throughout the rest of this history the word "plantation" will often be used in the contemporary sense of "a place that is planted."

16. Some authorities believe that the Wateree and the Catawba were displaced to the Kershaw County area by subsequent warfare, while other authorities contend that, as

descendants of the Woodlands Indians, they may have maintained some local presence for ages. For a compilation of documents and material related to the Wateree Indians, see Wes White (Tauchiary), with Charles W. Carroll, "A History of the Wateree Indians: 1566–1770," a manuscript in the Camden Archives.

17. The discussions of English contacts have purposely omitted John Lederer, whose name is mentioned often in early histories of this area. More-recent scholarship indicates that Lederer did not himself travel local parts of the Carolina interior and did not have the firsthand contacts he claimed with native people of interest to this history.

Chapter 3. Axes and Boundaries

1. Systematic archaeological study has not been conducted along the local shores of the Lynches River, although early stone relics and pottery from the area as well as nineteenth-century memoirs reveal a Native American presence. Located between other known settlements, however, the area no doubt attracted migratory or hunting camps over various periods of time. A small number of Kadapaw (possibly a variant of "Catawba") Indians lived in the area by the 1800s and called the Lynches the "Kadapaw."

2. For the standard scholarly local histories, see Kirkland and Kennedy, *Historic Camden: Colonial and Revolutionary* and *Historic Camden: Nineteenth Century.* These works have several times been reprinted by the Kershaw County Historical Society, Camden, S.C., and sometimes appear as parts 1 and 2 or as volumes I and II. For a combined, fuller index, see McKain, *Index to Historic Camden.*

3. Meriwether, *Expansion,* 99.

4. Accounts refer to a fierce battle and peace treaty between the Catawba and the Cherokee, prior to white settlement, which resulted in the tribes' keeping the Catawba/Wateree River as a boundary between them. See Alexander Gregg, *History of the Old Cheraws* (1867; repr., Spartanburg, S.C.: Reprint Co., 1965), 3–4. Some accounts say that the boundary was the Broad River. The tribes are said to have piled stones as a monument to their dead and in recognition of their agreement. Perhaps such a monument appears on Dr. William Blanding's circa 1845 map in Squier and Davis, "Ancient Works," one reprint of which is in Bierer, *Discovering South Carolina,* 42. On the map a hilltop west of the Wateree indicates piled rocks, marked "Indian Grave." Bierer, 49, says that the site is Buck Hill and includes a photograph of rocks there.

5. The traders were often referred to as "fur traders" since peltry was the most lucrative aspect of their business. In Carolina this mainly included deerskins.

6. John Lawson, *A New Voyage to Carolina* (London, 1709; electronic ed., North Carolina Collection, University of North Carolina at Chapel Hill), 184–85.

7. Some accounts report that they allied with the Spanish in this offensive.

8. The 627-acre Congaree Creek Heritage Preserve, bordering the Congaree River and Cayce opposite Columbia, documents the long history of that area. Two miles north of the "Old Fort," in 1748 the British built a second Fort Congaree to protect against Ohio Iroquois raiders. During the Revolutionary-era Fort Granby was established.

9. In the Revolution the Catawba supported the patriots; during the Civil War they fought as Confederate soldiers; and they have served as other American citizens have since that time.

10. The surveys were completed on July 3–4, 1775, one year prior to the signing of the Declaration of Independence.

11. Nine townships were established in South Carolina. In addition to Fredericksburg, these were Amelia, Kingston, New Windsor, Orangeburg, Purrysburgh, Queensborough, Saxe Gotha, and Williamsburg,

12. The area nominally lay within Prince Frederick's Parish, formed in 1734 to include the interior of Carolina, with a single parish church at coastal Georgetown.

13. A hand-drawn copy of the plat was executed by Thomas J. Kirkland, whose maps illustrate (without acknowledgment to him) both histories by Kirkland and Kennedy. Various drafts of these maps are in the Thomas J. Kirkland Papers, South Caroliniana Library, University of South Carolina, Columbia.

14. In the outlying areas drawn on his plat, St. Julian's shortened perspectives of distances, omission of distinctive meandering necks of the Wateree, and distancing of creeks along the river reveal his presentation of these features to be representative and generalized rather than specifically surveyed.

15. Edward B. Latimer, "Some Creeks Named by William Saunders," in *Names in South Carolina,* ed. Neuffer, 9:5–6.

16. Ibid. Latimer cites a source stating that Saunders came to the state in "about . . . 1735." (St. Julian's survey is dated 1734.)

17. Kirkland and Kennedy, *Historic Camden: Colonial and Revolutionary,* 42–43. Ex post facto law voided prior and future purchases of lands from Indians.

18. Strouds were highly desired trade-cloths because they could support ornamental beadwork, could be fringed, or could be made into clothing, shawls, or blankets. White blankets could be dyed to taste.

19. Brown must not have thought his deal a danger, however, for he remained committed to his same community and to his Indian wife and children, even when other traders followed changing times and moved westward. In 1735 new settlers moving into the Congarees protested that Brown's trading post was a "nuisance" because of the people it attracted.

20. Kirkland and Kennedy, *Historic Camden: Colonial and Revolutionary,* 67.

21. Ibid., 68; Meriwether, *Expansion,* 100. The men were a hardy group, however. According to records in the South Carolina Department of Archives and History (hereafter SCDAH), they all were alive to pursue titles at the end of ten years when the quitrent exemption expired. They all filed surveys about midcentury when settlers were arriving in large numbers. By then at least two of them had leased out their land and finalized its sale after receiving titles.

22. Kirkland and Kennedy, *Historic Camden: Colonial and Revolutionary,* 40. Here mapmakers continued for some time to mark the location of an "Indian town," at the site where later cotton mills operated and beside present Kendall Lake, earlier known as Factory Pond. The curious fact that Factory Pond appears to have had its name before the first manufacturing facility was erected there may suggest that the name actually attaches to a colonial meaning of "factory"—a trading post for a trader, or "factor." Such could be consistent with the site's long association with an Indian village. Area property was first owned by William Ancrum and Lambert Lance, partners in the Charleston

firm that Joseph Kershaw later represented in his Pine Tree Hill store, the nucleus of early Camden.

23. Kirkland and Kennedy, *Historic Camden: Colonial and Revolutionary,* 67–71, includes a map by the authors. See also Meriwether, *Expansion,* 99–109; and Janie Revill, *Sumter District* (Columbia, S.C.: State, 1968), 14–18.

24. Revill, *Sumter District,* 20.

25. A legend is frequently retold that the Jumping Gully in the Wateree Swamp received its name when the Tory Daniel McGirtt escaped from patriot pursuers by jumping over the gully astride his beloved steed Gray Goose. In fact, the name Jumping Gully is found on maps predating the Revolution. Part of the legend is that McGirtt, a devoted horseman, was a loyal patriot until efforts were made to appropriate his horse for military purposes.

26. William Faden, *A Map of South Carolina and a Part of Georgia* (London: William Faden, 1780), in the Historical Map Collection of the University of Alabama.

27. Many stories describe how creeks were named. Oral tradition says a respected and much-frequented midwife (a "granny-woman") had her home-section ("quarter") on Granny's Quarter Creek. The old term may refer to a hunting camp or trader's post, as Lawson also uses "quarters" for a shelter used by travelers in the owner's absence. Ideas that the name refers to "slave quarters" can be dismissed by the fact that the name was in use prior to plantations in the area. Speculation has been made that "Granny" is a misspelling of "Gray," the name of an early resident (or Graves, such as Graves Ford of the Wateree). Mills's 1825 map named the location "Gray's Quarters." However, the misspelling is a cartographer's error since the stricter authorities of land deeds consistently use a form of "Grannies" (Grannies', Granny's, Granny, Grany's, Grany, Granney, Granney's, Graney, Graney's, Grannie, etc.).

Beaver Creek, White Oak Creek, Flat Creek, and Gum Swamp derived names descriptive of their settings, while Spears and Wrights were early settlers whose names lingered. Camp Creek has been variously reported to be the seasonal site of an Indian camp and a frontier hunting camp. The story is also told that country folk coming to Camden to trade regularly camped there overnight, just outside Camden, before proceeding into town early in the morning to transact their business.

Jumping Run (Gully) west of the Wateree once adjoined another branch, Swimming Run, and the two crossing the road from the Congarees no doubt described conditions that horsemen expected at those points. Sawney's Creek has been suggested in association with the Indian tribe Shawnee, though no close connection has been found as the tribe was not locally present. "Sawney," a colloquial reference to Scots-Irish ancestry, may refer to the nationality of the settlers along the creek.

Chapter 4. Powder Horns and Homesteads

1. The French and Indian War, the last of four conflicts between Britain and France and various allies, was the only one of those to begin in America. Born of conflict between the French and their Indian allies versus the British colonists and their Indian allies, it had spread to Europe by 1756 and involved the major nations on the Continent. Europeans called this conflict, which ended in 1763, the Seven Years' War or the Great

War for Empire. The concluding treaty, signed in Paris, essentially removed the French from North America. British-colonial relations after 1763, however, created conditions that would plunge Britain into yet another war—this time against its own colonies in North America.

2. Although legendary status has over the years simplified the relationship into special bonds of "friendship" and "sympathy" between peaceful whites and protective Indians, the complex associations between the Catawba and Camden area leaders are more fully documented in James H. Merrell, *The Indians' New World: Catawbas and Their Neighbors from European Contact through the Era of Removal* (New York: W. W. Norton, 1989).

3. Kirkland and Kennedy, *Historic Camden: Colonial and Revolutionary,* 72–73.

4. Revill, *Sumter District,* 15.

5. Meriwether, *Expansion,* 103.

6. Ibid.

7. Ibid.

8. William M. Shannon, circa 1870, is believed to be the author of a speech on old Camden to the local bar association. A copy of the manuscript transcribed in 2000 by Mrs. Carolyn Floyd Beck, with Leroy Gardner, is held in the Camden Archives. It presents two possible dates for Quaker arrival, citing the historian David Ramsay for 1750 and "tradition" for 1745. Writing later, Shannon uses 1750. See Shannon, *Old Times in Camden,* 1.

9. Kirkland and Kennedy, *Historic Camden: Colonial and Revolutionary,* 74. Further, they add names "suggestive of Quakerism" and locate some of the properties acquired by members of the colony. They point out also that James and John Adamson are sometimes thought to belong to the group, but as "fighting" Quakers because of respective activity in Indian and Revolutionary conflicts.

10. Meriwether, *Expansion,* 103.

11. Warren B. Smith, *White Servitude in South Carolina* (Columbia: University of South Carolina Press, 1961), 41.

12. Meriwether, *Expansion,* 103.

13. Smith, *White Servitude,* 41, identifies Wyly's connection with the Melones and with Hugh Cunhary, who received a Craven County grant the same year. Smith also identifies two other 1755 grantees as out-of-time apprentices bound in Ireland: John Dowling, to Robert Milhous; and Denis Hagen, to Robert Belton. Dowling received fifty acres in Craven County, and Hagen received the same amount on the Santee River.

14. Meriwether, *Expansion,* 106.

15. Bees were not native to America. Estate inventories indicate that some beekeeping was practiced in the Kershaw County area by the late 1700s and possibly during the colonial era.

16. Gregg, *History of the Old Cheraws,* 109.

17. Ibid., 109–10.

18. Ernst and Merrens, "Camden Turrets," 561.

19. James M. Burgess, *Chronicles of St. Mark's Parish* (Columbia, S.C.: Charles A. Calvo, 1888), 12.

20. The garrison at the second Fort Congaree, near the old fort in the area of present Columbia, left in 1754 to join Washington and were in the defeat at Fort Necessity. It was the only time in his career that Washington surrendered an army under his command.

21. Thomas J. Kirkland Papers, South Caroliniana Library. We are grateful to the South Caroliniana Library for permission to cite and/or quote from papers in its collections.

22. Meriwether, *Expansion,* 107.

23. Ibid., 105–6.

24. Merrell, *Indians' New World,* 195.

25. Ibid., 200.

26. Lieutenant James Adamson of the Pine Tree colony was among those killed by the Cherokee at Fort Loudon, Tenn.

27. A copy of Wyly's "Map of the Catawba Indians," 1764, is reproduced in Merrell, *Indians' New World,* 201.

28. The Treaty of Augusta ended the Cherokee War and settled some other Indian matters.

29. In 2009 King Hagler was inducted into the South Carolina Hall of Fame. The image representing him there is a silhouette of the weathervane effigy preserved in the Camden Archives. In 1995 an exact copy replaced the aging effigy on the town clock tower on Broad Street, Camden. The image is incorporated in the county seal on the front of the Kershaw County Courthouse, and it has so long been included in other logos that it has become a county icon.

Chapter 5. "A mix'd Medley"

1. *The Carolina Backcountry on the Eve of the Revolution: The Journal and Other Writings of Charles Woodmason, Anglican Itinerant,* edited by Richard Hooker. Copyright 1953 by the University of North Carolina Press, renewed 1981 by Richard Hooker. Published for the Omohundro Institute of Early American History and Culture. Quotations from this book used by permission of the publisher (www.uncpress.unc.edu). This collection of Reverend Charles Woodmason's writings includes valuable annotations and an introduction by the editor.

2. A useful way of evaluating Woodmason's material is to consider the purpose and intended audience of an individual piece of writing. His journal served as a mileage log and travel record but also included first impressions as well as occasional reflections during various emotional moods. It was personal, frankly spoken writing intended for his own reading, and perhaps for communicating his experiences with a sympathetic, like-minded friend or relative in England. Its apparent inconsistencies of attitudes thus reflect natural variations of private human thoughts over time. Other writings include public sermons strongly denouncing the evils and immoralities he perceived, some sermons targeting dissenting religions and nonscriptural sects he encountered. His correspondences with officials in London and authorities in Carolina use firm but reasoned arguments of persuasion, and they sometimes produced effective results on behalf of colonial causes. It is highly unlikely that some personally invective pieces, such as "A Letter to John Chesnut" and "A Burlesque Sermon," were ever made public. Instead, as satire, they more likely served as a private method of anger control and personal defense against injustices he perceived against his person. At one point in his journal, 47, Woodmason

reacts with wit when avenging another disadvantageous situation: "What I could not effect by Force—or Reason—I have done by Sarcasm."

3. Hooker, *Carolina Backcountry*, 7.

4. Ibid., 6–7, 9. The image of the interior as "wild country" endangered by heretical extremists had been fostered only five years earlier by a bizarre incident in another settlement. In 1761 at Saxe Gotha in the fork of the Broad and Congaree rivers, followers of Jacob Weber—who claimed to be God—murdered three people in an outburst of "religious" enthusiasm. Weber described one of the dead as the Devil. The resulting stain of the Weberite "heresy" or "delusion" influenced attitudes of many orthodox churchmen.

5. In 1759, at the end of present Meeting Street, Samuel Wyly conveyed four acres to the Quakers for "rent of one Pepper Corn . . . if . . . demanded." Here were established a meetinghouse and a burying ground, part of present Quaker Cemetery in Camden. A meetinghouse of the Presbyterians, used at times by Episcopal ministers also, was erected about that time near the present juncture of Meeting and Church streets, on property later conveyed to them by Joseph Kershaw. The old Presbyterian burying ground is now part of present Quaker Cemetery.

6. Hooker, *Carolina Backcountry*, 84–85.

7. Ibid., 20. Neither the specific Baptists (the most numerous of the backcountry groups) nor the individual Methodist about whom Woodmason complains can be certainly identified. "Methodist" did not bear its modern sense of a separate denomination, nor had the Methodist Society of the Anglican Church yet organized in this country. At the time there were "methodists" in the Anglican church, such as Reverend John Wesley in England or the evangelist George Whitfield, who spoke widely in America.

8. Ibid., 55, 33. Page references for quotations in each paragraph from this source will be grouped for ease.

9. Ibid., 34, 52.

10. Ibid., 15, 13, 16.

11. Ibid., 56, 23–24.

12. Richard Maxwell Brown, *The South Carolina Regulators* (Cambridge, Mass.: Harvard University Press, 1963), 29.

13. The lowcountry was charged with being little motivated to provide backcountry courts since Charlestonians would have lost the purchasing power of those who had to journey to their city during court sessions. Furthermore, improvements that might make the interior more inviting for settlement threatened to decrease the value of coastal lands.

14. Hooker, *Carolina Backcountry*, 10–11, 169–70. Woodmason decries the people as cowardly and in cahoots with the outlaws, not at that point recognizing their intimidation.

15. Ibid., 171–72.

16. Ibid., 42–44.

17. Ibid., 44–45.

18. Ibid., 49.

19. Because the March 17, 1768, *South Carolina Gazette* announced Samuel Wyly's death on February 13 at Pine Tree Hill, the historians surmise that the name was changed between February 13 and April 12, the date of the Act of Assembly. They concur with the tradition that the new name probably came at the suggestion of Joseph Kershaw. See Kirkland and Kennedy, *Historic Camden: Colonial and Revolutionary*, 94–95.

20. Brown, *South Carolina Regulators,* 46.

21. The Presbyterian meetinghouse at Camden had been closed to Woodmason's preaching since the four citizens who had built the church at their own expense, expecting to be repaid from pew rentals, found Presbyterians refusing to pay for pews as long as Woodmason officiated there.

22. The September 12, 1768, *South-Carolina Gazette* announced a Regulator meeting in Camden on October 5 to list grievances to carry en mass to the assembly. No such march materialized, but that fall in the election of 1768, Regulators traveled in large numbers to lowcountry polls to elect their own men to three seats in the assembly, which had forty-eight seats. Elected were Moses Kirkland, a Regulator leader; Tacitus Gaillard, a backcountry landholder; and Aaron Loocock, a Charleston merchant, Camden landowner, and partner in the firm of Joseph Kershaw and John Chesnut. What effect these representatives might have had is unknown. Governor Montagu dissolved the assembly on November 19 when that body defied him in opposing Parliament's Townshend duties.

23. Brown, *South Carolina Regulators,* 105.

24. Kirkland and Kennedy, *Historic Camden: Colonial and Revolutionary,* 95–96.

25. Jean Stephenson, *Scotch-Irish Migration to South Carolina, 1772: Rev. William Martin and His Five Shiploads of Settlers* (Strasburg, Va.: Shenandoah, 1971).

26. Walter Edgar, *Partisans and Redcoats: The Southern Conflict That Turned the Tide of the American Revolution* (New York: HarperCollins, 2001), 20–21.

27. Thomas J. Kirkland Papers, South Caroliniana Library.

28. McLaurin and Teal, *Just Mud,* 19. This history, 25–30, discusses the advanced pottery of hard-paste porcelain produced by the Bristol, England, factory owned by later county resident Richard Champion, who immigrated as a planter in 1784 but operated no pottery works here prior to his 1791 death. Kirkland and Kennedy, *Historic Camden: Nineteenth Century,* 14, point out that in 1766 the prospect of "pot works . . . set on foot in Carolina" was viewed with alarm by the English potter Josiah Wedgwood, who set about to prevent rival enterprise. McLaurin and Teal, 17, state that Wedgwood and other English potters, such as Champion, had already imported "Cherokee Clay" and produced "satisfactory pottery, including porcelain, from it." McLaurin and Teal speculate that Bartlam, before his move to Camden, communicated with Joseph Kershaw, a brickyard owner, about local clays. Bartlam's employee William Ellis came to Camden with him but moved on to begin a pottery in Salem, North Carolina.

29. In April 1776 Joseph Kershaw gave a visitor a local tour, including a ride "by Logtown to the Pottery." Dr. James Clitherall, journeying from Philadelphia to Charleston, recorded in his diary: "Here I saw some exceedingly good Pans, etc. which a Man who set up these found great demand for." McLaurin and Teal, *Just Mud,* 19–24, quotes the Clitherall diary and discusses Bartlam's pottery.

30. Kenneth E. Lewis, "Camden: A Frontier Town in Eighteenth Century South Carolina," in *Occasional Papers,* series 2 (Columbia: South Carolina Institute of Archaeology and Anthropology, 1976), 170–73.

31. Kirkland and Kennedy, *Historic Camden: Colonial and Revolutionary,* 99.

Chapter 6. Redcoats and Homespun

1. Kirkland and Kennedy, *Historic Camden: Colonial and Revolutionary,* 106–8. Jurors were Samuel Bradley, John Cantey, Samuel Cantey, Henry Cassels, Thomas Casity, Robert Carter, James Conyers, Edward Dickey, Sylvester Dunn, Joshua English, David Frierson, John Gamble, Moses Gordon, Henry Hunter, Isham Moore, David Neilson, John Payn, John Perkins Sr., Mathew Singleton (foreman), Jasper Sutton, David Wilson, and John Witherspoon.

2. Ibid., 109.

3. The Secret Committee actually predated the Provincial Congress, having been established by delegates at the General Meeting in Charles Town on July 6, 1774. Drawing membership from the backcountry as well as the lowcountry, the General Meeting was the first semblance of a true representative faction in South Carolina. When the Secret Committee seized official British communications to southern colonial governors authorizing use of military force against the colonists, they appropriated weapons and gunpowder from various colonial arsenals. See Edgar, *South Carolina,* 222.

4. Kirkland and Kennedy, *Historic Camden: Colonial and Revolutionary,* 120, asserts that two British agents, John Stuart and Alexander Cameron, set off the Cherokee uprising. Edgar, *South Carolina,* 208, identifies Stuart as a South Carolinian who served as superintendent for Indian affairs for the southern colonies and helped negotiate the Treaty of Augusta with the Cherokee in 1763; Edgar does not link Stuart with the 1776 uprising and does not mention Cameron at all. Richard Maxwell Brown, *The South Carolina Regulators* (Cambridge, Mass.: Harvard University Press, 1963), confirms Stuart as an Indian agent and links him with the Tories Moses Kirkland and Jacob Summeral but does not tie him to the 1776 Cherokee revolt; nor does Brown mention Cameron.

5. Scholarship on the Southern Campaign increased over several years from 2002 with a series of seminars conducted in Camden and sponsored by Historic Camden Revolutionary War Site and the Kershaw County Historical Society with scholarly presentations, discussions, and field trips to area sites. Growing collections of knowledge have expanded with electronic publishing; a newsletter, *Southern Campaigns of the American Revolution* (edited by Charles Baxley); and efforts to establish an interpretative park at the site of the Battle of Camden. David Reuwer edits *American Revolution* magazine.

6. Kirkland and Kennedy, *Historic Camden: Colonial and Revolutionary,* 128–33. These pages contain the complete 1780 pay bill that includes the names of slave owners who furnished laborers for the project. Owners were compensated; therefore, their furnishing labor does not prove anti-British sentiment. Working under James Brown, an engineer and master carpenter, were his black carpenters and other slaves belonging to John Adamson, William Ancrum, Abraham Belton, James Bettie, Burwell Boykin, Samuel Boykin, Archibald Brown, James Cary, Nathaniel Cary, John Chesnut, Joseph Clay, Joshua Dinkins, Samuel Elbert, Joshua English, Robert English, Joseph Habbersham, John Hope, John Hutchins, Ely Kershaw, Joseph Kershaw, Wm. Lang, William LeConte, John May, George McIntosh, Malachi Murphy, David Nelson, Charles Ogilvie, John Pain, John Platt, Isabella Reed, James Seesom, James Whitaker, Richard Whitaker, William Whitaker Jr., William Whitaker Sr., and John Wyly. Some

of these—Joseph and Ely Kershaw, John Chesnut, and Samuel Boykin—supported the patriots. Others such as James Cary supported the Crown. Of those likely Quakers who had to factor in peaceful religious convictions were the patriot John Wyly and the Loyalists John Adamson, Joshua English, and Robert English.

7. When the British took Camden, they converted the magazine to a star-shaped fortification and used it as a redoubt to guard the road from Charleston. Rawdon partly destroyed the position when he prepared to evacuate Camden, and Greene, fearing possible British return, completed the destruction.

8. Many of Cary's papers are in the Thomas Pittman Collection, North Carolina Archives.

9. Kirkland and Kennedy, *Historic Camden: Colonial and Revolutionary,* 126–33, gives details on attempts to fortify the town prior to British arrival, as well as their alterations when they took over. Joseph Kershaw began his house in the late 1770s but had not completed all details when the British commandeered it as headquarters. The square frame structure was a facsimile of a Charleston Georgian mansion with a brick basement at ground level, giving it the look of a three-and-one-half-story edifice. Situated on one of Camden's highest elevations, it was the town's most imposing structure, and its two-story front portico afforded a commanding view of the surrounding area.

10. Ibid., 214.

11. Banastre Tarleton Symposium, Historic Camden Revolutionary War Site, 2002.

12. Kirkland and Kennedy, *Historic Camden: Colonial and Revolutionary,* 208.

13. Decades later Jackson recalled military activity he said he witnessed from his upper-floor imprisonment when the British marched out to fight the Americans at Hobkirk Hill. Ibid., 209, cites a W. McCain who claimed that, as a prisoner in the second story of the jail on the corner of Broad and King streets, he observed the Battle of Hobkirk's Hill. McCain stated that the optimism of the prisoners turned to fear when the British captured the field, and prisoners anticipated death from angry returning soldiers.

14. Ibid., 139–40.

15. Ibid., 367, 143–44.

16. Ibid., 209–10.

17. Robert Stansbury Lambert, *South Carolina Loyalists in the American Revolution* (Columbia: University of South Carolina Press, 1987), 298.

18. Ibid., 186, states regarding Joseph Kershaw's Charleston partner: "The merchant Aaron Loocock had contributed a good deal of money and service to the rebel cause; now after taking British protection and accepting appointment to the street commission, he sailed for England where he spent the remainder of the war."

19. Samuel Mathis Papers, South Caroliniana Library. Some excerpts of the diary are printed in Kirkland and Kennedy, *Historic Camden: Colonial and Revolutionary,* 399–403. Mathis also wrote a separate account of the Battle of Hobkirk's Hill, having walked over the site afterward and having collected information from men who were present.

20. Kathleen Lewis Sloan, introduction to Julian Stevenson Bolick, *A Fairfield Sketchbook* (Winnsboro, S.C.: Fairfield County Historical Society, 2000), 4.

21. Lambert, *South Carolina Loyalists,* 119.

22. Sloan, introduction, 4.

23. Banastre Tarleton Symposium.

24. Many historians have examined Gates's judgment in every detail. John R. Maass, *Horatio Gates and the Battle of Camden—"That Unhappy Affair" August 16, 1780* (Camden, S.C.: Kershaw County Historical Society, 2001), evaluates a number of those who have attempted to explain Gates and the Battle of Camden.

25. Details of the Gates Ford location, and of other Revolutionary sites in the county, are described and mapped in *Guide to Selected Historical Sites in Kershaw County.*

26. Characteristics of guerrilla warfare are observed in the relative ease with which Taylor captured the approaching convoy because his partisan troops' appearance was in "similitude . . . with the homespun dresses of the Loyalists" (Banastre Tarleton, *Campaigns of 1780–81 in Southern America* [London, 1787], 134).

27. Edward McCrady, *The History of South Carolina in the Revolution* (New York, 1901), 681.

28. Kirkland and Kennedy, *Historic Camden: Colonial and Revolutionary,* 219.

29. Lyman C. Draper Collection, University of Wisconsin, Madison; microfilm, South Caroliniana Library.

30. In various published accounts an imaginative story appears that "'Scape O'er" was the correct spelling of the swamp at the headwaters of the Black River and the old Kershaw County boundary, its name being said to have originated from "escapes over" the swamp by Revolutionary partisans. However, "Scape Whore" was a map and deed location before the Revolution, appearing thus on the Mouzon map made in 1771. The origin of the colorful name is unknown but frequently speculated. "Scrape" and "Scrap" are other spellings found, as are "Hoar," "Hore," "Oar," "Ore," etc.

31. Jenkins, *Experience, Labours, and Sufferings,* 22.

32. Kirkland and Kennedy, *Historic Camden: Colonial and Revolutionary,* 402. The nineteenth-century neighborhood that developed on the old battlefield was called Hobkirk Hill, which name it presently bears. At the time of the battle, tradition is that the hill was known by the name of a resident, probably Thomas Hobkirk (ibid., 225n). Mathis and others of the time called it "Hobkirk's" Hill.

33. Stephen E. Haller, *William Washington: Cavalryman of the Revolution* (Bowie, Md.: Heritage Books, 2001), 128.

34. Kirkland and Kennedy, *Historic Camden: Colonial and Revolutionary,* 227.

35. Ibid., 229.

36. Ibid., 231.

37. Military historians may offer many reasons for the outcome of the battle—the British ability to move, undetected, to the base of the hill; Rawdon's boldness; Gunby's gaffe. Greene's opinion that Gunby was solely responsible for the loss was corroborated by a court of inquiry held when the army stopped at Rugeley's.

38. Kirkland and Kennedy, *Historic Camden: Colonial and Revolutionary,* 242.

39. Ibid., 267–71.

40. Ibid., 410. James Kershaw, the son of Joseph Kershaw, noted in his diary of July 6, 1800, a visit from the lawyer Stephen Boykin, with deputies Thomas Ballard and John McCaa, "to demand Cato [Guinea Cato] the property of James Cary, held in possession by my father. Answer, would not deliver him unless compelled by law."

41. JoAnne McCormick, "Civil Procedure in the Camden Circuit Court, 1772–1790," in *South Carolina Legal History,* Proceedings of the Reynolds Conference (Columbia: University of South Carolina Press, 1980), 241–54.

Chapter 7. New Ways

1. Edgar, *South Carolina,* 245.

2. Kirkland and Kennedy, *Historic Camden: Colonial and Revolutionary,* 322.

3. Throughout this chapter, for simplicity, general references are made to "court records" or "legislative records" without citing specific references to particular area courts. The text discusses the changing names of court jurisdictions, so that dates of records will indicate their jurisdictions—Camden District, Lancaster County, Kershaw County, Saint Mark's Parish, etc. Many of the documents are in records of the Kershaw County Court at Camden, most of which have also been microfilmed and are available with additional records of the courts and of the legislature at SCDAH in Columbia. In addition information has been gleaned from numerous unfilmed records there, including petitions, depositions, arrest warrants, reports, and the like. References gleaned from "account books" include various papers in the South Caroliniana Library. Contemporary newspapers and business directories were also consulted.

4. In varying degrees an expectation was held for some time that, as conditions became more settled, slavery would gradually be abolished. South Carolina in 1792 passed "an Act to prohibit the Importation of Slaves from Africa, or other places beyond the sea, into this state, for two years." In 1795 delegates of several abolitionist societies in convention in Philadelphia petitioned the state to take certain steps to abolish all slave traffic and prepare slaves for eventual freedom. By then, however, the recent invention of the cotton gin had increased demand for slave labor, and petitions were numerous from slave owners requesting to bring into the state additional slaves they owned outside its boundaries.

5. Born in Virginia in 1763, Bonds Conway came to Camden in 1792 as a slave of Edwin Conway assigned to his son Peter. With written permission to hire himself out, Bonds Conway accumulated his own money, which Zachariah Cantey used to purchase him in 1793, subsequently freeing him. From that time on, Bonds Conway earned his living as a skilled carpenter, and he acquired the entire block of King, Market, York, and Lyttleton streets. A cottage-style home he built circa 1812, the Bonds Conway House, was purchased by the Kershaw County Historical Society in 1977 and moved to its present location, 811 Fair Street. Restoration was completed in 1980 for the house to serve as society headquarters. An image of the house forms the society's logo.

6. In that time without newspapers or courthouses, congregational meetings also filled secular functions. The reading of will citations and announcements of auctions to settle estates was a traditional public responsibility of a preacher. Records of wills and estates therefore verify some of these actions and thus identify some of the preachers and congregational gatherings within the Kershaw County area.

7. At the outbreak of hostilities, Anglican ministers had returned to England, but in Baltimore in 1784 a religious society that had originally formed to revitalize the Church of England now instead organized a new and separate denomination, the Methodist Episcopal Church in America. While technically the early preachers in the local area were

"Methodist Episcopals," they were commonly called simply "Methodists," which is the term used here. The Episcopal Church, retaining Anglican worship traditions, did not reestablish itself locally until the next century.

8. By various sources the fading of local Quaker presence is attributed to a combination of influences, including migration, intermarriage, pressures of war, and attrition. Some of the Camden Quakers as early as the 1760s migrated to join the colony at Bush River (Newberry County), and the two meetings maintained connections. Quakers early opposed slavery, and many at Bush River, among others, moved away from it to Ohio in the early 1800s. Bush River minutes in 1806 advise trustees to sell a meetinghouse lot in Camden. Bush River ceased meetings in 1822.

9. This meetinghouse had been built in the early 1770s. Kirkland and Kennedy, *Historic Camden: Nineteenth Century,* 280–82, addresses some conflicting evidence regarding its denomination, concluding that it belonged to the Presbyterians but was also used at times by Episcopalian itinerants.

10. James Kershaw's diary refers to a town meeting on September 15, 1794, to "consider removal of ye place of Burial." Property set aside for an Episcopal church at the northwest corner of Bull and Broad streets had gone unused as a building lot, though it had been used for burials. Graves from "the Episcopal burying ground" were moved from this site, in the main part of town, to the expanded area of the Quaker burying ground at the edge of town. Kershaw mentions on October 12, 1798, the burial of Mrs. Thomas Broom at the "New Ground." Kirkland and Kennedy, *Historic Camden: Colonial and Revolutionary,* 404–13, reprints sample portions of James Kershaw's diary. The original, also consulted, is in the James Kershaw Papers, South Caroliniana Library.

11. Inabinet, *Lyttleton Street United Methodist Church,* 52.

12. Keith Krawczynski, ed., "William Drayton's Journal of a 1784 Tour of the South Carolina Backcountry," *South Carolina Historical Magazine* 97 (July 1996): 201–2. The journal writer is not Judge William Henry Drayton, already deceased, but a former justice of the peace of Berkeley County in prewar years who held a number of legal positions and in 1789 was associate judge of the S.C. Supreme Court.

13. The wills and estate papers of the Camden District Court from 1781 to 1787 were later filed with Kershaw County records. General sessions, criminal court, and other records for various years of the Camden District Court are at the SCDAH.

14. Of these four old county names, all except Claremont survive as names for modern counties, although all areas have changed. Claremont became part of Sumter County in 1800. Existing records for present Kershaw County from 1785 to 1791 are generally found in the accounts of other early county courts, filed with records of Fairfield, Lancaster, Richland, and Sumter counties. Some early records were lost, especially during disruptions of the Civil War.

15. The selection in 1786 of a capital at present Columbia, on the Broad River, was one such move.

16. The names of the appointees in the four counties in 1785 are found on the General Assembly Special Committee "Report Listing the Justices of the Peace in Camden District and Parts of Cheraw District and Their Subordinate Counties," SCDAH.

17. Harvey Teal gave the authors this information, which he compiled from Frances M. Hutson, *Journal of the Constitutional Convention of South Carolina May 10, 1790–June*

3, 1790 (Columbia, S.C.: State Printing, 1946). The group met for nineteen days, but little detail is provided about opinions of individuals.

18. The following year, from the west of the Wateree, Arthur Brown Ross and Reuben Starke were commissioners from Kershaw County appointed to serve with commissioners from Fairfield County to determine the boundary line between the two counties.

19. Most court issues related to slaves as property. Misdeeds were generally considered the right and responsibility of the master to address, judge, and punish. In community trials judging slaves, masters were generally part of the process. James Kershaw's diary refers to his sitting on the trial of Punch for "conjuration." In another incident, without trial, he has three slaves whipped for stealing another planter's hogs. Instances referring to the discipline of slaves are notably fewer in Kershaw's diary than in the earlier Revolutionary diary of Samuel Mathis. See Kershaw and Mathis papers, South Caroliniana Library.

20. Edgar, *South Carolina,* 246.

21. Kirkland and Kennedy, *Historic Camden: Colonial and Revolutionary,* 393.

22. James Kershaw later served as a county judge. His diary says that he was sworn in on August 7, 1798, and that Stephen Boykin became the new clerk. Kershaw on February 8, 1799, states that he gave his bond for the office, guaranteed by John Adamson, Dan Carpenter, and John Kershaw.

23. Kirkland and Kennedy, *Historic Camden: Colonial and Revolutionary,* 227.

24. On February 23, 1789, a legislative committee report discussed grievances against the county courts of citizens of Camden, Camden District, and Claremont and Clarendon counties. Committee members concluded that "suspension of County Courts . . . ought not be made without mature deliberation, but as a considerable number of the Inhabitants . . . have signed the said Petition," they recommended that a "Bill be brought in to suspend the Jurisdiction of the County Courts under certain restrictions," thus giving time for further discussion.

25. Seven indentures all entered consecutively on record on April 7, 1790, may have been payoffs from losing bettors in a horse race. Large sums, secured by slaves and/or land, were to be paid, for reasons unnamed, to three men—Douglas Starke, John Blanton, and Willis Whitaker—whose names have been linked in other contexts with turf interests. All from Camden District, the planters signing the indentures and their penal sums in pounds sterling were John Adamson, 464; Thomas Ballard, 250; Arthur Cunningham, 442; Robert Lee, 514; Middleton McDonald, 192; Reuben Perry, 510; and Reuben Starke, 142. Witnesses were singularly or in various combinations these three men: William Brown, Zach Cantey, and Douglas McCrae. (As comparison for relative value, in 1789 Henry Rugeley of Fairfield County paid 550 pounds sterling for a centrally located Camden business-residential town lot and a plantation of 150 acres on the northeast side of the Wateree River.) An old local legend, written down by Wm. D. Trantham Jr. and surviving in manuscript form in the Trantham-Bauskett-Nelson Papers in the Camden Archives, tells the story of the losing "Godolphin Filly" in one of the high-waging horse races among area planters about 1850.

26. Kirkland and Kennedy, *Historic Camden: Colonial and Revolutionary,* 337.

27. Edgar, *South Carolina,* 248.

28. Kershaw's Charleston partners William Ancrum and Aaron Loocock also had property losses, but as Loyalists. They were so classified and their property confiscated since they had been among Charleston citizens presenting a congratulatory address to Clinton and Arbuthnot on the capture of that city. Kershaw's brother William had been paroled at Charleston, imprisoned in Camden, and afterward, he said, with no means left to provide for his family, had accepted British protection and gone to Charleston, where he operated a store, which was confiscated after the war. Joseph Kershaw's wife and children remained in the Camden area under the care of her young, paroled brother, Samuel Mathis, whose diary shows shipments to the family from William (W. K.) from Charleston ("from Town"). The third Kershaw brother, Ely, who in 1766 was granted the land on which the town of Cheraw developed, moved to Camden, where he was in business with Joseph by 1774. Both brothers were imprisoned by the British and expatriated to Bermuda, where Ely died of dysentery aboard ship in the harbor of Saint George.

29. Cary's claims in British Public Records present his Tory sufferings at the hands of the Americans. Besides his capture at Cary's Fort the day before the Battle of Camden and his release at Fishing Creek, Cary had been subjected to other attacks. In December 1780 Rawden wrote Cornwallis reporting "the attempt of a party of Rebels to carry off Colonel Cary." Departing with the British in 1781, Cary lost his home, land (1,302 acres in the vicinity of Camden and 700 acres with "no improvements" in Johnston County, North Carolina), and "crops of flax, indigo, madder, and cotton; herds of 26 horses, 109 cows, 35 sheep, 363 hogs; and 14 slaves" (although at one time slaves reportedly numbered 42). In a July 5, 1782, letter to Cornwallis, Cary, then an evacuee, referred to having been "twice plundered by the Rebels they got from me most of my personal Property by plundering, [and] some of my Negros (slaves) they murdered, as they could not lay their barbarous Hands on me."

30. McRa(e), from the Pee Dee, may have been a nonresidential partner (at least some of the time) and may not have moved to Camden until 1794. See Kirkland and Kennedy, *Historic Camden: Colonial and Revolutionary*, 409.

31. Land records, SCDAH.

32. Kirkland and Kennedy, *Historic Camden: Colonial and Revolutionary*, 406.

33. Two copies of this 1793 petition of free people of color to the General Assembly are found on microfilm at the SCDAH. Some signatures are light and some spellings variant, but the names appear to be as follows, alphabetized: Jesse Anderson, John B(i/u)rd, David Coal, George Coal, William Coal, (Brev?Serv?)ard Going, Edward Going (Senr), Isaac Going, Levi Going, William H(e)arriss, Aaron Jones, Ba(ss/fh?) Jones, Arche Morriss, Henry Morriss, John Morris (Junr), John Morris (Senr), (Sidon?) Morris, William Morriss (Junr), William Morris (Senr), Samuel Morris, J. Shampai(g)n, William S(h/t?)andley, and Brenig Woodward. No indication is given to the areas of residence, but an accompanying list of names testifying to the character of petitioners is headed by Richard Winn of Fairfield County. Some of the names, such as John Cook, are found in the upper part of the Kershaw County area and around Camden. The appeal further states that the petitioners "are generally a Poor needy People, have frequently large Families to maintain" and are "but a small removed from Slavery." In introduction the petition says that "they conceived their ancestors merited the Publick

confidence and obtained the Title of a Free People by rendering some particular Service to their Country" for which the "Government thought just and right to notice and to reward their Fidelity with Emancipation, and other singular Priviledges."

34. Kirkland and Kennedy, *Historic Camden: Nineteenth Century*, 423.

35. Georgetown Road was the one major transportation route that passed through the full length of the county area without passing through Camden.

36. A road from Camden extended to Chesnut's Ferry on the east bank; on the west bank a road from Chesnut's Ferry extended to Colonel's Creek. On the east side of the river, Chesnut Ferry Road linked with the Camden Ferry Road via the old Road to Rocky Mount, which followed the river.

37. English was shortly afterward allowed to open a road from his ferry to the main Charleston Road.

38. In 1791 notice was also made of "McCullum's Ferry on Great Lynches," possibly a private venture and further up on the river.

39. Since the first bridge over the Wateree was built in 1827 at the ferry site of its day, the standing pier of the old bridge on the west bank of the Wateree (a short distance north of the I-20 bridge) is presumably about three hundred yards south of the Revolutionary-era ferry landing, the road to which was guarded by Cary's Fort on an overlooking bluff. The standing pier, in woodlands, is not seen from the I-20 bridge, although the bridge is easily viewed from the area of the pier.

40. Kirkland and Kennedy, *Historic Camden: Nineteenth Century*, 15. Watson's memoir was compiled by William Reed Dean and published in 1863.

41. No laws questioned conflicts of interest for public representatives simultaneously employed in related private industries. Details on the canal-building era and its works related to the Kershaw County area are found in Arthur P. Wade, "Mount Dearborn: The National Armory at Rocky Mount, South Carolina, 1802–1829," *South Carolina Historical Magazine* (July/October 1980): 207–341.

42. Ibid., 209. Washington is quoted from his letter to Secretary of War James McHenry of December 13, 1798.

43. Names and locations are gleaned from deeds, wills, petitions, and orders for overseers of roads.

44. Other investors who applied to be added to the new charter were John Adamson, Jonathan Belton, Burwell Boykin, Joseph Brevard, Daniel Brown, Dan Carpenter, Benjamin Carter, Richard L. Champion, James Chesnut, John Chesnut, James English, William Lang, William Langley, Samuel Mathis, and John McCaa.

45. The "Hessian" engineer Senf had originally come to America with General John Burgoyne's British troops, but he switched sides after being captured at Saratoga and served with Greene. He mapped the Battle of Camden and from 1793 was engineer of a landmark undertaking, the Santee Canal.

46. The Bonds Conway House, circa 1812, is today headquarters for the Kershaw County Historical Society at 811 Fair Street, Camden. An image of the house, which was moved to its present site after its purchase in 1977, serves as the society's logo. Built as a home by Bonds Conway, the house preserves the original architectural details of the master craftsman, whose descendants remain among the interested contributors to the society's preservation of the historic home.

47. The distinction between an "inn" and a "tavern" was frequently blurred in references, and one name or the other was likely to be used for the same establishment.

48. Guinea Catoe was no doubt a skilled worker, for when attempts were made on behalf of his original owner, Colonel James Cary, to reclaim him, James Kershaw refused, according to his July 6, 1800, diary.

49. In 1793 George Brown rented the brew house, and in 1794 William Mayrant purchased the brewing instructions, according to Kershaw's diary.

50. A native of the bordering Salem section at one time part of Kershaw County, Carter had enlisted in the Continental army when he was a student in Charlotte, North Carolina, and had been present under Gates at the Battle of Camden.

51. In 1768 the patent for hard-paste pottery was first granted to its originator, the chemist William Cookworthy, from whom the patent and factory producing it were purchased by Richard Champion in 1770 when the operation moved from Plymouth to Bristol. When Champion attempted to renew the patent in 1775, his efforts were strongly opposed by rival pottery manufacturer Josiah Wedgwood. The legal struggle to defend the patent was so costly that Champion sold the formula to a group of Staffordshire potters and turned his face to new opportunities in America. The products of Champion's factory ranged from simple tableware to highly decorative pieces. The Camden Archives owns examples of dinnerware, and the Mint Museum in Charlotte, North Carolina, owns biscuit plaques and a mourning statue entitled "Grief" in memory of Champion's late daughter Eliza. Champion was enthusiastic about America even before his decision to move here, evidenced by plaques with portraits of Ben Franklin and George Washington.

52. Another son, George L. Champion, was considered a local crackpot in the early 1800s because he vehemently opposed public development of canals, insisting instead that steam railroads would be the wave of the future.

53. Kirkland and Kennedy, *Historic Camden: Nineteenth Century,* 263–70.

54. James Kershaw mentions having borrowed "Mrs. Jarvois's Piano Fork" in 1795.

55. Donald Jackson and Dorothy Twohig, eds., *The Diaries of George Washington,* in *The Papers of George Washington* (Charlottesville: University Press of Virginia, 1979), from American Memory collection, Library of Congress.

56. Among sources is Kirkland and Kennedy, *Historic Camden: Colonial and Revolutionary,* 306–13.

57. That memory of Washington's visit survived long in local interest is shown in the January 8, 1878, *Camden Journal,* quoting the *Blue Ridge (N.C.) Blade:* "We were shown, last week, by Dr. J. M. Happoldt, of this place, a quilt under which General Washington slept. This quilt was made by Mrs. Sarah Reid, wife of Capt. Reid, of Camden, S.C., in the year 1775, and Mrs. J. M. Happoldt is a granddaughter of Mrs. Reid, into whose possession the quilt passed as a family relic. Capt. John Reid kept a public house at Camden, at which Gen. Washington put up on his way to Charlotte, N.C., and during his stay covered with this quilt. Capt. Reid fought in the battle at Ramsour's Mill, N.C., in 1812."

58. De Kalb was originally interred in a field behind "the Blue House" where he died. The house was located at the northwest intersection of Meeting and Broad. The original marker over his grave is preserved in a wall at the entrance to the Robert Mills Courthouse. The reinterment of De Kalb on DeKalb Street will be discussed in the following chapter.

59. These observations were taking place during the Reign of Terror, when the liberties seized at the beginning of the French Revolution were being suppressed in a bloody chaos.

60. Officers elected for the Kershaw County Regiment were Lieutenant Colonel Zachariah Cantey and Majors Willis Whitaker and Thomas Ballard; elected for the Camden Militia were Captain David Bush, Lieutenant James Brown, and Ensign James Cain.

Chapter 8. Cotton and Complexities

1. For census data in this chapter, see Kershaw County in Federal Censuses of South Carolina, 4 issues: 1800, 1810, 1820, 1830 (Camden, S.C., Kershaw County Historical Society, 1970–94); *South Carolina State Census, 1839: A Schedule of the White Population of Kershaw District, South Carolina* (Camden, S.C.: Kershaw County Historical Society, 1997); *Kershaw County, South Carolina, Census with Expanded Genealogical Information, 1850* (Camden, S.C.: Catawba-Wateree Genealogical Society, 1997); *Return of Crops and Other Statistics of Kershaw County, South Carolina, 1868* (Camden, S.C.: Kershaw County Historical Society, 1998).

2. Anne Mims Wright, comp., "Diary of Arthur Brown Ross," in *A Record of the Descendants of Isaac Ross and Jean Brown,* ed. Anne Mims Wright (Atlanta: Conger, 1977), reprinted in *Messenger* (Catawba-Wateree Genealogical Society, June–September 1990).

3. The word "planter" is used here in the sense of "one who plants," including both small and large agriculturalists. Although some writers limit use of the word "planter" to only those of large operations and use "farmer" to refer to small agriculturalists, such distinctions were inconsistent in contemporary time and with present historians.

4. A student of church history for various denominations will find much material to study within Kershaw District. The general coverage given in this book has not attempted to broach distinctions within denominations and those influences on individual churches, nor has discussion been attempted of associational developments, also of significance. Methodists of the time were Methodist-Episcopal, but for ease here they are called by the general name, as widely referred. Information in the following section has been gathered from Works Progress Administration (WPA) church records (South Caroliniana Library) and a wide variety of primary and secondary sources, including deeds, newspaper articles, church records, church histories, and denominational histories. See files and published works at the Camden Archives.

5. Jenkins, *Experience, Labours, and Sufferings,* 115–16.

6. Most church minute books have been microfilmed since the authors examined originals and are now more widely available. Authors read minutes of Flat Rock Baptist and Bethsada (Primitive) Baptist and other records at the South Caroliniana Library (which also has church records of the WPA Writers' Project). Authors read Camden Baptist, Camden (Lyttleton Street) Methodist, and Bethesda Presbyterian minutes at those locations. (Camden Baptist minutes are now at Furman University.) Authors read photostats of Mt. Moriah and a typescript of Grace Episcopal records. Publications of various churches also quote from surviving records, and miscellaneous information is found in files at the Camden Archives.

7. Kirkland Papers, South Caroliniana Library.

8. Ibid.

9. A copy of Blanding's sketch, in private possession, is in the Camden Archives and has been reprinted in Inabinet, *Lyttleton Street United Methodist Church,* 14.

10. Ibid., 68.

11. For a list of free black and slave members, see Inabinet, *His People,* 115–17.

12. Inabinet, *Lyttleton Street United Methodist Church,* 70–74.

13. Margaret Maxwell Martin, "Methodism in Camden," *Southern Christian Advocate,* November 4, 1853.

14. From 1816 forward in this history, local newspapers have proved invaluable sources to the authors, who have read many sequences of them extensively and chronologically in order to gather impressions of the times as well as to find specific pieces of information. Sequential and thorough attention to overall coverage increases the usefulness of newspapers as primary sources, for in them over time is the opportunity for errors to be corrected and alternative opinions to be expressed. The authors usually identify these sources, by newspaper name and date, in their narrative rather than in separate citations.

15. See chap. 2, n. 2.

16. Earle E. Spamer, Academy of Natural Sciences in Philadelphia, to the authors, February 24, 2003; Smithsonian staff search report to the authors, 2003. The Rehoboth Antiquarian Society at the Blanding Public Library and Carpenter Museum in Blanding's native community, Rehoboth, Massachusetts, where he died in 1857, reported that they do not own material identifiable from Kershaw District, South Carolina. A letter from the society reached the Camden Archives with a copy of a sketch, in private possession, that Blanding made of the Methodist church at Camden. Blanding's name is preserved in having been given to the northern Blanding turtle (*Emys blandingii*), a yellow-throated, long-necked wetlands variety, subject of a tracking project in 2000 to encourage its protection.

17. The discovery took place at the Adamson mounds. In 1849, when Dr. Blanding was living in Rehoboth, his sister Lucy Carpenter visited Camden and wrote her brother of a trip to (Adamson) mounds, where she found items of interest, including a large urn. The following year her kinswoman Rebecca Lee Bonney wrote Lucy Carpenter about finds that family members continued to make at the mounds and about a party of small boys collecting relics for "Dr. Parsons." See Blanding family papers and Bonney family papers, South Caroliniana Library.

18. Harvey S. Teal's extensive study of South Carolina photographers does not give evidence of photography being used in this period for purposes aside from human portraits. Teal in 2008 told the authors that I. B. Alexander probably did not photograph antiquities. However, Alexander's son William S. Alexander was an outstanding photographer in the postbellum period who may have taken some photos of antiquities. A well-known photograph he took of Adamson Mound is mislabeled "Taylor's mound" (Mulberry) on reproductions. An Alexander descendant married Norman S. Fohl, a noted local relics collector and antiques dealer.

19. William Gilmore Simms, *Book of My Lady: A Melange* (Philadelphia: Key & Biddle, 1833).

20. The unsettled treaty led to a renewal of Catawba claims in the twentieth century. In 1993 Congress restored the Catawba Indian Nation as a federally recognized tribe and awarded $50 million in settlement of its claim.

21. Note, appearing to be from an oral interview, Kirkland Papers.

22. The diaries are, respectively, in the William Blanding Papers and the James Kershaw Papers, South Caroliniana Library.

23. Abram Blanding and Robert Mills were two of the members of the board making the 1822 report to the legislature by the Board of Public Works. See David Kohn, ed., *Internal Improvement in South Carolina, 1817–1828* (Washington, D.C., 1938), 145–70.

24. The 1992 *Guide to Historical Sites in Kershaw County* reproduces a modern highway map numbered to match corresponding numbers added to a reproduced 1825 Mills map, with accompanying text and photographs for fifty-seven sites. A 1993 supplement adds the Benjamin McKoy House.

25. Esther S. Davis, *Memories of Mulberry* (Camden, S.C.: privately printed, n.d.). The writer of the most detailed local memoir that describes a grand plantation's antebellum way of life was the granddaughter of Colonel James and Mary C. Chesnut; the daughter of Mary Cox Chesnut and Dr. George Reynolds; and the wife of Reverend J. Bruce Davis. She explained household operations, occupations of skilled craftsmen, and other endeavors that managed a lifestyle characterized by "order, neatness, and an abundant hospitality." See chapter 9 for other writings of Esther Davis.

26. Kirkwood began in 1818 around Kirkwood Spring and developed into an area of popular health and tourist resorts in the late 1800s and early 1900s.

27. Rosser H. Taylor, *Ante-Bellum South Carolina: A Social and Cultural History* (Chapel Hill: University of North Carolina Press, 1942), 75.

28. Ibid., 74.

29. The petition of October 27, 1830, on behalf of Squires McDonald was signed by John Ballowd, John J. Blair, J. F. Bryant, D(rury) Campbell, J. W. Cantey, John Cantey, Thomas Lang, Hugh McCall, William McWillie, William Nixon, and William B. Parker. Four years later John Chesnut and James W. Cantey were on McDonald's bond when "Mary Ann Cunningham" brought suit against him for "pursuing . . . and pushing her with a hoe" and no action was taken. He may be the Squire McDonald briefly mentioned in the writing of Mary Chesnut.

30. Federal Writers' Project, United States Works Progress Administration, Manuscript Division, Library of Congress. WPA writers in Kershaw County concentrated on transcriptions of court and church records rather than interviewing.

31. See chapter 9 regarding Viola B. Muse's interview at Palatka, Florida, with Randall Lee, born in Camden, probably a slave of Dr. John Milling on Sanders Creek; and Stiles M. Scruggs's interview at Columbia, South Carolina, with the Reverend James H. Johnson, born "at the town servants' quarters of Alfred Brevart [Dr. Alfred Brevard] at Camden."

32. E. Louise, *Elizabeth Clevland Hardcastle, 1741–1808: A Lady of Color in the South Carolina Low Country* (Columbia, S.C.: Phoenix, 2001), 420–29. Andrew Dibble married Ellie Naomi Naudin of Camden, a granddaughter of Bonds Conway, and established a prominent line.

33. Taylor, *Ante-Bellum South Carolina,* 45.

34. Kirkland and Kennedy, *Historic Camden: Nineteenth Century,* 228.

35. Ibid., 228–33.

36. Ibid., 233–34.

37. Taylor, *Ante-Bellum South Carolina,* 7.

38. Kirkland and Kennedy, *Historic Camden: Nineteenth Century,* cite Reverend Brantley's name as Samuel, but Orphan Society records and records of the Camden Baptist Church list it as William.

39. Steen, *Stoneboro,* 87.

40. 1850 Kershaw County, S.C., Census Expanded with Genealogy, Catawba-Wateree SCGS (1997), 134–35.

41. Cunningham, *Liberty Hill,* 107–8.

42. Louise, *Elizabeth Clevland Hardcastle,* 335.

43. Some historians use ten slaves as designation for a planter, and some use twenty. The number of fifteen slaves reasonably averages those differences.

44. Kirkland and Kennedy, *Historic Camden: Colonial and Revolutionary,* 348. She is also noted as the grandmother of Mary Boykin Chesnut.

45. Priscilla T. Oliver, foreword to *The Fifth Federal Census 1930 South Carolina, Kershaw District* (Camden, S.C.: Kershaw County Historical Society, 1994), ii.

46. L. Glen Inabinet, "'The July Fourth Incident' of 1816: An Insurrection Plotted by Slaves in Camden, South Carolina," in *South Carolina Legal History,* Proceedings of the Reynolds Conference (Columbia: University of South Carolina Press, 1980), 209–21. The incident occurred prior to the more widely known lowcountry plot led by Denmark Vesey in 1822, and the Camden trial served as a precedent in the Vesey proceedings. The slave who warned Chesnut was later awarded his freedom and a pension by the state legislature, although for safety his name was kept secret. Inabinet located his manumission record and learned his name—Scipio. The Camden attorney Francis Deliesseline described most conspirators as motivated by "wild and frantic ideas of the rights of man, and the misconceived injunctions and examples of Holy Writ." Some were religious, could read and write, and had been regarded as good servants. Isaac, for example, had been a drummer in Captain Levy's company and marched with militiamen to the defense of Charleston in the War of 1812.

47. Blanding Family Papers, South Caroliniana Library. The William Blandings were not slave owners.

48. Oliver, foreword, I.

49. Wright, "Diary of Arthur Brown Ross."

50. Circumstantial evidence connects the Camden planter and banker Lewis Ciples in some way with a family of free persons of color (names listed in report to the twenty-eighth Congress) who migrated in a different direction, from South Carolina to Monrovia, Liberia, in 1833 as part of "back to Africa" efforts sponsored by the American Colonization Society. Among the arrival records of the ship *Hercules* is found a free-born household headed by thirty-two-year-old Lewis Ciples (Cyples), his wife, Susan, and three children, among whom was six-year-old Lewis Ciples Jr. The father was described as a tailor, his wife as a seamstress, and both could write; young Ciples could spell. The rarity of the Ciples surname is discussed by Joan Inabinet, *A Wateree River Plantation Journal* (Camden, S.C.: Kershaw County Historical Society, 1997).

51. Allen H. Stokes Jr., *Gold Rush Letters from William Lemmond: A 49er from Carolina* (Camden, S.C.: Kershaw County Historical Society, 1999).

52. Similarities of mill names operating in different areas can be confusing, as can multiple name changes over time for the same mill seat. Researchers and genealogists assuming locations by mill names must take precautions. As only one example, Schrock's Mill is a long-used name in the eastern area (for a mill, a community, and a voting district), and in 1813 a separate Schrock's mill operated in a distant area on Sanders Creek.

53. Teal, *Rides about Camden.* The series is reprinted in this booklet.

54. Kirkland and Kennedy, *Historic Camden: Nineteenth Century,* 33.

55. Inabinet, *Lyttleton Street United Methodist Church,* 89.

56. References have been gathered from a number of sources, including newspapers, court records, maps, voting rosters, directories, tax records, and miscellaneous papers such as letters and business ledgers, some in private hands and others at the South Caroliniana Library, Camden Archives, and SCDAH.

57. Harvey S. Teal, ed., *Kershaw County/District Business Directory, 1854–1900* (Camden, S.C.: Kershaw County Historical Society, 1999), 5–7.

58. Teal and Robert J. Stets, eds. *South Carolina Postal History and Illustrated Catalog of Postmarks, 1760–1860* (Columbia, S.C.: privately printed, 1989), 81

59. Names are given here as found on the map, despite various uses of possessive endings. Variable spellings for each locale are found throughout contemporary and later references and should be anticipated.

60. Kirkland Papers.

61. These private papers are in the possession of the authors.

62. Some merchants overlap the rough division of time suggested here, and since it is not possible to pinpoint the beginnings of some individual merchant enterprises, the time references should be considered general.

63. Camden Medical Association Papers, Camden Archives.

64. P. Thornton, *The Southern Gardener and Receipt Book,* repr. ed. in the Antique American Cookbooks series (Birmingham: Oxmoor, 1984). An illustrated introduction by Shirley Abbott, 1–22, focuses on the lives of Phineas and Elizabeth (Williams) Thornton and the community of Camden in their time.

65. The reference book, written by John C. Gunn and first copyrighted in 1840, appears in various local advertisements and references. The copy from which the following passage, 295–96, was quoted, was the 1849 edition, published in Louisville by Allston Mygatt. The copy that came to hand belonged to an antebellum family in the upper part of Kershaw District and had apparently been well used, for hand-stitched repairs had been made to hold together a part of the leather spine.

66. Kirkland and Kennedy, *Historic Camden: Nineteenth Century,* 64–82, devotes a chapter to the pomp and circumstance of this visit, long recalled in local memory. On entering Kershaw District, Lafayette first encamped at Lovick Young's on Lynches Creek, reaching Camden on March 8, 1825. Still standing is "the Lafayette Cedar," an aged tree grown from one of the decorative plantings outside Lafayette Hall, the home where the general was welcomed and now the site of the Kershaw County Courthouse. Another

relic is the Masonic "Lafayette Trowel" used by the general to lay the cornerstone of the De Kalb monument and afterward in cornerstone ceremonies of numerous other local public buildings and monuments.

67. Stones of the abandoned canals were dug out and used by local farmers in later years. Materials were also claimed and removed for use as fill in the building of the Wateree Dam in the early 1900s.

68. In 1787 Christian Senf drew a map for the Company for Opening the Catawba and Wateree River for Navigation, proposing a canal at Love's Shoals with its lower end opposite a branch that today empties into Lake Wateree. The route of this map, too, is sometimes confused with the location of the state's canal. The private company apparently did some digging for a canal in the area, reportedly in 1811 or even earlier. Senf was also the engineer of a canal at Pine Tree Creek.

69. Kohn, *Internal Improvement.* These and many of the following facts are gleaned from this source.

70. The information regarding the Irish workers on the Wateree Canal is largely anecdotal rather than documentary.

71. Richard Sanders Allen, *Covered Bridges of the South* (New York: Bonanza Books, 1970), 4.

72. In 2002 the authors were taken to the east side of the river by Ralph and Darlene Cantey to view remains on the opposite bank. The authors were also taken to the site of the pier on the west bank by the landowner Claude Campbell, who had lately uncovered it when clearing overgrowth that had long obscured it from view.

73. The very early and continued use of this area as a crossing point had been encouraged by a shallow, rocky bottom that made for easy foot passage in low water. Cureton and Blair were two of the proprietors of the Boat Yard on the river further north of town and would have been pleased to remove obstacles that at times required boats to stop at the rival Camden Ferry Landing.

74. Kirkland and Kennedy, *Historic Camden: Nineteenth Century,* 328, lists these names.

Chapter 9. Broken Ties

1. C. Vann Woodward and Elisabeth Muhlenfeld, eds., *The Private Mary Chesnut: The Unpublished Civil War Diaries* (New York: Oxford University Press, 1948), 3.

2. Teal, *Kershaw County Confederate Miscellany,* 2, 16–18.

3. Woodward and Muhlenfeld, *Private Mary Chesnut,* 5.

4. Woodward, ed., *Mary Chesnut's Civil War,* 46.

5. Rives Lang Beaty, ed., "Recollections of Harriet DuBose Kershaw Lang," *South Carolina Historical Magazine* 59 (July 1958): 159–70, quoted by permission of the South Carolina Historical Society. The writer of the memoir is hereafter referred to as Harriet Lang.

6. Kirkland and Kennedy, *Historic Camden: Nineteenth Century,* 159.

7. Edward M. Boykin, *The Falling Flag* (New York: R. J. Hale, 1874), 66.

8. D. Augustus Dickert, *History of Kershaw's Brigade,* ed. Mack Wyckoff (Wilmington, N.C.: Broadfoot, 1990).

9. The Camden Archives houses microfilmed newspapers as well as memoirs, letters, and other accounts in the files of the United Daughters of the Confederacy, the Catawba-Wateree Genealogical Society, and miscellaneous families.

10. Warren, who before the war encouraged fellow citizens "to nerve your hearts and bare your arms to strike for your altars and fires, be prepared to do your duty," also alluded to the possibility of being "called upon to die upon the altar of our country." He was killed leading his troops against Little Round Top at Gettysburg. See death notice, July 17, 1863, *Camden Confederate.*

11. His staff included Colonel E. B. C. Cash.

12. Quoted in Kirkland and Kennedy, *Historic Camden: Nineteenth Century,* 161–63. In the years after the war, Mrs. Davis kept a private school in her home. She is referred to later in this chapter as Esther Davis.

13. Beaty, "Harriet Lang," 196.

14. Kirkland and Kennedy, *Historic Camden: Nineteenth Century,* 160. The churches' bells were not, however, actually used for such a purpose. These bells were eventually returned to their towers. The July 31, 1863, *Confederate* reported that the church bells donated twelve or fifteen months earlier were not needed to be cast into cannons, and in fact, already "the one belonging to the Methodist church has resumed its old station." The December 11, 1863, issue mentioned that the Episcopal Church bell had been heard for the first time in nearly two years.

15. Beaty, "Harriet Lang," 164.

16. Kelly is sometimes said to have been a wounded Confederate evading Yankee captors. Kelly has also been said to have been a man so heartsick with war experiences that he chose to live as a hermit.

17. John C. West, *A Texan in Search of a Fight* (Waco: Texian, 1969), 146–47. West, a Texas transplant from Kershaw District, was a soldier in Hood's Fourth Texas Brigade, Company E.

18. Kirkland and Kennedy, *Historic Camden: Nineteenth Century,* 161–63.

19. Richard Harwell and Philip N. Racine, eds., *The Fiery Trail: A Union Officer's Account of Sherman's Last Campaigns* (Knoxville: University of Tennessee Press, 1986), 142–43.

20. Ibid., 144.

21. Bessie Clark Whitaker as told to Bertie Zemp, Anne Whitaker Adams Collection, Camden Archives.

22. Harwell and Racine, *Fiery Trail,* 145.

23. One account is Oscar J. Smyrl, "The War between the States and Its Aftermath," in *Kershaw County Legacy,* ed. Inabinet and Inabinet, 17–19.

24. Harwell and Racine, *Fiery Trail,* 145–49.

25. Kirkland and Kennedy, *Historic Camden: Nineteenth Century,* 164, state that the bridge was burned by Union troops and trace some conflicting traditions that the Confederates may have set fire to the Cornwallis House before it fell into enemy hands.

26. *Camden Journal and Confederate,* March 10, 1865.

27. Kirkland and Kennedy, *Historic Camden: Nineteenth Century,* 163–75.

28. Harvey Teal, Kershaw County Historical Society meeting and tour of sites, November 4, 2000. Teal, *Kershaw County Confederate Miscellany,* 67–68, states that the name West's Crossroads apparently was a creation of the federal army since no local maps or other references used that name.

29. War of the Rebellion, Official Records of the Union and Confederate Armies. All of the records relating to Kershaw County have been reprinted in Teal, *Kershaw County Confederate Miscellany,* 56–86.

30. Harwell and Racine, *Fiery Trail,* 148.

31. Official Records, in Teal, *Kershaw County Confederate Miscellany.*

32. Harwell and Racine, *Fiery Trail,* 150–51.

33. Woodward, *Mary Chesnut's Civil War,* 742.

34. Beaty, "Harriet Lang," 198–99.

35. Federal Writers' Project.

36. Marszalek, *Diary of Emma Holmes,* 434.

37. Teal, *Kershaw County Confederate Miscellany,* 83.

38. Marszalek, *Diary of Emma Holmes,* 434.

39. Williamson, *After Slavery,* 24.

40. Marszalek, *Diary of Emma Holmes,* 434.

41. Harvey S. Teal, "Experiencing History: A Visit to a Railroad Stonehenge," University South Caroliniana Society *Newsletter,* Spring 1997.

42. Teal, *Kershaw County Confederate Miscellany,* 52–54, provides one militiaman's firsthand account of the activities surrounding Potter's raid into Kershaw District and the clash at Boykin's Mill.

43. Marszalek, *Diary of Emma Holmes,* 434; Beaty, "Harriet Lang," 199–200.

44. Williamson, *After Slavery,* 25; Edgar, *South Carolina,* 374.

45. David Duncan Wallace, *South Carolina, A Short History, 1520–1948* (Columbia: University of South Carolina Press, 1969), 554.

46. Woodward, *Mary Chesnut's Civil War,* 830.

47. Boykin, *Falling Flag,* 64–66.

48. Most of these obituaries have been compiled from local newspapers and family files in cooperation with the Catawba-Wateree Genealogical Society and are in the Camden Archives.

49. Kirkland and Kennedy, *Historic Camden: Nineteenth Century,* provides more extensive information on these men. Chesnut and Kershaw in 1868–76 were "the political leaders of the state." Kennedy in 1880 was elected lieutenant governor, and under appointment by President Cleveland he served as U.S. consul general at Shanghai, China, from 1884 to 1888.

50. Erected in 1910, the fountain was originally located at the Broad and DeKalb intersection and then was moved several times before it was refurbished and installed as a working fountain at its present location.

51. Felix DeWeldon's most famous sculpture is *Raising the Flag at Iwo Jima,* a memorial near the Arlington National Cemetery near Washington, D.C. The Kirkland memorial, as stated on its base, was "Dedicated to National Unity and the Brotherhood of Man."

52. Tradition has it that Boykin was the sharpshooter who felled Stevens. See Richard Manning Boykin, *Captain Alexander Hamilton Boykin* (New York, 1942), 185.

Chapter 10. Festering Controls

1. Williamson, *After Slavery,* 40.

2. Edgar, *South Carolina,* 379.

3. Beaty, "Harriet Lang," 204.

4. Kirkland and Kennedy, *Historic Camden: Nineteenth Century,* 197–98.

5. Some local individuals quietly flouted resistance with seeming compliance by signing oaths by mark rather than signature. The authors have seen a few surviving local oaths that were signed with "X" by persons otherwise known to be literate and capable of writing their own names.

6. In March 1865 Congress created the Bureau of Refugees, Freedmen and Abandoned Lands. Established within the War Department, the Freedmen's Bureau, as it became known, was to exist for one year from the end of the war. Managed by a presidentially appointed commissioner and ten assistants, the bureau was a primitive welfare agency distributing food, clothing, and fuel to the impecunious of both races. Commissioner Oliver O. Howard was given control of all confiscated land in the South.

7. Kirkland and Kennedy, *Historic Camden: Nineteenth Century,* 198.

8. All quotes by Matheson are from an interview for the Federal Writers' Project.

9. Under slavery only 60 percent of black Americans counted toward congressional apportionment. The "three-fifths" clause was a compromise at the 1789 constitutional convention.

10. Harvey S. Teal, *Public Schools, 1868–1870: Education during Reconstruction in Kershaw County, S.C.* (Camden, S.C.: Image Printing, 2004), 10.

11. The Second Military District was established on March 2, 1867, and consisted of South Carolina and North Carolina; General Daniel Sickles was given command.

12. When Congress in 1866 extended the existence of the Freedmen's Bureau to 1868, it approved additional assistant commissioners. It also authorized the retention of army officers mustered out of the regular service. It seems probable that this was the case with Samuel Place. Another provision of the same act allowed the sale of Confederate public land for black schools. This might explain the presence of Jackson School for blacks, which was built on a public park square in Camden.

13. The straight-out concept was to promote straight-ticket voting of Democrats only; it rebuked the concepts of fusion and cooperation.

14. The printed trial report is in the South Caroliniana Library.

15. The U.S. Supreme Court in *Ex parte Milligan,* December term 1866, condemned the practice of trying civilians in military tribunals when civilian courts were available. However, Congress differed with the ruling, and it was seldom upheld.

16. Kirkland and Kennedy, *Historic Camden: Nineteenth Century,* 200–201.

17. Samuel R. Adams to Robert K. Scott, May 26, 1868, Governors' Papers, SCDAH.

18. Kirkland and Kennedy, *Historic Camden: Nineteenth Century,* 202. There were attacks against Republicans statewide, and in addition to Dill, a representative from Abbeville and a senator from Orangeburg were murdered.

19. Copies of letters from M. P. "Pink" Kelley (Kelly) of Kershaw District to his wife, Eliza, July 4 to 19, 1868, from "Charleston Prison" were given to Joan Inabinet by their owner, Mrs. LaVerne Duncan of Clovis, New Mexico. A Confederate States of America veteran in Hampton's Brigade, Kelley was a vigilante with that unit during Sherman's invasion, and contents of the letters suggest that he was incarcerated in the roundup following the Dill shooting. The letters corroborate what the newspaper said of the arrests. On July 4 Kelley wrote his wife that he did not know what charges had been made against him, but "I think it verry hard and unjust to keep a man in prison for something he noed nothing about." The other letters maintain his innocence and deny any knowledge of the charges. On July 14 he wrote, "I understand that Mr. B. Albert Gardner Kelley & A. A. Boykin has gon home & I hope I will get off Soon." Two days later the *Journal* reported, "Alexander A. Boykin, Henry Boykin, and Burrell Albert, arrested by the military authorities for supposed complicity in the 'Dill' murder have been released and returned to their homes." Kelley and all others were released, no record existing that any information emerged.

20. Edgar, *South Carolina,* 398. He describes the attacks as "not coordinated but rather the work of individual dens of the Ku Klux Klan (KKK) formed to neutralize the Union League."

21. Carol K. Rockroth Bleser, *The Promised Land: The History of the South Carolina Land Commission 1869–89* (Columbia: University of South Carolina Press, 1969), 167. The counties were Charleston, Chesterfield, Colleton, Marion, and Richland.

22. Joan A. Inabinet, *A Wateree River Plantation Journal: "Rosny," from 1815* (Camden, S.C.: Kershaw County Historical Society, 1997).

23. Bleser, *Promised Land,* 42–43.

24. According to his obituary (*Columbia Record,* March 2, 1935), Major Samuel R. Adams was a civil engineer with Sherman and after the war was provost marshal in Camden, where he "was acclaimed by Kershaw county people for the manner in which he handled the delicate negro question and the Ku Klux Klan." Adams remained after Reconstruction ended and "was one of the contractors who built the Washington and Chesapeake railroad and the Three C's road . . . now a branch of the Southern railway. He also built the dam and canal that furnished the water to the Hermitage cotton mill of Camden." Besides "highway construction and other building work in the Camden section" and membership on the county board of commissioners, he was owner of "the big Adams mill pond and plantation, east of Camden [now Goodale State Park]. He was identified with social and club life of Camden and was prominent in Masonic circles. He was not looked upon as a former Union soldier and former provost marshal. The fact that he had fought against the Confederacy never proved embarrassing to him. Confederate veterans were his warmest friends."

25. Bleser, *Promised Land,* 47.

26. Edgar, *South Carolina,* 399.

27. Kirkland and Kennedy, *Historic Camden: Nineteenth Century,* 208–9.

28. Marszalek, *Diary of Emma Holmes,* 466, 460, 461–62.

29. Ibid., 460, 472.

30. William M. Shannon, manuscript, Camden Archives.

31. All quotes by Lee are from an interview for the Federal Writers' Project.

32. The January 18, 1867, *Camden Journal* reported a current migration of freedmen from South Carolina. Between 1860 and 1870 Kershaw District lost 93 "colored" people and 1,221 whites. The state as a whole gained 3,494 "colored" people and lost 1,633 whites.

33. Beaty, "Harriet Lang," 204.

34. Teal, *Return of Crops and Other Statistics of Kershaw County,* 2.

35. Daniel Whitfield Gardner, a veteran from the Bethune area, in his reminiscence of the war stated that in 1861 he had remained home to run his father-in-law's turpentine business to allow his father to enlist. However, Gardner himself enlisted on April 20, 1862, under Lieutenant B. S. Lucas and became company clerk in Captain Blair's Company A.

36. Transcribed by Dallas Phelps, Wateree-–Catawba Genealogical Society, Camden Archives.

37. W. E. Johnson Papers (copy), Camden Archives.

38. Fragment of an 1876 issue, month and day unknown.

39. Teal, *Public Schools.* A list of white and African American schools, students, and teachers is included.

40. A school named Jackson has continued to occupy the site since that time. The name continues in use for the elementary school at the site in 2010. Jackson will remain the name when the school moves to a new building on U.S. Highway 1 east of Camden in 2010–11.

41. Teal, *Public Schools.*

42. Inabinet, *Lyttleton Street United Methodist Church,* 99.

43. Inabinet, *His People,* 47–49.

44. Cunningham, *Liberty Hill,* 23.

45. Anniversary program, May 20, 2001, in church files, Camden Archives.

46. WPA Church Record Survey, 1936.

47. The November 14 *Camden Journal* reported the arrest of the two appointed election managers at Lizenby's precinct for default.

48. Edgar, *South Carolina,* 401.

49. "The Iron Man," WPA news brief, Caroliniana Library.

50. Gene Osborn, "The Torch and Its Work: Some Few of the Incendiary Fires in South Carolina," *Carolina Herald and Newsletter* 32 (January–March 2004).

51. Kirkland and Kennedy, *Historic Camden: Nineteenth Century,* 222.

52. Edgar, *South Carolina,* 404, cites a difference of 1,134 votes; Kirkland and Kennedy, *Historic Camden: Nineteenth Century,* 223, cites a difference of 1,323.

53. Laws that differentiate treatment based on race have over time become identified with the label "Jim Crow," a slur associated with minstrel-show racial stereotypes.

Chapter 11. Iron Rails and Soil Rows

1. President Rutherford B. Hayes used federal troops to end the violence that had spread across eleven states and shut down two-thirds of the nation's rail traffic. An estimated five hundred thousand workers from other industries had joined the striking railroad workers, and over one hundred people had been killed before federal intervention.

2. Edgar, *South Carolina,* 426.

3. John R. Welsh, "Welsh's Station in Kershaw County," in *Names in South Carolina,* ed. Neuffer, 15:56–57.

4. Melverda O. Gaskin, "Last of Local Railway Disappearing," *Kershaw News Era,* January 7, 1990. All in-text references to Gaskin are from this newspaper article. These stations were added over time. The article was written when the railway through Kershaw County was being dismantled, its use having dwindled after World War II when "the highway system began to mushroom" and trucking companies could deliver freight straight to destinations.

5. Questions raised by the newspaper editor T. Hal Clarke about financial accounting (or the lack of it) related to the Wateree Bridge were part of political tensions at the time of the Cash-Shannon duel.

6. Joan Inabinet, "Lewis P. Anderson," in *Kershaw County Legacy,* ed. Inabinet and Inabinet, 73–74. All in-text references to this interview are from this source.

7. Nancy Higgins, "Magisterial Memories: Judge [Edgar] Marsh Recalls Tales of Camden's 'Good Old Days,'" *Chronicle-Independent,* February 21, 1983.

8. Julian B. Rush to Mrs. Boykin, January 21, 1975, files of the Kershaw County Historical Society, Camden, S.C. The letter states that he was born on October 17, 1886, and includes the note, "Please overlook all mistakes as I had to learn to write left handed after losing my right arm."

9. "Dr. Kelly Says Indians Who Built Mound Were of Lamar Village Culture," *Camden Chronicle,* September 5, 1952.

10. Warrants were issued against former governor F. J. Moses, the former clerk of the house, and the former speaker and president pro tem of the senate. Former state treasurer Cardozo and former governor Chamberlain both left the state to avoid arrest.

11. Commissioners of elections were the Democrats A. W. Burnet and J. D. Shaw and the Republican Daniel Hoskins.

12. The *Camden Journal,* January 2, 1879, reported Demus Brownfield arresting two men for illegal acts of intimidation during the 1878 elections.

13. The *Camden Journal,* October 10, 1878, referred to the "colored militia company" as the "Ellis Light Infantry" and listed the following officers of the sixty-man unit: Lemon Thomas, captain; Theodore Campbell, first lieutenant; John Reed, second lieutenant; and Scipio Timbers, third lieutenant.

14. Some articles of the time reflect contemporary tensions by calling attention to race not merely with generic group identifiers (white or black or "colored") but with individual attention to skin tone. Salmond, for example, was described as "the color of a ginger cake."

15. During the Civil War the federal government issued "greenbacks," paper money not backed by specie (gold or silver). Farmers and debtors had benefited from inflation caused by more money in circulation. Bankers and other creditors who wanted a more restrictive currency succeeded in persuading Congress in 1875 to pass the Specie Resumption Act, which withdrew the last of the greenbacks. The Greenback Party, organized by those who desired the government to reissue greenbacks, was seen as favoring "the little man."

16. Thomas Ancrum, "Many Very Interesting Events of Former Years in Life of Camden Related by a Camden Native," *Camden Chronicle,* May 22, 1953. All in-text references to Ancrum are from this source.

17. Thomas J. Kirkland, "Tillman and I, Etc. after Thoughts," manuscript commenting on his series of four articles written after Ben Tillman's death and widely published in the *Columbia State* and reprinted in various newspapers entitled "Tillman and I," Kirkland Papers, Camden Archives. In the manuscript Kirkland comments, "The four articles . . . were portions of a single paper sent complete to the State more than a month ago and by it divided into weekly installments. It was not prepared for publication but only as a record for my family, hence its egotistic cast."

18. Elizabeth Hough, "Confederate Memorial Associations," in *Kershaw County Legacy*, ed. Inabinet and Inabinet, 13–14.

19. The memorial was removed to its present location, the center of the southwestern corner of Monument Square (for a number of years called Monumental Square).

20. Teal, *Kershaw County Confederate Miscellany*, 5–15.

21. The Southern and Northern Methodists had separated prior to the Civil War, like other denominations, and did not reunite until the formation of the United Methodist Church in 1968.

22. References that the graded system began operation under the organization of A. C. Moore in fall 1888 are supported by the June 10, 1898, *Chronicle:* "Six of the eleven of the present graduating class entered the school in Grade 1 . . . under the very efficient charge of Miss Lizzie Stone[y] when the Graded School System was really first established here, with A. C. Moore as Superintendent, and Mrs. Shannon as the first president. This class, therefore, a majority of whom have known no other schooling, may be considered the first fruits of the system as conducted here in Camden." Students graduated then at the end of tenth grade. Moore was afterward a professor of botany at South Carolina College.

23. In 1888 former Confederate major W. Z. (Zack) Leitner, South Carolina secretary of state and former state senator, died. Later his home, the residence on Monument Square built by John N. Gamewell, was sold to public school trustees and served as Camden High School from 1903 until 1919.

24. The McCandless schoolhouse was moved and made into a residence at 410 Laurens, retaining floor marks where teachers' desks stood.

25. Joan A. Inabinet, ed., *A History of Camden High School, Incorporating Jackson High School* (Camden, S.C.: Camden High School, 1991), provides researched information on Camden schools, black and white, from the beginning of the graded school system.

26. Kennedy served as superintendent of the Camden-area system from 1893 until 1912. Included in this system were Camden, Factory School, Malvern Hill School, Jackson School (black), and Knights Hill School (black).

27. J. W. Gardner, unpublished journal (1885–1901), Camden Archives.

28. Watts-Kirkland Family Papers, Camden Archives.

29. The 1893 depression was the most severe up to that time. Most farmers and debtors called for an inflation that would bring higher prices for crop yields. The coinage of silver, added to gold coinage, would have put more money in circulation and increased the prices of goods and services—hence inflation; but in the long run this would also have increased farmers' costs for purchasing farm equipment, seeds, and fertilizers.

30. Kirkland and Kennedy, *Historic Camden: Nineteenth Century*, 34. Camden Cotton Mill was sold in 1905. H. G. Carrison became president of the new corporation, Hermitage Cotton Mill.

31. Jean Wells, "Hermitage Mill," in *Legacy II,* ed. Inabinet and Inabinet, 56. Mrs. Wells and students interviewed a member of the family who owned Hermitage Mill.

32. Marion H. Heyman, "Some Impressions of Camden prior to and after Turn of Century," *Camden Chronicle,* March 19, 1953. All in-text references to Heyman are from this newspaper article.

33. "Our Town," *Camden News,* April 1945—newsprint supplement for servicemen, copy in Camden Archives. All in-text references to this article are from this source.

34. Nan Hough Forester, "Memories: Longtime Camden Resident Recalls Growing Up Here," *Chronicle-Independent,* May 4, 1983. All in-text references to Forester are from these memoirs.

35. The *Camden Chronicle,* September 6, 1901, reported that the "North Western Railroad" was building a twenty-four by ninety-four-foot freight depot "near the Three C's depot, on the north side of DeKalb street and not far from the office building of the Cotton Seed Oil Mill."

36. The original part of the Shannon house that became Hobkirk Inn is today a private residence at 1919 Lyttleton Street.

37. "There Was No Place Like Cousin Callie's Uphton Court," *Chronicle-Independent,* March 25, 1983, excerpts of Mrs. W. D. Tran(t)ham's article in the June 29, 1964, *Camden Chronicle.*

38. Daniels, *Nothing Could Be Finer,* 9.

39. Ibid., 5.

40. Viola C. Floyd, *Lancaster County Tours* (Lancaster, S.C.: Lancaster County Historical Commission, 1956), 90.

41. Gardner, *Murder and Mayhem,* 189.

42. Scott Pruden, "Liberty Hill 29074," *Chronicle-Independent,* January 22, 1993. Mary Cunningham's father, Charles D. Cunningham, was Liberty Hill postmaster from 1918 until 1942.

43. In the December 30, 1904, *Camden Chronicle,* J. E. Creed advertised a "Big Sale at Cantey Hill," stating, "The price of cotton has gone down and I am going to sell goods the same way." A. D. Kennedy's advertisement immediately below Creed's stated that cotton had declined fifteen dollars a bale.

44. Watts-Kirkland Family Papers, Camden Archives.

45. In a later interview W. T. Ratcliffe, the mill owner and grandson of its builder, said that the capacity of the water-powered sawmill was about 10 percent that of a modern diesel-powered one (*Camden Chronicle,* September 12, 1962).

46. Frank M. Heath, "Camden's First Football Team," *Camden Chronicle,* November 20, 1942.

47. Johnson, *Gridiron Legends,* 122. This work not only contains a century of scores and photographs but also reprints stories from the press.

48. Kirkland and Kennedy, *Historic Camden: Colonial and Revolutionary,* 33; F. N. McCorkle, "History of Camden Was Subject of Talk," *Camden Chronicle,* September 20, 1940.

49. McCorkle, "History of Camden."

50. Jean Pruett, "Camden Street Names," in *Names in South Carolina,* ed. Neuffer, 26:10.

51. Kirkland and Kennedy, *Historic Camden: Nineteenth Century,* 234.

52. A number of other accounts have been written regarding this event. See Harris H. Mullen, *The Cash-Shannon Duel: Also Duels around Camden, the Code of Honor* (Tampa: Trend House, 1963); and John Hammond Moore, "The Cash-Shannon Duel," manuscript, South Caroliniana Library.

53. Kirkland and Kennedy, *Historic Camden: Nineteenth Century,* 225–26.

54. Ibid., 225–26.

55. *Kershaw Gazette,* March 29 and April 5, 1883. The former stated that Bristow had "been visited frequently by the white ministers in town, and regularly by one or two of the colored preachers." The latter reported that when Sheriff Doby and a reporter went to Bristow's cell, he was "in conversation with Rev. Monroe Boykin and Rev. Townsend."

56. *Camden Chronicle,* September 3, 1897. Mormon elders, appealing for protection from the state attorney general's office, emphasized that they did not practice polygamy, nor was it preached by their elders. In various parts of the country, members of the Church of Jesus Christ of Latter-day Saints were being opposed because of the perception that they practiced polygamy.

57. Teal and Wallace, *South Carolina Dispensary.*

58. Halsall's son-in-law John McKain Smyrl, in the grocery business with him, later became the county dispenser and operated a state distillery at Smyrl Hill (area of present Ehrenclou Drive near Chesnut Ferry Road).

59. A number of state and local newspapers of varying dates have been gleaned for these details. Camden also had a beer dispensary by 1904, for which purpose the old post office on Rutledge Street was renovated.

60. Inabinet, *Lyttleton Street United Methodist Church,* 121.

61. The "lockup" was separated from public functions. A fragment of an 1883 *Kershaw Gazette* includes "The New Police Station," approving the town council's "having removed the guardhouse from its former inappropriate place and having built a more comfortable and a more convenient place in rear of the market. The old brick engine house has been partitioned so as to set apart the south end for a 'lock-up' for violators of the laws of the town." The facility contained two cells, each about nine feet square, and represented "a great improvement, as the old cells, where they were located, were an eyesore and a nuisance." The old firehouse building on Rutledge Street retained cells at the rear.

62. In fact, in 1897 the General Assembly had reduced penalties for violating the concealed-weapons law, which in essence encouraged the carrying of weapons. From the evidence of shootings during the two decades preceding the Great War, it appears that many citizens carried weapons.

Chapter 12. Uneven Steps

1. Edgar, *South Carolina,* 450–51.

2. The Southern's acquisition of the route within Kershaw County began with the purchase of the Three C's in 1898 to Camden. The transfer of the South Carolina Railroad below Camden seems to have been accomplished by 1902.

3. Present Route 261 to Boykin follows the route of old 521, which was rerouted to its present location, following the straight bed of the old dismantled Northwestern railroad.

4. By the 1872 schedule, the train left Camden at 7:20 A.M., arriving in Columbia at 11:55; the return train left Columbia at 2:10 P.M., arriving in Camden at 6:55. Trains changed at Kingville before crossing the Wateree River at Wateree Junction. In 1900 passengers could leave Camden at 8:22 A.M. and arrive in Columbia at 9:45; a return schedule allowed a traveler to return to Camden by 7:40 P.M. The January 25, 1901, *Camden Chronicle* mentioned that the American Bridge Company, at that time building the steel bridge for the railroad over the Wateree River, would next go to Egypt to build thirty-four viaducts for the Uganda Railroad.

5. Collected from various references on miscellaneous writings of Louise Pettus, Viola C. Floyd, Miles Gardner, and *Kershaw News-Era.* Kershaw's First Baptist was originally organized on the town's northeastern outskirts as Laurel Hill Baptist in 1881. The Methodist church and the Presbyterian church were both organized in 1891, the latter with sixteen charter members.

6. Neighbors brought an injunction "because the chemicals used in separating the gold from the ore ran down the streams and killed all the vegetation" (*Camden Chronicle,* May 30, 1913).

7. Steen, *Stoneboro,* 115–27.

8. Harvey S. Teal, "What a Railroad Brought to Kershaw County," *Update,* Kershaw County Historical Society, Camden, S.C., 2 parts, June and October 2002. All in-text references to Teal's article are to this source.

9. Harriet Mays, "Bethune History Given by Native," *Camden Chronicle,* November 13, 1970.

10. Patrick and Middendorf in Chesterfield County, also on the route between Columbia and Cheraw, were named for Seaboard bankers. In Kershaw County, Cassatt was named for Alexander Johnston Cassatt, who began his career in 1861 as a civil engineer with the Pennsylvania Railroad and served as president from 1889. A life-sized statue of him was erected in 1910 in Pennsylvania Station in New York. See Clyde Williams Jr., "Who Was Cassatt?," manuscript, Camden Archives.

11. Letter quoted from Thomas Ancrum, in undated clipping, Camden Archives. This is the source of information he supplied on Lugoff for "Camden Names" to Neuffer, *Names in South Carolina,* 13:9.

12. "Some Interesting Chit-Chat," undated clipping, Camden Archives.

13. The July 29, 1904, *Camden Chronicle* reported that the fire at Lafayette Hall spread considerably before it was discovered. Owned by Baron Egmont von Tresckow, the building was being run as a commercial hotel by Mr. and Mrs. Scott Brown.

14. Kirkland and Kennedy, *Historic Camden: Nineteenth Century,* 34. The January 4, 1901, *Camden Chronicle* reported that South Carolina led the nation in the construction of cotton mills with thirty-one new mills; fourteen others "made increases and enlargements." In its enumeration of the state's new mills, the capitalization of the DeKalb Cotton Mill is listed at two hundred thousand dollars.

15. Smyrl was sometimes familiarly called "John Mac," and his surname at times was perceived to be "McSmyrl." He used that spelling in advertising, and bottles for his Wateree Corn Whiskey are marked "John McSmyrl." See Teal and Wallace, *South Carolina Dispensary.*

16. Ken DuBose and Boo DuBose, "'Village' Conditions at Turn of Century Less than Perfect," *Chronicle-Independent,* May 4, 1983.

17. Oscar J. Smyrl, "The War between the States and Its Aftermath," in *Legacy II,* ed. Inabinet and Inabinet, 19.

18. Woody and Beard, *South Carolina Postcards, Volume VII* and *South Carolina Postcards, Volume VIII.* Davie Beard is a local collector.

19. Gardner, *Murder and Mayhem,* 191–92.

20. *Guide to Historical Sites in Kershaw County,* 79.

21. The *Camden Chronicle,* May 15, 1915, reported that the Daughters of the American Revolution preserved the "famous old court house for the town when it was about to be sold for brick." The mission of the organization then was education and "wiping out illiteracy." In 1912 Camden High School was operating in the old Gamewell-Leitner House on Monument Square.

22. Daniels, *Nothing Could Be Finer,* 2.

23. The April 10, 1914, *Camden Chronicle* referred to a "recent near panic" at the opera house that demonstrated the need for changes. Some disorder resulted when 150 children tried to leave when one side exit was obstructed by a platform used as a stage and the other side exit was dangerous. Also reported were that "the front doors open inward" and that the theater was on the second floor; the "present building is a menace to life and limb."

24. Gardner, *Murder and Mayhem,* 153–59.

25. Ibid., 166–69.

26. Bridge Papers, Camden Archives.

27. The *Camden Chronicle,* August 4, 1916, stated that in the Santee and Wateree swamps there was an estimated half-million dollars worth of cotton that had "floated away from various mill warehouses which were destroyed by the floods." Catawba Indians reportedly located over one hundred bales from "an eddy opposite their reservation on the Catawba River."

28. *Camden Chronicle,* August 11, 1916. South Carolina railroad inspectors examining the Seaboard trestle were told by engineers that they had to go down fifty feet to get a solid foundation for the concrete piers. The trestle was expected to be finished within thirty days.

29. *Camden Chronicle,* August 4, 1916. A problem following the floods was a proliferation of mosquitoes and the fear of malaria and other diseases. W. D. Whitaker, Camden's street commissioner, made a supply of crude oil at the old power plant available to the public at no charge. Whitaker said, "By freely using this oil in the damp places and ditches it will help a great deal."

30. The published suit is in the Kirkland Papers, South Caroliniana Library.

31. Mendel L. Smith, speaker of the house and candidate for governor (against Blease), was elected judge of the Fifth Judicial Circuit. The vacancy occurred when Judge Ernest Gary died. Smith's papers are at the South Caroliniana Library.

32. Coleman L. Blease, during his governorship, had alarmed many by his actions. He had granted 1,624 pardons and paroles and had disbanded the state militia, leaving the state unprotected for weeks. When Blease was informed of efforts under way to impeach

him, he resigned on January 12. Lieutenant Governor Charles A. Smith was sworn in ten minutes later.

33. There were numerous reasons for the success of the vote on Prohibition. Aside from the moral and religious ones, with a war going on in Europe and America on the verge of entering it, there was a move toward conservation. Grain that did not go into alcoholic beverages could be used as food for people and animals. Furthermore, since Germany—viewed as the aggressor in the war—had a high stake in the beer industry, Americans could derive a measure of satisfaction by shutting down use of that product.

34. The August 21, 1914, *Camden Chronicle* printed the farewell. Former governor Tillman, who had served in the United States Senate since his election in 1894, announced his intention to retire when his term ended in 1919; however, he died in 1918 while still in office.

35. In 1915, when the state militia was reorganized, the Kershaw Guards, who had been Company A, Second Infantry since 1903, became Company M, First Infantry and were part of the Third Battalion.

36. Estimates of water consumption needs were based on household and business requirements that differed greatly from present ones.

37. The *Camden Chronicle,* April 24, 1914, described the placement of cluster lights "on Broad from Lafayette on the North to York on the South, and on DeKalb from Lyttleton on the East to Broad on the West, alternating on each side of the pavement at distances of 100 feet apart."

38. Examinations were publicly announced for available positions. One of the reforms following President Garfield's assassination was the passage of the Pendleton Civil Service Act. The classification of thousands of civil service jobs would be filled not by patronage but by merit. Thus, mail carriers were chosen from those who successfully passed the civil service examination.

39. Use of this building as the public library ended when the new facility of the Kershaw County Library opened just south of it on Broad Street, but the Carnegie building was converted and later expanded to house the present Camden Archives and Museum, which had its origin in a collection begun in the old Camden Library there.

40. The August 18, 1916, *Camden Chronicle* advertised a "fully loaded 6-passenger" Anderson, "the Sensible Car," for $1,250 at McDowell Brothers in Camden (agents for Kershaw and Sumter counties). Kershaw Motor Company of Camden offered a Ford Runabout for $345 or a Ford Touring Car for $360.

Chapter 13. Bridging Isolation

1. The June 29, 1917, *Camden Chronicle* included a complete list of "Kershaw County Boys Who Have Enrolled for Service in Uncle Sam's Fighting Forces," divided into whites and blacks and listed alphabetically by place of registration. Since names of places are also precincts, they are probably the residential areas of enrollees. At the end of the war the December 20, 1918, *Camden Chronicle* listed the killed, wounded, and missing in action in France.

2. Concerned about adult illiteracy, in 1914 Miss Wil Lou Gray, rural school supervisor of Laurens County, organized the first night school in South Carolina. Before going

to an educational position in Maryland in 1917, she organized rural night schools, educational tours, and historical pageants in South Carolina. In 1918 she returned to her home state to head the South Carolina Illiteracy Commission and then become the first adult-education director for South Carolina, from which the landmark Opportunity School program began for family literacy.

3. Ironically only four months earlier the January 19, 1917, *Camden Chronicle* reported that Kershaw students had won a debate with Camden students at the Kershaw school auditorium. The topic was "Resolved That the deportation of the Negro from America would be beneficial to the South," and the Kershaw students were assigned the affirmative.

4. In the early days of automobile travel, similar travails were typical in other places as well. A letter was printed in the May 11, 1917, *Camden Chronicle* from Camden tourists Mr. and Mrs. Paul Rehnborg, who had returned to their home in Connecticut:

> Richmond to Fredericksburg [was] particularly bad. At Fredericksburg we learned that road (the National W. A. Highway) through Dumphries Swamp was impassable. Some cars had come through but only with the help of 4 to 6 mule teams, so we put our car and ourselves on Rappahanock [*sic*] River steamer for Baltimore and continued our trip from there. Pennsylvania roads are all fine macadam, so are New Jersey. From New York up, they have the finest Tarvia roads. We camped out all the way and spent two days camping and fishing on the river above Fredericksburg while waiting for steamer.

5. "Just below" is a description in relative comparison to previous bridges. The bridge site can be viewed to the north of the present U.S. Highway 1 bridge, from which at normal water levels some of the concrete of the old piers can be seen at the bank's western edge.

6. Kershaw County residents could purchase ticket books in advance at reduced prices.

7. The swinging bridge appears to have been in the area of Eagle's Nest. Some of the elderly residents of the upper county area recall having heard of it.

8. In January 1918, for the first time in twenty-eight years, Factory Pond was frozen over, and icy conditions remained for several days.

9. At the time in South Carolina liquor sales were legal only when ordered by individuals from out of state and received by them under a "gallon a month" restriction. Liquor that had been seized at the station was being sold by a local grocer, who flavored it with ginger and sold it by the drink.

10. President Wilson supported the amendment to conserve grain for the war effort.

11. Interview with Thomas McLester, Camden, 2006.

12. Hudson was transferred to the state mental hospital. Latta was named to the Law Enforcement Hall of Fame decades later.

13. Montgomery, *Camden Heritage,* 90.

14. African Americans were among board members of the Jeanes Fund, unlike boards of similar funds, and helped make financial decisions. Carol Sears Botsch, in the political science department at the University of South Carolina, Aiken, states in her study "The Jeanes Fund in South Carolina":

Miss Jeanes had insisted that Booker T. Washington sit on the board, and that he have the authority to pick other members. He selected other African-Americans to serve, selecting men who favored industrial education for blacks, rather than educating blacks for the professions, which might challenge the social and economic status quo. The monies were invested in secure government bonds, and when interest rates fell in the 1930s, rural schools had to depend on other foundations and federal aid to supplement. With these additional funds, the Fund was able to increase the low salaries of the Jeanes supervisors and employ them for a longer period of months each year. The fund merged with several other educational funds in the late 1930s, including the Virginia Randolph Fund, which had been created with monies raised by the Jeanes Supervisors. The result of this merger was the Southern Education Foundation.

15. Belk's father allowed publication of the comrade's letter. See *Camden Chronicle,* June 18, 1920.

16. The original name of James Leroy Belk Post 17 when it was first headquartered at Camden was Kershaw Post 17, but soon confusion resulted in references and mailings with a newer post at the town of Kershaw. At Kershaw, Post 63 took the name of the Walter Johnson Post. Many years later additional posts organized in the county: Sanders-Stoney Post 203 at Camden, Bethune Memorial Post 155 at Bethune, and Larry Jeffers Post 195 at Lugoff-Elgin.

17. The list of names honored annually at the combined memorial services of the American Legion posts of Kershaw County includes World War I active-duty wartime deaths. The names were matched with local cemetery records.

18. *Camden Chronicle,* December 3, 1920.

19. Ibid., June 23, 1929. "Uncle Wash Drakeford," who had accompanied his master Colonel William Drakeford through the war, died at eighty-seven years old at his home fifteen miles north of Camden. He had remained "bright and alert" until a few weeks before his death. "He could read and write from what had been taught him in slavery and around the camp fires during the war. He used remarkably correct English and could express himself in a clear manner."

Chapter 14. Inns, Farms, and Mill Whistles

1. The first group of women named, in the order listed (perhaps the order of registering), were as follows: Mrs. Lucy W. Kennedy, Miss Olive W. Whitredge, Miss Rosa Gaskin, Mrs. J. E. Gaskin, Mrs. Lydia V. Elliott, Mrs. Lottie Kirkley, Miss Minnie Hough, Mrs. Sue Bethune, Mrs. Katie Bethune, Mrs. M. C. Miller, Mrs. Edna Z. Team, Miss M. E. Gerald, Mrs. B. B. Kennedy, Mrs. S. A. Burrier, Mrs. M. N. Carrison, Mrs. Sadie J. Eichel, Miss Rosa Lee Jacobson, Miss C. Wolfe, Miss Celeste F. Mumford, Miss Elizabeth Carrison, Mrs. Mary E. Boykin, Mrs. Mai Wells Boykin, Mrs. Ida S. Heath, Mrs. Rhetta Burnett Corbett, Mrs. Helen Alexander Savage, Mrs. Harriett Burnett Whitaker, Mrs. Alice Corbett Marye, Miss Ethel Caroline Yates, Mrs. Blanche Gregory, Mrs. Ella Raley, Mrs. Rhodie Honeycutt, Mrs. M. E. Lorick, Mrs. Bessie Lorick, Mrs. Mary G. Perry, Mrs. B. R. Wolfe, Miss Sara F. Wolfe, Mrs. M. E. Blackwell, Mrs. Alethia Huckabee Truesdell, Miss Willie Watkins, Miss Charlotte D. Kershaw, Mrs. Josephine K. deLoach, Mrs. Josephine Watkins, Mrs. Nellie Simpson Pearce, Mrs. S. E. Hough,

Mrs. Louise W. Lenoir, Mrs. Carrie W. Burnett, Mrs. Annie Huckabee Miller, Mrs. Laura J. Mitcham, Mrs. Cleo Mitcham Buddin, Mrs. Margaret J. Mills, Mrs. Alice Dupre Chewning, Miss Margaret Smith Burnett, Mrs. Margaret O. Latham, Miss Lal R. Blakeney, Mrs. Estelle C. Harding, Miss Mary D. Villepigue, Mrs. Blanche Clyburn, Miss Lena M. Lineberger, Miss Minnie A. Alexander, Miss Willie S. Alexander, Mrs. Ida I. Marshall, and Mrs. Bessie McLean King. Those registrants in the second group were Addie E. Grigsby, Lillian M. Grigsby, Bessie L McCaskill, Roma Lyles, Floride S. Parker, Kate B. Ward, Emma W. Alexander, Rose E. Alexander, and Callie Williams.

It might appear that the names in the September 17, 1920, *Camden Chronicle* were published as potential encouragement to other women to register. On October 8, however, the later article omitted courtesy titles when naming nine more registrants of like status and was positioned side by side with a report of "Three Women Arrested" at a house of ill repute "in the lower section of the city." This might appear to be a reminder, as women at the time were being warned, that public exposure could result in embarrassing company.

2. A longtime assistant in the clerk of court's office before her appointment, she in later years married the widowed clerk of court James H. Clyburn and later, after his death, was herself elected clerk of court.

3. In 1929 Kathleen B. Watts was elected county superintendent of education.

4. Mary Blakeney Zemp Letters, transcribed by Elizabeth Goude Patterson, Caroliniana Library.

5. J. W. Maynard was named cotton grader at Camden in September 1920.

6. County agent John W. Sanders was soon inviting farmers to join hands with the American Products Export and Import Corporation for "a better and broader cotton market."

7. A letter sent out by national Ku Klux Klan leader W. J. Simmons and printed without comment in the November 5, 1920, *Camden Chronicle* protested that such persons were not part of the "real" KKK, which, the writer said, was "sworn to uphold the law," not to break it.

8. Some farmers even made their own molasses, growing and cooking the syrup of the cane they ground.

9. Arsenic tended to build up in clay-heavy soils more than in sandy ones. One of the causes of soil infertility in the 1930s was thought to be buildup of arsenic in cotton fields that had been repeatedly dusted in the 1920s.

10. Before Prohibition it was considered unsafe for women to be in the downtown area on Saturday, especially later in the day, as public drunkenness was common.

11. Clyde T. Mounter, *The Quiet Revolution: A Seventy-five Year History of Women's Extension Clubs in South Carolina* (Easley, S.C.: Martin Printing, 1995), 25.

12. Broadus Mitchell, *The Rise of Cotton Mills in the South* (Baltimore: Johns Hopkins University Press, 1921), 231.

13. Jean Wells, "Hermitage Mills," in *Legacy II,* ed. Inabinet and Inabinet, 56, says that Pitts became paymaster in 1908 and served as president from 1909, based on Pitts family interview. An article reprinted from the *Hermitage Citizen* of July 1920 in the July 30 *Camden Chronicle* states: "In 1905 the present Hermitage Mill was organized with

H. G. Carrison as president; C. H. Yates, vice president and secretary; and R. B. Pitts, manager. In December 1911 Mr. R. B. Pitts took charge as president and treasurer, which position he still holds."

14. Wells, "Hermitage Mills," 56.

15. Henry P. Kendall, "The Kendall Company," speech at the Newcomen Society, Boston, 1953.

16. This meeting has sometimes been reported as having taken place in April, but a report of its taking place on March 5 appeared in the March 12, 1920, *Camden Chronicle,* and election results for mayor and alderman at the first meeting were named in that issue.

17. At the next meeting, the new village preacher, the Reverend W. E. Furcron, was named an ex-officio member of the governing board. The same alderman were reelected for a second six-month term, except that when Ike DeBruhl moved, he was replaced by Jess Moore.

18. A colloquial name for the business-residential area was "Potlikker," for the cooking odors from homes and eating establishments there. The name was widely used for a number of years.

19. *The Kershaw County, South Carolina, Cemetery Survey,* vol. 1, quotes the death date from his tombstone in the Cedars Cemetery in Camden as July 4, 1926, but the year should be 1927, evidenced by the unfolding of events as reported in the *Camden Chronicle.*

20. Daniels, *Nothing Could Be Finer,* 91.

21. Nancy Higgins, "Minnie Baum's Seen 'Great Progress,'" *Camden Chronicle,* July 27, 1981.

22. Daniels, *Nothing Could Be Finer,* 85.

23. Stephen Lough, "The Kirkwood Hotel," in *Legacy II,* ed. Inabinet and Inabinet, 62.

24. Karl P. Abbott, *Open for the Season* (New York: Doubleday, 1950), 182.

25. Margaret Pokrant, "The Kirkwood Hotel," in *Legacy II,* ed. Inabinet and Inabinet, 64.

26. Oliver, *Living in Camden,* 27.

27. Gila Holland, "White Oak Basket Weaving," in *Legacy II,* ed. Inabinet and Inabinet, 24, cover photograph.

28. Oliver, *Living in Camden,* 26.

29. Interview with Shannon DuBose, Camden, 2004.

30. In April 1932, for example, the club met at the home of Mrs. Charles Salmon to study the work of Edward MacDowell for their program: "Mrs. Dan Murchison read a sketch of MacDowell's life and interpreted his 'Woodland Sketches.' The sketches were rendered on the piano by Mrs. James Gandy. Mrs. Edward DuBose gave a most interesting talk on the MacDowell colony at Peterborough, N.H."

31. The letters, in the possession of Joan A. Inabinet, are addressed to Mrs. Edwin Farmer. Because she signed only with affectionate names (e.g., "Your Only Child"), the young woman's complete identity cannot be determined. A comment in one letter suggests that she was acquainted with Mrs. MacDowell.

32. In 1929 Laighton's memoir of his life and home, *Ninety Years at the Isles of Shoals,* was first published by Andover Press in Andover, Massachusetts, when he was ninety years of age. Mentions are included of Adams, Marvin, and the Camden inn. Laighton was a guest at the Hobkirk Inn and present at his deathbed when Marvin died. Laighton died in Portsmouth shortly before his one hundredth birthday.

33. In 1919 Galsworthy was in Camden visiting Mr. and Mrs. Ralph Ellis.

34. Throughout the 1920s the Tuskegee Institute's annually collected statistics on lynchings in the South were printed on the front page of the *Camden Chronicle* in early January. The incidents were not local.

35. In addition to his business and real estate investments, Kirkbride had other interests and an international background. The *Camden Chronicle* also reported a literary accomplishment. The *Stamford, Conn., Advocate* reported "a favorable reception" to the opening of *The Lion's Whelp,* a "comedy drama in four acts," written by Mr. William H. Kirkbride, whose winter home was Camden and who was spending the summer at Dublin, New Hampshire. The play was "set in one of the shires of England and in the Canadian Northwest," countries where the American-born playwright had spent a good deal of time.

36. Daniels, *Nothing Could Be Finer,* 76.

37. Jeff McMahan, *A History of the Camden Hunt 1926–1996* (Camden, S.C.: privately printed, 1996), 5. Peck Woods and Weeks Woods were areas hunted when the sporting enthusiast William H. Kirkbride was owner.

38. Abbott, *Open for the Season,* 191–93. Versions of this tale grew into local fireside hunting lore, different storytellers at times claiming to have been the one to capture the tail and be startled by the reaction of the hunt club.

39. Mary Blakeney Zemp's August 6, 1922, letter describes the view at a distance on "a lovely ride yesterday . . . beyond Cantey Hill, where we got a beautiful view of the lake made by damming the Wateree near Great Falls. I had no idea there was such scenery in our old county. It reminded us of pictures of scenes in Switzerland, and was well worth the ride of 15 miles or more" (Mary Blakeney Zemp Letters, Caroliniana Library).

40. *Camden Chronicle,* March 27, 1978.

41. The shop was named for their infant daughter, whom in later years they accompanied for a time to Hollywood to advance her career as a child movie star.

42. Mary Blakeney Zemp Letters, Caroliniana Library. A March 25, 1923, letter from her states: "I have never known an evangelist to create as much interest as Billy Sunday is doing, not only in Columbia, but throughout the state, especially in the counties near Columbia. He came to Camden . . . to the largest audience I have ever seen here. . . . My honest opinion is that the man is called of God for the biggest work that can be undertaken."

43. The article stated, "The capture was made just outside the city limits at a wayside store run by Villepigue. . . . The officers had their eyes on the place for a long time and had made repeated efforts at a capture, but each time had failed. The whiskey was not sold from the store, but in a house just to the rear, in which Villepigue resides, but says he did not own."

44. The sales practices were described to the authors by former customers and by a Dusty Bend bootlegger's daughter.

45. Johnston, *History and Homes of Liberty Hill,* I.

46. Abbott, *Open for the Season,* 187–88.

47. In 1920 Camden trustees purchased the large old Reynolds home at the corner of Chesnut and Lyttleton to refit as an enlarged school for Camden High. However, the building burned to the ground on January 1, 1921, with no insurance. Camden High students on a split schedule shared the brick Camden Graded School building on Laurens Street until 1922, when a new graded school was built facing Lyttleton on the Reynolds site and the high school took over the brick building.

48. According to the 1925 Camden city directory and other sources, that year W. A. Clarke, whose home was in Columbia, was principal of Camden High School. CHS teachers included Agnes Corbett, Louise Johnson, Eileen Little, Harry W. Muldrow, (Mrs.) Phoebe Schenk, Alberta Team, Lottie M. Vaughan, and Henrietta Zemp. Additional white teachers in Camden were Brucie Barnes, Mary F. Blackwell, Beulah Blyther, Elah Belle Blyther, Margaret Boton, Mary E. Brasington, Margaret Burnet, Dorothy Burns, Agnes DePass, Alex L. Geisenheimer, (Mrs.) Emily L. Guy, Sue Haile, Marjorie Hannah, Louise Hirsch, Henrietta Johnson, (Mrs.) Selma McKain, (Mrs.) Leslie McLeod, Willie Belle Mackey, (Mrs.) Margaret Mills, Eleanor Mitchell, (Mrs.) Anna E. Montgomery, George W. Nicholson, Ada Phelps, (Mrs.) Susie C. Taylor, Sarah Wolfe, and Ellie Zemp. In 1925 the principal of the Mill (Mills Village) School, located midway between Wateree and Hermitage mills, was Ernestine Bateman, and the teachers included (Mrs.) Bessie L. McCaskill, Lillian Patterson, (Mrs.) Lula Pearce, and Miss Annie L. Woodward. Teaching kindergarten at the Wateree Mills Club Room was Helen Phelps.

49. Teachers known to have been at Jackson High in the mid-1920s included Katie C. Powell, Addie M. Thomas, Julia Thomas, and Angie S. Thompson. Additional teachers identified by the 1925 city directory as "colored" lived and taught in various schools of the community at the time. They were Katie L. Boykin, Mamie Boykin, Eunice Carroll, Josie D. Collins, Josie Gettys, Peola Jones, Jennie E. Meeks, Willie Mouzon, Sallie Payton, Alta M. Thompson, and Wilhelmina B. Williams.

50. In 1925 Browning Home was the residence of Principal Rachel Erwin, Assistant Superintendent Florence Allinson, and Financial Secretary Lois C. McEwen, as well as the following white teachers: Hattie Johnson, Janie Few, Eva May Giger, Carrie Hall, Louella Johnson, Etta Morley, Lucile Papejoy, and Ruth Wildy. Local teachers identified by the city directory as "colored" were Rachel Brown, Ellie N. Dibble, Elise Myers, and Mattie J. Williams, whose homes were in the community.

51. Mary Blakeney Zemp Letters, Caroliniana Library. A letter from her dated May 19, 1923, states, regarding effects of the fire:

> These last two days have been like a dreadful dream . . . the whole town has been like a pall had fallen upon it. I went to the funeral of the 65 [*sic*] buried in one grave yesterday, and it was the most pathetic experience imaginable. The Humphries family is peculiarly bereaved—both the father and mother . . . and burned too badly to be recognized. In trying to save others, Tom was so badly burned that he died at the hospital last night, and today his funeral was held at Beulah Church. . . . There were five funerals today. . . . We were all so demoralized that we can scarcely think of anything but the terrible accident, and while everyone

> tried to avoid discussing it so much, we always find ourselves returning to the subject. . . . You cannot think of the terrible sorrow those wives and mothers are feeling as they relate the experiences of seeing their loved ones either burning or being crushed to death. . . . Stoney Campbell . . . got his wife out through a window and returned for his only child . . . to see her crushed under other bodies, and in trying to pull her out, heard her bones break, and left her to die without further suffering. This is one of the awful experiences we hear on all sides. I must not write more of this.

The authors have interviewed several survivors and witnesses, and contemporary local, state, and national newspapers contain lengthy accounts. A number of articles and memoirs are collected in the Camden Archives. The earliest separate publication is J. O. Moselely, *The Terrible Cleveland Fire: Its Victims and Survivors* (Charleston, S.C.: Southern Printing & Publishing, [1923]).

52. Of the dead listed on the memorial, ten were surnamed Dixon; eight, Davis; eight, McLeod; seven, Hendrix; five, McCaskill; four, Brown; four, Phillips; three, Croft; three, Hinson; three, Humphries; three, West; two, Arrants; two, Campbell; two, Sowell; two, Trapp. Surnames listed once were Barnes, Bowen, Godwin, Johnson, Pearce, Rush, Smith, Truesdel, and Wade (the nursemaid Sadie Wade, designated as "colored"). Surnames suggest family relationships, although marriage connections among the victims made family ties even more involved.

53. The Charlotte Thompson School opened in November to serve three districts and to replace four rural schools—Boykin, Cleveland, McLeod, and Stockton. The only one of the three Cleveland School teachers who elected to teach at the new school that survivors afterward attended was Miss Esther Garvin (later Bruce), who had escaped the fire by jumping out of the window. Mrs. Bruce, who taught in area schools past midcentury, was a kind and soft-spoken woman known to admonish misbehaving students gently: "People should be kind to one another. You don't know what can happen."

Chapter 15. Empty Pockets

1. On June 9, 1933, the *Camden Chronicle* reported "Terrific Sand Storm Tuesday Afternoon" when Camden and environs were "visited by high winds, accompanied by the densest cloud of dust ever seen here. It became so dark that automobiles had to turn on their lights for safety, and out on the highways they were compelled to stop by the roadside. A slight shower of rain soon followed, accompanied by considerable electricity. . . . The rain was not heavy enough to do very much good to vegetation and crops are still suffering from the drouth [*sic*]."

2. The bonds were retired in 1941.

3. Mendel Smith Papers, Caroliniana Library.

4. The January 27, 1933, *Camden Chronicle* quoted the *Calhoun Times* regarding state commander Hobson Hilton's speech at an American Legion meeting in Saint Matthews:

> He carries an empty sleeve, and was introduced as having won his spurs on the battlefield. . . . He is, when aroused, a capital talker. He exploded the soft doctrine that radicalism must not be preached. . . . He rasped the wild and brutal beasts of

> Wall Street and the international bankers, for all this propaganda to dam up the stream of governmental help to the veterans. You could almost see the blood under the epidermis as he skinned those plutocrats above. This war, he shouted, fought largely to save their money, spawned 23.000 of these million and multi-millionaires, who have robbed the government out of four billions of dollars in taxes during the last few years. Five per cent of their breed own 95 per cent of the wealth of the country, and yet they are clandestinely and selfishly scheming to beat the poor ex-service men out of their just dues. "We propose to fight them to a finish and we have the fighting organization to do it." He also warned Congress that "we have the strength and propose to use it."

5. On October 1, 1930, a law went into effect with requirements for a test of driving ability and a fee of fifty cents for a driver's license. However, all persons who currently held one of the old licenses that had been issued free without a driving test would automatically receive one of the new licenses—provided that driver was at least twelve years of age.

6. The South Carolina Council of Farm Women was organized in 1921.

7. In 1931 Zemp installed there the milling equipment he had moved from his father-in-law G. H. Lenoir's Lakewood operation, where floods in 1929 had blown out the dam, which was not replaced. The Lakewood Milling Company had been noted for making a fine grade of flour. Damage occurred throughout the county during the weather extremes of 1929–30.

8. *Camden Chronicle,* August 21, 1963.

9. The tradition of weekly social receptions continued until the death of Mrs. Kerr in 1936, when her obituary in the October 30 *Camden Chronicle* described her as "the first tourist settler in Camden." She and her husband (who predeceased her) had been coming to Camden for more than four decades, having originally registered in the 1890s at the Hobkirk Inn, then managed by Eldredge. They purchased as a home one of the former residences of John J. Cantey and made it a showplace with gardens laid out by Samuel Russell.

10. Mrs. C. M. Wilder of Savannah, Georgia, was the publicist in her place in 1932, although Mrs. Winkler returned the following year. William Garrard was the publicist in 1935.

11. The April 29, 1932, *Camden Chronicle* called E. T. Start "a photographer of international reputation . . . who has made a life-long study of his profession." He was noted for photographs of presidents, nationally known celebrities, sports, and nature. Many of the familiar local postcard images and publicity photos of the time were made by Start. The *Chronicle* stated that Start first came to Camden with T. E. Krumbholz when the Kirkwood Inn was built. He and his wife had a winter home in Camden on North Broad Street and a summer home in New York. Start told the *Chronicle* on February 17, 1933, that he was the last survivor of the original staff that had opened the Kirkwood for business thirty years earlier. See also Harvey S. Teal, *Partners with the Sun: South Carolina Photographers 1840–1940* (Columbia: University of South Carolina Press, 2001), 221–23.

12. At the ribbon-cutting ceremony opening the highway at Cheraw on September 17, 1931, a crowd of four thousand heard a message on the occasion broadcast by telephone

over loudspeakers. The orator, whom they cheered, was New York's governor Franklin Delano Roosevelt, introduced as "the next president of the United States." Roosevelt had not yet been formally nominated.

13. The name of the present Sunnyhill subdivision, begun north of Camden in the 1960s, was chosen through related business interests to recall the old plantation name, but it is not located near the site of the old Sunny Hill home. The original house, home of the early Mickle family, stood on a ridge twelve miles north of Camden. It was here that the diarist Emma Holmes of the Civil War era tutored the Mickle children. Leonard purchased Sunny Hill from its final family owner, John Belton Mickle, who lived his last years until 1937 on Union Street in Camden. In June 1947 fire leveled Sunny Hill Plantation, leaving only a chimney standing. Neighbors and plantation workers kept the fire from spreading to ten adjoining structures, including the caretaker's lodge, "fine modern stables," a water and light power house, kennels, and a tank containing one thousand gallons of fuel oil. The loss of the sixteen-room house and its surrounding landscaped grounds was estimated at $125,000. Leonard purchased adjoining Chancefield from another winter resident, Walton Ferguson Jr., from New York, who gave that name to the tract he had purchased, including the Sanders Creek site known as Vaughan's Mill, later Holland's Mill. Later, Ferguson's widow, the former Dorothy Herron Taylor, and children for various years resided seasonally at the Chancefield house, which Ferguson had built.

14. Facing concerns of extinction of the most popular game birds, in 1931 regulations forbade the baiting of fields for dove shooting and shortened the season to one month in order to restore numbers of mourning doves. The daily bag limit was reduced from twenty-five to eighteen in 1932. The *State* obituary that year of Lemuel Whit Boykin, a seventy-one-year- old native of the Boykin community, stated about one of the old-time hunters who had witnessed changes in the game population in his lifetime: "Brought up in the country, Whit Boykin was an expert woodsman and a phenomenal shot, and he brought hunting and fishing to the point of an art. His experiences by field and flood, told in his gripping and inimitable style, have delighted innumerable hearers around campfire and dining table. In more recent years, seeing the ever increasing scarcity of game, he had been deeply interested in conservation."

15. In 1899, some thirty years earlier, R. A. Carpenter was foreman of the construction crew that had constructed the Seaboard freight station at Camden. When he resigned from Seaboard, he entered the lumber business and operated mills in Pageland and Jefferson before coming to Camden.

16. The lecture took place in February 1933. Earle Sumner Draper, whose firm had helped design several Charlotte suburbs, was soon at work in a new federal position as director of town planning and housing with the Tennessee Valley Authority.

17. A core of the northern players was hired or reimbursed by the resorts, much in the way tennis instructors and golf pros blended into the athletic and social setting of hotel life. Discreet arrangements preserved a resort ambiance of polo as a sport for gentlemen rather than professionals.

18. Although assistance at the Children's Home (which was later named the Margaret C. Mayfield Children's Home) was extended regardless of race, only white children lived at the home.

19. Johnson, *Gridiron Legends,* 18.

20. The station's call letters were derived from South Carolina's slogan in recent years advertising the health advantages of produce grown in the state's soil: "Wonderful Iodine State."

21. *Chronicle-Independent,* May 4, 1983.

22. The second and only other airship of its design, the *Macon,* also came to deadly end in 1935, leading to the demise of the dirigible program.

23. Donald Leroy "Roy" Truesdell (Truesdale), a Lugoff native, was the most recent Kershaw County recipient of the Medal of Honor. The Marine corporal lost his right hand on patrol "in active operations against armed bandit forces" in northern Nicaragua in 1934 when he protected several men in his command by picking up and attempting to throw away a detonated grenade that endangered them.

24. South Carolina voted against ending national Prohibition, but when the end came, the state law reverted to the 1895 constitution allowing the sale of beer and wine in taverns and places serving food, but not in bars. Liquor sales in the meantime were restricted to limited amounts ordered and purchased by individuals from out-of-state dealers.

25. Near the end of the decade Mrs. Morrison and Mrs. Samuel Russell were leaders in organizing a little theater, the Playmaker's Guild, in Camden.

26. "Old-Timer Recalls Bi-Centennial," *Camden News,* January 31, 1957.

27. The pageant *Camden, Yesterday and Today* had been scheduled for presentation on Wednesday. Unless its ending had been changed since the original production in 1925, like *Birth of a Nation* it culminated with the end of Reconstruction. The pageant by "colored citizens" on Thursday was said to have presented a continuation of time to the present. Script details of this pageant, its authorship, and its title have not been located.

28. Several slightly different versions of the map are in existence, as the artist(s) altered or added sections for individual clients. Some of the black and white versions were hand-colored. Some of the maps were made into wall hangings, and a number were framed and hung as artwork. The latest version, reprinted about the early 1960s, added identifications of individuals and views.

29. The Reconstruction Finance Corporation, government owned and funded, was created by Congress in 1932 to grant emergency loans to railroads and financial institutions. The premise was that stabilizing these key businesses would trickle down benefits to smaller businesses as well.

30. Jack Irby Hayes Jr., *South Carolina and the New Deal* (Columbia: University of South Carolina Press, 2001), 40.

31. It was pointed out at the time that "Kershaw County is fortunate in having her records intact," as so many other areas had records burned by Sherman or lost in other ways. Three copies of the will transcripts were made—one left on file in the probate judge's office, one at the library of the University of South Carolina (now at SCDAH), and one at the Camden Public Library (today in the Camden Archives). Some of the final binding work was completed under FERA. The transcripts were later microfilmed as well. Kershaw County's records that were referred to might have been more accurately described as relatively intact.

32. Harvey S. Teal examined the Department of Public Welfare records at the state archives for 1934–42 and collected over eight hundred names from Kershaw County

hired by the CCC during those years (*Camden Chronicle-Independent,* November 22, 2005). These records do not include the year prior to that time when the county emergency relief council was in charge of CCC selections, during which time numbers can be derived only from other sources, such as newspaper accounts.

33. For several months, until other CCC camps were organized, guardsmen were without a place to conduct their own military training.

34. Some of the CCC work in this area involved construction of the Myrtle Beach State Park, completed in early 1934, and completion of the Intracoastal Waterway, dedicated at Socastee in 1936.

35. The nursery along U.S. Highway 1 west of Camden near the Wateree River operated to propagate and distribute millions of seedling trees. With walkways, benches, and picnic tables added to the site by CCC workers, the site served as a small wayside park, which was popular with locals and travelers. Among other wayside parks, CCC workers developed a sizable area near Midway School.

36. Firetower Road off Highway 521 (North Broad Street) denotes the site.

37. In 1946 the Buffalo fire tower was completed, the last of six towers that covered the entire county.

38. The guitarist Munroe Tucker, one of the CCC campers, wrote a song about the terrific rain and windstorm at the Blaney camp. Called "Falling Tents," the song was published in the *Chronicle.*

39. The memorial tablet, preserved in the Memorial Room of American Legion Post 17, Camden, is one of the few artifacts of the CCC camps in Kershaw County.

40. The 1938 state highway map labeled the site CCC Camp Hilton as "Abandoned."

41. Microfilm copies of camp newspapers at South Caroliniana Library.

42. Harvey S. Teal, interview, 2006.

43. Cunningham, *Liberty Hill,* 126.

44. At the time Teal was told that in Kershaw County only he and one farmer in West Wateree had refused to sign the contract, according to what Harvey S. Teal told the authors in 2006.

45. Some results of the NRA codes did last, such as compulsory education and the end of child labor in the mills, although the latter step had already been taken in some but not all southern mills. What in present times seems an obvious benefit had been only slowly accepted by some mill workers, who considered family unity and choice to be traditional rights. When Colonel Leroy Springs was challenged for alleged child labor violations in his mills, which included the mill at Kershaw, he countered that since his workers lacked birth certificates, he had no way of knowing their real ages.

46. In his career Bassett won over one hundred steeplechase races. He was inducted into the National Museum and Racing Hall of Fame in 1972.

47. The innkeeper Karl P. Abbott, *Open for the Season,* 196, describes a party thrown for Governor Blackwell by northern guests at the Kirkwood Hotel after one of the races. The fifteen-foot-long centerpiece on the banquet table was "an authentic reproduction of the Springdale Steeplechase Course, complete with miniature hurdles and gallery, toy horses, and riders." The evening included "mellow candlelight, mellow laughter, and mellow bourbon flowing freely. Prohibition was on, but there was always private stock."

The previous governor, John G. Richards, who was opposed to alcohol, gambling, and Sunday entertainments, was far less popular with the winter colony.

48. The tradition clings in the Kirkwood section of Camden, where some of the homes still have stables and a few of the streets are purposely unpaved to protect hooves. Signs there whimsically read, "Horses, keep off the sidewalks."

49. As has been reported, the background of the book drew heavily from a manuscript of real-life tales of black residents on his plantation, which Dixie Boykin had compiled and given to Kirkbride for use in his planned novel. The two continued to collaborate on the material after the publication of *Dark Surrender.* After the hoped-for movie did not materialize, Boykin and Kirkbride went to New York with an added musical score in hopes of getting a stage play produced. None of these original materials is known to exist today. Ronald de L. Kirkbride's *Dark Surrender* was reprinted in London by Arthur Baker in 1950, a facsimile of the original publication. The authors of this history have interviewed, among others, a niece of Boykin and a son of Kirkbride.

50. The prevalence of families named Boone led to the name of Boonetown, which was often pronounced "Bone" by the family and others. Both the Boonetown and Bonetown spellings are found in early writings, but the latter has invited many colorful stories of origin and has retained general preference in colloquial usage.

51. Vaughan was later killed during World War II when the plane he was piloting went down in a training accident.

52. Savage, *Mysterious Carolina Bays.*

53. The gate columns, "Monumental Gateway to World War Vetrens [*sic*]," are indicated on a map dated May 26, 1936, "Map of Camden South Carolina, Showing Various Points of Historical Interest," by A. P. Boykin (Caroliniana Library). Plaques were added, and the columns were dedicated on May 30, 1941 (*Camden Chronicle,* May 23 and June 6, 1941).

54. By state law a female could wed at fourteen with parental consent or at eighteen without it, although any male under twenty-one had to have parental consent to marry.

Chapter 16. Wings of War

1. Kershaw County was divided into two districts. The board for District 1 included Deas Boykin of Boykin and Marvin Reasonover and John Whitaker Jr. of Camden; board members for District 2 were Gordon T. Bell of Lugoff and M. G. King of Bethune, as well as W. L. DePass, Oscar J. Smyrl, and Dr. Carl A. West, all of Camden.

2. Owned auxiliary landing fields, variously called by number and name, included the following: 1. Bateman Field, five miles from the main Woodward Field; 2. Trotter Field near Lockhart Road, about ten flight miles north of Camden; and 3. Stevens Field at Kershaw. After the Southern Aviation School closed and World War II ended, officials signed deeds on July 18, 1947, conveying ownership of the former SAS properties to Camden and Kershaw County. Woodward Field remained in operation as today's Woodward Airport. The town of Kershaw obtained Stevens Field, where the Kershaw Airport operated for a time, although in 1998 it was acquired to become part of Carolina Motorsports Park, a road-racing course. Trotter Field, mostly covered with rock and asphalt, was sold in a government surplus sale in spring 1947 and is presently a residential

and tree-farm area. It has been reported that during maneuvers and SAS emergencies some other farm fields in the county were also used for temporary landings, but ownership was not acquired. Also the military base at Shaw Field in Sumter County maintained an auxiliary landing strip, Rembert Field, on Highway 54 in Kershaw County, where steel mesh landing mats were laid down for practice with hasty combat-condition landings and takeoffs.

3. "The old Carpenter house" purchased for use as a club for instructors at the Southern Aviation School was on Greene Street, part of the area that figured in the Battle of Hobkirk Hill. The core of the house was built about 1830 by Judge T. J. Withers at 2031 Lyttleton Street (a location earlier called Gander Hill), from which site it had been moved along the ridge in about 1920 by D. E. Norton to replace the John McCaa house, which had burned. The high-rise here was earlier known as Gunby Terrace. The SAS Instructors' Club was in a convenient location since it was only a short walk across Broad Street to the former Kirkwood golf course, then operated by local citizens organized as the Country Club. For some time known as the Magnolias, the house has recently been referred to again as Gander Hill.

4. Martin Cahn, "Trained at Camden's SAS, British Cadet Still Recalls First Solo Flight Here," *Chronicle-Independent,* March 28, 2003.

5. In October 1942 Grace Episcopal Church dedicated a communion plate, "an exquisite solid silver paten" given by Mr. and Mrs. A. A. Pritchard of Dover, Kent, England, as a memorial to their son. The city of Camden also designated as Pritchard Court a newly opened commercial lane east of the post office. The Pritchard Building on that court housed American Legion Post 17 from 1948 to 1952.

6. Daniels, *Nothing Could Be Finer,* 161–62, recounts a colorful episode when Patton wore his pistols to a Thanksgiving luncheon at Mulberry Plantation.

7. According to the army, the October to November dates were chosen to minimize effects on farming since most crops would have been harvested by the maneuver dates. One effect was, however, that as a combination of the maneuvers and the number of immature birds reported, the quail-hunting season was canceled in fourteen counties, including Kershaw.

8. During the actual maneuvers, residents were requested to provide sleeping accommodations for no more than seventy-five cents per night or for free, if possible.

9. Charles W. McGuirt, *Alice the Elephant and Other Stories of Growing Up in Rural South Carolina* (Camden, S.C.: Midlands Printing, 2004). The author weaves his memories of Alice into colorful episodes of his boyhood on a farm adjoining Chancefield.

10. The brick columns were removed during midcentury widening of U.S. Highway 1, and for a long time the whereabouts of the bronze markers were unknown. In 2006 one of the plaques was discovered in the basement of the Kershaw County Courthouse. The Kershaw County Marine Corps League restored and rededicated the plaque, mounting it on an interior wall in the courthouse. Its origin was not known at the time of the rededication.

11. One such article was in the December 6, 1956, *Camden News.* Two Kershaw County men in service at Pearl Harbor when it was attacked were William Rufus Teal of Cassatt, at Schofield Barracks, and Mrs. Margaret Mayfield's son Captain Daniel B. Miller, on a ship in the harbor. Both survived.

12. Wartime marriages also included those of couples who met because of military circumstances. The Lugoff teenager Alice Reynolds met her future husband, William Franklin King, while he was a Fort Jackson soldier on maneuvers in the Camden area. She later recalled, "I remember parachuters getting stuck in the trees. I met and corresponded with a number of the soldiers who came to Camden. They would throw their addresses out to us on rocks." Paul F. White Sr. met his future wife, Mary M. Richey of Camden, in 1943 when he was a Link trainer instructor at Southern Aviation School. He later recalled regarding that year, "Out of my department of 12, six married Camden ladies." Dances and other socials brought together visiting soldiers and young women of Kershaw County. Church and Red Cross "pen pal" correspondence introduced some young couples by mail.

13. The relocation of the eastern bridge approach wiped out of existence the small wayside park that was the state's first forest nursery.

14. In 1945 the American Legion sold its two-story Legion Hall at 537 DeKalb Street to Gus and Christopher Beleos, owners of the Home Furnishing Company. The American Legion moved in August to the former George Stewart printing plant, formerly part of Electric Maid Bakery, on Pritchard Square. Equipment from the former Legion Hall and the old Rutledge Street armory were moved to the new building for a service center.

15. Correspondence in the authors' possession from Dr. George S. Rhame to the nurse Mrs. Harry (Minnie) Baum in 1942 includes a typed list of seven air-raid-related first-aid stations, thus named: Children's Home, Old Armory, Rear of Court House, Mr. Lee Little's Garage, Saint Mary's Hall, W. L. DePass Residence Sr., and Wateree Mill.

16. In November 1947 a two-story house that had been one of the Kirkwood cottages on Greene Street was destroyed in a fire described as "one of the most destructive to visit this community in decades." It was the home of Mr. and Mrs. W. P. (Elizabeth) Thomas.

17. The name "Country Club" or "Camden Country Club" appeared for decades in tourist and social columns in connection with golfing facilities at the Kirkwood Hotel, especially in reference to the separate clubhouse on the hotel grounds where sports and social activities were organized. The present Camden Country Club claims 1903 as the date of origin. As early as the 1905 Sanborn map, a large, separate building to the east of the main building is labeled "Country Club." In 1942 the name was carried over and used to refer to the organization of private citizens who were operating the golf club at the Kirkwood. In 1952 the modern Camden Country Club was organized.

18. The other two cities, Bennettsville and Orangeburg, also had schools to train pilots.

19. The October 31, 1946, *Camden Chronicle* reported the county's first casualty to be returned home. Private First Class David W. Reynolds, to be buried at Smyrna Church in West Wateree, had been killed in action two years earlier, October 8, 1944, in Germany.

20. "S.A.S. at Camden had over one hundred civilian Flight Instructors, and they trained over 6,000 student Cadets (including 300 British Cadets). The School was a noteworthy example of Civilian all-out participation in war-time Aviation" (Paul F. White Sr., "Brief History of the 64th AAFFTD, Southern Aviation School, Camden, S.C.," August 20, 1991, Camden Archives). SAS at Camden was the home base of the Sixty-fourth Army Air Forces Flight Training Detachment.

21. The formal Japanese surrender was made on September 2. Some American servicemen faced additional long months of transition and occupation duty.

22. Racial composition of war statistics were twelve blacks and eighty-seven whites, in contrast to nearly evenly divided statistics in World War I.

23. Veterans were urged to register their discharges at the county courthouse, where they were kept in a separate book.

24. The "bad nerves" of a number of veterans in response to loud or unexpected explosions were one reason that Camden in 1945 banned traditional Christmas fireworks in the city limits and extended the ban the following year. Local pastors also numbered among those who believed that explosives were contrary to the peaceful sanctity of a religious holiday. Support for the ban intensified when a stock of fireworks ignited at a Kershaw filling station and lunchroom in 1946, killing four former servicemen and injuring others. The tragedy caught public attention, and the following year South Carolina passed a statewide "anti-fireworks law."

25. In April 1946 the first floor of the Kirkwood annex was in temporary use as a golf club for the Camden Country Club, and the second floor had fifteen "finely appointed" guest rooms, a number of them with private baths. Hair announced his plans, "as soon as material is available," to extend two brick wings from the original core he purchased that month from Elihu and Carl Schlosburg, who had acquired it earlier for such an intended purpose. Hair hired an architect and displayed a scale model at the Chamber of Commerce of his intended revision, seventy rooms and two twelve-unit apartment sections. Work began with energy but slowed and stopped. Vandals destroyed some of the improvements, Hair died, and the overgrown grounds and building shell became an eyesore and community fire hazard. In 1951 an adjacent property owner bought the Kirkwood place and dismantled the remains. A marker indicates the location of the old hotel.

26. The company also experimented with the manufacture of a four-wheel riding lawn mower but found no market for such a product (Joe Upchurch Jr., interview, 2006).

27. When soybeans had been introduced locally about twenty-five years earlier, the beans shattered out, making harvesting difficult. When a shatter-proof bean was developed, the crop became more desirable.

28. Papers of Henry Savage Jr., South Caroliniana Library. Savage was the first mayor elected after the city changed to the city-manager form of government in 1948.

29. The *Camden Bulletin,* July 29, 1949, reported that the strike had been called by the Builders Trade Union.

30. Two of the old spans dated to 1899. The third and heavier span was built in 1916.

31. Had the safety requirement not been met, federal highway funds would have been lost.

32. The King Haiglar Apartments were constructed where the King Haiglar (variously spelled at times) Inn had stood. Originally the home of the nineteenth-century silversmith Alexander Young, who had his shop on the bottom floor, the house was later enlarged to about twenty rooms and occupied by the growing family of Henry Savage Sr. He sold it in 1926 to Wheeler P. Thomas, who converted it to an inn. It was lost to fire in December 1928.

33. Between Camden and the airport, the section had continued to grow since World War I, according to the January 30, 1948, *Camden Chronicle,* "first with the opening of DuBose Park, and later subdivisions at the Bellshaw farm, Lewisville and the airport section." J. P. Lewis opened the Lewisville development about 1945.

34. In 1948 the Jaycees funded the installation of several fire hydrants along U.S. Highway 1 in East Camden, outside the city limits. It was well past 2000 before installation of sewage lines began.

35. Trustees were Reverend Leslie W. Edwards, chairman; R. E. Perry, vice chairman; Mrs. William Hayes, secretary-treasurer; Mrs. John T. Stevens; and Mayor L. F. Truesdale.

36. Churchill introduced the term in his "Sinews of Peace" speech at Westminster College in Fulton, Missouri, on March 5, 1946.

37. Credit for coining the name of that elongated period of international tension between Russia and the United States is given in part to Bernard Baruch.

38. Developed early in World War II to control malaria, typhus, and other insect-borne human diseases, DDT was widely used thereafter until environmental concerns increased. Its use was limited by the U.S. government in 1969 and banned after 1972. Henry Savage Jr., who suffered chronic bronchitis, wrote on June 8, 1970, to the S.C. Board of Health regarding air pollution problems. He cited the Health Department's mosquito spraying in Camden, which, he said, rarely reached breeding places so that "the human residents get the gas while the mosquitoes remain secure in their leafy retreat."

39. Origins of the historic name Magazine Hill, so called for the Revolutionary War powder magazine at its foot, were obscured in the years that the city used the area as a trash dump. Many a child of the era thought that the name referred to the fact that the site was where families carried refuse, such as old magazines, for burning. Then sights of smoke and scents of burning were common in the area. Today part of Historic Camden Revolutionary War Site covers the reclaimed site.

40. The October 3, 1947, *Camden Chronicle* described the city's recent destruction by fire of a pest house, an old structure opposite the fairgrounds (present site of Rhame Arena, Broad and Bull streets) "that had been a refuge for a man allegedly suffering from an incurable and infectious disease." The use of pest houses in earlier times to isolate the improvident unhealthy is discussed in Joan Inabinet, "The Greatest Modern Improvement," in *Kershaw County Legacy,* ed. Inabinet and Inabinet, 37. The 1925 city directory gives the address of the "City Pest House" at 502 Broad Street.

41. In May 1948 nine registered nurses received diplomas from the Camden Hospital School of Nursing. In January 1948 nineteen practical nurses graduated in a ceremony at Browning Home Auditorium at Mather Academy, addressed by Jackson High principal P. B. Mdodana. The latter group had completed a course offered through the Vocational Department of the State Department of Education of South Carolina and taught by Nurse L. N. Crawford.

42. At their annual meeting in January 1948, the Camden Hospital Board of Directors reelected H. G. Carrison, Henry Savage Jr., and George R. Darden as president, vice president, and secretary, respectively. Carrison was only the third president; William Shannon served from 1913 (the hospital's first year) to 1921, and Dr. John Corbett served

from 1921 to 1946, at which time Carrison succeeded him. In 1948 Darden was hired as Camden Hospital superintendent, replacing George Ryan, who had been acting superintendent since the death of Mannes Baum. Seven directors, including Carrison, were serving on the board at the time it was enlarged; the others were A. Sam Karesh, R. M. Kennedy Jr., Dr. C. A. West, Dr. A. B. Whitaker, John Whitaker Jr., and W. Robin Zemp. The six directors added to the board included females and representatives of various parts of the county. They were L. D. Boykin of Boykin, Loring Davis of Bethune, Mrs. Marie L. Gaither of Camden, N. P. Gettys of Lugoff, William Hayes of Kershaw, and Mrs. R. B. Pitts of Camden.

43. The members were as follows: Bethune—Mrs. Fred Burrison, John Dan McLaughlin and Ellis Padgett; Blaney—Miss Isaiah Bowen, Dr. W. D. Grigsby, and Edward L. Sessions; Camden—Julian Burns, Mrs. Esther Mahaffey, and Austin Sheheen; Kershaw—J. R. Burns, T. V. Hough, and J. P. Truesdale.

44. Churches promoting the survey were Bethel AME, the Church of God, Edwards Chapel AMEZ, Macedonia Methodist, Mt. Moriah Baptist, Second Presbyterian, Sardis Baptist, Smyrl Hill Baptist, Smyrna Methodist, Saint Mark Church of God, Saint Paul Methodist, Trinity Methodist, Wesley Chapel Methodist, and the Browning Home & Mather Academy. Chairman of the survey was Trinity's Reverend W. R. Gregg, and Reverend M. A. Sanders Jr. was secretary.

45. In 1945 First Baptist purchased the three-story Baruch home, also known in recent years as Ivy Lodge, adjoining its sanctuary and began using the aged structure as a Sunday school annex. For some time church members corresponded with the Baruchs, hoping the philanthropic family would help preserve the home or assist in its removal. In spring 1946 Baruch visited his home place, and he was present in 1949 when a historical marker was erected, but he declined to contribute to its preservation. The upkeep of a 150-year-old house being too costly for the church, which also had need for the space, the house was demolished in 1951 after completion of a new educational building.

46. The brothers Carl, Elihu, and Leon Schlosburg were by various associations involved in several hostelry and entertainment enterprises. They closed their Sarsfield Club operations in summers and took their staff to operate the Ocean Strand Hotel at Crescent Beach (now part of North Myrtle Beach). In early 1947 Leon, assisted by his son Marion, became resident manager of the Sarsfield Hotel, DeKalb Street in Camden, when the brothers completed renovation of the former Camden Hotel (Hotel Camden), which had been operated for seventeen years by the Sterne family. The Sarsfield Coffee Shop, distinctive for a "metropolitan" look, opened in October. In 1949 the Sarsfield Hotel enlarged to fifty rooms.

47. See the appendix.

48. In 1949 the Kershaw County committee appointed to study districts and make school consolidation plans included the following: J. G. Richards, Camden superintendent; Ford B. Stanton, Midway superintendent; Mrs. Mary B. DuVal of Boykin, Camden teacher; Earl Truesdale, Lugoff; Jesse Ross, Blaney; T. C. Hoffman, Wateree Dam; J. E. Baker, Bethune; L. C. Clyburn, Westville; and Tom Corbett, Antioch.

49. Organizations of public teachers met regularly. In 1945 P. D. Baird of Pine Tree Hill School was president of the Kershaw County Teachers Education Association, and T. E. McLester of Jackson High was president of the Kershaw County Negro Teachers.

In 1947 a new group, the Teachers Council of the Camden City Schools, was organized under President Mary B. DuVal. Minutes of the KCTEA during postwar years show that local teachers voiced opinions on state and national educational aid, accreditation standards, salary improvements, retirement and sick leave benefits, class size reductions, district consolidations, and tax assessment systems.

50. By fall 1947 a number of county school lunchrooms operated under well-trained managers, and grammar-school children received good substantial lunches for fifteen cents each. Mrs. Mattie R. West was county supervisor. The schools and their managers included the following: Antioch, Aleyss Rogers; Baron DeKalb, Miss Mamie Smyrl; Bethune, Mrs. Bernie Hilton; Blaney, Mrs. Mattie Ross; Camden Grammar, Mrs. Charley Holland; Camden High, Mrs. W. B. Vereen; Midway, Mrs. C. L. McGuirt; Mt. Pisgah, Mrs. C. R. Griggin; and Pine Grove, Mrs. Annie Branham. School lunch programs often received surplus commodities from the federal government. In spring 1948 the fifty-five schools in Kershaw County received 798 bushels of Washington state apples; the county received one railroad car of the fifty-five freight cars the federal government sent South Carolina. The U.S. Department of Agriculture distributed four thousand bags of cabbage to all of the school lunch rooms, the Children's Home, and Camden Hospital. County schools and other institutions received USDA commodities with a wholesale value of thirty-two thousand dollars during the fiscal year 1947–48.

51. The Camden teacher Eugene McGrew, himself a veteran, was appointed as supervisor of trade and industrial education for fifteen counties.

52. A nursery school and a kindergarten were also operated on campus to give Mather students training in teaching.

53. Katie Lou Croft, "Proposals for Continuous Curriculum Development at Mather Academy," Ph.D. diss., Columbia University Teachers College, 1950.

54. Members of the Kershaw County Library Commission in 1947 were as follows: Mrs. O. J. Smyrl (chair), Reverend A. D. McArn, and Mrs. E. C. von Tresckow—all of Camden; Mrs. C. B. Mitchell—Bethune; Mrs. C. R. Bowen—Blaney; Mrs. Deas Boykin—Boykin; Reverend A. B. Davis—Kershaw; Mrs. R. J. Wardlaw—Liberty Hill; and Mrs. J. Team Gettys—Lugoff.

Chapter 17. Cultural Crossroads

1. The following summer Pastor Millard H. Osborne installed outdoor speakers of the type used at drive-in theaters and offered drive-in services.

2. Although registration was mandatory at age eighteen, a man could not be drafted for one year. However, between ages nineteen and twenty-six he could be "ordered into uniform and kept in service for 21 months." Congress had also given the president authority to activate the reserves and National Guardsmen for the same length of time. Local boards had the power to grant deferments. Controversy arose during the Korean War with charges that National Guard recruiters enticed young men to join the guard on the basis of increased chance of avoiding or deferring overseas service.

3. *Camden News,* May 10, 1956. The state forester reported that Kershaw County led the state in the planting of forest tree seedlings with over two million during the previous winter. By 1966 the state Commission of Forestry ranked Kershaw County fourth in the state in pulpwood production.

4. When he died in 2003, Holland was the longest-serving active lawmaker in South Carolina. He served Kershaw County in the S.C. House twelve years and in the S.C. Senate thirty-three years.

5. This building served its purpose until desegregation dissolved separate library facilities for the races. It was subsequently modified to serve various school and community purposes, and later it was renovated and enlarged as Camden Police Department headquarters.

6. In 1954 John Carl West, future governor of South Carolina, ran for his first public office. According to his biography at the South Caroliniana Library, where his papers are housed, "West's real entrance into politics resulted from his concern about the cramped and inadequate facilities of Camden Hospital, which came to his attention in 1952 when his three-year-old son was taken there with convulsions. West agreed to join a committee devoted to upgrading or replacing the existing hospital. When the effort ran into opposition, West ran for the state Senate in 1954 on the hospital issue, winning his seat by only three votes."

7. Brown, from Barnwell County, was nicknamed "the Bishop of Barnwell." Frequent references to his tight-knit supporters as "the Barnwell ring" echoed in numerous allusions to "ring" politics in Kershaw County by candidates who wished to be perceived as independent of such influences.

8. Although there had been no overt clashes within the county, tension was often evident. According to a *Camden Chronicle* report, a Saturday night (August 12, 1950) motorcade of "some 20 vehicles" carrying hooded Klansmen reportedly entered Camden from the Bishopville Highway. Led by a vehicle with an American flag and a red lighted cross, the convoy passed through the business district "with horns and sirens blaring" and then exited as they had arrived. The same caravan visited "Negro sections" of Bishopville before proceeding to Lynchburg. DeKalb magistrate John C. Langford issued a warrant charging "conspiracy to incite mob violence" against the Ku Klux Klan leader for South Carolina, who allegedly was present at the incident between Bethune and Bishopville. A Sumter man issued a complaint that he had been dragged from his vehicle by robed Klansmen and badly beaten. Incidents outside the county had spillover effects in local tension.

9. *Camden News,* March 29, 1956; Statement of Principle, adopted at the first meeting of the Kershaw County Citizens Council.

10. In the 1954 World Series, Doby played center field for the Cleveland Indians against the New York Giants. In 1962 he joined Don Newcombe as the first former major leaguers to play for a professional Japanese team, the Chunichi Dragons. Brook Benton, born Willie Peay in Lugoff, was a nationally popular recording star in the music industry.

11. The following information is related from the manuscript account in the Savage Papers, Caroliniana Library.

12. In early 1957 the Camden City Council adopted a resolution requiring all city employees to take an oath that they were "not now and will not become members of the KKK." J. H. Bickley of Marion, grand dragon of the KKK of South Carolina, wrote to Mayor Savage and members of the council: "I have made true statements to the press that the KKK did not have any connection or active part in anything claimed of Klan activities in that community."

13. The Smiths leased the facility in 1976 and closed it in 1985, as an alternative to a major investment to provide needed upgrades. Because of "a demand in the community for affordable housing," the Smiths teamed with Lem Wooten and converted the property into Blaney Hills subdivision. The streets in the development were named for the drag strip's most successful drivers.

14. In December emergency funds were appropriated to rebuild Blaney High School and to proceed with plans to build a new Camden High School, minus auditorium and gym. The following month the investigation of the Blaney arson case caused tempers to flair, resulting in uncharacteristic behavior by some prominent citizens. In an unfortunate private encounter in downtown Camden, the county school board chairman struck Camden's mayor, who was acting as a lawyer in another case for some Blaney citizens.

Chapter 18. Landmarks and Interstate

1. For several months in 2003–4, McKissick Museum in Columbia featured a major exhibit of Kershaw County pottery collected for the society's publication of McLaurin, Porter, and Teal's *"Just Mud"* (2002). The exhibit included relics of Indian and colonial pottery found in the county and many examples of the utilitarian and art pottery produced at Bethune from the mid-1920s to 1980. The name of the first Bethune pottery is uncertain, perhaps Augustine. Other names are better known: Bethune Pottery, Cole Pottery, Brown Pottery, and Guy Pottery. At least fifteen potters worked in the five potteries, which operated at various times. Their works were sold to tourists along U.S. Highway 1 and shipped across the United States. Leroy Stephens currently makes and sells yard and garden ornaments near Bethune, and Otis Norris makes and sells household and art pottery at his Sandhills Pottery in McBee. Their businesses are among those that continue to use Bethune clay.

SELECTED BIBLIOGRAPHY

As an aid to readers who wish to read further about Kershaw County and conduct research projects of their own, the list below selects works cited in the writing of this history that largely focus on the county as a whole or that cover several topics or areas of county interest. The list also includes works the authors have cited in more than one chapter of this history, suggesting broader usefulness to researchers. Space does not permit the inclusion of the many helpful church and organization histories, family genealogies, single biographies, and treatments of individual topics that the authors consulted; or the inclusion of many individual sites throughout the county where personal observations enhanced information-gathering. A number of individuals interviewed are named in the acknowledgments. Chapter endnotes cite additional valuable works on specific subjects.

Libraries, Archives, and Museums

Camden Archives and Museum. Camden, S.C.
Historic Camden Revolutionary War Site. Camden, S.C.
Kershaw County Courthouse and Government Center. Camden, S.C.
Kershaw County Historical Society. Camden, S.C.
Kershaw County Visitors Center. Camden, S.C.
Library of Congress. Washington, D.C., Federal Writers' Project, United States Works Progress Administration
National Equestrian Museum. Camden, S.C.
South Carolina Department of Archives and History. Columbia, S.C.
South Carolina Historical Society. Charleston, S.C.
South Caroliniana Library. University of South Carolina. Columbia, S.C.

Published Sources

Books and Articles

Beaty, Rives Lang, ed. "Recollections of Harriet DuBose Kershaw Lang." *South Carolina Historical Magazine* 59 (July 1958): 159–70.
Bierer, Bert W. *Discovering South Carolina.* Columbia, S.C.: State Printing, 1969.
Cunningham, Mary Ellen. *Long Ago at Liberty Hill—An Historical Sketch.* Camden, S.C.: Midlands Printing, 1997.
Daniels, Jack H. *Nothing Could Be Finer: A Fifty Year History of the Heyday of Polo and Winter Resorts in Camden 1898–1948.* Camden, S.C.: John Culler, 1996.
Edgar, Walter. *South Carolina: A History.* Columbia: University of South Carolina Press, 1998.

Ernst, Joseph A., and H. Roy Merrens. "'Camden Turrets Pierce the Skies!' The Urban Process in the Southern Colonies during the Eighteenth Century." *William and Mary Quarterly* 30 (October 1973): 549–73.

Gardner, Miles. *Murder and Mayhem in Old Kershaw.* Spartanburg, S.C.: Reprint Co., 2004.

A Guide to Selected Historical Sites in Kershaw County/District, South Carolina. Camden, S.C.: Kershaw County Historical Society, 1992.

Holcomb, Brent H., *Marriage and Death Notices from Camden, South Carolina, Newspapers 1816–1865.* Easley, S.C.: Southern Historical Press, 1978.

Holcomb, Brent H., ed. *Kershaw County, South Carolina, Minutes of the County Court 1791–1799.* Columbia: South Carolina Magazine of Ancestral Research, 1986.

Holcomb, Brent H., and Elmer O. Parker. *Camden District, S.C., Wills and Administrations, 1781–1787 (1770–1796).* Easley, S.C.: Southern Historical Press, 1978.

Hooker, Richard J., ed. *The Carolina Backcountry on the Eve of the Revolution: The Journal and Other Writings of Charles Woodmason, Anglican Itinerant.* Chapel Hill: University of North Carolina Press, 1953.

Inabinet, Joan A. *His People: A History of the Camden (First) Baptist Church.* Camden, S.C.: Pine Tree, 1985.

———. *Lyttleton Street United Methodist Church of Camden, S.C.: A History.* Camden, S.C.: Pine Tree, 2003.

Inabinet, L. Glen, and Joan A. Inabinet, eds. *Kershaw County Legacy: A Commemorative History.* Camden, S.C.: Kershaw County Historical Society, 1976.

———. *Legacy II: Kershaw County History and Heritage.* Camden, S.C.: Kershaw County Historical Society, 1983.

Jenkins, James. *Experience, Labours, and Sufferings of Rev. James Jenkins of the South Carolina Conference.* 1842. Repr., Columbia, S.C.: State Commercial Printing, 1958.

Johnson, Bill, comp. *Gridiron Legends: The Camden Bulldogs.* Edited by Joan A. Inabinet. Camden, S.C.: Pine Tree, 1991.

Johnston, Louise. *History and Homes of Liberty Hill, South Carolina.* Camden, S.C.: Midlands Printing, 1992.

Kershaw County in Federal Censuses of South Carolina. 4 issues: 1800, 1810, 1820, 1830. Camden, S.C.: Kershaw County Historical Society, 1970–94.

Kershaw County, South Carolina, Cemetery Survey. 3 vols. Camden, S.C.: Kershaw County Historical Society, 1991.

Kershaw County, South Carolina, Census with Expanded Genealogical Information, 1850. Camden, S.C.: Catawba-Wateree Genealogical Society, 1997.

Kirkland, Thomas J., and Robert M. Kennedy. *Historic Camden: Colonial and Revolutionary.* Columbia, S.C.: State, 1905.

———. *Historic Camden: Nineteenth Century.* Columbia, S.C.: State, 1926.

Marszalek, John F., ed. *The Diary of Miss Emma Holmes, 1861–1866.* Baton Rouge: Louisiana State University Press, 1979.

McKain, James D. *Index to Historic Camden, Colonial and Revolutionary and Nineteenth Century.* Columbia, S.C.: SCMAR, 1995.

McLaurin, Arthur Porter, and Harvey Stuart Teal. *"Just Mud": Kershaw County, South Carolina, Pottery to 1980*. Camden, S.C.: Kershaw County Historical Society, 2002.

Meriwether, Robert L. *The Expansion of South Carolina: 1729–1765*. Kingsport, Tenn.: Southern Publishers, 1940.

Montgomery, Rachel. *Camden Heritage: Yesterday and Today.* Columbia, S.C.: R. L. Bryan, 1971.

Moore, John Hammond, ed. *South Carolina Newspapers.* Columbia: University of South Carolina Press in cooperation with the Thomas Cooper Library, 1988.

Neuffer, Claude Henry, ed. *Names in South Carolina.* 24 vols. Columbia: University of South Carolina, Department of English, 1954–77.

Oliver, Priscilla Ann Trantham. *Living in Camden: Scenes since* Historic Camden. Camden, S.C.: Kershaw County Historical Society, 1995.

Savage, Henry, Jr. *The Mysterious Carolina Bays.* Columbia: University of South Carolina Press, 1962.

Shannon, William M. *Old Times in Camden: Pen Pictures of the Past.* Edited by Harvey S. Teal. Camden, S.C.: Kershaw County Historical Society, 1996.

South Carolina State Census, 1839: A Schedule of the White Population of Kershaw District, South Carolina. Camden, S.C.: Kershaw County Historical Society, 1997.

Squier, E. G., and E. H. Davis. "Ancient Works, Wateree District, S.C." In *Ancient Monuments of the Mississippi Valley: Comprising the Results of Extensive Original Surveys and Explorations.* Vol. 1 of *Smithsonian Contributions to Knowledge,* 105–8. Washington, D.C.: Smithsonian Institution, 1848.

Steen, Andrea Deborah VanLandingham. *Stoneboro: An Historical Sketch of a South Carolina Community.* Spartanburg, S.C.: Reprint Co., 1998.

Sweet, Ethel Wylly, Robert M. Smith Jr., and Henry D. Boykin II. *Camden: Homes and Heritage.* Camden. S.C.: Kershaw County Historical Society, 1978.

Sweet, Ethel Wylly, Molly Nettles, and Glen Inabinet. *A Guide to Historic Sites in Camden, South Carolina.* Camden, S.C.: Camden District Heritage Foundation, [1985].

Teal, Harvey S., ed. *Kershaw County Confederate Miscellany.* Camden, S.C.: Kershaw County Historical Society, 2000.

———, ed. *Return of Crops and Other Statistics of Kershaw County, South Carolina, 1868.* Camden, S.C.: Kershaw County Historical Society, 1998.

———, ed. *Rides about Camden, 1853 & 1873.* Camden, S.C.: Kershaw County Historical Society, 1996.

Teal, Harvey S., and Rita Foster Wallace. *The South Carolina Dispensary & Embossed S.C. Whiskey Bottles & Jugs 1865–1915.* Camden, S.C.: Midlands Printing, 2005.

Williamson, Joel. *After Slavery: The Negro in South Carolina during Reconstruction, 1861–1877.* New York: W. W. Norton, 1975.

Woodward, C. Vann, ed. *Mary Chesnut's Civil War.* New Haven, Conn.: Yale University Press, 1981.

Woody, Howard, and Davie Beard. *South Carolina Postcards.* Vol. 7: *Kershaw County.* Charleston, S.C.: Arcadia, 2002.

———. *South Carolina Postcards.* Vol. 8: *Camden.* Charleston, S.C.: Arcadia, 2003.

Newspapers and Periodicals

Bethune Observer. Bethune, S.C. 1914–23.
Camden Chronicle. Camden, S.C. 1891–1981.
Camden Confederate. Camden, S.C. 1861–63.
Camden Gazette. Camden, S.C. 1816–18.
Camden Independent. Camden, S.C. 1978–81.
Camden Journal (also published under similar titles, such as *Camden Weekly Journal*). Camden, S.C. 1826–91.
Camden News. Camden, S.C. 1956–58.
Camden Weekly Confederate. Camden, S.C. 1864.
Chronicle-Independent. Camden, S.C. 1981– .
Kershaw Gazette. Kershaw, S.C. 1873–87.
Southern Campaigns of the American Revolution. Online journal. 2004– .
Wateree Messenger. Camden, S.C. 1888–1935.

INDEX

ABOUT THE AUTHORS

A native of Camden and graduate of Winthrop College and the University of South Carolina, JOAN A. INABINET is a retired high school English teacher. Now a freelance writer and editor, she is a former president and board member of the Kershaw County Historical Society, for which she serves as newsletter and Web site editor. She has written or edited seven previous local history works, two in collaboration with her husband, L. Glen Inabinet.

L. GLEN INABINET taught history at Camden High School for thirty years. A native of Orangeburg, South Carolina, and a graduate of the University of South Carolina, he is a freelance writer, editor, and photographer and a past president and board member of the Kershaw County Historical Society and the Confederation of South Carolina Local Historical Societies. The Inabinets have three children and remain active members of many community and historical organizations.

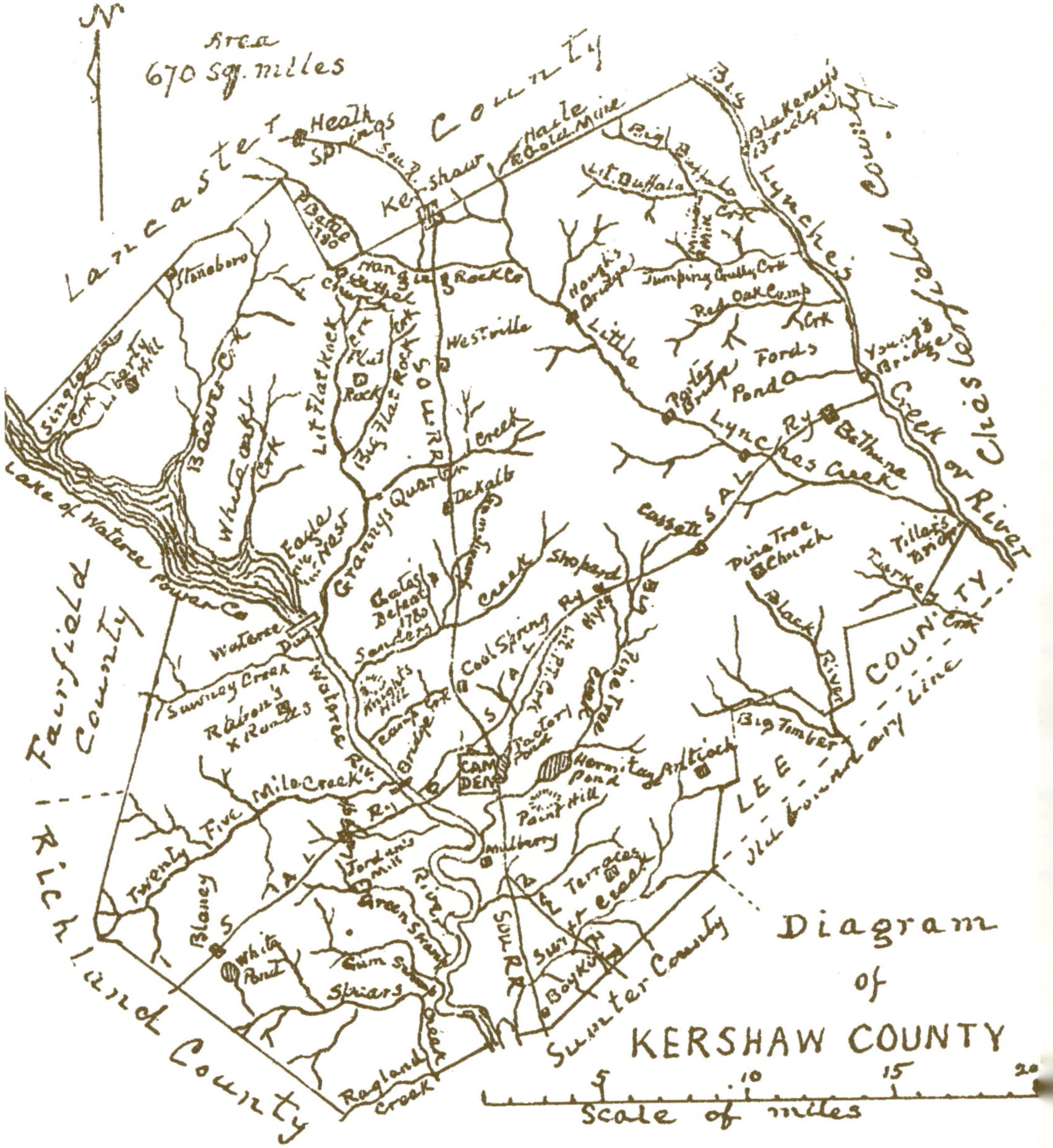

Diagram of KERSHAW COUNTY

N

Area 670 Sq. miles

Lancaster County

Fairfield County

Richland County

Sumter County

Chesterfield County

LEE COUNTY

Old Boundary Line

Heath Springs

Kershaw

Hale Gold Mine

Big Lynches

Blakeney's Bridge

Big Buffalo

Lit. Buffala

Battle 1780

Hangiag Rock Cr

Stoneboro

Liberty Hill

Singleton Crk

Beaver Crk

White Oak Crk

Lit. Flat Rock

Flat Rock

Big Flat Rock Crk

Westville

Jumping Gully Crk

Red Oak Camp

Lynches Creek or River

Young's Bridge

Ford's Pond

Lyn Ry

Bethune

Lynches Creek

Lake of Wateree

Eagle Nest

Granny's Quarter

DeKalb

Cassett

S A L

Pine Tree Church

Tillars Bridge

Turkey Crk

Black River

Gates' Defeat 1780

Sanders Creek

Shepard

Wateree Dam

Sawney Creek

Rabon's X Roads

Knights Hill

Cool Spring Ry

Factory Pond

Pine Tree Creek

Hermitage Pond

Antioch

Big Timber

CAMDEN

Wateree River

Twenty Five Mile Creek

Mulberry

Pine Hill

Jordan's Mill

Terrates

Swift Creek

Blaney

White Pond

Green Swamp

Gum Swamp

Spears Creek

Boykin

SOU. RR

Ragland Creek

5 10 15 20

Scale of miles